Clinical Aspects of
Child and Adolescent Development

Clinical Aspects of Child and Adolescent Development

An Introductory Synthesis of Developmental Concepts and Clinical Experience

MELVIN LEWIS, MB., B.S. (London) F.R.C.Psych., D.C.H.

Professor of Pediatrics and Psychiatry
Yale Child Study Center

and

FRED R. VOLKMAR, M.D.

Harris Associate Professor of Child Psychiatry,
Pediatrics, and Psychology
Yale Child Study Center

Third Edition

LEA & FEBIGER *Philadelphia • London*

Williams & Wilkins
Rose Tree Corporate Center, Building II
1400 North Providence Road, Suite 5025
Media, PA 19063-2043 USA

Library of Congress Cataloging in Publication Data

Lewis, Melvin, 1926–
    Clinical aspects of child and adolescent development: an
introductory synthesis of developmental concepts and clinical
experience / Melvin Lewis and Fred R. Volkmar.—3rd ed.
      p. cm.
    Rev. ed. of: Clinical aspects of child development. 2nd ed. 1982.
    Includes bibliographies and index.
    ISBN 0-8121-1218-0
    1. Child development. 2. Sick children—Psychology. 3. Child
psychiatry. I. Lewis, Melvin, 1926– Clinical aspects of child
development. II. Volkmar, Fred R. III. Title.
    [DNLM: 1. Adolescence. 2. Adolescent Psychiatry. 3. Child
Development. 4. Child Psychiatry. WS 105 L671c]
RJ131.L42   1989
155.4′024616—dc20
DNLM/DLC
for Library of Congress   89-7955
                                                  CIP

First Edition, 1971
Reprinted 1973
Reprinted 1974
Reprinted 1976
Reprinted 1978
Second Edition, 1982
Reprinted 1985
Third Edition, 1990

PRINTED IN THE UNITED STATES OF AMERICA

Print number: 5 4 3

To Dorothy, Gillian, and Eric
and
To Lisa, Lucy, and Emily

Preface

to First Edition

This book is written primarily for medical students. Other students may also find it useful. Its goal is to provide the student with an introductory synthesis of certain basic psychological concepts and their use in understanding the wide range of behavior seen during the stage of human development we call childhood. To the extent that sound diagnosis and treatment are based upon the principles and findings in child development, this book will also serve as a basis from which principles of management may be inferred. However, no attempt is made here to describe specific techniques of management.

Many medical students have an urge to learn "first things first," and since they want to become doctors, "first" to their minds means basic functioning, normal and abnormal. It is recognized that to teach a course of normal development without any reference to deviant or pathologic patterns is often thought at best to lack correlation and at worst to be quite irrelevant. On the other hand, to teach psychopathology before the student has an idea of normal psychologic development is to leave the student floundering in a sea of symptoms and signs, with no normal reference points by which he can chart his course.

The obvious resolution is to teach normality and abnormality simultaneously. An attempt, therefore, is made here to paint in broad strokes the essential framework, or skeleton, for such a resolution. At the same time, this overview should enable the student to fill in for himself the gaps in his knowledge, the gaps in the teacher's knowledge, and the gaps in any course on the subject. In working toward this goal I, of course, have had to be selective in the material used.

Others will differ from me in the selection and emphasis made. I have changed the balance several times myself. Each year students come to medical school better informed. Curricula in many medical schools are themselves in a state of flux. Further, the introduction of new findings and new concepts and the challenge to old beliefs are changing the face of medicine more rapidly than ever before. Nevertheless, I have tried to present the broad range of material fairly and consistently within a more or less unified theoretical frame of reference.

This brings me to a special characteristic of this book. The original literature is now so large that it cannot be encompassed by one person. Moreover, the mere physical act of trying to retrieve original works, papers, and other material from a library is enormously time-consuming, if not actually frustrating. Yet, if the medical student reads only someone else's synthesis, he is the poorer for the development of his own ideas.

In an effort to reduce this difficulty, a series of "notes" consisting of more or less extensive, but hopefully always relevant, quotations from the literature are appended to the end of each chapter. In this way I hope the student will at least get a taste of the joy of reading an original contribution, and perhaps be encouraged to make further explorations as he proceeds in his studies.

Implicit in this book is a particular pedagogical concept. This concept views medical education as a kind of spiral process, in which the student first goes once over lightly, and relatively briefly, the broad sweep of the curriculum. At subsequent periods he can then go over similar ground, this time with more familiarity and greater depth. This concept underlies some of the thinking, for example, of the new curriculum at Yale University School of Medicine. It is hoped, therefore, that this text will form the basis for such a first go-around by the student interested in human behavior. As such, it is purposefully brief. In fact, it contains the essential information and concepts presented in a 36-hour course consisting of lectures, demonstrations, interviews, clinical exercises, and seminars given during the first nine weeks of medical school. It may also serve as a "refresher" course when the student returns to the basic sciences in the "track system" now in use in the clinical years.

Many colleagues and friends have helped me in the preparation of this book, and of course the literature belongs to us all. If I have not assiduously acknowledged every thought, concept, or finding uttered or written by everyone I have listened to or read over the years, it is because I have come to regard many of them now as part of the common domain of accepted knowledge. Yet, I have tried to indicate certain landmarks in the literature that might be used as a guide for those who wish to explore the subject further.

My thanks go especially to my wife, Dorothy, for her ideas, her stimulation, and her encouragement. I also wish to thank Herbert D. Kleber, M.D., Ernesto E. Pollitt, Ph.D., Milton J.E. Senn, M.D., and Randall M. Zusman, medical student, for their helpful criticisms and suggestions. My particular thanks go to my secretary, Mrs. Arthur Eberlein, for her unflagging enthusiasm and helpful suggestions as well as her astonishing capacity to keep things in order and correct my errors. Lastly, I thank Lea & Febiger for their unfailing courtesy and cooperation.

New Haven, Connecticut   Melvin Lewis

Preface

For this third edition, the book is divided into six parts. Part One consists of brief capsule or summary reviews of certain essential human functions seen in longitudinal perspective during childhood. The functions selected include biological development, perception, attention and memory, attachment behavior, cognitive development, language development, psychosexual and aggressive drive development, affect development, moral development, psychosocial development, family development, and temperament.

Part Two consists of a description of the child seen in cross section at various stages of development, when these various functions coalesce to form the whole child. Where possible, clinical correlations are described.

Part Three describes the effects of illness, hospitalization, dying, and death in the context of development, and includes a chapter on child and adolescent psychiatric consultation and liaison in pediatrics.

Part Four is an introduction to clinical psychiatric diagnosis that draws on all of the preceding chapters.

Part Five provides a development perspective on selected categories of psychopathology in childhood and adolescence.

Part Six offers a brief developmental perspective on two forms of treatment: one psychodynamic (individual psychotherapy), the other psychopharmacologic.

An epilogue on society, development, and psychopathology has been added, and the rest has been extensively revised and updated throughout.

Because the goal is to provide a short introductory synthesis for the clinician, oversimplification is inevitable. Some attempt has been made to correct for this oversimplification by increasing the number and range of Notes (readings from original sources).

Because the child and adolescent are here looked at, first, in longitudinal and then in cross-sectional perspective, as well as under stress and in the context of psychiatric evaluation and psychiatric illness, repetition is also inevitable. We have tried to keep such repetition to a minimum.

What is the theoretical framework for this book? Until a new creative genius gives us the gift of a new vision of nature that will reshape our overview of life, the way Darwin, Freud, and Watson and Crick have done, we must struggle with the multiple theories we now have to account for human behavior. Explorations of the biology of the cell and the psychology of the unconscious continue to account for bits of human behavior, in some cases better than in others. We do not yet have a unified theory of human behavior although we do have some fragile and tantalizing wisps of connections that several authors have tried to elucidate (Heilbrunn, 1979; Kendel, 1979; Meyersburg and Post, 1979).

Scientists observe first and then try to account for those observations by inferring a law or constructing a model. If the law or the model is a good one, then consequences of that law or model will predict certain new events or phenomena and will "explain" certain other previously known but perhaps disparate facts. The more scientists can use measurement and the experimental method, the more confident they can be about their theories. Unfortunately, when a theory exists for which there is no relatively satisfactory scientific test that includes measurement (there is no absolutely ultimate test for truth), there is the risk of authoritarianism—a thing is held true because someone said it was so.

In the chapters that follow, we have tried to present some of the scientific findings that support a few of our theories of human behavior, at the same time keeping open the question of the validity of those theories that are still for the most part at the level of observation, inference, and speculation. Our reason for including the latter "unproven" theories is that in clinical practice we must often decide on the basis of experience and judgment when we do not have the necessary scientific knowledge. In doing this we hope we have avoided the risk of authoritarianism.

Last, this book continues to strive toward its overall aim: to be useful to all who wish to review and utilize basic developmental concepts and findings relevant to clinical psychiatric and psychologic work with children.

We wish to thank Ms. Ann Chieppo for typing the manuscript with devotion, care, and attention and Ms. Demetra Parthenios for her assistance in the final stages of manuscript preparation. Special thanks and love go to Dorothy Otnow Lewis for her passionate advocacy, clarity, and uncompromising regard for scientific evidence. Finally, as before, we thank Ken Bussy and his colleagues at Lea & Febiger for their patience, support, and unfailing courtesy.

Melvin Lewis
New Haven, Connecticut   Fred R. Volkmar

REFERENCES

Heilbrunn, G. (1979), Biologic correlates of psychoanalytic concepts. *J. Am. Psychoanal. Assoc.*, 27:597–626.

Kendel, E.R. (1979), Psychotherapy and the single synapse. *N. Engl. J. Med.*, 301:1028–1037.

Meyersburg, H.A., and Post, R.M. (1979), An holistic developmental view of neural and psychological processes. *Br. J. Psychiatry*, 135:139–155.

Acknowledgments

We would like to express our thanks to the following individuals and publishers for permission to use the material quoted in the Notes.

Note 1
H.A. Meyersburg; R.M. Post; British Journal of Psychiatry

Note 2
J. Bowlby; Basic Books, Inc.

Note 3
M.D.S. Ainsworth; S.M. Bell; Child Development

Note 4
J. Bowlby; American Journal of Psychiatry

Note 5
J. Piaget; International Universities Press, Inc.

Note 6
E.H. Lenneberg; John Wiley & Sons, Inc.

Note 7
N. Geschwind; W.H. Freeman & Co.

Note 8
Sigmund Freud Copyrights; The Institute of Psycho-Analysis; The Hogarth Press Ltd.; Basic Books, Inc.

Note 9
B. Bornstein; International Universities Press, Inc.

Note 11
E.E. Maccoby; C.N. Jacklin; Stanford University Press

Note 12
S. Feshbach; John Wiley & Sons, Inc.

Note 13
A. Freud; International Universities Press, Inc.

Note 14
J. Piaget; Macmillan Publishing Co., Inc.

Note 15
L. Kohlberg; Russell Sage Foundation

Note 16
C. Gilligan; American Journal of Orthopsychiatry

Note 17
E. Erikson; W.W. Norton

Note 18
T. Lidz; John Wiley & Sons, Inc.

Note 19
AACAP Committee on Rights and Legal Matters; American Academy of Child and Adolescent Psychiatry

Note 20
A. Thomas; S. Chess; H.G. Birch; New York University Press

Note 21
S. Chess; A. Thomas; Guilford Press

Note 22
T. Benedek; Little, Brown and Company

Note 23
H. Hartmann; International Universities Press, Inc.

Note 24
M.J.E. Senn; Josiah Macy, Jr. Foundation

Note 25
M.E. Lamb; John Wiley & Sons, Inc.

Note 26
A. Gesell; C.S. Amatruda; Paul Hoeber Medical Division, Harper & Row

Note 27
E.H. Erikson; International Universities Press, Inc.

Note 28
J. Bowlby; Penguin Books Ltd.

Note 29
R.A. Spitz; International Universities Press, Inc.

Note 30
J. Piaget; International Universities Press, Inc.

Note 31
D.W. Winnicott; Tavistock Publications Ltd.

Note 32
A. Freud; D. Burlingham; International Universities Press, Inc.

Note 33
Sigmund Freud Copyrights; The Institute of Psycho-Analysis; The Hogarth Press Ltd.; W.W. Norton

Note 34
J. Piaget; B. Inhelder; Basic Books, Inc.

Note 35
G.H.J. Pearson; Bulletin of the Philadelphia Association for Psychoanalysis

Note 36
M. Rutter; J. Tizard; K. Whitmore; Longman Group Limited

Note 37
L.E. Peller; The Psychoanalytic Study of the Child; International Universities Press, Inc.

Note 38
J. Piaget; Basic Books, Inc.

Note 39
E.H. Erikson; W.W. Norton & Co., Inc.

Note 40
P.H. Mussen; M.C. Jones; Child Development

Note 41
D.G. Prugh; E.M. Staub; H.H. Sands; R.M. Kurschbaum; E.A. Lenihan; American Journal of Orthopsychiatry

Contents

Part Three
DEVELOPMENTAL PERSPECTIVES ON PEDIATRIC DISORDERS

Part Four
INTRODUCTION TO CLINICAL PSYCHIATRIC DIAGNOSIS

Part Five
**HISTORIC AND DEVELOPMENTAL PERSPECTIVES IN CHILD AND
ADOLESCENT PSYCHOPATHOLOGY**

Part Six
DEVELOPMENTAL PERSPECTIVES ON TREATMENT

Part One
Longitudinal Perspectives

1
BIOLOGICAL DEVELOPMENT

It has long been known that the highest integrative functions are contained in the cerebral cortex (Sherrington, 1906). Our mind is a function of our brain and, in the last analysis, all psychological disturbances reflect changes in neuronal and synaptic function (Kendel, 1979). At the same time, there is a sequence of development in many biological structures and functions. This chapter therefore will focus on some of the more prominent developmental sequences and their possible relationships to behavior.

BRAIN MATURATION

During the fetal period, the development of the brain, as measured by volume percentage, proceeds (surprisingly) in a caudo-cranial direction (Tanner, 1970). Thus at birth, midbrain and spinal cord are more advanced than pons, medulla, and cerebrum. The cerebellum, which is least advanced at birth, grows rapidly from just before birth to about age 1. Cortical synaptic density appears to increase during infancy, reaching a maximum of about 50% *above* the adult mean at age 1 to 2, and thereafter declines until about age 16, when it remains constant until about age 75 (Huttenlocher, 1979). This phenomenon may help explain why immature brains may recover more completely from injury than fully matured brains. Thus a young child who has a severe injury to the speech areas of the brain may recover his or her speech within a few days, whereas an adult with the same injury may remain permanently aphasic. The apparent excess of synapses may also

account for the plasticity in the developing child. For example, children can more easily learn to speak second languages without an accent than can adults.

Among the primary areas, the motor area is the most advanced part of the cortex during the first two years of life. Development subsequently spreads out from each of the primary areas (sensory, visual, and auditory). Subsequent development within the motor and sensory areas then proceeds in a cephalocaudal direction—arms first, then legs. Visual association areas develop somewhat ahead of auditory areas, suggesting that infants understand what they see before they understand what they hear. At 1 month of age, the primary motor area appears to be functioning, and by 3 months of age all the primary cortical areas serving such functions as vision and learning appear to be relatively mature. By 2 years of age, the primary sensory area has essentially caught up with the motor area (Tanner, 1970).

Further development of the brain occurs during the second decade of life (Anokhin, 1964). For example, a massive reduction in the amplitude and duration of the delta electroencephalogram (EEG) of deep (stage 4) sleep occurs. Cerebral oxygen consumption also declines during this second decade, perhaps by 25% or even 50% (Chugani H, Phelps ME, Mazziotta JC, 1986). This decline might be a result of the dimunition in the density of synapses (so-called "fine tuning" of the brain) in the human frontal cortex that occurs during this same period (Huttenlocher, 1979). All three processes (i.e., changes in

3

stage 4 EEG waves, cerebral oxygen consumption, and synaptic density) follow a similar pattern: Each increases from birth to 2 to 5 years, when each reaches a maximum that is about twice the adult level. This high level is maintained between 5 and 10 years. A decline then occurs until the regular adult level is reached at about age 20. The decline is steepest between 10 and 15 years, i.e., at adolescence.

MYELINATION

Myelination in the brain continues to develop through adolescence and possibly into adulthood (Yakovlev and Lecours, 1967). Myelination tends to occur in arcs or functional units rather than in geographical areas (Anokhin, 1964). Thus the reticular formation, which is concerned with the maintenance of attention and consciousness, continues to myelinate as a system through to puberty and possibly beyond. Myelination also seems to occur in waves, starting in one system and then being overtaken later by myelination in another system (Bekoff and Fox, 1972). Ultimately, all the areas concerned with emotions become active. Heilbrunn (1979) has stated that the "central stations" concerned with emotions include (1) the medial portion of the amygdalate nucleus and areas in the hypothalamus—for rage, (2) the anterior cingulate gyrus—for fear, (3) the central gray—for rage and fear, (4) the lateral amygdalate—for complacency and fearlessness, and (5) the limbic system—for appetitive, pleasurable, and sexual impulses. A ventral branch originating in the reticular formation and innervating the hypothalamus regulates motivational activities, and a dorsal pathway originating in the locus ceruleus and innervating the hippocampus regulates cognitive functions. The locus ceruleus, the site in the pons of a major concentration of noradrenergic neurons, appears to coordinate all the pleasure centers (Cooper et al., 1974). Tracts from the locus ceruleus ascend to the thalamus, hypothalamus, cerebral cortex, cerebellar cortex, and spinal cord. Cells of the

aversive systems originating in the raphe nuclei extend through the mesencephalon (Stein and Berger, 1975). The hippocampi appear to be the site for memory formation, and the temporal cortex is involved in recall of past events.

Myelination correlates with a number of behaviors. For example, a delay in myelination may account for the fact that the smile of premature infants is delayed up to 10 weeks later than the smile of normal infants of the same postnatal age (Bronson, 1969). Other behavioral correlations have been described or speculated about by Meyersburg and Post (1979; see Note 1).

NEURON AND NEUROTRANSMITTER DEVELOPMENT

Brain development begins in a germinal zone within the primordial brain with epidermal neuroblasts dividing to generate postmitotic neurons. These immature neurons then migrate on a genetically determined schedule to different regions of the brain. For example, early ependymal cells in the embryonic cerebral ventricle divide and migrate radially in an orderly fashion along a scaffolding of shafts of radial glial cells (Rakie, 1988). The full complement of cortical neurons are laid down during the first half of gestation. Cortical neurons constitute about two thirds of our total neurons and about 75% of our synapses. Cell-to-cell interactions, neurotransmitters, and environmental factors influence this development. Primitive caudal regional cells are laid down first, followed by more recently evolved structures such as the cerebral cortex. There, in turn, the youngest neurons are layered, from within out, onto the surface of the brain. These neurons arriving later have to pass earlier neurons in order to arrive at their more superficial location.

Clusters of neurons also form in the brain stem, migrate as a group, and coalesce to form such bodies as the locus ceruleus, raphe nuclei, and substantia nigra. Other groups, or systems, of neurons include the early formed modulatory group in the midbrain and brain stem (with arborization to the forebrain), the reticular core, and the GABAergic neurons in the cortex, cerebellum, corpus striatum, and spinal cord.

Once the neurons are in place, neurotransmitter differentiation occurs. Noradrenergic, dopaminergic, serotoninergic, and cholinergic activity characterizes the reticular core neurons. Of note, the levels of biogenic amine metabolized in the cerebral spinal fluid (CSF) are highest in infants and decline with age. Similarly, platelet monoamine oxidase normally decreases during childhood and adolescence.

A major location of noradrenergic neurons that synthesize and secrete norepinephrine is the locus ceruleus, which in turn innervates the cerebral cortex, limbic system, midbrain, and cerebellum. This noradrenergic system develops early, perhaps in the middle of the first trimester of pregnancy, and constitutes a critical early juncture in the development of the cortex. Noradrenergic neurons modulate arousal, anxiety, and affective state. Interestingly, early basic infant behavioral reactions, e.g., fear of strangers and separation anxiety, similarly are manifested by marked arousal and anxiety. The locus ceruleus also appears to be involved in the etiology of depression and other mental disorders throughout the life cycle, from the cradle to the grave (e.g., Alzheimer's disease).

The dopaminergic (DA) system, located in the striatal-limbic system, may be involved in such conditions as Tourette's disorder, which has its onset usually around 7 years of age. In addition, at about the age of 7 years, when DA levels in the forebrain are at their height, clinicians can also diagnose the early onset of schizophrenia. The dopaminergic system might also be involved in the syndrome of attention deficit hyperactivity disorder (ADHD). Stimulants such as methylphenidate (Ritalin), which increase the release and inhibit the reuptake of dopamine and norepinephrine, thus increasing the levels of both neurotransmitter substances, reduce the level of hyperactivity and increase attention in children who have ADHD. Conversely, neuroleptic medications such as haloperidol (Haldol) act, in part, to block the effects of dopamine and are used in the treatment of schizophrenia and autism. Curiously, Tourette's disorder and ADHD occur more commonly in boys than in girls, perhaps reflecting sex differences in the clearance of DA metabolites (5-hydroxyindoleacetic acid [5-HIAA] and homovanillic acid [HVA]). Boys have a higher accumulation of the DA metabolite and a lower accumulation of the indolamine serotonin (5HT) metabolite.

Cholinergic pathways in the cerebral cortex and hippocampal formation may have a spurt in development in the postnatal period, coinciding with the appearance at about 1 year of enhanced memory and speech in infants.

GABAergic neurons, which are found in the cerebral cortex, cerebellum, corpus striatum, and spinal cord, but are not part of the reticular core, are formed later. These cells are inhibitory, especially for the pyramidal cells, and are implicated in sedation and seizure susceptibility.

The opioid system appears to be involved in pain perception and stress-induced analgesia. Profound disruption of this system might be involved in various self-injurious behaviors seen in certain syndromes of childhood.

The concept of a developmental organization of neurotransmitters is supported by other findings (Himmich, 1971; Coyle and Axelrod, 1972; Coyle, 1985). For example, it has been reported that dopamine-beta-hydroxylase (DBH) activity is low during the first year of life and increases 10-fold from birth to the second decade (Molinoff et al., 1970) and that the levels of DBH in the newborn correlate with the scores of irritability, unsociable responses, 1-year anomaly scores, and activity levels at birth, 5 months, and 12 months, respectively (Rapoport et al., 1977).

Developmental change is also noticeable in the observation that neurons can express non-adrenergic phenotypes early in development and only later exhibit cholinergic function (Landis and Keefe, 1983).

Some investigators have reported that high levels of CSF homovanillic acid (HVA) are found in neuropsychiatrically disturbed children but not in adult psychiatric patients and that this phenomenon may represent a developmental change in dopamine receptor sensitivity or the maturation of other neuromodulators (Leckman et al., 1980).

Animal studies have also suggested that two kinds of dopamine receptors exist in the basal ganglia of mammalian species, one excitatory and the other inhibitory, and that these tracts may complete their development at different stages (Rosengarten and Friedhoff, 1979), giving rise to different patterns of vulnerability at different stages of life. A ribonucleic acid (RNA) developmental life curve has also been described. The amount of cellular RNA increases from the third to the fortieth year, then maintains a plateau between ages 40 and 60, after which it decreases sharply. Concomitantly, there is a constant increase of ribonuclease which destroys RNA, accounting perhaps in part for the difficulty of remembering recent events during old age (Heilbrunn, 1979).

Neuroendocrine control undergoes a similar developmental sequence. For example, the hypothalamic-pituitary gonadotropin-gonadal axis first appears to be functioning during fetal life and early infancy. During childhood it then is suppressed to a low level of activity. Finally, at puberty, the system is reactivated. Thus the 10 years or so between late infancy and the onset of puberty can be viewed as an interval of functional gonadotropin-releasing hormone (GnRH) insufficiency, ending when GnRH secretion by neurosecretory neurons is reactivated (Grumbach, 1980). The GnRH neurons, located in the medial basal hypothalamus in the region of the arcuate nucleus, seem to be controlled by extrahypothalamic neural pathways and brain monoamines.

PSYCHOIMMUNOLOGY

Animal studies suggest a developmental relationship between immune function and various emotional states, e.g., depression-like states. In humans, the developing immune system in childhood, particularly in infancy,

may be especially vulnerable to environmental influences and may result in long-term effects on immune capacity (Schliefer et al., 1986). In adolescents, academic stress in some individuals leads to a decrease in salivary secretory immunoglobulins (Jemmott et al., 1983). Other kinds of stresses, particularly acute stress, may cause an increase in cortisol, catecholamine, prolactin secretion, and growth hormone, and a decrease in testosterone. The catecholamine increase may in turn decrease insulin release and promote gluconeogenesis and glycogenolysis in the liver. These specific psychoimmune responses and changes in children and adolescents who suffer from diabetes may lead to an increase in blood glucose, which in turn may alter insulin requirements. Abnormal immune responses (e.g., autoimmunity) have also been found in some children with autistic disorder (Weizman et al., 1982).

EEG DEVELOPMENT

EEG patterns show a developmental progression. Interestingly, birth in itself does not seem to affect neurological maturation. The EEG of an infant born at 28 weeks is much the same 6 weeks later as that of an infant born at 34 weeks (Dreyfus-Brisac, 1966). However, the interaction with the environment is thought to bring about some developmental shift, even in this largely maturational sequence of EEG change in the premature infant. Thus the intermittent sharp-and-slow bursts (the so-called *trace-alternant*) EEG, representing unmodulated cortical activity, disappears earlier in the premature infant than it does in the full-term infant of comparable gestational age. Presumably the change in early quiet-sleep EEG reflects the organization that takes place after birth.

At about 3 months of age, when the smile response generally occurs (the "first organizer," as described by Spitz [1965]), there is another associated EEG change: the onset of sleep EEG changes from a simple direct change (waking →REM state) to a stepwise change (waking →stage 1 nonREM stage 2 nonREM →REM sleep) (Metcalf and Jordan, 1971). There is some evidence to suggest that waking EEG changes also occur at about the ages of 2 years, 6 years, and 11 years, which happen to be the ages at which important cognitive changes occur (Gibbs and Knott, 1949). For example, sleep spindles in the EEG during stage 2 sleep decrease between 6 and 12 months of age, at about the time that an increase in memory occurs and so-called stranger anxiety becomes manifest (Tanguay et al., 1975). An individual's characteristic pattern (usually about 8 to 13 c/sec) becomes established by about 15 or 16 years of age.

Electroencephalogram (EEG) studies have also shown that different regions of the cerebral hemispheres develop at different rates and ages (Thatcher, Walker, and Giudice, 1987). Five growth periods in intrahemispheric corticocortical coupling have been identified between birth and adulthood, and there appears to be a sequencing of different anatomic systems during postnatal corticol development. The timing of these EEG changes appears to overlap nicely with the timing of Piaget's description and theory of cognitive changes in development.

GENETIC FACTORS IN DEVELOPMENT

Genetic factors play an important role in development. Torgerson and Kringlen (1978) studied the development of temperamental characteristics in 53 same-sexed twins. They studied such temperamental attributes as activity level, rhythmicity, approach/withdrawal, adaptability, intensity, threshold, mood, distractibility, and attention span/persistence. Monozygotic twins were found to be temperamentally more similar than dizygotic twins, particularly in activity level, approach/withdrawal, and threshold. The evidence suggested that this phenomenon was a genetic effect. Cantwell (1976) reviewed the evidence for the role of genetic factors in the hyperkinetic syndrome (hyperactivity, impulsivity, distractibility, and excitability) and

found that evidence from family studies, adoptive studies, and twin studies suggested a polygenic inheritance mechanism for the disorder, i.e., multiple gene sites appear to be involved. Genetic disorders, of course, account for a large number of syndromes in childhood. For example, of the half million moderately and severely mentally retarded children, nearly 50% have a genetic disorder (Crandall, 1977). Other disorders in which genetic factors play an important role include dyslexia (Hallgren, 1950), enuresis (Hallgren, 1957), stuttering (Carter, 1969), schizophrenia and manic depression. The genetic marker for some cases of manic depression, for example, is tied to chromosome 11. At least one gene in the chromosome 11 region (the tyrosine hydroxylase gene) is present in dopamine synthesis, which is thought to be involved in manic-depression.

ENVIRONMENT AND BIOLOGICAL DEVELOPMENT

It is important to note that the genetic factors previously mentioned do not operate in a void: the environment is an essential element in the final expression of a trait or disorder. Genetic and experiential factors act to produce a reaction range so that even individuals with the same genetic endowment may exhibit a variety of outcomes. For example, in studies of children of schizophrenics, genetic theory and empirical data suggest that children with severely affected parents and with many affected relatives will have the highest risks, whereas children with only one mildly affected parent may have risks that approach the population base rates (Hanson et al., 1977). Yet as Hanson et al. point out, some children of diagnosed schizophrenics will have *no* genetic risk for schizophrenia, and some of those who do will still enjoy a life of adequate mental health, even without intervention. In fact, the concordance rate for schizophrenia in identical twins is only about 50%. Thus environmental factors seem to be as important as genetic factors in the emergence of the schizophrenia syndrome. So far, no specific environmental factor is known.

Environmental factors may affect biological development in other ways. For example, psychosocial stimulation may have a profound effect on biogenic amine metabolism, which in turn may affect behavior and emotions (Axelrod et al., 1970). Although much of this knowledge is still at the level of research, increasingly it is influencing clinical approaches to child and adolescent development.

BRAIN DAMAGE AND BRAIN DEVELOPMENT

Damage to the brain in children clearly affects behavior. Many premature infants who suffer hemorrhages into the ventricles may subsequently develop learning difficulties and CNS deficits. Brain damage in general is accompanied by a much increased rate of psychiatric disorder, and the rate of disorder is in proportion to the extent of damage. Thus psychiatric disorder is significantly more common in children with bilateral brain lesions than in children whose conditions are confined to one side of the brain (Rutter et al., 1970). At the same time, the range of psychiatric disorders in brain-damaged children is heterogeneous, without specific features for the most part (Rutter, 1977), although recent work on the localization of cognitive operations and contrasting left and right hemisphere abilities does pinpoint the cause of certain specific disabilities (Posner et al., 1988; Kosslyn, 1988).

STATE AND EARLY DEVELOPMENT

The organization of behavior in the infant also appears to be partially dependent on the state of the infant. Brazelton has noted that "an infant who manifests all states of consciousness and who can change state appropriately with or without environmental stimulation indicates a greater capacity for organization and control than an infant who cannot demonstrate this range of behavior or who is 'locked into' a state in an obligatory way" (Eagle and Brazelton, 1977 p. 43).

It is important to distinguish between the term state as used simply to connote in general regularly occurring clusters of behavior and the term state as used to mean specifically a manifestation of central nervous system arousal. In the latter use of the term, the very fluctuations, or rhythms, of state are themselves important data about CNS integration, not just confounding variables. Behavior in the infant, then, is a function of the state of the organism, the specific stimuli acting on the organism, and the environment in which these act (Escalona, 1962). In turn, state includes:

1. the infant's position at the time of stimulation;
2. the response characteristics of an infant to state;
3. the baseline level of behavioral activities of the infant at the time of observation;
4. the maturational level of competence;
5. various time-elapsed variables, such as time since last feeding and time since last startle response.

State is also considered to be a rhythmic process, with a temporal component. This time dimension is important in considering the phasic aspects of states of hunger or sleep, or of alertness, or of endocrine activity (Anders, 1978) (Fig. 1–1).

THEORETICAL MODELS OF DEVELOPMENT

How does development proceed? For present purposes, we may classify theories of child development into two classes: reactive and structural. Reactive theories postulate that the child's mind begins as a *tabula rasa* and that the child then reacts to the environment. Major examples of this type of theory include stimulus-response theory, learning theories, classical conditioning therapy, and operant conditioning theory. The clinical implications for treatment that flow from reactive theories are that symptoms are regarded as learned behavior; i.e., the symptom is the disorder and that through relearning and/or environmental change the symptom is removed and therefore the disease is cured.

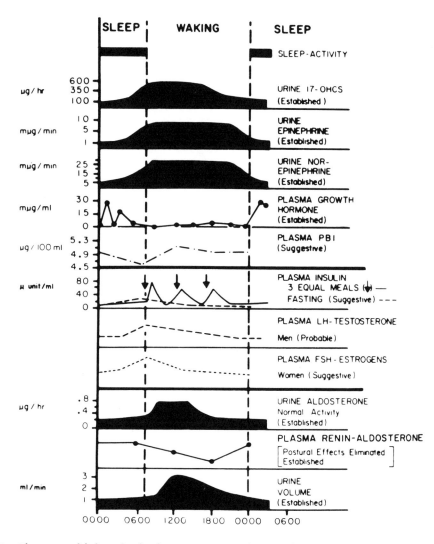

Fig. 1–1.   Phase map of daily cycle of endocrine measures and urine volume in man in relation to habitual sleep and feeding schedule. (Reprinted by permission of publisher from: Psychosomatics and chronobiology, by G. Curtis, *Psychosomatic Medicine,* 34:235. Copyright 1972 by Elsevier North Holland, Inc.)

Structural theories postulate that there is a genetically determined capacity for the development of patterns, or systems, of behavior and that the child interacts with his or her environment from the very beginning. The continuing sequence of behavior patterns that then emerge is described as stages that are qualitatively different from each other. Major examples of structural theories include the general theories of Bowlby, Freud, and Erikson and Piaget's special theory of cognitive development. The clinical aspects of some structural theories will be discussed shortly.

The clinical implications for treatment that flow from structural theories are that some kind of reorganization within the child is required; e.g., resolution of intrapsychic conflict, alteration of the family homeostasis, and acquisition of new schema.

The concept of stages is important in structural theories because it enables one to analyze behavior, just as classification in biology serves as a basis for subsequent analysis and understanding. The criteria for stages include the following:

1. A stage, or structure, is characterized

Note 1

H.A. Meyersburg and R.M. Post (1979), *Br. J. Psychiatry* 135–139.

TEMPORAL CORRESPONDENCE OF SEVERAL NEUROLOGICAL AND PSYCHOLOGICAL DEVELOPMENTAL SEQUENCES

FIRST DECADE — *SUCCEEDING DECADES*

MONTHS OF FIRST YEAR — *FIRST YEAR*

Column scale: −9 −6 −2 0 1 2 3 4 5 6 7 8 9 10 11 12 | 2nd yr. | 3rd yr. | 4th yr. | 5th yr. | 6th yr. | 7th yr. | 8th yr. | 9th yr. | 10th yr. | 2nd | 3rd | 4th | 5th | 6th | 7th & beyond

MYELINATION CYCLE

STRIATO ACOUSTIC SYSTEM
MOTOR ROOTS
OPTIC RADIATIONS & TRACTS
SENSORY ROOTS AND TRACTS

YAKOVLEV & LECOURS

PYRAMIDAL TRACTS & STRIATUM
CEREBELLAR PEDUNCLES
LIMBIC SYSTEM
ACOUSTIC RADIATIONS
GREAT CEREBRAL COMMISSURES
RETICULAR FORMATION
INTRACORTICAL NEUROPIL ASSOCIATION AREAS ?! — ?! — ?!

NEUROMOTOR

Tonic Neck Reflex | Head Balanced | Sits | Creeps | Stands Alone | Walks | Runs | Rides tricycle | Stands on one foot | Skips

FREUD

ORAL | ANAL | PHALLIC OEDIPAL LATENCY | ADOLESCENCE | ADULTHOOD
Delay of the Drives Leads to Secondary Thinking

PIAGET

SENSORI-MOTOR PERIOD | PERIOD OF PRE-OPERATIONAL THOUGHT | STAGE OF CONCRETE OPERATIONS | FORMAL OPERATIONS
1st Abstraction
1st Internalized Thinking

SPITZ

- INFANT MATERNAL DIALOGUE →
- PRIMAL CAVITY PREOBJECT
- OBJECT SPECIFICITY
- Smiling Response (1st Organizer of the Psyche)
- Stranger Anxiety (2nd Organizer of the Psyche)
- "No" Response (3rd Organizer of the Psyche)

MAHLER

SEPARATION INDIVIDUATION PROCESS

- Autistic Phase Hatching Period
- Practising
- Rapprochement (Refueling)
- Object Constancy (Libidinal)
- Omnipotence
- Separation
- Resolution of Omnipotence

ERICKSON

ORAL-RESPIRATORY SENSORY STAGE (SUCKING)	MUSCULAR-ANAL INCORPORATIVE MODE (BITING)	LOCOMOTOR-GENITAL	LATENCY	PUBERTY & ADOLESCENCE	YOUNG ADULT-HOOD	ADULTHOOD	MATURITY	POST-MATURITY
Trust vs. Mistrust	Autonomy vs. Shame & Doubt	Initiative vs. Guilt	Industry vs. Inferiority	Identity vs. Role Confusion	True Genitality	Intimacy vs. Isolation	Generativity vs. Stagnation	Ego Integrity vs. Despair

as a whole ("the final form of equilibrium") and not just as the juxtaposition of parts. The concept of definable stages means behavioral characteristics that have some degree of stability and autonomy.

2. There is an invariant sequence, or constant order of succession, from one stage to another.

3. While multiple and interrelated lines of stage development are present, each line may also have its own rate of development ("level of preparation, level of completion"), giving rise to a multi-leveled organism at any given moment.

4. Each successive stage in normal development represents an advance from the previous stage.

5. Each later stage supersedes all earlier stages in that structures constructed at a given age become an integral part of structures that follow.

6. The change is qualitative, and not just quantitative.

7. Each stage proceeds in the direction of increasing complexity of organization, increasing differentiation and integration.

8. Biogenetic, environmental, experiential, and psychological factors interact to facilitate the developmental progress, coping, and adaptation.

9. There are presumed critical, or sensitive, periods during which conditions are optimal for the normal development of important functions, such as attachment, gender identity, and language.

Is development a continuous process? Certain phenomena, such as the enhancement of memory between 8 and 12 months of age and the shift from a perceptual mode to a symbolic-linguistic mode at about 17 months, seem to emerge more or less suddenly, perhaps more in relation to maturation of special areas in the central nervous system than to the mother-child bond (Kagan, 1979). Kagan argues that such phenomena suggest the possibility of some discontinuities in development and that the experiences of the average infant with its parents might not, af-

ter all, have long-lasting cumulative effects. Nevertheless, many experienced clinicians firmly believe that the kind of care-taking the infant receives in the first year *is* very important in terms of his or her ultimate cognitive and emotional development. In any case, quality of care does appear to be an important determinant of infant characteristics.

In the chapters that follow we concentrate on some of the major structural theories of development. At the same time, we remember that there is a biological aspect and social context for all human behavior and that in medicine we observe at least three dimensions: "the patient as a living organism, the patient as a member of society, and the patient as a person" (Tosteson, 1979, p. 691).

REFERENCES

Anders, T. (1978), State and rhythmic processes. *J. Am. Acad. Child Psychiatry*, 17:401–420.

Anokhin, P.K. (1964), Systemogenesis as a general regulation of brain development. *Prog. Brain Res.*, 9:54–86.

Axelrod, J., et al. (1970), Changes in enzymes involved in the biosynthesis and metabolism of noradrenaline and adrenaline after psychosocial stimulation. *Nature*, 225:1059–1060.

Bekoff, M., and Fox, M. (1972), Postnatal neural ontogeny: environment-dependent and/or environment-expectant. *Dev. Psychobiol.*, 5:323–341.

Bronson, G. (1969), Vision in infancy: Structure-function relationships. In: *Brain and Early Behavior Development*, ed. R.J. Robinson. New York: Academic Press.

Cantwell, D.P. (1976), Genetic factors in the hyperkinetic syndrome. *J. Am. Acad. Child Psychiatry*, 15:214–223.

Carter, C.O. (1969), Genetics of common disorders. *Br. Med. Bull.*, 25:52–57.

Chugani, H.T., Phelps, M.E., and Mazziotta, J.C. (1987), Positron emission tomography study of human brain functional development. *Ann. Neurol.*, 22:487–497.

Cools, A.R., and Van Rossum, J.M. (1976), Excitation-mediating and inhibition-mediating dopamine receptors. *Psychopharmacologia*, 45:243–254.

Cooper, J.R., Bloom, F.E., and Roth, R.H. (1974), *The Biochemical Basis of Neuropharmacology*. New York: Oxford University Press.

Coyle, J.T. (1985), Introduction to the world of neurotransmitters and neuroreceptors. In: *Annual Review*, ed. R.F. Hales and A.J. Frances. Washington, D.C.: American Psychiatric Press, 4:3–97.

Coyle, J.T., and Axelrod, J. (1972), Tyrosine hydroxylase in the rat brain: Developmental characteristics. *J. Neurochem.*, 19:1117–1123.

Crandall, B.F. (1977), Genetic disorders and mental retardation. *J. Am. Acad. Child Psychiatry*, 16:88–108.

Curtis, G. (1972), Psychosomatics and chronobiology. *Psychosom. Med.*, 34:235–256.

Dreyfus-Brisac, C. (1966), The bioelectrical development of the central nervous system during early life. In: *Human Development*, ed. F. Falkner. London: Saunders.

Eagle, D.B., and Brazelton, T.B. (1977), The infant and risk-assessment and implications for intervention. In: *Child Psychiatry: Treatment and Research*, ed. M.F. McMillan and S. Henao. New York: Brunner/Mazel.

Escalona. S. (1962), The study of individual differences and the problem of state. *J. Am. Acad. Child Psychiatry*, 2:11–37.

Gibbs, F.A., and Knott, J.R. (1949), Growth of the electrical activity of the cortex. *Electroencephalogr. Clin. Neurophysiol.*, 1:223–229.

Grumbach, M.M. (1980), The neuroendocrinology of puberty. *Hosp. Pract.*, 15:51–60.

Hallgren, B. (1950), Specific dyslexia ("congenital word-blindness"): A clinical and genetic study. *Acta Psychiatr. Neurol. Scand.*, (Suppl.) 65.

Hallgren, B. (1957), Enuresis: A clinical and genetic study. *Acta Psychiatr. Neurol. Scand.*, 32(Suppl. 114):1–159.

Hanson, D.R., Gottesman, I.I., and Meehl, P.E. (1977), Genetic theories and the validation of psychiatric diagnoses: implications for the study of children of schizophrenics. *J. Abnorm. Psychol.*, 86:575–588.

Heilbrunn, G. (1979), Biologic correlates of psychoanalytic concepts. *J. Am. Psychoanal. Assoc.*, 27:597–626.

Himmich, W.A. (1971), Biochemical processes in behavioral development: Biochemical processes of nervous system development. In: *The Biopsychology of Development*, ed. E. Tobach et al. New York: Academic Press.

Huttenlocher, P. (1979), News release, July 16, 1979, quoted in *Pediatr. Currents*, 28(9):72.

Huttenlocher, P.R. (1979), *Brain Res.*, 163:195.

Jemmott, J.B., Borysenko, J., Borysenko, M., et al. (1983), Academic stress, power motivation, and decrease in secretion rate of salivary secretory immunoglobulin. *Lancet*, 1:1400.

Kagan, J. (1979), The form of early development. *Arch. Gen. Psychiatry*, 36:1047–1054.

Kendel, E.R. (1979), Psychotherapy and the single synapse. *N. Engl. J. Med.*, 301:1028–1037.

Kosslyn, S.M. (1988), Aspects of a cognitive neuroscience of mental imagery. *Science*, 240:1621–1626.

Landis, S.C., and Keefe D. (1983), Evidence for neurotransmitter plasticity in vivo: Developmental changes in properties of cholinergic sympathetic neurons. *Dev. Biol.*, 98:349–372.

Leckman, J.F., Cohen, D.J., Shaywitz, B.A., Caparulo, B.K., Heninger, G.R., and Bowers, M.B., Jr. (1980), CSF monoamine metabolites in child and adult psychiatric patients: A developmental perspective. *Arch. Gen. Psychiatry*, 37:677–681.

Metcalf, D.R., and Jordan K. (1971), EEG ontogenesis in normal children. In: *Drugs, Development and Cerebral Function*, ed. W.L. Smith. Springfield, Ill.: Charles C Thomas, pp. 125–144.

Meyersburg, H.A., and Post, R.M. (1979), An holistic developmental view of neural and psychological processes. *Br. J. Psychiatry*, 135:139–155.

Molinoff, P.B., Brimijoin, W.S., Weinshilboum, R.M., et al. (1970), Neurally mediated increase in dopamine-beta-hydroxylase activity. *Proc. Natl. Acad. Sci. U.S.A.*, 66:453–458.

Posner, M.I., Petersen, S.E., Fox, P.T., and Raichle, M.E. (1988), Localization of cognitive operations in the human brain. *Science*, 240:1627–1631.

Rakie, P. (1988), Specification of cerebral cortical areas. *Science*, 241:170–176.

Rapoport, J.L., Pandoni, C., Renfield, M., et al. (1977), Newborn dopamine-beta-hydroxylase, minor physical anomalies and infant temperament. *Am. J. Psychiatry*, 34:676–679.

Rosengarten, H., and Friedhoff, A.J. (1979), Enduring changes in dopamine receptor cells of pups from drug administration to pregnant and nursing rats. *Science*, 203:1133–1135.

Rutter, M. (1977), Brain damage syndromes in childhood: Concepts and findings. *J. Child Psychol. Psychiatry*, 18:1–21.

Rutter, M., Graham, P., and Yule, W. (1970), A Neuropsychiatric Study in Childhood. *Clinics in Developmental Medicine*, Nos. 35, 36. S.I.M.H. London: Heinemann.

Schleifer, S.J., Scott, B., Stein, M., and Keller, S.E. (1986), Behavioral and developmental aspects of immunity. *J. Am. Acad. Child Psychiatry*, 26:751–763.

Sherrington, C.S. (1961), *Integrative Action of the Nervous System* (1906). New Haven, Conn.: Yale University Press.

Spitz, R. (1965), *The First Year of Life*. New York: International Universities Press.

Stein, L., and Berger, B.D. (1975), Noradrenergic reward mechanisms, recovery of function, and schizophrenia. In: *The Chemistry of Mood, Motivation and Memory*, ed. J.L. McGaugh. Advances in Behavioral Biology, Vol. 4. New York: Plenum Publishing Corporation, pp. 81–103.

Tanguay, P.E., Ornitz, E.M., and Kaplan. A. (1975), Evolution of sleep spindles in childhood. *Electroencephalogr. Clin. Neurophysiol.*, 38:175–181.

Tanner, J.M. (1970), Physical growth. In: *Carmichael's Manual of Child Psychology*, ed. P.H. Mussen. New York: John Wiley & Sons.

Thatcher, R.W., Walker, R.A., and Yuidice, S. (1987), Human cerebral hemispheres develop at different rates and ages. *Science*, 236:1110–1113.

Torgerson, A.M., and Kringlen, E. (1978), Genetic aspects of temperamental differences in infants: A study of same-sexed twins. *J. Am. Acad. Child Psychiatry*, 17:433–444.

Tosteson, D.C. (1979), Learning in medicine. *N. Engl. J. Med.*, 301:690–694.

Weizman, A., Weizman, R., Szekely, G.A., Wijsenbeek, H., and Livni, E. (1982), Abnormal immune response to brain tissue antigen in the syndrome of autism. *Am. J. Psychiatr.*, 139:1462–1465.

Yakovlev, P.I., and Lecours, A.R. (1967), The myelogenetic cycles of regional maturation of the brain. In: *Regional Development of the Brain*, ed. A. Kinkowski. Oxford: Blackwell.

2

PERCEPTION, ATTENTION, AND MEMORY

Shortly before the turn of the century, William James (1890–1950) described the world of the infant as "one great blooming, buzzing confusion"; this view minimized the capacities of the infant to perceive and attend to stimuli. Over the last 20 years, increasingly innovative experimental techniques have shown that even from the first weeks of life, sophisticated capacities to perceive, attend to, and remember stimuli can be demonstrated (Bower, 1972). Both perception and attention reveal a developmental sequence (Nurcombe, 1990).

VISION

Within a few hours after birth infants tend actively to pay more attention to high-contrast stimuli (Kessen, 1967) and soon begin to scan for such contrasts. One-month-old infants pay more attention initially to the edges and contours of the head and face and subsequently, within a month or two, begin to look at eyes, then the mouth (at 5 months), and finally the face (preferably a smiling face) as a whole (Gibson, 1969). Thus, vision is an important biological component in the development of attachment.

Infants probably perceive depth (the "visual cliff" experiment) by 2 months (Campos, Langer, and Krowitz, 1970), at about the same time they are able to converge their eyes. Color, too, is perceived at approximately the same time (Bornstein, 1975). Visual acuity in 2-week-olds starts off at 20/800

(Fantz, Ordy, and Udelf, 1962) and reaches 20/20 by 5 years of age.

Infants at 1 week of age appear to be attracted to strongly patterned visual stimuli, such as horizontal shapes, concentric circles, and face-like mosaics. Pattern is preferred over color, brightness, or size, and infants appear to be attracted to complex patterns rather than simple ones, and by moving objects rather than stationary ones (Fagan, 1979; Fantz et al., 1975: Kessen and Bornstein, 1978). Perceptual abilities become increasingly sophisticated, so that by 8 months of age, they are able to perceive different dimensions of stimuli such as shape and color, as well as depth. These characteristics again contribute to the attachment. Thus it so happens that the one object that has all the characteristics just mentioned—i.e., is (1) in almost constant motion, (2) emits a great deal of highly varied stimuli, (3) appeals to a number of different sensory modalities, (4) is quite complex, (5) possesses a distinctive pattern, and (6) is also responsive to the infant's own behavior—is the human object and the human *face* in particular.

Older children of 10 to 12 weeks soon become habituated and lose interest, and their visual attention wanders if the stimulus is simply repeated and nothing new is introduced. These changes seem to coincide with brain maturation, as reflected in such changes as the appearance of alpha rhythms (Ellington, 1967).

HEARING

Infants hear at birth. Auditory acuity improves rapidly over the first few days, with the infant preferring an intermittent tone to a continuous one (Brackbill et al., 1966). Improvement in acuity continues to occur over the first two years. The 1-week-old infant can recognize his or her mother's voice, to which the infant responds more readily than to the voice of a stranger (Mills and Melhush, 1974). Most infants can probably locate the direction of the source of a sound at birth. Soft or continuous sounds are particularly effective in eliciting the infant's head turning or eye movements towards the stimulus (Muir and Field, 1979). By 3 months of age, head turning toward the direction of a sound is typical. The infant, in effect, seems to be especially "tuned" for human speech virtually at birth (Ferald, 1984).

Certainly, the infant can distinguish human speech sounds practically at birth (Eimas et al., 1971). The number and rate of subsequent categorical sound distinctions may vary according to the language the infant hears. Some early distinctions atrophy and disappear if the language does not require them, and presumably new distinctions can be learned when acquiring a new language.

TASTE, SMELL, AND TOUCH

Newborns discriminate sweet tastes at birth (Nowlis and Kessen, 1976) and also have a sense of smell (Engen, Lipsitt and Kaye, 1963). Newborns can discriminate the four basic tastes (sugar, acid, salt, and bitter) and have been shown to adapt rates of sucking in response to sucrose solutions in different concentrations (Kobre and Lipsett, 1972). Similarly, tactile discrimination increases gradually. It is clear that newborns do respond to pain, e.g., related to circumcision (Porter, Porges, and Marshall, 1988); cutaneous sensitivity is apparent from the eighth week of intrauterine development.

The newborn and young infant thus appear to be organized in such a way as to explore and learn about the environment in a remarkably rapid and efficient manner.

ATTENTION

Attentional capacities also show a developmental sequence, with increasingly sophisticated patterns of attending evident as infants become more alert and mobile (Kagan and Lewis, 1965). Capacities to attend at 4 months of age can be related to developmental status at 1 year (Ruddy and Bornstein, 1982). Capacities for internal representation, e.g., in relation to memory and language, are related to attentional abilities.

Attention is more than just being locked in, or riveted, to a single stimulus such as a mesmerizing source of light which, for the sake of illustration, we can call television. Although duration of attention is an important dimension, even if it is a mindless attention, it is only one of many dimensions of attention. Other dimensions besides (1) duration, or span, include the ability to (2) differentiate among stimuli, (3) order them in relation to a particular goal, (4) selectively dampen out unwanted stimuli, (5) remember in sequence chains of stimuli and relate them to each other, (6) coordinate stimuli received through different sensory pathways, and (7) coordinate responses in different effector pathways.

Then again, each of these seven major dimensions, or components, of attention is subject to variation from child to child and from time to time in any given child by such factors as motivation, intelligence, the complexity of the task requiring attention, and fatigue. Furthermore, each of these factors, especially motivation and intelligence, is a complex phenomenon. Thus when we say a child is having an attentional problem, such a statement is, at best, a global statement and requires further analysis.

Attentional problems are prominent in such conditions as attention deficit, hyperactivity disorder, learning disorders, and even in autism.

MEMORY

The processes of perceiving, paying attention, recognizing patterns, filtering and retaining selective information (encoding), and recalling that information (retrieval) are all components of memory. Memory develops in spurts, perhaps in relation to central nervous system maturation.

Infants soon recognize and remember mother's voice, face, smell, taste, and touch. Initially memory is short. A 1-month-old can remember a mobile for about 24 hours (Weizmann, Cohen, and Pratt, 1971). By 5 or 6 months an infant can remember for several weeks an object seen only for a few minutes (Cohen and Gelber, 1975). Memory subsequently increases in duration as memories increasingly accumulate and memory becomes less context dependent. Evidence of memory is seen in such phenomena as object permanence, stranger reaction, attachment behaviors, and separation anxiety. Memories of the past gradually lead to predictions of the future, e.g., the infant begins to predict and anticipate that mother is about to leave by observing the mother's preparatory actions.

The process of memory storage is an active one, and not simply a matter of warehousing. Perceived items (up to about 5 to 9 at a time), if they are attended to and registered, can be remembered for a short while (about 30 seconds), constituting so-called short-term memory. Short-term memory items may then be encoded and stored for later retrieval, constituting so-called long-term memory.

Memory for pattern recognition appears to require an intact parietal lobe, thalamus, and midbrain (Petersen, 1985; Posner et al., 1988). Visual word forms are developed in the occipital lobe (Posner et al., 1988). The left hemisphere seems to be better than the right hemisphere for mental imagery and arranging shapes (Kosslyn, 1988). Semantic language tasks are processed in the anterior left frontal lobe. Words presented in auditory form are processed in the left temporoparietal cortex (Geschwind, 1965). Auditory memory and attention, e.g., digit span memory, seem to

involve the left supramarginal and angular gyri. Gradually with maturation, the child acquires more efficient strategies, especially for episodic memory, which consists of the automatic storage and retrieval of spatially located, temporally ordered, person experiences. Young children, aged 4 to 6 years, generally are able to locate events spatially but are not very good at dating events in time, whereas older children from 10 years of age onward generally have acquired the concept of historical time and sequence and can usually then order events temporally (Goldstone and Goldfarb, 1966).

By and large, children's short-term memory for things that they understand may be as good or better than adults' short-term memory (Loftus and Davies, 1984; Johnson and Foley, 1984), but children do fall prey, perhaps more easily than do adults, to suggestions they understand. Memory tends to improve with age up to adulthood (Brown, 1975). Children seem to notice items that adults might consider irrelevant, yet they tend to make more errors of omission than do adults (Neisser, 1984). Children sometimes try to fill in gaps in their memories by confabulating. Perhaps because children lack previous knowledge, they have difficulty relating events and organizing disparate elements into a cohesive whole (Johnson and Foley, 1984).

The issue of memory in infants and children is important clinically in such psychiatric disorders as post-traumatic stress disorder (Terr, 1988) and in children's accounts of alleged sexual abuse (Schetky and Green, 1988).

Finally, Piaget has commented that we reconstruct the past as a function of the present and that there may be no such thing as pure memories, i.e., all memories of early childhood, to a greater or lesser extent, may be "created" (reconstructed) from later material, with inferences and fantasies interwoven. Piaget once gave a fascinating example from his own memories of early childhood (Bringuier, 1980):

. . . I have a childhood memory of my own that would be absolutely splendid if it were authentic, because it goes back to an age when one doesn't have memories of childhood. I was still in a baby carriage, taken out by a nurse, and she took me down the Champs-Elysees, near the Rond-Point. I was the object of an attempted kidnapping. Someone tried to grab me out of the buggy. The straps held me in, and the nurse scuffled with the man, who scratched her forehead; something worse might have happened if a policeman hadn't come by just then. I can seen him now as if it were yesterday—that was when they wore the little cape that comes down to here (he motions with his hand) and carried a little white stick, and all that, and the man fled. That's the story. As a child I had the glorious memory of having been the object of an attempted kidnapping. Then—I must have been about fifteen—my parents received a letter from the nurse, saying that she had just converted and wanted to confess all her sins, and that she had invented the kidnapping story herself, and she had scratched her own forehead, and that she now offered to return the watch she'd been given in recognition of her courage. In other words, there wasn't an iota of truth in the memory. And I have a very vivid memory of the experience, even today. I can tell you just where it happened on Champs-Elysees, and I can still see the whole thing.

REFERENCES

Bornstein, M.H. (1975), Qualities of color vision in infancy. *J. Exp. Child Psychol.*, 19:401–419.

Bower, T.G.R. (1972), *Development in Infancy*. 2nd ed. San Francisco: Freeman.

Brackbill, Y., Adams, G., Crowell, D.H., and Gray, M.C. (1966), Arousal levels in newborn and preschool children under continuous stimulation. *J. Exp. Child Psychol.*, 3:176–188.

Bringuier, J.C. (1980), Conversations with Jean Piaget. Chicago: University of Chicago Press, p. 120.

Brown, A.L. (1975), The development of memory: knowing about and knowing how to know. In: *Advances in Child Development and Behavior* (Vol 10).

Campos, J.J., Langer, A., and Krowitz, A. (1970), Cardiac responses on the visual cliff in prelocomotor human infants. *Science*, 170:196–197.

Cohen, L.J., and Gelber, E. (1975), Infant visual memory. In: *Infant Perception: From Sensation to Cognition*. (Vol. 1) eds. L.J. Cohen and P. Salapatek. New York: Academic Press.

Eimas, P.D., Sequeland, E.R., Jusczyk, P., and Vigonto, J. (1971), Speech perception in infants. *Science*, 171:303–306.

Ellington, R.J. (1967), Study of brain electrical activity in infants. In: *Advances in Child Development and Behavior*, ed. L.P. Lipsitt and G.C. Spiker. New York: Academic Press.

Engen, T., Lipsitt, L.P., and Kaye, H. (1963), Olfactory responses and adaptation in the human neonate. *J. Comp. Physiol. Psychol.*, 56:73–77.

Fagan, J.F. (1979), The origins of facial pattern recognition. In: *Psychological Development from Infancy: Image to Intention*. ed. M.H. Bornstein and W. Kessen. New York: John Wiley & Sons.

Fantz, R.L., Ordy, J.M., and Udelf, M.S. (1962), Maturation of pattern vision in infants during the first six months. *J. Comp. Physiol. Psychol.*, 55:907–917.

Fantz, R.L., Fagan, J.F., and Mirander, S.B. (1975), Early perceptual development as shown by visual discrimination, selectivity, and memory with varying stimulus and population parameters. In: *Infant Perception: From Sensation to Cognition: Basic Visual Processes* (Vol I), ed. L. Cohen and P. Salapatek. New York: Academic Press.

Ferald, A. (1984), The perceptual and affective salience of mothers' speech to infants. In: *The Origin and Growth of Communication*. ed. L.C. Feagaus, R. Garvey, M.T. Golinkoff, C. Greenberg, J.N. Hardin. Norwood, NJ: Ablex.

Geschwind, N. (1965), Disconnexion syndromes in animals and man. Part I. *Brain*, 88:237.

Gibson, E.J. (1969), *Principles of Perceptual Learning and Development*. New York: Appleton-Century-Crofts.

Goldstone, S., and Goldfarb, J.L. (1966), The perception of time by children. In: *Perceptual Development in Children*. ed. A.H. Kidd and J.L. Rivoire. New York: International Universities Press.

James, W. (1890/1950), *The Principles of Psychology*. (Vol. 1) New York: Dover Publications.

Johnson, M.K., and Foley, M.A. (1984), Differentiating fact from fantasy: The reliability of children's memory. *J. Soc. Issues*, 40:33–50.

Kagan, J., and Lewis, M. (1965), Studies of attention in the human infant. *Merrill-Palmer Q.*, 2:95–122.

Kessen, W. (1967), Sucking and looking: Two organized congenital patterns of behavior in the newborn. In: *Early Behavior: Comparative and Developmental Approaches*. ed. H.W. Stevenson, E.H. Hess, and H.L. Rheingold. New York: John Wiley & Sons.

Kessen, W., and Bornstein, M.H. (1978), Discriminability of brightness change for infants. *J. Exp. Child, Psychol.*, 25:526–530.

Kobre, K.R., and Lipsitt, L.P. (1972), A negative contrast effect in newborns. *J. Exp. Child Psychol.*, 14:81–91.

Kosslyn, S.M. (1988), Aspects of a cognitive neuroscience of mental imagery. *Science*, 240:1621–1626.

Loftus, E. (1980), *Memory*. Reading, MA: Addison-Wesley.

Loftus, E.F., and Davies, G.M. (1984), Distortion in memory of children. *J. Soc. Issues*, 40:51–67.

Mills, M., and Melhush, E (1974), Recognition of mother's voice in early infancy. *Nature*, 252:123–124.

Muir, D., and Field, J. (1979), Newborn infants orient to sounds. *Child Dev.*, 50:431–436.

Neisser, Y. (1984), The control of information pickup in selective looking. In: *Perception and its Development: A Tribute to Eleanor Gibson*. ed. A.D. Pick. Hillsdale NJ: Lawrence Erlbaum, pp. 201–219.

Nowlis, G.H., and Kessen, W. (1976), Human newborns differentiate differing concentrations of sucrose and glucose. *Science*, 191:865–866.

Nurcombe, B. (1986), The child as witness: Competence and credibility. *J. Am. Acad. Child Psychiatry*, 25:473–480.

Nurcombe, B. (1990), The development of attention,

perception, and memory. In: *Child and Adolescent Psychiatry: A Comprehensive Textbook.* ed. M. Lewis. New York: John Wiley & Sons.

Petersen, S.E., Robinson, D.L., and Keys, W. (1985), Pulvinar nuclei of the behaving rhesus monkey; visual responses and their modulation. *J. Neurophysiol.*, 54:867.

Porter, F.L., Porges, S.Q., and Marchall, R.E. (1988), Newborn pain cries and vagal tone: Parallel changes in response to circumcision. *Child Dev.*, 59:495–505.

Posner, M.I., Petersen, S.E., Fox, P.T., and Raichle M.E. (1988), Localisation of cognitive operations in the human brain. *Science*, 240:1627–1637.

Ruddy, M.H., and Bornstein, M.H. (1982), Cognitive correlations of infant attention and maternal stimulation over the first year of life. *Child Dev.*, 53:183–188.

Schetky, D.H., and Green, A.H. (1988), *Child Sexual Abuse.* New York: Brunner/Mazel.

Terr, L. (1988), What happens to early memories of trauma? A study of twenty children under age five at the time of documented traumatic events. *J. Am. Acad. Child Adol. Psychiatry*, 27:96–104.

Weizmann, F., Cohen, L., and Pratt, J. (1971), Novelty, familiarity and the development of infant attention. *Dev. Psychol.*, 4:149–154.

3

ATTACHMENT BEHAVIOR

In the study of the origin of man, parenting and social relationships, monogamous pair bonding, specialized sexual-reproductive behavior, and bipedality have been proposed as vital precursors for the development of brain and human intelligence (Lovejoy, 1981). Embedded in this pivotal capacity for social relationships in general and the nuclear family in particular is the ability to form attachments. From the time of birth, infants are remarkably social creatures. The preadaptation of infants for social interaction and the complex processes underlying the development of attachments are presumably some of the evolved characteristics on which infant survival is based (Freedman, 1974).

Mutual, synchronous interaction with a stable and responsive caregiver is important for the infant's development. The infant often sets the pace for this interaction (Schaffer, 1977), in which the mothering person is an almost equal partner. The infant at birth is preadapted, so to speak, for survival and sociability. The infant sees, hears, sucks, and grasps in highly specific ways from the beginning (Bornstein and Kessen, 1979). The development of these functions depends upon the mutual, synchronous interactions between the infant and another person over time, with the infant often setting the pace for this interaction (Schaffer, 1977). Thus the infant appears to have innate active functions that (1) perform selectively, (2) have intrinsic rhythms and changes of state, and (3) are modifiable through interaction with another person. The mothering person is an almost equal partner in this interaction.

Klaus and Kennell (1976) have emphasized the importance of early contact between parents and neonate for the formation of attachment. They once stated that the mother and father must have close contact with the neonate during the sensitive period of the first minutes and hours of life. During this time the mother and father appear to exhibit species-specific responses to the infant when they are first exposed to the neonate, and the infant responds to the mother with some signal, such as a body movement or an eye movement.

Subsequent studies have confirmed the ease with which bonding can occur in the first few hours of life (Hales et al., 1977). However, the full process of attachment and relationships is not confined to the first few minutes of life, or even the first six months. Rather, the process is long and complex, with many fail-safe mechanisms built in that, on the whole, guarantee survival and attachment (Lamb, 1982; Klaus and Kennell, 1982; Korsch, 1983). All this is part of a new direction in the progress of the concept of attachment, in which the role of maternal attachment to the infant during the newborn period (particularly in relation to the care of the premature infant) is now considered as important as the infant's attachment to the mother (Barnett et al., 1970; Klaus et al., 1972). Interference in this interaction may be a factor in child abuse (Klaus and Kennell, 1976), divorce, and subsequent giving up of the infant (Leifer et al., 1972). Fathers can be, and are, involved in attachment as much as mothers (Parke, 1978; Pruett, 1987).

In their original work, Bowlby (1958; 1969) and Ainsworth (1963; 1973), drawing on ethology, evolutionary theory, psychoanalysis, cognitive-developmental theory, and control-systems theory, described and conceptualized how this earliest ,bond, or attachment, between an infant and another person is formed. From the beginning, other individuals, usually the parents, will exercise an attention-compelling influence on the infant that is unrivaled by any other single feature of the environment. By the same token, parents are attracted to the infant, leading to a situation in which an enmeshing of parent-infant interaction patterns occurs. There is then a progression in the infant from responding to rather primitive stimulus configurations that he or she abstracts from the total sensory input, to taking in people as a whole. Because the infant is exposed to just a few specific individuals initially, their characteristics are learned first.

The motivation is the process of learning itself; the more the infant seems interested in things, the more he or she wants to see; and since human beings appear to be by far the most interesting objects, those are the objects the infant wants to see more of.

What is the evidence for this?

Visual fixation occurs within a few hours after birth. During the first months of life the eyes are locked at a focal distance of about 8 inches; images nearer or farther are blurred. As it happens, 8 inches is about the distance of the mother's face during feeding. As noted previously (p. 14), the human face becomes the first object to acquire substantial visual meaning for the child. Faces begin to function as "social releasers" at around 3 months of age (Spitz, 1965), stimulating bids for social interaction on the part of the infant; this is also about the time that infants begin to vocalize responsively and when temporal regularities in mother-infant gaze appear (Jaffe, Stern, and Perry, 1973). Other sensory modalities are intimately involved in early mother-child interaction. In other words, all the infant's sensory systems are "go" and are functioning at birth or shortly thereafter, and

all contribute to the infant's attachment to the mother.

The infant's contribution to these processes has become increasingly clear (Bell and Harper, 1977). Individual differences can be observed in the newborn nursery and may contribute to patterns of interaction and attachment. Fries and Woolf (1953) have described some of these individual differences as "congenital activity types," and Chess and Thomas (1977) have elaborated the concept of "temperament" in the child. These inborn characteristics of each child do result, given an average expectable environment, in individual, intrinsic personality characteristics, a fact that parents have known for centuries.

In essence, the infant appears to be programmed to respond to, learn about, and become attached to that aspect of his or her environment that is most likely to ensure survival—namely, another person, particularly the mothering person. The strength of this process is suggested by the observation that even neglected or abused infants typically form attachments (Egeland and Sroufe, 1981) as do infants with Down Syndrome (Berry, Gunn, and Andrews, 1980).

Attachment, then, is an affectional tie that one person forms to another person, binding them together in space and enduring over time. Attachment is discriminating and specific. One may be attached to more than one person, but there is usually a gradient in the strength of such multiple attachments (Schaffer and Emerson, 1964b). Attachment implies affect, predominantly affection or love.

Bonding implies a selective attachment (Cohen, 1974) that is maintained even in the absence of the person with whom the bond exists.

Attachment behavior is behavior that promotes proximity to or contact with the specific figure or figures to whom the person is attached. Attachment behavior includes signals (crying, smiling, vocalizing), locomotions (looking, following, approaching), and contacts (clambering up, embracing, and clinging). Sucking, clinging, following, crying, and smiling become incorporated by 8 or 9 months. Attachment behavior is strongest in toddlers; bonding is most secure in older children (Rutter, 1976).

Bowlby (1958; 1969) in particular and later Ainsworth (1963; 1973) developed the idea that the act of smiling in infancy may be one of a group of "innate release mechanisms" that release a particular protective response in the mother. Thus at about 6 to 8 weeks, the infant first recognizes the facial configuration of the smile in the mother and can be said to imprint the mother as the person to whom he will turn. In turn, the mother is affected by this recognition of her by the infant in a way that increases her affectionate bond to the infant. At this point, mothers often experience a sense of being recognized by their child. The reciprocal behavior of the parents is the "caretaking behavior." Bowlby also proposed that the evolutionary function of the attachment behavior is to protect the infant from danger, especially the danger of attack by predators. The system may be activated by the hormonal state, environmental stimulus situation, and CNS excitation. The system is terminated in response to a specific terminating signal (e.g., attachment achieved) or by habituation. The attachment behavior system is in equilibrium with other important behavior systems, e.g., exploratory behavior, which is elicited by stimuli that have novelty and complexity or change (any of which may draw the infant away from the mother).

At least 15 kinds of attachment behavior have been described (Ainsworth, 1963):

1. Differential crying: The infant cries when held by someone other than the mother and stops crying when taken by her.
2. Differential smiling: The infant smiles more readily and more frequently in interaction with the mother than in interaction with another person.
3. Differential vocalization: The infant vocalizes more readily and more frequently in interaction with the mother than in interaction with another person.
4. Visual-motor orientation: The infant,

when apart from his mother but able to see her, keeps his eyes more or less continuously oriented toward her.
5. Greeting responses: On the mother's return after an absence, the infant smiles and shows general attachment.
6. Lifting of arms in greeting.
7. Hand clapping in greeting.
8. Crying when the mother leaves.
9. Scrambling over the mother: The infant climbs over the mother, exploring her person and clothes.
10. Following the mother: Once able to crawl, the infant attempts to follow the mother when she leaves the room.
11. Burying the face in the mother's lap.
12. Clinging: The infant clings tightly to the mother when apprehensive.
13. Kissing: The infant returns the mother's kiss.
14. Exploration from the mother with the mother as a secure base: The infant makes short excursions away from the mother but returns to her from time to time.
15. Flight to the mother as to a haven of safety.

These attachment behaviors may vary in intensity and, in certain pathological states, such as infantile autism, they may be absent or deviant.

WHEN DOES ATTACHMENT OCCUR?

The proportion of the life cycle during which attachment behavior is seen is highly species-specific and is sometimes sex-specific. Ethological work, starting with Lorenz's early work (1935), has suggested that some species, particularly those that are able to walk shortly after birth, are particularly likely to imprint or latch onto the first moving object they see, typically the mother. Subsequently, they follow her, and only her. Other species, whose young have a prolonged period of care prior to the ability to move independently, exhibit a more gradual formation of attachment to the mother. Sex effects are also noted. In female sheep, for example, attachment to the mother may continue into old age, so that a flock of sheep consists of young sheep who follow their mothers, who follow the grandmothers, who follow the great-grandmothers, and so on. Male sheep, however, break away from their mothers at adolescence, and become attached to older males. In geese, on the other hand, attachment ends by the end of the second or third winter, in both males and females. Examples of the evidence for attachment behavior in primates other than humans are found in the work of Harlow (with monkeys) and Goodall (with chimpanzees).

Attachment behavior in the human is modified by an important human characteristic: the extreme biological helplessness of the human infant. Yet during the first few days of life babies are soothed by being picked up, talked to, and cuddled, and they soon enjoy watching people, independent of being fed (although *not* being hungry helps). The human infant can distinguish his or her mother as a person by about 4 months of age, long before he or she can move toward her or cling to her. The infant can smile and vocalize and can follow her readily.

Ainsworth (1963) showed that by 6 months of age most infants in her study cried when their mothers left the room, and greeted their mothers with smiles, crows of delight, and lifting of the arms when the mothers returned—all examples of attachment behavior. This behavior increased in vigor between 6 and 9 months of age, so that when their mothers returned, the infants would quickly crawl toward them to reestablish proximity. Furthermore, clinging to the mother was shown to become especially evident after 9 months of age, particularly if the infant was alarmed by the presence of a stranger. This phenomenon has been confirmed in studies by Schaffer and Emerson (1964a) in Scotland.

Attachment during the first half-year is more or less indiscriminate; almost anyone can satisfy the infant's need for attention. After 6 months of age, a change occurs; people *other* than the mother *upset* the infant when they approach him or her. The infant shows so-called stranger anxiety. There is now a significant emotional relationship between the infant and the mothering adult or adults. Actually, the age range when this relationship occurs is probably from 5 to 12 months. In stranger anxiety, the infant's recognition of incongruity of perceptions means that he or she now can recall a representation of the familiar face when looking at the stranger's face. At this point the specific mother-child or, rather, child-mother bond becomes a very specific entity. The image of the mother now has some constancy, or permanence, in the infant's mind, and this image can be retrieved and called upon for reassurance. "Mother" has become an internalized object, a memory, that can be recalled and used as a basis for comparison.

Most infants are attached both to people other than the mother (although they are usually most strongly attached to the mother) and to inanimate objects. In general, these multiple attachments have similar goals, i.e., to achieve security. Both multiple attachments to people and attachments to inanimate objects appear to be associated with a *strong* tie to the mother.

On the other hand, infants who are *not* strongly attached to one mothering person (e.g., institutionalized infants) often have general impairment in their development of human attachments exhibiting either indiscriminant oversociability or social unresponsiveness; they are also *rarely* attached to inanimate objects such as cuddly toys. The fewer the caretakers, the greater the likelihood of attachment. That is, the more the care approximates to the strong "one mother" type of attachment, the better it is for the infant in terms of his or her attachments. Autistic children often exhibit failures in attachment, apparently on a biological basis (see pp. 348–350).

CONSEQUENCES OF ATTACHMENT

There are certain consequences of attachment. We will consider two: (1) *generaliza-*

tion to other people and (2) development of *schema* (see p. 31 for a definition) as a prerequisite for stranger anxiety and separation anxiety.

Generalization

Rheingold (1965) studied 16 six-month-old infants in an institution in which many volunteers cared for the children. For 8 babies Rheingold herself played the role of mother, 8 hours a day, 5 days a week, for 8 weeks (e.g., she bathed, diapered, played with, and smiled at the babies). Thus *one* person gave these babies *extra nurturance.* The other 8 babies were kept to the regular institutional routine, in which several different women cared for each child. All 16 babies were tested each week for the 8-week period and then each week for 4 weeks after the 8 weeks. The tests were of the babies' social responsiveness to three different groups of people: (1) the experimenter, (2) the examiner who gave the tests, and (3) a stranger (at the end of the 8 weeks).

The results of this study were that the 8 babies who had the special care showed more social responsiveness *not only* to the mother surrogate but *also* to the examiner than did the control group. That is to say, *generalization* had occurred.

Thus if an infant makes a set of responses to one class of objects, or people, he is likely to make them to similar objects, or people, provided that they are not too dissimilar from the original ones.

Development of Schema as a Prerequisite for Stranger Anxiety and Separation Anxiety

Stranger Anxiety. At 6 to 8 months of age, the infant has developed such a good schema of the mother's face that a stranger's face is now a discrepant one. One could, therefore, call stranger anxiety *a reaction to a discrepancy that is beyond the infant's capacity to assimilate or to make some other constructive response to,* such as asking, "Who is that?" (which the infant cannot do at 6 months but can do later).

Of course, by a later date the infant has also been exposed to many strange faces, so that he has also had opportunities to generalize and to form new schema. Later the strange face is also less discrepant and thus causes less anxiety. As a matter of fact, stranger anxiety is rare in institutionalized infants, who see a constant stream of strange faces, and it diminishes spontaneously in normal infants.

There is some evidence for a genetic factor in stranger anxiety; this evidence is found in a twin study carried out by Freedman (1965). Identical twins were compared with fraternal twins for the intensity of the fear of strangers. Freedman found that there was a greater concordance in the timing as well as the intensity of the fear of strangers between identical twins than between fraternal twins. There is also a sex difference. Schaffer (1966) found that stranger anxiety began earlier in girls than in boys.

Separation Anxiety. Separation anxiety, which begins at about 10 months and wanes at about 18 months, has two components: (1) the discrepancy produced when the child is placed in a strange environment without his mother and (2) the child's inability to make a relevant response that will bring him to his mother. The closer the attachment of the baby to the mother, the more frequent and intense is the separation anxiety.

Let us look at these two components of separation anxiety, particularly the child's inability to make a relevant response that will bring him to his mother.

Rheingold put a group of 10-month-old infants one by one in a strange room under four conditions: (1) with the mother, (2) with a stranger, (3) with toys, and (4) alone. Rheingold found that when the mother was present, nothing much happened and that when the infant was put in a *strange room and was without the mother* the infant cried (toys or strangers were of no help). When an infant was placed in a room with the mother—a room that had an open door that led to the strange, empty room in which the infant had cried—the infant crawled into the empty room, *but he did not cry, even though he was alone.* Instead, the infant stayed for a short period, looked around, and then crawled back to talk to the mother. The infant could now do something effective when he or she became anxious by the discrepant environment.

What the evidence adds up to is that once the mother's absence is no longer a discrepant event or once the child can do something about the mother's absence, separation anxiety, like stranger anxiety, should also vanish. It is of interest that the greater the number of figures to whom a child was attached, the more intense the attachment to mother as the principal figure was likely to be. Incidentally, the intensity and consistency with which attachment behavior is shown vary from day to day, and even from hour to hour. Hour-to-hour variation is due to such organismic factors as hunger, fatigue, illness, unhappiness, and pain, all of which lead to increased crying and following. Environmental factors, such as the presence of a stranger, arouse alarm, especially after 40 weeks of age. This alarm in turn intensifies attachment behavior.

The subsequent course of attachment behavior is something like this:

During the second year, the child begins to protest impending separation. Parents in turn often anticipate the protest, and try to hide from the child signs that they are about to leave.

By the end of the third year, most children are able to accept the mother's temporary absence, to engage in play with other children, and to be sufficiently comforted by a secondary attachment figure (e.g., a nursery school teacher) provided that (1) the figure is a familiar person, (2) the child knows where mother is, and (3) the child is not upset for any other reason, such as illness. Note again that the child's attachment to other children and teachers has nothing to do with having physiological needs met.

Attachment behavior after the age of 3 is less urgent and less frequent but still important. Rutter (1976), after reviewing the evidence, concludes that children may have difficulty in developing stable selective attachments for the first time after the age of 3 or 4 years.

Attachment persists through to age 6 or even older, when it is expressed sometimes as a wish to hold a parent's hand when going on an outing. It probably exists all through childhood, adolescence, adulthood, and even old age; daughters remain attached to their mothers, older people attach themselves to younger people, adults attach themselves to a group. These attachment behaviors intensify at times of stress, such as sickness and death, when people are drawn close to people they trust. Bowlby emphasizes that this reaction is an intensification of attachment behavior and *not* regression in the psychoanalytic sense.

Attachment behavior also has a strong affective component. The attachment figure is loved by the infant, and the sight or return of the mother is greeted with joy. Threat of loss creates anxiety and anger.

Detachment may occur following prolonged separation. When young children are admitted to the hospital and thus undergo separation, they may first react with acute distress and crying ("protest"), then with misery and apathy ("despair"), and finally with apparent disinterest ("detachment") (Bowlby, 1975). Single separation experiences rarely have long-term consequences. Long-term consequences follow acute stresses only if they are also associated with chronic stresses (Rutter, 1972). At the same time, recurrent stressful separations, such as recurrent hospital admissions, are associated with an increased risk of psychiatric disorders (Quinton and Rutter, 1976).

Major patterns of attachment in response to the "strange" situation have been described (Table 3–1) (Sroufe, 1983; Main and Solomon, 1986):

Table 3–1.   Major Attachment Patterns

Type
1. Securely attached
2. Anxious avoidant
3. Anxious resistant
4. Disorganized

The anxious avoidant child expects to be rebuffed, rejected, or abused, and tries to avert these experiences by becoming independent, sometimes at the expense of being too narcissistic.

The anxious resistant child tends to be a clinging child.

Interestingly, each pattern, once formed, seems to persist through childhood (Table 3–2) at least during the first five years of life.

What is of special interest is the developmental pathway taken by each of the patterns of attachment, each of which is formed during infancy.

SUMMARY OF PHASES IN THE DEVELOPMENT OF ATTACHMENT

First Phase: Undiscriminating Social Responsiveness (0 to 3 months)

From the beginning the infant has some capacity to respond differentially to different stimuli, and thus to discriminate them (Table 3–3). Further, the range of stimuli to which the infant is most responsive includes the range commonly emanating from human adults, including visual stimuli, auditory stimuli, and stimuli associated with feeding. Yet the infant does not initially discriminate between the persons presenting these stimuli.

When the infant does begin to discriminate between persons, he or she does so more readily through some modalities than others, e.g., tactile-kinesthetic discrimination first, then auditory discrimination, and the visual discriminations at approximately 8 weeks.

Second Phase: Discriminating Social Responsiveness (3 to 8 months)

The infant discriminates between familiar figures (mother and one or two others) and those who are relatively unfamiliar.

The first subphase includes discrimination and differential responses to figures close at hand, e.g., differential smiling, vocalization, and crying.

The second subphase includes discrimination between figures at a distance, e.g., as evidenced by differential greeting and crying when a particular figure leaves the room.

Third Phase of Active Initiative in Seeking Proximity and Contact (7 months to 3 years)

At about 7 months, a striking increase occurs in the infant's initiative in promoting proximity and contact. Voluntary movements of the infant's hands and arms are now conspicuous in his or her attachment behavior. Following, approaching, clinging, and similar behaviors become more significant. The infant is now attached.

In psychoanalytic theory, the infant at this stage is said to have an anaclitic-type of object relation. In cognitive-developmental theory, the infant at this stage is said to be at the fourth subphase of sensorimotor development and to have acquired "object permanence."

It is interesting to note here that Spitz talked of "organizers" as a concept to account for the factors that govern the process of transition from one level of development to the next.

1. The smiling response is the visible manifestation of a certain degree of organization in the psychic apparatus.

Table 3–2. Persisting Patterns of Attachment

1 yr:	secure	avoidant	resistant
4½ yrs:	cooperative	emotionally insulated	tense
	popular	hostile	impulsive
	resilient	antisocial	easily frustrated
	resourceful		passive
			helpless

Table 3–3.   Undiscriminating Social Behaviors

Primitive Behaviors	Orienting Behaviors	Signaling Behaviors
Sucking	Visual fixation	Smiling
Grasping	Visual tracking	Crying
	Listening	Vocalization
	Rooting	
	Postural adjustment	

2. The second organizer is the 8-month anxiety, which marks a new stage in development.
3. The third organizer is the achievement of the sign of negation and of the word "no." In Spitz's view it is the first abstraction, or symbol, formed by the child, usually at the beginning of the second year (around 15 months), when the infant turns his or her head away to refuse food (a response that has its origins in the rooting reflex).

Fourth Phase: Goal-Directed Partnership (3 years)

The infant in the fourth phase infers something about the mother's "set goals" and attempts to alter her set goals to fit better with his or her goals in regard to contact, proximity, and interaction (provided the mother does not dissemble about what her set goals are, e.g., to leave the infant at nursery school).

NECESSARY CONDITIONS FOR THE DEVELOPMENT OF ATTACHMENT

The following conditions are prerequisites for the development of attachment:
1. "Sufficient" interaction with the mother.
2. The ability of the infant to discriminate the mother or other attachment figure from other persons.
3. The ability of the infant to begin to conceive of a person as having a permanent and independent existence even when that person is not present to the infant's perception.

An infant's goal-corrected behavior probably becomes increasingly smooth and effective in parallel with the later stages of development of the concept of the object which, according to Piaget, is completed at about 18 months. Piaget suggested that the concept of *persons* as permanent objects evolves in homologous stages but in advance of the development of things as permanent objects, presumably because an infant finds people the most interesting external prototypes of objects.

FACTORS THAT INFLUENCE THE DEVELOPMENT OF ATTACHMENT

The following factors influence the development of attachment:
1. Sensitive phases in the development of infant-mother attachment. The sensitive phase during which attachments are most readily formed spans a period of months in the middle of the first year. It probably starts in the neonatal period. Provence and Lipton (1962) showed that infants kept in an institution until they are 8 to 24 months old find it difficult to become attached to a foster mother later, and that age range seems to be the upper limit of the sensitive phase for becoming attached for the first time.
2. Infant-care practices (e.g., feeding practices).
3. Maternal care, infant behavior, and mother-infant interaction. The mother's contribution to attachment is affected by such factors as her hormonal state, her parity and experience, and her personality. The infant's contribution is affected by such factors as wakefulness and activity level, crying, temperament, and biologic endowment.

4. Maternal deprivation (e.g., placement in an institution or severe maternal depression).

Strong attachments occur under the following five conditions:

    (a) When the interaction has a certain degree of intensity, as when a sensitive, responsive parent gives a great deal of attention to the child, talks with the child and, especially, plays with the child (Stayton and Ainsworth, 1973).

    (b) When the parent responds regularly and readily to the child's needs as signalled, for example, by crying. The child is likely to become strongly attached to a parent who can recognize and respond to the child's signals.

    (c) When the number of caretakers is limited. The fewer the caretakers, the greater the attachment.

    (d) When the child's own contribution is strong; that is, when his needs and signals are strong.

    (e) When the child is in the early sensitive phase (of imprinting), i.e., during the first two years.

Curiously, parental rejection, even to the extent of physical abuse, appears to increase the attachment behavior of the child. In 1963 Kovak and Hess did an experiment with chicks that confirms the existence of that phenomenon. First these investigators determined the critical attachment phase for imprinting in the chicks. Then they gave the chicks who were in this critical phase electrical shocks while the chicks were with their parents. (They did not give shocks to a control group.) They gave shocks to a group of chicks at a later time, well beyond the critical attachment phase. The chicks who were given shocks during the critical attachment phase actually followed their parents significantly more than did those who were not given shocks. The chicks who were given shocks after the critical attachment phase avoided their parents, presumably because they associated their parents with the shocks. Thus it appeared that the chicks who experienced pain during the phases when they depended on their parents to a tremendous degree for survival sought to get even closer to their parents.

Interestingly, infants in institutions have also been found to show more clinging and following behavior but to be less likely to show bonding and deep, lasting relationships than 4-year-olds reared in families (Tizard and Rees, 1975).

Attachment theory, detailed as it is, is still incomplete in that it does not account for a large area of functioning and behavior, even within the line of the development of the affectional tie between child and adult (Kagan, 1984). However, it is a promising avenue of inquiry. Attachment theory is important because it provides a basis for proper care of the premature infant, suggests principles for adoption practices, and provides clues for understanding child abuse and delinquency.

ATTACHMENT BEHAVIOR AND REGRESSION

Studies on attachment (Bowlby, 1969; Ainsworth, 1973) also raise interesting questions about behavior that is sometimes thought of as regression. The observation of interest here is that attachment behaviors, such as crying and clinging, become more prominent at times of stress, including separation, sickness, and death, particularly when there is no alternative solution. Clinically, one might ordinarily regard this behavior as regression. However, it is important to emphasize, as Bowlby does, that such behaviors may represent instead an intensification of attachment behavior, and not regression. The significance of this difference is twofold. First, intensification of attachment behavior must be recognized as a normal phenomenon and should be distinguished from pathologic or pathogenic regression. Second, even when regression does occur, it may at times similarly represent a return to an earlier, more stable level of organization and may therefore represent, in essence, a normal, and potentially adaptive, activity.

Note 2

From *Attachment and Loss*, Volume 1, *Attachment* by John Bowlby. © 1969 by the Tavistock Institute of Human Relations, Basic Books, Inc., Publishers, New York. Reprinted by permission.

So far as can be seen at present, the development of attachment behavior in human infants, though much slower, is of a piece with that seen in sub-human mammals. Much evidence supports that conclusion and none contradict it.

Present knowledge of the development of attachment behavior in humans can be summarized briefly under the same eight heads that were used. . . . to describe present knowledge of imprinting in birds:

   i. In human infants social responses of every kind are first elicited by a wide array of stimuli and are later elicited by a much narrower array, confined after some months to stimuli arising from one or a few particular individuals.

   ii. There is evidence of a marked bias to respond socially to certain kinds of stimuli more than to others.

   iii. The more experience of social interaction an infant has with a person the stronger his attachment to that person becomes.

   iv. The fact that learning to discriminate certain faces commonly follows periods of attentive staring and listening suggests that exposure learning may be playing a part.

   v. In most infants attachment behavior to a preferred figure develops during the first year of life. It seems probable that there is a sensitivity period in that year during which attachment behavior develops most readily.

   vi. It is unlikely that any sensitive phase begins before about six weeks and it may be some weeks later.

   vii. After about six months, and markedly so after eight or nine months, babies are more likely to respond to strange figures with fear responses, and more likely also to respond to them with strong fear responses, that they are when they are younger. Because of the growing frequency and strength of such fear responses, the development of attachment to a new figure becomes increasingly difficult towards the end of the first year and subsequently.

   viii. Once a child has become strongly attached to a particular figure, he tends to prefer that figure to all others, and such preference tends to persist despite separation.

We may conclude, therefore, that, so far as is at present known, the way in which attachment behavior develops in the human infant and becomes focused on a discriminated figure is sufficiently like the way in which it develops in other mammals, and in birds, for it to be included, legitimately, under the heading of imprinting—so long as that term is used in its current generic sense. Indeed, to do otherwise would be to create a wholly unwarranted gap between the human case and that of other species.

Note 3

From M.D.S. Ainsworth, and S.M. Bell (1970), Attachment, exploration and separation: Illustrated by the behavior of one-year-olds in a strange situation. *Child Development*, 41:49–67. Copyright © 1970, The Society for Research in Child Development, Inc. Reprinted by permission of publisher.

The following propositions are suggested as essential to a comprehensive concept of attachment. They are based on an ethological-evolutionary point of view, and have been formulated on the basis of reports of a broad range of investigations, including naturalistic studies of mother-infant interaction, and studies of mother-child separation and reunion in both human and nonhuman primates, as well as the illustrative strange-situation study reported here.

   1. Attachment is not coincident with attachment behavior. Attachment behavior may be heightened or diminished by conditions—environmental and intraorganismic—which may be specified empirically. Despite situationally determined waxing and waning of attachment behavior, the individual is nevertheless predisposed intermittently to seek proximity to the object of attachment. It is this predisposition—which may be conceived as having an inner, structural basis—that is the attachment. Its manifestations are accessible to observation over time; a short time-sample may, however, be misleading.

   2. Attachment behavior is heightened in situations perceived as threatening, whether it is an external danger or an actual or im-

pending separation from the attachment object that constitutes the threat.

3. When strongly activated, attachment behavior is incompatible with exploratory behavior. On the other hand, the state of being attached, together with the presence of the attachment object, may support and facilitate exploratory behaviors. Provided that there is no threat of separation, the infant is likely to be able to use his mother as a secure base from which to explore, manifesting no alarm in even a strange situation as long as she is present. Under these circumstances the relative absence of attachment behavior—of proximity-promoting behavior—can not be considered an index of a weak attachment.

4. Although attachment behavior may diminish or even disappear in the course of a prolonged absence from the object of attachment, the attachment is not necessarily diminished; attachment behavior is likely to reemerge in full or heightened strength upon reunion, with or without delay.

5. Although individual differences have not been stressed in this discussion, the incidence of ambivalent (contact-resisting) and probably defensive (proximity-avoiding) patterns of behavior in the reunion episodes of the strange situation is a reflection of the fact that attachment relations are qualitatively different from one attached pair to another. These qualitative differences, together with the sensitivity of attachment behavior to situational determinants, make it very difficult to assess the strength or intensity of an attachment. It is suggested that, in the present state of our knowledge, it is wiser to explore qualitative differences, and their correlates and antecedents, than to attempt premature quantifications of strength of attachment.

Note 4

From J. Bowlby (1988), Developmental psychiatry comes of age. *Am. J. Psychiatry* 145:1–10, pp. 2 and 3.

(1) . . . Emotionally significant bonds between individuals have basic survival functions and therefore a primary status. 2) They can be understood by postulating cybernetic systems situated within the CNS of each partner that have the effect of maintaining proximity or ready accessibility of each partner to the other. 3) In order for the systems to operate efficiently, each partner builds in his or her mind working models of self and of other and of the patterns of interaction that have developed between them. 4) Present knowledge requires that a theory of developmental pathways should replace theories that invoke specific phases of development in which it is postulated a person may become fixated and/or to which he or she may regress.

The bonds with which developmental psychiatry is principally concerned are those of child to parent and the complementary bond of parent to child. The key hypothesis is that variations in the way these bonds develop and become organized during the infancy and childhood of different individuals are major determinants of whether a person grows up to be mentally healthy . . .

When individuals of any age are feeling secure they are likely to explore away from their attachment figure. When alarmed, anxious, tired, or unwell they feel an urge toward proximity. Thus, we see the typical pattern of interaction between child and parent known as exploration from a secure base. Provided the parent is known to be accessible and will be responsive when called upon, a healthy child feels secure enough to explore. At first these explorations are limited both in time and space. Around the middle of the 3rd year, however, a secure child begins to become confident enough to increase time and distance away—first to half-days and later to whole days. As he or she grows into adolescence, the excursions are extended to weeks or months, but a secure home base remains indispensable nonetheless for optimal functioning and mental health. No concept within the attachment framework is more central to developmental psychiatry than that of the secure base.

REFERENCES

Ainsworth, M.D.S. (1963), The development of infant-mother interaction among the Ganda. In: *Determinants of Infant Behavior* (Vol. 2), ed. B.M. Foss. London: Methuen, pp. 67–112.

Ainsworth, M.D.S. (1973), The development of infant-mother attachment. In: *Review of Child Development Research* (Vol. 3), ed. B.M. Caldwell and H.N. Ricciuti. Chicago: University of Chicago Press, pp. 1–94.

Ainsworth, M.D.S., and Bell, S.M. (1970), Attachment, exploration and separation: Illustrated by the behavior of one-year-olds in a strange situation. *Child Dev.*, 41:49–67.

Barnett, C., et al. (1970), Neonatal separation: Maternal side of interactional deprivation. *Pediatrics*, 46:197–205.

Bell, R.Q., and Harper, L.V. (1977), *Child Effects on Adults*. Hillsdale: Lawrence Erlbaum Associates.

Berry, P., Gunn, P., and Andrews, R. (1980), Behavior of Down's syndrome infants in a strange situation. *Am. J. Mental Defic.*, 85:213–218.

Bornstein, M.D., and Kessen, W. (Eds.) (1979), *Psychological Development from Infancy: Image to Intention*. Hillsdale, N.J.: Lawrence Erlbaum Associates.

Bowlby, J. (1958), The nature of the child's tie to his mother. *Int. J. Psychoanal.*, 39:350–373.

Bowlby, J. (1969), Attachment. In: *Attachment and Loss*, (Vol. 1). New York: Basic Books.

Bowlby, J. (1975), Separation: Anxiety and Anger. In: *Attachment and Loss*, (Vol. 2). Harmondsworth: Penguin.

Chess, S., and Thomas A. (1977), Temperamental individuality from childhood to adolescence. *J. Am. Acad. Child Psychiatry*, 16:218–226.

Cohen, L.J. (1974), The operational definition of human attachment. *Psychol. Bull.*, 81:107–217.

Egeland, B., and Sroufe, L.A. (1981), Attachment and early maltreatment. *Child Devel.*, 52:44–52.

Fagan, J.F. (1979), The origins of facial pattern recognition. In: *Psychological Development from Infancy*, ed. M.H. Bornstein and W. Kessler. Hillsdale, N.J.: Lawrence Erlbaum Associates.

Fantz, R.L. (1975), Early visual selectivity. In: *Infant Perception: From Sensation to Cognition*, ed. L.B. Cohen and P.H. Salapatek. New York: Academic Press.

Freedman, D.G. (1965), Hereditary control of early social behavior. In: *Determinants of Infant Behavior*, (Vol. 3), ed. B.M. Foss. New York: John Wiley & Sons, Inc., pp. 149–159.

Freedman, D.G. (1974), *Human Infancy: An Evolutionary Perspective*. Hillsdale: Lawrence Erlbaum Associates.

Fries, M.E., and Woolf, F.J. (1953), Some hypotheses on the role of the congenital activity type in personality development. *Psychoanal. Study Child*, 8:48–62.

Hales, D., Lozoff, B., Sosa, R., and Kennell, J. (1977), Defining the limits of the sensitive period. *Dev. Med. Child Neurol.*, 19:454.

Jaffe, F., Stern, M., and Perry, M. (1973), Conversational coupling and gaze behavior in pre-linguistic human development. *J. Psycholinguist Res.*, 2:321–329.

Kagan, J. (1984), *The Nature of the Child*. New York: Basic Books.

Klaus, M.H., and Kennell, J.H. (1976), *Maternal-Infant Bonding*. St. Louis: C.V. Mosby Co.

Klaus, M.H., et al. (1972), Maternal attachment: Importance of the first postpartum days. *N. Engl. J. Med.*, 286:460–463.

Klaus, M.H., and Kennell, J.H. (1982), In: *Parent-Infant Bonding*, St. Louis, C.V. Mosby.

Korsch, B.M. (1983), More on parent-infant bonding. *J. Pediatr.*, 102:249–250.

Kovach, J.K., and Hess, E.H. (1963), Imprinting: Effects of painful stimulation upon the following response. *J. Comp. Physiol. Psychol.*, 56:461.

Lamb, M.E. (1982), The bonding phenomena: Misinterpretations and their implications. *J. Pediatr.*, 101:555.

Leifer, A., Leiderman, P.H., Barnett, C., and Williams, J. (1972), Effects of mother-infant separation on maternal attachment. *Child Dev.*, 43:1203–1218.

Lorenz, K.Z. (1935), Der Kumpan in der Umvelt des Vogels. *J. Ornithol. Berl.*, 83. English translation in *Instinctive Behavior*, ed. C.H. Schiller. New York: International Universities Press.

Lovejoy, C.O. (1981), The origin of man. *Science*, 211:341–350.

Main, M., and Solomon, J. (1986), Discovery of an insecure disorganized/disoriented attachment pattern. In: *Affective Development in Infancy*, ed. T.B. Brazelton and M.W. Yogman. Norwood, NJ: Ablex, pp. 95–124.

Parke, R.D. (1978), Perspectives on father-infant interaction. In: *The Handbook of Infant Development*, ed. J.D. Osofsky, New York: John Wiley & Sons, Inc.

Provence, S., and Lipton, R.C. (1962), *Infants in Institutions*. New York: International Universities Press.

Pruett, K.D. (1987), *The Nurturing Father*. New York: Warner Books.

Quinton, D., and Rutter, M. (1976), Early hospital admissions and later disturbances of behavior: an attempted replication of Douglas' findings. *Dev. Med. Child Neurol.*, 18:447–459.

Rheingold, H.L. (1965), The modification of social responsiveness in institutional babies. *Monogr. Soc. Res. Child Dev.*, 21:2, #63.

Rutter, M. (1972), *Maternal Deprivation Reassessed*. Harmondsworth: Penguin.

Rutter, M. (1976), Separation, loss and family relationships. In: *Child Psychiatry*, ed. M. Rutter and L. Hersov. Oxford: Blackwell.

Schaffer, H.R. (1966), The onset of fear of strangers and the incongruity hypothesis. *J. Child Psychol. Psychiatry*, 7:95–106.

Schaffer, H.R. (1977), Introduction: Early interactive development. In: *Studies in Mother-Infant Interaction*, ed. H.R Schaffer, London: Academic Press.

Schaffer, H.R., and Emerson, P.E. (1964a), The development of social attachments in infancy. *Monogr. Soc. Res. Child Dev.*, 29:1–77.

Schaffer, H.R., and Emerson, P.E. (1964b), Patterns of response to physical contact in early human development. *J. Child Psychol. Psychiatry*, 5:1–13.

Spitz, R.A. (1965), *The First Year of Life*. New York: International Universities Press.

Sroufe, L.A. (1983), Individual patterns of adaptation from infancy to preschool. In: *Minnesota Symposium on Child Psychology* (Vol. 16), ed. M. Perlmutter. Hillsdale, N.J.: Lawrence Erlbaum Associates.

Stayton, D.J., and Ainsworth, M.D. (1973), Individual differences in infant responses to brief, everyday separations as related to other infant and maternal behaviors. *Dev. Psychol.*, 9:226–235.

Tizard, B., and Rees, J. (1975), The effect of early institutional rearing on the behavior problems and affectional relationships of four-year-old children. *J. Child Psychol. Psychiatry*, 16:61–74.

4

COGNITIVE DEVELOPMENT

Some of the earliest manifestations of thinking in the infant involve the body. The infant reacts to a *sensory* stimulus with a *motor* reaction: place a finger in the infant's hand, and the infant grasps; place a nipple in his or her mouth, and the infant sucks; place a pattern in front of the infant's eyes, and he or she looks. This sensorimotor pattern is the earliest kind of thinking, and it starts with those innate patterns of behavior that were just noted: grasping, sucking, looking, and gross body activity.

The basic element in Piaget's theory of the child's cognitive development is the *schema*, which consists of a pattern of behavior in response to a particular stimulus from the environment. However, the schema is more than just a response, because the child also acts upon the environment. For example, the infant sucks in response to a nipple. The schema of sucking then becomes increasingly complex as the child reacts to and acts upon a wider range of environmental stimuli. Thus when the child can put a thumb into his or her mouth, the schema of sucking evoked by a nipple is gradually broadened to include this new and similar but not identical stimulus, the thumb. The new object (the thumb) is said to be *assimilated* (see Note 5) into the original schema. At the same time, the infant has to modify his or her sucking behavior slightly because the thumb is different in shape, taste, and other characteristics from the nipple. This act of modification, which Piaget calls *accommodation*, results in a new equilibrium. These two processes, assimila-

tion and accommodation thus proceed in ever increasing complexities.

Four major stages of development are described in Piaget's theory:

1. A sensorimotor stage—from about birth to 18 months.
2. A preoperational stage—from 18 months to 7 years.
3. A stage of concrete operation—from 7 years to adolescence.
4. A stage of abstract operations—adolescence.

Each of these stages is subdivided. Clearly, Piaget is presenting a developmental theory, or system, with stage sequences. However, what moves a child from one stage to the next, beyond the intellectual effort required to resolve a cognitive discrepancy, is still unclear, even in Piaget's theory. Although Piaget has a great deal to say about cognition, he has relatively little to say about affects or about the later influence of the environment on thinking.

SENSORIMOTOR STAGE

In the *sensorimotor stage* (0 to 18 months of age), there are six substages. They can be described as follows:

1. In the first month, the infant exercises a function, such as looking or grasping, simply because it exists.
2. During the next 3 to 4 months (from 1 to 4½ months of age) new schemas are acquired. They are usually centered on the infant's own body (e.g., his thumb) (so-called primary circular reactions).

31

3. Sometime between 4½ months to 8 or 9 months of age, the infant tries to produce an effect upon the object he sees or grasps, i.e., he now involves events or objects in the external environment (e.g., a rattle) (secondary circular reactions).

4. By 8 or 9 months to 11 or 11½ months of age, the infant begins to be aware of the existence of unperceived objects hidden, say, behind a pillow or in peek-a-boo games. This is also the time of so-called stranger anxiety. The mental image of the object has now achieved some degree of permanence in the infant's mind (object permanence).

5. In the first half of the second year (11 or 12 months to 18 months of age) the child explores more thoroughly an object and its spatial relationship, e.g., by putting smaller objects into and taking them out of larger ones.

   (a) The child initiates changes that produce variations in the event itself, e.g., dropping, for example, bread and then toys from different heights or different positions.

   (b) The child actively searches for novel events (tertiary circular reactions).

6. By the end of the second year (18 months to 2 years of age), the child shows some evidence of reasoning; mental trial and error replaces trial and error in action, e.g., the child uses one toy as an instrument to get another.

The use of toys and play for a child is essentially a form of thinking. If one gives a 2-year-old some beads, a box lid, and a Teddy bear, the child will soon place the beads on the box lid and set the Teddy bear beside it. The child will then pick up the beads, one by one, and put them to the mouth of the Teddy bear. In this way, the child recalls in play his experience of eating. The box lid and the beads seem to symbolize the plate and the food, and the Teddy bear seems to represent the child. Thus these external objects are organized in such a way as to represent the child's internal symbolization of eating.

In playing in this way, the child clarifies for himself or herself the mental representation of eating and is able to develop it further. Piaget calls this evocation of past activity in the present *deferred imitation*, a characteristic of symbolic thought.

By this time, words have emerged. At this stage, language is first of all an accompaniment to action that is derived from or based on deferred imitations. Gradually, a change occurs, and language, like play, becomes the verbal representation of a past action. The word then begins to function as a sign. At this stage, however, the child's language is still a private one; the child does not at first use adult meanings, syntax, and so on. In fact, it is very difficult for the 2-year-old to conceptualize; the child may know Tom, Dick, Harry, and Daddy, but he or she cannot understand man as an abstract concept. If the child says the word man, he or she means a particular person (usually the father). According to Piaget, it is not until the child is about 7 or 8 years old that his or her image and private language give way to the public verbal sign. At that age the *verbal sign*, rather than the image, is the signifier used in thought.

Deferred imitation, symbolic play, graphic imagery, mental image, and language constitute what Piaget calls the semiotic function, by which he means the ability to represent something (the signified) by means of something else (the signifier). The semiotic function is consolidated between 2 and 4 years of age.

PREOPERATIONAL STAGE

The *preoperational stage*, occurring roughly between the ages of 2 and 7, clearly reflects progress over the preceding stage of sensorimotor intelligence. Two substages are described: the stage of symbolic activity and make-believe play and the stage of decentration.

Symbolic Activity and Make-Believe Play (2 to 4 Years)

One can see in this substage the development of symbolic thought and of representation. Language becomes increasingly important as the child learns to distinguish between actual objects and the labels used to represent them. As a result, the child gradually becomes able to reason symbolically rather than motorically, as was the case in the sensorimotor period, when he or she was limited to the pursuit of concrete goals through action. Despite these significant advances, however, striking cognitive limitations to preoperational thinking distinguish it from the logical thought processes that emerge in the subsequent stages of concrete and, ultimately, formal operations.

There are a number of hallmarks of preoperational thinking. Principally, the child in the preoperational stage is unable to reason logically or deductively; rather, his judgments are dominated by his *perceptions* of events, objects, and experiences. A further limitation is that the child can attend to only one perceptual dimension or attribute at a time, to the exclusion of all others. The concept of *time* is also not available to a child at this stage. The child can recognize sequences and daily routines (e.g., mealtime, play time, sleep time, day and night, and Daddy's or Mommy's going and coming), but he has no concept of an hour, a minute, a week, or a month.

The preoperational child is also extremely egocentric. By that Piaget does not mean that the child is selfish per se. Rather, Piaget employs the term egocentric to refer to a certain cognitive limitation of the preoperational stage, namely, that the young child is conceptually unable to view events and experiences from any point of view but his or her own. The child is clearly the center of his or her own representational world. Similarly, the child is unable to differentiate clearly between self and the world, between the subjective realm of thoughts and feelings and the objective realm of external reality.

In addition, at the preoperational stage the child's reasoning is neither inductive nor deductive but what Piaget terms transductive. That is, the young child tends to relate the particular to the particular in an alogical manner. Events may be viewed as related not because of any inherent cause-and-effect relationship but simply on the basis of spatial and/or temporal contiguity or juxtaposition. Furthermore, the child at this stage is unaware of and therefore unconcerned about possible contradictions in his or her logic.

Let us look at Piaget's example of transduction in a 2-year-old child who makes the statement: "Daddy's getting hot water, so he's going to shave" (Piaget, 1951). The child is attempting to make an inference although he or she does not have the concepts yet to carry out the reasoning process. The child does have certain preconcepts: i.e., symbols that are neither general nor particular. For example, the child's symbol (preconcept) of *shaving* has in it Daddy, face, hot water, razor, soap, and bathroom, and the child's symbol (preconcept) of *hot water* has in it washing, face, soap, bathroom, and so the child makes the inference, "hot water is shaving."

The child does *not*, however, have a true concept (general symbol) of *shaving*, which would have in it a number of exemplars, such as shaving with hot water, shaving with an electric razor, and shaving with a brush. Nor does he or she have the true concept (general symbol) of *hot water*, which would have in it such exemplars as hot water for shaving, hot water for making tea, and hot water for washing.

The child in Piaget's example is simply reasoning from preconcept to preconcept (i.e., if x, than y) although there is not necessarily any relationship between the two preconcepts. That is what is meant by transduction, one of several forms of thinking at this stage.

Let us look at some of the other forms of thinking Piaget describes for the preoperational stage:

1. *Juxtaposition*, which simply means that parts are collected together, or juxtaposed, but are not related to each other.

For example, Piaget asked a 4-year-old child, "What makes . . . [an] . . . engine go?" The child answered, "The smoke." Piaget then asked, "What smoke?" And the child replied, "The smoke from the funnel." Here the child juxtaposed "smoke" and "engine" as cause and effect, without any knowledge of their actual relationship.

One sees juxtaposition in the child's drawings at the preoperational stage. For example, a child's drawing of a bicycle might consist of a picture such as that shown in Figure 4–1. The chain, cogwheel, and pedals are seen as necessary for the wheels to turn, but how they are actually related, attached, and work is a mystery to the child. The child concentrates on the parts, or details, of the experience without being able to relate the parts into a whole.

2. *Syncretism* is the term used when the child relates everything to everything else. The child concentrates on the whole of the experience without relating the whole to the parts. For example, Piaget asked a 4-year-old, "How does the bicycle go?" The child answered, "With wheels." Piaget than asked, "And the wheels?" and the child answered, "They are round." Piaget then asked him, "How do they turn?" You can guess what the child said: "It's the bicycle that makes them turn."

3. *Concentration* denotes the child's tendency to concentrate on one aspect of

a changing relationship to the exclusion of other aspects (Piaget, 1952). For example:

A row of eggs in egg cups is arranged as follows:

A 4-year-old child is asked if there is the same number of eggs as egg cups. He usually says yes. The eggs and the egg cups then are rearranged as follows:

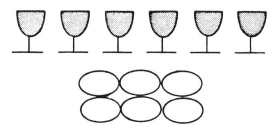

And the child is asked if they are the same now. The child usually answers no, explaining that there are more egg cups than eggs.

But if the eggs and egg cups are rearranged as follows,

the child will say that there are now more *eggs.* That is to say, the young child can concentrate on the arrangement of the eggs or on the arrangement of the egg cups, but not on both.

In addition, whichever is spread

apart more is an aspect of the relationship that dominates the child's thinking. That is, the child concentrates only on the aspect *spread apart*, which gives the appearance of an increase in number, and he or she cannot notice that the number of parts has not changed, that only their arrangement has changed.

4. Piaget calls this inability to manipulate mental representations in a rapid and flexible way *static representation*.

5. Another characteristic of the preoperational stage is *egocentrism* (Piaget, 1951), in which the child credits inanimate things with having feelings like his or her own and in which the child believes that thoughts have the power to change things. The child believes things exist because someone (e.g., mother) put them there, and he or she does not yet have any notion of a viewpoint other than his own. An example of potentially exasperating egocentrism occurs when a child makes up a new word and assumes that everyone knows what he or she is talking about. The child may, for example, talk of "stocks," an ordinary word but one that he or she has coined to mean socks and stockings.

Here are some other examples provided by Piaget:

—A 3½-year-old said, "The stairs are horrid; they hit me." (This could also be seen as an example of animism, which will be described shortly.)

—A 3-year-old girl heard a car that was moving on a road at a right angle to the road she was on, and she became frightened. She said, "I don't want the car to come here. I want it to go there." It so happened that the car went in the direction she wished. At that, she said, "You see, it's gone over there because I didn't want it to come here."

—A 6-year-old was asked, "Why are there waves on the lake?" Her reply was, "Because they've been put there."

6. Another characteristic Piaget describes

is the *animistic thinking* of the young child. The young child believes that virtually anything that moves is alive. Things such as stones or clouds are invested with feelings and motives. At the same time, mental events such as dreams are viewed as things that come in from the outside.

Let us now discuss animism in more detail to illustrate two other points besides the concept itself: (1) the *detailed complexity* that is involved in the apparently simple concept of animism and (2) *Piaget's method.*

Let us take the example of the child's concept of the sun and the moon. Here are a 6-year-old's responses to various questions Piaget asked:

Questions and answers about the sun:
—How did the sun begin? . . . *It was when life began.*
—Has there always been a sun? . . . *No.*
—How did it begin? . . . *Because it knew that life had begun.*
—What is it made of? . . . *Of fire.*
—But how? . . . *Because there was a fire up there.*
—Where did the fire come from? . . . *From the sky.*
—How was the fire made in the sky? . . . *It was lighted by a match.*
—Where did it come from, this match? . . . *God threw it away.*
Questions and answers about the moon:
—How did the moon begin? . . *Because we began to be alive.*
—What did that do? . . . *It made the moon get bigger.*
—Is the moon alive? . . . *No . . . Yes.*
—Why? . . . *Because we are alive.*

The child just quoted believes that the sun and moon are *alive* (animism) and that the sun resulted from the actions of an outside agent (artificialism). The child also believes there is some connection between human activities and activities of things (participation). Such is the *first stage* of the child's understanding of the origins of the sun and the moon.

Now let us look at the responses of an 8-year-old.

——How did the sun begin? . . . *It was a big cloud that made it.*

——Where did the cloud come from? . . . *From the smoke.*

——And where did the smoke come from? . . . *From houses.*

——How did the clouds make the sun shine? . . . *It's a light which makes it shine.*

——What light? . . . *A big light. It is someone in Heaven who has set fire to it.*

In the last three answers there is still evidence of artificialism, but in the first answer the child invokes only natural phenomena to explain the sun's origin. That is, in this second stage of the child's understanding of the origins of the sun and the moon, the artificialism and the animism are less blatant. In the third stage, the child gives up the notions of artificialism, animism, and participation and attributes the sun's formation to natural processes, however crudely he or she understands them.

The foregoing discussion gives a glimpse of Piaget's method. It is a clinical method rather than a fixed-questionnaire method. Neither is it a naturalistic method of simply observing the child's spontaneous utterances. It is clinical in the sense that the child's responses are followed up with nonleading questions. It has much in common with the *clinical interview*, in that it opens up things in an exploratory way. This fact is not surprising because Piaget really first came across the clinical method when he visited Bleuler, the Swiss psychiatrist well known for his study of schizophrenia.

Decentration (4 to 7 years)

The second substage of preoperational thinking occurs from 4 to 7 years of age, when an increased accommodation to reality, with progressive "decentering" from the child's own interests, perception, and points of view, gradually takes over. The decentering comes about partly because of the child's increased social involvement (e.g., at school). Social interaction virtually demands that the child use language, and he or she discovers that what one thinks is not necessarily the same as what one's peers think. The child begins to see himself or herself and the surrounding world from other points of view.

CONCRETE OPERATIONS

Let us take a close look now at the stage of *concrete operations*, from 7 to 11 years of age. The child at this stage is no longer bound by the configuration perceived at a given moment. He or she can now take into account two variables at once (e.g., height and width). Piaget (1952) performed what is now a classic experiment. One form of Piaget's experiment is as follows: A child is first asked to make sure that the amount of water in two identical beakers is the same:

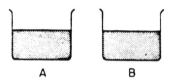

Water from one of the beakers is then transferred into a tall cylinder:

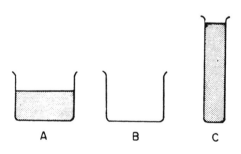

And the child is asked, "Is the amount of water the same?"

A child who is in the *preoperational* stage will say *no*, and then, if asked, will say why. He or she will say that either the water in the cylinder has more "because it's higher," or the water in the beaker has more "Because it's wider."

A child who is at the stage of *concrete operations* will be able to say, "*Yes*, the amount of water is the same," and if asked why, he or she will be able to say, "Because it's narrower [in the cylinder] and wider [in the beaker]."

The child has, in fact, mastered what Piaget calls the concept of *conservation*. The child acquires the concept of conservation not only for volume but also for number, class, length, weight, and area.

These types of conservation occur at different ages. The conservation of *objects* occurs quite early, usually by the end of the sensorimotor period. *Quantity* is conserved at 6 to 8 years of age, and *weight* at 9 to 12 years of age. Probably the variation in age at which different conservations are achieved is related to how easily the property can be dissociated from the child's own action. According to Piaget (1958), "It is more difficult to . . . equalize . . . objects whose properties are less easy to dissociate from one's own action, such as weight, than to apply the same operation to properties which can be objectified more readily, such as length."

This example of unevenness in the ontogenetic emergence of certain logical operations Piaget calls *décalage;* conservation, for example, does not appear in "full bloom." In the stage of concrete operations the child cannot think about his or her own thinking; that would be too abstract for the child at this stage. Hence the child at this stage has difficulty conceptualizing his or her emotions, a difficulty that Susan Harter calls *affective décalage.*

The child under the age of 6 or 7 is, in fact, tied to his or her immediate perceptions upon seeing the same quantity of water transferred from a beaker to a taller cylinder. The child is not able at first to reason that although the shape of the container is different, the amount of water is the same. Instead, the child will be more influenced by his or her perception

of which looks more because of the particular dimension that affects him.

After the age of 6 or 7, the child is no longer bound by his or her perception and can apply reasoning. The age of 6 or 7 marks a key turning point in the child's thinking. It is the age at which the child starts first grade. It also corresponds in psychoanalytic theory to the time when the oedipal struggle is thought to be resolved and the superego consolidated. Now the child can more readily distinguish between fantasy and reality. An interesting graphic representation of this cognitive change may be found in the child's drawings (Figs. 4–2, 4–3, 4–4).

In short, the major advance in the concrete operations stage is that the child can apply basic logical principles to the realm of concrete experiences and events without letting his or her perceptions interfere. Gradually his or her logical thought processes become organized into an increasingly complex and integrated network through which he or she confronts and systematically responds to the world around him or her.

FORMAL OPERATIONS

Piaget observed that "the great novelty that characterizes adolescent thought and that starts around the age of 11 to 12, but probably does not reach its point of equilibrium until the age of 14 or 15 . . . consists in the possibility of manipulating ideas in themselves and no longer in merely manipulating objects" (Piaget, 1969, p. 12). The young adolescent can now use hypotheses, experiment, make deductions, and reason from the particular to the general. The adolescent is no longer tied to his or her environment.

In fact, the difference between the formal operations stage and the concrete operations stage is that in the concrete operations stage the child can make statements about the environment based on relationships between objects or classes of objects, whereas in the formal operations stage the adolescent can produce new statements by combining previously arrived at statements. That is, he or

Stage: Sensorimotor period (ages 0–2). The child is most concerned with acting upon his environment.
Goal: Kinesthetic pleasure.

Fig. 4–2.   Reproduced with permission of David Fassler.

she can make theoretical statements independent of specific content, and can apply this way of thinking to all kinds of data.

The result of this is a further release from the concrete world. To quote Piaget (1958) again: "The most distinctive property of formal thought is this reversal of direction between reality and possibility; instead of deriving a rudimentary type of theory from the empirical data, as is done in concrete inferences, formal thought begins with a theoretical synthesis implying that certain relations are necessary and this proceeds in the opposite direction" (p. 251).

Let us look in more detail at the stage of formal operations. Again, Piaget used the clinical method. The classic experiment involves a pendulum. The adolescent is given a pendulum (Fig. 4–5) and then is asked, "What determines how fast it swings?" In response, the adolescent:

1. begins by imagining a series of purely hypothetical possibilities,
2. then holds some factors constant while varying others,
3. then observes the results, without bias, and
4. then draws the correct conclusion, i.e., length is a necessary and sufficient determinant of the speed of oscillation: a short pendulum swings fast, a long pendulum swings slowly. In propositional

Stage: Preoperational stage (ages 2– 7). The child is busy constructing theories about his body.

Goal: The drawing is a representation of the child's theories (not of reality).

Fig. 4–3.   Reproduced with permission of David Fassler.

logic terms, this particular pattern (i.e., of length determining oscillation) is called reciprocal implications. As such it forms one of a set of 16 binary operations or logical relations, usually called functions. The names of the 16 binary operations are:

Negation
Conjunction
Inverse of implication
Inverse of converse implication
Conjunctive negation
Independence of variable A to variable B
Independence of variable B to variable A
Reciprocal implication
Reciprocal exclusion
Inverse of independence of variable A to variable B
Inverse of independence of variable B to variable A
Disjunction
Converse implication
Implication
Incompatibility
Tautology

The essence of a binary model is that only statements involving two values are made,

Stage: Concrete operations, or logical thinking (age 7 to 11). The child now draws what he *knows* to be there.

Goal: The child is now representing what he knows to be there.

"Transparencies"

Fig. 4–4. Reproduced with permission of David Fassler. The child draws a "transparency," i.e., what the child knows to be there and "sees" through the opaque object that is hiding the known item.

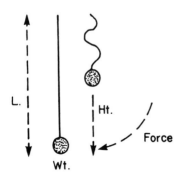

Fig. 4–5. Pendulum.

e.g., the pendulum is long or short. Following this arrival at the correct conclusions through the analytic use of these functions, the adolescent can then go further: he or she can now manipulate the conclusions to derive further concepts. These new manipulations are entirely mental operations, *completely* free from the original observations.

These new manipulations, or mental operations, are classified by Piaget into four groups that comprise the so-called INRC groups:

I = Identity
N = Negation
R = Reciprocity
C = Correlativity

The achievement of these formal operational cognitive structures represents the final stage in the process of human thought (but not, of course, in the *content* of human thought).

According to Ginsburg and Opper (1969), these logical models are in general:

1. unknown, i.e., unconscious to the adolescent
2. qualitative, not quantitative
3. abstractions, not protocols
4. an integrated system, in which each function operates in relation to all the others
5. ideal capabilities, not actual measures of performance
6. explanatory and, to some extent, predictive, i.e., given the knowledge of the structure of the adolescent's mental operations, one can predict in general terms how he or she will perform other, similar tasks.

The advent of formal operations provides the adolescent with capacities to conceptualize reality in sophisticated ways. These capacities have important implications for understanding adolescent idealism and morality (see pp. 214–220).

CRITIQUE OF PIAGET'S THEORY

Piaget's work was unappreciated in the United States for many years. This reflected his emphasis on the question of *why* and *how* intelligence developed rather than on *measurement* of intelligence *per se* and, in addition, his clinical approach was uncongenial to many American psychologists. Prior to the discovery of his work, descriptions of cognitive development were largely based on learning theory; Piaget's work highlighted the active engagement of the child as the organizer of his or her experience. It has had a profound impact on cognitive psychology.

This substantial body of work is, however, limited in several respects. Piaget's approach is less focused on the specific processes involved in intelligence as usually defined

(Siegler and Richards, 1982). His theory does not adequately deal with the question of how cognitive development comes about, e.g., in terms of the relative roles of (1) neurological maturation, (2) the social environment and education, (3) experience and experimentation, and (4) internal cognitive reorganization (equilibration) in response to contradiction and failure. The theory is only minimally concerned with the role of affect or motivation in the development of cognitive capacity. Studies of the theory have provided somewhat mixed support for Piaget's views.

Although the movement of children through the stages he outlined seems to conform to Piaget's predictions (Neimark, 1975), it is clear that modifications in the various situations used can result in responses that apparently contradict his theory, e.g., if familiar objects are used children may be able to perform more sophisticated cognitive tasks. Similarly, performance within a given stage is sometimes inconsistent across tasks, and the transitions between stages appear less discrete than Piaget's theory would predict (Siegler and Richards, 1982). Piaget minimized the ability of teachers or parents to accelerate development (what he termed "the American question"); it is clear, however, that children can be taught to engage in conservation tasks by helping them to attend to relevant stimuli (Gelman, 1969). A more recent approach has emphasized information processing as a model for children's cognitive development; this approach is more concerned with mechanisms and processes in the development of intelligence.

Despite these qualifications, Piaget's views have had profound significance for understanding cognitive development. At a theoretical level, his system has helped us understand the development of thought process and the particular difficulties the preoperational child has in resolving emotional as well as intellectual problems. For such a child, reality and fantasy may be poorly differentiated and affects more difficult to conceptualize (conserve). Second, at a practical level,

Piaget's system has implications for the way in which therapy is conducted with a child in the prelogical stage. Lastly, Piaget's system has proved to be a useful instrument in school consultation (Poulsen and Lubin, 1979) and pediatric care (Bibace and Walsh, 1980).

Note 5

From J. Piaget (1936), The origins of intelligence in children. (Margaret Cook, translator.) "Assimilation: Basic Facts of Psychic Life." International Universities Press.

Three circumstances induce us to consider assimilation the fundamental fact of psychic development. The first is that assimilation constitutes a process common to organized life and mental activity and is therefore an idea common to physiology and psychology. In effect, whatever the secret mechanism of biological assimilation may be, it is an empirical fact that an organ develops while functioning (by means of a certain useful exercise and fatigue). But when the organ in question affects the external behavior of the subject, this phenomenon of functional assimilation presents a physiological aspect inseparable from the psychological aspect; its parts are physiological whereas the reaction of the whole may be called psychic. Let us take for example the eye which develops under the influence of the use of vision (perception of lights, forms, etc.). From the physiological point of view it can be stated that light is nourishment for the eye (in particular in primitive cases of cutaneous sensibility in the lower invertebrates, in whom the eye amounts to an accumulation of pigment dependent on environing sources of life). Light is absorbed and assimilated by sensitive tissues and this action brings with it a correlative development of the organs affected. Such a process undoubtedly presupposes an aggregate of mechanisms whose start may be very complex. But, if we adhere to a global description—that of behavior and consequently of psychology—the things seen constitute nourishment essential to the eye since it is they which impose the continuous use to which the organs owe their development. The eye needs light images just as the whole body needs chemical nourishment, energy, etc. Among the aggregate of external realities assimilated by the organism there are some which are incorporated into the parts of the physico-chemical mechanisms, while others simply serve as functional and general nourishment. In the first case, there is physiological assimilation, whereas the second may be called

psychological assimilation. But the phenomenon is the same in both cases: the universe is embodied in the activity of the subject.

In the second place, assimilation reveals the primitive fact generally conceded to be the most elementary one of psychic life: repetition. How can we explain why the individual, on however high a level of behavior, tries to reproduce every experience he has lived? [This] is only comprehensible if the behavior which is repeated presents a functional meaning, that is to say, assumes a value for the subject himself. But whence comes this value? From functioning as such. Here again, functional assimilation is manifest as the basic fact.

In the third place, the concept of assimilation from the very first embodies in the mechanism of repetition the essential element which distinguishes activity from passive habit: the coordination of the new with the old which foretells the process of judgment. In effect, the reproduction characteristic of the act of assimilation always implies the incorporation of an actual fact into a given schema, this schema being constituted by the repetition itself. In this way assimilation is the greatest of all intellectual mechanisms and once more constitutes the relation to them, the truly basic fact. . . .

REFERENCES

Bibace, R., and Walsh, M.E. (1980), Development of children's concept of illness. *Pediatrics*, 66:912–917.

Gelman, R. (1969), Conservation acquisition: A problem of learning to attend to relevant attributes. *Cognitive Psychol.*, 7:167–187.

Neimark, E.D. (1975), Intellectual development in adolescence. In: *Review of Child Development Research*, Vol. 4. ed. F.D. Horowitz. Chicago: University of Chicago Press.

Ginsburg, H., Opper, S. (1969), *Piaget's Theory of Intellectual Development*. Englewood Cliffs, N.J.: Prentice-Hall, Inc.

Piaget, J. (1936), The origins of intelligence in children, trans. Margaret Cook. In: *The Essential Piaget*, ed. H.E. Gruber and J.J. Vonèche. New York: Basic Books, 1977, pp. 215–249.

Piaget, J. (1951), *Play, Dreams and Imitation in Childhood*, trans. C. Gattegno and F.M. Hodgson. New York: Norton.

Piaget, J. (with Alina Szeminska) (1952), *The Child's Conception of Number*, trans. C. Gattegno and F.M. Hodgson. London: Routledge & Kegan Paul.

Piaget, J. (1954), *The Child's Conception of Physical Causality*, trans. M. Cook. New York: Basic Books.

Piaget, J. (1958), *The Growth of Logical Thinking*. New York: Basic Books.

Piaget, J. (1969), The intellectual development of the adolescent. In: *Adolescence: Psychosocial Perspec-*

tives, ed. G. Caplan and S. Lebovici. New York: Basic Books, pp. 22–26.

Poulsen, M.K., and Lubin, G.I. (Eds.) (1979), *Piagetian Theory and Its Implications for Helping Professionals.* Proceedings, Eighth Interdisciplinary Conference, Vol. II, Co-sponsored by University Affiliated Program, Children's Hospital of Los Angeles and the University of Southern California Schools of Education and Religion. USC Bookstore, University Park, Los Angeles.

Siegler, R.S., and Richards, D.D. (1982), The development of intelligence. In: *Handbook of Human Intelligence.* ed. R.J. Sternberg. Cambridge: Cambridge University Press.

5

LANGUAGE DEVELOPMENT

Many species have the ability to communicate. Animals exhibit various forms of communication, such as signs signalling fear, alarm, and sexual excitement. Human language, however, has a number of unique characteristics; it has meaning, permits tremendous productivity and creativity, and can be independent of the constraints of the immediate situation (Brown, 1973). According to Lenneberg (1969), language has the following six characteristics:

1. It is present in all cultures.
2. Its onset is age-correlated.
3. There is only one acquisition strategy for infants everywhere.
4. It is based intrinsically upon the same formal operating characteristics, whatever its outward form.
5. These operating characteristics have apparently remained constant throughout recorded history.
6. It is a form of behavior that may be impaired specifically by circumscribed brain lesions.

Actual language begins when the brain has matured to two thirds of its full extent (the brain has reached about four fifths of its adult weight by age 3 [Marshall, 1968]). Conversely, when the brain is fully matured, language acquisition becomes more difficult. Bogen (1969) has also suggested that there are two distinct minds, each related to a particular hemisphere (the left for language and verbal activity; the right for nonlanguage and nonverbal functions, such as the capacity for apposing or comparing perceptions, schemas, and engrams) (see also Farah et al., 1985;

Kosslyn et al., 1985; Deleval et al., 1983). For example, musical capacity has been associated with the right hemisphere (Alajouanine, 1948; Critchley, 1953; Luria, 1966; Schlesinger, 1962). At the same time, under certain circumstances, the left cerebral hemisphere is sometimes better at mental imagery (Kosslyn, 1988).

Although a vast amount of information about the acquisition of language was obtained prior to the 1950's, this information mostly described the kinds of sounds or words children made and their errors in language use (Menyuk, 1971). Subsequent studies have focused on the processes by which children understand and learn language and the early processes that serve as its basis. There is considerable debate about whether language is best understood as a biologic phenomenon (Lenneberg, 1967), an innate given (Chomsky, 1957), or an acquired or learned function (Statts, 1971). Does cognitive development determine language (Piaget, 1923; Inhelder, 1971)? Or does language structure thought and culture (Vygotsky, 1962 [1934]; Luria, 1976; Whorf, 1956)? This search for an explanation of how language develops continues; in the meantime it remains a mystery. In any event, children seem to learn fundamental language rules rather than specific grammatical constructions (Brown, 1973).

The capacity to discriminate between different sounds is present in the newborn (Friedlander, 1970). Indeed, from the beginning the infant is virtually programmed to move in rhythm to the human voice (Condon and Sander, 1974), and will orient with eyes, head, and body to animate sound stimuli (Mills, 1974). Infants 1 to 4 months of age can perceive acoustical cues basic in speech, and are thus essentially prepared for hearing the components of language (Eimas, Siqueland, Jusczyk, and Vigorito, 1971; Aslin, Pisoni, and Jusczyk, 1983).

Subsequent language development correlates most closely with motor development although the two functions are not necessarily causally related in any specific way (see Note 6). Crying, which is present during fetal life, becomes differentiated during the first few months into recognized cries related to hunger, discomfort, pain, pleasure, and other stimuli (Wolff, 1969). As crying decreases, cooing increases and vowel sounds (e.g., "oo") begin to dominate. Consonants and babbling begin to appear at about 5 months of age and words at about 1 year of age, with a range of 8 to 18 months of age (Morley, 1965). At the same time, by 1 year of age the infant discriminates between and responds to differences in language, depending on who is speaking and how he or she is speaking (e.g., the intonation and the amount of repetition used). Comprehension during the first year of life is less readily studied; it does appear that even at 1 to 2 months of age infants can distinguish among various speech sounds (Eimas, 1985). By 8 to 12 months of age, infants can associate words with objects although they probably make considerable use of context and other cues. It does appear that in infancy, as indeed throughout life, receptive abilities are somewhat more advanced than expressive ones. Vocabulary gradually increases to about 200 words by age 2. Nouns appear first, then verbs, adjectives, and adverbs. Pronouns appear by about age 2, and conjunctions after age 2½. By this time, too, the child's understanding of language has increased immensely. The child's play at this stage in effect represents his or her "inner language." Between ages 2 and 4 the child has acquired, or learned, most of the fundamental (as opposed to the academic) rules of grammar although how he or she does it is not known. Characteristic errors are made

during this period as the child attempts to generalize rules (e.g., in relation to use of irregular verbs). Similarly, errors in articulation are typical during the preschool period ("wabbit" for "rabbit").

Although the basic capacity for, and form of, language remains more or less constant from culture to culture, the rate of acquisition of vocabulary and syntax is affected by the social environment. Interestingly, the earliest production of human sounds is relatively unaffected by reduced speech in the parents, as occurs in, for example, families with congenitally deaf mothers (Lenneberg et al., 1965), and subsequent emergence of language and stage sequences may occur at the usual times even under such an adverse circumstance.

The child apparently has a built-in capacity to abstract various universal relationships and regularities in the particular language he or she hears, and he or she uses this capacity to construct an operation by means of which he or she can apply its principles for the formulation of an infinite number of sentences. Such an operation for language is obviously far more economical and powerful than anything the child might accrue or learn from simple imitation. Moreover, the capacity for this operational work seems not only to be related to the child's general cognitive capacities but also to be an integral part of the child's uniquely human cognition. Thus, a simple learning theory (stimulus-response) model does not appear adequate to account for the complexity of children's language.

As the child develops and moves from stage to stage, he or she develops the capacity to react to increasingly complex stimuli, starting with intonation and moving through articulation of specific sounds to special syntactical and semantic stimuli. In this way, the child learns a linguistic code. All children appear to follow the same sequence in the development of phonology, syntax, and semantics.* Chomsky's theory of generative trans-

---

*Phonology = the sound structure of morphemes, phonemes, and words.
Syntax = categories, such as noun, verb, sentence.
Semantics = the meaning of words and utterances and the relationships between them.

formational grammar (1957) suggests that in some way, perhaps through "innate intellectual structures," the child develops a basic grammar that can generate an infinite number of sentences and an optional transformational grammar that transforms the basis of a sentence into its various forms (e.g., passive and interrogative).

Alternatively, these inner structures may derive from the sensorimotor schemas (Piaget, 1954). Indeed, the formation of such schemas during the long sensorimotor stage may be essential for the subsequent emergence of language and linguistic competence. Language in this view is one expression of what Piaget terms the semiotic function, which includes symbolic games, imagery, and imitation (Inhelder, 1971). Early schemas of experience precede symbolic language, and language comprehension precedes language production (children understand words and sentences long before they can say them) (Lovell and Dixon, 1967).

There is no satisfactory psychoanalytic theory for language acquisition (Wolff, 1967). The child begins to use language as a symbolic instrument, initially—and necessarily— through the help of the mothering person whom we can call "the mother." For example, the mother uses a word (e.g., "Dada" or "Mama," then "Daddy" or "Mommy") as a symbol, and in so doing she helps in the organization of the symbolizing process that is taking place within the infant. She does not create that process within the infant; she facilitates its development. Initially, of course, considerable overextension occurs; a child may call all men Daddy (or all four-legged animals doggie) until further accommodation of the concepts, or schemas, of Daddy (or doggie) occurs.

It is likely that the mother's spoken words initially are experienced by the infant as tones and rhythms, rather than as words with meanings, and as such are part of the unprecedented kinesthetic, tactile, visual, auditory, olfactory, and gustatory bombardment that the infant tries to assimilate and organize into schemas. Eventually, the child's percept of,

say, "mother" and the word "Mother," already linked, becomes better defined. In this sense mothers are sensitive language teachers of their children (Moerk, 1974). The sensitive timing, repetition, and associated pleasurable affects with which the mother uses words for labeling, shaping, and so on, serve to stimulate the development of language. (Curiously, mothers seem to talk more to their baby girls than to their baby boys [Halverson and Waldrop, 1970]).

Reinforcement may be more important for phonetic and semantic development than for syntactic development (Brown and Hanlon, 1970). The best stimulus for syntactical development appears to be a rich conversational interchange without any attempt to modify the child's utterances (Cazden, 1966).

Children continue to learn phonology, syntax, and semantics throughout the school years. The utterances of young children appear to depend on the support of the nonlinguistic environment. For example, if one asks a young child a question "out of the blue," one often draws a blank (Bloom, 1975). Young children tend to respond more readily when they are asked to talk about events that are in a more immediately perceived context (Brown and Bellugi, 1964).

Linguistic shifts occur continuously. For example, at about age 6 or 7, children shift from making syntagmatic responses to making paradigmatic responses (Francis, 1972). Syntagmatic associations are response items that are in a grammatical class different from that of the stimulus (i.e., the words just "go together," e.g., hot–bath, or apple–eat), whereas paradigmatic associations are response items that belong to the same grammatical class as the stimulus (e.g., hot–cold, or apple–pear). In addition, prior to age 6 or 7 children link temporal succession to succession of enunciation, e.g., a young child will interpret the sentence "The girl goes upstairs when the boy has parked the car" to mean that the girl goes upstairs first and the boy parks the car afterward (Ferreiro, 1971). After age 6 to 7, the child is no longer tied to this concrete perception of sequence. Furthermore, sometime between ages 5 and 10, children become more conscious of the structure of the language they use (Nelson, 1977).

Finally, the child is able to speak and understand language independently of the context in which it occurs. At about age 12, when the child is in the stage of logical operations, language becomes a means of knowing.

Several external factors may influence this early development, particularly early symbolic language development. Infants who have been "maternally deprived," and perhaps particularly deprived of verbal stimulation (Langmeir and Matejcek, 1975), have an incomplete development of the capacity to symbolize, especially the capacity for language and abstract thinking (Provence and Lipton, 1962).

More recently, attention has been paid to the long-range effects of patterns of care in the neonatal period. For example, Ringler and his colleagues (1975) have demonstrated that the amount of mother-child contact in the neonatal period influences the amount and kind of speech patterns used by mothers interacting with their children as late as 2 years of age. Specifically, they found that mothers who had had an additional 16 hours of contact with their infants (i.e., besides the usual minimum contact in the first 3 days after birth) used significantly more questions, adjectives, and words per proposition, and fewer command words and content words when talking with their children than did the mothers in the control group. Ringler and his colleagues suggested that this difference in maternal language stimulation, brought about by hospital care practices, might be an important factor in shaping linguistic behavior in the young child.

Certain other environmental and child-rearing practices also influence language development and, consequently, social development. For example, twins who are reared in close proximity and without much adult stimulation will develop idioglossia. Luria and Yudovich (1959) gave a dramatic example of gross speech retardation in their study of two 5-year-old identical twin boys: "As a rule,

our twins' speech acquired meaning only in a concrete-active situation. Outside this situation a word either did not possess any kind of permanent meaning, or only indicated what they were talking about without disclosing sufficiently clearly in what sense it was being used" (p. 40). When the twins were separated and placed in a special social situation in which they were compelled to speak with others in order to communicate with them, a rapid development of speech occurred.

Hearing children reared by deaf parents are able to develop adequate spoken language when oral stimuli are provided by others and the parents use gestures (Critchley, 1967). Children reared in bilingual households have no difficulty in developing speech, unless they are of low intelligence or social prejudices are present (Peal and Lambert, 1962; Soffietti, 1955).

The role of physical deprivation in the development of language is less clear. The lack of clarity has to do principally with the difficult methodologic problems of researching the subject. All that can be said with certainty is that factors such as severe malnutrition, associated as they often are with multiple physical insults, produce a language deficiency that is not easily reversed by nutritional rehabilitation (Lefevre, 1975).

Delayed speech and language development may occur with mental retardation, deafness, cerebral palsy, developmental disorders, and infantile autism. Congenitally deaf children, as would be expected, have considerable difficulty in learning language; interestingly even before they are exposed to conventional sign language they often spontaneously develop relatively complicated systems of gestural communication (Goldin-Meadow and Mylander, 1983). Before age 4, injury to the left hemisphere may result in transient aphasia; however, language development will resume if the right hemisphere is intact. Persisting language impairment does not usually occur after unilateral lesions in the first few years of life (Lenneberg, 1967). Disease or injury to the left hemisphere that

Note 6

From E.H. Lenneberg (1967), *Biochemical Foundation of Language*. New York: John Wiley & Sons, Inc., pp. 128–130.

DEVELOPMENTAL MILESTONES IN MOTOR AND LANGUAGE DEVELOPMENT

At the completion of:	*Motor Development*	*Vocalization and Language*
12 weeks	Supports head when in prone position; weight is on elbows; hands mostly open; no grasp reflex	Markedly less crying than at 8 weeks; when talked to and nodded at, smiles, followed by squealing, gurgling sounds usually called *cooing*, vowel-like in character and pitch-modulated; sustains cooing for 15–20 seconds
16 weeks	Plays with a rattle placed in hands (by shaking it and staring at it), head self-supported; tonic neck reflex subsiding	Responds to human sounds more definitely: turns head; eyes seem to search for speaker; occasionally some chuckling sounds
20 weeks	Sits with props	The vowel-like cooing sounds begin to be interspersed with more consonantal sounds; labial fricatives, spirants, and nasals are common; acoustically, all vocalizations are different from the sounds of the mature language of the environment
6 months	Sitting: bends forward and uses hands for support; can bear weight when put into standing position, but cannot yet stand with holding on; reaching: unilateral; grasp: no thumb apposition yet; releases cube when given another	Cooing changing into babbling resembling one-syllable utterances; neither vowels nor consonants have fixed recurrences; most common utterances sound somewhat like ma, mu, da, or di
8 months	Stands holding on; grasps with thumb apposition; picks up pellet with thumb and finger tips	Reduplication (or more continuous repetitions) becomes frequent; intonation patterns become distinct; utterances can signal emphasis and emotions
10 months	Creeps efficiently; takes side-steps, holding on; pulls to standing position	Vocalizations are mixed with sound-play such as gurgling or bubble-blowing; appears to wish to imitate sounds, but the imitations are never quite successful; beginning to differentiate between words heard by making differential adjustment
12 months	Walks when held by one hand; walks on feet and hands—knees in air; mouthing of objects almost stopped; seats self on floor	Identical sound sequences are replicated with higher relative frequency of occurrence, and words (mamma or dadda) are emerging; definite signs of understanding some words and simple commands (show me your eyes)
18 months	Grasp, prehension, and release fully developed; gait stiff, propulsive, and precipitated; sits on child's chair with only fair aim; creeps downstairs backward; has difficulty building tower of 3 cubes	Has a definite repertoire of words—more than three, but less than 50; still much babbling but now of several syllables with intricate intonation pattern; no attempt at communicating information and no frustration for not being understood; words may include items such as thank you or come here, but there is little ability to join any of the lexical items into spontaneous two-item phrases; understanding is progressing rapidly

occurs after the early teens may result in permanent loss of language. At this age, the brain has fully matured, and further development does not occur (Geschwind, 1972; see Note 7).

Note 7

When a word is heard, the output from the primary auditory area of the cortex is received by Wernicke's areas. If the word is to be spoken, the pattern is transmitted from Wernicke's area to Broca's area, where the articulatory form is aroused and passed on to the motor area that controls the movement of the muscles of speech. If the spoken word is to be spelled, the auditory pattern is passed to the angular gyrus, where it elicits the visual pattern. When a word is read, the output from the primary visual areas passes to the angular gyrus, which in turn arouses the corresponding auditory form of the word in Wernicke's area. It should be noted that in most people comprehension of a written word involves arousal of the auditory form in Wernicke's area. Wernicke argued that this was the result of the way most people learn written language. He thought, however, that in people who were born deaf but had learned to read, Wernicke's area would not be in the circuit.

According to this model, if Wernicke's area is damaged, the person would have difficulty comprehending both spoken and written language. He should be unable to speak, repeat, and write correctly. The fact that in such cases speech is fluent and well articulated suggests that Broca's area is intact but receives inadequate information. If the damage were in Broca's area, the effect of the le-

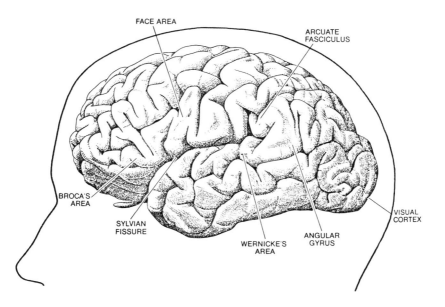

PRIMARY LANGUAGE AREAS of the human brain are thought to be located in the left hemisphere, because only rarely does damage to the right hemisphere cause language disorders. Broca's area, which is adjacent to the region of the motor cortex that controls the movement of the muscles of the lips, the jaw, the tongue, the soft palate and the vocal cords, apparently incorporates programs for the coordination of these muscles in speech. Damage to Broca's area results in slow and labored speech, but comprehension of language remains intact. Wernicke's area lies between Heschl's gyrus, which is the primary receiver of auditory stimuli, and the angular gyrus, which acts as a way station between the auditory and the visual region. When Wernicke's area is damaged, speech is fluent but has little content and comprehension is usually lost. Wernicke and Broca areas are joined by a nerve bundle called the arcuate fasciculus. When it is damaged, speech is fluent but abnormal, and patient can comprehend words but cannot repeat them.

sion would be to disrupt articulation. Speech would be slow and labored but comprehension should remain intact.

REFERENCES

Alajouanine, T. (1948), Aphasia and artistic realization. *Brain*, 71:229–241.

Aslin, R.N., Pisoni, D.B., and Jusczyk, P.W. (1983), Auditory development and speech perception in infancy. In: *Handbook of Child Psychology*, Vol. 2, ed. P. Mussen. New York: John Wiley & Sons, Inc.

Bloom, L. (1975), Language development review. In: *Review of Child Development Research*, ed. F.R. Horowitz. Chicago: University of Chicago Press, 4:245–303.

Bogen, J.E. (1969), The other side of the brain. *Bull. Los Angeles Neurol. Soc.*, 34:135–162.

Brown, R. (1973), *A First Language: The Early Stages*. Cambridge, Mass.: Harvard University Press.

Brown, R., and Bellugi, N. (1964), Three processes in the child's acquisition of syntax. *Harvard Educ. Rev.*, 34:133–151.

Brown, R. and Hanlon, C. (1970), Derivational complexity and order of acquisitions of speech. In: *Cognition and the Development of Language*, ed. J.R. Hayes. New York: John Wiley & Sons, Inc.

Cazden, C. (1966), Subcultural differences in child language: An interdisciplinary review. *Merrill-Palmer Q.*, 12:185–219.

Chomsky, N. (1957), *Syntactic Structures*. The Hague: Mouton.

Condon, W.S., and Sander, L.W. (1974), Neonate movement is synchronised with adult speech: Interactional participation and language acquisition. *Science*, 183:99–101.

Critchley, E. (1953), *The Parietal Lobes*. London: E. Arnold.

Critchley, E. (1967), Language development of hearing children in a deaf environment. *Dev. Med. Child Neurol.*, 9:274–280.

Deleval, J., DeMol, J., and Noterman, J. (1983), Loss of mental images. *Acta Neurol. Belg.*, 83:61–70.

Eimas, P.D. (1985), The perception of speech in early infancy. *Sci. Am.*, 252:46–52.

Eimas, P.D., Siqueland, E.R., Jusczyk, P., and Vigorito, J. (1971), Speech perception in infants. *Science*, 171:303–306.

Farah, M.J., Gazzaniga, M.S., Holtaman, J.D., and Kosslyn, S.M. (1985), A left hemisphere basis for visual mental imagery. *Neuropsychologia*, 23:115–118.

Ferreiro, E. (1971), *Les relations temporelles dans la langue de l'enfant*. Geneva: Droz.

Francis, H. (1972), Toward an explanation of paradigmatic-syntagmatic shift. *Child Dev.*, 43:949–959.

Friedlander, B.Z. (1970), Receptive language development in infancy: Issues and problems. *Merrill-Palmer Q.*, 16:7.

Geschwind, N. (1976), Language and the brain. In: *Progress in Psychobiology*, ed. R.F. Thompson. San Francisco: Freeman, pp. 341–348.

Goldin-Meadow, S., and Mylander, C. (1983), Gestural communication in deaf children: Noneffect of parental input on language development. *Science*, 221:372–374.

Halverson, C.F., and Waldrop, M.F. (1970), Maternal behavior towards own and other preschool children: The problem of "ownness." *Child Dev.*, 41:839.

Inhelder, B. (1971), The sensory-motor origins of knowledge. In: *Early Childhood: The Development of Self-Regulatory Mechanisms*, ed. D.N. Walcher and D.L. Peters. New York: Academic Press, pp. 141–155.

Kosslyn, S.M. (1988), Aspects of a cognitive neuroscience of mental imagery. *Science*, 240:1621–1626.

Kosslyn, S.M., Holtzman, J.D., Farah, M.J., and Gazzaniga, M.S. (1985), A computational analysis of mental image generation: evidence from functional dissociations in split-brain patients. *J. Exp. Psychol. Gen.*, 114:311.

Langmeir, J., and Matejcek, Z. (1975), *Psychological Deprivation in Children*, 3rd Ed. New York: Halsted Press.

Lefevre, A.B. (1975), Language development in malnourished children. In: *Foundations of Language Development*, ed. E.H. Lenneberg and E. Lenneberg. New York: Academic Press, 2:279–296.

Lenneberg, E.H. (1967), *Biological Foundations of Language*. New York: John Wiley & Sons, Inc.

Lenneberg, E.H. (1969), On explaining language. *Science*, 164:635–643.

Lenneberg, E.H., Rebelsky, F.G., and Nichols, I.A. (1965), The vocalizations of infants born to deaf and hearing parents. *Hum. Dev.*, 8:23–37.

Lovell, K., and Dixon, E.M. (1967), The growth of the control of grammar in imitation, comprehension and production. *J. Child Psychol.*, 8:31.

Luria, A.R. (1966), *Higher Cortical Functions in Man*. New York: Basic Books.

Luria, A.R. (1976), *Cognitive Development*. Cambridge, Mass.: Harvard University Press.

Luria, A.R., and Yudovich, F.I. (1959), *Speech and the Developmental Process in the Child*. London: Staples Press.

Marshall, W.A. (1968), *Development of the Brain*. Edinburgh: Oliver & Boyd.

Menyuk, P. (1971), *The Acquisition and Development of Language*. Englewood Cliffs: Prentice-Hall.

Mills, M. (1974), Recognition of mother's voice in early infancy. *Nature*, 31.

Moerk, E. (1974), Changes in verbal child-mother interactions with increasing language skills of the child. *J. Psycholinguist. Res.*, 3:101–116.

Morley, M.E. (1965), *The Development and Disorders of Speech in Childhood*, 2nd Ed. Edinburgh: E. & S. Livingston.

Nelson, K.E. (1977), Aspects of language acquisition and use from 2 to age 20. *J. Am. Acad. Child Psychiatry*, 16:584–607.

Peal, E., and Lambert, W.E. (1962), The relationship of bilingualism to intelligence. *Psychol. Monogr.*, 76 (27).

Piaget, J. (1923), *The Language and Thought of the Child*. London: Routledge & Kegan Paul.

Piaget, J. (1954), Language and thought from a genetic point of view. *Acta Psychol.*, 10:88–98.

Provence, S., and Lipton, R.C. (1962), *Infants in Institutions*. New York: International Universities Press.

Ringler, N.M., et al. (1975), Mother-to-child speech at 2 years. *J. Pediatr.*, 86:141–144.

Schlesinger, B. (1962), *Higher Cerebral Functions and Their Clinical Disorders.* New York: Grune & Stratton.

Soffietti, J.P. (1955), Bilingualism and biculturalism. *J. Educ. Psychol.*, 46:222–227.

Statts, A. (1971), Linguistic-mentalistic theory versus an explanatory S-R learning theory of language development. In: *The Ontogenesis of Grammar*, ed. D.I. Slobin. New York: Academic Press.

Vygotsky, L.S. (1962), *Thought and Language.* New York and Cambridge, Mass.: Wiley and MIT Press. (Original Russian edition, 1934.)

Whorf, B.L. (1956), Language, mind and reality. In: *Language, Thought and Reality*, ed. J.B. Carroll. Cambridge, Mass.: MIT Press, pp. 246–270.

Wolff, P. (1967), Cognitive considerations for a psychoanalytic theory of language acquisition. In: *Motives and Thought: Psychoanalytic Essays in Honor of David Rappaport*, ed. R. Holt. New York: International Universities Press, pp. 300–343.

Wolff, P. (1969), The natural history of crying and other vocalizations of early infancy. In: *Determinants of Infant Behavior*, ed. B.M. Foss. London: Methuen, p. 81.

6

PSYCHOSEXUAL DEVELOPMENT

The link between hormonal conditions, brain functions, and sexual behavior provides the foundation for any consideration of psychosexual development (Hamburg and Lunde, 1966). Psychological influences also play a major role (Maccoby and Jacklin, 1974). It is important to distinguish among genetic (chromosomal) sex, sex role (culturally based expectations), and core gender identity (the inner sex of sexual identity).

Genetic (chromosomal) sex is determined when the ovum is fertilized. The XY-bearing sperm is male, the XX female. Gonadal and hormonal sex determinations in turn depend on the presence of H-Y antigen. The embryonic gonad *without* H-Y antigen tends to form an ovary. H-Y antigen is required to produce a testis. Thus the fetus tends to develop along female lines if there are no testes and their accompanying hormones. Testicular differentiation occurs during the seventh week of gestation, whereas ovarian differentiation occurs at about 11 or 12 weeks. Testicular hormones that bring about masculinization include testosterone and a glycoprotein. At age 7 adrenal androgen levels increase in both boys and girls. At puberty, from about age 11 to 17, testosterone increases in males, while estradiol increases in females until adult levels are reached at about age 19. However, there is a considerable range in both the onset of puberty and its duration in both sexes.

Biologic factors may play a part in some of the differences seen in the behaviors and roles of males and females. Girls with congenital adrenal hyperplasia, for example,

seem to engage more energetically in rough outdoor play and appear to be less interested in doll play (Erhardt and Baker, 1974). Erhardt and Meyer-Bahlberg (1979) studied the effects of prenatal sex hormones, particularly prenatal androgens, on development of the central nervous system with particular reference to psychologic differentiation. They found in essence that the cumulative evidence suggests some effect on sex-dimorphic behavior, including childhood rehearsing of parenting.

Sexual identity (gender), however, is almost entirely a function of how the parents perceive the child's external genitalia and consequently assign a sex to the infant, and how they subsequently raise the child in the context of social expectations. Sexual orientation and preference, too, at least among males, do not seem to be correlated with hormonal (androgen/estrogen) balance.

Sex-typing of behavior probably occurs as a result of an interaction among biologic, cognitive, social learning, and psychodynamic (psychoanalytic) factors.

The first systematic psychoanalytic account of the psychosexual development of children was attempted by Freud in "Three Essays on the Theory of Sexuality" (S. Freud, 1905). An instinct, or drive, in psychoanalysis was defined as "the psychical representative of an endosomatic, continuously flowing source of stimulation" or as "an elementary urge, rooted in bodily tensions, which environmental influences may deflect from its course and modify in many ways but probaby cannot eradicate" (Waelder, 1960). The sexual drive was said to change in its objects and its aims as the individual proceeded in his or her development. A sequence of development in sexuality was proposed, while sexual development was seen as intimately involved in all the many other simultaneous lines of development (A. Freud, 1965). At the same time, an organic substructure was thought to be the basis of these provisional ideas, making it "probable that it is special substances and chemical processes which perform the operations of sexuality . . ." (S. Freud, 1914, p. 78) and that "deeper research will one day trace the path further and discover an organic basis for the mental event" (S. Freud, 1900, pp. 41–42).

Four major psychoanalytic sources of evidence are available for study, all of them at the level of clinical inference. Historically, the first source was in the recovery or reconstruction of what psychoanalysts believed to be early infantile feelings that occurred during the psychoanalysis of adults (e.g., S. Freud, 1909a). Second, remnants of such infantile sexuality have been inferred in normal adult behavior and in certain psychological disturbances in adults, such as the sexual perversions, eating disturbances, gastrointestinal disturbances, and certain characterological disorders (e.g., Abraham, 1921, 1925, 1934). Third, the analysis of children provided additional anecdotal data (e.g., Bornstein, 1949; S. Freud, 1909b). Fourth, and more recently, direct observation of children has added a new dimension to psychoanalytic data (e.g., Spitz, 1965). It should be remembered, however, that just as certain behavior in children may represent infantile sexuality even though it does not look "sexual," other phenomena that may involve the sex organs may not necessarily represent psychosexual behavior. For example, penile erections in infants and children may occur regularly in association with REM sleep and may represent a metabolic change rather than any particular sexual wish or fantasy (Fisher et al., 1965).

PSYCHOANALYTIC THEORY

In psychoanalytic theory, the sexual aim of a young infant is simple: to obtain a feeling of pleasure and satisfaction and the relief from discomfort by the most immediate means possible. The young infant derives pleasure from a wide variety of visual, tactile, kinesthetic, and auditory stimuli, but by far the most sensitive and apparently the greatest source of pleasure appears to be in the region of the mouth. The object of the sexual instinct is the infant himself or herself, seen in autoerotic activities, such as mouthing and sucking at the breast, fist, or thumb. Questions have been raised about some of the viewpoints subsumed under the heading of orality (Sandler and Dare, 1970). Moreover, Freud did note that "the phylogenetic foundation has so much the upper hand over personal accidental experience that it makes no difference whether a child is really suckled at the breast or has been brought up on the bottle and never enjoyed the tenderness of a mother's care. In both cases the child's development takes the same path. . . ." (S. Freud, 1940, pp. 188 ff.). Lastly, it is important to note that certain genetic factors and biological orienting patterns are in operation prior to any psychologic mechanisms. For example, the suck reflex is coordinated to the cyclic flow of breast milk (Dubignon and Campbell, 1969), and by 6 days of age the infant can selectively orient to smell, preferring his own mother's milk (MacFarlane, 1975).

As the infant develops and as speech and the capacity for symbol formation emerge, the child begins to experience feelings about his or her separateness and worth. He or she develops a sense of autonomy which has to be reconciled with ambivalent feelings, all at about the same time that he or she is acquiring new skills, only one of which is sphincter control. During this process, according to psychoanalytic theory, the anal mucosa is said to become erotogenized and may serve in part the aims of the ambivalent feelings just mentioned. Indeed, the young child may express his or her ambivalence in the (pleasurable) holding in and letting go of feces during bowel movements. However, this ambivalence may also be expressed in the controlling and clinging behavior seen in some 2- and 3-year-old children. The central role of the anal mucosa at this stage has probably been exaggerated, reflecting the practices that prevailed at the time Freud made his observations more than current behavior.

When the child is between 3 and 6 years of age, behavior that is more clearly recognizable as "sexual" appears. The child at this stage is very much aware of the anatomical differences between the sexes and is curious about pregnancy, childbirth, and death. Sometimes this interest is represented in the play of the child. For example, play with toys that involve filling and emptying, opening and shutting, fitting in and throwing way, and building up and knocking down has been interpreted as representing a curiosity about the body and sexual functions. The opportunities for the sequential development of play in childhood thus become as important for the sexual development of the child as they are for other purposes (e.g., problem solving, mastery of body skills, functional pleasure in play, coping with anxiety, facilitating relationships with people, and communication). The child at this stage is said to experience intense sexual and aggressive urges toward both parents, but the aim is less well defined. Boys and girls may become absorbed by fairy-tale or television characters that serve to represent children's own fantasies. Such fantasies also emerge in the dreams of children. Children of this age may also play at being mothers and fathers or doctors and nurses—working toward a partial fulfillment of their sexual aims, which at this time may be partially fused with their aggressive fantasies. Boys and girls may inflict pain on each other in keeping with their understanding of the sexual act as an act of violence. They may also be quite exhibitionistic and possessive, especially of the parent of the opposite sex. Hostility to the same-sex parent seems to be influenced by certain characteristic family patterns of relationships present in a particular society (Honigmann, 1954).

Between 6 and 12 years of age, during the elementary-school years, concepts of inevitability regarding birth, death, and sex differences become clarified, and the sense of time and the ability to differentiate between fantasy and reality become established. Defense mechanisms, which in general bar from consciousness certain unacceptable impulses and fantasies and at the same time provide some substitute gratification, are strengthened. The child consolidates earlier reactions, such as shame against exhibitionistic urges, disgust against messiness, and a sense of guilt that contains sexual and aggressive wishes. The child's play at this time is usually characterized by organization, whether in a board game or team game. Sex play, far from being dormant, continues actively, especially with voyeuristic tendencies and the urge to touch. The sex play often may be more discreet at this age (that is, adults may see it less often) yet it may also be quite overt, with much interest and curiosity (Reese, 1966). The object of the sexual instinct may be a peer, but the actual playmate may be of either sex.

When puberty comes, the young adolescent struggles to achieve mastery of his or her body and of sexual and aggressive urges at the same time that he or she is trying to separate from his or her family, find new and appealing sexual objects, and achieve a sense of identity. In the course of this struggle, the sexual behavior of the adolescent may range from an indiscriminate regression (toward expressions of earlier forms of the sexual drive, manifested in impulsive behavior, messiness, and alternating labile affects) to petting and mutual masturbation, which may be heterosexual or homosexual and, eventually, intercourse. Sometimes earlier aims and objects are temporarily gratified and used, for example, in isolated acts of fellatio or in exhibitionistic behavior. Adolescents who are in poor control may sexually molest a young child, especially during babysitting.

Ultimately, a mature primacy of the genital zone is established, with an appropriate heterosexual object choice and an appropriate achievement of the new sexual aims of a love relationship, sexual intercourse, orgasm, discharge, and childbirth.

CRITIQUE OF PSYCHOANALYTIC THEORY

Rutter (1971, 1976) reviewed the scientific literature on normal psychosexual development and concluded that Freud's description of the oral and anal stages is too narrow and somewhat misleading, that the oedipal situation is not universal, that Freud's description of the latency period is wrong in most respects, and that Freud's concept of an innate sex drive that has a quantifiable energy component is only a half-truth. Rutter noted that at present there is insufficient evidence to decide among the various psychologic theories of sexual development. Rutter does not mince words. However, even though the level of scientific reliability and validity in psychoanalytic research is generally low, Rutter may be ignoring the levels of abstraction in psychoanalytic writings (Waelder, 1962; Achenbach and Lewis, 1971). The "artificial structure of hypothesis" (S. Freud, 1920, p. 60) that psychoanalysts use in their metapsychology may indeed be "blown away" by the answers provided by biology (S. Freud, 1920, p. 60). In the meantime, however, the clinical data derived from the psychoanalytic situation should be placed in escrow, so to speak, pending confirmation or refutation by accepted scientific methods.

Recently, however, other questions have been raised about Freud's theory of infantile sexuality. For example, some scholars now believe Freud was wrong in assuming that his patients' accounts of their being sexually abused by a parent (often the father) in early childhood were only fantasy (Klein and Tribich, 1980; Masson, 1981; Krull, 1986). The evidence in Freud's own reports, including the Dora case (S. Freud, 1905/1906), reveals abundant information about sexually destructive behavior by the parents toward the child, and overwhelming data gathered since the 1960s attest to the greater numbers of children who are in fact abused by their parents. The importance of this new challenge is that it draws attention back to the real world in which the child lives as an important element

in the development of the child, a hitherto neglected area in psychoanalysis.

ALTERNATIVE VIEWPOINTS

Other approaches have been used to account for sex differences. Kohlberg (1978), for example, attempted to expand upon Piaget's theories and suggested that gender identity develops along with cognitive development and that children tend to behave in ways that are consistent with the image of themselves. Sex-typing of behavior occurs, however, long before gender constancy is achieved around 3½ years of age. In contrast, social learning theorists, such as Mischel (1970), have suggested that imitation of same-sexed models through a process of socialization and reinforcement is a major mechanism. Yet even here we regularly observe phenomena that detract from social learning as a complete explantion. For example, infants do not always chose a same-sex model, and even when they do the resemblance may not be very striking. Moreover, the pathologic forms of psychosexual development do not appear to be directly associated with either the parental model or the modes of reinforcement used.

Maccoby and Jacklin (1974) conducted an extensive analysis of available research on sex differences (see Note 11). They noted that the available research suggests that the similarities between the sexes are more pronounced than the differences, i.e., perhaps the issue should be viewed as why girls and boys are so alike rather than why they are different. They also note the tremendous range of expression in sex-typed behaviors, so that for any given behavior, considerable overlap between the sexes often is observed. They note that one of the most consistent differences between the sexes is the greater aggressiveness of boys as compared to girls.

SEXUAL PREFERENCE

Saghir and Robins (1973) have provided considerable support for a childhood behavioral pattern associated with both male and female homosexuality. Of the males studied, 67% of the 89 homosexuals versus 3% of the heterosexuals reported that they had played mostly with girls and were considered "sissy" or effeminate during boyhood. The prehomosexual female sample (N = 56) included a significantly higher proportion of "tomboys," both in childhood (70% versus 16%) and adolescence (35% versus 0%), with lack of interest in doll play discriminating prehomosexual from preheterosexual "tomboys."

Green (1979), in a review of some of the retrospective and prospective research regarding sexual preference, noted that Whitham (1977), who had studied 107 exclusively homosexual males and compared them to exclusively heterosexual males, had found that 47% of the homosexuals recalled being more interested in doll play than other boys their age, 44% recalled liking to cross-dress more, and 42% recalled preferring girls' games and having a female peer group. In contrast, such behaviors were recalled by fewer than 1% of the heterosexuals. Of course, heterosexuals might simply repress such memories to a greater extent.

Green (1979) noted that "feminine boyhood behavior, as defined by clothing, toy, peer group, activity, and role-playing preferences, does not consistently predict later homosexual orientation. However, from preliminary data, it does appear to load in favor of such an outcome in some persons" (Green, 1979, pp. 107 ff.). Green went on to note that his

. . . data so far indicate a moderate amount of homosexual fantasy, arousability, and overt behavior in a sample of boys who were previously "feminine." However, of considerable importance is the current variation in sexual orientation in these boys. One mid-adolescent is a "drag queen" and has had an extensive series of same-sex partners. One is genuinely bisexual, with an equal distribution of erotic fantasies and overt behaviors involving males and females. One prepubertal boy reports erections in response to fantasies or pictures of nude males but not females, although he had had no interpersonal genital experience. Others report an exclusively heterosexual orientation.

This variation in outcome is noteworthy. Clearly all boys who show behaviorial patterns considered

"feminine" are not prehomosexual. Parents of boys whose behavior does not fit the conventional stereotype of "masculinity" should not be rendered anxious by the belief that their children are prehomosexual. . . . However, many parents do become grief-striken if they believe their children are or will become homosexual (Green, 1979, p. 108).

Green therefore feels it is important to stress the markedly atypical early childhood behavior of the sample described here and the considerable variability in their later sexual behaviors. Because there is a wide range of ultimate behaviors, caution is needed in making any prediction about outcome.

Note 8

From S. Freud (1905), *Three Essays on the Theory of Sexuality,* Standard Edition. London: The Hogarth Press, 1953, pp. 125–243.

Summary[1]

. . . We started out from the aberration of the sexual instinct in respect of its object and its aim and we were faced by the question of whether these arise from an innate disposition or are acquired as a result of experiences in life. We arrived at an answer to this question from an understanding, derived from psychoanalytic investigation, of the workings of the sexual instinct in psychoneurotics, a numerous class of people and one not far removed from the healthy. We found that in them tendencies to every kind of perversion can be shown to exist as unconscious forces and betray their presence as factors leading to the formation of symptoms. It was thus possible to say that neurosis is, as it were, the negative of perversion. In view of what was now seen to be the wide dissemination of tendencies to perversion we were driven to the conclusion that a disposition to perversions is an original and universal disposition of the human sexual instinct and that normal sexual behavior is developed out of it as a result of organic changes and psychical inhibitions occurring in the course of maturation; we hoped to be able to show the presence of this original disposition in childhood. Among the forces restricting the direction taken by the sexual instinct we laid emphasis upon shame, disgust, pity and the structures of morality and authority erected by society. We were thus led to regard any established aberration from normal sexuality as an instance of developmental in-

---

[1]All footnotes omitted.

hibition and infantilism. Though it was necessary to place in the foreground the importance of the variations in the original disposition, a cooperative and not an opposing relation was to be assumed as existing between them and the influences of actual life. It appeared, on the other hand, that since the original disposition is necessarily a complex one, the sexual instinct itself must be something put together from various factors, and that in the perversions it falls apart, as it were, into its components. The perversions were thus seen to be on the one hand inhibitions, and on the other hand dissociations, of normal development. Both these aspects were brought together in the supposition that the sexual instinct of adults arises from a combination of a number of impulses of childhood into a unity, an impulsion with a single aim. . . .

. . . We found it a regrettable thing that the existence of the sexual instinct in childhood has been denied and that the sexual manifestations not infrequently to be observed in children have been described as irregularities. It seemed to us on the contrary that children bring germs of sexual activity with them into the world, that they already enjoy sexual satisfaction when they begin to take nourishment and that they persistently seek to repeat the experience in the familiar activity of "thumb-sucking." The sexual activity of children, however, does not, it appeared, develop *pari passu* with their other functions, but, after a short period of efflorescence from the ages of two to five, enters upon the so-called period of latency. During that period the production of sexual excitation is not by any means stopped but continues and produces a store of energy which is employed to a great extent for purposes other than sexual—namely, on the one hand in contributing the sexual components to social feelings and on the other hand (through repression and reaction-forming) in building up the subsequently developed barriers against sexuality. On this view, the forces destined to retain the sexual instinct upon certain lines are built up in childhood chiefly at the cost of perverse sexual impulses and with the assistance of education. A certain portion of the infantile sexual impulses would seem to evade these uses and succeed in expressing itself as sexual activity. We next found that sexual excitation in children springs from a multiplicity of forces. Satisfaction arises first and foremost from the appropriate sensory excitation of what we have described as erotogenic zones. It seems probable that any part of the skin

and any sense-organ—probably, indeed, *any* organ—can function as an erotogenic zone, though there are some particularly marked erotogenic zones whose excitation would seem to be secured from the very first by certain organic contrivances. It further appears that sexual excitation arises as a by-product, as it were, of a large number of processes that occur in the organisms, as soon as they reach a certain degree of intensity, and most especially of any relatively powerful emotion, even though it is of a distressing nature. The excitations from all these sources are not yet combined; but each follows its own separate aim, which is merely the attainment of a certain sort of pleasure. In childhood, therefore, the sexual instinct is not unified and is at first without an object, that is, auto-erotic.

The erotogenic zone of the genitals begins to make itself noticeable, it seems, even during the years of childhood. This may happen in two ways. Either, like any other erotogenic zone, it yields satisfaction in response to appropriate sensory stimulation; or, in a manner which is not quite understandable, when satisfaction is derived from other sources, a sexual excitation is simultaneously produced which has a special relation to the genital zone. We were reluctantly obliged to admit that we could not satisfactorily explain the relation between sexual satisfaction and sexual excitation, or that between the activity of the genital zone and the activity of the other sources of sexuality.

We found from the study of neurotic disorders that beginnings of an organization of the sexual instinctual components can be detected in the sexual life of children from its very beginning. During a first, very early phase, oral erotism occupies most of the picture. A second of these pregenital organizations is characterized by the predominance of sadism and anal erotism. It is not until a third phase has been reached that the genital zones proper contribute their share in determining sexual life, and in children this last phase is developed only so far as to a primacy of the phallus.

We were then obliged to recognize, as one of our most surprising findings, that this early efflorescence of infantile sexual life (between the ages of two and five) already gives rise to the choice of an object, with all the wealth of mental activities which such a process involved. Thus, in spite of the lack of synthesis between the different instinctual components and the uncertainty of the sexual aim, the phase of development corresponding to that period must be regarded as an important precursor of the subsequent final sexual organization.

The fact that the onset of sexual development in human beings occurs in two phases, i.e. that the development is interrupted by the period of latency, seemed to call for particular notice. This appears to be one of the necessary conditions of the aptitude of men for developing a higher civilization, but also of their tendency to neurosis. So far as we know, nothing analogous is to be found in man's animal relatives. It would seem that the origin of this peculiarity of man must be looked for in the prehistory of the human species.

It was not possible to say what amount of sexual activity can occur in childhood without being described as abnormal or detrimental to further development. The nature of these sexual manifestations was found to be predominantly masturbatory. Experience further showed that the external influences of seduction are capable of provoking interruptions of the latency period or even its cessation, and that in this connection the sexual instinct of children proves in fact to be polymorphously perverse; it seems, moreover, that any such premature sexual activity diminishes a child's educability. . . .

Note 9

From B. Bornstein (1949), The analysis of a phobic
    child. *The Psychoanalytic Study of the Child,*
    III/IV, New York: International Universities
    Press, Inc., pp. 181–226.

Frankie, a 5½-year-old boy of superior intelligence who was eager to learn, was brought into analysis because of a severe school phobia. He liked to play with the other children and was friendly and amenable with them, but shy and withdrawn in the presence of any stranger. He became panic-stricken if his mother or nurse were out of sight. Even when left with his father in his own home, he was occasionally overwhelmed by attacks of anxiety. His phobic symptom had existed for more than 2 years. . . .

When Frankie was 2, it became especially difficult to put him to bed at night. Regularly, he screamed for an hour before he fell asleep, and also whenever he awoke during the night. A third screaming period occurred at the age of 4½ years and was stopped only after the nurse threatened to punish him. . . .

The child's anxiety reached its peak when he was brought to nursery school at the age of 3 years and 9 months. At that time, his sister's nurse had

just left the home, and he had to share his own nurse with the baby (aged 9 months). He went to school for only 2 days. Each time, he had to be taken home because of his wild attacks of fear and screaming, and nothing could make him return to school. . . .

The analyst suggested that treatment be postponed until after a period of preparation for analysis in which the school was to cooperate with the analysts. . . .

Frankie started his first session by building a hospital which was separated into a "lady department," a "baby department," and a "men's department." In the lobby, a lonely boy of 4 was seated all by himself, on a chair placed in an elevated position. The child's father was upstairs visiting "a lady" who, he informed us, when questioned, "is sick or maybe she's got a baby, maybe— I don't know, never mind." He made the point that newborn babies and mothers were separated in this hospital. Casting himself in the roles of a doctor and a nurse, he attended to the babies in a loving way, fed and cleaned them. However, toward the end of the play, a fire broke out. All the babies were burnt to death and the boy in the lobby was also in danger. He wanted to run home, but remembered that nobody would be there. Subsequently he joined the fire department, but it was not quite clear as to whether the firemen had started the fire or put it out. Frankie announced: "Ladies, the babies are dead; maybe we can save you!" Actually only those lady patients who had no babies were rescued by him. The one whom he several times—by a slip of the tongue— had addressed as "Mommy," however, was killed in the fire. No particular attention was given to the men's department. Most of the men had died anyway.

This game, which was repeated in the analysis for many weeks, betrayed the intensity of the boy's fury against his mother and sister. He could not forgive his mother for her unfaithfulness. He took her going to the hospital as a desertion of him and a sign of her lack of love. She must suffer the same tortures which he had suffered when she left him. He said, as it were: "I don't love you either; I hate you, I don't need you, you may die in the hospital. If you hadn't had a baby I would love you." . . .

Frankie, who so thoroughly punished his mother by the withdrawal of his love, naturally lived in continual fear of retaliation. He could not stay at home or go out without his mother because he needed the presence of just that person against whom his aggressive impulses were directed. The presence of the ambivalently loved person prevents the phobic from being overwhelmed by his forbidden impulses and assures him that his aggressive intentions have not come true. But while the unconscious hatred directed at the protecting person is usually difficult to uncover in the analysis of adults, it was still very close to the surface in this 5½-year-old boy. . . .

The danger which threatened the mother from relations with men would result in what was the gravest danger to him: The arrival of a new baby. He had to guard against a repetition of this traumatic experience.

It was this concern that was responsible for the insomnia which became acute at this point of his analysis. There had been previous occurrences of insomnia when he was 2½ and again when he was 4½. Now again it took him hours to fall asleep. He listened silently and anxiously to the noises at night. Whenever his parents spent an evening at home, he ran back and forth between the living room and his bedroom. He wanted to know, as he expressed it, what plans they were making. They might eat something special and he wanted to share it. Or someone might come and hurt his Mommy. Ideas about the problem of procreation filled the hours of his severe insomnia. . . .

One element which was already present in his wild performances became the predominant and all-important feature: a strong inclination to gain pleasure by use of his eyes. This voyeuristic element led him to a new impersonation, that of an omniscient God.

In this new role he made the analyst a frightened, sleeping child into whose ears God whispered dreams of wild colliding horses, of violent scenes in which "Daddy throws Mommy out of the window so that she had to go to the hospital for eighteen days." The "sleeping games" revealed his suspicions of something frightful happening between his father and mother during the night— something he would have liked to observe. As God, he had the right to see and watch everything. His new role of God provided him with a greater power than he had previously enjoyed as attacker, judge, or policeman—roles in which he had experienced the triumph of the conqueror, but also suffered the pain of the conquered. . . .

Later, however, when he realized that God was not only his own creation but a concept shared by others and that he could not rule "his" God to the extent necessary to be protected from anxiety, he replaced his fantasy of an omniscient God by an imaginary television apparatus which belonged exclusively to his fantasy and thus was completely at the disposal of his wishes and plans. ("God sees everything, but the television apparatus sees only if I turn it on.") The television apparatus brought the child closer to reality. When he was God, he made the analyst dream about those frightful scenes between his parents, while with the introduction of his imaginary television apparatus, he himself attempted to face those scenes. The analyst was made a co-observer of eating scenes for which Frankie provided the music (another auditory manifestation) while explaining the observed events to the analyst. He reassured the analyst many times that the observations were "make believe" and actually he never again reached the previously described state of excitement and anxiety. By means of his invention of the television apparatus, he removed himself not only from the scenes he imagined, but also from the feelings of desire and concomitant guilt which those scenes aroused. . . .

The following is one of the scenes observed through the apparatus: Father was in the restaurant and ordered the most delicious food for Mother from the restaurant owner. Then he had a secret talk with the owner. As soon as Mother had eaten, she collapsed and died; the food was poisoned. (In his thoughts, eating was linked with being impregnated, for which Frankie had not yet forgiven his mother, and for which he still punished her by death.) Father and the owner of the restaurant were unconcerned by her death; they continued their pleasant talk and play, shoving Mother under the table.* Some drawings of this time show God and God's wife feasting at a dinner

---

*The scene is rich in its overdetermined factors; it permits the reconstruction of Frankie's oedipus complex. The element, "Mother is shoved under the table," refers to the child's resentment against his mother, who did not pay any attention to him when he, sitting under the table, tried to disturb his parents' meal. The next element, "Father and restaurant owner confer about the food for Mother (from which she dies)," is an indication of Frankie's wish to participate in his father's sexual activities. Frankie's position as restaurant owner was evident in many daydreams: he possessed "all the restaurants in New York." This detail makes us anticipate that Frankie's hostility toward his mother contained also some envy of her role as father's wife. Owner and father-Frankie and father do together what otherwise mother and father do. We shall see later how strong the child's desire was to take the passive role with the father.

table, disturbed by "little gnomes" who alternately attack God and his wife.

These games helped the investigation and understanding of a past period of his life: We had reason to assume that when he was 4½, his screaming attacks had reappeared as his reaction to audible primal scene experiences. His father once wrote us that in former times, "in his prankish days," he used to pinch his wife and throw her into the air "all in fun and for exercise . . . I can imagine what it must have seemed like to someone who heard it but did not see what actually happened." Frankie's running back and forth between his bedroom and the living room occurred in reaction to auditory stimuli and continued until his nurse quenched his active interest and nightly curiosity by a threatening and punishing attitude.

With the process of internalization of his conflicts the actually threatening nurse was replaced by imaginary objects, mainly wolves, who stood guard under his bed and kept him from getting up and investigating what might be happening in the parental bedroom.

These imaginary wolves under the bed were able, like the God he had played, to see what he did and to surmise his intentions. As soon as he put out hand or foot to go into his parents' bedroom,* the wolves would snap at him; "but they would let me go to the bathroom." For a protection from their attacks the boy armed himself with many weapons, preferably with a long stick, in order to beat the wolves down when they raised their heads. He maintained that they observed all his movements, and he in turn countered with an equally watchful attitude. His configuration of the wolves contained as elements the punitive and protective parent figures as well as his own impulses. The wolves punish his intentions and prevent their fulfillment. Their symbolic role as superego was strikingly confirmed in a drawing which Frankie called the WOLVES' STATUE. It showed an oversized wolf (in human form) with outstretched arms, floating above Frankie in his bed, under which a number of smaller-sized wolves (also in human form) were engaged in mysterious activities, obviously of a sexual nature. In his comments on this picture, Frankie said: "It shows what the wolves hope for, what they will look like some day."

---

*The element of uncovering the hands and feet is overdetermined and it is obviously a presentation of its opposite, i.e., a reverse of the original warning against touching his genital under the bedcover.

The dread of wolves which had haunted the child for weeks finally led to the analysis of his castration fear. In his stories and in his play, the mother's attackers who previously had been punished by death, now were punished by almost undisguised castration. In his pictures he endowed God with monstrously elongated arms and legs, only to cut off these limbs with scissors. Immediately after such operation he tried to undo this symbolic act of castration by drawing innumerable new arms and legs. Frankie derived reassurance from the idea that destruction is not necessarily irrevocable and consequently dared to express the thoughts of castration without any symbolic disguise. Mother's attackers were imprisoned and he, as a doctor, subjected the prisoners to operations which usually threw him into a state of exaltation. Playing the doctor, he exclaimed: "Those criminals, they have to be operated on. Off with their wee-wees. It has to come off!" In his play he guarded himself against any awareness of his fear by identifying himself with the person performing the act of castration. His fear of the anticipated retaliation found expression in his behavior toward his pediatrician. Frankie had always been a difficult patient, but during this period he absolutely refused to be examined, and assaulted the doctor by throwing blocks or potatoes which he carefully had stored under his bed for this purpose.

Note 10

Herbert (later to become famous under the pseudonym "Little Hans"), the 5-year-old son of Max Graf, a musicologist and critic in Vienna, suffered for months from a fear that horses on the street might bite him. Under the supervision of Sigmund Freud, Max Graf tried to treat his son by the then new treatment of psychoanalysis. Unfortunately, the symptoms did not subside. Herbert was then brought to see Dr. Freud toward the end of March, 1908. Freud, after some pleasantries, described to Herbert the essence of what later became known as the Oedipus Complex. Herbert, like all normal boys, was destined to become fond of his mother and would then fear his father's anger. Herbert was astonished, and on his way home asked his father, "Does the professor talk to God, as he can tell all that beforehand?"

Note 11

From E.E. Maccoby and C.N. Jacklin (1974),

The Psychology of Sex Differences, Stanford: Stanford University Press, pp. 360, 363.

In previous chapters we have discussed three kinds of factors that affect the development of sex differences: genetic factors, "shaping" of boy-like and girl-like behavior by parents and other socializing agents, and the child's spontaneous learning of behavior appropriate for his sex through imitation. Anyone who would hope to explain the acquisition of sex-typed behavior through one or two of these processes alone would be doomed to disappointment. Not only do the three kinds of processes exert their own direct influence, but they interact with one another.

Biologic factors have been most clearly implicated in sex differences in aggression and visual-spatial ability. We have argued that the male's greater aggression has a biologic component, citing in support the fact that (1) the sex difference manifests itself in similar ways in man and subhuman primates; (2) it is cross-culturally universal; and (3) levels of aggression are responsive to sex hormones. We have also found, surprisingly, that there is no good evidence that adults reinforce boys' aggression more than girls' aggression; in fact, the contrary may be true.

How then does psychologic sex differentiation come about? The psychoanalytic theory of identification would have it that the child identifies with the same-sex parent and learns the details of a sex role through imitation of this parent. Social-learning theory also emphasizes imitation, but argues that children are more often reinforced when they imitate a same-sex rather than opposite-sex model, so that they acquire a generalized tendency to imitate not only the same-sex parent but other same-sex models as well.

We have found several problems with these theories. The first is that children have not been shown to resemble closely the same-sex parent in their behavior. In fact, the rather meager evidence suggests that a boy resembles other children's fathers as much as he does his own, at least with respect to most of the behaviors and attributes measured so far. The same applies to girls' resemblance to their mothers. When people believe they see parent-child resemblance, we suspect they are often noticing physical resemblance rather than behavioral resemblance.

A second problem is that when offered an opportunity to imitate either a male or female model, children (at least those under 6 or 7) do not characteristically select the model whose sex matches their own; their choices are fairly random in this regard. Yet their behavior is clearly sex-typed at a much earlier age than the age at which choice of same-sex models begins to occur. A final problem is that children's sex-typed behavior does not closely resemble that of adult models. Boys select an all-male play group, but they do not observe their fathers avoiding the company of females. Boys choose to play with trucks and cars, even though they may have seen their mothers driving the family car more frequently than their fathers; girls play hopscotch and jacks (highly sex-typed games), although these games are totally absent from their mother's observable behavior.

REFERENCES

Abraham, K. (1949), The influence of oral eroticism on character disorders (1934); Contribution to the theory of the anal character (1921); Character formation on the genital level of the libido (1925). In: *Selected Papers on Psychoanalysis.* London: The Hogarth Press.

Achenbach, T.M., and Lewis, M. (1971), A proposed model for clinical research and its application to encopresis and enuresis. *J. Am. Acad. Child Psychiatry,* 10:535–554.

Bornstein, B. (1949), The analysis of a phobic child. *Psychoanal. Study Child,* 3/4:181–226.

Dubignon, J., and Campbell, D. (1969), Sucking in the newborn during a feed. *J. Exp. Child Psychol.,* 7:282–298.

Erhardt, A.A., and Baker, S.W. (1974), Fetal androgens, human central nervous system differentiation, and behavioral sex differences. In Sex Differences in Behavior. ed. R.C. Friedman and R.M. Vanderwiele. New York: John Wiley & Sons, Inc.

Erhardt, A.A., and Meyer-Bahlberg, H.F.L. (1979), Prenatal sex hormones and the developing brain: Effects on psychosexual differentiation and cognitive functioning. *Annu. Rev. Med.,* 30:417–430.

Fisher, C., et al. (1965), Cycle of penile erection synonymous with dreaming (REM) sleep. *Arch. Gen. Psychiatry,* 12:29–45.

Freud, S. (1900), *The Interpretation of Dreams,* Standard Edition, 4, 5 (1953). London: The Hogarth Press, pp. 41–42.

Freud, S. (1905), *Three Essays on Sexuality,* Standard Edition, 7 (1953). London: The Hogarth Press.

Freud, S. (1905), *Fragment of an analysis of a case of hysteria,* Standard Edition, 7 (1953), ed. J. Strachey. London: Hogarth Press.

Freud, S. (1909a), *Notes Upon a Case of Obsessional Neurosis,* Standard Edition, 10 (1955). London: The Hogarth Press.

Freud, S. (1909b), *Analysis of a Phobia in a Five-Year-Old Boy,* Standard Edition, 10 (1955). London: The Hogarth Press.

Freud, S. (1914), *On Narcissism: An Introduction*, Standard Edition, 14 (1975). London: The Hogarth Press.

Freud, S. (1920), *Beyond the Pleasure Principle*, Standard Edition, 18 (1955). London: The Hogarth Press.

Freud, S. (1940), *An Outline of Psycho-Analysis*, Standard Edition, 23 (1969). London: The Hogarth Press, pp. 188–189.

Green, R. (1979), Childhood cross-gender behavior and subsequent sexual preference. *Am. J. Psychiatry*, 136:106–108.

Hamburg, D.A., and Lunde, D.T. (1966), Sex hormones in the development of sex differences in human behavior. In: *The Development of Sex Differences*, ed. E.E Maccoby. Stanford, Calif.: Stanford University Press, pp. 1–24.

Honigmann, J.J. (1954), *Culture as Personality*. New York: Harper.

Klein, M., and Tribich, D. (1980), On Freud's blindness, *Colloquium*, 3:52–59.

Kohlberg, L. (1978), Revisions in the theory and practice of moral development. In: *New Directions in Child Development: Moral Development*, ed. W. Damon. San Francisco: Jossey-Bass.

Krull, M. (1986), *Freud and his Father*. New York: W.W. Norton (English edition).

MacFarlane, J.A. (1975), Olfaction in the development of social preference in the human neonate. In: *Parent-Infant Interaction*. CIBA Symposium No. 333. ASP.

Maccoby, E.E., and Jacklin, C.N. (1974), *The Psychology of Sex Differences*. Stanford: Stanford University Press.

Masson, J.M. (1981), The seduction hypothesis in the light of new documents. Paper presented at the Western New England Psychoanalytical Society, New Haven, CT, June 6, 1981.

Mischel, W. (1970), Sex-typing and socialization. In: *Carmichael's Manual of Child Psychology*, (Vol. 2), ed. P.H. Mussen. New York: John Wiley & Sons, Inc., pp. 3–72.

Reese, H.W. (1966), Attitudes toward the opposite sex in late childhood. *Merrill-Palmer Q.*, 12:157–163.

Rutter, M. (1971), Normal psychosexual development. *J. Child Psychol. Psychiatry*, 11:259–283.

Rutter, M. (1976), Other family influences. In: *Child Psychiatry*, ed. M. Rutter and L. Hersov. Oxford: Blackwell, pp. 74–108.

Saghir, M., and Robins, E. (1973), *Male and Female Homosexuality*. Baltimore: Williams & Wilkins.

Sandler, J., and Dare, C. (1970), The psychoanalytic concept of orality. *J. Psychosom. Res.*, 14:211–222.

Spitz, R.A. (1965), *The First Year of Life*. New York: International Universities Press.

Waelder, R. (1960), *Basic Theory of Psychoanalysis*. New York: International Universities Press.

Waelder, R. (1962), Review of psychoanalysis, scientific method, and philosophy. *J. Am. Psychoanal. Assoc.*, 10:617–632.

Whitham, F. (1977), Childhood indicators of male homosexuality. *Arch. Sex. Behav.*, 6:89–96.

7

AGGRESSION

DEFINITION

Aggression has not been satisfactorily defined; it has been used to refer to such varied levels as descriptive (apparent fighting); motivational (conscious or unconscious, either with intent to injure or simply as instrumental in achieving some goal); and theoretical construct (the "aggressive drive"). Injurious or destructive behavior also may or may not be associated with such affects as rage and anger. Such affects in turn may result in harmful behavior, either as their primary aim or in an effort to reduce the intensity of the affect. Sometimes the welling-up of anger is necessary to energize, so to speak, an assertive act. Even at the manifest descriptive level, there is often confusion between what is a normal assertive act and what is an aggressive act. To confuse the matter further, some psychoanalysts have assumed that the energy for self-assertive, nonhostile, adaptive behavior is derived almost exclusively from "aggressive drive energy" (Hartmann et al., 1949).

Aggressive behavior, then, may be either associated with the drive to achieve a goal, which in itself is not destructive, or motivated by actual hostile, destructive intentions (Sears et al., 1957). The original source of either kind of aggression may be primarily "instinctual" in the psychoanalytic sense, i.e., the "aggressive drive" (Freud, 1920), or it may be "innate" in the ethological sense (Storr, 1968). Aggression may be heightened by frustration (Dollard et al., 1939), or reinforced in social learning (Miller, 1941; Feshbach, 1964).

Several attempts have been made to define and classify aggression, without much agreement. Moyer (1967) has provided one useful classification for mammalian aggression in general (see Note 12). Washman and Flynn (1962) also have suggested a distinction between affective and predatory aggression. Affective aggression involves defensive postures and autonomic arousal, and it is motivated by a desire to avoid. Predatory aggression involves active stalking and directed attack, and it is usually motivated by appetitive needs.

BIOLOGICAL PERSPECTIVES

Neurotransmitters have a role in the regulation of aggression, and research is beginning to suggest possible mechanisms (Alpert et al., 1981). The centers in the brain that appear to generate aggressive behavior are located in the hypothalamus, posterior cingulate gyrus, central gray, and the dorsomedial half of the amygdala. The parts of the limbic system that are involved in rage behavior include the amygdala and the hippocampus in the temporal lobe, hypothalamus, cingulate gyri and cingulum, septum pellucidum and septal area, and related portions of the thalamus, basal ganglia, orbital region of the frontal lobe, and midbrain (Fig. 7–1).

Moyer (1971) suggested that predatory aggression is related to hypothalamic and amygdala function, that fear-induced aggression is related to the amygdala, septum, and hypothalamus, and that irritable aggression occurs via the hypothalamus, amygdala, and caudate nucleus. Maternal aggression (in response to

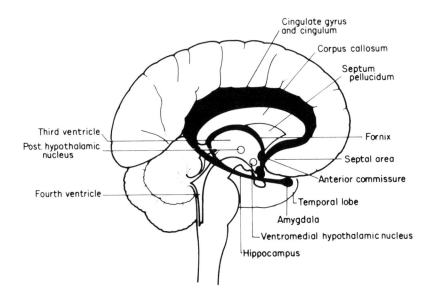

Fig. 7–1.   F.A. Elliott (1978), Neurological factors in violent behavior (the dyscontrol syndrome). Reprinted by permission from the figure on page 65, Chapter 5, in *Violence and Responsibility: The Individual, the Family and Society* by Robert L. Sadoff, Ed. Copyright 1978, Spectrum Publications, Inc., New York.

a perceived threat to the mother's offspring) is related to estrogens. Territorial aggression and aggression stimulated by the appearance of a competitive male are mediated by androgens. Instrumental aggression is learned through rewards for aggressive behavior.

The level of aggression is clearly responsive to sex hormones (Money and Ehrhardt, 1968). Differences in the frequency of aggressive behavior between males and females may be related to prenatal variations in hormone levels (Reinisch, 1981). A higher level of androgen in young girls is associated with a greater interest in rough play (Ehrhardt and Baker, 1974), whereas boys whose mothers had less progesterone and more estrogen during pregnancy appear to be less aggressive (Yalom et al., 1973). Testosterone may act on the fetal brain to facilitate particularly the learning of aggressive patterns of behavior (Hamburg, 1974). In women, premenstrual tension may lower the threshold for violence. One study of women in prison found that 62% of their violent crimes had been committed during the premenstrual week (Morton et al., 1953). In a study by Mattsson et al. (1980), 40 male delinquent recidivists had a slightly

higher mean plasma testosterone (T) level than a group of normal adolescents of the same age and pubertal stage. Furthermore, delinquents who had committed armed robbery tended to have higher mean T levels than less violent offenders.

Whereas the Y chromosome present in males presumably accounts for certain aspects of "maleness," an extra Y chromosome (XYY syndrome) does not produce more "maleness" or more aggression. In fact, XYY males who are unusually tall, have severe acne, and have a below-average IQ are usually isolated and tend to daydream (Owen, 1972). Further, while the incidence of XYY males in the prison population is about 2% compared to about 0.11% in the general population, the crimes they commit are not especially violent or aggressive (Hook, 1973).

Severe aggression against the self is found in children with Lesch-Nyhan syndrome (Lesch and Nyhan, 1964). This rare inborn error of purine metabolism is sex-linked, affecting only boys. The boys bite their lips and/or cheeks, and some have virtually amputated their fingers, even though they experience pain. Physical restraint is required to prevent self-destructive behavior. These children are also mentally retarded, and have choreoathetosis (Nyhan, 1978).

PSYCHOLOGICAL PERSPECTIVES

Increased aggressiveness in boys is found in all cultures, and this sex difference is present from early life. Boys also elicit more aggressive responses from other children (Hutt, 1972). The trait of aggressiveness tends to be more stable over time in boys than in girls (Kagan and Moss, 1962). Aggressive behavior is common in preschool children and then declines until adolescence, when it rises again (Werry and Quay, 1971). Adolescent boys give significantly more aggressive projective test responses than do girls (Rosenzweig, 1970). Aggressivity may be a result of polygenetic influences expressed in the individual temperament of a given child (Thomas et al., 1963).

Aggression, rather broadly defined, has been a major focus of psychoanalytic theory. "Aggressive drive" is said to serve the adaptive needs and functions of the child at the same time that it finds an avenue for discharge through these functions. Some psychoanalysts think that aggression at all times has direction in that it is primarily object seeking (Fairbairn, 1952). The concepts of amount and direction are implied when the term cathexis is used in psychoanalytic theory. Later in development, aggressive drive is said to be fused with the sexual drive (Hartmann et al., 1949). Aggression is said in psychoanalytic theory to be "neutralized" when it serves conflict-free, adaptive ends, notably in intellectual functioning and problem solving. Sublimation through, for example, artistic work, is then perhaps a special case of the general process of neutralization by which unbound aggression is modified and used to serve higher purposes, including socialization. Aggression is needed to achieve whatever mastery of the external world is possible for an individual. Aggression is also pleasurable.

Aggression in the assertive sense seems to have a developmental sequence. Observations of young infants suggest that from the very moment of independent life the infant assertively exercises certain rudimentary functions that in part serve to facilitate adaptation. Such functions have been said to represent "primary autonomous apparatuses" (Hartmann, 1950). Perhaps it would be more correct to say that the adaptive aspect of these functions is rudimentary (the functions themselves may be quite complex), and the functions are rudimentary only insofar as they are manifested during the earliest period of development. Examples of such functions are the rooting reflex, the grasp reflex, the tonic neck reflex, and certain behavioral reactions, such as anticipatory posturing and changes in activity that represent attention following an external stimulus, whether it is visual, auditory, or tactile. All these functions may operate in the service of adaptation and survival. Thus, the newborn infant alerts with human holding (Korner and Thoman, 1970) and quiets with picking up and rocking (Korner and Thoman, 1972). In short, the infant is a sucking, looking, grasping, learning individual. In some cases the survival value of these functions is readily seen; in others it is less obvious. Anticipatory posturing and changes in attention states, reflected in changes in activity, clearly serve to alert the infant to his environment. In doing so they actively serve the adaptive and survival interests of the infant. It remains unclear to what extent these activities are best considered aggressive. For example, in one study of infants under the age of 5 months who were in an institution, those infants who were most active were least likely to show developmental retardation (Schaffer, 1966).

Each of these functions, or activities, results in and is enhanced by the infant's experiencing a measure of control (to whatever extent control is possible in the infant) over his or her environment. An early measure of control, for example, is the extent to which the infant is able to mentally assimilate the nipple, the breast, or the mother through the exercise of sensorimotor activities. Subsequent activities, such as crawling, walking, and so on, similarly require energy to function; and each activity in turn can act as a motor pathway for the adaptive efforts of the infant as well as for the discharge of aggression. Later, play, symbolic language, and intellectual development serve similar adaptive and aggressive purposes.

Aggression in the hostile sense similarly seems to show a developmental progression. The young infant may seem to turn his aggression inward (e.g., he may bang his head) or outward (e.g., he may have temper tantrums or show destructive behavior). When the 2- or 3-year-old child is able to manipulate his bowel and bladder functions, they too may be used to discharge aggression outwardly, albeit in such indirect forms as soiling and wetting. Goodenough (1931) studied aggressive behavior in preschoolers. She noted that tantrums peaked at around age 2 and then decreased in frequency while acts of retaliation increased with age during the preschool period. Increased demands from parents, e.g., for toilet training, etc., may contribute to the tantrums of the toddler; an alternative view would emphasize the importance of emergent language skills as a means of expressing aggression in more socially appropriate ways. Clinicians have observed that once a child acquires language, the frequency of temper tantrums decreases. Later, the child may discharge his aggression in more subtle forms, and in doing so his or her behavior is no different from that seen in many adults. The child may, for example, manage not to hear the request of an adult, whether parent or teacher. The child's aggression also may be disguised by slyness or by such reaction formations as shyness and embarrassment. Occasionally, a child will remove himself or herself from any situation that invites his or her own aggression, or the child may deny to himself or herself as well as others that he or she has even had an aggressive wish. At other times, the child may cunningly stick to the letter of a rule; e.g., he or she may do something that is allowed in one situation but that in the present context is

clearly an aggressive act. The young school-age child may deal with aggression by turning it into its opposite, e.g., the child may be too sweet or too good.

As social conflict with hostile aggression develops, such aggression is dealt with in part by defense mechanisms, including repression, displacement, projection, and various reaction formations, particularly guilt. A child, for example, may feel guilt about a hostile wish, then blame another person for his or her aggressive behavior, and subsequently identify with that person. Or the child may attempt to rationalize his or her actions. A 7- or 8-year-old child may begin to attempt to exercise his or her capacity for moral judgment (see pp. 80–81) to help control hostility and aggression.

At the same time, aggressive behavior itself may be a defense. Thus aggressive behavior may be used to ward off depression, giving rise to a so-called masked depression (Burks and Harrison, 1962).

VARIATIONS OF AGGRESSIVE DRIVE DEVELOPMENT AND BEHAVIOR

What factors influence aggressive drive development? Observations in the newborn nursery reveal that there is an enormous range of activity among infants in a standard environment, suggesting that there are variations in aggressive drive endowment. There also seems to be a reciprocal relation between aggression and dependency. For example, the active exploratory behavior of an infant may be in conflict with the attachment behavior of the same infant, who seeks proximity and the gratification of his or her dependency needs. In some children, the more the child remains dependent, the more aggression will be latent, producing in some instances a fantasy life filled with aggression. On the other hand, perhaps this realm of fantasy life is essential, given the prolonged period of relative biological helplessness during human development. Aggressive expression is thus thought by some to be a necessary human need (Storr, 1970). Aggression has been noted to have important adaptive aspects in nonhuman primates (Suomi, 1977).

Excessive, overt stimulation may give rise to frustration and heightened aggressive tension, leading to such affects as rage and hate. Covert stimulation may take place as the result of spankings. Actual child abuse may be a forerunner of hostile aggressive behavior in children. Parents who punish frequently or severely tend to have children who are more aggressive (Feshbach, 1970). Parental role models and permissiveness in regard to aggressive behavior between siblings at home, reinforced by peer relationships outside the home, may facilitate the development of aggression through learning and may pave the way toward producing an aggressive child. Suppressive parental attitudes may exceed the child's capacity to control himself or herself, leading to behavior that is beyond the tolerance of the parents. Weak emotional ties between parent and child may result in inadequate love to bind the aggression; the child, for example, may have little incentive or wish to please and may act on his or her aggressive impulses with little, if any, feeling of guilt. Similarly, conflict in the mother and father about their own aggressive impulses may lead them to become more or less paralyzed when it is necessary to control the child and set limits. Such parents are prone to react excessively, and often inconsistently, usually on the basis of their own needs rather than those of the child. Violence on television may contribute to aggressive behavior in young school-age children, at least in terms of immediate effects (U.S. Public Health Service Report, 1972; Friedrich and Stein, 1973).

Aggressive behavior as a disorder in children can be the manifestation of a variety of underlying causes, including genetic disorders, brain damage, borderline or psychotic states, abuse, neglect, abandonment, and inadequate parental models (Lewis et al., 1979a). Loss of the father as a result of divorce may lead to aggressive behavior, especially in boys (Tuckman and Regan, 1966). Aggressive disorders are more common in boys from lower socioeconomic backgrounds, and the disorders are often accompanied by academic difficulties and anxiety (Wolff, 1961; 1967; 1971).

Violence in children and adolescents, except in self-defense, is usually abnormal (Lewis et al., 1979a). Organic brain conditions, such as psychomotor epilepsy and episodic dyscontrol, may underlie violent behavior. The organic dyscontrol syndrome (Mark and Ervin, 1970), thought to be more common in males, occurs most frequently during adolescence and early adulthood. Genetic factors may determine whether a lesion produces temporal lobe epilepsy or dyscontrol (Elliott, 1978). In some instances, perinatal trauma, head injury, infantile convulsions, or infectious illness may be associated with temper tantrums in infancy and childhood, and then by intense explosions of rage and by pathologic intoxication in adolescence. Children with 6- and 14-per-second spikes plus other EEG abnormalities exhibit significantly more aggressive behavior than comparison groups without the 6- and 14-per-second spikes, showing extreme outbursts of rage and violent acts with minimal provocation (Walter et al., 1960). There are no identifiable significant neuropsychiatric differences between adolescents who commit severely violent sexual acts and adolescents who commit severely violent nonsexual acts (Lewis et al., 1979b).

Children and adolescents who commit the most violent offense of murder are similarly found to have multiple vulnerabilities, including neurologic impairment, psychiatric illness, individual multiple psychotic symptoms, cognitive deficits, and parental abusiveness, both physical and sexual (Lewis et al., 1988). The interactive effect of these intrinsic vulnerabilities, child abuse, and parenteral violence is a powerful factor in the etiology of extreme aggression in children and adolescents.

What can be seen from the foregoing review is that the theory of "aggression" is surprisingly undeveloped. Part of the difficulty lies in the different levels of conceptualization. Clinically, the manifest "aggressive" behavior of the child should not be taken at its face value, but rather should be examined for its biological, motivational, and sociocultural roots and influences.

Note 12

Feshbach, S. (1970), Aggression. In: *Carmichael's Manual of Child Psychology* (Vol. 2). ed. P.H. Mussen. New York: John Wiley & Sons, Inc., p. 175. (After K.E. Moyer (1967), Kinds of aggression and their physiological basis. Report No. 67–12. Department of Psychology, Carnegie-Mellon University, Pittsburgh, Pa.)

1. Predatory aggression. Here the eliciting stimulus is the presence of a natural object of prey.

2. Intermale, spontaneous aggression. The release of this aggressive pattern is typically the presence of a male of the same species, and a male to which the attacker has not become habituated.

3. Terror-induced aggression. This type of aggression is always preceded by escape attempts and usually occurs under conditions of confinement in which the animal is cornered by some threatening agent.

4. Irritable aggression. This response is elicited by a wide range of stimuli and is characterized by an affective display. It is not preceded by attempts to escape.

5. Territorial defense. The stimulus situation eliciting this behavior entails an area which the animal has established as its "territory" and an intruder, typically but not necessarily an animal of the same species.

6. Defense of the young. This form of aggression among mammals is usually displayed by the female. The stimulus complex evoking the aggression consists of the presence of the young and the proximity of a threatening agent to the young of the animal.

7. Instrumental aggression. Any of the preceding classes of aggression may produce a stimulus change resulting in reinforcement of the behavior. Instrumental aggression is characterized by the increase in the probability of an aggressive response to a particular stimulus situation as a result of prior reinforcement.

REFERENCES

Alpert, J.E., Cohen, D.J., Shaywitz, B.A., and Piccirillo, M. (1981), Neurochemical and behavioral organization: Disorders of attention, activity and aggression. In: *Vulnerabilities to Delinquency*, ed. D.O. Lewis. New York: Spectrum.

Burks, H., and Harrison, S. (1962), Aggressive behavior as a means of avoiding depression. *Am. J. Orthopsychiatry*, 32:416.

Dollard, J., Doob, L.W., Miller, N.E., Mowrer, O.H., and Sears, R.R. (1939), *Frustration and Aggression*. New Haven: Yale University Press.

Ehrhardt, A., and Baker, S. (1974), Fetal androgens, human central nervous system differentiation and behavior sex differences. In: *Sex Differences in Behavior*, ed. R. Friedman, R. Richart, and R.L.V. Wiele. New York: John Wiley & Sons, Inc.

Elliott, F.A. (1978), Neurological factors in violent behavior (the dyscontrol syndrome). In: *Violence and Responsibility*, ed. R.L. Sadoff. New York: Spectrum, pp. 59–86.

Fairbairn, W.R.D. (1952), *An Object-Relations Theory of the Personality*. New York: Basic Books.

Feshbach, S. (1964), The function of aggression and the regulation of aggressive drive. *Psychol. Rev.*, 71:257–272.

Feshbach, S. (1970), Aggression. In: *Carmichael's Manual of Child Psychology* (Vol. 2), ed. P.H. Mussen. New York: John Wiley & Sons, Inc., pp. 159–259.

Freud, S. (1920), *Beyond the Pleasure Principle*, Standard Edition, 18 (1955). London: The Hogarth Press.

Friedrich, L.K., and Stein, A.H. (1973), Aggressive and prosocial television programs and the natural behavior of preschool children. *Monogr. Soc. Res. Child Dev.*, 38. No. 4.

Goodenough, F.L. (1931), *Anger in Young Children*. Minneapolis: University of Minnesota Press.

Hamburg, D. (1974), Ethological perspectives on human aggressive behavior. In: *Ethology and Psychiatry*, ed. N. White. Toronto: University of Toronto Press, pp. 209–219.

Hartmann, H. (1950), Comments on the psychoanalytic theory of the ego. *Psychoanal. Study Child*, 5:74–96.

Hartmann, H., Kris, E., and Loewenstein, R.M. (1949), Notes on the theory of aggression: I. Introduction. *Psychoanal. Study Child*, 3/4:9–12.

Hook, E.B. (1973), Behavioral implications of the human XYY genotype. *Science*, 179:139–150.

Hutt, C. (1972), Sexual differentiation in human development. In: *Gender Differences: Their Ontogeny and Significance*, ed. C. Orensted and C.C. Taylor. London: Churchill-Livingstone.

Kagan, J., and Moss, H.A. (1962), *Birth to Maturity*. New York: John Wiley & Sons, Inc.

Korner, A.F., and Thoman, E.B. (1970), Visual alertness in neonates as evoked by maternal care. *J. Exp. Child Psychol.*, 10:67–68.

Korner, A.F., and Thoman, E.B. (1972), The relative efficacy of contact and vestibular proprioceptive stimulation in soothing neonates. *Child Dev.*, 43:443–453.

Lesch, M., and Nyhan, W.L. (1964), A familial disorder of uric acid metabolism and central nervous system function. *Am. J. Med.*, 36:561.

Lewis, D.O., Pincus, J.H., Bard, B., et al. (1988), Neuropsychiatric, psychoeducational and family characteristics of 16 juveniles condemned to death in the United States. *Am. J. Psychiatry*, 145:584–589.

Lewis, D.O., Shanok S.S., Pincus, J.H., and Glaser, G.

(1979a), Violent juvenile delinquents: Psychiatric, neurological, psychological and abuse factors. *J. Am. Acad. Child Psychiatry*, 18:307–319.

Lewis, D.O., Shanok, S.S., and Pincus, J.H. (1979b), Juvenile male sexual offenders. *Am. J. Psychiatry*, 136:1194–1196.

Lorenz, K. (1966), *On Aggression*. New York: Harcourt, Brace & World.

Mark, V.H., and Ervin, F.R. (1970), *Violence and the Brain*. New York: Harper & Row.

Mattsson, Å., Schelling, D., Olwens, D., Löw, D., and Svensson, J. (1980), Plasma testosterone, aggressive behavior, and personality dimensions in young male delinquents. *J. Am. Acad. Child Psychiatry*, 19:476–490.

Miller, N.E. (1941), The frustration-aggression hypothesis. *Psychol. Rev.*, 48:337–342.

Money, J., and Ehrhardt, A.A. (1968), Pre-natal hormone exposure: Possible effects on behavior in man. In: *Endocrinology and Human Behavior*, ed. R.P. Michael. London: Oxford University Press.

Morton, J.H., Addison, H., Addison, R.G., Hunt, L., and Sullivan, H. (1953), A clinical study of pre-menstrual tension. *Am. J. Obstet Gynecol.*, 65:1182–1191.

Moyer, K.E. (1967), Quoted in Feshbach, S. (1970), Aggression. In: *Carmichael's Manual of Child Psychology* (Vol. 2), ed. P.H. Mussen. New York: John Wiley & Sons, Inc., p. 175.

Moyer, K.E. (1971), *The Physiology of Hostility.* Chicago: Markham.

Nielson, J., and Christensen, A.L. (1974), Thirty-five males with double Y chromosome. *Psychol. Med.*, 4:28–37.

Nyhan, W.L. (1978), The Lesch-Nyhan syndrome. *Dev. Med Child Neurol.*, 20:376.

Owen, D.R. (1972), The 47 XYY male: A review. *Psychol. Bull.* 78:209–233.

Reinisch, J.M. (1981), Prenatal exposure to synthetic progestins increases potential for aggression in humans. *Science*, 221:1171–1173.

Rosenzweig, S. (1970), Sex differences in reaction to frustration among adolescents. In: *The Psychopathology of Adolescence*, eds. J. Zubin and A.M. Freedman. New York: Grune and Stratton, pp. 90–102.

Schaffer. E.G. (1966), Activity level as a constitutional determinant of infantile reaction to deprivation. *Child Dev.*, 37:595–602.

Sears, R.R., Maccoby, E.E., and Levin, H. (1957), *Patterns of Child Rearing*. Evanston, Ill.: Row, Peterson.

Storr, A. (1968), *Human Aggression*. New York: Atheneum. (Bantam Books, 1970.)

Suomi, S. (1977), Development of attachment and other social behaviors in rhesus monkeys. In: *Attachment Behavior*, eds. T. Alloway, P. Pliner, and I. Kramer. New York: Plenum Publishing.

Thomas, A., Birch H.G., Chess, S., Hertzig, M.E., and Korn, S. (1963), *Behavioral Individuality in Early Childhood*. New York: New York University Press.

Tuckman, J., and Regan, R.A. (1966), Intactness of the home and behavioral problems in children. *J. Child Psychol. Psychiatry*, 7:225–233.

U.S. Public Health Service Report to the Surgeon General (1972), *Television and Growing Up: The Impact of Televised Violence*. Washington, D.C.: U.S. Government Printing Office.

Walter, R.D., Colbert, E.G., Koegler, R.R., Palmer, J.O., and Bond, P.M. (1960), A controlled study of the 14- and 6-per-second EEG pattern. *Arch. Gen. Psychiatry*, 2:559–566.

Wasman, M., and Flynn, J.P. (1962), Directed attack elicited from hypothalamus. *Arch. Neurol.*, 6:220–227.

Werry, J.S., and Quay, H.C. (1971), The prevalence of behavior symptoms in young elementary school children. *Am. J. Orthopsychiatry*, 41:136–143.

Wolff, S. (1961), Symptomatology and outcome of preschool children with behavior disorders attending a child guidance clinic. *J. Child Psychol. Psychiatry*, 2:269–276.

Wolff, S. (1967), Behavioral characteristics of primary school children referred to a psychiatric department. *Br. J. Psychiatry*, 113:885–893.

Wolff, S. (1971), Dimensions and clusters of symptoms in disturbed children. *Br. J. Psychiatry*, 118:421–427.

Yalom, I., Green, R., and Fisk, N. (1973), Prenatal exposure to female hormones: Effect on psychosexual development. *Arch. Gen. Psychiatry*, 28:554–561.

8

AFFECT DEVELOPMENT

The expression of affects, or emotions, which may be positive (e.g., feelings of happiness, joy, exhilaration, pride, and love) or negative (e.g., feelings of anxiety, anger, sadness, shame, guilt, disgust, and fear), appears to develop in the first place from early body behaviors such as smiling and crying. However, even these early behaviors are not simple and, as in the case of crying, may already be highly differentiated at birth (Wolff, 1969).

Although anxiety and depression appear to be complex affects, they, along with other affects, can be recognized by well-defined patterns of facial expression. Patterns of facial expression have been described for such emotions as happiness, surprise, fear, distress, anger, sadness, disgust, and shame (Eckman and Friesen, 1975; Izard, 1971). These patterns are exhibited in infancy (Izard, 1977). Within the next 2 to 4 years, children acquire progressively increased skills in both perception and expression of emotion; typically the capacity to discriminate affective expressions is advanced over the ability to produce them. (Odom and Lemond, 1972).

These early body behaviors and affects soon undergo a complex development that involves neurologic maturation, temperament, cognition, learning, and experience in the context of specific environmental situations and responses. There appears to be a progressive differentiation from more or less global affective states, such as a generalized excitement, to more specific emotions, such as anger and fear, that appear some time after 6 months of age. Some affects, such as guilt, may not be expressed until the second year

70

(see p. 182). (see p. 182). By the time a child is in nursery school the child not only has a wide range of affects, but is also aware of these affects both in himself or herself and in others. The child also develops the capacity to label emotions. Subsequent development varies with each affect and also varies according to the different experiences of the child.

PLEASURE

The smile is probably the earliest indication of pleasure. Newborns will exhibit the neonatal or "reflex" smile (really a half smile that does not involve the eye muscles) (Korner, 1969). Social smiling appears between the 4th and 6th weeks of life; it involves the entire face and occurs in response to social stimulation (Sroufe and Water, 1976). Laughter occurs after smiling, again in response to stimulation. Baby games such as peek-a-boo become effective elicitors of laughter and pleasure. Smiling and laughter appear to be manifestations of heightened arousal; older infants will laugh when they master a task.

ANGER

Anger is a prominent affect in 2-year-olds, manifested by temper tantrums. As language develops, the child is able to express anger verbally, although boys still continue to express their anger physically. The most common cause of early temper outburst is some conflict with parental authority; later outbursts may arise from conflicts with peers, especially during the nursery school years when conflicts about play may arise.

DEPRESSION

Depressive affect, manifested by crying, withdrawal, reduced activity, lack of responsiveness, and a sad appearance, may be seen in infants who have been maternally deprived, neglected, or abused. Similar symptoms may be seen throughout childhood. Depressive affect occurs in about 12% of 10-year-olds, and increases to about 20% in 14- and 15-year-old adolescents (Rutter, Tizard and Whitmore, 1970). An older child may feel rejected, and may have a low self-esteem. During adolescence the prevalence and severity of major depressive disorder increase markedly, with some preponderance in girls, culminating in depression being twice as common in adult women as in adult men. Depression in adolescents is often accompanied by suicidal thoughts.

ANXIETY

Anxiety in children appears to develop in part out of a biologically determined pattern of response to situations that are potentially dangerous to survival. These include strangers, unfamiliar or discrepant situations, the unknown, being alone, being isolated, being abandoned, darkness, heights, loud noises, objects that loom large or approach too rapidly, and loss of support or nurturance. These situations may have been associated through evolution with the approach of predators or other hazards. Some of these situations may be ameliorated by experience, the level of arousal, the reassuring presence of the mother, and the infant's response options (e.g., whether he or she can crawl back to mother). Many anxieties change or even disappear as the infant's experience broadens and cognitive development occurs.

The general behavioral manifestations of anxiety in children include fidgetiness, shyness, compulsive symptoms, and an anxious appearance.

The physiologic changes that accompany anxiety have been reviewed by Lader (1980) and summarized by Werry (1986) as follows:

1. **Cardiovascular:** increased pulse rate, vasoconstriction in the fingers, raised blood pressure.
2. **Pupillary:** longer dilatation duration under stress.
3. **Respiratory:** increased respiratory rate, less efficient utilization of inspired oxygen.
4. **Musculoskeletal:** increased amplitude of finger tremor, raised muscle tension.
5. **Electroencephalogram** (EEG): decreased amounts of alpha and increased beta rhythms, diminished contingent negative variation (CNV).
6. **Endocrine:** elevated blood cortisol, urinary 17-hydroxy corticosteroids and aldosterone, blood and urinary catecholamines.
7. **Palmar sweat glands:** increased conductance, increased spontaneous fluctuations in conductance, slower habituation to novel stimuli.

These changes in essence produce a state of "over-alertness, over-arousal, and over-preparedness" (Lader, 1980; p. 238).

Fears and Anxiety

Not surprisingly, most children show some fears (Jersild and Holmes, 1935). However, the fears change over the course of development. Young infants react with anxiety to sudden stimulus change. During the first year, stranger anxiety (fear of the stranger, "8-month anxiety") and separation anxiety reactions are common. Preschool children fear animals, the dark, natural phenomena such as thunder and lightning, and frightening dreams with ghosts and monsters. Grade-school children fear bodily injury. Older children and adolescents develop anxiety about school performance (Hill, 1972; Sarason, 1975) and social relations. Adults may continue to experience anxiety in relation to achievement (test anxiety, fear of failure), social acceptance (social anxiety), physical danger, dread of being alone (Bernstein and Allen, 1969), and death. Although many childhood fears and anxieties abate with maturation and development, there is at present little longitudinal research on prediction and outcome of the various fears and anxieties (Campbell, 1986).

PSYCHOANALYTIC CONCEPTUALIZATION

Psychoanalytic explanations of affects in general and anxiety in particular involve the concept of signals. For example, Ego is said to develop "signal anxiety" in the face of an impending "danger situation," which may be real or fantasized. Danger situations are thought to follow a developmental sequence: The infant fears first the loss of the mothering person, then the loss of the love of the mothering person, followed by fear of bodily harm, and the fear of Superego guilt or of Ego disintegration. The purpose of the signal anxiety, which is an unpleasurable experience, is to mobilize mechanisms of defense to prevent the individual from being flooded with overwhelming anxiety. The defense mechanisms in turn also follow, to some extent, a developmental sequence, starting with projection, introjection and projective identification, repression and denial, moving on to reaction formations, turning against the self, isolation and undoing, on to defenses typically seen in adolescence, e.g., intellectualization. Other affects, such as depression, may have similar signal functions.

A multiple layering of affects and defenses is thought to occur, e.g., reaction formations and guilt may be mobilized to deal with anxiety aroused by an unacceptable aggressive urge; the guilt may in turn become too uncomfortable, necessitating the mobilization of rage to ward off the guilt; the rage in turn may be dealt with by further defense mechanisms, e.g., displacement, projection, undoing, isolation, and so on. The almost impossible task of scientifically verifying this sequence is readily apparent. Further, the theory does not explain how perceptions and fantasies are transposed into anxiety or other affects.

ETHOLOGIC CONCEPTUALIZATION

Charles Darwin (1872) first noted that patterns of affective expression are universal and recognized readily across vastly different cultures (Izard, 1971); Darwin also noted similarities in affective displays across species and the potential adaptive function of affective displays. Ethologists stress the adaptive or protective functions of affect. For example, fear responses become prominent just at the point where infants are able to move independently and thus are able to move away from threatening stimuli. Similarly, the separation anxiety that occurs when attachment figures become unavailable may serve to restore attachment; this kind of separation anxiety may, in some instances, later become the basis for "school phobia." Repeated separations and threats of abandonment may initially give rise to anger and subsequently result in the "affectionless character." Actual losses may be followed by grief, mourning, and the affect of depression (Bowlby, 1973).

COGNITIVE CONCEPTUALIZATION

Attempts have been made to account for affective development on the basis of both cognitive processes and learning theory. The interrelation between affects and cognition is best seen in the "fear-of-strangers" reaction. Kagan (1974), for example, has suggested that when the infant experiences a cognitive discrepancy on seeing an unfamiliar face, fear gives rise to the "fear-of-strangers" reaction.

Affective responses may also be learned. For example, certain fears can be acquired through conditioning, although the theory is far from settled (Rutter, 1980). Then again, a child may respond to stress with passivity and a feeling of having no control, leading to a cognitive set of "learned helplessness," which may predispose the child to depression (Seligman, 1976). This learned helplessness may be more prominent in girls, possibly as a result of feedback implying intellectual failings a girl may receive from teachers. Thus learned helplessness may contribute to the finding that adult women are more prone to depression than men.

Although affects serve an adaptive function, they may also be disorganizing. Excessive amounts of affects such as anxiety, fear, anger, and depression may lead to dysfunction and breakdown. At the other end of the spectrum, affective deprivation may result in an emotionally blunted personality, with lack of curiosity, fewer expressions of pleasure and, in some cases, apparent fearlessness. Neither cognitive processes nor learning theory can totally account for the developmental course nor the universal nature of affective expression. For example, stranger anxiety cannot be explained on the basis of conditioning; the smile of blind infants (Fraiberg, 1974) cannot be explained on the basis of imitation. Individual differences in affective expression are significant, even in children at the same age and developmental level. Precise mechanisms that account for the complex range of affective experience, e.g., empathy, jealousy, and admiration, have yet to be identified.

Numerous questions arise from these concepts, and much research is required to elucidate the answers (Emde, 1980).

REFERENCES

Bernstein, D.A., and Allen, G.J., (1969), Fear survey schedule II. Normative data and factor analyses based upon a large college sample. *Behav. Res. Ther.*, 7:403–407.

Bowlby, J. (1973), *Attachment and Loss, Vol. 2, Separation: Anxiety and Anger.* London: Hogarth Press.

Campbell, S.B. (1986), Developmental issues in childhood anxiety. In: *Anxiety Disorders of Childhood*, ed. R. Gittelman. New York: The Guilford Press, pp. 24–57.

Darwin, C. (1872/1975), *The Expression of Emotions in Man and Animals.* Chicago: University of Chicago Press.

Eckman, P., and Friesen, W. (1975), *Unmasking the Face.* Englewood Cliffs, N.J.: Prentice-Hall.

Emde, R. (1980), Toward a psychoanalytic theory of affect: In: *The Course of Life Vol I: Infancy and Early Childhood*, ed. S.I. Greenspan and G.H. Pollock. Washington, D.C.: D.H.H.S. Publication No. (ADM) 80-786, U.S. Government Printing Office.

Fraiberg, S. (1974), Blind infants and their mothers: An examination of the sign system. In: *The Effect of the Infant on the Caregiver*, eds. M. Lewis and L. Rosenblum. New York: John Wiley & Sons.

Hill, K.T. (1972), Anxiety in the evaluative context. In: *The Young Child: Reviews of Research* (Vol 2), ed. W.W. Hartup. Washington, DC: Natural Association for the Education of Young Children.

Izard, C. (1971), *The Face of Emotion.* New York: Meredith.

Izard, C. (1977), *Human Emotions.* New York: Plenum Publishing.

Jersild, A.T., and Holmes, F.B. (1935), *Children's Fears.* New York: Teachers College, Columbia University.

Kagan, J. (1974), Discrepancy, temperament, and infant distress. In: ed. M. Lewis, and L.A. Rosenblum. pp. 229–248.

Korner, A.F. (1969), Neonatal startles, smiles, erections, and reflect such as related to state, sex, and individuality. *Child Dev.*, 40:1039–1053.

Lader, M.H. (1980), The psychophysiology of anxiety. In *Handbook of Biological Psychiatry, Part II: Brain Mechanisms and Abnormal Behavior—Psychophysiology*, ed. H.M. VanPraag, M.H. Lader, O.J. Rafaelsen, and E.J. Sachar. New York: Marcel Dekker.

Odom, R.D., and Lemond, C.M. (1972), Developmental differences in the perception and production of facial expression. *Child Dev.*, 43:359–369.

Rutter, M. (1980) (Ed.), *Scientific Foundations of Developmental Psychiatry.* London: Heinemann.

Rutter, M., Tizard, J., and Whitmore, K. (Eds.) (1970), *Education, Health and Behavior.* London: Longmans.

Sarason, I.G. (1975), Test anxiety, attention, and the general problem of anxiety. In: *Stress and Anxiety* (Vol 1). ed. C.D. Spielbergen and I.G. Sarason. Washington, DC: Hemisphere.

Seligman, M.E.P. (1976), Depression and learned helplessness. In: *Research in Neurosis.* ed. H.M. van Praaj. Utrecht: Bohn, Scheltema and Holkema, pp. 72–107.

Sroufe, A.L.A., and Waters, E. (1976), The ontogenesis of smiling and laughter: A perspective on the organization and of development in infancy. *Psych. Rev.*, 83:173–189.

Werry, S. (1986), Diagnosis and assessment. In: *Anxiety Disorders of Childhood.* ed. R. Gittelman. New York: The Guilford Press, pp. 73–100.

Wolff, P.H. (1969), The natural history of crying and other vocalizations in early infancy. In: *Determinants of Infant Behavior* (Vol. 4), ed. B.M. Foss. London: Methuen.

9

PSYCHOANALYTIC LINES OF DEVELOPMENT

Psychoanalysis has had a profound impact on child psychiatry and child development. In his work with neurotic adults, Sigmund Freud became concerned with the effects of early childhood experience on later development. Based on psychoanalyses of adults, and later, of children, Freud's theory came to include both a general theory of mental functioning (metapsychology) as well as a clinical theory applicable to mental disorders. Freud changed his theory significantly during his lifetime. Initially, psychoanalytic theory was concerned with concepts of energy and "cathexis," then with a distinction between the conscious and unconscious contents of the mind, and finally, with a specific model of the mind that posited structures of ego, id, and superego. Subsequent to Freud's death, there was a strong emphasis on the ego and its functions (ego psychology); more recently the role of object relations and "self" psychology have been emphasized. Although Freud's direct clinical work with children was quite limited, his daughter Anna elaborated a psychoanalytic model of development in childhood.

A comprehensive view of inferred intrapsychic development using the idea of "development lines" has been conceptualized by Anna Freud (1965; see Note 13). Six lines of development have been described:

1. from dependency to adult object relationships;
2. from suckling to rational eating;
3. from wetting and soiling to bladder and bowel control;
4. from irresponsibility to responsibility in body management;
5. from egocentricity to companionship;
6. from body to toy and from play to work.

Other lines of development, such as from cooing to complex sentences and from early schema to abstract thoughts, could also be described (see the earlier chapters). The following brief summary outlines the major elements in the six lines just listed.

FROM DEPENDENCY TO ADULT OBJECT RELATIONSHIPS

This phase starts with the infant in a state of more or less "biological unity" with the mother. In the first month or two the infant is said to be in a normal autistic phase, virtually oblivious to the environment. During the next 6 months the infant's behavior is conceptualized as being in a normal symbiotic phase, in which the infant behaves as though he or she and the mother were an omnipotent system: a dual unity within one common boundary. By 9 months, separation-individuation is said to occur; that is, the infant shows some separate functioning in the presence of and with the emotional availability of the mother. However, the relationship is still regarded as a need-fulfilling, "part-object," anaclitic relationship, i.e., the "object" (the mother) exists for the infant only inasmuch as and so long as it (she) satisfies a need. From

18 months to 36 months, "object constancy" is achieved. During this period the child's relationship with adults is highly ambivalent, with much clinging, dominating, and torturing ("the anal sadistic stage").

From 3 to 6 years, the child is said to be in an object-centered, phallic-oedipal phase, characterized by possessiveness of the parent of the opposite sex, jealousy and rivalry of the parent of the same sex, curiosity, and exhibitionism.

From 6 to 11 years, the child is in so-called latency, with libido transfer to teachers and other adults, fantasies of disillusionment and denigration of the parents ("family romance" fantasies), and aim-inhibited interests.

During preadolescence, a return to earlier part-object, need-fulfilling, ambivalent attitudes occurs. At adolescence a struggle with infantile object ties reemerges, accompanied by strong defenses against pregenitality as the adolescent strives toward genital supremacy with objects of the opposite sex outside the family. While the term "object" is used by psychoanalysts to signify a person, the use of the term by itself does not confer any greater scientific precision. Moreover, it is somewhat misleading in that the first "objects" are really *people*.

FROM SUCKLING TO RATIONAL EATING

This line, according to Freud, begins with nursing, followed by weaning at about 3 to 4 months and the change to self-feeding at about 10 months. The equation food = mother still dominates. By age 3, "disagreements" with mother occur about the amount and intake of food ("table manners") and about eating sweets. Various food fads emerge. Gradually, the equation food = mother fades, to be replaced by certain irrational attitudes toward eating, e.g., fears of being poisoned (orally impregnated), and of getting fat (pregnant), and fears related to intake and output (anal birth), as well as a variety of reaction formations against cannibalistic and sadistic fantasies that have been

inferred or interpreted as being present in the course of the psychoanalytic treatment of children. Finally, these sexualized attitudes give way to a rational attitude toward food. The data for these ideas are largely anecdotal, and have not been validated by rigorous scientific research.

FROM WETTING AND SOILING TO BLADDER AND BOWEL CONTROL

This line starts with the child's freedom to wet and soil and continues until the parents decide to intervene. Subsequently, feces are endowed with interest, love, and aggression as the infant offers feces as gifts or as the child soils as an act of aggression. The infant then identifies with his or her parents' wishes and he or she internalizes controls, a phenomenon that often is accompanied by reaction formations, e.g., disgust against the desire to mess. Finally, autonomous control is fully established. Again, this psychoanalytic interpretation of motives and wishes has not been independently validated.

FROM IRRESPONSIBILITY TO RESPONSIBILITY IN BODY MANAGEMENT

This line extends from the early establishment of the pain barrier and a narcissistic interest in the body through a recognition of external dangers to, finally, a voluntary endorsement of health rules.

FROM EGOCENTRICITY TO COMPANIONSHIP

Initially, other children are perceived for the most part as disturbers of the mother-child relationship. Then other children are related to as mere inanimate objects. By age 3, other children are seen as helpmates, at least for the duration of the task at hand. Finally, other children are recognized as human objects in their own right, and true sharing, admiring, fearing, and empathy develop.

FROM BODY TO TOY AND FROM PLAY TO WORK

Initially, the infant plays only with his or her own body and, by extension, the mother's body. Then the infant becomes attached to a particular transitional object (see Note 31), which gradually becomes any soft and cuddly toy, especially at bedtime. Gradually, the child turns to toys that may represent the body. A pleasure in mobile toys can be observed. Often toys are used to express ambivalent fantasies. Later, toys (e.g., dolls) serve as displacement objects for oedipal feelings. Finally, play becomes an end in itself, with pleasure in the finished product. The ability to play in this way is the forerunner of the ability to work, marked by a capacity to delay, control, inhibit, and modify impulses in the light of social reality.

The "meaning" of the concept of developmental lines is elusive until it is realized that the concept is part of a metapsychologic profile. In turn, the metapsychologic profile is an integration of empirical observations and psychoanalytic theory, including structural, dynamic, genetic, economic, and adaptive metapsychologic points of view. These five points of view all have a developmental perspective. The strength (and limitation) of the profile lies in its view of the person as a complex organism. However, the very complexity of the psychoanalytic view of the person makes the profile cumbersome to use. Moreover, some of the concepts lack clarity, and assessment and measurement in many, if not all, of the developmental lines are difficult. The reliability of statements is low, and prediction is hazardous. Nevertheless, some child psychoanalysts still find this concept useful in, for example, assessing a child's readiness for nursery school, arriving at a diagnosis, or deciding whether psychoanalytic treatment is indicated. In clinical practice, however, most such assessments are usually made on a simpler basis.

Note 13

From A. Freud (1965), *Normality and Pathology in Childhood.* New York: International Universities Press, pp. 64–68.

Prototype of a Developmental Line: From Dependency to Emotional Self-Reliance and Adult Object Relationships

To serve as the prototype for all others, there is one basic developmental line which has received attention from analysts from the beginning. This is the sequence which leads from the newborn's utter dependence on maternal care to the young adult's emotional and material self-reliance—a sequence for which the successive stages of libido development (oral, anal, phallic) merely form the inborn, maturational base. The steps on this way are well documented from the analyses of adults and children, as well as from direct analytic infant observation. They can be listed, roughly, as follows:

1. The biological unity between the mother-infant couple, with the mother's narcissism extending to the child, and the child including the mother in his internal "narcissistic milieu" (Hoffer, 1952), the whole period being further subdivided (according to Margaret Mahler, 1952) into the autistic, symbiotic, and separation-individuation phases with significant danger points for developmental disturbances lodged in each individual phase;

2. the part object (Melanie Klein, 1957), or need-fulfilling, anaclitic relationship, which is based on the urgency of the child's body needs and drive derivatives and is intermittent and fluctuating, since object cathexis is sent out under the impact of imperative desires and withdrawn again when satisfaction has been reached;

3. the stage of object constancy, which enables a positive inner image of the object to be maintained, irrespective of either satisfactions or dissatisfactions;

4. the ambivalent relationship of the preoedipal, anal-sadistic stage, characterized by the ego attitudes of clinging, torturing, dominating, and controlling the love objects;

5. the completely object-centered phallic-oedipal phase, characterized by possessiveness of the parent of the opposite sex (or vice versa), jealousy of and rivalry with the parent of the same sex, protectiveness, curiosity, bids for admiration, and exhibitionistic attitudes; in girls a phallic-oedipal (masculine) relationship to the mother preceding the oedipal relationship to the father;

6. the latency period, i.e., the postoedipal lessening of drive urgency and the transfer of libido

from the parental figures to contemporaries, community groups, teachers, leaders, impersonal ideals, and aim-inhibited, sublimated interests, with fantasy manifestations giving evidence of disillusionment with and denigration of the parents ("family romance," twin fantasies, etc.);

7. the preadolescent prelude to the "adolescent revolt," i.e., a return to early attitudes and behavior, especially of the part-object, need-fulfilling, and ambivalent type;

8. the adolescent struggle around denying, reversing, loosening, and shedding the tie to the infantile objects, defending against pregenitality, and finally establishing genital supremacy with libidinal cathexis transferred to objects of the opposite sex, outside the family.

While the details of these positions have long been common knowledge in analytic circles, their relevance for practical problems is being explored increasingly in recent years. As regards, for example, the much-discussed consequences of a child's separation from the mother, the parents or the home, a mere glance at the unfolding of the developmental line will be sufficient to show convincingly why the common reactions to, respectively, the pathological consequences of such happenings are as varied as they are, following the varying psychic reality of the child on the different levels. Infringements of the biological mother-infant tie (phase 1), for whatever reason they are undertaken, will thus give rise to separation anxiety (Bowlby, 1960) proper; failure of the mother to play her part as a reliable need-fulfilling and comfort-giving agency (phase 2) will cause breakdowns in individuation (Mahler, 1952) or anaclitic depression (Spitz, 1946), or other manifestations of deprivation (Alpert, 1959), or precocious ego development (James, 1960), or what has been called a "false self" (Winnicott, 1955). Unsatisfactory libidinal relations to unstable or otherwise unsuitable love objects during anal sadism (phase 4) will disturb the balance fusion between libido and aggression and give rise to uncontrollable aggressivity, destructiveness, etc. (A. Freud, 1949). It is only after object constancy (phase 3) has been reached that the external absence of the object is substituted for, at least in part, by the presence of an internal image which remains stable; on the strength of this achievement temporary separations can be lengthened, commensurate with the advances in object constancy. Thus, even if it remains impossible to name the chronological age when separations can be tolerated, according to

the developmental line it can be stated when they become phase-adequate and nontraumatic, a point of practical importance for the purposes of holidays for the parents, hospitalization of the child, convalescence, entry into nursery school, etc.*

There are other practical lessons which have been learned from the same developmental sequence:

that the clinging attitudes of the toddler (phase 4) are the result of preoedipal ambivalence, not of maternal spoiling;

that it is unrealistic on the part of parents to expect of the preoedipal period (up to the end of phase 4) the mutuality in object relations which belongs to the next level (phase 5) only;

that no child can be fully integrated in group life before libido has been transferred from the parents to the community (phase 6). Where the passing of the oedipus complex is delayed and phase 5 is protracted as the result of an infantile neurosis, disturbances in adaptation to the group, lack of interest, school phobias (in day school), extreme homesickness (in boarding school) will be the order of the day;

that reactions to adoption are most severe in the latter part of the latency period (phase 6) when, according to the normal disillusionment with the parents, all children feel as if adopted and the feelings about the reality of adoption merge with the occurrence of the "family romance";

that sublimations, foreshadowed on the oedipal level (phase 5) and developed during latency (phase 6), may be lost during preadolescence (phase 7), not through any developmental or educational failure but owing to the phase-adequate regression to early levels (phases 2, 3, and 4);

that it is as unrealistic on the part of the parents to oppose the loosening of the tie to the family of the young person's battle against pregenital impulses in adolescence (phase 8) as it is to break the biological tie in phase 1 or to oppose pregenital autoeroticism in phases 1, 2, 3, 4, and 7.

REFERENCES TO NOTE 13

Alpert, A. (1959), Reversibility of pathological fixations associated with maternal deprivation in infancy. *Psychoanal. Study Child*, 14:169–185.

---

*If, by "mourning" we understand not the various manifestations of anxiety, distress, and malfunction which accompany object loss in the earliest phases but the painful, gradual process of detaching libido from an internal image, this, of course, cannot be expected to occur before object constancy (phase 3) has been established.

Bowlby, J. (1960), Separation anxiety. *Int. J. Psychoanal.*, 41:89–113.

Freud, A. (1949), Aggression in relation to emotional development. *Psychoanal. Study Child*, 3/4:37–42.

Hoffer, W. (1952), The mutual influences in the development of ego and id: Earliest stages. *Psychoanal. Study Child*, 7:31–41.

James, M. (1960), Premature ego development: Some observations upon disturbances in the first three years of life. *Int. J. Psychoanal.*, 41:288–294.

Klein, M. (1957), *Envy and Gratitude*. London: Tavistock.

Mahler, M.S. (1952), On child psychosis and schizophrenia: Autistic and symbiotic infantile psychoses. *Psychoanal. Study Child*, 7:286–305.

Spitz, R.A. (1946), Anaclitic depression. *Psychoanal. Study Child*, 2:313–342.

Winnicott, D.W. (1955), Metapsychological and clinical aspects of regression with the psycho-analytical set-up. *Int. J. Psychoanal.*, 36:16–26.

REFERENCE

Freud, A. (1965), *Normality and Pathology in Childhood*. New York: International Universities Press.

10

MORAL DEVELOPMENT

Moral behavior derives in part from the basic cultural rules governing social action that the child assimilates and internalizes, and moral development is the increase in the degree to which the internalization and accommodation of these basic cultural rules have occurred. From an evolutionary perspective, it has survival value (Fishbein, 1976). The process of internalization of values is usually assumed to be influenced by punishment and reward, identification with parents as models, and role-taking opportunities during play with peers. The degree to which internalization has taken place may be measured by the child's ability to resist temptation to break a rule (e.g., against cheating) when detection or punishment may *not* be a factor, the emotion of guilt, and the child's capacity to judge behavior. This capacity is complicated because it involves:

1. intelligence;
2. the capacity to anticipate future events;
3. the capacity for empathy with another person;
4. the ability to maintain attention and not give in to an impulse;
5. control of fantasies (especially aggressive fantasies);
6. a sense of self-esteem and confidence in oneself.

Fear of punishment is prominent in young children. Next to develop is an urge to confess. By age 12 or 13, most children seem to react directly to guilt and internal self-criticism when faced with the fact of their transgression, although this reaction often occurs at a much earlier age.

The reaction of guilt is caused in part by the threat of loss of love and in part by the threat of punishment. What also correlates with internal guilt is the remorse that is initially induced when a parent points out through reasoning—and within the limits of the child's understanding at any given stage of development—the harm that may be caused to others by a particular act of aggression.

Cheating in one situation does not necessarily imply that cheating will occur in another situation. Further, children are not "cheaters" or "honest"; there is a bell-shaped curve with an average of moderate cheating in the middle. Cheating may also depend on the effort required and risk of detection involved; i.e., noncheaters may simply be more cautious rather than more honest. The most influential factors determining resistance to temptation to cheat or disobey in preadolescents are situational (Kohlberg, 1964).

In Piaget's view, the cognitive limitations of the child 3 to 8 years old lead him to equate moral rules with physical laws, so that he views moral rules as fixed, eternal things. Perhaps this is because the child under the age of 8 cannot distinguish between subjective and objective aspects of his experience—what Piaget terms the child's realism. Another reason may be that the child under the age of 8 cannot distinguish his own perspective on events from the perspectives of others—what Piaget terms egocentrism. Piaget describes the development of moral judgment in terms of six aspects, all of which are related to, and seem to reflect, cognitive development. In general, all six dimensions reveal a development from judging in terms of immediate external physical consequences toward judging in terms of subjective or internal values. The six dimensions are (Kohlberg, 1964): intentionality in judgment, relativism in judgment, independence of sanctions, use of reciprocity, use of punishment to make restitution and to reform, and naturalistic views of misfortune.

INTENTIONALITY IN JUDGMENT

Young children tend to judge an act as bad mainly in terms of its actual *physical* consequences, whereas older children judge an act as bad in terms of the *intent* to do harm. Thus when children are asked who is worse, a child who breaks five cups while helping his mother set the table or a child who breaks one cup while stealing some jam, 4-year-olds say that the child who committed the larger accidental damage is worse, and 9-year-olds say that the "thief" is worse.

RELATIVISM IN JUDGMENT

Young children view acts as either totally right or totally wrong, and they assume that an adult is always right, whereas older children are aware of possible diversity in views of right and wrong. This point is illustrated by the responses of children who are told the following story: A lazy child had been forbidden by his teacher to get any help in his homework. But a friend helped the lazy child. The children told this story are then asked such questions as, Did the helping child think he was right or wrong for helping? Did the lazy child think he was right or wrong for accepting help? What does the teacher think? Six-year-olds say that the helping child would have thought he was wrong to help, and they expect everyone to agree with this single-minded judgment. Nine-year-olds realize that there might be more than one way to view the moral issues involved.

INDEPENDENCE OF SANCTIONS

The young child says an act is bad because it will elicit punishment, whereas an older child says an act is bad because it violates a rule or does harm to others. This point is illustrated by the responses of children who are told the following story: A child was being helpful by watching his baby brother while his mother was out. When his mother returned, she spanked the child. Four- or 5-year-olds say that the child must have done something bad to get punished; 7- or 8-year-olds say that the child was good, not bad, even though he was punished. Thus it can be seen that older children can separate issues.

USE OF RECIPROCITY

Four-year-old children do not use reciprocity as a reason for consideration of others, whereas children of 7 and older frequently do. Even 7-year-olds show mainly selfish and concrete reciprocity concerns. This point is illustrated by the responses of a group of 10-year-olds who were asked, "What does the Golden Rule say to do if a boy came up and hit you?" Most of the 10-year-olds interpreted the Golden Rule in terms of concrete reciprocity and say, "Hit him back. Do unto others as they do unto you." But by age 11 to 13, most children can clearly judge in terms of ideal reciprocity, in terms of putting oneself in someone else's shoes.

USE OF PUNISHMENT TO MAKE RESTITUTION AND TO REFORM

Young children advocate severe, painful punishment for misdeeds; older children favor milder punishments that will also lead to some reform of the person involved.

NATURALISTIC VIEWS OF MISFORTUNE

Children of 6 or 7 view accidents that follow misdeeds as punishment willed by God ("immanent justice"); older children do not make this connection.

To summarize Piaget's views on the moral judgments of the child (Piaget, 1977; see Note 14), moral development can be viewed in the context of the major stages of cognitive development:

1. *Preoperational Stage.* The morality of constraints—rules of behavior are viewed as natural laws handed down to the child by his or her parents. Violation brings retribution or unquestioned punishment, and no account is taken of motives.
2. *Stage of Concrete Operations.* Rules of behavior become a matter of mutual acceptance, with complete equality of treatment, but no account is taken of special circumstances.
3. *Stage of Formal Operations.* The morality of cooperation—rules can be constructed as required by the needs of the group so long as they can be agreed upon. Motives are now taken into account, and circumstances may temper the administration of justice.

As the child advances through these stages, a progressive decentering occurs, and moral judgments shift toward inner orientation and self-control.

Building on Piaget's views, Kohlberg (1964; see Note 15) has suggested three major levels of development of moral judgment:

1. *Level 1. Premorality (or Preconventional Morality)*
   a. Type 1. Punishment and obedience orientation (i.e., obedience to parents' superior force)
   b. Type 2. Naive instrumental hedonism (i.e., agreement to obey only in return for some reward)
2. *Level II: Morality of Conventional Role-Conformity*
   a. Type 3. Good-boy morality of maintaining good relations, approval of others (i.e., conformity to rules in order to please and gain approval)
   b. Type 4. Authority maintaining morality (i.e., adherence to rules for the sake of upholding social order)
3. *Level III: Morality of Self-Accepted Moral Principles*
   a. Type 5. Morality of social contract, of individual rights, and of, for example, democratically accepted law (with a reliance on a legalistic "social contract")
   b. Type 6. Morality of individual principles of conscience (there is voluntary compliance based on ethical principles; this level is probably not reached until early adolescence, and it may not be reached at all)

Interestingly, Jurkovic (1980) noted that delinquents differ in their level of moral development just as they do in their personality and behavioral style. Indeed, "not only do they vary from one another in stages of moral development, but they also fluctuate in their own reasoning level on differential moral problems" (p. 724)

Numerous criticisms have been made of Kohlberg's work. Certain of the stages, especially the later stages, have not been reliably replicated, and many believe that the descriptions of some of these stages are too politicized in favor of a liberal viewpoint. Others think that the stages described are, in any event, bound by culture, the historic moment, middle class status, the nature of the experimental situation used, and the male sex of the subjects. As a result of these criticisms, Kohlberg (1978) and Colby (1978) subsequently identified two types of reasoning at each stage: type A emphasizes literal interpretation of the rules and roles of society, whereas type B is a more consolidated form and refers to the intent of normative standards. However, in general, Kohlberg essentially held to the same hierarchical sequence and idealized end point.

More recently, Gilligan (1982a; see also Note 16) offered a different view of moral development in which an expanding connection with and concern for others were thought to represent an alternative developmental pathway and goal. This alternative and equally valid pathway has been demonstrated more often in girls than in boys, i.e., in general, girls seem to have "a greater sense of connection and concern with relationships more than with rules" (p. 202). Moral *behavior* and moral reasoning are not, necessarily, the same (Mischel and Mischel, 1976).

Note 14

Reprinted with permission of Macmillan Publishing Co., Inc. from "Egocentric thought in the child," in *The Moral Judgement of the Child*, by J. Piaget. First Free Press Paperback Edition, 1965.

The Idea of Justice

To bring our inquiry to a close, let us examine the answers given to a question which sums up all that we have been talking about. We asked the children, either at the end or at the beginning of our interrogatories, to give us themselves examples of what they regarded as unfair.*

The answers we obtained were of four kinds: (1) Behavior that goes against commands received from the adult—lying, stealing, breakages, in a word, everything that is forbidden. (2) Behavior that goes against the rules of a game. (3) Behavior that goes against equality (inequality in punishment as in treatment). (4) Acts of injustice connected with adult society (economic or political injustice). Now, statistically, the results show very clearly as functions of age:

	Forbidden	Games	Inequality	Social Injustice
6–8	64%	9%	27%	—
9–12	7%	9%	73%	11%

Here is an example of the identification of what is unfair with what is forbidden:

Age 6: "A little girl who has a broken plate," "to burst a balloon," "children who make a noise with their feet during prayers," "telling lies," "something not true," "It's not fair to steal," etc. . . .

Here are examples of inequalities:

Age 6: "Giving a big cake to one and a little one to another."

Age 10: "When you both do the same work and

---

*As a matter of fact, this term is not understood by all, but it can always be replaced by "not fair" (Fr. *pas juste*).

don't get the same reward." "Two children both do what they are told, and one gets more than the other." "To scold one child and not the other if they have both disobeyed."

Age 12: "A referee who takes sides."

And some example of social injustice:

Age 12: "A mistress preferring a pupil because he is stronger, or cleverer, or better dressed."

"A mother who won't allow her children to play with children who are less well dressed."

"Children who leave a little girl out of their games, who is not so well dressed as they are."

These obviously spontaneous remarks, taken together with the rest of our inquiry, allow us to conclude, insofar as one can talk of stages in the moral life, the existence of three great periods in the development of the sense of justice in the child. One period, lasting up to the age of 7–8, during which justice is subordinated to adult authority; a period contained approximately between 8–11, and which is that of progressive equalitarianism; and finally a period which sets in toward 11–12, and during which purely equalitarian justice is tempered by considerations of equity.

The first is characterized by the nondifferentiation of the notions of just and unjust from those of duty and disobedience: whatever conforms to the dictates of the adult authority is just. As a matter of fact even at this stage the child already looks upon some kinds of treatment as unjust, those, namely, in which the adult does not carry out the rules he has himself laid down for children (e.g., punishing for a fault that has not been committed, forbidding what has previously been allowed, etc.). But if the adult sticks to his own rules, everything he prescribes is just. In the domain of retributive justice, every punishment is accepted as perfectly legitimate, as necessary, and even as constituting the essence of morality; if lying were not punished, one would be allowed to tell lies, etc. In the stories where we have brought retributive justice into conflict with equality, the child belonging to this stage sets the necessity for punishment above equality of any sort. In the choice of punishments, expiation takes precedence over punishment by reciprocity, the very principle of the latter type of punishment not being exactly understood by the child. In the domain of immanent justice, more than three-quarters of the subjects under 8 believe in an automatic justice which emanates from physical nature and inanimate objects. If obedience and equality are brought into conflict, the child is always in favor of obedience: authority takes precedence over justice. Finally, in the domain of justice between children, the need for equality is already felt, but is yielded to only where it cannot possibly come into conflict with authority. For instance, the act of hitting back, which is regarded by the child of 10 as one of elementary justice, is considered "naughty" by children of 6 and 7, though, of course, they are always doing it in practice. (It will be remembered that the heteronomous rule, whatever may be the respect in which it is held mentally, is not necessarily observed in real life.) On the other hand, even in the relations between children, the authority of older ones will outweigh equality. . . .

The second period does not appear on the plane of reflection and moral judgment until about the age of 7 or 8. But it is obvious that this comes slightly later than what happens with regard to practice. This period may be defined by the progressive development of autonomy and the priority of equality over authority. In the domain of retributive justice, the idea of expiratory punishment is no longer accepted with the same docility as before, and the only punishments accepted as really legitimate are those based upon reciprocity. Belief in immanent justice is perceptibly on the decrease and moral action is sought for its own sake, independently of reward or punishment. In matters of distributive justice, equality rules supreme. In conflicts between punishment and equality, equality outweighs every other consideration. The same holds good a fortiori of conflicts with authority. Finally, in the relations between children, equalitarianism obtains progressively with increasing age.

Toward 11–12 we see a new attitude emerge, which may be said to be characterized by the feeling of equity, and which is nothing but a development of equalitarianism in the direction of relativity. Instead of looking for equality in identity, the child no longer thinks of the equal rights of individuals except in relation to the particular situation of each. In the domain of retributive justice this comes to the same thing as not applying the same punishment to all, but taking into account the [extenuating] circumstances of some. In the domain of distributive justice it means no longer thinking of a law as identical for all but taking account of the personal circumstances of each (favoring the younger ones, etc.). Far from leading to privileges, such an attitude tends to make equality more effectual than it was before.

Note 15

From L. Kohlberg (1964), Development of moral character. In: *Review of Child Development Research* (Vol. I), ed. M.L. Hoffman and L.W. Hoffman. New York: Russell Sage Foundation, pp. 400–404.

In an initial study of 72 boys of ages ten to sixteen, with Piaget procedures, six types of moral judgment were defined after extensive study. . . .

Each of the six general types of moral orientation could be defined in terms of its specific stance on 32 aspects of morality. In addition to areas suggested by the Piaget dimensions, the aspects ranged from "Motives for Moral Action" to "Universality of Moral Judgment," from "Concepts of Rights" to "Basis of Respect for Social Authority." As an example, the six types were defined as follows with regard to Aspect 10, "Motivation for Rule Obedience or Moral Action":

Stage 1. Obey rules to avoid punishment.

Stage 2. Conform to obtain rewards, have favors returned, and so on.

Stage 3. Conform to avoid disapproval, dislike by others.

Stage 4. Conform to avoid censure by legitimate authorities and resultant guilt.

Stage 5. Conform to maintain the respect of the impartial spectator judging in terms of community welfare.

Stage 6. Conform to avoid self-condemnation.

Aspect 10: Motivation for Moral Action
Stage 1: Punishment—Age 10:

(Should Joe tell on his older brother to his father?)

"In one way it would be right to tell on his brother or his father might get mad at him and spank him. In another way it would be right to keep quiet or his brother might beat him up."

Stage 2: Exchange and Reward—Jimmy, Age 13:

(Should Joe tell on his older brother to his father?)

"I think he should keep quiet. He might want to go someplace like that, and if he squeals on Alex, Alex might squeal on him."

Stage 3: Disapproval Concern—Andy, Age 16:

(Should Joe keep quiet about what his brother did?)

"If my father finds out later, he won't trust me. My brother wouldn't either, but I wouldn't have a *conscience* that he (my brother) didn't."

"I try to do things for my parents; they've always done things for me. I try to do everything my mother says; I try to please her. Like she wants me to be a doctor, and I want to, too, and she's helping me to get up there."

Stage 6: Self-condemnation Concern—Bill, Age 16:

(Should the husband steal the expensive black market drug needed to save his wife's life?)

"Lawfully no, but morally speaking, I think I would have done it. It would be awfully hard to live with myself afterward, knowing that I could have done something which would have saved her life and yet didn't for fear of punishment to myself.

The stages just listed would be generally taken to reflect moral internalization rather than cognitive development. Cognitive development is more immediately apparent in the following stages of thought about Aspect 3, "The Basis of Moral Worth of a Human Life":

Stage 1. The value of a human life is confused with the value of physical objects and is based on the social status or physical attributes of its possessor.

Stage 2. The value of human life is seen as instrumental to the satisfaction of the needs of its possessor or of other persons.

Stage 3. The value of a human life is based on the empathy and affection of family members and others toward its possessor.

Stage 4. Life is conceived as sacred in terms of its place in a categorical moral or religious order of rights and duties.

Stage 5. Life is valued both in terms of its relation to community welfare and in terms of life being a universal human right.

Stage 6. Belief in the sacredness of human life as representing a universal human value of respect for the individual.

Aspect 3: Basis of Moral Worth of a Human Life
Stage 1: Life's Value Based on Physical and Status Aspects—Tommy, Age 10:

(Why should the druggist give the drug to the dying woman when her husband couldn't pay for it?)

"If someone important is in a plane and is allergic to heights and the stewardess won't give him medicine because she's only got enough for one and she's got a sick one, a friend, in back, they'd probably put the stewardess in a lady's jail because she didn't help the important one."

(Is it better to save the life of one important person or a lot of unimportant people?)

"All the people that aren't important because one man just has one house, maybe a lot of furniture, but a whole bunch of people have an awful lot of furniture and some of these poor people might have a lot of money and it doesn't look it."

Stage 2: Life's Value as Instrumental to Need-Satisfaction—Tommy at age 13:

(Should the doctor "mercy-kill" a fatally ill woman requesting death because of her pain?)

"Maybe it would be good to put her out of her pain, she'd be better off that way. But the husband wouldn't want it, it's not like an animal. If a pet dies you can get along without it—it isn't something you really need. Well, you can get a new wife, but it's not really the same."

Stage 4: Life Sacred Because of a Social and Religious Order—John, Age 16:

(Should the doctor "mercy-kill" the woman?)

"The doctor wouldn't have the right to take a life, no human has the right. He can't create life, he shouldn't destroy it."

Stage 6: Life's Value as Expressing the Sacredness of the Individual—Steve, Age 16:

(Should the husband steal the expensive drug to save his wife?)

"By the law of society he was wrong but by the law of nature or of God the druggist was wrong and the husband was justified. Human life is above financial gain. Regardless of who was dying, if it was a total stranger, man has a duty to save him from dying."

. . . The age trends for the six stages, considered as including all aspects of morality, are indicated in the accompanying figure. It is evident that the first two types decrease with age, the next two increase until age thirteen and then stabilize, and the last two continue to increase from age thirteen to age sixteen. These age trends indicate that large groups of moral concepts and attitudes acquire meaning only in late childhood and adolescence and require the extensive background of cognitive growth and social experience associated with the age factor.

There are two possible interpretations of these age findings. Both common sense and most psychological theory would view such age differences as the effect of increased learning of the verbal morality characteristic of the adult American culture. Some patterns of moral verbalization are presumably easier to learn than others, are perhaps explicitly taught earlier, and hence are characteristic of younger ages.

Developmental theories suggest a second inter-

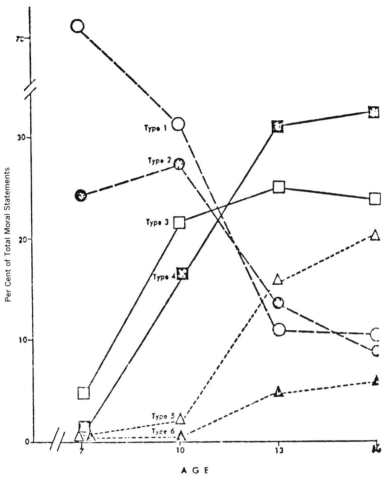

A G E

Mean Per Cent of Total Moral Statements of Each of Six Moral Types at Four Ages

pretation. The stages of moral thinking may not directly represent learning of patterns of verbalization in the culture. Instead, they may represent spontaneous products of the child's effort to make sense out of his experience in a complex social world, each arising sequentially from its predecessors.

As an example, Tommy, the ten-year-old exemplar of a Stage 1 conception of life's value, implies that one should decide whose life to save in terms of the amount of furniture owned. While Tommy's response probably reflects his parent's high concern about acquiring or preserving furniture, his derivation of the value of life from the value of furniture is his own. The naive or primitive

quality of Tommy's belief arises from a characteristic failure of younger children (usually under eight) to distinguish the value of an object to its owner and its (moral) value to others (moral "egocentrism") . . . when Tommy made this distinction three years later, he set off on quite a different path in considering the value of a life, one based on its replaceability in terms of the needs of others. Each line of thinking reflects his organization of values presented to him by his world in terms of assumptions characteristic of his current development level.

The writer has been led to accept this second, or developmental, interpretation by evidence suggesting that his stages form an invariant developmental sequence. This evidence suggests that the use of a more advanced stage of thought depends upon earlier attainment of each preceding stage and that each involves a restructuring and displacement of previous stages of thought. . . .

Note 16

From C. Gilligan (1982), New Maps of Development: New Visions of Maturity. *Am. J. Orthopsychiatr.*, pp. 199–211.

. . . Two children—Amy and Jake—were in the same sixth grade class at school and participated in a study designed to explore different conceptions of morality and self. The sample selected for study was chosen to focus the variables of gender and age while maximizing developmental potential by holding constant, at a high level, the factors of intelligence, education, and social class that have been associated with moral development, at least as measured by existing scales. The children in question were both bright and articulate and, at least in their 11-year-old aspirations, resisted easy categories of sex-role stereotyping since Amy aspired to become a scientist while Jake preferred English to math. Yet their moral judgments seemed initially to confirm previous findings of differences between the sexes, suggesting that the edge girls have on moral development during the early school years gives way at puberty with the ascendance of formal logical thought in boys.

The dilemma these children were asked to resolve was one in the series devised by Kohlberg to measure moral development in adolescence by presenting a conflict between moral norms and exploring the logic of its resolution. In this particular dilemma, a man named Heinz considers whether or not to steal a drug, which he cannot afford to buy, in order to save the life of his wife. In the standard format of Kohlberg's interviewing procedure, the description of the dilemma itself—Heinz's predicament, the wife's disease, the druggist's refusal to lower his price—is followed by the question, should Heinz steal the drug? Then the reasons for and against stealing are explored through a series of further questions, conceived as probes and designed to reveal the underlying structure of moral thought.

Jake

Jake, at 11, is clear from the outset that Heinz should steal the drug. Constructing the dilemma as Kohlberg did as a conflict between the values of property and life, he discerns the logical priority of life and uses that logic to justify his choice:

For one thing, a human life is worth more than money, and if the druggist only makes $1000, he is still going to live, but if Heinz doesn't steal the drug, his wife is going to die. (Why is life worth more than money?) Because the druggist can get a thousand dollars later from rich people with cancer, but Heinz can't get his wife again. (Why not?) Because people are all different, and so you couldn't get Heinz's wife again.

Asked if Heinz should steal the drug if he does not love his wife, Jake replies that he should, saying that not only is there "a difference between hating and killing," but also, if Heinz were caught, "the judge would probably think it was the right thing to do." Asked about the fact that, in stealing, Heinz would be breaking the law, he says that "the laws have mistakes and you can't go writing up a law for everything that you can imagine."

Thus, while taking the law into account and recognizing its function in maintaining social order (the judge, he says, "should give Heinz the lightest possible sentence"), he also sees the law as manmade and therefore subject to error and change. Yet his judgment that Heinz should steal the drug, like his view of the law as having mistakes, rests on the assumption of agreement, as societal consensus around moral values that allows one to know and expect others will recognize "the right thing to do."

Fascinated by the power of logic, this 11-year-old boy locates truth in math which, he says, is "the only thing that is totally logical." Considering the moral dilemma to be "sort of like a math problem with humans," he sets it up as an equation and proceeds to work out the solution. Since his solution is rationally derived, he assumes that anyone following reason would arrive at the same conclusion and thus that a judge would also consider stealing to be the right thing for Heinz to do. Yet he is also aware of the limits of logic; asked whether there is a right answer to moral problems, he says that "there can only be right and wrong in judgment," since the parameters of action are variable and complex. Illustrating how actions undertaken with the best of intentions can eventuate in the most disastrous of consequences, he says

. . . like if you give an old lady your seat on the trolley, if you are in a trolley crash and that seat goes through the window, it might be that reason that the old lady dies.

Theories of developmental psychology illuminate well the position of this child, standing at the juncture of childhood and adolescence, at what

Piaget described as the pinnacle of childhood intelligence, and beginning through thought to discover a wider universe of possibility. The moment of preadolescence is caught by the conjunction of formal operational thought with a description of self still anchored in the factual parameters of his childhood world, his age, his town, his father's occupation, the substance of his likes, dislikes, and beliefs. Yet as his self-description radiates the self-confidence of a child who has arrived, in Erikson's terms, at a favorable balance of industry over inferiority—competent, sure of himself, and knowing well the rules of the game—so his emergent capacity for formal thought, his ability to think about thinking and to reason things out in a logical way, frees him from dependence on authority and allows him to find solutions to problems by himself.

This emergent autonomy then charts the trajectory that Kohlberg's six stages of moral development trace, a three-level progression from an egocentric understanding of fairness based on individual need (stages one and two), to a conception of fairness anchored in the shared conventions of societal agreement (stages three and four), and finally to a principled understanding of fairness that rests on the free-standing logic of equality and reciprocity (stages five and six). While Jake's judgments at 11 are scored as conventional on Kohlberg's scale, a mixture of stages three and four, his ability to bring deductive logic to bear on the solution of moral dilemmas, to differentiate morality from law, and to see how laws can be considered to have mistakes, points toward the principled conception of justice that Kohlberg equates with moral maturity.

Amy

In contrast, Amy's response to the dilemma conveys a very different impression, an image of development stunted by a failure of logic, an inability to think for herself. Asked if Heinz should steal the drug, she replies in a way that seems evasive and unsure:

Well, I don't think so. I think there might be other ways besides stealing it, like if he could borrow the money or make a loan or something, but he really shouldn't steal the drug, but his wife shouldn't die either.

Asked why he should not steal the drug, she considers neither property nor law but rather the effect that theft could have on the relationship between Heinz and his wife. If he stole the drug, she explains,

. . . he might save his wife then, but if he did, he might have to go to jail, and then his wife might get sicker again, and he couldn't get more of the drug, and it might not be good. So, they should really just talk it out and find some other way to make the money.

Seeing in the dilemma not a math problem with humans but a narrative of relationships that extends over time, she envisions the wife's continuing need for her husband and the husband's continuing concern for his wife and seeks to respond to the druggist's need in a way that would sustain rather than sever connection. As she ties the wife's survival to the preservation of relationships, so she considers the value of her life in context of relationships, saying that it would be wrong to let her die because, "if she died, it hurts a lot of people and it hurts her." Since her moral judgment is grounded in the belief that "if somebody has something that would keep somebody alive, then it's not right not to give it to them," she considers the problem in the dilemma to arise not from the druggist's assertion of rights but from his failure of response.

While the interviewer proceeds with the series of questions that follow Kohlberg's construction of the dilemma, Amy's answers remain essentially unchanged, the various probes serving neither to elucidate nor to modify her initial response. Whether or not Heinz loves his wife, he still shouldn't steal or let her die; if it were a stranger dying instead, she says that "if the stranger didn't have anybody near or anyone she knew," then Heinz should try to save her life but he shouldn't steal the drug. But as the interviewer conveys through the repetition of questions that the answers she has given are not heard or not right, Amy's confidence begins to diminish and her replies become more constrained and unsure. Asked again why Heinz should not steal the drug, she simply repeats, "Because it's not right." Asked again to explain why, she states again that theft would not be a good solution, adding lamely, that, "if he took it, he might not know how to give it to his wife, and so his wife might still die." Failing to see the dilemma as a self-contained problem in moral logic, she does not discern the internal structure of its resolution; as she constructs the problem differently herself, Kohlberg's conception completely evades her.

Instead, seeing a world comprised of relationships rather than to people standing alone, a world that coheres through human connection rather than through systems of rules, she finds the puzzle in the dilemma to lie in the failure of the druggist to respond to the wife. Saying that "it is not right for someone to die when their life could be saved," she assumes that if the druggist were to see the consequences of his refusal to lower his price, he would realize that "he should just give it to the wife and then have the husband pay back the money later." Thus she considers the solution to the dilemma to lie in making the wife's condition more salient to the druggist or, that failing, in appealing to others who are in a position to help.

Just as Jake is confident the judge would agree that stealing is the right thing for Heinz to do, so Amy is confident that "if Heinz and the druggist had talked it out long enough, they could reach something besides stealing." As he considers the law to "have mistakes," so she sees this drama as a mistake, believing that "the world should just share things more and then people wouldn't have to steal." Both children thus recognize the need for agreement but see it as mediated in different ways: he impersonally through systems of logic and law, she personally through communication in relationship. As he relies on the conventions of logic to deduce the solution to this dilemma, assuming these conventions to be shared, so she relies on a process of communication, assuming connection and believing that her voice will be heard. Yet while his assumptions about agreement are confirmed by the convergence in logic between his answers and the questions posed, her assumptions are belied by the failure in communication, the interviewer's inability to understand her response.

. . .Thus in Kohlberg's dilemma these two children see two very different moral problems—Jake a conflict between life and property that can be resolved by logical deduction, Amy a fracture of human relationship that must be mended with its own thread. Asking different questions that arise from different conceptions of the moral domain, they arrive at answers that fundamentally diverge, and the arrangement of these answers as successive stages on a scale of increasing moral maturity calibrated by the logic of the boy's response misses the different truth revealed in the judgment of the girl. To the question, "What does he see that she does not?", Kohlberg's theory provides a ready response, manifest in the scoring of his judgments a full stage higher than hers in moral maturity; to the question, "What does she see that he does

not?", Kohlberg's theory has nothing to say. Since most of her responses fall through the sieve of Kohlberg's scoring system, her responses appear from his perspective to lie outside the moral domain.

. . . In this way, these two 11-year-old children, both highly intelligent, though perceptive about life in different ways, display different modes of moral understanding, different ways of thinking about conflict and choice. Jake, in resolving the dilemma, follows the construction that Kohlberg has posed. Relying on theft to avoid confrontation and turning to the law to mediate the dispute, he transposes a hierarchy of power into a hierarchy of values by recasting a conflict between people into a conflict of claims. Thus abstracting the moral problem from the interpersonal situation, he finds in the logic of fairness an objective means of deciding who will win the dispute. But this hierarchical ordering, with its imagery of winning and losing and the potential for violence which it contains, gives way in Amy's construction of the dilemma to a network of connection, a network sustained by a process of communication. With this shift, the moral problem changes from one of unfair domination, the imposition of property over life, to one of unnecessary exclusion, the failure of the druggist to respond to the wife.

. . . We are attuned to a hierarchical ordering that represents development as a progress of separation, a chronicle of individual success. In contrast, the understanding of development as a progress of human relationships, a narrative of expanding connection, is an unimagined representation. The image of network or web thus seems more readily to connote entrapment rather than an alternative and nonhierarchical vision of human connection.

REFERENCES

Colby A. (1978), Evolution of a moral-developmental theory. In: *New Directions in Child Development: Moral Development*, ed. W. Damon. San Francisco: Jossey-Bass.

Fishbein, H.D. (1976), *Evolution, Development, and Children's Learning*. Palisades: Goodyear.

Gilligan, C. (1982a), *In a Different Voice: Psychological Theory and Women's Development*. Cambridge, Harvard University Press.

Jurkovic, G.J. (1980), The juvenile delinquent as a moral philosopher. A structural-developmental perspective. *Psychol. Bull.*, 88:709–727.

Kohlberg, L. (1964), Development of moral character.

In: *Review of Child Development Research* (Vol. I), ed. M.L. Hoffman and L.W. Hoffman. New York: Russell Sage Foundation, pp. 400–404.

Kohlberg, L. (1978), Revisions in the theory and practice of moral development. In: *New Directions in Child Development: Moral Development,* ed. W. Damon. San Francisco: Jossey-Bass.

Mischel, W., and Mischel, H. (1976), A cognitive-social learning approach to morality and self regulation. In: *Moral Development and Behavior,* ed. T. Lickona. New York: Holt, Rinehart, and Winston.

Piaget, J. (1977), Egocentric thought in the child. In: *The Essential Piaget,* ed. H.E. Gruber and J.J. Vonèche. New York: Basic Books, pp. 186–188.

11

PSYCHOSOCIAL DEVELOPMENT

A broader, psychosocial perspective of the life cycle has been described by Erikson (1959), who propounded what he called the epigenetic principle: anything that grows has a *ground plan* and out of this plan the *parts* arise, each part having its *time* of special ascendancy until all parts have arisen to form a *functioning whole.*

Each item of the healthy personality to be discussed is *systematically related to all other items:* all items depend on the *proper development in the proper sequence of each item,* and each item *exists in some form before its decisive and critical time arrives* (see Table 11–1). Each stage becomes a *crisis* because of a *radical change in perspective.*

In order to do Erikson justice, the description of his theory that follows will quote extensively from his monograph "Identity and the Life Cycle" (Erikson, 1959; see Note 17).

BASIC TRUST VS. BASIC MISTRUST

This is an "incorporative oral stage" of receiving and accepting, with a mutuality between mother and child, as well as an "active incorporative stage," with biting, and so on. It includes conscious experiencing and ways of behaving and unconscious inner states. Erikson described how mothers create a sense of trust in their children by a kind of caring that combines sensitive care of the baby's individual needs along with a firm sense of personal trustworthiness.

AUTONOMY VS. SHAME AND DOUBT

In this stage Erikson believed that the maturation of the muscle system and the ability to coordinate such conflicting action patterns as 'holding on' and 'letting go' were important to the child, along with the child's investment in his or her autonomous will. The so-called anal zone was thought by Erikson to lend itself more than any other to the expression of stubborn insistence on conflicting impulses because:

1. It is the modal zone for two contradic-

Table 11–1. Diagram Illustrating Progressive Differentiation of Parts*

First Stage (about first year)	BASIC TRUST	Earlier form of AUTONOMY	Earlier form of INITIATIVE
Second Stage (about second and third years)	Later form of BASIC TRUST	AUTONOMY	Earlier form of INITATIVE
Third Stage (about fourth and fifth years)	Later form of BASIC TRUST	Later form of AUTONOMY	INITIATIVE

*From E. Erikson (1959), *Identity and the Life Cycle.* New York: W.W. Norton, 1979. By permission.

tory modes, i.e., retention and elimination.

2. The sphincters are part of the muscle system, which in general alternates between rigidity and relaxation, flexion and extension.

The whole stage, then, becomes a battle for autonomy. While standing on his or her own two feet, the child delineates "I" and "you," "we" and "mine." The child here is apt to both hoard things and discard them, to both cling to possessions and throw them out the window. Erikson conceptualized a sense of autonomy and pride arising from a sense of self-control without loss of self-esteem. Concomitantly, a sense of doubt and shame might arise from a sense of muscular and anal impotence, loss of self-control, and parental overcontrol.

"To develop autonomy, a firmly developed and a convincingly continued stage of early trust is necessary. . . . At around 8 months the child seems to be somehow more aware, as it were, of this separateness; this prepares him for the impending sense of autonomy.

"Shame supposes that one is completely exposed and conscious of being looked at—in a word, self-conscious. One is visible and not ready to be visible.

". . . be firm and tolerant with the child at this stage, and he will be firm and tolerant with himself. He will feel pride in being an autonomous person; he will grant autonomy to others; and now and again he will even let himself get away with something."

INITIATIVE VS. GUILT

By age 4 to 5, the child knows that he or she *is* a person, and tries to discover what kind of a person he or she will be. Like his or her parents? Powerful? Beautiful? Dangerous?

The child at this stage:

1. moves around freely and more violently,
2. has a greater command of language and asks many questions,
3. is highly imaginative, a trait that leads

at times to a sense of guilt, as though the fantasy itself were a crime.

The child seems to "grow together" psychologically and physically, and is "self activated." Not only can the child walk and run, he or she tries to find out what *can* be done with the ability and what *may* be done with it. The child at this stage makes comparisons (e.g., about sexual differences).

There is what Erikson calls an *intrusive mode*, characterized by (1) intrusion into other *bodies* by *attack*, (2) intrusion into other *people's ears and minds* by *aggressive talking*, (3) intrusion into *space* by vigorous *locomotion*, and (4) intrusion into the *unknown* by *consuming curiosity*.

The child at this stage feels ashamed that certain fantasies or behavior will be discovered. He or she also begins to feel guilty automatically, even for thoughts and for deeds that nobody has watched. Yet at the same time the child is ready to learn quickly and avidly, and to become grown up (in regard to responsibility, discipline, and performance). The child now is willing to make things together, to collaborate with other children for the purpose of constructing and planning (instead of bossing and coercing), to profit by his or her association with teachers and ideal prototypes, and to feel equal to others in worth.

INDUSTRY VS. INFERIORITY

This stage differs from others in that it does not consist of a swing from a violent inner upheaval to a new mastery. The violent drives are said to be normally dormant at this time. It is a stage of "outer hindrances." The child sooner or later becomes dissatisfied and disgruntled; he or she may have a sense of not being useful and may feel unable to make things and to make them well, even perfectly. "It is as if he knows . . . (Erikson says) . . . he must begin to be somewhat of a worker and potential provider before becoming a biological parent." The dangers at this stage are:

1. that the child will develop a sense of

inferiority, a feeling that he or she will
never be any good;

2. that the child's sense of identity
(through identification) will remain prematurely fixed on being nothing but a
good little worker or a good little
helper, which may not be all he or she
could be;

3. that the child may never acquire the
enjoyment of work and the pride of doing at least one kind of thing well.

In summary, this is a socially decisive
stage. A sense of division of labor and of
equality of opportunity develops at this time,
and the ground is set for the child's sense of
identity.

IDENTITY VS. IDENTITY DIFFUSION

The concept of ego identity is one of Erikson's major contributions, and it is necessary here to quote him directly. Ego identity
is more than the sum of childhood identification; "It is the inner capital accrued from
all those experiences of each successive
stage . . . when successful identification led
to a successful alignment of the individual's
basic drives with his endowment and his opportunities. . . . The sense of ego identity,
then, is the accrued confidence that one's
ability to maintain inner sameness and continuity (one's ego in the psychological sense)
is matched by the sameness and continuity of
one's meaning for others . . . Thus, self esteem, confirmed at the end of each major
crisis, grows to be a conviction that one is
learning effective steps toward a tangible future, that one is developing a defined personality within a social reality which one understands . . . Accruing ego identity gains
real strength only from wholehearted and
consistent recognition of real accomplishment . . . The danger of this stage is identity
diffusion. . . ."

To continue in Erikson's words,

To say . . . that the identity crisis is *psycho* and
social means that:

1. It is a subjective sense as well as an observable quality of personal sameness and con-

tinuity, paired with some belief in the sameness and continuity of some shared world
image . . .

2. It is a state of being and becoming that can
have a highly conscious . . . quality and yet
remain, in its motivational aspects, quite unconscious and beset with dynamics of conflict . . .

3. It is characteristic of a developmental period
[adolescence and youth].

4. It is dependent on the *past* for the resource
of strong identifications in childhood, while
it relies on new models encountered in
youth, and depends for its conclusion on
workable roles offered in young adulthood.
In fact, each subsequent stage of adulthood
must contribute to its preservation and re-
newal . . . Psychosocial identity . . . also
has a *psycho-historical* side. The study of
psychosocial identity . . . depends on . . .

   (1) the personal coherence of the individual
and role integration in his group;

   (2) his guiding images and the ideologies of
his time;

   (3) his life history—and the historical moment . . .

The unconscious complexities . . . can be
grouped thus:

1. Every person and every group harbors
a *negative identity* as the sum of all
those identifications and identity fragments which the individual had to sub-
merge in himself as undesirable or ir-
reconcilable or which his group has
taught him to perceive as the mask of
fatal "difference" in sex role or race, in
class or religion . . .

2. In some young people, in some classes,
at some periods in history, the personal
identity crisis will be noiseless and contained within the rituals of passage
marking a second birth; while in other
people, classes, and periods, the crisis
will be clearly marked off as a critical
period intensified by collective strife or
epidemic tension. Thus the nature of
the identity conflict often depends on
the latent panic or, indeed, the intrinsic
promise pervading a historical period. . . . Psychosocial identity . . .
is . . . situated in three orders in which
man lives at all times:

   (1) The *somatic order*, by which an or-

ganism gets to maintain its integrity in a continuous reciprocal adaptation of the *milieu intérieur* and other organisms.

(2) The *personal order*—that is, the integration of "inner" and "outer" world in individual experience and behavior.

(3) The *social order*, jointly maintained by personal organisms sharing a geographic-historical setting . . .

How is Erikson's contribution assessed today? Rapaport (1959) made the following observations on Erikson's theory:

1. It outlines the universal sequences of phases of psychosocial development.
2. The phases, for the first time in the history of psychoanalytic theory, span the whole life cycle.
3. Each phase is characterized by a phase-specific developmental task.
4. There is a mutual coordination between the developing individual and his social environment.
5. At the same time, each society has its own way to meet each phase of the development of its members through specific institutions, such as parental care, schools, and teachers.
6. The individual is *genetically* a social person, society merely influencing the manner in which he or she solves developmental tasks.
7. The particular way society's caretaking institutions influence the functioning of various modes (e.g., retentive and intrusive) leads to a change of function, which eventually results in the characteristic behavior of the individual.
8. The theory as a theory is not always clear in terms of its level of abstraction.
9. Erikson relates his ego theory to Freud's id psychology of drive development.

Piaget (1960) noted that "the great merit of Erikson's stages . . . is precisely that he attempted, by situating the Freudian mechanisms within more general types of conduct

(walking, exploring, etc.), to postulate continual integration of previous acquisitions at subsequent levels" (p. 13).

Erikson is not a scientist in the measuring, experimental sense. Rather, he is a perceptive observer. He began writing about ego identity in the late 1940s and early 1950s, and the body of his work stems from that period. Possibly his key concept is that of identity, which comprises a conscious sense of individual identity, an unconscious striving for a continuity of personal character, a criterion for the work of ego synthesis, and the maintenance of an inner solidarity with a group's ideals and identities.

Erikson has also approached his subject through biography (he has written about Shaw, Ghandi, Luther, and himself, including his analysis with Anna Freud), clinical work with children, and theory. Many people, especially such authors as Lifton and Kenniston, have moved farther in the direction of psychohistory. Others seem to equate Erikson with "ego psychology," and have subsequently concentrated their interest on "ego functions," particularly cognitive development.

Some of Erikson's theories have not held up under scientific scrutiny; for example, his theory of sex differences in children's play (among them, that boys tend to build towers and girls tend to build enclosures). Clinicians who work with children have found many of Erikson's concepts (e.g., of basic trust and identity) useful, albeit mostly at a general, somewhat global level. Still others have taken issue with some of Erikson's concepts (e.g., that of identity diffusion). For example, followers of Erikson have attempted to derive the diagnostic category of identity disorder (DSM-III-R, 313.82*), which is said to consist of (1) severe/subjective distress regarding uncertainty about a variety of identity-related issues (e.g., long-term goals, career choice, friendship patterns, sexual orientation, religious orientation identification, systems of

---

*Here and elsewhere in this book, the numbers in parentheses refer to the DSM-III(R) classification of the disorder being discussed.

Note 17. ERIKSON'S LIFE-CYCLE CHART

	1.	2.	3.	4.	5.	6.	7.	8.
I. INFANCY	Trust vs. Mistrust				Unipolarity vs. Premature Self-Differentiation			
II. EARLY CHILDHOOD		Autonomy vs. Shame, Doubt			Bipolarity vs. Autism			
III. PLAY AGE			Initiative vs. Guilt		Play Identification vs. (oedipal) Fantasy Identities			
IV. SCHOOL AGE				Industry vs. Inferiority	Work Identification vs. Identity Foreclosure			
V. ADOLESCENCE	Time Perspective vs. Time Diffusion	Self-Certainty vs. Identity Consciousness	Role Experimentation vs. Negative Identity	Anticipation of Achievement vs. Work Paralysis	Identity vs. Identity Diffusion	Sexual Identity vs. Bisexual Diffusion	Leadership Polarization vs. Authority Diffusion	Ideological Polarization vs. Diffusion of Ideals
VI. YOUNG ADULT					Solidarity vs. Social Isolation	Intimacy vs. Isolation		
VII. ADULTHOOD							Generativity vs. Self-Absorption	
VIII. MATURE AGE								Integrity vs. Disgust, Despair

moral values, and group loyalties) and (2) subsequent impairment of social or occupational (including academic) functioning, both of more than 3 months' duration and not due to any other mental disorder. However, those who disagree with this categorization, such as Rutter and Shaffer (1980), have stated that there is now "a substantial body of research of many different kinds which runs counter to the views of adolescence which seem to underlie this concept" (see also Rutter, 1979). More empirical research is needed before the issue can be settled.

Note 17

From E. Erikson (1959), *Identity and the Life Cycle*. New York: W.W. Norton, 1979. By permission.

REFERENCES

DSM-III-R (1987), *Diagnostic and Statistical Manual of Mental Disorders*. Washington, D.C.: American Psychiatric Association, pp. 89–91.

Erikson, E.H. (1959), Identity and the life cycle. *Psychol. Issues,* 1:101–172.

Piaget, J. (1960), The general problem of the psychobiological development of the child. In: *Discussions on Child Development* (Vol. 4), ed. J. Tanner and B. Inhelder. New York: International Universities Press, pp. 3–27.

Rapaport, D. (1959), Introduction: A historical survey of psychoanalytic ego psychology. *Psychol. Issues,* 1:5–17.

Rutter, M. (1979), *Changing Youth in a Changing Society: Patterns of Adolescent Development and Disorder*. London: Nuffield Provincial Hospitals Trust. Cambridge, Harvard University Press, 1980.

Rutter, M., and Shaffer, D. (1980), DSM-III: A step forward or back in terms of the classification of child psychiatric disorder? *J. Am. Acad. Child Psychiatry,* 19:371–393.

12

FAMILY DEVELOPMENT

A family is a matrix of a special group with a special bond to live together, employing transactions, role divisions, and other communications, for the purpose of nurturance, socialization, and "enculturation" (Tseng and McDermott, 1979) (see also Note 18). Socialization begins at birth (Schaffer, 1979). Parent and infant form a dyad, and their interactive behavior has a temporal patterning. Brazelton and his colleagues (1974) have described, for example, the cyclical nature of the interactions between young infants and their mothers. The infant is equipped at birth with the means to begin coping with other people in his or her environment, and he or she seems virtually to be preadapted for social interchange. At the same time, the parents seem to sense the infant's rhythms and cycles, and they try to synchronize their behavior with the infant's. Socialization has begun, and it continues to develop within the context of the family. "Enculturation" occurs through language use, ways of relating, values, unconscious beliefs, and role expectations (Lidz, 1968).

In any event, the family is constantly changing both within itself and in relation to society. Within the family, individuals may be in various transition states, such as being the youngest, being the oldest, leaving home, getting married, beginning parenthood, dying. In the context of society, the family both contributes and reacts to such changes as industrialization, economic depression, overpopulation, migration, political climate, educational and welfare policies, cultural forces, and religious toleration. These intrafamilial and societal factors interact.

According to Hareven (1977), a "typical" developmental sequence in American families in the 1970s was marrying early, having children early, and having few children. Today, however, many middle class women are marrying later in life. The "typical" family experiences a compact period of parenthood in the middle years of life and then a longer period (about one third of adult life) without children. Finally, there is often a period of living alone following the death of a spouse, most frequently the husband (Glick, 1955).

Normally, children thrive when they develop within a healthy family. At the same time, the traditional family is not the only healthy setting in which the development of the child may proceed. In the United States nearly 50% of all children born today will spend an extended portion of their lives with only one parent before they reach age 18. The divorce rate was nearly twice as high in 1978 as in 1970 (it increased most drastically in the 30- to 44-age bracket); and from 1970 to 1981 the divorce rate more than doubled (Bureau of the Census, 1982). Projections suggest that by 1990, 30% of children in this country will live in a family that has experienced divorce (Wallerstein and Corbin, In Press). From 1970 to 1978 there was an increase of 184% in the number of single black women who headed households (Bureau of the Census, 1978).

SINGLE PARENTHOOD, LATCHKEY CHILDREN, AND DAY CARE

Single parenthood is a growing trend in the United States today. In 1982, 22.5% of all children in the United States were living in single-parent homes (Bureau of the Census, 1982). More and more single adolescents as well as single older women are giving birth to children. In the last 20 years the proportion of births among unmarried women rose from 5% in 1960 to 19% in 1982.* Looked at another way, the majority of poor families with children are headed by women (Moynihan, 1985). There has, in fact, been a major growth in families headed by women with no husband present—nearly 10 million households, amounting to almost 12% of all households. Beyond that, the Bureau of Labor Statistics reported in 1985 that 46% of all mothers with children under 3 are in the work force. The likelihood is that more and more families will be headed by a single parent who has to go to work. When a mother goes to work, 40 or 50 hours of work are added to the family system (Hunt and Hunt, 1977), and when she is a single parent, few if any other adults are available to share this extra allotment of work. The impact of maternal employment on the child depends on various factors such as income level, sex of the child, and degree of support for the mother. The impact of father absence depends on the age and sex of the child; early loss of the father appears to have a more detrimental effect (Hetherington, 1972).

Who takes care of the children? Sometimes there is only a young preadolescent sibling, 12 or 14 years of age; sometimes the children are just left to fend for themselves. The best estimates are that there are 2 to 5 million "latchkey" children between 6 and 13 years of age, and probably as many as 8 to 10 million "latchkey" children altogether under the age of 18 years.

Unfortunately, there are scarcely any controlled data on the safety, health, education, or welfare of these children as they grow up, much less on their emotional health. The variables are many: much depends on the needs of the children, the strengths and weaknesses of the families, and the support system available. The issue is large enough for society as

a whole to consider. Some of these children may be at risk for subsequent disorders, including the risk for violence and delinquency.

At present we have no perfect solutions for this problem. One partial contribution is day care. A wide range of standards exists among day care centers, and the outcome for the children is immensely variable. Clarke-Stewart (1982) noted, for example, that physical development is accelerated in children of poor families who use day care, but not in middle class children who use day care. At the same time, children in day care manage as well emotionally as, and in some cases better than, children at home. Day care children are usually quite well attached to their mothers. Because different children have different needs, thought must be given to the match between child and day care center, beyond the basic issue of adequate minimal standards for all day care centers. Some programs, like Head Start, are sometimes outstanding, but Head Start can handle only 20% of the eligible children.

Although day care is an important alternative for these children, it is not the full answer and, in any case, has many problems of its own to be solved, among them the issues of safety and minimal standards.

Questions about the advantages or disadvantages of "multiple mothering" arise when one considers the need for a steady relationship with one person. When there is one major mother figure and one or more mother surrogates (as occurs when a mother goes out to work and the child is cared for by a mother surrogate), no harm is done, provided the mother surrogate is a suitable person. Again, when there are several almost primary mother figures (up to four or five, as in extended families), children respond very well. However, when there are many different mother substitutes, each of whom may be inadequate and one of whom is intensely attached to the child, the child may suffer. This situation occurs in many institutions.

HOMOSEXUAL PARENTS AND CHILD DEVELOPMENT

Another variant of the traditional family is the rearing of a child by homosexual parents.

---

*National Center for Health Statistics, 1985.

There are about 1.5 million lesbian parents in the United States (Hunter and Polikof, 1976). What is known about the effects on the child? The question is important, because in the absence of knowledge, myth prevails. Such myths include notions that homosexuality is pathologic, that homosexuals will act out sexually in front of or with children, that the child will become confused in his or her gender identity, and that the child will become homosexual.

Lesbian mothers are in fact perfectly successful in maternal roles (Hoeffer, 1981; Kirkpatrick, Smith and Roy, 1981). Lesbian mothers, like heterosexual mothers, are greatly concerned about the care of their children (Pagelow, 1980), and are also concerned that their children have adequate male figures with whom to identify (Kirkpatrick et al., 1981). The lesbian partner is often viewed as an aunt or big sister, and household chores are shared equally (Hall, 1987).

Lesbian mothers are similar to heterosexual mothers too in their encouragment of non-sex-type toys for both boys and girls (Hoeffer, 1981). There is no evidence that lesbian mothers prefer their children to become homosexual; rather, acceptance of a child's object choice seems to be more common.

In general, the rearing of children in all-female households does not in itself lead to disorders of gender identity or homosexuality. Green (1978), in a study of 37 children raised by homosexual and transsexual parents, suggested that the children in general develop appropriate sexual identities and assume usual heterosexual attitudes, as do children reared in heterosexual-mother households. Golombok, Spencer, and Rutter (1983), in a controlled study of 37 children aged 5 to 17 years, found no evidence of incestuous advances to children and no evidence of inappropriate gender identity. All the children reported that "they were glad to be the sex that they were and none would prefer to be the opposite sex." In essence, the study found no differences in gender identity, sex-role behavior, or sexual orientation between children brought up in lesbian households and those brought up in heterosexual single-parent households. "Rearing in a lesbian household per se did not lead to atypical pyschosexual development or constitute a psychiatric risk factor."

THE FAMILY LIFE CYCLE

Returning to the development of the family, one particular definable developmental stage within the family is that of parenthood, which is a process having an early, a middle, and a late phase with respect to the developing child (Benedek, 1970). The early phase of parenthood extends from conception to adolescence. The middle phase of parenthood begins when the child begins to mature sexually as he or she starts to take a sexual interest in another person, and it continues through marriage and childbearing. The onset of old age marks the beginning of the late phase of parenthood, when the now "adult child" beomes a need-fulfilling person for the aged parent, thus completing the cycle.

At each stage of the cycle, parents seem to relive and to rework through those conflicts that they experienced when they were at the stage of development their child is now in. However, each parent is also at his or her stage of adult development, and thus there are a myriad of possible combinations of developmental levels. The principle of developmental phases is one way of understanding the complexity of both nuclear and extended family relationships.

Significant changes occur in patterns of parent-child interaction over the course of the family life cycle (Maccoby, 1984). Predominant issues shift in relation to the child's increasing abilities and capacities for autonomy. For example, methods of discipline gradually shift from authoritarian control and limit setting in the preschool years toward patterns of mutual discussion and reasoning with the school age child (Maccoby, 1984). The amount of time parents spend in direct child care also varies with parents spending proportionally less time with school age children.

Although the division of labor between parents is shifting away from the "traditional" model, in many intact families the father has particular responsibility for aspects of discipline and tend to encourage more independence as well as more traditional sex-typed behaviors (Hetherington, Cox, and Cox, 1978).

Sibling relationships provide a unique contribution to the family and provide opportunities for emotional, social, and cognitive growth. The addition of a sibling to the family produces major changes in the child's life. Sibling relationships differ from peer relationships in numerous ways, e.g., amount of shared experience, and provide special opportunities for the sibship in social interaction, resolution of conflict, and negotiation of issues of dependency (Bryant, 1982).

Children have roles to play within the family. They may satisfy various needs of the parents and may provide opportunities for the parents to rework various developmental tasks as the parents experience the children at different developmental stages. Children may also play pathologic roles in a family, including those of scapegoat, baby, pet, and peacemaker (Rollins et al., 1973). Children with adverse temperamental features are most likely to be selected for scapegoating by parents at times of stress (Rutter et al., 1977). Children also take on what Anthony (1973) calls a "family likeness," displaying personality characteristics, coping styles, prejudices, and defense characteristics similar to those of other members of the family. Projective identification (Klein, 1946) and externalization (Brodey, 1959) are some of the processes by which this process is hypothesized to occur. Projective identification is the term used to describe putting part of oneself or part of one's impulses and feelings into another person, leading to an identification with that other person based on attributing to him or her some of one's own qualities. Child abuse may be one consequence of this mechanism.

CHILD ABUSE

In 1985, one out of 33 children aged 3 to 17 years living with two parents at home was reported to be the victim of severe violence, giving rise to a total of one million or more children each year who are abused. Of these one million children, between 2,000 and 5,000 die each year as a result of the abuse (AMA, 1986; Gelles and Straus, 1985). Some violence occurs in 62% of all families. The number of reported cases has been increasing every year. Among reported child abuse cases, 48% are in poor, single-parent households.

Abuse most commonly affects children under the age of 5, but may occur throughout childhood and adolescence. Hyperactive children are especially vulnerable. The most common perpetrator is the child's mother, average age of 26, who is living in a poor home and is socially isolated. Role reversal is a common phenomenon: often the parent was abused as a child.

By and large the outlook for many abused children and their families is not good. Lynch and Roberts (1982), among others, have noted a high prevalence of abnormality in follow-up of abused children, and a failure to thrive that often accompanies child abuse. Martin et al. (1974) also found 53% of their sample of abused children to have some neurologic abnormality. Martin and Beezley (1977) studied the behavior of children 4½ years after abuse, and found that over half were described as having low self-esteem and having types of behavior that made peers, parents, and teachers reject them. Often by the time they reach primary school these children are socially isolated and identified as hostile by their teachers. Even if the abused child is placed outside his biologic family, he is still in a high-risk group for both fostering and adoption breakdown. Many abused children grow up to be abusing adults.

A related phenomenon is sexual abuse. Currently in our society we are seeing an increase in the number of reports of sexual abuse of children. From 1980 to 1985 reports of sexual abuse increased by 55%. The incidence is estimated at 100,000 to 250,000 cases per year (AMA, 1986). Each year 5,000 cases of incest are reported. Eighty percent of reported sexual abuses of children involve middle class individuals. In most instances the abuser is known to the child and uses enticement or bribery to get the child to comply. This way of taking advantage of the child's immaturity and vulnerability has an important aftermath for the child, who at a later time may feel guilty and at fault. The child may also realize later that he or she has been tricked or betrayed. In cases where there is a use of force, or even just an accompanying threat of violence, the child also feels that his or her body has been damaged, and this is followed by a loss of self-esteem, with subsequent depression and anxiety. Such a child needs an opportunity to talk to a skilled person, alone. The therapist can determine the validity of the child's account when the child begins to describe multiple episodes, perhaps each escalating in degree over a period of time, with explicit detail. There is usually an initial period of secrecy to which the child has been sworn or instructed by the abuser, and this too later engenders guilt in the child. Such children need psychotherapeutic intervention. Yet surprisingly, the child's needs are often ignored by parents and professionals, and treatment is not given. Attention must be paid to the psychologic needs of these children (Finkelhov, 1986; Schetky and Green, 1988).

SUMMARY

The essential elements of what a family has to offer a child remain important, no matter how varied the setting. These elements include a loving relationship, opportunities for attachment, continuity of care and affection, adequate stimulation, and a steady relationship with one person (Rutter, 1972).

A loving relationship means that the infant experiences someone who holds him or her in high esteem, who is delighted with the infant, and who gives the child a warm feeling. Such a person readily and generously meets the infant's inner needs, protects him or her, and ensures that the child receives the necessary stimulation.

Strong attachments occur when the interaction has a certain degree of intensity, as it has when a parent (or other adult) gives a great deal of attention to the child, feeds the child, talks with the child, plays with the child (especially), and responds regularly and readily to the child's needs—signalled by, say, crying. The parent who recognizes and responds to the different signals of a child is one to whom the child is likely to become strongly attached. Stronger attachments generally occur if (1) the number of caretakers is limited (the fewer the caretakers, the stronger the attachments), (2) the attachments occur during the early sensitive period, especially the first two years, and (3) the child's own contribution to the attachment process is strong, especially in regard to the strength of the child's needs and signals.

Criteria for what constitutes the optimum continuity of care have yet to be established. Questions about how much of what kinds of stimulation are essential for a child also remain unanswered.

Although numerous attempts have been made to classify families (Fisher, 1977; Fleck, 1983), none of them has been universally accepted. What is abundantly clear from the literature on the family is that the development of the child must be considered in the context of the development of the family in which the child is reared, and that family developmental psychopathology and family therapy are important areas of clinical knowledge (McDermott, 1981).

Note 18

From T. Lidz (1970), The family as the developmental setting. In: *The Child and His Family*, ed. E.J. Anthony and C. Koupernik, pp. 19–40, Copyright © 1970, John Wiley & Sons, Inc. Reprinted by permission of John Wiley & Sons, Inc.

The family is . . . a very special type of group with characteristics imposed upon it by the biological differences of its members as well as by the particular purposes it serves. Recognition of these characteristics leads to an appreciation of some requisites of its structure. . . .

1. The nuclear family is composed of two generations each with different needs, prerogatives,

and obligations. The parents, having grown up in two different families, seek to merge themselves and their backgrounds into a new unit that satisfies the needs of both and completes their personalities in a relationship that seeks permanence. The new unit differs to a greater or lesser degree from their families of origin and thus requires malleability in both partners. The new relationship requires the intrapsychic reorganization of each spouse to take cognizance of the partner. Stated in very simple terms, the ego functioning of each is modified by the presence of an alterego including the id, ego, and superego requirements of the alterego. Wishes and desires of a spouse that can be set aside must be differentiated from needs that cannot be neglected.

The parents are properly dependent upon one another, and children must be dependent upon parents, but parents cannot properly be dependent upon immature children. The parents serve as guides, educators, and models for offspring. They provide nurturance and give of themselves so that the children can develop. Though individuals, as parents they function as a coalition, dividing roles and tasks in which they support one another. As basic love objects and objects for identification for their children, who the parents are, how they behave, and how they interrelate with one another and not simply what they do to their child and for their child are of utmost importance to the child's personality development.

The children, in contrast to their parents, receive their primary training in group living within the family, remaining dependent upon the parents for many years, forming intense emotional bonds to them, and developing by assimilating from their parents and introjecting their characteristics, and yet must so learn to live within the family that they are able to emerge from it to live in the broader society; or, at least, to start families of their own as members of the parental generation.

2. The family is also divided into two genders with differing but complementary functions and role allocations as well as anatomical differences. The primary female role derives from women's biological structure and is related to the nurture of children and the maintenance of a home needed for that purpose, which leads to an emphasis upon interest in interpersonal relationships and emotional harmony—an expressive-affectional role. The male role, also originally related to man's physique, is concerned with the support and protection of a family and establishing its position in the larger society—an instrumental-adaptive role.

3. The relationships between family members are held firm by erotic and affectional ties. The parents who seek to form a permanent union are permitted and even expected to have sexual re-

lationships. While all direct sexual relationships within the family are prohibited to the children, erogenous gratification from parental figures that accompanies nurturant care is needed and fostered; but it must be progressively frustrated as the need for such primary care diminishes lest the bonds to the family become too firm and prevent the child's investment of interest and energy in the extrafamilial world. The de-erotization of the child's relationships to other family members is a primary task of the family. . . .

4. The family forms a shelter for its members within the larger society. Theoretically, at least, members receive affection and status by ascription rather than by achievement, which provides a modicum of emotional security in the face of the demands of the outside world. However, the family must reflect and transmit the societal ways, including child-rearing techniques appropriate to each developmental phase, and the culture's meaning and value system, and so forth, to assure that the children will be able to function when they emerge from the family into the broader society.

These fundamental characteristics of the nuclear family, and correlaries derived from them, set requisites for the parents and their marital relationship if it is to provide a suitable setting for the harmonious development of their offspring and to foster their children's development into reasonably integrated adults capable of independent existence. . . .

The family must foster and direct the child's development by carrying out a number of interrelated functions. . . . (1) the parental nurturant functions that must meet the child's needs and supplement his immature capacities in a different manner at each phase of his development; (2) the dynamic organization of the family which forms the framework for the structuring of the child's personality or, perhaps stated more correctly, channels and directs the child into becoming an integrated individual . . . (3) the family as the primary social system in which the child learns the basic social roles, the value of social institutions, and the basic mores of the society; and (4) the task of the parents to transmit to the child the essential instrumental techniques of the culture, including its language.

Note 19

From AACAP Committee on Rights and Legal Matters, Sub-Committee on Guidelines for Evaluation of Child Sexual Abuse (1988), Guidelines for the Clinical Evaluation of Child and Adolescent Sexual Abuse by the American Academy of Child and Adolescent Psychiatry's Committee on Rights and Legal

Matters. Diane H. Schetky, M.D., Chair and John Sikorski, M.D., Co-Chair. With permission from the American Academy of Child and Adolescent Psychiatry, Washington, D.C. Approved by the Council of the AACAP, June 10, 1988.

Introduction

The explosion of cases involving allegations of child* sexual abuse exceeds the resources available to deal with the problem. Many clinicians lack specific training in this area, and the legal profession is often confronted with an array of self-identified experts who have emerged to fill the void. Unfortunately, these evaluations often use inadequate diagnostic techniques or fail to evaluate the child within the context of the family. If conclusions are drawn on the basis of inadequate or insufficient information, children may be harmed, parent-child relationships seriously damaged, and these cases contaminated to the point that courts and other professionals have great difficulty sorting out what did or did not occur.

The purpose of the clinical evaluation of child sexual abuse is to determine whether (1) abuse has occurred; (2) the child needs protection; and (3) the child needs treatment for medical or emotional problems. Guidelines for validating child and adolescent abuse have not yet been fully defined. The following guidelines have been developed to assist clinicians performing these evaluations:

1. *The choice of clinician to evaluate the child for sexual abuse.*

   Persons doing evaluations must be professionals with special skills and experience in child and adolescent sexual abuse, and evaluations ideally should be performed under the direction of an experienced child and adolescent psychiatrist or psychologist. We recognize that in many cases this may not be possible. Clinicians performing these evaluations should possess sound knowledge of child development, family dynamics related to sexual abuse, effects of sexual abuse on the child, and the assessment of children, adolescents and families. Further, they should be trained in the diagnostic evaluation of both children and adults. They should be comfortable with testifying in court and prepared and willing to do so.

   It is important to establish that specialized training has been obtained either during the professional's formal training program or at a later time.

   The evaluator and the child's or adolescent's therapist should be two different in-

dividuals. This clarifies roles and preserves confidentiality in treatment.

2. *The number of times the child is interviewed.*

   The child should be seen for the minimum number of times necessary and by the fewest number of people as is necessary. We urge that agencies share information to avoid duplication of efforts and unnecessary stress for the child. The development of teams which integrate local police and reporting agencies is an ideal approach toward encouraging cooperation among agencies. Multiple interviews may be viewed by the child as a demand for more information and may encourage confabulation.

3. *The location of the interview.*

   The interview should take place in a relaxed environment, preferably not in an emergency ward or in a place with the trappings of authority such as a police department or a principal's office. The child should be allowed privacy without interrupting phone calls or people coming in and out of the room.

4. *Obtaining the history.*

   Gathering a history on the child or adolescent from parents or caregivers is an important part of the evaluation and should include: developmental history, cognitive assessment, history of prior abuse or other traumas, relevant medical history, behavioral changes, history of the parents' abuse as children, and the family's attitudes toward sex and modesty. Prior psychiatric disorders in the child or parent, impressions of the child's credibility, and allegiances to respective parents are also relevant.

5. *Interviewing both parents in intrafamilial abuse.*

   It is important to obtain a history from the perspective of each parent. The clinician needs to be able to consider all sides of the story, and any other stresses besides sexual abuse, that could account for the child's symptoms. Sufficient time should be spent with each parent alone. This should include a psychiatric assessment of each parent, especially if there is concern that the allegation may be false, or when a parent was abused as a child.

6. *Use of guardian ad litem.*

   If custody is an issue, a guardian ad litem for the child should be appointed to represent the child's best interests, preventing parents from subjecting the child to multiple evaluations in the hope of finding an expert

---

*Unless indicated otherwise, "child" refers to infants, children, and adolescents.

who will support one or another's contentions.

7. *Considering false allegations.*

The possibility of false allegations needs to be considered, particularly if allegations are coming from the parent rather than the child, if parents are engaged in a dispute over custody or visitation, and/or if the child is a preschooler. Under such circumstances, the clinician should consider observing the child separately with each parent. Before these observations, the clinician should meet alone with the child to establish trust and ensure that the child will feel some degree of control over the interview with the alleged offender. If the child is too upset by the proposed visit, and there is risk of traumatizing the child, the clinician may decide that the visit with the alleged offender should not occur. Resistance from a parent alone is not a reason to avoid this part of the evaluation.

False allegations may arise in other situations as well, such as the misinterpretation of a child's statement or behavior by relatives or caretakers. Adolescents may also occasionally make false allegations out of vindictiveness or to cover their own sexuality. Children who have experienced prior sexual abuse may sometimes misinterpret actions of adults or accuse the wrong person of abuse.

8. *Modifications in the clinical evaluation.*

The magnitude of the charges involved in alleged child sexual abuse, and their ramifications in terms of legal sequelae and impact on the family, require diagnostic evaluations with certain modifications. These evaluations differ from the usual psychiatric evaluation because the examiner is being asked to determine whether certain events occurred, and to determine at least one individual's credibility. It is essential that the clinician maintain emotional neutrality, approach the case with an open mind, adopt a non-judgmental stance and seek out the unique particulars of each case. Great care must be taken to avoid leading questions and coercive techniques; the child must be allowed to tell his story in his own words. The clinician needs to focus on detailed descriptions of discrete events and pinpoint them to time, place and frequency. It is useful to go over events more than once as accounts may change or new information may emerge. Finally, these evaluations differ from usual clinical evaluations in that more effort needs to be invested in obtaining corroborating information from other sources. This may include medical or school reports, prior psychiatric evaluations and talking with significant others.

9. *Assessing the child's credibility.*

Factors enhancing the child's credibility include detailed descriptions in the child's own language and from the child's point of view; spontaneity; an appropriate degree of anxiety, inclusion of idiosyncratic or sensorimotor detail; consistency of allegations over time (minor details and descriptive terms may change but the child's account of events should remain basically the same); behavioral changes consistent with the abuse; absence of motivation or undue influence for fabrication; and corroborating evidence. The evaluator needs to be aware of the child's cognitive and emotional development and how this may affect the interpretation and the recall of events.

10. *Anatomically correct dolls.*

In these assessments it is not necessary to use anatomically correct dolls. They may be useful for eliciting the child's terminology for anatomical parts, and for allowing the child who cannot tell or draw what happened, to demonstrate what happened. Care should be taken not to use these dolls in a way to instruct, coach or lead the child. Further, they should not be used as a short cut to a more comprehensive evaluation of the child and the child's family. The examiner should anticipate being asked in court why they were or were not used, and may need to remind the court that such aids alone do not provide reliable answers. (California has barred the admissibility of evidence obtained through use of anatomically correct dolls until such a time that the procedure has been accepted as reliable in the scientific community in which it was developed.)

11. *The use of children's drawings.*

Children's drawings are helpful in assessing child sexual abuse. These include spontaneous drawings, or asking the child to draw a male and female, kinetic family drawings, self-portraits, what happened and where it happened, or even a picture of the alleged offender. The usefulness of drawings lies in the affect and information they elicit and certain findings which may be suggestive of sexual abuse such as depiction of genitalia or avoidance of sexual features altogether. However, as with any other tool, they should be interpreted by an experienced clinician and in the context of the overall clinical picture.

12. *Videotaping.*

Videotaping, when possible, can serve several useful purposes including (1) preserving the child's initial statements; (2) avoiding duplication of efforts by sharing the video with others involved in the investigation; (3) encouraging the defendant to plead guilty, thereby sparing the child from testifying in court; (4) presenting the video to the grand jury in lieu of the child; and (5) as a teaching tool to help the interviewer and others improve techniques.

In making a videotape, the following concerns, disadvantages or risks should be taken into consideration: Videos can be used to harass or intimidate the child on cross-examination, or viewers may regard the testimony as more credible because it was given on video. Videos might be shown out of context or fall into the hands of those who have no professional obligations of confidentiality or concern for the child's best interest. Clinicians should familiarize themselves with laws in their states relative to admissibility of videotaped testimony.

The child should always be informed as to the purpose of the videotape and about who is present if a one-way mirror is being used. Parental consent and the child's assent should be obtained prior to videotaping.

13. *Psychological testing.*

Testing alone does not diagnose sexual abuse either in the victim or offender. It is helpful as a part of the evaluation of the alleged offender, and in cases of possible false allegations, it may be helpful to have testing of both parents. In all fairness, if testing is done on one parent, it should probably be done on the other as well. Testing of the victim may be indicated if there are questions about intelligence or thought processes.

14. *Reporting.*

Child sexual abuse must be reported in accord with ethical and legal requirements in each state. Clinicians should be aware of these requirements. The parent(s) and child should be informed as clinically indicated, and to the extent that the child's best interests are protected. Once the report is made and the legal or child protective services investigation begins, it often becomes difficult to obtain a history from the accused parent, who may become defensive.

15. *The medical evaluation.*

Every child who may have been sexually abused should have a physical examination. The medical exam gathers medicolegal evidence and treats any problems related to the abuse. It can be informative and can reassure the child or adolescent. Preferably, the examinaton should be performed by a pediatrician or family physician known to the child or by a pediatric gynecologist. The physician should know the ramifications of an examination carried out in this context. Such evaluations require special training which many physicians in the community have not yet obtained. Thus it is important to determine the qualifications of the physicians planning to do the physical exam. When possible, the child should be allowed to choose the sex of the examining physician. It is recommended that a trusted, supportive adult remain with the child during the evaluation.

Whenever there is the possibility of obtaining forensic evidence, the exam should take place promptly. If the child has been raped, or there is possibility of acute trauma or infection, or the abuse occurred within 72 hours of the disclosure, the child should be examined as soon as possible in order to obtain forensic evidence. Preferably, the child should be seen in a physician's office rather than the emergency ward. The genital exam may be conducted in the context of an overall physical so as to deemphasize it, and the child should be informed of what the physician is doing and be told afterwards what the findings are. It should be remembered that a negative genital exam does not rule out sexual abuse. The child's emotional state and degree of relaxation may affect the findings on both vaginal and rectal exams. If the child refuses to cooperate with the physical exam for reasons of trauma, consideration should be given to deferring the exam until such a time when, with benefit of counseling, the child is seemed able to cooperate.

If a child is already being evaluated by a mental health professional, the physician doing the physical exam should be sensitive to the child and minimize questions about the abuse so as to avoid contaminating the child's data and duplicating interviews.

16. *Formulating recommendations.*

The clinician needs to decide, based on history, an evaluation of child and parents, and a review of corroborating evidence, whether or not any sexual abuse occurred. A carefully written report should document the basis for these determinations. The next question concerns the immediate disposition of the child and whether it is safe to allow the child to return home. This decision is usually made by protective services, but the clinician's opinion is helpful. the decision will take into consideration whether or not the family believes and can protect the child, what the child's wishes are (depending on the age of the child) and, if living in the home, whether the offender is willing to take responsibility for his or her actions and seek help. Prior psychiatric problems which may have predisposed the abuse need to be sorted out from reactions to the abuse and its aftermath. Diagnostic impressions should be made and decisions need to be made as to what sort of treatment is recommended and for whom. This may include a range or combination of treatment modalities including individual, family, group and couples therapy, as well as behavioral and pharmacological approaches to the offender.

In some cases the evaluator may not be able to determine whether sexual abuse occurred. There are a number of reasons why this may be the case, including contamination by too many evaluations, particularly biased or leading ones. In addition, the child may be too young to verbalize what occurred, the abuse may have happened too long ago, or the child may have been subjected to the undue influence of competing parents and no longer knows what to believe. In such cases, the clinician must attempt to offer the child reasonable protection while also preserving parent-child ties.

The effects of child sexual abuse are diagnosable in the same sense that other medical conditions are diagnosable—on the basis of history, physical examination and the judicious use of various tests. Rarely is one finding along diagnostic of sexual abuse; rather, findings must be interpreted within the total context of a thorough evaluation. However, if the case proceeds one may be expected to explain opinions in terms of reasonable degree of medical certainty.

REFERENCES

AMA Council on Scientific Affairs (1986), AMA diagnostic and treatment guidelines concerning child abuse and neglect. *Connecticut Medicine*, 50:122–128.

Anthony, E.J. (1973), A working model for family studies. In: *The Child and His Family*, ed. E.J. Anthony and C. Koupernik. New York: John Wiley & Sons, Inc., pp. 3–20.

Benedek, T. (1970), Parenthood during the life cycle. In: *Parenthood: Its Psychology and Psychopathology,* ed. E.J. Anthony and T. Benedek. Boston: Little, Brown, pp. 185–206.

Brazelton, T.B., Koslonski,B., and Main, M. (1974), The origins of reciprocity: The early mother-infant interaction. In: *The Effect of the Infant on Its Caretaker,* ed. M. Lewis and L. Rosenblum. New York: John Wiley & Sons, Inc.

Brodey, W.M. (1959), Some family operations and schizophrenia. *Arch Gen. Psychiatry,* 1:379–402.

Bryant, B.K. (1982), Sibling relationships in middle childhood. In *Sibling Relationships: Their Nature and Significance Across the Lifespan,* ed. M. Lamb and B. Sutton-Smith. Hillsdale: Erlbaum.

Bureau of the Census (1978), Washington, D.C.: U.S. Government Printing Office. Publication No. 657.004/145.

Clarke-Stewart, A. (1982), *Day Care.* Boston: Harvard University Press.

Finkelhov, D. (1986), *A Sourcebook on Child Sexual Abuse.* Beverly Hills: Sage Publications.

Fisher, L. (1977), On the classification of families. *Arch. Gen Psychiatry,* 34:424–433.

Fleck, S. (1983), A holistic approach to family therapy and the axes of DSM-III. *Arch. Gen. Psychiatry,* 40:901–906.

Gelles, R.J. and Straus, M.A. (1985), National Family Violence Surveys. Presented at the National Conference on Child Abuse and Neglect. Chicago, November 11, 1985.

Glick, P. (1955), The life cycle of the family. *Marr. Fam. Living,* 18:3–9.

Golombok, S., Spencer, A., and Rutter, M. (1983), Children in lesbian and single-parent households: Psychosexual and psychiatric appraisal. *J. Child. Psychol. Psychiatry,* 24:551–572.

Green, R. (1978), Sexual identity of 37 children raised by homosexual or transsexual parents. *Am. J. Psychiatry,* 135:692–697.

Hall, M. (1978), Lesbian families: Cultural and clinical issues. *Social Casework,* 23:380–385.

Hareven, T.K. (1977), Family time and historical time. *Daedalus,* 107:57–70.

Hetherington, E.M. (1972), Effect of father absence on personality development in adolescent daughters. *Dev. Psychol.,* 7:313–326.

Hetherington, E.M., Cox, M., and Cox, R. (1982), Effects of divorce on parents and children. In: *Nontraditional Families: Parenting and Child Development,* ed. M. Lamb. Hillsdale: Erlbaum.

Hoeffer, B. (1981), Children's acquisition of sex-role behavior in lesbian mother families. *Am. J. Orthopsychiatry,* 51:536–544.

Hunt and Hunt (1977), Quoted in Galinsky, E.: Work and family in the 80's: The parent perspective. Family Resource Coalition Report, 1984, 3:2–4.

Hunter, N., and Polikoff, N. (1976), Custody rights of lesbian mothers: Legal theory and litigation strategy. *Buffalo Law Review,* 25:691.

Kirkpatrick, M., Smith, K., and Roy, R. (1981), Lesbian mothers and their children: A comparative study. *Am. J. Orthopsychiatry* 51:545–551.

Klein,M. (1946), Notes on some schizoid mechanisms. *Int. J. Psychoanal.,* 27:99–110.

Lidz, T. (1968), *The Person*. New York: Basic Books.

Lidz, T. (1970), The family as the developmental setting. In: *The Child and His Family*, ed. E.J. Anthony and C. Koupernik. New York: John Wiley & Sons, Inc., pp. 19–40.

Lynch, M.A., and Roberts, J. (1982), Developmental progress of young children from abusing families. In: *Consequences of Child Abuse*. London: Academic Press.

McDermott, J.F., Jr. (1981), Indications for family therapy: question or non-question? *J. Am. Acad. Child Psychiatry*, 20:409–419.

Maccoby, E.E. (1984), Middle childhood in the context of the family. In: *Development During Middle Childhood: The Years from Six to Twelve*, ed. W.A. Collines. Washington, D.C.: National Academy Press.

Martin, H.P., and Beezley, P. (1977), Behavioral observations of abused children. *Dev. Med. Child Neurol.*, 19:373–387.

Martin, H.P.,Beezley, P., Conway, E.F., and Kempe, C.H. (1974), The development of abused children. In: *Advances in Pediatrics* I (Vol 21), ed. I. Schulman. Chicago: Yearbook Medical.

Moynihan, D.P. (1985), *Family and Nation*. Harcourt Brace Jovanovich. Washington DC: National Center for Health Statistics, 1985.

Mueller, E., and Silverman, N. (1989), Peer relations in maltreated children. In: *Child Maltreatment: Theory and Research on the Causes and Consequences of Child Abuse and Neglect*, ed. D. Cicchetti and V. Carlson. Cambridge: Cambridge University Press.

Pagelow, M. (1980), Heterosexual and lesbian single mothers: A comparison of problems, coping and solutions. *J. Homosex.*, 5:189–204.

Rollins, N., Lord, J.P., Walsh, E., and Weil, G.E. (1973), Some roles children play in their families. *J. Am. Acad. Child Psychiatry*, 12:511–530.

Rutter, M. (1972), *Maternal Deprivation Reassessed*. Harmondsworth: Penguin.

Rutter, M. (1989), Intergenerational continuities and discontinuities in serious parenting difficulties. In: *Child Maltreatment: Theory and Research on the Causes and Consequences of Child Abuse and Neglect*, ed. D. Cicchetti and V. Carlson. Cambridge: Cambridge University Press.

Rutter, M., Quinton, D., and Yule, B. (1977), *Family Pathology and Disorders in Children*. London: John Wiley & Sons, Inc.

Schaffer, H.R. (1979), Acquiring the concept of dialogue. In: *Psychological Development from Infancy*, ed. M.H. Bornstein and W. Kessen. Hillsdale, N.J.: Lawrence Erlbaum Associates, pp. 279–306.

Schetky, D.H., and Green, A.H. (1988), Child Sexual Abuse. A Handbook of Health Care and Legal Professionals. New York: Brunner/Mazel Inc.

Solomon, M.A. (1974), Typologies of family homeostasis: Implications for diagnosis and treatment. *Family Therapy*, 1:9–18.

Tseng, W.S., and McDermott, J.F. (1979), Triaxial family classification. *J. Am. Acad. Child Psychiatry*, 18:22–43.

Wallerstein, J.S. and Corbin, S.B. (In Press), The child and the vicissitudes of divorce. In: *Child's Psychiatry: A Comprehensive Textbook*, ed. M. Lewis. New York: John Wiley & Sons.

13

TEMPERAMENT

In the course of their clinical observations and research, Chess and Thomas became fascinated with what they perceived as the individual behavior or personality styles that characterized each child—or rather, the peculiar shaping and reshaping of these styles as the child and his or her family develop. This phenomenon came to be known as the temperament of the child and, subsequently, in 1956, Chess and Thomas, together with the late Dr. Herbert Birch, launched their New York Longitudinal Study (Thomas and Chess, 1987; Chess and Thomas, 1984).

BEHAVIORAL CATEGORIES OF TEMPERAMENT

Chess and Thomas identified nine categories of behavior that constitute the individual's temperament (Table 13–1).

Their descriptions of items of enquiry of parents used for assessing each of the aforementioned categories included the following:

Table 13–1. Categories of Behavior in Temperament Assessment

1. Activity level
2. Rhythmicity (hunger, elimination, sleep/wake)
3. Approach or withdrawal responses
4. Adaptability to a change in the environment
5. Threshold of responsiveness
6. Intensity of any given reaction
7. Mood (quantity and quality)
8. Degree of distractibility
9. Persistence in the face of obstacles

From Chess, S., and Thomas, A. (1986), *Temperament in Clinical Practice*, New York: Guilford Press.

Activity level may be estimated from a child's behavior preferences. Would the child rather sit quietly for a long time engrossed in some task, or does she prefer to seek out opportunities for active physical play? How well does the child fare in routines that require sitting still for extended periods of time? For example, can she sit through an entire meal without seeking an opportunity to move about? Must a long train or automobile ride be broken up by frequent stops because of the child's restlessness?

Rhythmicity can be explored through questions about the child's habits and their regularity. For instance, does the child get sleepy at regular and predictable times? Does she have any characteristic routines relating to hunger, such as taking a snack immediately after school or during the evening? Are the bowel movements regular?

Approach/withdrawal, or the youngster's pattern of response to new events or new people, can be explored in many ways. Questions can be directed at the nature of the child's reaction to new clothing, new neighborhood children, a new school, and a new teacher. What is the child's attitude when a family excursion to a new place is being planned? Will she try new foods or new activities easily or not?

Adaptability can be identified through a consideration of the way the child reacts to changes in environment. Does the child adjust easily and fit quickly into changed family patterns? Is she willing to go along with other children's preferences, or does she always insist on pursuing only her own interests?

Threshold level is more difficult to explore in an older child than in a young one. However, it is sometimes possible to obtain information on an unusual feature of threshold, such as sensitivity to noise, to visual stimuli, or to rough clothing, or remarkable unresponsiveness to such stimuli.

The *intensity of reactions* can be ascertained by finding out how the child displays disappointment or pleasure. If something pleasant happens does the child tend to be mildly enthusiastic, average in the expression of joy, or ecstatic? When unhappy, does the child fuss quietly or bellow with rage or distress?

Quality of mood can usually be estimated by parental description of their offspring's overall expressions of mood. Is the child predominantly happy or contented, or is she a frequent complainer and more often unhappy than not?

Distractibility, even when not a presenting problem, will declare itself in the parents' descriptions of ordinary routines. Does the child start off to do something and then often get sidetracked by something her brother is doing, by a coin collection, or by any number of several circumstances that catch the eye or ear? Or, on the contrary, since the child is engaged in an activity, is she impervious of what is going on around her?

Data on persistence and attention span are usually easier to obtain for the older child than for the infant. The degree of persistence in the face of difficulty can be ascertained with regard to games, puzzles, athletic activities such as learning to ride a bicycle, and schoolwork. Similarly, after the initial difficulty in mastering these activities has been overcome, the length of the child's attention span for and concentration on these same kinds of activities can be ascertained (Chess and Thomas, 1986, pp. 120–121).

The idea of the child as an active person had, of course, been promulgated in some form by others. Rousseau, for example, in his book *Emile* in 1762, conceived of the child as a separate person who actively discovered the world and constructed his or her own knowledge—a forerunner of modern Piagetian views of the construction of reality in the child. Rousseau was, in fact, probably the first to introduce the ideas of development and developmental stages. (The term "maturation" was later introduced by Gesell in the 1930s and 1940s.) Freud too had laid the framework for an understanding of the active internal processes at work within the mind of the child. What is new here is not only the child's active contribution to his or her own actual life experiences and conflicts in the course of the child's interaction with parents and other individuals, but the notion of genotypical variations in style originating in the genotype of an individual and brought out and modified by the individual child's active interaction with his or her environment. In other words, here, as in breeds found in some

other species, we can see a variety of strains among human beings (such as fearful, shy, and timid; or bold, outgoing, and aggressive), with each strain modified and capable of being shaped by experience, teaching, and learning. (Interestingly, such "strains" have been suggested by previous investigators. Jung, for example, suggested two types, the introvert and the extrovert; however, the scientific data for such strains were previously found lacking.)

All of us are aware of an individual who attacks a new experience with gusto and enthusiasm, or one who cautiously, perhaps fearfully, dips but one toe at a time to test the water. The goal for the child is, or should be, mastery. How does a particular child go about achieving this goal? What may interfere with the accomplishment of the task? How may the child be helped in this endeavor? The central concept Chess and Thomas devised to study and understand these questions was that of the "goodness of fit" in the complex interactions over time between the child's temperament and the environment.

GOODNESS OF FIT

The concept of goodness of fit essentially means a compatibility between the child's capacities and temperament, and the demands and expectations of the environment. In a sense, this is an evolutionary concept, reminiscent of the Darwinian theory that postulates that those organisms whose characteristics are most adaptive to their environment (i.e., who show a goodness of fit) have the best chance to survive and flourish. Moreover, multiple kinds of interactions between the organism and the environment may be adaptive; there is no one, fixed, "right" interaction.

Sometimes the individual can modify his or her behavioral patterns to achieve a better fit with the environment. Sometimes the demands and expectations of the environment need to be modified and shaped to achieve a better, more compatible fit between the environment (the parent) and the individual (child or adolescent). Insight and understanding into one's temperament, whether one is a child, adolescent, or adult, can be beneficial in achieving the best possible match between people who have to relate to each other and "fit" together in the interests of the optimal development of each individual.

These two concepts, temperament and goodness of fit, give clinicians an additional general way of understanding the various and varying difficulties children of the same family have with their parents (and vice versa). These two concepts also specifically offer clinicians the opportunity to identify certain particular temperamental characterstics that predict to some degree the possibility of a "poor fit" between the child and his or her caretakers. This represents a practical approach that adds to our way of assessing behavior and the difficulties that may arise between child and parent.

Chess and Thomas found that about 1 in 10 children had a "difficult" temperament, and about 1 in 6 was in the "slow-to-warm-up" group. About two fifths of the children studied had an "easy" temperament.

Parents worry a great deal about their children, especially the difficult child. They may also feel guilty and believe that they have caused the difficulty. Often this is far from the truth, and the parents can be reassured and helped to learn better ways of handling the child with a difficult temperament.

Neither temperament nor development is confined to children. Chess and Thomas recognized this in their descriptions of temperament during adult development, and in the even greater complexity of "fits" that may occur.

Studies have suggested that temperament derives, in part, from genetic influences (Torgeson and Kringlen, 1978). Some evidence (Kagan, Reznik, Clarke, Snidman, and Carcia-Coll, 1984) suggests that temperament is relatively stable, at least over the preschool

period. Studies from different parts of the world have revealed associations between temperament and activity levels, sociability, (including different reactions to the strange and unfamiliar), parent-child interaction, school performance, differences in mother-child interactions, and accident rates in children; some cultural differences have also been noted (Caudill and Weinstein, 1969).

CONTINUITY AND OUTCOME

The New York Longitudinal Study is an exemplary study of the enormous complexity of an interactional model. Limitations of the study include the reliance on parental report (as opposed to direct observation). Some of the terms proposed clearly imply value judgments and may be somewhat misleading in that some parents might perceive as "difficult" a baby which other parents would find "easy." Other studies (Field and Greenberg, 1982; Hubert, Wachs, and Peters-Martin, 1982) have questioned the stability of measures of temperament and their variability across settings. However, the study does suggest the importance of enduring patterns of behavior and interactional processes over development which, in turn, suggests the potential for therapeutic intervention.

SUMMARY

All these ideas challenged some previously held views on the causes of various developmental and clinical phenomena. Until the 1950s the prevailing explanations, when no actual organic brain damage was present, were largely based on either psychoanalytic assumptions and inferences or behavioral and learning therapy notions. However, Thomas, Chess, and Birch changed the balance when they added the important idea that the child, far from being a passive recipient, or simply a responder to various stimuli, was an active initiator and contributor to his or her own experience and development. They found too that this activity on the part of the child was determined to an extent by the child's temperament, and that the child's particular developmental characteristics contributed in important ways to some of the behavior disorders observed in children.

Temperament is not a theory of development; rather it is but one attribute of an individual—albeit an important one. Therapists do not confine their approach to treatment primarily to issues of temperament. In any event, most treatments in child and adolescent psychiatry now include multiple approaches. Nevertheless, individuals in whom temperamental issues are prominent and important in the development of the behavioral difficulties are often brought to the attention of teachers, nurses, pediatricians, and child psychiatrists, and can be helped by the appreciation of these concepts (Chess and Thomas, 1986).

Note 20

From A. Thomas, S. Chess, and H.G. Birch (1968), *Temperament and Behavior Disorders in Children.* New York: New York University Press, pp. 182–183.

As in the case when any significant influencing variable is identified, there is an understandable temptation to make temperament the heart and body of a general theory. To do so would be to repeat a frequent approach in psychiatry, which, over the years, has been beset by general theories of behavior based upon fragments rather than the totality of influencing mechanisms. A one-sided emphasis on temperament would merely repeat and perpetuate such a tendency and would be antithetical to our viewpoint, which insists that we recognize temperament as only one attribute of the organism . . . the relevance of the concept of temperament to general psychiatric theory lies neither in its sole pertinence for behavior disorders, nor in its displacment of other conceptualizations, but in the fact that it must be incorporated into any general theory of normal and aberrant behavioral development if the theory is to be complete.

Note 21

From S. Chess and A. Thomas (1986), Temperamental categories and their definitions. In: *Temperament in Clinical Practice*, ed. S. Chess and A. Thomas. New York: Guilford Press, pp. 273–281.

1. *Activity level.* The motor component present in a given child's functioning and the diurnal proportion of active and inactive periods. Protocol data on motility during bathing, eating, playing, dressing, and handling, as well as information concerning the sleep–wake cycle, reaching, crawling, and walking, are used in scoring this category.

Examples in infancy of statements indicating high activity are, "He moves a great deal in his sleep and must be re-covered several times each night," "She kicks and splashes so much in the bath that the floor must be mopped afterward," or "He has recently learned to turn over and now he does it constantly." Examples of statements indicating low activity would be, "In the morning I find him lying in the same place he was when he fell asleep," or "She can turn over but she doesn't do it much."

At toddler age, examples might be as follows for high activity: "When a friend from nursery school comes to visit, she immediately starts a game of running around wildly," or for low activity, "Given a choice of activities, he usually selects something quiet such as drawing or looking at a picture book."

In middle childhood, statements indicating high activity might be, "When he comes home from school he is outside immediately playing an active game," or "In the house she is constantly doing acrobatics—even while doing her homework. She is in constant motion." A statement indicating a low activity level might be, "Typically she gets involved with a tremendous jigsaw puzzle and sits quietly working at it for hours."

2. *Rhythmicity (regularity).* The predictability and/or unpredictability in time of any function. It can be analyzed in relation to the sleep–wake cycle, hunger, feeding pattern, and elimination schedule.

In infancy, statements illustrative of high regularity are, "Unless she is sick, her bowel movement comes predictably once a day immediately after her breakfast," or "Nap time never changes no matter where we are, and he sleeps from 1 to $2\frac{1}{2}$ hours without fail." Examples of statements showing irregularity are, "I wouldn't know when to start toilet training since bowel movements come at any time and he has from 1 to 3 a day," or "At feedings, sometimes she drains the bottle but other times she is done after only 2 ounces or so."

In the toddler period, high rhythmicity would be exemplified by reports such as, "Her big meal is always at lunch time," while a statement indicating low rhythmicity would be, "Sometimes he falls asleep right after dinner and on other days he keeps going till 9 or 10 p.m.—there is no predicting."

In middle childhood, examples of statements of high regularity are, "He awakens like clockwork each morning; I never need to wake him for school," or "She comes in from play at the same time each day without being called; she says she feels hungry." A statement indicating irregularity might be, "If he hasn't finished his homework by bedtime, he just continues since he never gets sleepy at the same hour at night."

3. *Approach or withdrawal.* The nature of the initial response to a new stimulus, be it a new food, a new toy, or a new person. Approach responses are positive, whether displayed by mood expression (smiling, verbalization, and the like) or motor activity (swallowing a new food, reaching for a new toy, active play, and so on). Withdrawal reactions are negative, whether displayed by mood expression (crying, fussing, grimacing, verbalization, or the like) or motor activity (moving away, spitting new food out, pushing new toy away, and so forth).

Statements showing high approach in infancy: "He always smiles at a stranger," "She loves new toys," or "He is interested in tasting anything new we give him." High withdrawal would be illustrated by, "He ignores a new toy until it has been around for several days," and "When I introduce a new food, her first reaction is to spit it out."

In the toddler period, a statement illustrating high approach would be, "We went to her new play group yesterday; as always she plunged right in." High withdrawal in the same situation might be shown by, "We started a new play group two weeks ago. Although it meets three times a week, he remained on the side for the first whole week and only last week did he begin to participate in activities."

In later childhood, a statement of high approach might be, "He came home from his new school the first day talking as if everybody was his best friend and phoned one of his classmates immediately." A high-withdrawal illustration would be, "The class just started to learn fractions. As usual, she is all confused and is sure she will never learn. I reminded her that she always says that with a new subject but later she masters it well."

4. *Adaptability.* Responses to new or altered situations. One is not concerned with the nature of the initial responses, but with the ease with which they are modified in desired directions.

Illustrations in infancy of high adaptability are, "When he first was given cereal, he spit it out but it took only two or three times and he was eating it with gusto," or "She used to tell her new stuffed bear 'I don't like you' but after a few days she began to play with it and now it's her best friend." Low adaptability in infancy would be illustrated by, "Every time I put her into her snow suit she screams and struggles till we are outside— and that has been going on for three months."

At toddler age, high adaptability would be exemplified by, "She got her first tricycle and couldn't master it, called it 'stupid.' But then I noticed her practicing on it every day and by a week she was out pedaling happily with her friends." A statement illustrating low adaptability would be, "It took him all fall to go contentedly to nursery school and each time he gets a cold and is out for several days, he becomes reluctant to go again."

In midde childhood, a statement of high adaptabilty might be, "He went to a tennis camp this summer. Although it was a totally new type of schedule and he felt uncomfortable at first, he became easily involved and felt comfortable within the first week." A low-adaptable child would be exemplified by, "She started a new school with a different way of teaching. Although it is now three months, she still gets confused and wants explanations in the old fashion."

5. *Threshold of responsiveness.* The intensity level of stimulation that is necessary to evoke a discernible response, irrespective of the specific form that the response may take, or the sensory modality affected. The behaviors utilized are those concerning reactions to sensory stimuli, environmental objects, and social contacts.

In infancy, statement illustrating low threshold would be, "If a door closes even softly, he startles and looks up," or "She loves fruit but if I put even a little cereal with it she won't eat it." Reports of high-threshold behavior are, "He can bang his head and raise a bump but he doesn't cry or change his behavior," or "I can't tell from her action when she is wet or soiled, I have to check by looking."

At toddler age, examples of low threshold would be, "She likes her eggs scrambled one particular way; it they are a shade harder or softer she won't eat them," or "He complains about any pants if the waistband is the slightest bit tight." High-threshold examples might be, "She never complains of feeling cold even though she may be shivering and her lips are blue," or "Whether clothing texture is smooth or rough doesn't make any difference; he seems comfortable in every type."

In middle childhood, statements exemplifying low threshold are, "She is the first one in any group to notice an odor or feel a change in the room temperature," or "He is very alert to people's expressions and comments when I look tired." Examples of high threshold are, "He came home from playing soccer with a blistered heel and he hadn't noticed it or felt any discomfort," or "One of the lights went out while she was doing her homework and she didn't notice it, just went on with her work."

6. *Intensity of reaction.* The energy level of response, irrespective of its quality or direction.

Examples of high intensity in infancy are, "When she is hungry she cries loudly from the beginning—there is no mild fussing at all," or "If he hears music be bubbles with loud laughter and bounces in time to it." Examples of low intensity would be, "He had an ear infection and his eardrums were bulging but he behaved only slightly less frisky than usual and whimpered a bit," or "If he hears a loud noise he fusses but doesn't cry."

In the toddler period, statements indicating high intensity might be, "As soon as she has trouble with a puzzle she screams and throws the pieces," or "When I make his favorite dessert, he jumps with joy and runs shouting to tell his sister." Examples of low intensity are, "If another child takes her toy she grabs it back but doesn't cry," or "If his clothing is uncomfortable he tells me quietly while insisting that it be changed."

In middle childhood, illustrations of high intensity are, "They call him a sore loser because he yells that his opponent is a cheater, and he throws things around in anger," or "In the restaurant she couldn't get the food she wanted and screamed and made a huge fuss." Examples of low intensity might be, "She was taken to a musical show for her birthday. Although she had chosen it herself and told her friends about it, she was deadpan during the performance," or "I know he was very upset at failing the test, but outwardly he appeared only a little subdued."

7. *Quality of mood.* The amount of pleasant, joyful, and friendly behavior, as contrasted with unpleasant, crying, and unfriendly behavior.

In infancy, examples of negative mood might be, "Every time he sees food he doesn't like, he whines and fusses until I take it off the table," or "Each night when put to sleep he cries at least 5 to 10 minutes." Illustrations of positive mood are, "When he sees me take out his bottle of juice, he begins to smile and coo," or "If he is not laughing and smiling I know he's getting sick."

At the toddler period, examples of negative mood would be, "She typically comes home from nursery school full of complaints about the other children," or "At night he regularly feels cheated—for example, he wants one more story, and at no time does he go to bed pleasantly." Positive mood statements are, "He got new shoes and he ran around bubbling with pleasure and showing everyone he met," or "It's a pleasure to come home; she tells me all the nice things she did with smiles of enjoyment."

In middle childhood, statements showing negative mood might be, "School just started last week

and he has already accumulated grievances about each teacher," or "We went shopping for new pants and shirts but she found something wrong with everything we looked at—there's no pleasing her." Positive mood would be exemplified by, "The class went on an excursion and her teacher commented on how cooperative and helpfully she behaved," or "He never objects to home chores, just takes out the garbage and does whatever he is asked with a smile."

8. *Distractibility.* The effectiveness of extraneous environmental stimuli in interfering with or in altering the direction of the ongoing behavior.

An example in infancy of high distractibility would be, "He likes to poke objects into the electric outlets but his attention can easily be shifted by offering a toy," or "If someone passes by while she is nursing, she not only looks but stops sucking until the person has gone." Statements illustrating low distractibility would be, "She has learned to push a little table around the house and if it gets stuck she cannot be sidetracked but keeps trying," or "When he is hungry and it takes a while to get his food ready, it is not possible to get him involved in play—he just keeps crying until he is fed."

In the toddler period, high distractibility might be demonstrated by, "She's not a nagger. If she wants special cookies she sees in the supermarket she will ask once or twice, but then accept a substitute," or "His room is strewn with toys—he scarcely has begun one when his eye is caught by another and he keeps changing, forgetting to put anything back." Low distractibility would be shown by, "He got a new kind of interlocking blocks and we couldn't get him to leave them even when his best friend came to play," or "If she decides she wants to go out to play and it is raining, she will fuss and won't accept any substitute."

In middle childhood, statements of high distractibility would be, "His homework takes a long time as his attention repeatedly is sidetracked," or "She is constantly losing something, as she gets involved with something else and forgets it." Low distractibility might be shown by, "His friends ask him to come to play hockey but if he is making a model airplane, they can't pull him away," or "Once she starts reading a book, we can't get her attention until she gets to the end of a chapter."

9. *Attention span and persistence.* Two categories that are related. Attention span concerns the length of time a particular activity is pursued by the child. Persistence refers to the continuation of an activity in the face of obstacles to the maintenance of the activity direction.

In infancy examples of high persistence would be, "Even though we can get him sidetracked by a toy, as soon as we stop playing with him he returns to his own task of poking at the electric outlet," while long attention span would be illustrated by, "If I give her some magazines she will contentedly tear up paper for as long as a half hour." A statement indicating low persistence would be, 'If the bead doesn't go on the string immediately, she gives up," while short attention span would be shown by, "Although she loves her teddy bear, she only plays with it for a few minutes at a time."

In the toddler period high persistence would be indicated by a statement such as, "If he is pushing his wagon about and it gets stuck he struggles and yells until it moves again or else he comes for help—he doesn't give up," while long attention span would be shown by, "She can be engrossed playing in the sand box for almost an hour." A statement of low persistence would be, "He asked to be taught to draw a dog but lost interest after the first try," and this would also indicate short attention span.

In middle childhood, a statement illustrating high persistence and long attention would be, "She couldn't understand her grammar homework at first but she stubbornly kept at it until she had mastered it even though it took two hours." Short attention span but high persistence would be illustrated by, "She wouldn't give up until she had learned her part in the play, but she worked at memorizing for only about 15 minutes at a time." A statement indicating short attention span and low persistence would be, "He decided to learn how to figure skate but after five minutes he gave up trying."

Three temperamental constellations of functional significance have been defined by qualitative analysis of the data and factor analysis. The first group is characterized by regularity, positive approach responses to new stimuli, high adaptability to change, and mild or moderately intense mood that is preponderantly positive. These children quickly develop regular sleep and feeding schedules, take to most new foods easily, smile at strangers, adapt easily to a new school, accept most frustration with little fuss, and accept the rules of new games with no trouble. Such a youngster is aptly called an easy child, and is usually a joy to his or her parents, pediatricians, and teachers. This group comprises about 40% of our NYLS sample.

In the toddler period, middle childhood, and adolescence such children are quickly at ease in a new school or with new people and are welcomed by others because they are good-natured and helpful. In response to the positive welcome they receive, their own sense of ease tends to be reinforced and they continue to welcome new experiences.

At the opposite end of the temperamental spectrum is the group with irregularity in biological functions, negative withdrawal responses to new stimuli, nonadaptability or slow adaptability to change, and intense mood expressions that are frequently negative. These children show irregular sleep and feeding schedules, slow acceptance of new foods, prolonged adjustment periods to new routines, people, or situations, and relatively frequent and loud periods of crying. Laughter, also, is characteristically loud. Frustration typically produces a violent tantrum. These are characteristics of the difficult child, and mothers and pediatricians find such youngsters· troublesome indeed. This group comprises about 10% of our NYLS sample.

Given sufficient time, these children do adapt well, especially if places and people and environmental circumstances remain constant. However, should there be a total change in surroundings and type of expectations in the developmental periods of toddler, middle childhood, and/or adolescence, the difficult child constellation is likely to come into evidence again.

The third noteworthy temperamental constellation is marked by a combination of negative responses of mild intensity to new stimuli with slow adaptability after repeated contact. In contrast to the difficult children, these youngsters are characterized by mild intensity of reactions, whether positive or negative, and by less tendency to show irregularity of biological functions. The negative mild responses to new stimuli can be seen in the first encounter with the bath, a new food, a stranger, a new place, or a new school situation. If given the opportunity to reexperience such new situations over time and without pressure, such a child gradually comes to show quiet and positive interest and involvement. A youngster with this characteristic sequence of response is referred to as the slow-to-warm-up child, an apt if inelegant designation. About 15% of our NYLS sample falls into this category.

These children, adolescents, and young adults are shy and need time to become comfortable in situations of new developmental demands. Their moderate or low intensity of mood expression may protect against stormy interactions, but under some circumstances in later childhood, adolescence, or adulthood may lead to the acceptance of a side-line position.

As can be seen from the above percentages, not all children fit into one of these three temperamental groups. This results from the varying and different combinations of temperamental traits that are manifested by individual children. Also, among those children who do fit one of these three patterns, there is a wide range in degree of manifestation. Some are extremely easy children in practically all situations; others are relatively easy and not always so. A few children are extremely difficult with all new situations and demands; others show only some of these characteristics and relatively mildly. For some children it is highly predictable that they will warm up slowly in any new situation; others warm up slowly with certain types of new stimuli or demands, but warm up quickly in others.

It should be emphasized that the various temperamental constellations all represent variations within normal limits. Any child may be easy, difficult, or slow-to-warm-up temperamentally, or may have a high or low activity level, distractibility, and low persistence or the opposite, or any other relatively extreme rating score in a sample of children for a specific temperamental attribute. However, such an amodal rating is not a criterion of psychopathology, but rather an indication of the wide range of behaviorial styles exhibited by normal children.

In adolescence and adulthood also, temperamental traits may be present in varying combinations and may not fit into an easy-to-difficult spectrum.

Whether there has been continuity from infancy on or change in temperamental expression with the passage of years, the importance of temperamental individuality has to do with the interactions of that particular stage of life in the particular environment of that episode.

REFERENCES

Caudill, W.A., and Weinstein, H. (1969), Maternal care and infant behavior in Japan and America. *Psychiatry*, 32:12–43.

Chess, S., and Thomas, A. (1984), *Origins and Evolutions of Behavioral Disorders: Infancy to Early Adult Life*. New York: Brunner/Mazel.

Chess, S., and Thomas, A. (1986), *Temperament in Clinical Practice*. New York: Guilford Press.

Field, T., and Greenberg, R. (1982), Temperament ratings by parents and teachers of infants, toddlers, and preschool children. *Child Dev.*, 53:160–163.

Hubert, N.C., Wachs, T.D., and Peters-Martins, P. (1982), The study of early temperament: Measurement and conceptual issues. *Child Dev.*, 49:571–600.

Kagan, J., Reznik, R.J., Clarke, C., Snidman, N., and Garcia-Coll, C. (1984), Behavioral inhibition to the unfamiliar. *Child Dev.*, 55:2212–2225.

Thomas, A., and Chess, S. (1987), *Temperament and Development*. New York: Brunner/Mazel.

Torgesen, A.M., and Kringlen, E. (1978), Genetic aspects of temperamental differences in infants: A study of same-sexed twins. *J. Am. Acad. Child. Psychiatry*, 17:433–444.

Part Two

Cross-Sectional Perspectives

14

PRIOR TO BIRTH

PRENATAL DEVELOPMENT

The psychologic development of the child has its antecedents during the prenatal period (Hutt et al., 1968; Lecaneut, 1986; Madison, 1986; Schmidt et al., 1985; Prechtl, 1985). The fetus can react to loud sounds by gross motor activity (Bernard and Sontag, 1947). Actual behavior conditioning of the fetus may even be possible, although this has not yet been convincingly demonstrated (Spelt, 1948). Nevertheless, certain behavior does occur in the fetus (Hooker, 1952), including a sucking reflex at about 20 weeks. Mothers report that the fetus responds with vigorous movements when it hears the mother's voice, or becomes soothed by the mother's heartbeat or the rhythm of her body when she walks slowly and rhythmically. At about the third month, responses become more localized (Humphrey, 1970). The important points here are that heredity and environment are already interacting and that it is conceivable that future psychologically motivated behavior can be influenced by manipulating the genetic and environmental variables. In any case, from the beginning the new organism in its own right exerts an influence on the world. For example, the quickening movements of the fetus evoke a response in the mother, representing an early contribution of the child to the mother-child interaction. Throughout development the child will continue to influence his or her environment through the child's own activity.

PRENATAL ENVIRONMENT

The environment of the prenatal child is of course intrauterine, but even this relatively homeostatic environment is to some extent influenced by the mother's physical and emotional state. Weight gain during pregnancy is important for fetal growth. The normal mother who eats her regular diet usually gains the minimum 25 pounds needed to allow her fetus to grow adequately and to prepare herself for the lactation period that may follow (Winick, 1981). Malnutrition, illness, radiation, drugs taken by the mother, and anxiety, on the other hand, may seriously affect the development of the fetus.

Smoking during pregnancy clearly affects birth weight; the more the woman smokes, the lower the birth weight (DHHS, 1981). Infants born to chronic smokers may show a withdrawal syndrome (Finnegan, 1981). Longer term effects on infant development are less clear (Lefkowitz, 1981).

Ingestion of alcohol during pregnancy may cause the fetal alcohol syndrome, characterized by a distinctive face, impaired growth, and mental retardation. Limb malformation, heart defects, urogenital abnormalities, and numerous other dysmorphoses may occur. Binge drinking during early gestation may be critical. The risk of defect from alcoholism in the pregnant mother may be as high as 35%. The incidence of fetal alcohol syndrome is about 1 to 2 per 1,000 live babies, perhaps making it the leading teratogenic cause of mental retardation in the United States, and possibly in the Western World. Women who

117

drink heavily may also be more likely to smoke during pregnancy (Rosett, et al., 1976).

Other potential adverse influences include exposure to certain drugs, radiation, and environmental teratogens. Viral infections throughout pregnancy are also particularly worrisome.

Prenatal sex hormones have a powerful effect on the developing brain and psychosexual differentiation (Ehrhardt and Meyer-Bahlburg, 1979; Imperato-McGinley, et al., 1979). Differences in the frequency of aggressive behavior may be related to prenatal variations in hormone levels (Reinisch, 1981).

THE MOTHER'S PERSONALITY

Four major factors of the mother's attitude influence her relationship with her child: *First is the mother's personality prior to, during, and after pregnancy.* Perhaps the single most important factor here is the nature and extent of the mother's own experience of being mothered. Persisting aspects of the mother's relationship with her own parents, her sense of feminine identification, and her relationship with the child's father are further variables to be considered. Many of these kinds of prevailing personality factors affect the mother's relationship to her child. Sometimes direct displacement of the mother's feelings and attitudes onto the child occurs. At other times the child is used as a weapon (or battlefield) in a continuing struggle with the father. At all times the mother's particular perceptual capacities, mothering skills, and ability to develop during the phase of motherhood affect the mother-child relationship (A. Freud, 1955).

ACCEPTANCE OF PREGNANCY

The Mother's Specific Attitudes Toward Pregnancy

Besides the fear or pleasure the mother may have eperienced in regard to being pregnant, she may have had hidden and complex motivations for becoming pregnant. For example, she may have wanted to please the grandparents of the expected child. Or she may have conceived a child in an unrealistic wish to save her marriage. Or she may have become pregnant in an attempt to deal with her anxiety about frigidity or sterility. Or she may have yearned for a child, in an unconscious fantasy in which she herself was the nurtured infant. Sometimes hostile attitudes toward the fetus are crystallized during a painful or physically traumatic labor.

REACTION TO PREGNANCY

The Acute Impact of the Normal Psychologic Reactions to Pregnancy

During the normal "crisis" of pregnancy the woman has been described as moving through a phase of enhanced preoccupation with herself ("cathexis of the self") until quickening brings about a new person ("object") with whom the woman forms a complex relationship (Bibring et al., 1961; see also Note 22). Moreover, this crisis in the mother is thought to continue beyond parturition, and it may influence the nature of the mother-child relationship. Sometimes unresolved psychologic reactions to pregnancy spill over and cause disturbances in the delicate balance of the earliest mother-child relationship. For example, the multiple stresses of childbirth may temporarily upset the mother's physiologic and psychic equilibrium, producing any kind and degree of psychiatric disorder (Normand, 1967). The specificity of the disorder in part depends upon such factors as the previous level of emotional maturity, including the sense of femininity, and the presence of certain unresolved conflicts, such as hostility toward the mother's own mother. However, hormonal changes after pregnancy can result in psychologic problems regardless of the mother's maturity. Typically, the onset of clinical symptoms occurs during the puerperium. Perhaps the most common symptoms are depressive ones. Many normal women experience postpartum blues (Markham, 1961). This depression may lead to some degree of withdrawal, accompanied by partial rejection of the baby. The withdrawal and rejection, in turn, may result in early feeding difficulties in the baby, leading to further rejection and the creation of a vicious cycle. In this way a physiologic and a consequent psychologic reaction to the pregnancy and labor may interfere with the normal development of the mother-child interaction. Certainly, depression in the mother is likely to give rise to psychiatric symptoms in the child (Cohler et al., 1974). We now know that genetic and physiologic predispositions to psychiatric disorders, particularly major depressive disorders, play major roles in the development of postpartum psychoses.

MOTHER'S LATENT EXPECTATIONS OF THE CHILD

A child may come to be used by the mother to express her own conscious or unconscious wishes. Occasionally, she may fantasize that she can remake herself in the child or at least "correct" (usually she over-corrects) the mistakes in the way she was brought up.

MODIFYING FACTORS

All the foregoing influences become even more complex if either parent is absent. The attitudes and expectations become more powerful when there are reinforcing reality factors, such as adoption, a difficult childbirth, brain damage, the fear of certain hereditary traits, illness, or an unwanted child. Pregnant women who want an abortion but cannot obtain one are more likely to experience child-rearing difficulties, and to produce a greater frequency of psychiatric problems in the young child (Forsmann and Thuwe, 1966) than are pregnant women who want their infant. Furthermore, none of these factors remains static: they are in a continuous state of flux. Some of these factors will be discussed later as they impinge on the child at different phases in his or her development, but one point must be emphasized here: the child

continues to make a contribution to any continuing conflict between the parent and child.

ROLE OF THE FATHER

The mother is, of course, only part of the child's environment, albeit usually the most important part in the child's early years. What has been said so far about the mother could also be said about the father (Earls, 1976; Osofsky, 1982). Fathers sometimes experience some of the physical symptoms of pregnancy (Shershefsky and Yarrow, 1973); in some cultures fathers literally experience the pangs of childbirth (couvade). Even when fathers do not have bodily concerns they may resent the increased preoccupation of the mother with the pregnancy and displace this resentment onto the child. The father may love the child as part of himself and as an aspect of his wife or their relationship. Alternatively, the father's ambivalence about the marriage or his lack of motivation for fatherhood may disrupt the father-child relationship. Occasionally, the father will become anxious because of the prospect of increased responsibility or because of identification with his own father (Zilboorg, 1931). Sometimes the father's ideas of what a mother's role and a father's role should be are in conflict with the mother's ideas on the subject. Then again, if the father is insecure in his work, he may be unable to meet the needs of the mother and child.

Studies have amply demonstrated the importance of the father in the development of the child, particularly during early childhood when a warm father-child relationship fosters well-adapted development (Lamb, 1975; Pruett, 1987). (See Note 25.)

GRANDPARENTS AND SIBLINGS

Grandparents, uncles and aunts, and siblings also form part of the child's environment. Grandparents and other members of the extended family are important parts of the child's life. The efforts of family members can be experienced as helpful and supportive or as intrusive. Often the advent of a baby will reawaken old conflicts and provide opportunities for their resolution.

An older sibling, especially of the same sex, who has been prepared for the new baby will generally have a positive sibling relationship. Sibling rivalry is more likely to occur when the older sibling has negative feelings toward the mother, especially when the mother decreases her attention to the older sibling (Dunn and Kendrick, 1979).

PERINATAL VARIABLES

Prematurity is an important factor in subsequent development. Prematurely born infants are poorly parented more frequently than are full-term infants (Klein and Stern, 1974), and they are more prone to abuse and/or neglect (Klaus and Kennell, 1970; Hunter et al., 1978). Minde and his colleagues (1980) have shown that a mother's activity with her premature infant in the neonatal nursery may be a good indicator of her initial adjustment to this infant and of her current emotional adjustment. Severe prematurity (birth weight less than 4½ pounds), severe complications of pregnancy and/or delivery, and severe familial stress make their contribution to behavior disorders in later life, even when social class factors are held constant (Drillien, 1965). Overactivity and restlessness are the most common behavior problems that are related to severe prematurity (i.e., a birth weight of 3 pounds or less).

On the other hand, not all psychiatrically disturbed children have low birth weights, and complications of birth do not necessarily result in psychiatric disorder. In a study in which the obstetric histories of 100 primary school-age children referred to a psychiatric department with reactive psychiatric disorders were compared with the obstetric histories of 100 matched controls, no significant differences were found between the two groups in maternal age, birth weight, factors suggestive of an abnormal fetus, complications of pregnancy, complications of delivery,

or the postnatal conditions of the child (Wolff, 1967).

SUMMARY

What was suggested in the preceding discussion is that the infant arrives in the world with an already complex development behind him or her, possessing an array of functions operating in ways that are peculiar to the infant and actively making a unique contribution. Far from being a *tabula rasa*, the infant at birth has certain behavioral characteristics, brought about even prenatally by the interaction of genes and the environment, which are unique to the infant. Furthermore, these functions operate in such a way that a state of partial adaptedness may be said to exist at birth.

Once outside the womb, the active infant encounters the mother more directly. The mother now constitutes what Hartmann has called the average expectable environment (Hartmann, 1939; see Note 23). The continuing mutual relationship between infant and mother enables the infant to survive and thrive. The personality of the mother continues to influence this relationship. More specifically, the particular impact of the events of pregnancy, labor, and birth of a live child upon the mother in turn causes her to influence her child in characteristic ways.

Children born into an environment that is more or less prepared for the child, an environment that is not "ideal" but is at least "good enough" will contribute to that environment. Furthermore, the mental activity of the infant can turn a good-enough environment ("the ordinary good mother is good enough") into an optimum environment (Winnicott, 1958).

ANTICIPATORY GUIDANCE

Attempts have been made to forestall some of the possible difficulties beween mother and infant by means of "anticipatory guidance," a method first conceptualized by Milton Senn (1947; see Note 24). Success in these attempts depends on the sensitivity and skill of the pediatrician on the one hand, and the capacity of the parent to change on the other hand. Unfortunately, many of the attitudes and fantasies just mentioned are often unconscious. Consequently, considerable resistance to any change is encountered in parents. Moreover, the indices for predicting which expectant mothers will have difficulties with their infants are not always sufficiently sensitive, except in extreme instances.

Note 22

From T. Benedek (1970), The psychobiology of pregnancy. In: *Parenthood*, ed. E.J. Anthony and T. Benedek. Boston: Little, Brown, pp. 137–151. Copyright 1970, Little, Brown and Company.

Pregnancy is a "critical phase" in the life of a woman. Using the term as ethologists use it, it implies that pregnancy, like puberty, is a biologically motivated step in the maturation of the individual which requires physiologic adjustments and psychologic adaptations to lead to a new level of integration that, normally, represents development. For a long time the significance of the psychobiological processes of pregnancy was neglected by psychoanalysts. Freud, impressed by the emotional calmness of pregnant women, considered pregnancy as a period during which the woman lives in the bliss of her basic wish being gratified; therefore, he assumed that pregnant women are not in need of or accessible to psychoanalytic therapy. Since then psychoanalytic investigations have revealed the two opposing poles which account for pregnancy as a critical phase. One is rooted in the drive organization of the female procreative function, the other in the emotional disequilibrium caused by the stresses of pregnancy and the danger of parturition.

Recently, Rheingold collected into a large volume references regarding women's "fear of being a woman," with emphasis on the fear of death connected with childbearing. . . . This concept is so deeply ingrained in the human mind that even Freud failed to recognize the emotional manifestations of the instinctual tendency to bear children in the drive organization of women. Helene Deutsch, in her major work, attributes "the devoted patience which women of uncounted generations have shown in the service of the species" to the necessity of women's socioeconomic dependence on man. . . . An ever-growing literature abounds in the discussion of this concept, drawing its arguments from folklore, religion, mythology, and from the history of civilizations. . . .

Against such telling evidence it may seem foolhardy to propose the results arrived at by psychoanalytic investigations. Yet it seems safe to do so since investigations have revealed the psychobiologic process of the female reproductive function without which mankind would not exist. . . .

In the perspective of the psychobiologic processes of pregnancy, one can evaluate the clinical significance of the developmental conflicts and their constellation in the personality organization of women; these conflicts, revived during pregnancy, influence women's feelings about motherhood and their attitude toward their child and/or children. Psychoanalyses of pregnant women or women in the postpartum period thus provide clues to the interactions of three generations in the psychology of parenthood. . . .

On the basis of psychoanalytic observations Helene Deutsch generalized that a deep-rooted passivity and a specific tendency toward introversion are characteristic qualities of the female psyche. . . Investigation of the sexual cycle has revealed that these propensities reappear in intensified form correlated with the specifically female gonadal hormone, lutein, during the postovulative phase of the cycle. Such observations justify the assumption that the emotional manifestations of the specific receptive tendency and the self-centered retentive tendency are the psychodynamic correlates of a biologic need for motherhood. Thus motherhood is not secondary, not a substitute for the missing penis, nor is it forced by men upon women "in the service of the species," but the manifestation of the all-pervading instinct for survival in the child that is the primary organizer of the woman's sexual drive, and by this also her personality. Thus the specific attributes of femininity originate in that indwelling quality of woman's psyche which is the manifestation and result of the central organization of receptive and retentive tendencies of the reproductive drive that becomes the source of motherliness. . . .

Pregnancy is a biologically normal but exceptional period in the life of women. At conception a "biologic symbiosis" begins that steers the woman between the happy fulfillment of her biologic destiny and its menacing failures. The heightened hormonal and metabolic processes which are necessary to maintain the normal growth of the fetus augment the vital energies of the mother. It is the interlocking physiologic processes between mother and fetus that make the pregnant woman's body abound in libidinous feelings. As metabolic and emotional processes replenish the libido reservoir of the pregnant woman, this supply of primary narcissism becomes a wellspring of her motherliness. Self-centered as it may appear, it increases her pleasure in bearing her child, stimulates her hopeful fantasies, diminishes her anxieties. One can, however, observe differences in women's reactions to this psychobiologic state. A woman whose personality organization makes her a natural mother enjoys the narcissistic state with vegetative calmness, while a less fortunate woman defends herself, often consciously, against that experience. As women succeed in adjusting to the hormonal influences of pregnancy, the initial fatigue, sleepiness, and some of the physical reactions such as vertigo or morning sickness diminish. Thus women are able to respond to their physical and emotional well-being by expanding and enjoying their activities. While the pregnant woman feels her growing capacity to love and to care for her child, she experiences a general improvement in her emotional state. Many neurotic women who suffer from severe anxiety states are free from them during pregnancy; others, in spite of morning sickness or in spite of realistic worries caused by the pregnancy, feel stable and have their best time while they are pregnant. Healthy women demonstrate during pregnancy just as during the high hormone phases of the cycle an increased integrative capacity of the ego.

Yet the drive organization which accounts for the gratification of pregnancy harbors its inherent dangers. It tests the physiologic and psychologic reserves of women. Realistic fears, insecurities motivated by conception out of wedlock, economic worries, unhappy marriages make the test more arduous. Yet even such pregnancies usually have a normal course. We might assume that such pregnancies, in our age of relatively free use of contraceptives, are often deliberately or unconsciously chosen for their drive gratification and therefore have a curative effect. To this assumption one might object, since we all know that the hope for a change for the better in an interpersonal relationship or in an external situation may enhance the gratification of pregnancy. To this, however, I would answer that the increased libidinal state of pregnancy enhances hope and by this might favorably influence not only the pregnancy but also the realities of the environmental situation. Whether the hope will be fulfilled or disappointed, the fact is that hope arising from the libidinal state of pregnancy is often the motivation of motherhood. The point to be emphasized is: *only if the psychosexual organization of the woman is loaded with conflicts toward motherhood do actual conditions stir up deeper conflicts and disturb the psychophysiologic balance of pregnancy.* . . .

Since the father's attitude toward the child might be influenced by the communicated experience of his wife, the emotional course of the pregnancy is largely responsible for the psychologic environment of the child; since it might con-

firm or undermine the meaning of the marriage, it may stabilize or disrupt the primary social unit, the family. . . .

Note 23

From H. Hartmann (1939), *Ego Psychology and the Problem of Adaptation.* (D. Rapaport, translator, 1958). New York: International Universities Press.

In his prolonged helplessness the human child is dependent on the family, that is, on a social structure which fulfills here—as elsewhere—"biological" functions also. . . .

The processes of adaptation are influenced both by the constitution and external environment, and more directly determined by the ontogenetic phase of the organism. . . .

No instinctual drive in man guarantees adaptation in and of itself, yet on the average the whole ensemble of instinctual drives, ego functions, ego apparatuses, and the principles of regulation, as they meet the average expectable environmental conditions, do have survival value. Of these elements, the function of the ego apparatuses . . . is "objectively" the most purposive. The proposition that the external world "compels" the organism to adapt can be maintained only if one already takes man's survival tendencies and potentialities for granted. . . .

A state of adaptedness exists before the intentional processes of adaptation begin. . . .

Note 24

From M.J.E. Senn (1947), Anticipatory guidance of the pregnant woman and her husband for their roles as parents. In: *Problems of Early Infancy* (Transactions of the First Conference). New York: Josiah Macy, Jr. Foundation, pp. 11–16.

At the New York Hospital pediatricians who are Fellows in Pediatric-Psychiatry interviewed women at various periods of pregnancy. . . . In the experiment as set up, the pediatrician who interviewed the parents prenatally was the physician who examined the baby in the newborn period, planned its feeding program, and provided general medical care. This pediatrician was also responsible for the care of the baby throughout infancy and early childhood.

This experiment at the New York Hospital has shown that both men and women approaching parenthood do desire to talk about the coming event, and are exceedingly pleased to have an opportunity to meet and talk with the pediatrician who will care for their baby throughout the early years of its life. In fact, many women who heard about the experiment demanded pediatric consultation before the birth of their baby. Unfortunately, this could be done only for relatively few women, as the experiment was set up on a limited scale.

It was brought out that the pregnant woman often is actually more apprehensive about her role as a mother than her ability to deliver a viable infant. She is anxious about her own health and the life of the fetus and fearful of her ability to come through labor without too much discomfort or delivery without dying in the process. Even with such great anxiety about labor and delivery, however, it is significant and interesting to learn that she has an almost equally great apprehension that she may somehow fail in her role as a mother in the years when she is to care for and guide her child.

The father also was invited to meet with the pediatrician and in every case he came for at least one prenatal interview.

At each interview the prospective parent or parents are encouraged to talk about the pregnancy, about their feelings generally, and to ask any questions concerning the infant and its care. The pediatrician's role is a dual one—that of listener and adviser. He describes techniques of baby care, breast feeding, breast care before and after the birth of the baby, weaning, supplementary and complementary formula feeding, and the preparation of foods. Practical advice is given as to what to purchase in the way of equipment. The advantages of breast feeding are mentioned but there is no attempt made to "sell" breast feeding to the exclusion of bottle feeding, lest the parents be overcome with guilt or other adverse emotions in those instances where breast feeding is attempted and is unsuccessful. The psychological concomitants of infant feeding are stressed repeatedly. In the interviews talk about the baby and its care is purposely limited to the newborn period, that is, the first month of life, lest the parents become confused and confounded by the manifold material discussed.

As a result of the prenatal pediatric interviews, the incidence of breast feeding can be kept above 80%. Furthermore, the mother is able to prepare for the neonatal care well in advance, so that she can spend a good part of her time caring for the infant without feeling guilty about other duties which are neglected or taken over by substitutes. The mother has learned techniques of infant care and thereby is relaxed in her relationship to the new baby, her husband and others in the household. Where there are other children, both parents have been prepared for the usual sibling rivalry feelings and can protect the siblings as much as possible from the trauma incident to the birth of the new baby. The father is able to accept the role a mother-substitute and as housewife-substi-

tute because he has been told what the reality situation would be like in the household after the birth of the new baby, and to act in a supportive way to his wife not only during the pregnancy, but also through the neonatal period when the mother and newborn return to the home. Where other persons in the family have to be considered, either physically or psychologically, the prospective parents are encouraged to make arrangements for their temporary care outside the family well in advance of the birth of the baby so that their presence does not influence adversely the convalescence of the mother or the early life of the baby.

In conclusion, the experiment of interviewing pregnant women and their husbands in terms of their function as parents has demonstrated to pediatricians that their role as physician-guide to the mother could best begin before the birth of the infant, through what may be called "anticipatory guidance," and that modern pediatrics should train physicians so that this role might be filled with optimum benefit to parent and child alike.

Note 25

From M.E. Lamb (1975), The Role of the Father in Child Development. New York: John Wiley & Sons, Inc.

Infants appear to relate to their mothers mainly as attachment figures (sources of security), whereas the fathers are not only attachment figures quite as satisfactory as the mothers but also are the focus of more frequent distal affiliative behaviors as well. At least in part, this may relate to differences in the types of interaction that the parents initiate.

Further evidence that mothers and fathers assume different roles in relation to their infants is apparent in the analysis of the play and physical contact. Whereas the fathers did not play more often with the infants than the mothers did, the type of play in which they engaged differed. The fathers were more likely to engage in idiosyncratic and rough-and-tumble types of play, and it may be because of the greater variety and unpredictability of the play with the fathers that the response to play with them was more positive than with the mothers. Similar reasons may account for the fact that the response to play with both parents was more positive than with the visitor, whose play was clearly more stereotyped.

The analysis of physical-contact interaction yields additional information regarding the manner in which the mothers and fathers may be differentiated in the eyes of their infants. The mothers held the infants far more than the fathers did, but this was usually for caretaking or controlling the infant's activities. They seldom picked up or held the infants for play, whereas infants were held by their fathers most often for this purpose. It was this that accounted for the fact that the response to physical contact with the fathers was more positive than with the mothers.

In sum these results certainly suggest that to regard fathers as occasional mother substitutes is to disregard the fact that there are substantial and, I believe, important differences in the character of mother–infant and father–infant interaction (Lamb, 1975). The results suggest that, when both parents are present, fathers are more salient persons than mothers: They are more likely to engage in unusual and more enjoyable types of play and, hence, appear to maintain the infants' attention more than the mothers do. Nevertheless the role of father as playmate does not appear to prevent his being seen as an attachment figure as well; indeed he is apparently seen in his role as often as mother (at least at the times when the observations were made; it is conceivable that, at other times of the day, this would not be true). Unfortunately the present study does not permit us to determine to what extent the father–infant interaction observed was supported by the presence of the mother; in her absence, would the father–infant interaction have been the same? We intend to focus further attention on this question.

REFERENCES

Benedek, T. (1970), The psychobiology of pregnancy. In: *Parenthood*, ed. E.J. Anthony and T. Benedek. Boston, Little, Brown & Co., pp. 137–151.

Bernard, J., and Sontag, L.W. (1947), Fetal reactivity and sound. *J. Genet. Psychol.*, 70:205–210.

Bibring, G.L., Dwyer, T.F., Huntington, D.S., and Valenstein, A.F. (1961), A study of the psychological processes in pregnancy and of the earliest mother-child relationship. *Psychoanal. Study Child*, 16:9–72.

Cohler, B.J., Grunebaum, H.U., Weiss, J.L., Gallant, D.H., and Abernethy, V. (1974), Social relations, stress and psychiatric hospitalization among mothers of young children. *Soc. Psychiatry*, 9:7–12.

D.H.H.S. (1981), *The Health Consequences of Smoking for Women—A Report of the Surgeon General*. Rockville, MD: U.S. Dept. of Health and Human Services, Public Health Service, Office of Smoking and Health.

Drillien, C.M. (1965), The effect of obstetrical hazard on the later development of the child. In: *Recent Advances in Paediatrics*, ed. D. Gairdner. London: Churchill, pp. 82–109.

Dunn, J., and Kendrick, C. (1979), Interaction between young siblings in the context of family relationship. In: *The Child and Its Family*, ed. M. Lewis and L.A. Rosenblum. New York: Plenum Publishing Corp.

Earls, F. (1976), The fathers (not the mothers): Their importance and influence with infants and young children. *Psychiatry*, 39:209–226.

Ehrhardt, A.A., and Meyer-Bahlburg, H.F.L. (1979), Prenatal sex hormones and the developing brain: Effects on psychosexual differentiation and cognitive function. *Ann. Rev. Med.*, 30:417–430.

Finnegan, L.P. (1981), The effects of narcotics and alcohol on pregnancy and the newborn. *Ann. N.Y. Acad. Sci.*, 362:136–157.

Forsmann, H., and Thuwe, I. (1966), One hundred and twenty children born after application for therapeutic abortion refused. *Acta Psychiatr. Scand.*, 42:71–88.

Freud, A. (1954), Safeguarding the emotional health of our children: An inquiry into the concept of the rejecting mother. In: *National Conferences of Social Work: Casework Papers*, 1955. New York: Family Service Association of America, p. 5.

Hartmann, H. (1939), *Ego Psychology and the Problem of Adaptation*, trans. D. Rapaport. New York: International Universities Press.

Herzog, J. (1982), Patterns of expectant fatherhood: A study of the fathers of a group of premature infants. In: *Father and Child: Developmental and Clinical Perspectives*. ed. S. Cathard and A. Guraitt. Boston: Little, Brown and Co.

Hooker, D. (1952), *The Prenatal Origin of Behavior*. Lawrence, Ka.: University of Kansas Press.

Humphrey, T. (1970), The development of human fetal activity and its relation to postnatal behavior. In: *Advances in Child Development and Behavior*. ed. H.W. Reese and L.P. Lipsitt. New York: Academic Press.

Hunter, R.S., Kilstrom, N., Kraybill, E.N., and Loda, F. (1978), Antecedents of child abuse and neglect in premature infants: A prospective study in a newborn intensive care unit. *Pediatrics*, 61:629–635.

Hutt, S.J., et al. (1968), Auditory responsivity in the human neonate. *Nature*, 218:888–890.

Imperato-McGinley, J., Peterson, R.E., Gautier, T., and Sturla, E. (1979), Androgens and the evolution of male-gender identity among male pseudohermaphrodites with 5OC-reductase deficiency. *N. Engl. J. Med.*, 300:1233–1237.

Klaus, M.H., and Kennell, J.H. (1970), Mothers separated from their newborn infants. *Pediatr. Clin. North Am.*, 17:1015–1037.

Klein, M., and Stern, L. (1974), Low birthweight and the battered child syndrome. *Am. J. Dis. Child*, 122:15–18.

Lamb, M.E. (1975), Fathers: Forgotten contributors to child development. *Hum. Dev.*, 18:245–266.

Lecaneut, J.P., et al. (1986), Fetal response to acoustic stimulation depends on heart rate, variability patterns, stimulus intensity, and repetition. *Early Hum. Dev.* 13:269–285.

Lefkowitz, M.M. (1981), Smoking during pregnancy: Long-term effects on offspring. *Devel. Psychol.*, 17:192–194.

Madison, L.S., et al. (1986), Fetal response decrement: True habituation? *J. Dev. Behav. Pediatr.*, 7:14–20.

Markham, S. (1961), A comparative evaluation of psychotic and non-psychotic reactions to childbirth. *Am. J. Orthopsychiatry*, 31:565.

Minde, K.K., Marton, P., Manning, D., and Hines, B. (1980), Some determinants of mother-infant interaction in the premature nursery. *J. Am. Acad. Child Psychiatry*, 19:1–21.

Normand, W.C. (1967), Post-partum disorders. In: *Com-*

prehensive Textbook of Psychiatry, ed. A.M. Freedman and H.I. Kaplan. Baltimore: Williams & Wilkins, pp. 1161–1163.

Osofsky, H. (1982). Expectant and new fatherhood as a developmental phase. *Bull. Menninger Clin.* 46:209.

Prechtl, H.F. (1985), Ultrasound studies of human fetal behavior. *Early Hum. Dev.*, 12:91–98.

Pruett, K.D. (1987), The Nurturing Father. New York: Warner Books Inc.

Reinisch, J.M. (1981), Prenatal exposure to synthetic progestins increases potential for aggression in humans. *Science*, 2:1121–1173.

Rosett, H.L., Ouellette, E.M., and Weiner, L. (1976), A pilot prospective study of the fetal alcohol syndrome at the Boston City Hospital: Part I. Maternal Drinking. *Ann. N.Y. Acad. Sci.*, 273:118–122.

Schmidt, W., et al. (1985), Fetal behavioral states and controlled sound stimulation. *Early Hum. Dev.*, 12:145–153.

Senn, M.J.E. (1947), Anticipatory guidance of the pregnant woman and her husband for their roles as parents. In: *Problems of Early Infancy* (Transactions of the First Conference). New York: Josiah Macy, Jr. Foundation, pp. 11–16.

Shereshefsky, P.M., and Yarrow, L.J. (1973), *Psychological aspects of a first pregnancy and early postnatal adaptation*. New York: Raven Press.

Spelt, D.K. (1948), Conditioned responses in the human fetus *in utero*. *Psychol. Bull.*, 35:712–713.

Winick, M. (1981), Food and the fetus. *Nat. Hist.*, 90:76–81.

Winnicott, D.W. (1958), Mind and its relaton to the psychesoma. In: *Collected Papers Through Paediatrics to Psycho-Analysis*. London: Tavistock, p. 245.

Wolff, S. (1967), The contribution of obstetric complications to the etiology of behavior disorders in childhood. *J. Child Psychol. Psychiatry*, 8:57–66.

Zilboorg, G. (1931), Depressive reactions related to parenthood. *Am. J. Psychiatry*, 87:927.

Zilboorg, G. (1957), The clinical issues of post-partum psychopathological reactions. *Am. J. Obstet. Gynecol.*, 73:305.

15

EARLY INFANCY—THE FIRST YEAR

CONCEPT OF DEVELOPMENT

Development is a complex process that occurs throughout the life cycle; it is defined as the totality of full blossoming and the multiple, interrelated, uses of functions and skills. It is usual to refer to the sequential emergence and linear growth of capacities as maturation; in reality the development of any specific function or skill reflects the interaction of biological endowment and experience. The development of the embryo and fetus has often been taken as a model for subsequent development with processes of differentiation and integration acting in a reciprocal fashion (Werner, 1948). For example, as in development of the embryo, the development of motor skills proceeds in a cephalocaudal (head to tail) and proximodistal (center outward) fashion; head control is achieved before trunk control and arm control is achieved before hand control.

The human genotype provides considerable developmental potential and sets certain limitations on development. Different aspects of development depend in different proportions on biologic endowment or experience (Waddington, 1966). Even the baby with an optimal biologic endowment will not develop well if cared for in an inappropriate environment; conversely, the baby with significant biological disability will typically not achieve usual levels of functioning even when cared for in a highly appropriate environment. As noted by Erikson (1959), human development appears to follow the epigenetic principle that states the development has a

ground plan and that out of this plan the *parts* arise with each part having its *time* of ascendancy until all parts have arisen to form a *functioning whole*.

Various models of development have been postulated. Typically these assume a succession of *stages* of development with each successive stage building on the previous one and replacing it. Changes between stages are both qualitative and quantitative. Each stage in development is hypothesized to involve progressive structuralization and differentiation. Development can be viewed either as the whole or some sector of the whole such as "cognitive development." Although this latter view is common, it is important to note that, in reality, children develop as wholes rather than as parts and that any division of development is, of necessity, somewhat arbitrary. Given a nurturing and appropriately stimulating environment, there is an inevitable thrust toward development.

CRITICAL PERIOD

Implicit in the stage concept of development are the issues of transitions between stages and the concept of "critical periods." The notion of "critical periods" is analogous to the critical period in embryogenesis, during which certain organs are irreversibly laid down at specific times and cannot be formed at other times. For example, the drug thalidomide interferes with the morphogenesis of limbs during the critical period of their development. The concept of critical periods has had to be modified with reference to psychologic development, given the complex variables involved in the development of any given function, the unitary functioning of the individual, and the observation that some degree of recovery is usually observed even with the grossest possible insults to the developing child. The notion of "sensitive periods" (Wolff and Feinbloom, 1969) has been proposed to refer to those periods in development that are particularly optimal for development of a specific skill; this concept is probably more applicable to psychologic development. Such periods are ones for optimal acquisition of a skill as well as greatest vulnerability to its disruption. In a broad general way there seem to be critical periods in psychological development; for example, the first two years seem to be important for the development of the capacity to form relationships. The limitations of the notion of critical periods is suggested by various observations. For example, it had once been postulated that if a child does not learn to read during the critical formative school years he will have difficulty in learning to read at a later date. To some extent this postulate is true. However, the important emphasis here is in the ease of learning to read. Some illiterate adults inducted into the Armed Services have been taught to read although not well. Moreover, the factors resulting in adult illiteracy are multiple. Lastly, the critical period, if any, for learning to read may extend over a long period of time, so that even illiteracy of long duration may give way to the capacity to read if the conditions change.

Few functions exist in pure isolation, and most clinical phenomena have multiple determinants. For example, stimulus deprivation, somatic injury, malnutrition, and other factors at work during the sensitive period of the early years may produce as an end result a child who has failed to thrive and who appears to be arrested at a retarded level. Yet, it is still often difficult to assess the relative contribution of each of these antecedent factors, and usually impossible to say whether the function that appears to be affected (e.g.,

intellectual development) is affected critically or irreversibly.

The concept of a critical period may still be useful, however, particularly in very early development, when irreversibility may indeed be a factor. Perhaps the best example of the use of the critical period concept is in the studies of early separation of mother and child, when irreversibility is a strong possibility. For example, Spitz (1945), using the baby tests worked out by Hetzer and Wolf (1928), studied 130 children, 61 in a foundling home and 69 in a nursery. The significant differences between the two institutions were as follows: the foundling home had few toys, the children were isolated and virtually screened from the world; they lay supine in the hollow of their mattresses, and they lacked all human contact for most of the day, particularly from the age of 3 months onward. The nursery, on the other hand, provided each child with a mother who gave, and continued to give, the child everything a good mother has to give.

Spitz found that the Developmental Quotient of children in the foundling home dropped from 124 to 72 by the end of the first year of life, and the children showed seriously decreased resistance to disease and an appallingly high mortality. Children in the nursery gained slightly in their Developmental Quotient (101.5 to 105 by the end of the first year of life).

The rapid decline in the development of children in the foundling home occurred at approximately the same time that they were weaned, i.e., between their third and fourth months. At this time, even the human contact they had during nursing stopped. Their perceptual world was emptied of human partners.

Spitz concluded that it was the deprivation of maternal care, maternal stimulation, and maternal love that produced the clear evidence of damage to the foundling home infants, and that even when put in a more favorable environment after age 15 months, the damage could not be repaired by normal measures (Spitz, 1946). That is to say, the absence of adequate mothering during this critical period of development to all intents and purposes led to irreversible damage.

It would appear that this study supports the concept of a critical period. However, Spitz himself was also careful to state that "whether it [the psychosomatic damage] can be repaired by therapeutic measures remains to be investigated." The qualifications of degree of irreversibility and extent of therapeutic intervention therefore are further considerations in the definition of the concept of critical period.

This study was important also because it was one of the first to document the role of maternal deprivation in the etiology of childhood disorders. Since that time the concept of maternal deprivation has undergone much revision and refinement. For example, Langmeir and Matejcek (1975) have listed at least four major types of deprivation:

1. Stimulus deprivation, in which there is a lack of sensory and motor stimulation, particularly in the earliest stages of life.
2. Cognitive deprivation, in which the environment fails to provide sufficient structure, organization, and reasonable predictability of events, making it difficult for the child to make sense out of his or her experiences, particularly in terms of his or her behavior and the response from the environment.
3. Attachment deprivation, in which there is a failure of the reliable presence and responsiveness of a person to whom the child can focus his perceptual, cognitive, and affective activities; this failure leads to a failure to become attached.
4. Social deprivation, in which the absence of adequate socialization experiences gives rise to a series of impairments, including learning difficulties, a deformed value system, and an impaired facility for the performance of social functions and roles.

Rutter (1972), too, clarified the findings relating to maternal deprivation to the point that the global term should no longer be used. Instead, the effects of varying degrees, du-ration, and reasons for separation and loss must be assessed in the context of many other variables. These variables include the child's stage of development, experiences with brief, incremental, and happy separations, degree of attachment attained, experiences with frightening medical procedures, lack of toys or play opportunities, experiences with unfamiliar and/or unsympathetic staff or parents and inadequate preparation, and the child's having parents who have psychiatric disturbances. Among these variables, overt parental discord involving the child over a considerable period of time, parental psychiatric disturbance, and the degree of attachment formed are perhaps the most important.

A further example of the concept of a critical period can be seen in the special case of gender identification arising out of the development of object relations. According to Money et al. (1955), gender identification is generally irreversibly established by 2½ years of age. Wrong assignment of sex in the case of infants with intersex problems cannot usually be changed after that age (see p. 154).

With these concepts in mind, development will be described here from the standpoints of biological maturation, personality development, cognitive development, and psychosocial development.

MATURATION

One of the great services Arnold Gesell performed for pediatrics was to document in an orderly and detailed manner the sequence of skills that can be observed in a child as he or she advances in age (see Note 26). His work was avidly seized upon by pediatricians eager to reassure mothers that their children were normal. Unfortunately, the details of each step of maturation were sometimes taken as inviolable. The development of the child came to be viewed by some as an unfolding flower that only had to be watered and fed. Further, the precision with which each detail of any given stage was regarded in this viewpoint was unwarranted because it did not take into accout the enormous variation from child to child at any given age, and from time to time in a given child. By circular reasoning it became easy to equate age with explanation, e.g., the reason a 3 month old behaves this way is *because* most 3 month olds behave this way. This notion sidestepped basic issues of motivation and stimulation and failed to explain *why* children behaved in certain ways or *what* factors affected their behavior.

Nevertheless, important general sequences and milestones were described for the normal child, in a normal environment, and these normative sequences are worth noting.

Motor Sequence

Gesell and Amatruda (1941) observed that most children creep, can be pulled to their feet, and have a crude prehensory release by the time they are 10 months old. Within the next 2 months, they can walk with help, and can prehend a small pellet. By 2 years of age they are running with ease, although not with great skill. Probably as a result of better nutrition and health care, infants now appear to achieve motor skills at earlier ages than did babies 50 years ago.

Adaptive Sequence

Similarly, by 10 months of age a child can bring two cubes together as if to compare them and by 12 months can release a cube in a cup. By 2 years of age, a child can build a tower of six cubes and can imitate a circular motion with a crayon on paper.

Language Sequence

The sequence of emergence of actual sounds is broadly the same in all children everywhere (Lewis, 1963). Children vocalize and respond to sounds from birth, possibly even prenatally. The child can be soothed specifically by the mother's voice as early as the first few weeks. The early phonetic characteristics of discomfort cries of the infant appear to be the focal manifestations of total reaction to discomfort, determined in part by the physiologic contraction of his or her facial muscles. By about the sixth week, the infant

begins to utter repetitive strings of sound called babbling. In doing so, he or she finds satisfaction in producing at will those sounds which at first have occurred involuntarily, acquires skill in making sounds, and imitates as best he or she can the sound of others. The nearer the approximation of his or her sounds to those of the parents, the more marked will be the parents' approval of the child, and the greater will be the infant's incentive to repeat sounds. In this way the child acquires the phonetic pattern of the mother tongue. What is important here is that in these earliest weeks the frequency and variety of sounds already may be restricted through inadequate fostering by the caring adult. Accounts of how children learn to speak have been described by Lewis (1959), Howlin (980), Cromer (1980), and Cantwell and Baker (1987).

At 5 months most infants can discriminate "p" from "t," "b" from "g," and "i" from "a," and by 12 months can discriminate and respond differently to differences in tone, vocabulary, and the person who is speaking.

At 10 months most children heed their name when called and usually understand certain simple commands (although these responses may have more to do with the tone with which the command is said than with the word itself). Often the child can say a word, as well as say "Ma-ma" or "Da-da." Most children say their first words by the end of the first year. More words are added, until by age 2 years a child usually says two sentences and can say "I." Two thirds of children begin to use phrases by age 2 (Morley, 1965). By age 2, an average child can understand several hundred words (language comprehension usually precedes language production) and can use about 200 (Rutter and Bax, 1972). Nouns are used before verbs.

Personal-Social Development

A 10-month-old child can feed himself or herself a cracker (sloppily) and play "peek-a-boo," "pat-a-cake," and "so-big." By 12 months of age the child is finger feeding and somewhat cooperative in dressing. By 2 years of age, the child is able to verbalize his or her toileting needs. The child is also playing with elementary jigsaw puzzles, balls, and pull toys. He or she is picking things up, throwing them down, and imitating others.

ROLE OF ACTIVITY

It is important to keep in mind, however, that while the sequences just outlined are accurate, the timetable is immensely variable. Moreover, the child contributes to his or her own velocity of development. First of all, children start off with different innate capacities; some are active, some quiet, and some highly unpredictable. Fries attempted to classify children into various congenital activity types, suggesting that there was a continuity of a general activity level for given individuals (Fries and Woolf, 1953). Thomas et al. (1963), in their New York study, developed nine categories of behavioral style that were consistent for the individual infant (see p. 107). More significant is that the infant's level of activity is an important determinant of development. Babies who are constitutionally very active and mobile appear to suffer less from a period of understimulation during a hospital stay than do less active babies (Schaffer, 1966).

Some children by temperament are irritable and slow to adapt to novel circumstances, and others adapt readily to changes in the environment (Thomas et al., 1968). These characteristics interact with parental attributes. An important aspect of parenting is the parents' ability to understand the infant's clues (Bell and Ainsworth, 1972). Some parents prefer an active, alert child, whereas others prefer a quiet, passive child (Rutter, 1976). The possible combinations for mutual enhancements or mutual disharmonies are multiple, and these interactions change in time and according to different circumstances. Later in development, the interaction between intrinsic factors, including motor activity and sensitivity to discomfort on the one hand, and environmental factors, including stimulation and the ability to soothe the infant on the other hand, subtly contrib-

ute to the infant's identification processes (Ritvo and Solnit, 1958).

INFLUENCE OF THE INFANT ON THE MOTHER

Maternal behavior seems to be under the control of the stimulus-and-reinforcing conditions provided by the young infant in such a way that at first the mother's behavior is shaped by the infant's behavior. This phenomenon then affects how the mother shapes the infant's behavior (Moss, 1967). For example, eye-to-eye contact seems to foster positive feelings in the mother (Robson, 1967). These feelings in the mother have something to do with her "being recognized" in a highly personal and intimate way, and it is perhaps for this reason that mothers of blind children often feel rebuffed at first by their infants. Again, Bowlby (1958) believes that the smiling of an infant acts as a social releaser of instinctual responses in the mother, along with such other innate "releasers" as crying, following, clinging, and sucking. Lorenz (1966) has suggested that the human smile is also a ritualized form of aggression comparable to the "greeting" ceremonies that inhibit intraspecific fighting in many lower animals.

In effect, infant and parent constitute a dyad, in the context of which development occurs (Schaffer, 1977). Increasingly, recognition is being given to this dyad in developmental studies concerned with language development (Nelson, 1977), visual behavior (Stern, 1974), attention (Collins and Schaffer, 1975), and problem-solving (Kaye, 1976).

ROLE OF STIMULATION

At the same time, the amount and kind of stimulation a child receives greatly affect the degree of development and use of any particular skill that may appear on schedule and in its rudimentary form. The amount of stimulation provided by the adults is one of the major determinants of the infant's behavior (Schaffer and Emerson, 1964).

Stimulation and Language Development

Specific stimulation for language development mentioned earlier is a case in point. In a study of 75 family-reared children and 75 institutionalized infants, Provence and Lipton (1962) observed that the response of the parent contributes to the process of differentiation in the infant's mental functioning. The parent's repetition, labeling, and responses to the infant's reactions to his or her environment, to the infant's feelings, and to the infant's vocalizations are important to the infant's recognition of himself or herself, other persons, and the world. Further, responses from others are essential to the child's development of meaningful speech. For example, one of the ways in which the mother appears to influence the development of speech is through a process of "mutual imitation." Moreover, the mother's speech is "both a carrier of the emotions and an organizing influence on the infant's mental apparatus." The mother, through her way of responding to the infant in action, and especially in speech, identifies or "labels" many things for the infant (e.g., people, toys, the child, his or her feelings and actions, and the feelings and actions of others). The infant becomes able to identify many aspects of inner and outer reality because the mother provides the appropriate experiences.

On the other hand, for the institutionalized infant who is placed in a family at the end of the first year, there is a much later period when the speech is predominantly used to express a need or to repeat in a literal way some phrase or sentence learned by rote or from imitation of the parent. Provence and Lipton (1962) noted that ". . . it takes much longer before the [institutionalized] children verbalize their fantasies, comment upon their play, ask questions that express a wish to learn about things or talk about feelings. . . . In these [institutionalized] children one can demonstrate on the tests during and after the second year a greater facility in the aspects of language that represents a concreteness of thought (e.g., ability to name objects or pic-

tures) than in some of the speech that reflects a capacity for more abstract and flexible thought" (pp. 93–94). The institutionalized child's understanding of the adult's language is also retarded.

Stimulation and Visual Activity

Another specific stimulus that enhances development is the increased visual attention that comes about after extra handling of both institutionalized infants (White and Held, 1966) and noninstitutionalized infants. Korner and Grobstein (1966) have also observed that when a crying newborn is picked up and put to the shoulder, there is an increase in the frequency of eye opening, alertness, and scanning, as well as the obvious soothing effect. Calibration of the degree of attention to both visual and auditory stimulation in the newborn is achieved by using changes in the heart rate, motor responsivity, and other measurable responses (Lewis et al., 1966).

NEEDS OF THE INFANT

Clearly, the infant responds to an internal environment as well as to an external one. Initially, the infant's internal life appears to consist of felt needs. These needs seem to fall into two categories: immediate needs and long-range needs. The immediate needs are for the relief of hunger and discomfort, for sleep, and to suck. The infant appears to have little if any tolerance if these needs are unsatisfied.

The infant's long-range needs are for the warmth and security of a mothering person, adequate stimulation (an infant needs to be talked to), and graduated performance expectations, in which the mothering person has reasonable expectations for increasingly differentiated skills. Although the infant may appear to have greater tolerance if any of these long-range needs are not met, compared to the infant's intolerance when immediate needs are not met, serious character defects (e.g., development of an "affectionless character" as described by Bowlby, 1951) may appear later as a result of significant early deprivation in any of these areas.

Sleep

Sleep in the infant has certain interesting characteristics. During the first few weeks of life, the infant sleeps two thirds of the time, for approximately 50-minute periods. This sleep of the infant may represent a third state of being inasmuch as a major proportion of his or her sleep appears to be so-called "rapid eye movement (REM) sleep." The phenomenon of rapid eye movement associated with the periodic low-voltage phase that occurs in a regular electroencephalographic sleep cycle was first described by Aserinsky and Kleitman (1953). This phase of sleep appeared to have a periodicity in adults of 90 minutes and to last about 20 minutes. When adult subjects were awakened during this phase of REM sleep, a high incidence of dream recall was noted. Aserinsky and Kleitman postulated (1) a special inhibiting mechanism that blocked all motor movement except those of the eye and middle ear muscles and (2) occasional brief muscle twitches. When REM sleep was interrupted and the subject was deprived of REM sleep, there followed an increase in the number of times REM sleep appeared, an increase in the actual amount of REM sleep and an increase in the size and duration of the twitches. There was also a shift toward hyperexcitability in the behavior of the subject. Anxiety seems to be a naturally occurring phenomenon that possibly suppresses REM sleep.

The curious fact is that the infant seems to spend much of his or her sleep in the REM state (Dreyfus-Brisac et al., 1958) at a time in life when there is unlikely to be much content to the dreams, if indeed the infant dreams at all. A 10-week premature infant spends about 80% of sleeping time in the REM state, and a full-term infant spends about 50% of sleeping time in the REM state. Thereafter, the percentage of sleep spent in the REM state declines steadily, to the extent that at the end of the first year it is down to 35%, and by 5 years of age it is only 20%. A

shift toward a night pattern of sleeping occurs at about 16 weeks of age, although the infant at this state is still rarely awake for more than 3 hours at a time (Parmelee et al., 1964). A plausible hypothesis is that this REM state is regulated by as yet unknown biochemical mechanisms, and may well have important basic survival functions prior to any consequent hypothesized functions of dreaming. Whatever the function of REM sleep, an adequate amount of it appears to be an important need of the infant.

Full-term infants switch from active REM sleep to quiet non-REM (NREM) sleep about every 50 to 60 minutes, and neonates have a sleep-wake cycle of about 3 to 4 hours. During the first year, prolongations of daytime wakeful periods and night-time sleep periods occur, culminating in a true diurnal rhythm by about 4 years of age (Anders, 1978). Interestingly, active REM sleep and quiet NREM sleep rhythms seem to be determined by constitution (Ellingson, 1975), whereas sleep–wake rhythms seem to be more culturally determined.

Modes of Need Satisfaction

Most of the needs mentioned earlier are met within the mutual adaptation that occurs between the infant, who is born with a certain degree of preadaptiveness (Hartmann, 1939), and the "ordinary devoted mother" (Winnicott, 1945), who creates a sense of "basic" trust in her child. This sense of trust is engendered by the mother's appropriate and reliable response to her sensitive and accurate perception of the baby's needs (Erikson, 1959; see Note 27). Important modes of exchange and gratification should not be neglected during this early period. These modes include visual, auditory, tactile, and kinesthetic stimulation. Many of these modes of stimulation occur during feeding, but are by no means confined to the feeding situation.

Signs of Unmet Needs

If the needs of the infant are not met soon, signs of acute tension appear. And if there is a chronic deficiency of need fulfillment, signs of a disorder of development appear. The signs of acute tension in early infancy are diffuse; they may be restlessness, fretfulness, whining, crying, clinging, physical tenseness, and various visceral dysfunctions, such as vomiting or diarrhea, or a sleep disturbance. The extent and duration of the deprivation are significant factors. For example, weaning that is attempted too early or is done too abruptly may cause acute anxiety in the child.

More prolonged deprivations of one or more of the need-satisfying experiences at this stage may influence the development of the child in the direction of a personality that remains clinging and dependent, or that craves food and drink to console himself in times of stress, or that strives aggressively to win love, or that is chronically envious. Inconsistent gratifications may influence the child in the direction of an untrusting personality. Massive chronic early deprivation is found in children who develop the syndrome of "affectionless characters" (Bowlby, 1951; see Note 28) or who experience "failure to thrive" (Leonard et al., 1966) or, in some children, failure to grow in height. Complete loss of the mother in the second half of the first year without any replacement mothering gives rise to the syndrome of "anaclitic depression," the chief symptoms of which are a dejected expression and a reluctance for motility (Spitz, 1946). (See chapter 31 on Depressive Disorder.)

EARLY PERSONALITY DEVELOPMENT AND THE SENSE OF SELF

What has been said so far implies that the rudiments of the personality are present in the earliest period of life and that the development of the personality arises, in part, from the body and its needs. This section examines further the process by which the personality develops.

The infant's body is an obvious source of gratification as well as of discomfort. The infant actively touches his or her body frequently, at first through random movement and then through intentional action; for example, the infant puts his or her thumb or finger in the mouth, sometimes as early as age 3 to 6 weeks. (Reflex thumbsucking occurs in the fetus in utero.) Furthermore, the infant passively receives body comforts of a rich variety as he or she is fed, burped, diapered, cuddled, or whirled in the air. Indeed, the infant appears initially to perceive the environment only to the extent that it alters his or her body. Fingers and mouth are important at this stage. In the early months, the infant initially does not appear to discriminate between his or her own fingers and those of others, his or her own mouth and that of the mother. (Sometimes the infant puts food into the mother's mouth instead of his or her own, an action that is often mistaken as a sign of altruism or generosity.) Further, an external object exists for the infant (if it exists for the child at all) only as long as it gratifies a need. To the extent that the external environment and the internal life are as one to the infant, the infant is said by psychoanalysts to be in a state of "primary identification" (S. Freud, 1923). To the extent also that the infant is oblivious of the external world, the infant is said by some to be in a normal "autistic" state (Mahler, et al., 1975). The infant then gradually perceives the mother's face, although it is unlikely that his or her image of it is well formed initially. The image of the mother's face probably comes to be associated in the infant's mind with the need-fulfilling properties he attributes to the perceived mother. In psychoanalysis this stage is called the need-fulfilling (or part-object) stage of object relations. (The development of the infant's relationships with others is discussed subsequently.)

ORIGINS OF REALITY TESTING

The infant eventually discerns that some stimuli and sources of gratification can only come from the outside, indicating that he or she is beginning to distinguish between stimuli that come from within and stimuli that come from the outside. He or she is engaged in what is called reality testing. The function of reality testing is continually reinforced by the infant's widening experience that some things are present and some are not (experience the infant gains in peek-a-boo games) and that some feelings can be made to go away and others cannot. That is to say, the infant is becoming increasingly aware of the boundaries between himself and the external world and in doing so is becoming aware of himself or herself as a separate person. The development of self-concept in infancy is exemplified by reactions of infants to their own mirror image, which progress from a stage of watching the mother to a period of relating to the image as if it were another child to, finally, a phase of clear self-recognition (Harter, 1983). By 9 months of age, the infant probably has attained a rudimentary sense of self (Lewis and Brooks, 1976).

EARLY DEVELOPMENT OF DYADIC RELATIONSHIPS

Pattern recognition in the 3- to 6-month-old infant can be demonstrated by the fact that the infant smiles when he or she is shown a face mask that consists of a forehead, eyes, and a nose in motion (the motion distinguishes the features from the background) (Spitz, 1965; see Note 29). During this earliest period when the infant probably does not as yet have a full image of one particular face, he is said by psychoanalysts to be at the preobject, or part-object, stage of relations (Spitz, 1965).

The choice of the word "object" in psychoanalysis as a scientific term (e.g., "object relations," "object love") to represent the nature of the love relationship between two persons is unfortunate for two reasons. First, it implies that the psychoanalytic theory of relationships has been scientifically established, which is not the case; the term "object relations," therefore, is a pseudoscientific term. Second, the word "object" is generally used to refer to some *thing*. When it refers to some *person*, its use in psychoanalysis as a technical term obscures the very phenom-

enon we are trying to understand, namely, the nature of the relationship between two persons and not just the general relationship between any two nonspecific tangible things ("objects") in space.

Feature perception begins virtually at birth, and it is a complicated process. Investigations of the looking patterns of newborns, for example, suggest that infants may be able at birth to analyze extensive visual information in selected, organized ways (Kessen, 1967; Kessen and Bornstein, 1978).

What is striking now is the wealth of new data on the earliest dyadic relationship and the astonishing capacities of the newborn. At 1 week of age, the infant is attracted to strongly patterned stimuli, e.g., horizontal shapes, concentric circles, and face-like mosaics. Pattern is also preferred over color or brightness or size, again indicating some degree of form perception in the neonate. Infants also appear to be attracted by complex patterns rather than simple ones and by objects that are in motion rather than those that are stationary. It soon becomes clear that the infant prefers to look at an object that: (1) is in almost constant motion, (2) emits a great deal of highly varied stimuli, (3) appeals to several different sensory modalities, (4) is complex, (5) possesses a distinctive pattern, and (6) is responsive to the infant's own behavior (Fagan, 1979; Fantz, 1975).

If we look at these characteristics, we see at once that they are all contained in the mother's face—not her breast, but her face—suggesting that perhaps we should talk about the good face and the bad face! At any rate, there is a strong developmental biologic guarantee that, given a responsive adult, attachment will occur within the context of that dyadic relationship. Klaus and Kennell (1976) have suggested that the infant utilizes all these capacities in its earliest bonding behavior. At one time they even suggested that the neonate must have close contact with the mother and father as early as during the first minutes and hours of life, so that the adult can make a species-specific response to the infant that will set in motion the process of bonding. Certainly the general idea of early bonding has been reiterated by Hales and associates (1977) and others.

At present, however, the development of the long-term parent-child relationship is regarded as a more complex phenomenon. Further, the notion that the first few minutes or hours of life are critical is now regarded as an overstatement (Lamb, 1982; Korsch, 1983). Klaus and Kennell (1982) themselves have retracted their extreme earlier position and they too have noted that the human infant is highly adaptable and is able to utilize any one of a number of fail-safe routes to attachment.

Much of this research is consonant with the current trend in which the dyadic relationship is included in all studies of infant development, a point emphasized by Schaffer (1977) and others. Nevertheless, what is being suggested here is that even within the dyadic relationship there is a complex biologic component for the earliest adaptive behavior of the neonate and infant, and that this biologic component probably plays an important part in the subsequent formation of object relationships (or attachments) of the individual. It may even be that, in many instances, the major thrust of the infant's genetic programming again outweighs minor variations in parental behavior.

STRANGER ANXIETY

By the second half of the first year there are clear signs that the infant is now aware of a person as a whole object. He or she begins to imitate the other person and to show signs of anxiety when confronted with an unfamiliar person ("stranger anxiety"). This phenomenon was first described by Baldwin (1895), who called it organic bashfulness, and it has since then been the subject of continuous study (Rheingold, 1968; Stroufe, 1977). It is most prominent at about 8 months of age. Several inferences may be drawn from this phenomenon. First, because the infant can now differentiate between the mother's face and that of a stranger, he or she must by now have a better defined mental image of the mother—and one that the child can also retain; i,e., he or she clearly can use the function of memory. Recognition of facial representations between 5 and 7 months of age has been well documented (Fagan, 1979). Furthermore, the infant has clearly endowed that mental representation with certain attributes (e.g., security giving). These attributes, while first bestowed on the external object (the mother), must by now be a part of the more or less constant internalized mental representation of the mother. Kagan (1971) has offered a discrepancy hypothesis to account for stranger anxiety. In its most general terms, the hypothesis states that an event (such as the presentation of a stranger) that activates existing structures (the schema of a known person) but that cannot be assimilated to them creates arousal. If the discrepancy and the arousal are too great because of a failure of assimilation and accommodation, negative affect will occur.

EARLY RELATIONS AND "OBJECT CONSTANCY"

The fact that the infant now begins to relate to people as people—and not simply as "need-fulfilling objects"—is a further step in the development of his or her capacity for object relations. Moreover, the infant increasingly experiences the external object (the person) as being firmly separate from himself or herself. In addition, as already stated, the infant is now able to retain in his or her memory a constant image of this other person. At this point the infant is said to have reached, but not yet fully consolidated, what psychoanalysts call the stage of object constancy (see p. 75).

EARLY DEFENSE MECHANISMS

Psychoanalysts hypothesize that the infant appears now to have exercised at least two further processes or mechanisms: (1) projection of an internal state onto an external "object" and (2) introjection of that projected attribute to form an internalized mental representation of that "object." These two mechanisms may form the earliest "defense mechanisms" (S. Freud, 1926) the infant uses to deal with anxiety.

All these functions—the sense of self, the capacity to form relationships, the ability to test reality, and the use of defense mechanisms—are relatively enduring and autonomous, and in psychoanalytic theory they are referred to as psychic "structures" and are subsumed under the general heading of "ego functions." These terms, however, are essentially metaphors, and much misunderstanding arises when they are used concretely. It may be more accurate, for example, to think of such basic processes as regulation of visual attention as the earliest examples, or precursors of, defense mechanisms. It is rarely necessary to use these terms in either practical infant psychiatry or early infant development research. They are theoretical abstractions or, as Freud (1926) termed it, they comprise "the whole of our artificial structure of hypotheses" (p. 231).

BEGINNING OF THOUGHT

At the same time that the functions just discussed are developing, the signs of early cognitive development can be discerned. In the first month of life, the infant seems to exercise a function simply because it is there, but shows few signs of coordinated activity. The infant learns to recognize the nipple, but cannot coordinate his or her head and hand when the thumb falls out of the mouth. Although the infant seems to be a sucking, looking, listening, and grasping individual, it is impossible to know what he or she is aware of. In psychoanalytic theory, the infant is said to be in a state of "primary repression," in the sense that there is no obvious evidence yet of conscious thought. However, within a few months the infant finds that a chance action leads to a pleasurable experience, and the pleasurable experience may act as one of the earliest stimuli to repeat the action—in what Piaget calls a "primary circular reaction" (Piaget, 1952). Thus there is now evidence of

thinking, and it would appear that motor activity is one of the primary sources from which thinking develops. Piaget has emphasized the necessity of action for cognitive growth.

The first 8 months or so are particularly important from the point of view of later perceptual and intellectual development, because it is during this period that the child lays the foundations of cognitive functioning. The actual process by which reality data are treated or modified to become incorporated into the mind is just as important as any intrinsic connections in the external stimuli, because the infant becomes aware of these intrinsic connections only to the extent that he or she can assimilate them by means of his or her existing schema. The schema is, in fact, the basic cognitive structure in Piaget's account of cognitive development. A particular thing in the environment arouses a behavior pattern, or schema, in the child. This schema is then applied to an increasing variety of things. New things that are similar to the first thing become "assimilated" into the existing schema.

THUMB SUCKING

The phenomenon of thumb sucking can be examined from the cognitive viewpoint. Fortuitous or reflex thumb sucking may occur in the prenatal period. However, sometimes as early as the second month a more "systematic" thumb sucking occurs. It involves the coordination of hand and mouth and so indicates an assimilation with a previously existing schema of the breast or the nipple. In other words, the infant's previous sucking experience (the schema of, for example, the nipple) is now broadened to include a new but similar experience—the thumb. The thumb or, more specifically, the new motor act of bringing the thumb into the mouth and the new sensory experience of the thumb have now been assimilated into the existing schema with which it was initially matched.

If the new aspect of the environment encountered is too dissimilar from the existing schema, the existing schema in turn "accommodates," that is, the existing schema is modified. For example, an infant encountered an animal that he or she calls "doggie." The schema subsumed under the concept doggie will, for a while, assimilate all new and similar animals, and the infant will for a while call all animals doggie. Eventually an encounter with an animal that is sufficiently different will stimulate the child to modify his schema of doggie. The new schema will have "doggie" as a more specific concept, and animals other than dogs will be subsumed under different names. This modification of the schema is what Piaget means by accommodation. Assimilation and accommodation are reciprocal mental operations.

It is important to note that Piaget's account of cognitive development is based on the interaction between the individual and his environment; it is not a theory of simple innate maturation, nor does it follow a simple stimulus-contingency model. As a matter of fact, Piaget's theory grew out of his study of the reasoning process that underlay the wrong answers children gave to test questions. (Piaget was attempting to standardize Cyril Burt's tests of children in Binet's Laboratory School in Paris, where he had gone in 1917 at the age of 21 following his study of psychiatry at the Burghölzli Hospital in Zurich.) It was then that cognitive structure was first studied as an internal organization of patterns of thought, fulfilling the abstract criteria of development previously mentioned.

Some time during age 6 to 12 months, the infant enters what Piaget calls the substage of secondary circular reactions, when the infant begins to alter his or her environment intentionally to satisfy a need. The infant will, for example, shake a crib to produce movement in a mobile suspended above him. The infant may also believe, however, that any other movement he or she observes while shaking the crib is the result of his or her action. Moreover, the infant seems to believe that the very existence of objects, and their movements, is entirely dependent on the infant's actions and perceptions. What the infant at this stage cannot see does not exist for him or her.

The qualitative cognitive change that occurs in the evolution of secondary circular reactions may also be associated with neurophysiologic changes in the brain. Thus the change from primary to secondary circular reactions may be related to the way in which the slow delta activity seen in the EEG is interspersed with faster activity (Walter, 1956).

Toward the end of the infant's first year, an increasing coordination of schemas can be observed, and the child begins to be aware of the existence of unperceived objects. The infant may knock down a screen to get at a hidden toy, and he or she behaves as if aware that objects can be moved by external forces. Moreover, the child now begins to explore an object more fully, and the beginnings of an experimental approach can be seen, with the appearance of so-called tertiary circular reactions (see Note 30). In his or her reactions the child seeks or creates new situations to which he or she can react. The infant is learning about spatial relations by putting smaller objects into and taking them out of larger objects. However, the infant does not yet understand (for example) that a long toy must be rotated through a right angle in order to pull it through the bars of a playpen; the child will try to pull it through as it is. Curiously, it appears that perception often, if not usually, precedes action, at least after the foundations of the initial schemas have been laid. For example, a child often can discriminate sounds before he or she can articulate them (Berko and Brown, 1960) and can distinguish forms long before he or she can draw them (Ling, 1941).

Psychoanalysis is weak in regard to its theory of cognitive development. Essentially, two concepts are described: primary process thinking and secondary process thinking. Early primary process thinking is characterized by virtually no capacity to delay the urge for immediate gratification of a need, by rapid shifting from activity to activity in search of gratification (e.g., crying, thumb sucking, mouthing, and tongue protruding when trying to gratify hunger), and by the use of such preverbal processes as visual and auditory impressions. Primary process thinking is prominent in the first year of life. The psychoanalytic term "primary process" is thus used to cover two concepts. The first concept concerns the infant's "unpleasurable" tensions brought about by relatively unbound, intense drives and effects that are constantly seeking immediate and usually indiscriminate discharge. The second concept applies to an irrational, wishful type of thinking characterized by such mechanisms as condensation, displacement, and symbolic representation— the same mechanisms that Freud also hypothesized were the means ("dream work") by which the latent content of a dream were transformed into the dreamer's manifest content. It is not at all clear how these two uses of the concept are related.

As the infant's capacity to tolerate delay and frustration increases, and as the infant begins to use language and logic, a shift in the child's mode of thinking also occurs. Increasingly, the thinking of the child becomes more logical and less "magical." This shift is virtually complete (except in dreams) by the time the child is 6 or 7 years of age, when the child is at the stage of thinking that Piaget has called "concrete operations" (see p. 36). In the stage of concrete operations, the child can apply basic logical principles to his or her experience of the world, unencumbered by his or her immediate perceptions. Psychoanalysts call this new mode of tamed impulses (impulse delay) and logical thinking "secondary process."

INFANTILE FANTASY LIFE

What occurs in the infant's mind during the first 6 months is not known. It *looks* as though the infant is engaged in an active fantasy life, and narrative evidence gathered during psychoanalyses of adults has led to *inferences* that this fantasy life has certain general characteristics. However, one has no direct access to the infant's thoughts at this stage, and any attempt at description is limited by (1) the

boundaries of direct observation of infantile behavior, (2) the inferential nature of reconstruction from material derived from adult and child analyses, (3) the impossibility of recapturing a pure preverbal state, and (4) the handicap of sophisticated adult language.

Nevertheless, the urge to understand the infant has led to speculations about the early fantasy life. For example, Klein (1960) has suggested that in the first 3 or 4 months of life the infant is filled with fantasies of omnipotence. These fantasies are fostered by the repeated gratifications that follow the infant's active demands. For example, when the infant screams with hunger, a nipple is immediately and consistently placed in his or her mouth. At the same time, the infant is thought to experience every discomfort as inflicted by the outside, as though the infant were being persecuted. This attack gives rise to anxiety (Klein calls it persecutory anxiety). Further consequences of the fantasy of being persecuted include the creation and the welling-up of revengeful, destructive fantasies. Because the infant values highly what he or she perceives to be an attacking object (the nipple or the breast), the infant strives to "preserve" his or her source of gratification. The infant accomplishes this by splitting off feelings of love from feelings of hate. Some of the hate, which was first projected into the breast, is now turned inward and introjected in an effort to conserve an "ideal breast." The infant retains a feeling of gratitude, but sometimes experiences envy and often experiences greed. Klein calls this whole speculative complex the paranoid-schizoid position.

Klein postulates that at about 5 or 6 months of age, the infant becomes aware of and concerned about the harm his or her destructive impulses (some of which have been turned inward) and enormous greed might do, and this fear gives rise to a depressive anxiety, the so-called depressive position. The infant the tries to placate the mother and to make reparations by trying to please her.

None of the aforementioned has been validated by scientific research and it is much colored by the necessity of using adult language in describing very unadult experience.

INFANTILE ANXIETY

What can be said with less speculation and more certainty is that the infant appears to manifest signs of tension or anxiety and that the most common anxiety-evoking situation during the first 18 months is the threat of losing the mother. Anxiety initially seems to develop automatically whenever the infant is overwhelmed by internal or external stimuli that cannot be mastered or discharged. As the infant develops, anxiety is produced in anticipation of such a danger. This anticipatory anxiety seems to act as a signal to activate whatever mechanisms are available to the infant to reduce the danger. The advantage of signal anxiety over automatic anxiety is that signal anxiety is less massive, does not incapacitate, and is far more economical and adaptive than is automatic anxiety.

CHILD-REARING PRACTICES

The findings and concepts just described have significance for normal child-rearing practices and for the understanding of certain pathologic states. Thus each of the functions mentioned earlier requires specific conditions for its optimum development. A few of the minimal requirements are discussed in the following paragraphs.

The development of the sense of self requires consistent and gratifying responses from the adult, appropriate labeling of feelings and body parts, opportunities for body play and exploration, stimulation from the environment, and protection from overwhelming anxiety.

The development of the capacity for relationships requires the reliable presence of a mother or mothering person who perceives and responds to the infant's needs in an appropriate manner. The term reliable presence implies at the very least the absence of prolonged separations, especially during the critical period of attachment that becomes prom-

inent from 6 to 12 months of life and proceeds to object constancy from about age 8 months to 3 or 4. Prolonged separation may still be a hazard after that age, but it is less likely to cripple the development of relationships as severely as does separation during these early years. The term reliable presence also implies continuity of care, affection, and appropriate responsiveness.

The notion of the mother's perceiving and responding in an appropriate manner should not be construed as meaning that the mother must understand every need of her child precisely and meet each need exactly. This would be impossible and, in any case, would not promote development. The child learns what his or her needs are through the mother's approximate responses, and the child learns also to tolerate minor frustrations through the mother's unavoidably inexact or incomplete responses. However, the notion does imply that the mother protects the child from intolerable unpleasantness and anxiety and responds with appropriate measures to meet most of the child's needs. Thus the child crying from hunger is fed, and the child crying because of physical discomfort is diapered.

The development of the ability to test reality requires an environment that labels events correctly for the child, that provides the child with appropriate visual, auditory, tactile, and kinesthetic stimulation, and that reasonably gratifies the child.

The development of the capacity to tolerate frustrations and, later, to mobilize defenses against anxiety depends in part on the kind and degree of frustration to which the child is exposed. Frustration experiences within the infant's current capacity for delay can be increasingly tolerated. Frustration that is real and rational, and not created artificially, is better tolerated by the infant, and also facilitates reality testing. Because the infant may interpret reality frustrations as hostile attacks upon him or her, explanations of the reasons for the frustration may minimize the tendency to form such frightening fantasies, may reduce the anxiety that such fantasies arouse, and may promote the use of secondary process logic in dealing with anxiety. However, the young child usually requires additional support when the frustration exceeds the child's tolerance. For example, if separation from the mother is for too long, a substitute mothering person or substitutions for aspects of the mother are required.

The findings and concepts described earlier are also helpful in understanding certain pathologic states. For example, sometimes there is an intrinsic internal failure to form social relationships and to make meaningful patterns out of sensory stimuli, with a consequent handicap in dealing with the demands of the environment. The condition of infantile autism is an extreme example of this kind of failure, although other forms of pervasive developmental disorders have been described.

INFANTILE AUTISM

The syndrome of infantile autism, which was first described by Kanner (1943), occurs in about 4 or 5 children per 10,000, with boys affected three or four times as often as girls (Lotter, 1966). The onset is almost always before 36 months of age, and in many cases the condition can be diagnosed within the first year of life. Typically autistic children have little, if any, interest in their parents or in social interaction. Speech either does not develop at all or is replete with such disorders as echolalia, disordered naming, fragmentation, pronominal reversal, and "portmanteauisms." The child may also show difficulty in developing normal routines and has an inordinate desire for sameness. The child may also show no anticipatory or adaptive posturing, may seem unresponsive, and may avoid looking others straight in the eye. The child shows failure of attachment and often seems happiest when left alone or when whirled. Furthermore, he or she has a preference for inanimate things and lacks empathy. The child may strum his or her fingers toward the periphery of his or her gaze, but is not blind. The child may ignore loud sounds, but is not deaf. Sometimes the child is excessively

quiet; at other times the child screams, rocks, and bangs his or her head. Autistic children often show a special kind of defective cognitive development, and those who are significantly mentally retarded develop seizures more often than do children who are of normal intelligence (Rutter, 1970). The cognitive defect involves language ability, information processing, and temporal sequencing. A comprehensive definition of the syndrome of autism has been given by the National Society for Autistic Children (Ritvo and Freeman, 1978).

The likelihood is high that in autism a basic brain abnormality is present (see Chapter 28). Evidence of a genetic factor in some cases of autism is suggested by Folstein and Rutter's (1977) finding that more than one third of the monozygotic twins they studied were concordant for autism, whereas none of the dizygotic twins they studied were concordant for autism. Signs of brain damage or organic abnormalities are found with a greater frequency among autistic children than among normal children, and the characteristic perceptual, language, and speech difficulties seem to be specific to autism.

In many cases of autism, there have been complications during pregnancy. At the same time, no specific biologic markers or biochemical abnormalities have been identified. No factors in the child's psychologic environment have been shown to cause autism. Autism is not caused by a psychiatric disorder or a psychologic problem in the parents. However, secondary reactions on the part of parents who have to cope daily with a child who is emotionally draining and unresponsive may complicate the clinical picture.

Unfortunately, the prognosis for autism is guarded. Only 1 to 2% will be able to achieve personal and occupational self-sufficiency as adults; about two-thirds of individuals are in need of chronic care (DeMyer, et al., 1981). Autistic children with a low IQ do least well. The prognosis is poor for children who have not developed speech by the age of 5. Twenty-eight percent of autistic children develop epilepsy during adolescence (Rutter, 1970).

MATERNAL INSUFFICIENCY

The syndrome of infantile autism is an extreme example of a primary intrinsic failure in the infant's interaction with his environment. On the other hand, a number of other childhood symptoms primarily related to states of maternal insufficiency can occur. For example, the failure-to-thrive syndrome in infants and the symptom of accidental poisoning in childhood are typical results of a breakdown in mothering that may have occurred for a variety of reasons. Certain cases of child abuse fall into this category, as do children who present themselves frequently with injuries, sometimes quite consciously self-inflicted. The resources of the mothers in these families are often markedly depleted, and such mothers often feel unsupported and overwhelmed. Complete absence of any mothering at all, of course, leads to the syndrome of anaclitic depression, seen in some institutionalized infants.

Failure to thrive in infants, characterized by poor weight gain and growth below the third percentile following an initially normal weight and growth curve, and a tendency to avoid social interactions, may have many causes. One of these is a disturbance in the mother–child relationship (Patton and Gardner, 1962). In one study of 13 infants ranging in age from 10 weeks to 27 months, who had fallen progressively below the third percentile in weight, Leonard et al. (1966) found multiple problems in each of their families. None of the mothers reported receiving dependable and appropriate nurturing during their own childhoods, and many expressed current feelings of inadequacy. The fathers in these families were often absent, uninvolved in family life, and unsupportive. The infants themselves showed a wide range of abnormal behavior, ranging from unusual watchfulness and an unsmiling expression in the youngest infants, through to absence of any stranger anxiety in the 4- to 10-month-old infants, and

superficial personal-social relationships in the older infants. Leonard postulated that the selection of the particular child who failed to thrive might have been brought about by multiple factors, including the psychologic impact upon the mother of the complications of pregnancy that frequently occurred, the dissonance between the infant's temperament and the mother's personality, and the added burden that the infant represented to an already depleted mother. All these factors contain a component that represents the infant's role in shaping the very environmental factors that are so detrimental to his or her own development. What is of further interest in this study is the view of motherhood as an unfolding developmental plan that is activated by pregnancy and the birth of a child. The mothers in this study fell into the category of what Anna Freud has called "unwilling mothers" (A. Freud, 1955), although this alone did not answer the question of exactly which are the most significant psychologic factors that interfere with the normal, mutual thriving of mother and infant.

Some authors have suggested that nonorganic failure to thrive is caused by hyponutrition (Woolston, 1983), whereas others have suggested that the answer is still unknown (Goldbloom, 1982; Drotar, in press).

SOCIAL DEPRIVATION

Maternal deprivation, itself a complex concept (see Rutter, 1972), must also be seen in its social context. It has long been known that mothers in the lower socioeconomic bracket have an increased incidence of complications of pregnancy and birth (Baird, 1959; Drillien, 1959). From 1935 to 1983 the gap between the infant mortality rates for white and black infants has continued to widen (Table 15–1). The risks consequent upon the increased incidence of complications of pregnancy and labor (themselves due to multiple causes), and the increased incidence of postnatal disease (such as iron deficiency anemia), expose infants who are economically and socially disadvantaged or who are in an ethnic group

Table 15–1. Infant Mortality Rates (per 1,000 live births)

Infants	Year		
	1935	1980	1983
Black	83.2	21.4	19.2
White	51.9	11.0	9.7

exposed to discrimination to massively excessive risks for maldevelopment (Birch, 1968). For example, malnutrition alone reduces the child's responsiveness to stimulation, and this reduced responsiveness itself can induce apathy in the adult who is caring for the child. In this sense, the child adds to his or her own disadvantaged environment. This underlying mutual apathy may later result in an impairment of the capacity for satisfying relationships and, later still, learning (Cravioto et al., 1966).

Children reared in the lower socioeconomic environments also seem to have a greater exposure to external dangers. For example, there appears to be a greater incidence of burns and other accidents in children from the lower socioeconomic backgrounds (Spence et al., 1954). Moreover, many mothers in the lower socioeconomic classes are young and inexperienced and offer a different kind of mothering to an infant. Marked class differences have also been found in child-rearing methods, although the research findings are conflicting. For example, Sears found that middle class mothers are more permissive than those of the lower class (Sears et al., 1957) whereas Davis concluded that middle class mothers are more restrictive (Davis and Havighurst, 1947). Whiting and Child (1953) claimed that children of the American middle class are among the most restricted anywhere in the world. In socially and culturally deprived homes there is usually little space and few toys or books. Parents are often preoccupied with their own problems and may have little energy to invest in their children's achievements (Wolff, 1969).

In summary, physical, socioeconomic, cul-

tural, and educational factors in our society clearly have a significant impact upon the development of the child, and no study of the development of an individual is complete without an understanding of these factors (Eisenberg, 1968; National Institute of Child Health and Human Development, 1969).

Note 26

From A. Gesell and C.S. Amatruda (1964). *Developmental Diagnosis*, 2nd Ed. New York: Paul Hoeber Medical Division, Harper & Row, pp. 8–14.
Stages and Sequences of Development.

Before describing diagnostic procedures it will be profitable to take a bird's-eye view of the territory which is to be explored by the developmental examination. Development is a continuous process. Beginning with conception it proceeds stage by stage in orderly sequence, each stage representing a degree or level of maturity. There are so many such levels that we must select a few which will serve best as a frame of reference for purposes of diagnosis. We have determined upon the following Key Ages: 4, 16, 28, 40 weeks; 12, 18, 24, 36 months.

To appreciate the developmental significance of these key ages it is well to examine their position in the early cycle of human growth. This cycle is depicted in the five charts which follow (Figs. 15–1 through 15–5). The first chart gives a comprehensive view of the entire scope of development; it includes the fetal period, to indicate the continuity of the growth cycle.

The organization of behavior begins long before birth; and the general direction of this organization is from head to foot, from proximal to distal segments. Lips and tongue lead, eye muscles follow, then neck, shoulder, arms, hands, fingers, trunk, legs, feet. The chart reflects this law of developmental direction; it also suggests that the four distinguishable fields of behavior develop conjointly in close co-ordination.

In terse terms the trends of behavior development are as follows.

In the first quarter of the first year the infant gains control of his twelve oculomotor muscles.

In the second quarter (16–28 weeks) he comes into command of the muscles which support his head and move his arms. He reaches out for things.

In the third quarter (28–40 weeks) he gains command of his trunk and hands. He sits. He grasps, transfers and manipulates objects.

In the fourth quarter (40–52 weeks) he extends command to his legs and feet; to his forefingers and thumb. He pokes and plucks.

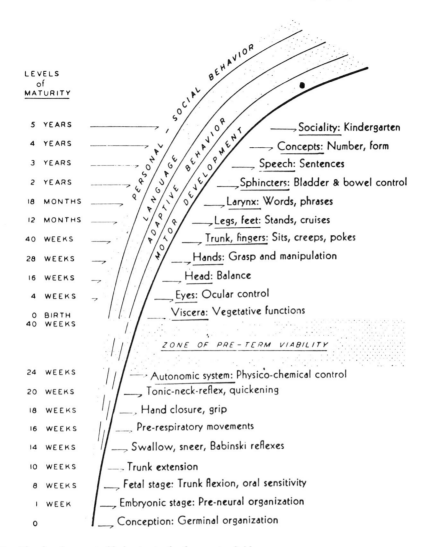

LEVELS
of
MATURITY

5 YEARS	Sociality: Kindergarten
4 YEARS	Concepts: Number, form
3 YEARS	Speech: Sentences
2 YEARS	Sphincters: Bladder & bowel control
18 MONTHS	Larynx: Words, phrases
12 MONTHS	Legs, feet: Stands, cruises
40 WEEKS	Trunk, fingers: Sits, creeps, pokes
28 WEEKS	Hands: Grasp and manipulation
16 WEEKS	Head: Balance
4 WEEKS	Eyes: Ocular control
0 BIRTH 40 WEEKS	Viscera: Vegetative functions

ZONE OF PRE-TERM VIABILITY

24 WEEKS	Autonomic system: Physico-chemical control
20 WEEKS	Tonic-neck-reflex, quickening
18 WEEKS	Hand closure, grip
16 WEEKS	Pre-respiratory movements
14 WEEKS	Swallow, sneer, Babinski reflexes
10 WEEKS	Trunk extension
8 WEEKS	Fetal stage: Trunk flexion, oral sensitivity
1 WEEK	Embryonic stage: Pre-neural organization
0	Conception: Germinal organization

Fig. 15–1.   The development of behavior in the four major fields.

In the second year he walks and runs; articulates words and phrases; acquires bowel and bladder control; attains a rudimentary sense of personal identity and of personal possession.

In the third year he speaks in sentences, using words as tools of thought; he shows a positive propensity to understand his environment and to comply with cultural demands. He is no longer a mere infant.

In the fourth year he asks innumerable questions, perceives analogies, displays an active tendency to conceptualize and generalize. He is nearly self-dependent in routines of home life.

At five he is well matured in motor control. He hops and skips. He talks without infantile articulation. He can narrate a long tale. He prefers associative play; he feels socialized pride in clothes and accomplishment. He is a self-assured, conforming citizen in his small world.

The remaining four charts diagram the sequences of development in Motor, Adaptive, Language, and Personal-Social fields of behavior. These four fields develop interdependently; and an adequate estimate of behavior maturity demands an appraisal of each major field. Each chart shows selected behavior patterns which illustrate the progressions of normal development. These patterns give a preliminary suggestion of the practical application of behavior norms.

Note 27

From E.H. Erikson (1959). Identity and the life cycle. *Psychol. Issues*, 1 (1):55–61.

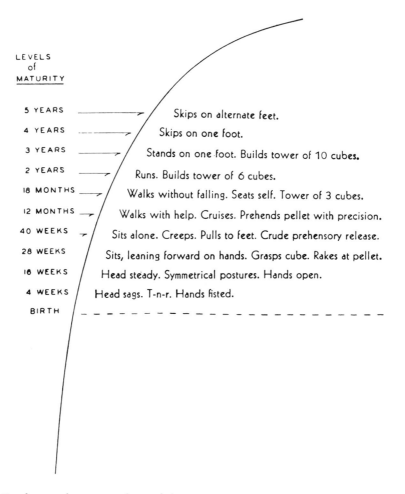

LEVELS
of
MATURITY

5 YEARS ——————→ Skips on alternate feet.

4 YEARS – – – – → Skips on one foot.

3 YEARS ——————→ Stands on one foot. Builds tower of 10 cubes.

2 YEARS ——————→ Runs. Builds tower of 6 cubes.

18 MONTHS ———→ Walks without falling. Seats self. Tower of 3 cubes.

12 MONTHS ——→ Walks with help. Cruises. Prehends pellet with precision.

40 WEEKS ——→ Sits alone. Creeps. Pulls to feet. Crude prehensory release.

28 WEEKS Sits, leaning forward on hands. Grasps cube. Rakes at pellet.

16 WEEKS Head steady. Symmetrical postures. Hands open.

4 WEEKS Head sags. T-n-r. Hands fisted.

BIRTH

Fig. 15–2. Developmental sequences of motor behavior.

The items on this chart include both gross motor and fine motor behavior patterns. To ascertain the maturity of postural control we institute formal postural tests which reveal the repertoire of the infant's behavior: supine, prone, sitting, and standing.

Fine motor control is evaluated in a similar manner. Small objects such as cubes, pellet and string elicit patterns of fine manual control.

Such tests illustrate the principles which also underlie the developmental diagnosis of behavior in the adaptive, language, and personal-social fields.

Basic Trust versus Basic Mistrust

I

For the first component of a healthy personality I nominate a sense of *basic trust*, which I think is an attitude toward oneself and the world derived from the experiences of the first year of life. by "trust" I mean what is commonly implied in reasonable trustfulness as far as others are concerned and a simple sense of trustworthiness as far as oneself is concerned. When I say "basic," I mean that neither this component nor any of those that follow are, either in childhood or in adulthood, especially conscious. In fact, all of these criteria, when developed in childhood and when integrated in adulthood, blend into the total personality. Their crises in childhood, however, and their impairment in adulthood are clearly cirumscribed.

In describing this growth and its crises as a development of a series of alternative basic methods, we take recourse to the term "a sense of." Like a "sense of health" or a "sense of not being well," such "senses" pervade surface and depth, consciousness and the unconscious. They are ways of conscious *experience*, accessible to introspection (where it develops); ways of *behaving*, observable by others; and unconscious *inner* states determin-

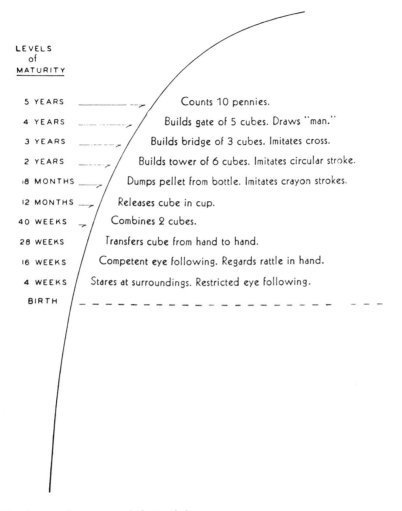

LEVELS
of
MATURITY

5 YEARS ———————→ Counts 10 pennies.

4 YEARS —————→ Builds gate of 5 cubes. Draws "man."

3 YEARS ————→ Builds bridge of 3 cubes. Imitates cross.

2 YEARS ———→ Builds tower of 6 cubes. Imitates circular stroke.

18 MONTHS ——→ Dumps pellet from bottle. Imitates crayon strokes.

12 MONTHS —→ Releases cube in cup.

40 WEEKS —→ Combines 2 cubes.

28 WEEKS Transfers cube from hand to hand.

16 WEEKS Competent eye following. Regards rattle in hand.

4 WEEKS Stares at surroundings. Restricted eye following.

BIRTH — — — — — — — — — — — — — — — — — —

Fig. 15–3. Developmental sequences of adaptive behavior.

To determine how the infant uses his motor equipment to exploit the environment we present him with a variety of simple objects. The small red cubes serve not only to test motor co-ordination, they reveal the child's capacity to put his motor equipment to constructive and adaptive ends. The cube tests create an objective opportunity for the examiner to observe adaptivity in action—motor co-ordination combined with judgment.

able by test and analysis. It is important to keep these three dimensions in mind, as we proceed.

In *adults* the impairment of basic trust is expressed in a *basic mistrust*. It characterizes individuals who withdraw into themselves in particular ways when at odds with themselves and with others. These ways, which often are not obvious, are more strikingly represented by individuals who regress into psychotic states in which they sometimes close up, refusing food and comfort, and becoming oblivious to companionship. In so far as we like to assist them with psychotherapy, we must try to reach them again in specific ways in order to convince them that they can trust the world and that they can trust themselves. . . .

As the newborn infant is separated from his symbiosis with the mother's body, his inborn and more or less coordinated ability to take in by mouth meets the mother's more or less coordinated ability and intention to feed him and to welcome him. At this point he lives through, and loves with, his mouth; and the mother lives through, and loves with, her breasts.

For the mother this is a late and complicated accomplishment, highly dependent on her development as a woman; on her unconscious attitude toward the child; on the way she has lived through pregnancy and delivery; on her and her community's attitude toward the act of nursing—and on the response of the newborn. To him the mouth

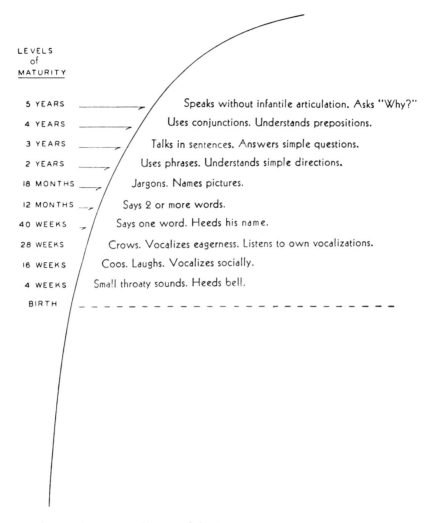

LEVELS
of
MATURITY

5 YEARS ——————→ Speaks without infantile articulation. Asks "Why?"

4 YEARS —————→ Uses conjunctions. Understands prepositions.

3 YEARS ————→ Talks in sentences. Answers simple questions.

2 YEARS ———→ Uses phrases. Understands simple directions.

18 MONTHS ——→ Jargons. Names pictures.

12 MONTHS —→ Says 2 or more words.

40 WEEKS → Says one word. Heeds his name.

28 WEEKS Crows. Vocalizes eagerness. Listens to own vocalizations.

16 WEEKS Coos. Laughs. Vocalizes socially.

4 WEEKS Small throaty sounds. Heeds bell.

BIRTH

Fig. 15–4.   Developmental sequences of language behavior.

Language maturity is estimated in terms of articulation, vocabulary, adaptive use and comprehension. During the course of a developmental examination spontaneous and responsive language behavior is observed. Valuable supplementary information may also be secured by questioning the adult familiar with the child's everyday behavior at home.

is the focus of a general first approach to life—the incorporative approach. In psychoanalysis this stage is usually referred to as the "oral" stage. . . .

During the "second oral" stage the ability and the pleasure in a more active and more directed incorporative approach ripen. The teeth develop and with hem the pleasure in biting on hard things, in biting *through* things, and in biting *off* things. This active-incorporative mode characterizes a variety of other activities (as did the first incorporative mode). The eyes, first part of a passive system of accepting impressions as they come along, have now learned to focus, to isolate, to "grasp" objects from the vaguer background and to follow

them. The organs of hearing similarly have learned to discern significant sounds, to localize them, and to guide an appropriate change in position (lifting and turning the head, lifting and turning the upper body). The arms have learned to reach out determinedly and the hands to grasp firmly. We are more interested here in the overall *configuration and final integration* of developing approaches to the world than *in the first appearances of specific abilities* which are so well described in the child development literature. . . .

The *crisis* of the oral stage (during the second part of the first year) is difficult to assess and more diffiult to verify. It seems to consist of the co-

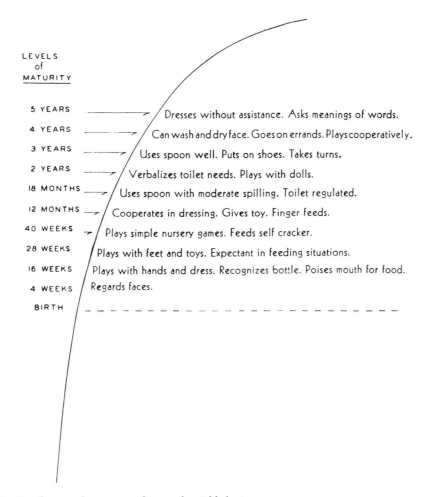

LEVELS
of
MATURITY

5 YEARS ——————————→ Dresses without assistance. Asks meanings of words.

4 YEARS ——————→ Can wash and dry face. Goes on errands. Plays cooperatively.

3 YEARS ———→ Uses spoon well. Puts on shoes. Takes turns.

2 YEARS ———→ Verbalizes toilet needs. Plays with dolls.

18 MONTHS ——→ Uses spoon with moderate spilling. Toilet regulated.

12 MONTHS —→ Cooperates in dressing. Gives toy. Finger feeds.

40 WEEKS →/ Plays simple nursery games. Feeds self cracker.

28 WEEKS Plays with feet and toys. Expectant in feeding situations.

16 WEEKS Plays with hands and dress. Recognizes bottle. Poises mouth for food.

4 WEEKS Regards faces.

BIRTH

Fig. 15–5.   Developmental sequences of personal-social behavior.

Personal-social behavior is greatly affected by the temperament of the child and by the kind of home in which he is reared. The range of individual variation is wide. Nevertheless maturity factors play a primary role in the socialization of the child. His social conduct is ascertained by incidental observation and by inquiry. The chart illustrates types of behavior which may be considered in evaluating the interaction of environmental influences and developmental readiness.

incidence in time of three developments: (1) a physiological one: the general tension associated with a more violent drive to incorporate, appropriate, and observe more actively (a tension to which is added the discomfort of "teething" and other changes in the oral machinery); (2) a psychological one: the infant's increasing awareness of himself as a distinct person; and (3) an environmental one: the mother's apparent turning away from the baby toward pursuits which she had given up during later pregnancy and postnatal care. . . .

What the child acquires at a given stage is a certain ratio between the positive and the negative which, if the balance is toward the positive, will help him to meet later crises with a better chance for unimpaired total development. The idea that at any stage a *goodness* is achieved which is impervious to new conflicts within and changes without is a projection on child development of that success ideology which so dangerously pervades our private and public daydreams and can make us inept in the face of a heightened struggle for a meaningful existence in our time. . . .

Note 28

From J. Bowlby (1951), Maternal care and mental health. World Health Organization, Monograph #2. Quoted in *Child Care and the Growth of Love*, ed. M. Fry. London: Penguin Books Ltd., 1953.

Prolonged breaks (in the mother-child relationship) during the first three years of life leave a characteristic impression on the child's personality. Such children appear emotionally withdrawn and isolated. They fail to develop loving ties with other children or with adults and consequently have no friendships worth the name. It is true that they are sometimes sociable in a superficial sense, but if this is scrutinised we find that there are no feelings, no roots in these relationships. This, I think, more than anything else, is the cause of their hard-boiledness. Parents and school teachers complain that nothing you say or do has any effect on the child. If you thrash him he cries for a bit, but there is no emotional response to being out of favour, such as is normal to the ordinary child. It appears to be of no essential consequence to these lost souls whether they are in favour or not. Since they are unable to make genuine emotional relations, the condition of relationship at a given moment lacks all significance for them. . . . During the last few years I have seen some sixteen cases of this affectionless type of persistent pilferer and in only two was a prolonged break absent. In all the others gross breaches of the mother-child relation had occurred during the first three years, and the child had become a persistent pilferer.

Note 29

From R.A. Spitz (1965), *The First Year of Life.* New York: International Universities Press, pp. 89–90.

An extremely simple experiment can be performed to show that what triggers the smile is a sign Gestalt which consists of a circumscribed part of the face. In this experiment contact is made with a three-month-old by smiling at him and nodding one's head; the infant will react by smiling, by becoming active and by wriggling.

One now turns one's head into profile, continuing to smile and to nod; the infant will stop smiling, his expression becomes bewildered. Developmentally advanced infants frequently seem to search with their glance somewhere in the region of the experimenter's ear, as if searching for the eye which disappeared; sensitive children appear to respond with a kind of shock, and it takes time to reestablish contact. This experiment shows that the three-month-old is still unable to recognize the human face in profile; in other words, the infant has not recognized the human partner at all; he has only perceived the sign Gestalt of forehead, eyes, and nose. When this Gestalt is modified through turning into profile, the percept is no longer recognized; it has lost its tenuous objectal quality.

Note 30

From J. Piaget (1952), *The Origins of Intelligence in Children.* New York: International Universities Press, pp. 266–269.

Tertiary circular reaction is quite different: if it also arises by way of differentiation, from the secondary circular schemata, this differentiation is no longer imposed by the environment but is, so to speak, accepted and even desired in itself. In effect, not succeeding in assimilating certain objects or situations to the schemata hitherto examined, the child manifests an unexpected behavior pattern: he tries, through a sort of experimentation, to find out in which respect the object or the event is new. In other words, he will not only submit to but even provoke new results instead of being satisfied merely to reproduce them once they have been revealed fortuitously. The child discovers in this way that which has been called in scientific language the "experimental in order to see." But, of course, the new result, though sought after for its own sake, demands to be reproduced and the initial experiment is immediately accompanied by circular reaction. But, there too, a difference contrasts these "tertiary" reactions to the "secondary" reactions. When the child repeats the movements which led him to the interesting result, he no longer repeats them just as they are but gradates and varies them, in such a way as to discover fluctuations in the result. The "experiment in order to see," consequently, from the very beginning, has the tendency to extend to the conquest of the external environment. . . .

Observation 141.—This first example will make us understand the transition between secondary and "tertiary" reactions: that of the well-known behavior pattern by means of which the child explores distant space and constructs his representation of movement, the behavior pattern of letting go or throwing objects in order subsequently to pick them up.

One recalls . . . how, at 0;10 (2) Laurent discovered in "exploring" a case of soap, the possibility of throwing this object and letting it fall. Now, what interested him at first was not the objective phenomenon of the fall—that is to say, the object's trajectory—but the very act of letting go. He therefore limited himself, at the beginning, merely to reproducing the result observed fortuitously, which still constitutes a "secondary" reaction, "derived" it is true, but of typical structure.

On the other hand, at 0;10 (10) the reaction changes and becomes "tertiary." That day Laurent manipulates a small piece of bread (without any alimentary interest; he has never eaten any and has no thought of tasting it) and lets it go continually. He even breaks off fragments which he lets drop. Now, in contradistinction to what has happened on the preceding days, he pays no attention to the act of letting go whereas he watches with great interest the body in motion; in particular, he looks at it for a long time when it has fallen, and picks it up when he can.

At 0;10 (11) Laurent is lying on his back but nevertheless resumes his experiments of the day before. He grasps in succession a celluloid swan, a box, etc., stretches out his arm and lets them fall. He distinctly varies the positions of the fall. Sometimes he stretches out his arm vertically, sometimes he holds it obliquely, in front of or behind his eyes, etc. When the object falls in a new position (for example on his pillow), he lets it fall two or three times more on the same place, as though to study the spatial relations; then he modifies the situation. At a certain moment the swan falls near his mouth: now, he does not suck it (even though this object habitually serves this purpose), but drops it three times more while merely making the gesture of opening his mouth. . . .

Observation 146.—At 1;2 (8) Jacqueline holds in her hands an object which is new to her; a round, flat box whih she turns all over, shakes, rubs against the bassinet, etc. She lets it go and tries to pick it up. But she only succeeds in touching it with her index finger, without grasping it. She nevertheless makes an attempt and presses on the edge. The box then tilts up and falls again. Jacqueline, very much interested in this fortuitous result, immediately applies herself to studying it. . . . Hitherto it is only a question of an attempt at assimilation . . . and of the fortuitous discovery of a new result, but this discovery, instead of giving rise to a simple circular reaction, is at once extended to "experiments in order to see."

In effect, Jacqueline immediately rests the box on the ground and pushes it as far as possible (it is noteworthy that care is taken to push the box far away in order to reproduce the same conditions as in the first attempt, as though this were a necessary condition for obtaining the result). Afterward Jacqueline puts her finger on the box and presses it. But as she places her finger on the center of the box she simply displaces it and makes it slide instead of tilting it up. She amuses herself with this game and keeps it up (resumes it after intervals, etc.) for several minutes. Then, changing the point of contact, she finally again places her finger on the edge of the box, which tilts it up. She repeats this many times, varying the conditions, but keeping track of her discovery: now she only presses on the edge!

REFERENCES

Anders, T. (1978), Home-recorded sleep in 2- and 9-month-old infants. *J. Am. Acad. Child. Psychiatry*, 17:421–432.

Aserinsky, E., and Kleitman, N. (1953), Regularly occurring periods of eye motility, and concomitant phenomena, during sleep. *Science*, 118:273–274.

Baird, D. (1959), The contribution of obstetric factors to serious physical and mental handicap in children. *J. Obstet. Gynecol.*, 66:743.

Baldwin, J.M. (1895), *Mental Development in the Child and the Race*. New York: Macmillan.

Bell, S.M., and Ainsworth, M.D.S. (1972), Infant crying and maternal responsiveness. *Child Dev.*, 43:1171–1190.

Bender, L. (1953), Childhood schizophrenia. *Psychiatr. Q.*, 27:663.

Berko, J., and Brown, R. (1960), Psycholinguistic research methods. In: *Handbook of Research Methods in Child Development*, ed. P. Mussen. New York: John Wiley & Sons, Inc.

Birch H.G. (1968), Health and the education of socially disadvantaged children. *Dev. Med. Child Neurol.*, 10:580–599.

Bowlby, J. (1951), Maternal care and mental health. Geneva: World Health Organization.

Bowlby, J. (1958), The nature of a child's tie to his mother. *Int. J. Psychoanal.*, 39:350–373.

Cantwell, D.P., and Baker, L. (1987), *Developmental Speech and Language Disorders*. New York: Guilford Press, pp. 17–36.

Collins, G.M., and Schaffer, H.R. (1975), Synchronization of visual attention in mother-infant pairs. *J. Child Psychol. Psychiatry*, 16:315–320.

Cravioto, J., DeLicardi, E.T., and Birch, H.G. (1966), Nutrition, growth and neuro-integrative development: An experimental and ecologic study. *Pediatrics*, 38:319.

Cromer, R.F. (1980), Normal language development: Recent progress. In: *Language and Language Disorders in Childhood*, ed. L.A. Hersov, M. Berger, and A.R. Nicol. New York: Pergamon Press, pp. 1–21.

Davis, A., and Havighurst, R.J. (1947), *Father of the Man*. Boston: Houghton Mifflin.

DeMyer, M.K., Hingtgen, J.N., and Jackson, R.K. (1981), Infantile autism reviewed: A decade of research. *Schizophr. Bull.*, 7:388–451.

Despert, J.L. (1947), The early recognition of childhood schizophrenia. *Med. Clin. North Am.*, May: 680.

Dreyfus-Brisac, C., Samson, D., Blanc, C., and Monod, N. (1958), L'électroencephalogramme de l'enfant normal demoins de 3 ans. *Etudes Neonatales*, 7:143.

Drillien, C.M. (1959), Physical and mental handicaps in the prematurely born. *J. Obstet. Gynaecol. Br. Empire*, 66:721–728.

Drotar, D. (in press), Failure to thrive. In: *Handbook of Pediatric Psychology*, ed. D.K. Routh. New York: Guilford Press.

Eisenberg, L. (1968), Racism, the family and society: A crisis in values. *Ment. Hygiene*, 52:512–520.

Ellingson, R. (1975), Ontogenesis of sleep in the human. In: *Experimental Study of Human Sleep*, ed. G.

Lairy and P. Salzarulo. Amsterdam: Elsevier, pp. 129–146.

Erikson, E.H. (1959), Identity and the life cycle. *Psychol. Issues*, 1:55–61.

Escalona, S.K. (1969), *The Roots of Individuality: Normal Patterns of Development in Infancy.* Chicago: Aldine, p. 547.

Fagan, J.F. (1979), The origins of facial pattern recognition. In: *Psychological Development from Infancy: Image to Intention*, ed. M.H. Bornstein and W. Kessen. New York: John Wiley & Sons, Inc., pp. 83–114.

Fantz, R.L. (1975), Early visual selectivity. In: *Infant Perception*, ed. L.B. Cohen and P. Salapatek. New York: Academic Press.

Folstein, S., and Rutter, M. (1977), Infantile autism: A genetic study of 21 pairs. *Child Psychol. Psychiatry*, 18:297.

Freud, A. (1955), Safeguarding the emotional health of our children: An inquiry into the concept of the rejecting mother. *National Conferences of Social Work: Casework Papers, 1956.* New York: Family Service Association of America, p. 9.

Freud, S. (1905), *Three Essays on Sexuality.* Standard Edition, 7 (1953). London: The Hogarth Press, p. 168.

Freud, S. (1923), *The Ego and the Id.* Standard Edition, 19 (1961). London: The Hogarth Press, pp. 12–59.

Freud, S. (1926), *Inhibitions, Symptoms and Anxiety.* Standard Edition, 20 (1959). London: The Hogarth Press, pp. 87–172.

Fries, M.E., and Woolf, F.J. (1953), Some hypotheses on the role of the congenital activity type in personality development. *Psychoanal. Study Child*, 8:48–62.

Gesell, A.O., and Amatruda, C.S. (1941), *Developmental Diagnosis*, 11th Ed., 1964. New York: Paul Hoeber Medical Division, Harper & Row, pp. 8–14.

Goldbloom, R.B. (1982), Failure to thrive. *Pediatr. Clin. North Am.*, 29:151.

Hales, D.J., Lzoff, B., Sosa, R., and Kennell, J. (1977), Defining the limits of the maternal sensitive period. *Dev. Med. Child Neurol.*, 29:454–461.

Harter, S. (1983), Developmental perspective on the self-system. In: *Handbook of Child Psychology*, Vol. 4, ed. E.M. Hetherington. New York: John Wiley & Sons, Inc.

Hartmann, H. (1939), *Ego Psychology and the Problem of Adaptation.* New York: International Universities Press.

Hetzer, H., and Wolf, K. (1928), Baby tests. *Zeitschrift für Psychologie*, p. 107.

Howlin, P. (1980), Language. In: *Scientific Foundations of Developmental Psychiatry*, ed. M. Rutter. London: Heinemann, pp. 198–219.

Kagan, J. (1971), *Change and Continuity in Infancy.* New York: John Wiley & Sons, Inc.

Kanner, L. (1943), Autistic disturbances of affective contact. *Nerv. Child*, 2:217.

Kaye, K. (1976), Infants' effects upon their mothers' teaching strategies. In: *The Social Context of Learning and Development*, ed. J.C. Glifewell. New York: Gardner.

Kessen, W. (1967), Sucking and looking: Two organized congenital patterns of behavior in the human newborn. In: *Early Behavior: Comparative and Developmental Approaches*, ed. H.W. Stevenson et al. New York: John Wiley & Sons, Inc.

Kessen, W., and Bornstein, M.H. (1978), Discriminability of brightness change for infants. *J. Exp. Child Psychol.*, 25:526–530.

Klaus, M.H., and Kennell, J.H. (1976), *Parent-Infant Bonding.* St. Louis: C.V. Mosby.

Klein, M. (1960), Our adult world and its roots in infancy. London: Tavistock, Pamphlet No. 2, p. 15.

Korner, A.F., and Grobstein, R. (1966), Visual alertness as related to soothing in neonates: Implications for maternal stimulation and early deprivation. *Child Dev.*, 37:867–876.

Korsch, B.M. (1983), More on infant bonding. *J. Pediatr.*, 102:249–250.

Lamb, M.E. (1982), Early contact and maternal-infant bonding: One decade later. *Pediatrics*, 70:763.

Langmeir, J., and Matejeck, Z. (1975), *Psychological Deprivation in Childhood*, 3rd Ed. trans. P. Auger. New York: Halsted Press.

Leonard, M.F., Rhymes, J.P., and Solnit, A.J. (1966), Failure to thrive in infants. *Am. J. Dis. Child.*, 3:600–612.

Lewis, M.M. (1959), *How Children Learn to Speak.* New York: Basic Books.

Lewis, M.M. (1963), *Language, Thought and Personality in Infancy and Childhood.* New York: Basic Books, pp. 15–24.

Lewis, M., and Brooks, J. (1976), Infants' social perception: A constructivist view. In: *Infant Perception: From Sensation to Cognition*, eds. L. Cohen and P. Salapatek. New York: Academic Press.

Lewis, M., Kagan, J., Campbell, H., and Kalafat, J. (1966), The cardiac response as a correlate of attention in infants. *Child Dev.*, 37:63–72.

Ling, B.C. (1941), Form discrimination as a learning cue in infants. *Comp. Psychol. Monogr.*, 17:2.

Lorenz, K. (1966), *On Aggression*, trans. M. Wilson. New York: Harcourt, Brace & World.

Lotter, V. (1966), Epidemiology of autistic conditions in young children. I. Prevalence. *Soc. Psychiatry*, 1:124–137.

Mahler, M.S., Pine, F., and Bergman, A. (1975), *The Psychological Birth of the Infant.* New York: Basic Books.

Money, J., Hampton, J.G., and Hampton, J.L. (1955), Hermaphroditism: Recommendations concerning assignment of sex, and psychological management. *Bull. Johns Hopkins Hosp.* 97:281.

Morley, M.E. (1965), *The Development and Disorders of Speech in Childhood*, 2nd Ed. Edinburgh: E. & S. Livingstone.

Moss, H.A. (1967), Sex, age and state as determinants of mother-infant interaction. *Merrill-Palmer Q.*, 13:19–36.

National Institute of Child Health and Human Development (1969), *Perspectives on Human Deprivation: Biological, Psychological and Sociological.* Washington, D.C.: U.S. Government Printing Office.

Nelson, K. (1977), First steps in language acquisition. *J. Am. Acad. Child Psychiatry*, 16:563–607.

Ornitz, E.M., and Ritvo, E.R. (1976), The syndrome of autism: A critical review. *Am. J. Psychiatry*, 133:609–621.

Parmelee, A.H., Wenner, W.H., and Schulz, H.R. (1964), Infant sleep patterns: From birth to 16 weeks of age. *J. Pediatr.*, 65:576.

Patton, R.G., and Gardner, L.I. (1962), Influence of family environment on growth: The syndrome of maternal deprivation. *Pediatrics*, 30:957–962.

Piaget, J. (1952), *The Origins of Intelligence in Children.* New York: International Universities Press.

Provence S., and Lipton, R. (1962), *Infants in Institutions.* New York: International Universities Press.

Putnam, M.D. (1955), Some observations on psychosis in early childhood. In: *Emotional Problems of Early Childhood*, ed. G. Caplan. New York: Basic Books, pp. 519–526.

Rank, B. (1955), Intensive study and treatment of preschool children who show marked personality deviations or "atypical development" and their parents. In: *Emotional Problems of Early Childhood*, ed. G. Caplan. New York: Basic Books, p. 491.

Rheingold, H.L. (1968), The effect of a strange environment on the behavior of infants. In: *Determinations of Infant Behavior* (Vol. 4), ed. B.M. Foss. London: Methuen.

Ritvo, E.R., and Freeman, B.J. (1978), Current research on the syndrome of autism. Introduction: The National Society for Autistic Children's definition of the syndrome of autism. *J. Am. Acad. Child Psychiatry*, 17:565–575.

Ritvo, S., and Solnit, A.J. (1958), Influences of early mother-child interaction on identification processes. *Psychoanal. Study Child*, 12:64.

Robson, K.S. (1967), The role of eye-to-eye contact in maternal-infant behavior. *J. Child Psychol. Psychiatry*, 8:13–25.

Rutter, M. (1970), Autistic children: Infancy to adulthood. *Semin. Psychiatry*, 2:435–450.

Rutter, M. (1972), *Maternal Deprivation Reassessed.* Harmondsworth: Penguin.

Rutter, M. (1976), Infantile autism and other child psychoses. In: *Child Psychiatry*, ed. M. Rutter and L. Hersov. Oxford, Blackwell, pp. 717–747.

Rutter, M., and Bax, M. (1972), Normal development of speech and language. In: *The Child with Delayed Speech*, ed. M. Rutter and J.A. Martin. *Clin. Dev. Med.*, No. 43. London: SIMP/Heinemann.

Rutter, M., Greenfield, D., and Lockyer, L. (1967), A five- to fifteen-year follow-up study of infantile psychosis. *Br. J. Psychiatry*, 113:1183–1199.

Schaffer, H.R. (1966), Activity level as a constitutional determinant of infantile reaction of deprivation. *Child Dev.*, 37:595.

Schaffer, H.R. (Ed.) (1977), *Studies in Mother-Infant Interaction.* London: Academic Press.

Schaffer, H.R., and Emerson, P.E. (1964), The development of social attachments in infancy. *Monogr. Soc. Res. Child Dev.*, 29 (3).

Sears, R.R., Maccoby, E.E., and Levin, H. (1957), *Patterns of Child Rearing.* New York: Row, Peterson.

Spence, J., Walton, W.S., Miller, F.J.W., and Courts, D.M. (1954), *A Thousand Families in Newcastle Upon Tyne.* London: Oxford University Press.

Spitz, R.A. (1945), Hospitalism: An inquiry into the genesis of psychiatric conditions in early childhood. *Psychoanal. Study Child*, 1:53–74.

Spitz, R.A. (1946), Hospitalism: A follow-up report. *Psychoanal. Study Child*, 2:113–117.

Spitz, R.A. (1946), Anaclitic depression: an inquiry into the genesis of psychiatric conditions in early childhood. *Psychoanal. Study Child*, 2:313–342.

Spitz, R.A. (1965), *The First Year of Life.* New York: International Universities Press.

Sroufe, L.A. (1977), Wariness of strangers and the study of infant development. *Child Dev.*, 48:731–746.

Stern, D.N. (1974), Mother and infant at play: The dyadic interaction involving facial, vocal and gaze behavior. In: *The Effect of the Infant on Its Caregiver*, ed. M. Lewis and L.A. Rosenblum. New York: John Wiley & Sons, Inc.

Thomas, A., Birch, H.G., Chess, S., et al. (1963), *Behavioral Individuality in Early Childhood.* New York: New York University Press.

Thomas, A., Chess, S., and Birch, H.G. (1968), *Temperament and Behavior Disorders in Children.* New York: New York University Press.

Waddington, C.H. (1966), *Principles of Development and Differentiation.* New York: Macmillan Publishing Co.

Walter, G. (1956), Electro-encephalographic development of children. In: *Discussions on Child Development*, ed. J.M. Tanner and B. Inhelder. London: Tavistock, p. 146.

Werner, H. (1948), *Comparative Psychology of Mental Development.* New York: Harper & Row.

White, B.L., and Held, R.M. (1966), Plasticity of sensori-motor development in the human infant. In: *The Causes of Behavior: Readings in Child Development and Educational Psychology*, 2nd Ed., ed. J.R. Rosenblith and W. Allinsmith. Boston: Allyn & Bacon, pp. 783–866.

Whiting, J.W.M., and Child, I.L. (1953), *Child Training and Personality: A Cross-Cultural Study.* New Haven: Yale University Press.

Winnicott, D.W. (1945), Primitive emotional development. *Collected Papers.* New York; Basic Books.

Wolff, P.H., and Feinbloom, R.I. (1969), Critical periods and cognitive development in the first 2 years. *Pediatrics*, 44:999–1006.

Wolff, S. (1969), *Children Under Stress.* London: Allen Lane, The Penguin Press.

Woolston, J.L. (1983), Eating disorders in infancy and early childhood. *J. Am. Acad. Child Psychiatry*, 22:114.

16

INFANCY—AGES 1 TO 3

MOTOR SEQUENCE

Motor skills become increasingly sophisticated so that by 3 years of age a child can stand on one foot, dance, and jump. He or she is also more dexterous than previously and can build a tower of 10 cubes. Ambidexterity gives way to lateralization some time during the third year, although handedness may not be firmly established for several years. Leg, eye, and ear dominance may also not become firmly established until the seventh, eighth, or ninth year or even later.

ADAPTIVE SEQUENCE

At 18 months the child can usually imitate a crayon stroke. By 2 years of age the child can imitate a circular stroke, and by 3 years he or she can imitate a cross. At 3 years of age he or she is also capable of building a bridge with three cubes.

LANGUAGE SEQUENCE

Most children talk fairly well by 3 years of age. They can talk in sentences although they do not always use the correct verb tenses and they often omit conjunctions. Nevertheless within the limits of his or her vocabulary and experience, a 3-year-old is usually quite capable of telling a simple story. The child can also communicate clearly using verbal language. If at 2 years of age most questions are "what" questions, by 3 years of age they are "where" and "who" questions, and by 4 years

of age the child begins to ask "why" (Watts, 1947).

Until about 2½ years of age normal children may repeat what is said to them. However, after that age such repetition is considered abnormal and is called echolalia. Echolalia is found most often in autism and mental retardation; it probably reflects the child's lack of understanding of language (Fay and Butler, 1971).

PERSONAL AND SOCIAL BEHAVIOR

By the age of 3, most children can take themselves to the toilet, feed themselves, and begin to dress themselves.

FANTASY LIFE AND PLAY

Once again, the maturation sequence described by Gesell (1941) can be considered only the skeleton of the child's psychologic development during these years. Fantasy life becomes more directly observable as the child becomes capable of symbolic play. During the first year of life play consisted of object manipulation and combination, e.g., banging blocks together. After the first birthday play materials can be used functionally, e.g., using a cup to feed a doll. Play style is then repetitious with few variations, little risk, no climax, and no real plot. Subsequently pretend play emerges and the child can use various play materials symbolically, e.g., a cup can become a boat, a bathtub, etc. (Rubin, Fein, and Vandenberg, 1983). By the end of the first year, most children have acquired a transitional object (Winnicott, 1951; see Note 31), which often is a piece of rag, a pillow, or a blanket to which the child has become very attached and to which he or she resorts for comfort. Such times may be at bedtime or following any stress, such as separation. The transitional object seems to represent a half-way step between attachment to himself or herself (e.g., the thumb) and attachment to the outside world (the mother). Often when the child holds the transitional object close to the nose, cheek, or mouth, he or she also manages to insert a finger into the nostril or mouth.

What is the clinical significance of the so-called transitional object? Sherman and her co-workers at Cornell University performed a study using data collected from parents of 171 normal children between 9 and 13 years of age from the middle to upper socioeconomic class (Sherman, et al., 1981). Their study did not substantiate earlier theoretic formulations on the use of treasured objects in relation to psychologic health or illness. In fact, they documented no significant differences between those children who continued to use a soft object after age 9 and those who never had a treasured object. This finding is interesting for two reasons: It underscores the necessity of testing a clinical hypothesis with scientific method (in this case an epidemiologic study) and highlights again "the diversity and richness of individual experience that falls within that larger category called 'normal' " (p. 383). We need reliable studies that establish what is normal behavior in a child. A recent study (Cohen and Clark, 1984) examined relationships between transitional object attachment in early childhood and personality characteristics in college student. Self report and parental reports were used and differences in personality profile were reported depending on whether or not the student had had a transitional object. While this observation is of interest reliance on self (and for that matter) parent report poses a problem for interpretation of the results given that both sources of information are potentially unreliable.

The play of a young child sometimes has as its underlying motif a working through of anxiety evoked by a fantasy or fear that the child will lose his or her mother's love. From about 18 months to 2½ or 3 years of age, this represents the most important and most common danger situation for the infant. As the child develops, other basic danger situations are perceived by the child, and each will be mentioned in sequence later.

RELATIONS WITH PARENTS

By the end of the second year, the manifestations of ambivalent behavior can be clearly seen in the child. For example, the child may attempt to control the mother through clinging, sometimes demanding behavior. As the child feels more autonomous, the negativistic behavior increases. Different styles of parent-child interaction are observed; some parents are more authoritarian, others more permissive, and yet others authoritative (Baumrind, 1967). Other parents may assume an uninvolved stance with the child (Maccoby and Martin, 1983). Children of authoritative parents (who combine warmth and discipline) are more self-reliant and responsible.

PEER RELATIONS

When he or she perceives others at all, the young infant seems to perceive them as disturbers of the relationship with the mother or father. Later, the child relates to other children more or less as to lifeless objects to be used, and only gradually becomes aware that they are alive and have feelings of their own. At first he or she uses other children simply as playmates, limiting the partnership to the period of time needed to perform a particular task. By 2½ to 3 years of age, however, the child is beginning to share with others, a task he or she will be helped to master in nursery shool. (The role of nursery school in education is discussed on page 197.)

Even by the end of the third year play

remains mostly self-contained. Although the child may want others to play with him or her, the play is rarely truly or continuously shared at this time. When a group of children of this age are observed playing, the activities of each child seem still to be more or less isolated. However, a tendency toward progressive social involvement can be observed. Thus a shift from solitary, independent play to parallel activity in which children play alongside but not with each other occurs during this period. Later, play occurs in which there is common activity, with sharing and taking turns, culminating in cooperative play in which there is a common goal, with each child playing a specified role (Parten, 1933).

PARENT DEVELOPMENT

The child's ambivalent behavior at this stage requires a shift in the mother's attitude to her child. She must now set limits for the child, at the same time as she must deal with the strong feelings that are now evoked in her. The two-way-street aspect of the dyadic relationship between mother and child is now more obvious and more demanding. Parents too are in a state of continuous development. Past unresolved feelings are evoked again at each stage of development of the child, while the parents are themselves currently developing and experiencing life differently as they grow older. Sometimes a mother may become depressed and may begin to fail in her mothering skills. The consequent failure of her infant to thrive may add to her feelings of inadequacy or guilt. This may lead to inadequate or inconsistent limits setting. Problems of poor impulse control in children often have their origins in this period, when internalization of controls firmly set from without should be occurring.

BODY IMAGE

During the second and third years, the child's concept of his or her body begins to take recognizable shape. The child at this stage often has a passionate interest in Band-

Aids. The child may become quite upset at a small graze and want to cover up the wound with a Band-Aid as if to hide the wound and prevent the loss of body fluid. It seems as though the child's idea of his or her body is that it is a kind of sac filled with fluid that sometimes oozes out. The child may have some vague ideas about the internal organs; for example, the child may think that his or her heart looks like the hearts seen on valentine cards.

Further evidence of the child's developing sense of body and feelings can be seen in other play typical of this stage. For example, play with toys that can be filled and emptied, opened and shut, fitted in, messed and cleaned, held on to (hoarded), and let go (thrown out) seems to reflect the child's interest in his or her body parts and their functions. Movable toys seem to help the child use with pleasure his or her increased ability to move around. Toys that can be built up and then knocked down seem to serve nicely as instruments for the expression of ambivalent feelings.

GENDER IDENTIFICATION

Early gender identification also occurs during this period. In a study of 76 hermaphroditic patients, Money and his colleagues (1955) showed that one cannot attribute psychologic maleness or femaleness to the chromosomal sex, gonadal sex, hormonal sex, internal accessory reproductive organs, or external genital morphology. Sex assignment and rearing are the crucial variables to the determination of gender role and orientation. Gender imprinting has begun by the first birthday, and the "critical period" is reached by about 18 months. By the age of 2½, gender role is already established in normal children. However, attitudes in the parents and certain specific external stresses may contribute to deviant sexual identity problems, such as transvestism (Stoller, 1967). The meaning of maleness and femaleness does not reach full maturity until after adolescence.

SENSE OF SELF

Literally standing on his or her own two feet, the child delineates "I" and "you" and increasingly expresses a sense of individuality and autonomy. The process by which the child achieves a sense of individuality and autonomy is not well understood. Mahler (1967) has attempted to delineate a series of phases during the first three years of life, starting with a "normal autistic phase" during the first two months of life. In the second month, a normal, undifferentiated "symbiotic phase" begins. It is a phase "in which the infant behaves as though he and his mother were an omnipotent system—a dual unit within one common boundary." This phase is said to reach its height at about 4 to 5 months of age. At about 9 months of age and onward, what Mahler calls the separation-individuation process takes place. This process consists essentially of the child's achievement of separate functioning in the presence and emotional availability of the mother. At about 18 months of age, the child appears to be at the peak of belief in his or her own magic omnipotence. During the second 18 months of life, individuation proceeds, culminating in the attainment of stable object constancy and a sense of autonomy. This model has yet to receive substantial empirical support.

OBJECT CONSTANCY

The term object constancy as used here is a psychoanalytic concept formulated by Hartmann (1952). It denotes the infant's ability to maintain constant relations with a person ("object") regardless of the state of need in the infant. In this sense, object constancy is different from what Piaget calls object permanence, which connotes the infant's ability to respond to items in the environment as if they possessed some permanence, a development that occurs perhaps around 5 or 6 months of age. A prerequisite for the development of object constancy is a lessening in the strength of the infant's needs or a greater control of those needs, which will enable the infant to retain a relationship with a person instead of shifting immediately to another person in search of immediate gratification (A. Freud, 1957). Anna Freud has noted that the very young infant is so dominated by his or her needs (the domination of the pleasure principle) that the infant cannot maintain an attachment to a nonsatisfying object for more than a given period. (The period may vary from several hours to several days.) Separation of the infant from the love object causes extreme distress to the infant from about 5 months to 2 years of age. As the child matures, however, and as the pleasure principle gives way to the reality principle, the child gradually develops the ability to retain attachments to and investments in the absent love object during separations of increasing length.

SENSE OF AUTONOMY

At this age the child also increasingly experiences a sense of individuality and self-control that leads to a feeling of achievement and pride and, in contrast, to a sense of shame and self-doubt when he or she has an "accident" and loses control (Erikson, 1959). Erikson has said also that it is necessary to "be firm and tolerant" with the child at this stage in order for the child to be firm and tolerant with himself or herself. "He will [then] feel pride in being an autonomous person; he will grant autonomy to others; and now and again he will even let himself get away with something." The wisdom of this advice is derived from experience, if not from scientific research.

COGNITIVE DEVELOPMENT

As long as the child feels that his or her thoughts are omnipotent, the child will also believe that others are omnipotent. Fraiberg (1959) described a 2-year-old girl who, on seeing the sun disappear in a spectacular sunset, turned to her father and said, "Do it again, Daddy!" However, by the end of the second year some symbolic representation also emerges. The child can now use "mental" trial and error instead of "action" trial and error. The child looks now for external causes of movements, and the child of course quite clearly distinguishes between the child and an object. Piaget has called this whole first period of cognitive functioning, which lasts until about 2 years of age, the sensorimotor stage, and he describes the infant's state during these first two years as egocentric. Egocentrism is used here not in the common sense, but to mean that initially the boundaries between objects and self are not differentiated; the child has little or no self-perception, and does not at first see his or her place in relation to the universe, which at that time does not exist for the child (Piaget, 1954) Piaget uses the term egocentric then in a purely epistemologic sense, without any affective or moral connotation. The child is egocentric to the extent that the child considers her or her own point of view as the only possible one. Indeed, the child who is egocentric is unaware that the other person has a point of view at all, and for this reason he or she is incapable of putting himself in someone else's place. A young child, for example, may make up a word and assume that everyone knows exactly what he or she means by that word. The child cannot conceive that the other person does not understand what that word means. (Egocentrism will be discussed again in reference to adolescence.)

Gradually the infant moves into a symbolic, preconceptual stage, so that by 3 years of age the child shows evidence of attempts at verbal reasoning, as well as symbolic activity in make-believe play. However, the child still tends to endow inanimate objects (e.g., thunderstorms, clouds, and the moon) with feeling (animism) (Piaget, 1929), and the child cannot yet understand the meaning of "I promise."

Toward the end of the sensorimotor stage, and as the child moves into the symbolic, preconceptual stage, problems can be solved by inventiveness. For example, the child can now rotate a stick through a 90-degree angle to bring it through the bars of the crib, and he or she can use one toy as an instrument to get another.

DEVELOPMENTAL TASKS

Some time between 1½ and 3 years of age it becomes clear that a child is tackling several developmental tasks. He or she is, first of all, achieving greater physical independence. The maturation of the neuromuscular system is central to a feeling of self-worth. The child has made a shift from a passive position to an active position. Furthermore, the child can now think better, using a language with symbols and concepts. Whereas the child earlier used the few words he or she had for the direct discharge of feelings (primary process), the child now uses language more independently, for what Hartmann (1939) has called the conflict-free ego sphere of functions and activities (secondary process). Along with this development, definite attitudes toward people are formed, especially toward those who set limits. It is toward such persons that the child behaves in a negativistic manner. Thus he or she often says, "I don't want to" and "No!" when a parent makes a request or sets a limit. It is as though the child is once more defining his or her autonomy through oppositional behavior. However, in some instances the behavior may be a manifestation of anxiety as the child struggles against a regressive pull. In other instances the behavior may be a direct discharge of aggression against the parent, especially if the mother-child relationship is an ambivalent one.

TOILET TRAINING

When the adaptive tasks and developmental achievements of the child between 1 and 3 years of age are considered, it becomes clear that while the child is adapting to his or her environment the environment is changing its attitudes and expectations of the child. Questions of discipline arise, particularly in regard to the child's aggressive behavior. Conflicts between parents and child are now more apparent. Toilet training may become one of the many possible sources of conflicts at this time. There are three requirements for toilet training: First, a child must be physiologically capable of controlling the anal or urethral sphincter. The age at which this control is achieved is different from child to child. Bladder control is usually achieved before bowel control which may be reached from 15 months to 2½ years of age. It often coincides with the maturation of the child's skill in walking. Second, the child must be psychologically capable of postponing the urge to urinate or defecate. That is to say, the child must have some capacity to recognize and delay as well as a wish to please the parents. Third, since initially the child usually needs help using the toilet, the child might be told to give a warning signal to an adult who is prepared to assist. Later, of course, the child will be able to go to the bathroom on his or her own. In general, all the parent has to do is wait until the child is ready and then encourage the child in a supportive way.

There are several possible outcomes of the toilet-training process. Children who have a satisfactory relationship with their parents usually have a strong wish to please their parents, to conform to their expectations, and to respond to the pleasure the parents show over the child's progress in toilet training. Sometimes the child identifies with the parents in their own reaction formations, such as disgust of feces. Occasionally, a child conforms out of fear. In such cases there is often an underlying rage and resentment that may be expressed as negativism, refusal to eat, or crying. Lastly, the child may object to the toilet training for a variety of reasons, and he or she may develop encopresis.

DIFFICULTIES IN THE PARENTS

Some of the problems in toilet training arise from the parent. The task of toilet training may awaken unresolved issues for the parent, e.g., around messiness or soiling. A mother may experience anxiety or a strong feeling of disgust when she sees the child freely soil or mess. She may rush the child,

punish the child, or simply frustrate him or her. Sometimes a mother wishes to show off how clean, or precocious, her child is, and will try to master her child's fumbling early attempts. Or she may express hostility toward the child through early forceful training. Occasionally, a mother may simply be ignorant of the requirements for toilet training or may be following a cultural or family pattern.

DIFFICULTIES IN THE CHILD

The child may not understand what the parents want, particularly if they themselves do not know what they want. Even when the parents are clear in their minds, the child may be confused by their behavior—first they praise him or her for the beautiful BM, then they promptly flush it down the toilet. In some cases the child may use bowel training as the issue over which he or she expresses earlier hostility toward the parents. Hostility is sometimes induced specifically in relation to toilet training. The birth of a sibling may occur around the time the child is being toilet trained. The child may then feel a loss of love or an impending loss of love, and express this feeling in a reluctance to be toilet trained, or may be confused about the origins of babies. Occasionally, actual separation and real loss may cause a relapse. An important factor is the child's ability to give up a pleasure for the sake of a greater social gain. Sometimes, too, a child is unwilling or unready to take this next step in development.

ENCOPRESIS

By 4 years of age, almost all children have achieved bowel control (Quay and Werry, 1972), although in one study of 10- to 12-year-olds, 1.3% of boys and 0.3% of girls still soiled once a month (Rutter et al., 1970). By 16 years of age the number of children with encopresis is virtually zero (Bellman, 1966). When soiling occurs after the age at which control is usually acquired, the child may not have acquired control for a variety of reasons, including poor training, a neurologic disorder, or mental retardation. The child who has achieved bowel control may temporarily relapse because of anxiety or rage from such causes as the birth of a sibling, parental discord, punitive child-rearing practices, illness, or hospitalization. When soiling occurs in association with a gastrointestinal disorder, the stools are often abnormal. Anthony (1957) has described three types of soiling: (1) continuous soiling, in which the child has never experienced control, (2) discontinuous soiling, in which there was a period of control prior to the episode of soiling, and (3) retentive soiling, in which the child stubbornly retains the stool and occasionally soils after a period of constipation. Other etiologic factors are a family history of soiling (which suggests a genetic factor) and a painful predisposing condition, such as an anal fissure. Thus the symptom of fecal soiling may have many causes, and it requires a careful diagnostic evaluation.

The following case example of fecal soiling may now be considered as a paradigm in the context of the developmental stage we are discussing. It should be remembered that the case is a single one, with its own peculiar characteristics, and that like all clinical cases, it is not a case purely of encopresis.

Mrs. D., a high-school graduate who had been married for 14 years, was a depressed, ineffective, and somewhat confused woman. Her depression had worsened considerably at the time of her mother's illness and subsequent death, which occurred when Harvey, her middle child, was in his first year of life. Mrs. D. had never been able to cope well. A visiting nurse once described Mrs. D's home as sparsely furnished and poorly kept. Mrs. D was unable to discipline her children, and the nurse noted at the time of her visit that both Harvey (by that time aged 5) and his younger sister Esther, were noticeably understimulated. Mrs. D. rarely interacted in a loving way with her children, and she seemed at times to be uninvolved. None of her children seemed at all eager to obey or please her; indeed, at times it looked as though her son Harvey wished to tease and provoke her.

Mr. and Mrs. D. communicated very little with each other. Mr. D. held two jobs, and he did not offer Mrs. D. much help in the rearing of the children.

When Harvey was 2 years of age, it was noted that he was constipated. He was often given suppositories. At the age of 2 years and 5 months, Harvey was hospitalized for a tonsillectomy and adenoidectomy. At this time, Harvey was still constipated; he strained at stool, holding himself rigid and soiling and screaming. He would not sit on the toilet; instead he stood up, stiffened and grew red in the face in an effort to hold back the feces. When he was 2½, his sister was born. Mrs. D. was depressed at the time and could not prepare him for the birth; Harvey reacted to it with intense jealousy and rage. At the age 4, Harvey was still constipated and his parents were now concerned that he might be retarded because his behavior was uncontrolled and babyish, and his speech was infantile and unclear. He also clung a great deal to his mother in a demanding, almost torturing, way.

When given psychologic tests, Harvey was shy and did not participate actively. He was shown to have an IQ of 83, with very poor performance on verbal items. There was no sign of organicity.

This case illustrates, among other things, the impact on the child of a depression in the mother. Mrs. D. was unable to provide the protective and facilitating function needed for the optimum development of her child. Thus Harvey was exposed to his mother's withdrawal, repeated enemas, a tonsillectomy, the birth of a sibling (for which he was poorly prepared), and repeated medical work-ups, including barium enemas, all before he was 5 years of age. Furthermore, each of these stresses (the repeated enemas, the tonsillectomy, the birth of a sibling, and so on) has a potential for trauma in its own right. Finally, it should be said that this case, like every other case, was not pure and simple. Harvey's father ran a diaper service, and he used the ready availability of clean diapers as an excuse to avoid confronting his son or his wife about Harvey's encopresis.

SEPARATION

Several types of external stress may influence the course of development at this stage. Among these stresses is separation, to which reference was made in regard to toilet training. Other effects of separation are examined in the present discussion. Separation from parents during early childhood is not a simple phenomenon (Yarrow, 1964; Rutter, 1976).

However, some general observations that have clinical significance can be made. During the first six months of life, if substitute mothering is provided, the child may experience little more upset over separation than would be expected from the change in routine that separation brings. However, from 6 months to about 4 years of age, after the child has formed a significant attachment to the mother, more serious reactions to separation occur. Indeed, the stronger the love tie, the greater the anxiety that separation produces. Other factors that influence the reaction to separation are the degree and duration of the separation, the way in which the separation is handled, the child's previous experiences of separation, the presence of other stresses (e.g., illness, pain, or the birth of a sibling), the child's innate individual tolerance, and subsequent experiences that may reinforce or mitigate the initial trauma.

Separation during these early years is usually accompanied by a short but significant period of grief (Freud and Burlingham, 1943; see Note 30). The child seems to experience the mother's absence as a confirmation of his or her negative wishes, or as a punishment for them, or even as a consequence of them. The child may feel guilty, and sometimes tries briefly to be extra good. The child also tries to deal with his or her feelings and fantasies through play, and at times his or her behavior regresses and symptoms appear. If the separation is prolonged and is more or less complete and if a substitute mother is not provided, the child may, after a "stage of protest" (Bowlby, 1961), sink into a state of despair and eventually become and remain depressed. The effects of separation can be mitigated by careful planning and anticipation for the child and by the availability of other important attachment figures, e.g., the father or other familiar adults.

SEPARATION AND REACTION TO HOSPITALIZATION

Separations are, of course, sometimes inevitable, as when a child has to go into the hospital. The reaction to separation during hospitalization is difficult to assess (Vernon et al., 1965; Rutter, 1972). The stress of physical illness is itself a major factor (it will be discussed in more detail in Chapter 20). Even in the well child, however, the hospital setting, with its unfamiliarity and the threat to bodily integrity that medical and surgical procedures pose, produces a reaction, particularly in relation to certain phase-specific anxieties (e.g., castration anxiety). The intensity of this reaction may be magnified when there is also a separation, particularly in the young child. Children between 7 and 12 months of age who have been hospitalized for less than 2 weeks show marked anxiety toward strangers, desperate clinging to their mothers, and loud crying when their mothers leave (Schaffer and Callender, 1959). Children 2 to 3 years of age show fear and anger at the time of their parents' departure, are acutely anxious with strangers, and manifest (1) depressive behavior (e.g., crying and withdrawal from people), (2) restlessness, hyperactivity, and rhythmic rocking, (3) regressive behavior (e.g., soiling and a refusal to chew solid food), and (4) physical disturbances (e.g., diarrhea and vomiting) (Prugh et al., 1953; see Note 35). Follow-up studies of children who had been hospitalized have shown that long-term effects are frequently seen, particularly the recurrent fear that their parents will leave them. Quinton and Rutter (1976) found, on the other hand, that single separation experiences at any age during childhood rarely have long-term consequences. Repeated hospitalization is associated with later psychiatric disorder, but the association is most marked in children who come from disadvantaged homes.

Separation may sometimes promote development. Lewis (1954) noted that children exposed to hostile mothers gained if they were placed in the care of sensitive substitute mothers (ordinarily the hostile mother would first be helped to resolve her destructive tendencies). Langford (1948) observed that many sick children in the hospital develop "constructive compensations" and come out more mature than they were before they were sick. This constructive growth experience was more likely to occur if the parent-child relationship was healthy and if the illness was handled well by parents, nurses, and physicians. A particular way in which a parent can help a child experience hospitalization as a constructive experience has been beautifully described by Robertson (1956). Further recent studies have confirmed the possibility that in older children hospitalization can have some positive effects (Solnit, 1960).

Many of the adverse reactions just described may be mitigated by specific measures (Wolff, 1973; Rutter, 1975). Having a parent room in, particularly for children under the age of 4, avoids, of course, any separation at all. Adequate preparation that offers the child explanations and opportunities for expressive play is helpful (Plank et al., 1959). Preadmission hospital visits by the child to become acquainted with the ward and the nurse and the elimination of unnecessary admission routines are also useful. The child is also comforted if he or she can bring along something familiar from home, and if the daily routines (e.g., for bathing, feeding, elimination, and sleeping) approximate as far as possible those to which the child is accustomed. If the mother cannot live in, frequent visits during which she actively participates in her child's care often allay the child's anxiety. The assignment to one nurse of the responsibility for the major care and attention to the child often reassures and comforts the child.

SEPARATION AND MATERNAL DEPRESSION

Psychologic separation may occur without the actual physical separation that occurs when a child enters the hospital. For example, a sense of separation and loss may be brought about in the child when the mother withdraws during a state of mourning and grief following a loss she has experienced, such as the loss of her husband through separation, divorce, illness, or death. Normally

the mother recovers from her grief, finds a new love object, and then reinvests her child with her maternal care. Less commonly, she attempts to substitute a child for her lost husband, with disastrous results for the child.

However, if the mother's grief continues as a state of depression, the child may be forced to deal with this state. Many children at this stage in their development cannot deal well with the loss that they feel. Instead, a child may initially deny the feelings and then deal with them on a "piecemeal" basis as he or she is faced with future developmental tasks that require the active presence of a mother. The adequacy with which a child deals with psychologic loss at this stage depends on such factors as (1) his or her developmental state, (2) the relationship that he or she had had with the "lost" mother, (3) the degree of loss (the death of the mother is the most severe degree), and (4) the support available from the environment.

If the mother's depression is chronic, a characteristic phenomenon may occur. The child may attempt to deal with the loss through identification with his or her concept of the depressed mother. The child, so to speak, internalizes impressions of what he or she considers to be certain aspects and attributes of the mother. The identification may form the basis of a true depression, in which the child feels a sense of blame and emptiness and at the same time experiences feelings of guilt and anxiety. The guilt and anxiety are thought to arise as reactions against rage and aggression, which are believed to have been turned inward against the hypothesized "introjected" mother. The child may attempt to ward off such feelings by increased motor activity and self-punishing behavior. Occasionally, the child exhibits a pseudodepression as he or she identifies with the outer characteristics of the depressed mother but does not internalize the aggression.

In any event, the young child appears not to mourn adequately, in part because his or her need for a full, loving relationship is vital at this stage and the interruption of continuity of affection and care, even though partial, may be too great an obstacle to overcome. Anna Freud (1965) has noted that "in the young child the capacity for outgoing love is still bound up inextricably with the reliable presence of the person who has been instrumental in calling forth this emotion and in interchange with whom it has developed." If the continuity of care and affection is broken, damage is "done to the personality by the loss of function and destruction of capacities which follow invariably on the emotional upheavals brought about by separation from, death or disappearances of the child's first love-objects."

Tolerance of the break in continuity and the consequent deprivation is low at this age, and a substitute mother is not usually available for, say, a mother who is mourning. This kind of experience of loss may permanently color the child's future love relationships.

CRUCIAL DEVELOPMENTAL TASKS

Perhaps the crux of this period of development is the child's move toward greater separation, independence, and autonomy at a time when he or she is capable of being demanding, intrusive, and negativistic. The extent to which the child successfully emerges from this stage depends on many factors, not the least of which are, on the one hand, the child's state of preparedness for the specific tasks just mentioned and, on the other hand, the degree to which the parents facilitate or hinder the child's progress.

PERVASIVE DEVELOPMENTAL DISORDER

Children with autism or other pervasive developmental disorders exhibit significant disruptions in the development of the crucial tasks of infancy. Parents of such children first become seriously concerned about their development as speech is either delayed or absent. However, a careful history typically reveals earlier delays in social and communicative development. For example, the autistic child usually has had little, if any, in-

terest in social interaction and failed to develop differential attachment to parents. These delays stand in marked contrast to the development of normal children who exhibit a profound interest in the social environment from the first days and weeks of life. Although early attempts were made to account for the syndrome of autism on the basis of deviant caretaking, it is now clear that it is the child (rather than the parents) who is disordered (see Chapter 28).

Apart from their obvious clinical importance, autism and related disorders are of interest for several reasons. Firstly, these disorders illustrate the importance of social factors in development (Cairns, 1979); the lack of the usual social motivational factors appears to have devastating consequences for the development of later communicative and cognitive skills. Secondly, these disorders illustrate the importance of viewing the infant as a partner in the parent-child dyad. Early notions of the pathogenesis of autism emphasized the role of parents in producing the syndrome; these notions rested on the observation that parent-child interaction was deviant in such cases. However, these views failed to consider the possibility that the deviance might arise from the child rather than from the parents. Finally, autism and related disorders are of particular importance to the extent to which they help clarify the biologic foundations of early human development.

NARCISSISTIC CHARACTER DISORDER

Some psychoanalysts believe that adults who suffer from a narcissistic character disorder had difficulty with this stage of separation-individuation.

According to one view (Kohut, 1971, 1980), the patient has a disorder inolving his or her sense of self, which arises during the separation-individuation phase (especially the so-called rapprochement phase) of development, when he or she received inadequate responses from the parents. This disorder is perpetuated either (1) as a draining, persistent, regressive need to seek a kind of accepting, affirming mirror of the child's sense of omnipotence or grandiosity, or (2) as a tendency to overidealize and merge with another person and thereby to overcome feelings of worthlessness or helplessness.

In either event, such a patient can tolerate neiher his or her own defects nor the less-than-ideal nature of others. The patient requires perfection in others and is easily overwhelmed and often chronically enraged—a rage that may be projected in the course of a projective identification. He or she may turn to drugs or other types of self-stimulating activities. Recurrent bouts of depression, low self-esteem, and preoccupation with bodily functions are common, and separations are difficult.

In another view (Kernberg, 1975), the patient has a grandiose image of self, again arising during the separation-individuation phase, but as a defense against early splitting of rage and envy directed toward internalized object representations. This may persist as a constant tendency toward splitting, seen often as rapid shifts between overidealization and devaluation of the object.

These hypotheses remain to be validated. To a considerable extent, these concepts are derived from work with adults that aims at reconstructing aspects of early childhood, for example, by recovering early childhood memories. It is unclear to what extent such reconstructions accurately recapture actual memories or events or subsequent versions of events.

ACCIDENTAL POISONING IN CHILDREN

A prototypical syndrome resulting from a failure of synchronization and mutual development between mother and child is so-called accidental poisoning in children. The poisoning act in early childhood can be viewed as the result of an interaction between certain developmental characteristics of the child and certain qualities of the mothering person. For example, in one study (Lewis et al., 1966), it was clear that in children under 18 months of age, their increased maturational ability for motor exploratory behavior was uncurtailed and uncontrolled, giving the impression of a heightened level of motor activity. At the same time, a state of depletion existed in the mothers, who were unable to cope without the support they had expected from their husbands or their mothers.

In that same study, in children between approximately 18 and 30 months of age, the developmental characteristic of negativism in the child was an important factor. The negativism seemed heightened in the child, perhaps because of frustration and the relative deprivation he or she endured while in the care of the depleted mother. The child's now heightened negativism seemed to combine with the apparent increase in motor activity that followed from poor internalization of controls to produce a situation in which the child could now deliberately do what he or she knew was not allowed, namely, swallow a forbidden substance. It was as though the child's wish and capacity to defy the mother were now greater than his or her wish to please her. Furthermore, there was in these children little incentive to delay the impulsive urge to imbibe the forbidden substance. Another interesting trait of this group of children was the developmental characteristics of imitation, which often expressed itself in the imitation of an older sibling. In some of these children, the increased motor activity also seemed to serve an adaptive purpose in that through such motor activity the child was attempting to ward off a depression that resulted from the maternal deprivation.

Children over about 30 months of age seemed to ingest poison more specifically as a reaction to loss. The poisoning act may have had the symbolic meaning of replenishment in response to the feeling of loss.

A 43-month-old girl ingested an antibacterial powder that was used for washing the diapers of her 9-month-old sister. This powder was unattractive visually, texturally, and to taste. In order to get her sister's special powder, the girl had to climb, open a cupboard door, and unscrew a cap.

The home was well organized, and the family was apparently functioning well. The parents seemed to be clear and consistent about teaching the child what was safe and what was dangerous, what was acceptable and unacceptable, and what the boundaries were in regard to safety in motility and behavior. Investigation revealed that a crucial factor in the poisoning act was the mother's reaction to her own mother's moving out of the home in order to take a job and to establish a life of her own. This loss, in addition to the birth of a second child, had depleted the mother's ability to give loving attention to the older child. The father, incidentally, was not used to helping; he had regularly retired to his hobby room after supper, leaving his mother-in-law to help his wife. The child reacted with increased negativism and what appeared to be a fierce determination to get what her infant sister had received.

In many of these children, a sense of loss appeared to be felt when their mother's capacity to love and attend to them diminished, perhaps because of illness, separation, or the birth of another child. The mother's state of depletion also interfered with his capacity to provide a safe environment for the child.

Another possible consequence of a weakened love tie is that the child has less incentive to control his or her body as well as impulses. Clinically, this consequence may express itself through such symptoms as bedwetting and fecal soiling, as an impairment in the child's capacity to play with other children, or as a tendency toward destructive behavior.

PERENNIAL DEVELOPMENTAL TASKS, ENVIRONMENTAL STRESSES, AND INDIVIDUAL CHARACTERISTICS

Throughout development the individual is probably reworking certain major perennial tasks. Outstanding among these tasks are learning to control his body and his impulses, achieving a sense of self, and evolving and resolving his or her feelings toward family and others. Furthermore, the vicissitudes of life are such that there is no shortage of events that serve to sharpen and shape the conflicts involved in each of these and many other de-

velopmental tasks. Separation and loss, particularly separation and loss during ages 1 to 3, are perhaps the most poignant events (they have already been discussed). However, it sometimes happens that a particular characteristic of the child placed him or her in the position of experiencing a seemingly normal environment as one that is adverse, and the child's development and resolution of any of the perennial tasks just mentioned suffer as a consequence of the vicissitudes that follow. To illustrate this phenomenon, the child who is mentally retarded will be discussed in the following section. (Mental retardation has been chosen for discussion at this developmental stage to underscore the clinical need for early diagnosis.)

THE MENTALLY RETARDED CHILD

Mental retardation is defined by significantly subaverage intellectual functioning with concurrent deficits in adaptive functioning (i.e., in abilities to meet age-expectable demands of daily life). An IQ score of less than 70 (i.e., greater than two standard deviations from the mean of 100) is usually taken as evidence of subaverage intellectual functioning although clinical judgements based on assessment using developmental tests can be used in younger children. Cases of severe and profound retardation are more likely to be recognized in the first years of life while mild retardation may not be diagnosed until school age (see Chapter 27). Given the difficulties intrinsic in the examination of infants and young children and the marked changes in thinking during the first years of life, it is not surprising that tests of infant "intelligence" are only very modestly related to subsequent IQ (Volkmar, 1989). It is also the case that observed "IQ" can change when social conditions change. In a classic study conducted at a time when most psychologists believed that the IQ was a measurable and "fixed" characteristic, Skeels and Dye (1939) demonstrated significant effects of environment on IQ. They transferred 13 apparently retarded children from their orphanage to become "house guests" at a state institution for the retarded. In the institution for the retarded they received considerable play and stimulation so that when they were reassessed every child had made IQ gains. These children were subsequently put up for adoption and grew up to become self-supporting, middle-class adults. A control group of 12 children the same age and with, originally, a higher mean IQ were left in the orphanage in which they received little individual attention; all but one of these children showed a decrease in IQ. At adult follow-up (Skeels, 1966), five of these individuals were in institutions, one had died, and five of the remaining six held unskilled jobs. This study dramatically demonstrates the impact of environment on intelligence.

Many conditions are associated with mental retardation (Masland et al., 1958; Bavin, 1968). Yannet (1956), for example, reported that mental retardation was an important symptom in more than 100 syndromes. Among the many causes is a genetic endowment that places the individual at the lower part of the normal distribution curve for intelligence (Penrose, 1963). Such a child is said to have "familial retardation." This group of children under the age of 18 years living in the United States comprises about 2,000,000 persons, of whom 65% are males, 35% females. The sex difference may be partly explained by the more difficult social role assigned to males, and by the lower tolerance for deviance that exists for males. It may also involve a genetic factor. The majority (75%) of mentally retarded people are normal in appearance, and the majority (75%) can do almost anything that does not require abstract thinking. The vast majority (80%) have no identifiable disorder, and they fall within the school-age range. The causes of the retardation in this group include parent-child interaction problems, physical trauma, psychosocial adversity, and genetic factors.

What particularly sets many mentally retarded children apart is not some postulated inherent defect or even their limited intellect, but rather the unfortunate socialization process they undergo in the course of their development. Even their low score on an intelligence test is a result of many factors, and perhaps the most important of these factors is, again, the child's social adjustment (Heber, 1962).

Both intellective and nonintellective factors play a role in the wide range of final socialization patterns achieved by retarded children. Among the nonintellective factors, personality and motivational and environmental factors seem to be the most significant ones (Zigler and Harter, 1969). For example, the retarded child may continuously experience failure, which may lead to his or her performing more poorly than if the child had had a number of successful experiences. The child performs poorly partly because he or she comes to distrust his or her own solutions to problems and relies instead on others. The child may also have experienced considerable deprivation in or out of an institution, leading to an exaggerated dependency. Curiously, retarded children in institutions take longer to solve concept-formation problems in a social setting with a warm, supportive experimenter than they do in a setting in which they cannot see the experimenter (Harter, 1967). It seems that the opportunity of meeting a need for warmth and support competes with the child's attention to a task and so leads to a poorer performance.

The child is, of course, especially prey to his parents' attitudes and feelings. Parents of a child who is retarded for no obvious organic cause only slowly, and painfully, become aware of their child's limitations. Every childbirth entails a risk, and the risk of having a child whose potential for what is called intelligence falls at the lower end of the normal distribution curve is a real one. Three types of parental reactions to retardation have been observed (Kanner, 1953). In one type, the parents exhibit a mature reaction in which feelings of loss, defeat, resentment, and guilt are experienced and worked through (Solnit and Stark, 1961). In a second type, the parents recognize but do not accept the defect. Parents in this group often engage in a pursuit of the "culprit." In a third type, the parents completely deny that their child is defective.

Although no amount of improving the social adaptation of the retarded child will transform him or her into an individual with superior or even average intelligence, the difference in intelligence should have nothing to do with the rights of the child as a human being in all dimensions (Zigler and Harter, 1969). Certainly the compounding of a retarded child's difficulties by the failure of society to make a partial adaptation to the child is neither necessary nor morally defensible.

Note 31

From D.W. Winnicot (1951), Transitional objects and transitional phenomena.[1] In: *Collected Papers*. London: Tavistock Publications Ltd., 1958, pp. 229–242.

. . . I have introduced the terms "transitional object" and "transitional phenomena" for designation of the intermediate area of experience, between the thumb and the teddy bear, between the oral erotism and true object relationship, between primary creative activity and projection of what had already been introjected, between primary unawareness of indebtedness and the acknowledgement of indebtedness. . . .

By this definition an infant's babbling or the way an older child goes over a repertoire of songs and tunes while preparing for sleep comes within the intermediate area as transitional phenomena, along with the use made of objects that are not part of the infant's body yet and not fully recognized as belonging to external reality. . . .

. . . there is the third part of the life of a human being, a part that we cannot ignore, an intermediate area of experiencing, to which inner reality and external life both contribute. It is an area which is not challenged, because no claim is made on its behalf except that it shall exist as a resting-place for the individual engaged in the perpetual human task of keeping inner and outer reality separate yet interrelated. . . .

In the case of some infants the thumb is placed in the mouth while fingers are made to caress the face by pronation and supination movements of the forearm. The mouth is then active in relation to the thumb, but not in relation to the fingers. The fingers caressing the upper lip, or some other part, may be or may become more important than the thumb engaging the mouth. Moreover this

caressing activity may be found alone, without the more direct thumb-mouth union. (Freud, 1905, Hoffer, 1949.)

In common experience one of the following occurs, complicating an autoerotic experience such as thumb-sucking:

1. with the other hand the baby takes an external object, say a part of a sheet or blanket, into the mouth along with the fingers; or
2. somehow or other the bit of cloth[2] is held and sucked, or not actually sucked. The objects used naturally include napkins and (later) handkerchiefs, and this depends on what is readily and reliably available; or
3. the baby starts from early months to pluck wool and to collect it and to use it for the caressing part of the activity.[3] Less commonly, the wool is swallowed, even causing trouble; or
4. mouthing, accompanied by sounds of "mum-mum", babbling, anal noises, the first musical notes and so on. . . .

All these things I am calling *transitional phenomena*. Also, out of all this (if we study any one infant) there may emerge some thing or some phenomenon—perhaps a bundle of wool or the corner of a blanket or eiderdown, or a word or tune, or a mannerism, which becomes vitally important to the infant for use at the time of going to sleep, and is a defence against anxiety, especially anxiety of depressive types. (Illingworth, 1951). Perhaps some soft object or cot cover has been found and used by the infant, and this then becomes what I am calling a *transitional object*. This object goes on being important. The parents get to know its value and carry it round when travelling. The mother lets it get dirty and even smelly, knowing that by washing it she introduces a break in continuity in the infant's experience, a break that may destroy the meaning and value of the object to the infant.

I suggest that the patterns of transitional phenomena begins to show at about 4-6-8-12 months. Purposely I leave room for wide variations.

Patterns set in infancy may persist into childhood, so that the original soft object continues to be absolutely necessary at bed-time or at time of loneliness or when a depressed mood threatens. In health, however, there is a gradual extension of range of interest, eventually the extended range is maintained, even when depressive anxiety is

---

1. Based on a paper read before the British Psycho-Analytical Society on 30th May, 1951. *Int. J. Psycho-Anal.*, Vol. XXXIV, 1953.

2. A recent example is the blanket-doll of the child in the film A Two-Year-Old Goes to Hospital by James Robertson (Tavistock Clinic. cf. also Robertson et al., 1952).

3. Here there could possibly be an explanation for the use of the term "wool-gathering", which means: inhibiting the transitional or intermediate area.

near. A need for a specific object or a behavior pattern that started at a very early date may reappear at a later age when deprivation threatens.

This first possession is used in conjunction with special techniques derived from very early infancy, which can include or exist apart from the more direct autoerotic activities. Gradually in the life of an infant teddies and dolls and hard toys are acquired. Boys to some extent tend to go over to use hard objects, whereas girls tend to proceed right ahead to the acquisition of a family. It is important to note, however, that *there is no noticeable difference between boy and girl in their use of the original Not-Me possession*, which I am calling the transitional object.

As the infant starts to use organized sounds (mum, ta, da) there may appear a "word" for the transitional object. The name given by the infant to these earliest objects is often significant, and it usually has a word used by the adults partly incorporated in it. For instance, "baa" may be the name, and the "b" may have come from the adult's use of the word "baby" or "bear". . . .

It is true that the piece of blanket (or whatever it is) is symbolical of some part-object, such as the breast. Nevertheless the point of it is not its symbolic value so much as its actuality. Its not being the breast (or the mother) is as important as the fact that it stands for the breast (or mother).

When symbolism is employed the infant is already clearly distinguishing between fantasy and fact, between inner objects and external objects, between primary creativity and perception. But the term transitional object, according to my suggestion, gives room for the process of becoming able to accept difference and similarity. I think there is use for a term for the root of symbolism in time, a term that describes the infant's journey from the purely subjective to objectivity; and it seems to me that the transitional object (piece of blanket, etc.) is what we see of this journey of progress towards experiencing. . . .

There are certain comments that can be made on the basis of accepted psychoanalytic theory.

1. The transitional object stands for the breast, or the object of the first relationship.
2. The transitional object antedates established reality-testing.
3. In relation to the transitional object the infant passes from (magical) omnipotent control to control by manipulation (involving muscle erotism and coordination pleasure).
4. The transitional object may eventually develop into a fetish object and so persist as a characteristic of the adult sexual life. (See Wulff's development of the theme.)
5. The transitional object may, because of anal-erotic organization, stand for faeces (but it

is not for this reason that it may become smelly and remain unwashed. . .)

The mother, at the beginning, by an almost 100 per cent adaptation affords the infant the opportunity or the *illusion* that her breast is part of the infant. It is, as it were, under magical control. The same can be said in terms of infant care in general, in the quiet times between excitements. Omnipotence is nearly a fact of experience. The mother's eventual task is gradually to disillusion the infant, but she has no hope of success unless at first she has been able to give sufficient opportunity for illusion. . . .

. . . The transitional phenomena represent the early stages of the use of illusion, without which there is no meaning for the human being in the idea of a relationship with an object that is perceived by others as external to that being.

The idea illustrated in Figure A is this: that at some theoretical point early in the development of every human individual an infant in a certain setting provided by the mother is capable of conceiving of the idea of something which would meet the growing need which arises out of instinctual tension. The infant cannot be said to know at first what is to be created. At this point in time the mother presents herself. In the ordinary way she gives her breast and her potential feeding urge. The mother's adaptation to the infant's needs, when good enough, gives the infant the *illusion* that there is an external reality that corresponds to the infant's own capacity to create. In other words, there is an overlap between what the mother supplies and what the child might conceive of. To the observer the child perceives what the mother actually presents, but this is not the whole truth. The infant perceives the breast only in so far as a breast could be created just there and then. There is no interchange between the mother and the infant. Psychologically the infant takes from a breast that is part of the infant, and the mother gives milk to an infant that is part of herself. In psychology, the idea of interchange is based on an illusion.

In Figure B a shape is given to the area of illusion, to illustrate what I consider to be the main function of the transitional object and of transitional phenomena. The transitional object and the transitional phenomena start each human being off with what will always be important for them, i.e., a neutral area of experience which will not be challenged.

. . . It is assumed here that the task of reality-acceptance is never completed, that no human being is free from the strain of relating inner and outer reality, and that relief from this strain is provided by an intermediate area of experience which is not challenged (arts, religion, etc.). (cf.

A   B

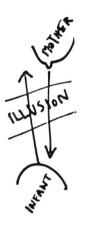

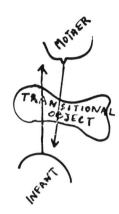

Riviere, 1936). This immediate area is in direct continuity with the play area of the small child who is "lost" in play.

In infancy this intermediate area is necessary for the initiation of a relationship between the child and the world, and is made possible by good enough mothering at the early critical phase. Essential to all this is continuity (in time) of the external emotional environment and of particular elements in the physical environment such as the transitional object or objects.

The transitional phenomena are allowable to the infant because of the parents' intuitive recognition of the strain inherent in objective perception, and we do not challenge the infant in regard to subjectivity or objectivity just here where there is the transitional object. . . .

. . . I do consider that transitional phenomena are healthy and universal.

1. Freud, Sigmund (1905). "Three Essays on the Theory of Sexuality.' Complete Psychological Works of Sigmund Freud. Vol. VII. London: Hogarth Press.
2. Hoffer, W. (1949). 'Mouth, Hand, and Ego-Integration.' *Psychoanal. Study Child*, Vol. III-IV. London: Imago.
3. Illingworth, R.S. (1951). 'Sleep Disturbances in Young Children.' *Br. Med. J.*
4. Riviere, J. (1936). 'On the Genesis of Physical Conflict in Earliest Infancy.' *Int. J. Psycho-Anal.*, Vol. XVII.
5. Robertson, J., Bowlby, J. and Rosenblith, Dina (1952). 'A Two-Year-Old Goes to Hospital.' *Psychoanal. Study Child*, Vol. VII. London: Imago.
6. Wulff, M. (1946). 'Fetishism and Object Choice in Early Childhood.' *Psychoanal. Quart.*, Vol. XV.

Note 32

From A. Freud and D. Burlingham (1942), *War and Children*. New York: International Universities Press, 1943.

Reactions to parting . . . (during the phase from about 6 months to 2 years of age) . . . are particularly violent. The child feels suddenly deserted by all the known persons in its world to whom it has learned to attach importance. Its new ability to love finds itself deprived of the accustomed objects, and its greed for affection remains unsatisfied. Its longing for its mother becomes intolerable and throws it into states of despair which are very similar to the despair and distress shown by babies who are hungry and whose food does not appear at the accustomed time. For several hours, the "hunger" for its mother, may over-ride all bodily sensations.

There are some children of this age who will refuse to eat or sleep. Very many of them will refuse to be handled or comforted by strangers. The children cling to some object or to some form of expression which means to them, at that moment, memory of the material presence of the mother. Some will cling to a toy which the mother has put into their hands at the moment of parting; others to some item of bedding or clothing which they have brought from home.

Some will monotonously repeat the word by which they are used to call their mothers, as for instance, Christine, seventeen months old, who said: "mum, mum, mum, mum, mum,". . . .

She repeated it continually in a deep voice for at least three days.

Observers seldom appreciate the depth and seriousness of this grief in a small child. Their judgment of it is misled for one main reason. This childish grief is short-lived. Mourning of equal intensity in an adult person would have to run its course throughout a year; the same process in the child between one and two years will normally be over in thirty-six to forty-eight hours. The difference in duration is due to certain psychological differences between the state of childhood and adultness. . . .

. . . A love object who does not give it immediate satisfaction is no good to it. Its memories of the past are spoilt by the disappointment which it feels at the present moment. It has no outlook into the future and it would be of no help to it if it had. Its needs are so urgent that they need immediate gratification; promises of pleasure are no help.

The little child will therefore, after a short while, turn away from the mother image in its mind and, though at first unwillingly, will accept the comfort which is offered. In some cases acceptance may come in slow stages. Christine, for instance, would at first only let herself be fondled or held by an unseen person. She would sit on somebody's lap, turn her head away, enjoy the familiar sensation of being held, and probably add to it in her own mind the imaginary picture of her own mother. Whenever she looked at the face of the person who held her she began to cry.

There are other children who are spared these violent reactions. They seem placid, dazed, and more or less indifferent. It takes a few days or even a week before this placidity is disturbed by a realisation of the fact that they are among strangers: all sorts of slighter depressive reactions and problems of behavior will then result. All children of this age, those with violent reactions as well as those where reaction is delayed, will show a tendency to fall ill under the new conditions; they will develop colds, sore throats, or slight intestinal troubles.

That the shock of parting at this stage is really serious is further proven by the observation that a number of these children fail to recognise their mothers when they are visited after they have "settled down" in their new surroundings. The mothers themselves realise that this lack of recognition is not due to any limitations of the faculty of memory as such. The same child who looks at its mother's face with stony indifference as if she were a complete stranger, will have no difficulty in recognising lifeless objects which have belonged to its past. When taken home again it will recognise the rooms, the position of the beds and will remember the contents of cupboards, etc.

. . . The mother has disappointed the child and left its longing for her unsatisfied; so it turns against her with resentment and rejects the memory of her person from its consciousness.

REFERENCES

Anthony, E.J. (1957), An experimental approach to the psychopathology of childhood: Encopresis. *Br. J. Med. Psychol.*, 30:146–175.

Bavin, J.T.R. (1968), The genetics of mental deficiency. In: *Foundations of Child Psychiatry*, ed. E. Miller. Oxford: Pergamon Press, pp. 457–488.

Baumrind, D. (1967), Child care practices anteceding three patterns of preschool behavior. *Genet. Psychol. Monogr.* 75:43–88.

Bellman, M. (1966), Studies on encopresis. *Acta Paediatr. Scand.*, (Suppl.) 170.

Bergman, R. (1968), A case of stuttering. *J. Am. Acad. Child Psychiatry*, 7:13–30.

Bowlby, J. (1961), Separation anxiety: A critical review of the literature. *J. Child Psychol. Psychiatry*, 1:251–269.

Cairns, R.B. (1979), *Social Development: The origins and plasticity of interchanges.* San Francisco, Plenum Publishing.

Cohen, J.N., and Clark, J.A. (1984), Transitional object attachments in early childhood and personality characteristics in later life. *J. Pers. Soc. Psych.*, 46:106–111.

Erikson, E.H. (1959), Identity and the life cycle. *Psychol. Issues*, 1 (1):65–74.

Fairbairn, W.R.D. (1952), *An Object-Relations Theory of the Personality.* New York: Basic Books, p. 176.

Fay, W.H., and Butler, B.V. (1971), Echo-reaction as an approach to semantic resolution. *J. Speech Hear. Disord.* 14:645–651.

Frailberg, S.H. (1959), *The Magic Years.* New York: Scribner's, p. 305.

Freud, A. (1957), The mutual influences in the development of ego and id. *Psychoanal. Study Child*, 7:42–50.

Freud, A. (1965), Continuity in theory from practice. In: *The Family and the Law*, ed. J. Goldstein and J. Katz. New York: Free Press, p. 1053.

Freud, A., and Burlingham, D. (1943), *War and Children.* New York: International Universities Press.

Freud, S. (1911), *Formulations on the Two Principles of Mental Functioning.* Standard Edition, 12 (1958). London: The Hogarth Press, pp. 213–226.

Gesell, A., and Amatruda, C.S. (1941), *Developmental Diagnosis.* New York: Paul Hoeber Medical Division, Harper & Row. (2nd Ed. 1964.)

Harter, S. (1967), Mental age, I.Q. and motivational factors in the discrimination learning set performances of normal and retarded children. *J. Exp. Child Psychol.*, 5:123–141.

Hartmann, H. (1939), *Ego Psychology and the Problem of Adaptation*, trans. D. Rapaport, New York: International Universities Press, 1958, p. 8.

Hartmann, H. (1952), The mutual influences in the development of ego and id. *Psychoanal. Study Child*, 7:7–70.

Hartmann, H. (1956), Notes on the reality principle. In: *Essays on Ego Psychology* (1964). New York: International Universities Press, pp. 241–264.

Hartmann, H., Kris, E., and Lowenstein, R.M. (1949), Notes on the theory of aggression. *Psychoanal. Study Child*, 3/4:9–36.

Heber, R.F. (1962), Mental retardation: Concept and

classification. In: *Readings on the Exceptional Child*, ed. P.E. Trapp and P. Himelstein. New York: Appleton-Century-Crofts, pp. 69–81.

Kanner, L. (1953), Parents' feelings about retarded children. *Am. J. Ment. Defic.*, 57:375–383.

Kernberg, O. (1975), *Borderline Conditions and Pathological Narcissism*. New York: Jason Aronson.

Kohut, H. (1971), *The Analysis of the Self*. New York: International Universities Press.

Kohut, H. (1980), Self Psychology: Reflections on the present and future. November 2, 1980, Boston Psychoanalytic Association Symposium on Reflections on Self Psychology.

Langford, W.S. (1948), Physical illness and convalescence: Their meaning to the child. *J. Pediatr.*, 33:242–250.

Lewis, H. (1954), *Deprived Children*. London: Oxford University Press.

Lewis, M., Solnit, A.J., Stark, M.H., Gabrielson, I.W., and Klatskin, E.H. (1966), An exploratory study of accidental ingestion of poisoning in young children. *J. Am. Acad. Child Psychiatry*, 5:255–271.

Maccoby, E.E., and Martin, J. (1983), Socialization in the context of the family: Parent-child interaction. In: *Handbook of Child Psychology*, Vol. 4, ed. E.M. Hetherington. New York: John Wiley & Sons, Inc., pp. 1–101.

Mahler, M.S. (1967), On human symbiosis and the vicissitudes of individualization. *Am. Psychoanal. Assoc.*, 15:710–762.

Masland, R.I., Sarason, S.B., and Gladwin, T. (1958), *Mental Subnormality: Biological, Psychological and Cultural Factors*. New York: Basic Books.

Money, J., Hampson, J.G., and Hampson, J.L. (1955), An examination of some basic sexual concepts: The evidence of human hermaphroditism. *Johns Hopkins Hosp. Bull.*, 97:301–319.

Parten, M.B. (1933), Social play among preschool children. *J. Abnorm. Soc. Psychol.*, 28:136–147.

Penrose, S.L. (1963), *The Biology of Mental Defect*. London: Sidgwick and Jackson.

Piaget, J. (1929), *The Child's Conception of the World*. New York: Harcourt, Brace & World.

Piaget, J. (1954), *The Construction of Reality in the Child*. New York: Basic Books, p. xii.

Plank, E.N., Caughey, P., and Lipson, M.J. (1959), A general hospital childcare program to counteract hospitalism. *Am. J. Orthopsychiatry*, 29:94–101.

Prugh, D.G., Staub, E., Sands, H., Kirshbaum, R., and Lenihan, E. (1953), A study of the emotional reaction of children and families to hospitalization and illness. *Am. J. Orthopsychiatry*, 23:70–106.

Quay, H.C., and Werry, J.S. (1972), *Psychopathological Disorder in Childhood*. New York: John Wiley & Sons.

Quinton, D., and Rutter, M. (1976), Early hospital admissions and later disturbances of behavior: An attempted replication of Douglas' findings. *Dev. Med. Child Neurol.*, 18:447–459.

Robertson, J. (1956), A mother's observations on the tonsillectomy of her four-year-old daughter, with comments by Anna Freud. *Psychoanal. Study Child*, 11:410–433.

Rubin, K.H., Fein, G.G., Vandenberg, B. (1983), Play. In: *Handbook of Child Psychology*. Vol. 4, ed. E.M. Hetherington. New York: John Wiley & Sons, Inc., pp. 693–774.

Rutter, M. (1972), *Maternal Deprivation Revisited*. Harmondsworth: Penguin.

Rutter, M. (1975), *Helping Troubled Children*. Harmondsworth: Penguin.

Rutter, M. (1976), Separation, loss and family relationships. In: *Child Psychiatry*, ed. M. Rutter and L. Hersov. Oxford: Blackwell, pp. 47–73.

Rutter, M., Tizard, J., and Whitmore, K. (eds.) (1970), *Education, Health and Behaviour*. London: Longmans.

Schaffer, H.R., and Callender, W.M. (1959), Psychologic effects of hospitalization in infancy. *Pediatrics*, 24:528–539.

Shaw, G.B. (1903), *Man and Superman*, Act III. New York: Penguin, 1946.

Sherman, M., Hertzig, M., Austrian R., and Shapiro, T. (1981), Treasured objects in shool-aged children. *Pediatrics*, 68:379–386.

Skeels, H.M. (1966), Adult status of children with contrasting early life experiences. *Monogr. Soc. Res. Child Dev.*, 31(3).

Skeels, H.M., and Dye, H.B. (1939), A study of the effects of differential stimulation on mentally retarded children. *Proc. Am. Assoc. Ment. Defic.*, 44:114–136.

Solnit, A.J. (1960), Hospitalization: an aid to physical and psychological health in childhood. *Am. J. Dis. Child.*, 9:153–163.

Solnit, A.J., and Stark, M.H. (1961), Mourning and the birth of a defective child. *Psychoanal. Study Child*, 16:523–537.

Stoller, R.J. (1967), Transvestites' women. *Am. J. Psychiatry*, 124:333–339.

Vernon, D.T.A., Foley, S.M., Sipowicz, R.R., and Schulman, J.L. (1965), *The Psychological Responses of Children to Hospitalization and Illness*. Springfield, Ill.: Charles C Thomas.

Volkmar, F.R. (1989), Infant Assessment. *Sem. Perinatol.*, 13:467–473.

Watts, A.F. (1947), *Language and Mental Development of Children*. London: Harrap.

Winnicott, D.W. (1951), Transitional objects and transitional phenomena. In: *Collected Papers*. London: Tavistock, 1958, pp. 229–242.

Wolff, S. (1973), *Children Under Stress*. Harmondsworth: Penguin.

Yannet, H. (1956), Classification and etiological factors in mental retardation. In: *Mental Retardation: Readings and Resources*, ed. J.H. Rothstein. New York: Holt, Rinehart & Winston, 1961.

Yarrow, L.J. (1964), Separation from parents during early childhood. In: *Review of Child Development Research*, Vol. I. M.L. Hoffman and L.W. Hoffman (Eds.) New York: Russell Sage Foundation.

Zigler, E.F., and Harter, S. (1969), The socialization of the mentally retarded. In: *Handbook of Socialization Theory and Research*, ed. D.A. Goslin. Chicago: Rand McNally.

17

EARLY CHILDHOOD—AGES 3 TO 6

MATURATION

Children become increasingly agile as they grow and develop during the period of early childhood—learning, for example, to skip on alternate feet. Their perceptual-motor skills also improve at this time: a child at 2 years of age can copy a circle, and a child at 3 years of age can copy a cross; by 5 years of age a child can copy a square and by 7 years of age a diamond. Memory and attention improve with age: by 6 years of age the child can count five digits forward and three digits backward. The use of language is, of course, extensive in early childhood and during this period the child learns to dress and to wash himself or herself without assistance.

CHILDHOOD SEXUAL THEORIES

At the same time, fantasy is now much more elaborate, and is influenced by such factors as (1) the child's growing awareness of sexual differences, pregnancy, childbirth, and death, (2) the child's life experiences, and (3) the persisting magical quality of his or her thinking. Children begin to form theories about sex (S. Freud, 1908). For example, the child at this stage often attempts to solve the problem of how conception occurs by postulating that something is swallowed. The child also seems to view sexual intercourse between the mother and father as an act of violence. Most children initially think that the baby is delivered through the anus, and later they think that the baby comes out through the navel.

MANIFESTATION OF SEXUAL THEORIES IN FOOD ATTITUDES

Some of the theories just mentioned may manifest themselves in certain irrational postures and feelings toward food. Avoidance of all food, or the fear of being poisoned, is sometimes related to a fear of pregnancy in the later years of this stage, when pregnancy is associated with oral intake. Occasionally, avoidance of food is based on the association of fatness with pregnancy, especially if the child has been told that a baby grows in the mother's stomach. More specific food aversions, such as to sausages or the yolk of an egg, often have more specific fantasies attached to them. That is to say, like all neurotic symptoms they may represent the forbidden wish as well as the defense against the wish, and may therefore be part of a reaction formation, such as disgust. They may represent an attempt to avoid direct expression of sadistic or cannibalistic fantasies, such as the fantasy of swallowing a penis or engulfing a newborn baby.

FAMILY ROMANCE

Every child also appears to develop some form of a family romance fantasy (S. Freud, 1909a). As the child becomes increasingly aware of the discrepancy between his or her idealized image of the parents and the actuality of the parents, the child become increasingly disillusioned with his or her parents. Part of the process of dealing with the disillusionment is the elaboration of a fantasy that the present parents are not really his or her parents and that the child "really" comes from, say, a royal family. This fantasized family, of course, can and does possess all the idealized characteristics previously attributed to the parents. At the same time, this splitting may also serve to lessen the guilt the child feels about the incestuous fantasies toward the parents at this time.

OEDIPAL FANTASIES

Fantasies also now appear to be more sex differentiated. The initial systematic description of these fantasies by Freud (1900) was late expanded in numerous case studies (e.g., Freud, 1905, 1909b, 1909c, 1918; Brunswick, 1940; Bornstein, 1949 [see Note 9], 1953). From these case studies it would appear that characteristic groups of drives, unconscious and conscious fantasies, and personal relationships occur in both boys and girls (see Note 33).

Before describing the psychoanalytic account of psychosexual development, it is important to note that many scientists think the concept of psychosexual stages is oversimplified to the point of being misleading (Rutter, 1971; White, 1960). Hypotheses involving unconscious feelings are difficult to test, as is the concept of the oedipus complex. In contrast to the psychoanalytic view, which emphasizes the predominant role of parents, social learning theorists (Mischel and Mischel, 1976) emphasize the many identifications children make with others, including, but not limited to, the parents. Therefore the discussion that follows must, from a strictly scientific viewpoint, be regarded as speculative (see Note 34).

PROTOTYPICAL FANTASIES OF BOYS

Boys at this stage tend to feel romantically attracted to their mothers, perhaps in the same way they imagine their fathers are. In such cases, the boy feels that his father is not only his rival but also an enemy who may hurt him. The form of the harm that a boy imagines

might befall him is determined in part by his current preoccupation with the anatomical differences between boys and girls and in part by any actual threats the boy may have received. Boys, for example, observing that girls do not have penises, may believe that girls once had penises and that the penises were removed; boys may then fear that the same fate may befall them (and some adults do try to stop boys from masturbating by telling them that their penises will be cut off).

In order to avoid being hurt, the boy normally gives up his active love for his mother and identifies with his father, thus resolving his oedipal conflict. However, occasionally he retains his active love for his mother and even goes so far as to accept a "castrated" position with respect to his father. In such cases the boy virtually offers himself to the father as a love object. This position has been called the passive oedipus conflict (Brunswick, 1940).

A 19-year-old student recalled during treatment that when he was 6 years old he used to take a bath with his sister. He remembered that he used to think that she had once had a penis and that it had been cut off. At the same time, he also demonstrated unwittingly how his current behavior was largely directed at giving others the impression that he was powerless, helpless, and a threat to no one. The two "events" thus seemed to be linked together in his mind, as though he were saying, "Leave me alone, you can pass me by; I've been done already." Interestingly, he simultaneously yearned for physical contact with men.

Mothers, of course, by and large do not treat their sons as they do their husbands. The son often is resentful of this and feels some degree of inadequacy—a feeling that is reinforced by his actual physical inferiority. In order to reassure himself and at the same time attract his mother's attention, the son may, even under normal circumstances, become self-conscious about his penis—or he may have a strong wish to exhibit his penis. Sometimes this wish takes a pathologic form, particularly if the parents heighten the conflict by their own behavior.

A 4-year-old boy was brought to the emergency room at 4 A.M. in an acute agitated state. For the previous four hours he had said there were spiders under his pajamas and there were shadows inside him. While in the waiting room he screamed as his aunt attempted to keep a coat over his completely nude body. He refused to wear any clothes at all, and he remained unashamedly naked.

On further study it was found that the boy and his mother slept in the same bed. There was a serious marital difficulty, which included a severe sexual problem and violent behavior between the parents, who slept apart.

Later it was learned that the boy's mother often allowed him to sit on her lap. He would feel her pelvis and ask her why she did not have the same feeling his father had. He would also be allowed to fondle his mother's breasts, and his mother noticed that he got an erection at the slightest touch—her touch. It became clear that this boy's fears about wearing his clothes were his way of reassuring himself and allaying his anxiety by keeping his genitals always in sight. For example, in a progressive play sequence the boy first exhibited his fear of spiders' crawling on his skin, then he touched his thigh and then his penis, and finally he wanted to look inside his trousers in search of his penis.

PROTOTYPICAL FANTASIES OF GIRLS

Girls during this period may tend to turn their love away from their mothers, at least to some extent, and to direct their attention increasingly to their fathers. Why this shift occurs is not entirely clear. One possible explanation is that the girl, unlike the boy, eventually does have to make a complete shift in the sex of her love object. In some cases this shift may be difficult to make, in part perhaps because of the nature or strength of the girl's tie to the mother. Probably the girl's active strivings toward the mother are never really given up but instead find their expression later, when the girl is able to complete his identification with her active mother at the time she herself is able to become a mother, to have a child of her own. In the meantime, however, the girl's wish to have a baby cannot be realized, and the girl seems to vacillate between loving her mother and loving her father and between wanting to be a girl and wanting to be a boy. She may envy the penis as a token of power, and may act on her envy by becoming a tomboy. Some-

times this tomboy behavior represents an attempt to deny her femininity. Occasionally, a girl will try to demean a boy by ridiculing him, to make him feel that he is stupid or repulsive. In some girls the disappointment about having female genitals may lead to a partial repudiation of the mother and a tendency instead to identify with the father. In other girls, the penis may be regarded as an abnormal growth on the body. Several circumstances may lead to this fantasy: (1) a girl may feel so secure about her femininity that it is the boy who looks odd to her, (2) the view of the penis as a growth may be a special case of the girl's wish to downgrade the boy's possession of a penis, and (3) in some families women may dominate and this circumstance may encourage the girls in the family to view males as defective.

The girl's vacillation is reinforced by the disappointment she feels at not having a baby by her father on the one hand and at not getting a penis from her mother on the other hand. Yet throughout this stage, the young girl is, of course, still dependent on her mother for the satisfaction of her daily needs, and so any jealousy of the mother because of the mother's place beside father is usually accompanied by anxiety. Thus any disapproval of the girl by the mother at this stage is acutely felt by the young girl, the more so because her thinking still lacks logic and she still tends to magically imbue the mother with omnipotent and dangerous power. Furthermore, in a sense any "punishment" is "immanently" justified, since the unconscious crime of a hostile wish against the mother has indeed been committed, and the line between a wish and an act performed is not always clear in the girl's mind at this stage. This vacillation of feelings leads to a characteristic ambivalence, found especially in women who have not adequately resolved their feelings toward their parents.

Both boys and girls feel guilty about their destructive wishes, and they are afraid of retaliation; boys at this stage more often fear physical injury, girls mostly seem to fear abandonment. According to Jones (1929), the fear of abandonment in girls may be related to an earlier fear of a loss of the personality itself and of the total annihilation of the capacity to be gratified—a condition for which the term aphánisis has been coined. Both boys and girls often seek, therefore, to reassure themselves. One common behavior pattern that serves this purpose is that of entering the parents' bedroom while the parents are together there. In so doing, the child not only is near the person he or she loves, but can also be reassured that the rival is still alive. Further, because the child's presence prevents intercourse, he or she may be attempting to prevent the birth of a sibling. More probably, however, the child is acting out fantasies of union with a parent and defending himself or herself against the fantasy, prevalent at this age, that parents hurt each other during intercourse.

SEDUCTION: REALITY AND FANTASY

Freud was initially convinced that his patients had been sexually molested by a parent. Later, he hypothesized that his patients' reports of such attacks during childhood resulted from the child's "phantasies" of being seduced and were not reports of actual events. However, some scholars now believe that Freud was right the first time; his patients possibly had been abused sexually by a parent, often the father (Klein and Tribich, 1980; Masson, 1981). The evidence in Freud's own case reports, including the Dora case (Freud, 1905), for example, reveals abundant information about destructive behavior by the parents toward the child, and a mass of data since the 1960s shows that large numbers of children are in fact abused by their parents.

RESOLUTION OF OEDIPAL FEELINGS

The resolution of these oedipal feelings appears to require some degree of identification with the parent of the same sex and some degree of internalization of the good and bad, loving and beloved, praising and forbidding, rewarding and punishing aspects of both parents, a process that takes place over a period of time and that consolidates the formation of what Freud conceptualized as the superego (S. Freud, 1924). In addition, it is hypothesized that a repression of direct sexual and aggressive fantasies in relation to either parent occurs—to the extent that there is an amnesia for these first few years of life. Thus in spite of evidence that the child's memory functions excellently during these early years, in later life few people can remember much about their first three or four years. However, whether this apparent amnesia reflects unconscious repression or immaturity of the central nervous system is unclear.

Sometimes a displacement of sexual and aggressive impulses occurs. A child may discharge his or her feelings onto another family member. Usually some sublimation occurs, as seen, for example, in boys who engage in competitive but less dangerous activities with their peers. This type of sublimation is discussed further in the next chapter (see Note 37).

FACTORS INFLUENCING OEDIPAL FANTASIES AND FEELINGS

The oedipal situation and its resolution just outlined represent the prototypical course (S. Freud, 1905; see Note 8). In actual life there are endless variations, and they are brought about by a host of factors. Parts of four major clusters of factors affect almost every child. First, of course, is the state of the preoedipal organization of the child. If the child has failed to achieve a sense of self or a feeling of trust, he or she is obviously less well prepared that he or she could be to resolve the problems and tasks of this period of life.

Sibling relationships affect the child's feelings. Sibling rivalry is usually caused by the way parents relate to their children, but once it exists it is a force in its own right (Levy, 1937; Hawkins, 1946).

Parents themselves are an obvious reality factor. The kinds of responses a parent makes to a child are determined in part by (1) the state of the marital relationship, (2) the specific relationship between a parent and a particular child, (3) the development and changing roles demanded of parents as the child develops and as they themselves grow older, and (4) the sometimes unwelcome resurgence of previously dormant conflicts, now activated by the child at a particular stage in development.

Last, a wide range of chance encounters my befall a child, including illness, separations, births, deaths, seduction, and divorce, each of which has its characteristic impact.

SUPEREGO

The modern concept of superego began with Freud's use of the term superego in his paper "The Ego and the Id" (Freud, 1923). The paper and the date are important because they mark a significant development in Freud's theory of the functioning of the mind. This development has come to be known as the structural theory, in which certain characteristics and modes of functioning are differentiated and clustered into three systems: id, ego, and superego. Several functions and elements of these systems were, in fact, described or foreshadowed in some of Freud's earlier works (Freud, 1910, 1914).

SUPEREGO DEVELOPMENT AND FUNCTION

The term superego denotes an abstract metaphor by which certain observable phenomena, such as the sense of guilt, can be understood and to a certain extent predicted. It does not denote an anatomic or a neurophysiologic entity.

From a developmental point of view, Freud argued that the superego prototypically arose from an identification with the father taken as a model, with desexualization and, perhaps, sublimation being part of that identification. When desexualization occurred, the usual power of positive, loving feelings (libidinal cathexis) to bind aggressive and destructive inclinations (aggressive cathexis)

was thought to be correspondingly weakened. This was said to result in a defusion or separation of sexual and aggressive drives, leaving the aggressive drive more mobile and available. This unbound aggressive drive was then hypothesized to be converted into the general harsh and cruel prohibitions of the now internalized object representations, expressed as various forms of moral sanctions, suh as "Thou shalt" (Freud, 1923). If the original object representation (parental figure) was perceived as harsh, then that quality would be internalized: "if the father was hard, violent and cruel, the superego takes over these attributes from him . . . the superego has become sadistic" (Freud, 1928). At the same time, the original severity of the superego did not—or not so much—represent the severity that had been experienced or anticipated from the object but expressed "the child's own aggressiveness toward the latter" (Freud, 1930). That is to say, identification with the real and attributed ethical and moral aspects of the parental figures was thought to have occurred. The identification had two aspects: one was an identification with the oedipal rival as a threatening, aggressive figure as a means of defense; the other was identification as a means of gratification—for example, a boy's merging with the father and thus sharing with him certain of his perceived attributes, such as his omnipotence. Thus an important motivation was the fear of loss of love, although avoidance of castration anxiety was thought to be the more common motivation that influenced superego organization (Freud, 1923).

The psychic energy that fueled superego functioning was conceptualized as deriving in the first place from the reservoir of energy conceptualized as id. However, the manner in which a major portion of superego formation occurred led, it was believed, to an overrepresentation of aggressive drive energy. Superego demands on ego functioning were thought to be as insistent and irrational as the original instinctual demands.

Following this classic view of the development of superego functioning, progressive phases were later hypothesized (Bornstein, 1951). For example, the superego was viewed as strict initially (e.g., at 6 to 8 years of age), with signs of a heightened ambivalence and a marked conflict over masturbation. Gradually, this struggle might abate so that in the second half of the latency period (e.g., at 8 to 10 years of age), the superego might be less strict and the sublimation more successful, and the child might begin to experience pleasure again from sexual gratification. Further development was also hypothesized to occur in which conscious or unconscious guilt was replaced by reasoned judgment. At the same time, regression in superego functioning theoretically could occur. It might manifest itself clinically as a resurgence of guilt having the quality of an instinctual urge, a strong need for punishment, or a tendency to externalize and project one's own guilt onto others. That tendency was thought to be represented in dreams, for example, as spoken words attributed to parental figures.

Again, the classic psychoanalytic view conceptualized superego functioning as an internalization of ideals and prohibitions previously attributed to the representation of the parental figures in external reality. The development of superego was thought to begin in the communications, conscious and unconscious, between parents and child during infancy. The influence of the society and culture could be transmitted in the early years largely through the way in which parents responded to and guided the child through the expected developmental phases. The more or less completed process would then provide a resolution of the oedipus complex, summarized in Freud's aphorism that the superego was the "heir of the oedipus complex." The major superego functions became self-observation, conscience, ego ideals, and repression. These superego functions might be reinforced by social sanctions (e.g., laws and moral codes), but would eventually assume a relative autonomy. Although more or less independent, superego functions would usually relate to the demands of id, reality, and ego. For example, ego defenses might repress guilt feelings and rationalize superego demands as well as meet the ideals presented.

Divergent Viewpoints

There are other psychoanalytic views of the development of superego, the most notable of which are those of Melanie Klein. Introjection as a process of superego formation was considered in the Kleinian view to constitute the first roots of superego, particularly during the paranoid-schizoid position, when ideal and persecutory objects were said to be introjected. The persecutory object was thought to be experienced as primitive and cruel, whereas the ideal object with which the ego was said to long to identify become the ego ideal. It, too, however, was described as harsh because of the high demands for perfection (Segal, 1964).

Klein (1960) postulated that feelings of guilt existed as early as the fifth or sixth month of life, when the boy was believed to become aware of and concerned about the harm his or her destructive impulses and greed might do, or might already have done, to the parental love objects. The baby was said to then experience an urge to make reparations. These feelings of guilt and the tendency to make reparations were thought to be experienced as predominantly depressive in nature, leading Klein to call this period of normal development the depressive position. Thus this self-critical and controlling function was what Klein believed to be superego and as such to operate early in life.

The superego during the depressive position was said to be experienced as an internal, ambivalently loved object, with injury to this object giving rise to feelings of guilt. However, the object was also thought to be loved and presumably felt by the child as helpful in the struggle against destructive impulses. Thus Klein (1955) believed that "the superego is something which is felt by the child to operate internally in a concrete way; that it consists of a variety of figures built up from his experiences and phantasies and that it is derived from the stages in which he has internalized (introjected) his parents" (p. 15). In this view, "the superego of the depressive position, among other features, accuses, complains, suffers and makes demands for reparation but, while still persecuting, is less harsh than the superego of the paranoid position" (Rosenfeld, 1955, p. 188).

Klein viewed internalization, and therefore superego formation, as beginning very early, with the first internalized object. In Klein's view (1958), "the superego precedes by some months the beginning of the Oedipus complex, a beginning which I date, together with that of the depressive position, in the second quarter of the first year" (p. 239).

Sexual Differences in Superego Formation

Because superego formation was seen as a function of oedipus complex resolution, and because the oedipal conflict and its resolution were thought to be different in boys and girls, differences in superego formation in the two sexes were postulated. Perhaps the most striking difference was Freud's (1925) conclusion that women were less moral than men. "For woman the level of what is ethically normal is different from what it is in men. Their superego is never so inexorable, so impersonal, so independent of its emotional origin as we require it to be in men . . . that they show less sense of justice than men, that they are less ready to submit to the great exigencies of life, that they are more often influenced in their judgments by feelings of affection or hostility—all these would be amply accounted for in the modification of the formation of their superego" (pp. 257 ff.). Obviously, there are serious questions about the validity of Freud's views on the development and psychologic characteristics of girls and women, particularly because disturbances of sexual identification seem more common in boys, rather than in girls who, presumably, must traverse a more complicated developmental pathway. Freud, of course, was significantly influenced by the traditional patriarchal and evolutionary values of his time (Schafer, 1974).

Deviations in Superego Functions

Superego deviations are said to be more likely to occur when preoedipal and oedipal development is deviant. Two particularly striking kinds of deviant development have been conceptualized: one in which the superego of the introjected parents is itself flawed, the other when a massive external event, such as the loss of a parent during the oedipal period, significantly alters the consolidation of the superego. In the case of parents who themselves have faulty values, the child is said to internalize these faulty values, leading to significant gaps in the child's superego—so-called superego lacunae (Johnson, 1949). In the case of the one-parent child, such deviations as a harsh, sadistic superego or a deficient superego are said to occur (Neubauer, 1960). In almost every case reported by Neubauer, the absent parent was either "immensely idealized or endowed with terribly sadistic attributes."

SPECIAL SITUATIONS

Other specific situations have fairly well-defined impacts on the oedipal conflict and its resolution. Two outstanding situations that have been carefully studied are the oedipal conflict in the adopted child and the oedipal conflict in the one-parent child. Although the impacts of these situations have certain characteristics, the outcome is still dependent on the balance of all the other variables just mentioned.

Adoption

Adoption can act as a powerful reality that reinforces the phase-specific fantasies just described. The adopted child finds it difficult then to deal with the heightened fantasy, and tends toward an action-oriented, repetitive behavior pattern than in effect plays out the child's fantasies. Unfortunately, the result is often one of multiple psychologic difficulties for the child.

Extrafamilial adoptees in the United States under the age of 18 constitute about 2% of the population (Brieland, 1965). However, a higher proportion of these children are referred for psychiatric help than would ordinarily be expected (Toussieng, 1966). The range of diagnostic categories of these children is broad, with perhaps a preponderance of children who tend to act out aggressively and sexually. The most powerful fantasies in the children are often woven around a search for the biologic parents, leading at times to actual explorations. The adopted child may continue to split the two sets of parents into "good" parents and "bad" parents, in either direction.

Many other factors, however, contribute to the psychologic problems of the adopted child. For example, the parents of the adopted child may have to deal continuously with their own reactions to their infertility and their own fantasies about the adopted child, who is often an illegitimate child. The continuous presence and behavior of the adopted child stimulate these fantasies in the parents, and their fantasies further interfere with the rearing skills of the parents (Schechter et al., 1964). For example, the idea of "the bad seed" is a prevalent shared fantasy, and it often leads to prophecy-fulfilling behavior in the child. The way in which a child is told about his or her adoption can be both an indicator of existing psychologic problems and a part of the cause of any future psychologic difficulties.

Some of the difficulties in telling a child about the adoption stem from emotional conflicts in the parents, but there are unresolved conceptual problems with even the best approach. Kirk (1964), for example, believes that the adoptive parents must face their own feelings and attitudes, especially those concerning their inability to produce children, and that the adoptive parents should discuss this subject openly with the child, along with the subject of the child's illegitimate birth. Peller (1961, 1963), feels that adoption should be a private matter within the family, and that "adoption day" should not be a matter of public pronouncement. Again, many workers feel that the child should be told about his or

her adopted status very early so that the child grows up with this knowledge and so that the child and parents can deal better with the many different aspects of the problem as the child's development proceeds. In this view, telling a child about adoption is a continuous process that has different meanings at different stages of development. Wittenborn (1957) found that children who were told of their adoption early tended to have higher IQs, to speak better, and to appear less clumsy than children who were not told early. However, as Lewis (1965) noted, the parents who felt comfortable telling their child early that he or she was adopted were also parents who had many good qualities, a factor that may have been more significant than the mere fact of early telling. Other workers favor postponing telling the child about the adoption until the child has accomplished some of the major tasks of development and has reached a period of relative emotional stability (between 6 and 10 years of age).

Neither method is simple, and many variables, such as the age and status of the siblings and the sociocultural environment, need to be considered. Moreover, much depends on how comfortable the parents feel about the position they have taken in the matter of talking with the child they have adopted and on their understanding of the kinds of problems that can arise.

Since the passage of the Children's Act of 1975 in Great Britain, British adopted persons over the age of 18 have had access to their birth records. Surprisingly, by 1980 only 1 to 2% of adopted adults had taken advantage of this legislation. The dire results that were prophesized did not materialize. However, there were some interesting sequelae. First, the number of babies available for adoption dropped from 21,299 in 1975 to 12,121 in 1978. This decline has been attributed to the inhibitory effect of the Children's Act on mothers who do not want to be traced at a later date. Second, some biologic mothers who had previously given their children for adoption began to come forward in an attempt to be found. In general, the act has allowed the truth to be found and feelings to be discussed openly. A study of 70 adolescents who took advantage of the law that enabled them to obtain information about their biologic parents revealed that most felt that they had a right to this information and that it was their parents' duty to give them the information, and that they were resentful of parents who were reluctant to give it. Many of these adolescents had felt confused and deprived when they were earlier denied the knowledge they later discovered for themselves (Triseliotis, 1973).

Most of the healthy, normal adoptees appeared to be more or less satisfied simply with the information they obtained (although they may have wished for more details). Less-well-adapted adoptees (those who had a poor self-image, who had an unsatisfactory home life, who had not been placed for adoption until after the age of 1, and who had an inadequate knowledge of their adoption) more often wanted to meet their biologic patents and were more often disappointed (Triseliotis, 1973).

In the United States, the Child Welfare League of America in 1976 reviewed 163 adoption agencies and found that more than 3,000 adult adoptees returned to these agencies in 1975. Two fifths (1,200) of these wished to learn the identity of or locate their natural families. Three fifths (1,800) wanted only identifying information.

The Committee on Adoption and Dependent Care (1981) of the American Academy of Pediatrics recommends that mature adoptees should have access to their birth records, but that an adult adoptee who wants this information should first have counseling with an adoption counselor to find out specifically what the adoptee wants to know and how his or her needs can best be satisfied.

The One-Parent Child

Having only one parent is another complication in reality that hampers the child's resolution of the oedipal conflict. In a detailed literature review of 10 reported cases and one current case presentation of a parent's being absent during the child's oedipal period, a pathogenic impact on the child's sexual identification and superego formation was inferred (Neubauer, 1960). For example, homosexuality occurred in some of the reported cases, with either a harsh, sadistic superego or a deficient superego that allowed incestuous acting out. However, it was not possible to distinguish between the effect of the parent's absence and the pathologic conditions of the remaining parent, who often appeared to be seductive. Furthermore, the timing of the loss and the sex of the missing parent and the child were significant variables that could not be adequately controlled in the reported studies, although the absent parent was said to be either "immensely idealized or endowed with terribly sadistic attributes." Idealization is a process by which the child denies what is disappointing about an object without withdrawing from the object (in this case the absent parent), in contrast to pure fantasy, in which the child simply turns disappointing parents into satisfactory ones (Hoffer, 1949). Children with one parent may have difficulty in achieving a satisfactory organization in the oedipal and postoedipal periods.

Herzog and Sudia (1968) emphasized that the effect of fatherlessness *in itself* is difficult to evaluate. Besides the attitudes and role of the mother in the fatherless home, the extent to which other male models influence the child is another important variable as are the reason for, and timing of, the absence. In addition, it simply cannot be said that a boy who, for example, is born out of wedlock, has no father for the first five years of his life, and is exposed to his mother's seductions will become a homosexual. He may (Leonardo da Vinci did), but who would say that to become a genius you must be born out of wedlock, have no father, and be open to your mother's seductions? (The origins of homosexuality are discussed on page 203. Additional information on homosexuality may be found on pp. 241 to 242, and on single parenthood on p. 96.)

PLAY CHARACTERISTICS

Some of the fantasies of this period and the psychologic mechanisms invoked to cope with them are represented in the child's normal play. The play is quite spontaneous; the child uses a wide range of feelings and fantasy themes. Role playing is highly characteristic, with a rich use of dolls, props, costumes and so on. Time sequences and duration, however, are largely disregarded. Some sharing of fantasies occurs, at least implicitly in the common activities of the children involved. Much of the play at this stage is clearly an attempt to copy adults, sometimes with envy, sometimes out of anger or fear. Occasionally, the play seems to be an attempt at self-reassurance as the child performs big and powerful roles (as a mother or father, a doctor or nurse), or clearly expresses a family romance. In any event, the play leads to a widening experience of the world, and as such dilutes the child's sense of sexual urgency in his or her relationship with the parents. At the same time, play is the child's first attempt to practice the skills he or she will need as an adult.

Functions of Play

Play is an essential occupation of children (Waelder, 1933). The pleasure in functioning and achieving in itself motivates the child toward further exploration as well as provides him or her with a sense of well-being. The term function pleasure was first used by Buhler (1930) to describe the pleasure infants show when they master simple motoric tasks. The child can now also actively repeat a gratifying experience. The representational aspect of play has already been mentioned. Erikson has described three spheres of activity in the child: the macrosphere, the autosphere, and the microsphere (Erikson, 1940). The macrosphere is the world at large in the child's experience (e.g., a visit to the dentist). The autosphere is the internal fantasy life of the child (e.g., "I am being attacked and will be hurt and mutilated"). The microsphere is the play world that the child creates, a world that is small, compact, manageable, and en-compassable. An example is the child who plays at being a dentist. The child turns a passive situation into one of active mastery, discharges some of his or her own revengeful aggressive fantasies, makes the situation come out differently, and repeats the situation at his or her bidding. The play performs a defense function (turning passivity into activity) and a discharge function (discharging aggressive drive). The play also gives a hint of a movement toward sublimation.

There is another important aspect of play as a developmental step. Play can be viewed as an intermediary step in the development of thought. If thought is conceptualized as a trial of action through controlled reason, it can be seen how the play of the child might facilitate that process. After all, play for the child is a process in which different solutions are tried out in controlled action in the world of play before being executed in modified form in the world at large. Gradually, this kind of "play" beomes internalized, and the process is entirely carried out at the mental level.

These conceptualizations of play are not the only ones (see also Brunner et al., 1976; Piaget, 1950; Vygotsky, 1967; Rubin et al., 1983). In a comprehensive review of the literature on children's play, Schwartzman (1979) listed approximately 800 references. Clearly many questions still need to be answered on the subject of children's play.

COGNITIVE DEVELOPMENT

A more detailed account of the structure of thought at this stage is given in the studies of Piaget (1926; see also Flavell, 1963). Piaget studied how the child progressively understands such concepts as (1) space, time, object, and causality, (2) spatial and numerical relations, and (3) conservation of length, area, and volume and the necessary processes that enable the child to understand how to classify. At this stage (2 to 7 years of age), which Piaget calls the preoperational stage, the child is aware of himself or herself as a separate person. The child is also aware that persons and things have a separate existence and are moved by forces other than the self. Children are quite capable of permanent intrapsychic representation of objects that are not perceptually present. In the symbolic and preconceptual period of the preoperational stage (approximately 2 to 4 years of age), the child can engage in symbolic activity in make-believe play and can also make attempts at verbal reasoning. Yet he or she may still endow inanimate objects with feeling (the animism mentioned earlier).

Some time during the second half of the preoperational stage Piaget describes an intuitive stage (approximately 4 to 7 years of age). In the intuitive stage there is an increased accommodation to reality (although the child is still bound to some extent to spatial relationships), a categorizing capacity that makes use of one characteristic of an object, and an inclination on the part of the child to follow his or her own line of thought when talking to another child, with very little actual exchange of information. The child can say 6 + 4 = 10, but is not capable of the reversible thinking that later will enable him to say 10 − 4 = 6. Piaget has noted several other characteristics of the child's thinking at this stage. For example, the child increasingly tries to verify his or her statements by trials of action, accommodating to what is then observed. The process of assimilation becomes in this way increasingly "decentered" from the child's interests although the child still tends to see things from his or her point of view only. To the extent that the child does this and finds it hard to take the view of another person, he or she is still egocentric.

At this stage, too, the child appears to think along the lines of immanent justice. That is, the child believes that punishment for wrong deeds is inevitable and inherent in the universe—a sort of early Hollywood type of thinking. An interesting clinical aspect of this kind of thinking is its persistent quality (hence the popularity of certain early Hollywood films?) and its impact on the child who is striving to deal with not only conscious but also unconscious real or imagined misdeeds.

Any punishment or, rather, any event that is seen by the child as a punishment is almost expected, is sometimes welcomed, and is often guilt-relieving. The child may observe this sense of relief and so develop a behavior pattern that actively seeks punishment because it is guilt-relieving. The child gets off the hook easily because he or she no longer has to suffer guilt.

SIGNS OF ANXIETY

Neither boys nor girls may be entirely successful in the resolution of their conflicts and may show signs of anxiety though a conduct disorder or by suffering from excessive guilt (see p. 182), especially about masturbation (see p. 183). Perhaps the most common conduct disturbance is a heightened aggressivity in play, in which a child may threaten others or hurt himself or herself. Occasionally, severe reaction formation against the wish to exhibit occur, with excessive shyness and withdrawal. Early learning difficulties may present themselves as the child imposes upon himself or herself an inhibition against discovering forbidden knowledge. Nail biting, tics, and other "nervous symptoms," such as nose picking, sniffing, and coughing, may also appear. Fears of the dark, animals, injury, doctors, and death may also occur, representing in part an underlying fear of being overwhelmed by the surge of unacceptable wishes and impulses.

DISORDERS OF AROUSAL

Disorders of arousal, associated with a shift from stage 3 or 4 NREM sleep in the direction of arousal, include night terrors, somnambulism and somniloquy, and bed-wetting. These disorders of arousal usually occur in the first three hours of sleep and are usually followed by retrograde amnesia for the episode. The actions often appear automatic and are not usually responsive to the immediate environment (Anders and Weinstein, 1972).

In night terrors, the child does not awaken completely, looks horrified, perspires, cries out, and often cannot be aroused from this state for 10 to 15 minutes. The child frequently has no memory of the event when fully awakened. Kales and his colleagues (1968) report an incidence of at least one episode of night terrors in 1 to 3% of all children between 5 and 12 years of age. Night terrors occur during arousal from stage 4 sleep.

Sleepwalking is also an arousal disorder. The child often has some awareness during the walking episode but usually has no memory of the event once awake. Sleepwalking is more common in boys than in girls, and it is commonly associated with night terrors. The walking usually lasts for a few minutes and occurs in stage 3 or stage 4 sleep. The delayed or impaired arousal out of this stage 3 or stage 4 sleep is thought to be the result of a delay in maturation (Broughton, 1968). Spontaneous remission usually occurs, but of those who remain sleepwalkers during young adulthood, about one third have been reported to be schizophrenic (Sours et al., 1963). Bedwetting is discussed later (p. 186).

ANXIETY DREAMS

Bad dreams (anxiety dreams) occur during REM sleep. They are normal, recurring psychic events that occur from infancy onward, and they appear to represent controlled anxiety. The bad dreams of children at this stage often involve a monster who may be coming in the window and is about to attack the child. At that point, the child suddenly wakes up, often with a pounding heart. A common underlying dream process (part of the "dream work") in such dreams is the projection and displacement of the child's own unacceptable aggressive fantasies onto the monster, who then turns around and threatens to attack the child.

The concept of dream work is a crucial one in psychoanalytic theory. Indeed, Freud regarded "The Interpretation of Dreams" as his most important work, stating that "insight such as this falls to one's lot but once in a lifetime" (S. Freud, 1900). Essentially the concept proposes a series of psychologic conflicts about forbidden wishes that arise during the sleeping state. The theory is too complex to be discussed adequately in this book, and it should be studied separately. Freud (1900) did note, however, that "even when investigation shows that the primary eliciting cause of a phenomenon is psychical, deeper research will one day trace the path further and discover an organic basis for the event" (pp. 41 ff.).

Interestingly, Hobson and McCarley (1977) have in fact suggested a biologic basis for dreaming. They postulate that the giant neurons of the pontine reticular function, the so-called FTG neurons, fire off during the desynchronized sleep state (D sleep) and bombard the forebrain, which then has to make sense of the messages received, resulting in the "dreamy" quality of dreams. FTG cell activity increases just before a REM period and peaks during REM sleep. FTG cells also activate cells in other parts of the brain, including the visual centers and the vestibular system.

Winston (1985) has also suggested that REM sleep permits a kind of "off line" processing which, without REM, would require a physically impractical demand on the prefrontal cortex. Winston then views the dream distortion not as the result of dream work disguising a dream wish, but rather as a reflection of the "normal associative process by which experience is interpreted and understood."

In any event, many psychoanalysts today realize that dreams and their interpretations are not necessarily the royal road to a knowledge of the unconscious that Freud first thought (Arlow and Brenner, 1988). In addition, Freud's *Interpretation of Dreams*, now almost 100 years old (Freud had virtually completed the book in 1896), can no longer be regarded as the most up-to-date account of dreams. The topic of dreams and dream interpretation now needs to be understood in a broadened biopsychosocial context.

Thus, one important aspect of these findings and theories is that a new dimension is added to our understanding of dreaming, if not to our understanding of the role of the forebrain in a particular dream. An important set of developmental and physiologic variables may have to be considered in any comprehensive account of the meaning of a dream. Although this does not specifically invalidate the psychoanalytic theory of manifest and latent dream content and intermediate dream work, it does considerably broaden the base for our understanding and open up new possibilities for dream exploration.

CHILD'S CONCEPT OF DREAMS

During the early part of this period, dreams themselves tend to be conceptualized by the child as external events, a process that Piaget calls realism (Piaget, 1951). However, the child soon begins to understand that dreams are not real external events. By their fifth birthday, most American middle-class children recognize that their dreams are not real events, and shortly afterward understand that dreams cannot be seen by others. By 6 years of age children are aware that dreams take place inside them, and by 7 years of age they are clearly aware that dreams are thoughts caused by themselves (Kohlberg, 1968).

GUILT

Guilt was mentioned earlier (p. 171) as another consequence of unresolved oedipal conflicts. In fact, guilt is a powerful affect at this stage, even with normal resolution of conflicts. If castration danger was the prototypical danger situation in the third and fourth years of life, guilt seems to be the overriding danger from about the fourth or fifth year onward, in greater or lesser degree. Erikson, for example, has described the developmental crisis at this stage as initiative versus guilt (Erikson, 1959). The child's imagination is exuberant to the point where the child can frighten himself or herself because he or she believes that a particular fantasy was virtually a committed crime. The child then feels guilty. He or she feels guilty even about mere thoughts, not to mention deeds that nobody may have seen. Rapaport (1967) tells the story of the little boy who goes toward a candy jar. Before the boy can lay a hand on the jar, he hears a great clap of thunder. He is momentarily taken aback, looks up, and says: "Good God, isn't one even permitted to think of it?" Yet, at the same time, the child is learning quickly, is desirous of sharing in obligations and being disciplined, and seems altogether more integrated.

Origin of Guilt

The origin of guilt is still to be explained. Children in their first year of life obey the commands of adults only for the duration of the command; there is very little carry-over to the next time the same situation arises (e.g., parents must repeatedly say to a child. "Stay away from the plug," as well as place covers over all electric outlets and physically intervene when necessary). Gradually the child internalizes these commands; 2-year-old children can be observed to repeat to themselves the commands they have heard repeatedly from their parents. Occasionally children seek reinforcement of these commands from their parents by acting provocatively, by asking questions, and by inviting their parents to see how good they have been.

Purpose of Guilt

Guilt, like anxiety, is an affect, and like all affects it appears to serve a purpose. The purpose, it would seem, is to provide a signal that a punishment will occur if certain behavior is persisted in, or committed at all. The stimulus for the child's response is the internalized real and imagined prohibitions of the parents (the superego described on pp. 174 ff.). Thus guilt arises essentially when there is a conflict between the child's wishes and the conscience. Like many affects, guilt may become acutely uncomfortable, causing the child to mobilize further defenses to ward off the guilt. Thus defenses may act against affects as well as against drives. Sometimes rage may be mobilized to deal with guilt. A multiple layering of such affects may thus occur.

The child's conscience requires reinforcement from the environment. The environment usually provides this reinforcing nutriment on the form of such social sanctions as marriage, parenthood, and normal social expectations in regard to ethics and morals, and so on. If this nutriment is lacking or faulty, the superego may become corrupted. If the parents themselves have faulty values, not only will the child internalize these values complete with their faults (see the discussion of superego lacunae, p. 204), but also the child's values will become further corrupted by the lack of adequate nutriments in the form of appropriate parental sanctions. On the other hand, certain strong moral attributes can be transmitted, particularly through specific family myths (Musto, 1969).

It would appear that these early prohibitions are in part internalizations of the child's perception of the parents' prohibitions, especially those that have been spoken aloud and heard by the child. However, in part they are also reinternalizations of the attributes and strictness that the child had previously externalized and projected onto the parents. Along with the spoken prohibitions of the parents is the implied threat of loss of the parents' love if the child disobeys. This threat is often conveyed by a glance, a change in receptivity, or gruffness. The child feels, or should feel, a consistency and firmness in the parents' command, and a sense of guilt about disobedience. If there is inconsistency, the child will sense the double message and will disobey. The parents will then be nonplussed at the child's "naughtiness" and, not recognizing their own inconsistency, may begin to punish the child, often by spanking.

Guilt is often expressed in a form of behavior that consistently provokes punishment. It is as though the punishment will be a just retribution for the forbidden unconscious crime. Through this punishment the child is temporarily relieved of the onerous feeling of guilt. Physical punishment administered at this time usually fits in with the child's fantasies and needs.

Guilt and Socialization

The internal problem of guilt is perhaps central to the external socialization of the child. In order to avoid the feeling of excessive guilt, the child may, for example, try to behave in accordance with accepted social rules of conduct. However, even this solution is tempered by intrapsychic, environmental, and developmental factors. Internally, the child's ability to postpone the urge for immediate gratification, the child's self-esteem, his or her ability to empathize with the feelings of others, as well as his or her intelligence and capacity for judgment—all these may modify the child's tolerance for guilt.

External modifying factors include (1) the varying impact of parental, peer, and societal sanctions; (2) the child's experiences of gratification or deprivation; and (3) the child's assessments (insofar as the child can make such assessments) of the risk of detection, the effort and ingenuity required, and the possible consequences versus the possible gains when he or she experiences the urge to cheat, lie, steal, or perform some other forbidden act.

From a cognitive-developmental point of view, the child's increasing ability to make a moral judgment parallels in part the level of cognitive development. For example, no matter what environmental influences are at work, a gradual shift takes place from making a judgment in terms of immediate external physical consequences to making a judgment in terms of subjective or internal purposes, norms, or values (Kohlberg, 1964). Most children understand the basic moral rules of society by the time they start first grade (Hartshorne and May, 1930). However, the way in which they make a moral judgment depends on the degree to which they have internalized specific moral values.

MASTURBATION

An almost universal source of guilt in the child is the urge to masturbate and the fantasies connected with masturbation. Although the term masturbation in its ordinary sense is understood to mean self-stimulation of the genitals, in its technical sense it means the gratification of the sexual drive by the self or an extension of the self. Because the sexual drive seems to have a sequence of development (S. Freud, 1905; see Note 8)—much as thinking, motility, and speech have a sequence of development—the self-gratification of the earliest manifestations of the sexual drive can also be considered as early forms of masturbation even though they are not genital. Thus, psychoanalysts consider the mouthing behavior of the infant as a rudimentary form of masturbation in that it is believed to be in part a manifestation of autoerotic activity in which the primitive so-called oral-stage sexual drive is being gratified by the self. The pleasures involved later in having a bowel movement may similarly also have a masturbatory component.

Penile erections occur in infancy, both spontaneously and in response to manipulation. Spontaneous early penile erections appear to be associated with REM sleep (Fischer et al., 1965). It is therefore plausible that such erections may represent a physiologic change as well as a psychic event.

Direct manipulation of the genitals reaches its first peak somewhere between 3 and 4 years of age, although accidental touching of the genitals may occur in very young infants. An interesting observation is that foundling-home infants deprived of object relations do not play with their genitals, even in their fourth year, whereas family-raised infants with good object relations play with their genitals toward the end of the first year (Spitz, 1962). More disguised masturbation takes place in the course of "horse play," as when the child contrives to rub the genital area against, say, the knee of an adult.

Girls appear to masturbate mostly through pressure of the thighs rather than direct fingering of the genitals. A possible hypothesis for this phenomenon is that the girl wishes to avoid exact tactile localization that might arouse anxiety about the absence of a penis (Brunswick, 1940). On the other hand, many girls masturbate by inserting foreign objects

into the vagina. Later, during adolescence, it appears that girls derive sexual gratification by stimulation in the region of the clitoris rather than the vagina, and this remains true of adult women, who achieve orgasm most regularly from stimulation in the region of the clitoris. In fact, it appears that in adults there is no such thing as a vaginal orgasm that is distinct from a clitoral orgasm (Sherfey, 1966). That is to say, clitoral and vaginal orgasms are not separate biologic entities, and regardless of where the female body is stimulated, there is absolutely no difference in the responses of the pelvic viscera provided the stimulation is sufficient to bring about orgasm (Masters and Johnson, 1966).

Origins of Masturbation

Several hypotheses have been offered about the origins of masturbatory activities and fantasies in the child. Brunswick (1940), for example, asserted that the early physical care of the child by the mother, a care that inevitably involves touching the genitals and that seems to be experienced by the child as a pleasurable seduction, constitutes a significant component of the basis for early childhood masturbation. Another stimulus to masturbate lies in the intense and jealous interest of the child in the sexual activity of the parents, which the child may have seen or about which he or she may have elaborated fantasies.

Masturbation Fantasies

During the act of masturbation the child may envisage what he or she fantasies takes place between the parents. The child may, for example, in keeping with his or her sexual theories, envisage either parent being suckled by the other, or, the child suckling either parent, or, the child being suckled. Such fantasies may be displaced, especially in girls, onto the image of suckling a doll. Occasionally, the child may fantasy a mutual touching of the genitals, much along the lines of his or her own experience of pleasure in touching the genitals or having the genitals touched, especially by the mother. Sometimes, in keeping with the child's interpretation of sexual intercourse as a sadomasochistic interaction, he or she may have accompanying fantasies of violence, often disguised as rockets blasting off, cars crashing into each other, or wars between armies.

Masturbation and Fantasies of Being Beaten

Sometimes a specific fantasy of being beaten occurs during masturbation (Freud, 1919). According to Freud, that fantasy first occurs before the fifth or sixth year, and it is accompanied by feelings of pleasure that have a masturbatory quality. Freud thought that the fantasies arose from the oedipal fantasies of the child and underwent a complicated series of changes. In boys, for example, the beating fantasy was thought to be passive from the beginning and to be derived from a feminine attitude to the father. The sequence of changes in the fantasy that Freud reconstructed were: "I am loved by my father," leading to the unconscious fantasy, "I am being beaten by my father," which resulted finally in the conscious masochistic fantasy, "I am being beaten by my mother." In girls, the first conscious form of the fantasy appeared to be sadistic (e.g., "A teacher is beating a number of boys."), but the satisfaction was still thought to be essentially masochistic. In both boys and girls, the fantasies appeared in part to be attempts to deal with their wish to be loved by their father.

Masturbation and Social Rules

Masturbation is a normal, even necessary, phenomenon, and so children of all ages need the opportunity to masturbate in private. Like eating habits and bowel training, however, the practice of masturbation is also usually subject to social rules in the interests of social relationships. It has even been suggested (although without supporting evidence) that cultures that permit the unrestricted gratification of the sexual urge during the elementary-school years and early puberty have a large proportion of people whose

level of personality development and intellectual functioning is lowered (Spitz, 1962). Compulsive masturbation is usually regarded as a sign of tension or disorder whose sources must be discovered and dealt with before the masturbation can be contained. Occasionally, a child becomes addicted to masturbation. Extreme anxiety and guilt are often engendered when the child is threatened with punishment or spanked for masturbating.

SPANKING

Spanking, however, does not usually eradicate this or any other behavior. Spanking may appear to have an effect at the time, but parents usually find that they must spank the child for the same misdeed again and again. When spanking does seem to have a more lasting effect, that effect is often the result of fear and a strong repression of the rage in the child. Occasionally, the child who has learned to control his or her impulses only through the mobilization of fear of a strong external punishment may repeatedly seek such punishment in order to dissipate any rising anxiety brought about by a threatened breakthrough of an impulse believed to be dangerous. Spanking may also reinforce the wish and the opportunities for the child to put feelings into actions. This acting out comes about partially through the child's identification with parents who also hit when they are desperate.

Sometimes spanking is sexually exciting. Parents who spank report that they try to hold themselves back, feel more and more provoked, and then suddenly let go. They say that after the discharge of their anger through physical activity (spanking), their relationship with the child is calm and loving, but the calm is usually short lived, and the cycle starts again. The parent, although he or she sees how ineffective spanking is, persists in spanking. The cycle of rising excitement, climax, discharge, and period of calm is suspiciously like a sexual gratification, which in some families seems to be the true, if unconscious, aim of the spanking.

Even the foregoing discussion does not touch on all the reasons that spanking is often the opposite of useful to the child in the long run. (Spanking often seems to be administered more because it is "useful" for the parents than because it is useful for the child.) For example, instead of the child's feeling guilty and learning internal ways to delay and divert the direct discharge of his or her impulses, a child may simply be let off the hook by a spanking: the child is immediately relieved of feelings of guilt and so is free to continue the activity, if he or she feels the external price to pay is not too high. For example, a child may reason that stealing an apple is worth the risk of a spanking and so feel free to steal. No internalization has occurred; wrong learning has taken place.

BED-WETTING

Enuresis is defined as the repetitive and inappropriate passage of urine past the age at which most children remain dry (usually 3 to 4 years of age). Enuresis is categorized as nocturnal or diurnal depending on whether it occurs during the night or day and as primary or secondary depending on whether bladder control had never been achieved (primary) or had once been achieved but was subsequently lost (secondary). Nocturnal enuresis is more common than diurnal and primary more common than secondary (Shaffer, 1985). Most children achieve night-time control by 3½ to 4 years of age (Shaffer, 1985). Some observers have stated that normal maturation in some children may not occur until puberty (Campbell, 1951). Curiously, the likelihood of remission does not increase steadily with age; rather, the likelihood of a child between 4 and 10 years of age becoming dry during any 12-month period remains constant at about 15%. An increase in prevalence often occurs after starting school, and about 25% of children who do acquire control subsequently lose control. The significance of these developmental differences is not clear. A family history of enuresis is sometimes seen among children who have enuresis. Enuresis

is also more common in disadvantaged children and in those living in institutions. In preschool children the problem is equally common in boys and girls; after age 7 boys begin to outnumber girls so that the disorder becomes twice as common in boys by age 11 (Shaffer, 1985). For a small percent of cases, the problem persists into adulthood.

Control usually comes about as a result of the interaction between this neuromuscular maturation and the psychologic capacity to postpone the urge to void. The psychologic capacity to delay an impulse is, in turn, part of the total psychologic development of the child and is derived from many sources. Some of these sources are all those factors that contribute toward such functions as relationships, motivation, and the capacity to deal with conflict.

Furthermore, because the total psychologic development of the child is integrally related to the environment, such factors as the attitudes of the child's parents and the hazards of illness, separation, and seduction also play a vital role in developing the capacity for impulse control.

Given this complex interaction of factors, it is not surprising that enuresis is a common symptom of early childhood, perhaps affecting at least 4% of children over 4 years of age (DSM-III-R, 1987).

Bed-wetting can, of course, be a symptom of many different kinds of organic disorders. Several clinical findings suggest that the cause is organic: (1) the wetting is diurnal as well as nocturnal, (2) there has never been a significantly long "dry" period, and (3) there are symptoms of an infection. Bed-wetting may occur also in children who have unusually small bladders (so-called primary enuresis) or a a result of a sleep disturbance. Some initial research seemed to suggest that enuretic episodes were more likely during arousal from nonREM sleep (usually stage 4) (Kales and Kales, 1974), and that it seemed to occur least often in REM sleep (Gastaut and Broughton, 1964). Subsequent studies (e.g., Mikkelsen et al., 1980) have, however, failed to confirm any clear-cut association with stage of sleep when the length of sleep stage is controlled for. Parents report that bed-wetting seems to occur in children who are sleeping heavily and are hard to awaken. However, Graham (1973) notes that parents have less cause to awaken children who are not bed-wetters, so that a valid comparison cannot usually be made. Although bed-wetting, sleepwalking, and nightmares occur during sudden intense arousal from slow-wave (stage 4) sleep, other "nervous" signs, such as teeth-grinding, occur during REM sleep (Reding et al., 1964).

Nevertheless, many children with enuresis do not have an organic basis for their symptom. Among these children, it is possible to group the factors as follows (Kolvin et al., 1972):

I. Developmental delay
   1. Slow maturation
   2. Inadequate training
   3. Insufficient stimulation
II. Psychologic conflict
   1. Temporary regressive phenomena
   2. Relatively stable neurotic symptom formation

The primary Group II causes of the enuresis tend to be intrapsychic and internalized in nature. Enuresis as a regressive phenomenon, for example, commonly occurs when a stress (such as illness, birth of a sibling, or separation and loss) is experienced before bladder control has been fully established. According to Katan (1946), enuresis as the expression of an internalized intrapsychic conflict tends to occur when fantasies common during this period of development (i.e., phase-specific fantasies) have been heightened by the interaction between internal and external events and produce anxiety of a degree that requires neurotic symptom formation.

For example, a common fantasy of the child during this period of development is that he or she will be harmed by persons of the opposite sex. This fear may arise as a fantasied consequence of destructive wishes toward the rival parent, or it may arise from an overwhelming sexual experience, which in many instances consists of a hostile seduction by the parent who (for example) handles the child's penis to direct the stream of his urine into the toilet. In the case of a boy, his fear of the mother may lead to a passive compliance in which urination is not within his control. In the case of a girl, her fear of the father as an aggressor may lead to a passive relinquishing of control (Gerard, 1939). In both instances, the bed-wetting also has a passive-aggressive revenge component. Furthermore, in many children who wet the bed the symptom is brought about by the same mechanisms that produce a conversion symptom, so that the child's wishes and his or her defense against the wishes are represented symbolically in the outpouring of urine.

What is alleged here is the interaction between a phase-specific fantasy and an external reality that is consonant with that fantasy, resulting in a conflict that expresses itself through a symptom in which all the factors are represented. Many of the beautiful anecdotal case descriptions by Gerard (1939), Katan (1946), and others, in which bed-wetting was attributed to intricate psychodynamic conflicts, today might be considered instances of a general developmental disorder (Shaffer and Gardner, 1981). In any event, controlled studies (e.g., Achenbach and Lewis, 1971) have not found evidence to support many of these psychodynamic hypotheses as being of primary etiologic importance.

MAJOR DEVELOPMENTAL THRUSTS

Several major developmental thrusts seem to be occurring during this stage of the child's life. The child's relationships are now more centered on identified people and bear witness to the exciting and anxiety-arousing fantasy life just described. Thus, in the child's manifest behavior, possessiveness of the parent of the opposite sex and jealousy and rivalry with the parent of the same sex can be observed. The child is also at times protective, curious, exhibitionistic, and compliment-seeking and, in the case of girls, is changing toward a somewhat masculine relationship with the mother. Children now begin to see other children as fellow children who have feelings, wishes, and rights of their own.

The child's increasing ability to take directions is matched by his or her better developed internal controls system. Play and other interactions with children shift from parallel play to cooperative play. Language and concept development reach a new level as the child observes and imitates others and acquires a sense of time. Curiosity about anatomic differences, pregnancy, childbirth, and death abounds, and masturbation is at its peak. During this stage the child strives to resolve individual, complex oedipal feelings with the early formation of a superego, and learns to accept his or her gender and sex role.

PHOBIC ORGANIZATION

At the same time, there appears to be a general tendency toward a phobic organization that is manifested in the numerous fears that occur at this stage (e.g., fear of the dark). The phobic nature of the defense organization at this time seems to be determined in part by a number of factors. One factor is the level of cognitive development, which may not yet permit more sophisticated mechanisms, such an intellectualization. Another factor is the general maturation and development of the psychic apparatus, which may not yet have provided the individual with a wide range of autonomous functions. A third factor thought to influence the development of phobias is the degree to which the child experiences a heightening of anxiety common at this developmental stage brought on by an event that is close to the prevailing fantasy. For example, tonsillectomy in a child who is concerned about mutilation of the body may heighten castration anxiety and stimulate specific defense mechanisms (Lipton, 1962).

DEFENSE HIERARCHY

Lewis (1971) postulated a sequential and hierarchical development of psychic defense structures that reflects in part maturation, development, and external events. A simplified schematic representation is shown in Table 17–1. In this diagram the vertical columns indicate the interacting forces of maturation, intrapsychic development, and external environment at each stage of development. This interaction would seem to determine, in part, the kind and degree of defense activity, shown in the bottom line of each vertical column. Thus, during infancy, projection, introjection, and projective identification seem to be prominent defense mechanisms reflecting the immature state of psychic organization. Later, between the ages of 3 to 6 ("early childhood"), the increased awareness and curiosity, the fears associated with body injury and castration, and the presence of specific real events, such as a tonsillectomy, may characteristically foster the use of phobic mechanisms. In the school-age child (ages 7 to 11) a more obsessional organization may be seen. Finally, during adolescence, the availability of formal operations may lend itself to intellectualization as a common defense mechanism.

Note 33

From S. Freud (1940). *An Outline of Psychoanalysis*. Reprinted from *The Standard Edition of the Complete Psychological Works of Sigmund Freud*. Translated and edited by James Strachey. By permission of Sigmund Freud Copyrights, The Institute of Psycho-Analysis, and the Hogarth Press Ltd., 1964, pp. 154–155.

. . . With the phallic phase and in the course of it the sexuality of early childhood reaches its height and approaches its dissolution. Thereafter boys and girls have different histories. Both have begun to put their intellectual activity at the service of sexual researches; both start off from the premiss of the universal presence of the penis. But now the paths of the sexes diverge. The boy enters the Oedipus phase; he begins to manipulate his penis and simultaneously has phantasies of carrying out some sort of activity with it in relation to his mother, till, owing to the combined effect of a threat of castration and the sight of the absence of a penis in females, he experiences the greatest trauma of his life and this introduces the period of latency with all its consequences. The girl, after vainly attempting to do the same as the boy, comes

Table 17–1. Development of Defense Hierarchy

		DEVELOPMENTAL STAGES		
Correlations	*Infancy*	*Early Childhood*	*School-Age Period*	*Adolescence*
Maturational skills	Biologic helplessness Limited awareness Limited motor control	Increased perceptual capacities Early motor control	Broad range of controlled perceptual, motor, and psychic activity	Extensive quantitative and qualitative changes in physical and psychologic changes associated with puberty
Psychologic development	Assimilation and accommodation Symbiotic state, need-satisfying object Loss of love anxiety	Preoperational thinking Object constancy Recognition of whole object Sexual development Castration anxiety	Concrete operations Autonomous ego development in latency Guilt	Formal operations Intrapsychic reorganization in the face of such adolescent tasks as identity crisis, body image changes, separation and object choice, or impulse control
Reinforcing parallel external events	Loss of the object	Fear of mutilation aggravated by actual event, e.g., tonsillectomy	School learning patterns	Career choice, move to college or military service
Simplified defense hierarchical sequence	Projection Injection Projective identification	Phobic organization	Obsessional organization	Intellectualization

to recognize her lack of a penis or rather the inferiority of her clitoris, with permanent effects on the development of her character; as a result of this first disappointment in rivalry, she often begins by turning away altogether from sexual life. . . .

Note 34

From: *The Psychology of the Child*, by Jean Piaget and Barbel Inhelder, translated from the French by Helen Weaver. © 1969 by Basic Books, Inc. © by Presses Universitaires de France. By permission of Basic Books, Inc. Publishers, New York.

. . . Yet . . . psychoanalysis . . . often sees nothing in affectivity but a series of repetitions or analogies with the past (new versions of the Oedipus complex, narcissism, etc.). It is true that Anna Freud* and E. Erikson† stressed "successive identifications" with elders who serve as models, thus liberating children from infantile choices (with the concomitant danger of identity diffusion according to Erikson), but they have neglected the role of the "concrete autonomy" acquired during later childhood and above all the role of cognitive constructions that pave the way for an anticipation of the future and a receptiveness to new values. . . .

REFERENCES

Achenbach, T., and Lewis M. (1971), A proposed model for clinical research and its application to encopresis and enuresis. *J. Am. Acad. Child Psychiatry* 10:535.

Anders, T., and Weinstein, O. (1972), Sleep and its disorders in infants and children: A review. *J. Pediatr.*, 50:311–324.

Arlow, J.A., and Brenner, C. (1988), The future of psychoanalysis. *Psychoanal. Q.* LVII:1–14.

Bornstein, B. (1949), The analysis of a phobic child: Some problems of theory and technique in child analysis. *Psychoanal. Study Child*, 3/4:181–226.

Bornstein, B. (1951), On latency. *Psychoanal. Study Child*, 6:279–285.

Bornstein, B. (1953), Fragment of an analysis of an obsessional child: The first six months of analysis. *Psychoanal. Study Child*, 8:313–332.

Brieland, D. (1965), Adoption research: An overview. In: *Perspectives on Adoption Research.* New York: Child Welfare League of America, p. 58.

Broughton, R.J. (1968). Sleep disorders: Disorders of arousal. *Science*, 159:1070–1078.

Brunner, J., Jolly, A., and Sylva, R. (Eds.) (1976), *Play: Its Role in Development and Evolution.* New York: Basic Books.

Brunswick R.M. (1940), The preoedipal phase of the libido development. *Psychoanal. Q.*, 19:293.

Buhler, C. (1930), *The First Year of Life.* New York: John Day.

Buhler, K. (1930), *The Mental Development of the Child.* New York: Harcourt, Brace & World.

Campbell, M. (1951), *Clinical Pediatric Urology.* Philadelphia: W.B. Saunders & Co., p. 801.

Child Welfare League of America, Inc. (1976), *The Sealed Adoption Record Controversy: Report of a Survey of Agency Policy, Practice and Opinion.* New York: Child Welfare League of America, Inc. Research Center.

Committee on Adoption and Dependent Care (1981), The role of the pediatrician in adoption with reference to "the right to know:" An update, *Pediatrics*, 67:305–306.

Erikson, E.H. (1940), Studies in the interpretation of play: I. Clinical observation of play disruption in young children. *Genetic Psychology Monographs*, p. 22. (Reprinted in *Contemporary Psychopathology*, ed. S.S. Tompkins. Cambridge, Harvard University Press, 1943, pp. 91–122.)

Erikson, E.H. (1959), Initiative versus guilt. *Identity and the Life Cycle. Psychol. Issues*, 1:74–82.

Fisher, C., Gross, J., and Zuch, J. (1965), Cycle of penile erection synonymous with dreaming (REM) sleep. *Arch. Gen. Psychiatry*, 12:29–45.

Flavell, J.H. (1963), *The Developmental Psychology of Jean Piaget.* New York: Van Nostrand, pp. 150–163.

Freud, S. (1900), *The Interpretation of Dreams.* Standard Edition, 4 (1953). London: The Hogarth Press, pp. 261–263.

Freud, S. (1905), *Fragment of an Analysis of a Case of Hysteria.* Standard Edition, 7, (1953). London: The Hogarth Press.

Freud, S. (1905), *Three Essays on the Theory of Sexuality.* Standard Edition, 7 (1953). London: The Hogarth Press, pp. 125–243.

Freud, S. (1908), *On the Sexual Theories of Children.* Standard Edition, 9 (1959). London: The Hogarth Press, pp. 205–226.

Freud, S. (1909a), *Family Romances.* Standard Edition, 9 (1959). London: The Hogarth Press, pp. 235–241.

Freud S. (1909b), *Analysis of a Phobia in a Five-Year-Old Boy.* Standard Edition, 10 (1955). London: The Hogarth Press, pp. 5–152.

Freud, S. (1909c), *Notes Upon a Case of Obsessional Neurosis.* Standard Edition, 10 (1955). London: The Hogarth Press, pp. 155–318.

Freud, S. (1914), *On Narcissism: an Introduction.* Standard Edition, 14 (1957). London: The Hogarth Press, pp. 73–104.

Freud, S. (1918), *From the History of an Infantile Neurosis.* Standard Edition, 17 (1955). London: The Hogarth Press, pp. 7–122.

Freud, S. (1919), *"A Child is Being Beaten": A Contribution to the Study of the Origin of Sexual Perversions.* Standard Edition, 17 (1955).

Freud, S. (1923), *The Ego and the Id.* Standard Edition, 19 (1961). London: The Hogarth Press, pp. 12–68.

Freud, S. (1924), *The Dissolution of the Oedipus Complex.* Standard Edition, 19 (1961). London: The Hogarth Press, pp. 171–179.

Freud, S. (1925), *Some Psychical Consequences of the*

---

*A. Freud, *The Ego and the Mechanisms of Defense* (rev. ed., New York: International Universities Press, 1967).

†E. Erikson, *Childhood and Society* (2nd ed.; New York: W.W. Norton, 1963).

Anatomical Distinction Between the Sexes. Standard Edition, 19 (1961). London: The Hogarth Press, pp. 243–258.

Freud, S. (1928), *Dostoevsky and Parricide.* Standard Edition, 21 (1961), London: The Hogarth Press, p. 185.

Freud, S. (1930), *Civilization and Its Discontents.* Standard Edition, 21 (1961). London: The Hogarth Press, pp. 64–148.

Gastaut, H., and Broughton, R.J. (1964), Conclusions concerning the mechanisms of enuresis nocturna. *E.E.G. Clin. Neurophysiol.,* 16:625.

Gerard, M. (1939), Enuresis: A study in etiology. *Am. J. Orthopsychiatry,* 9:48.

Graham, P.J. (1973), Depth of sleep and enuresis: A critical review. In: *Bladder Control and Enuresis,* Clinics in Dev. Med., Nos. 48/49, eds. I. Kolvin, R. MacKeith, and S.R. Meadow. London: SIMP/Heinemann.

Hartshorne, H., and May, M.A. (1928–1930), *Studies in the Nature of Character.* Vol. 1, *Studies in Deceit;* Vol. 2, *Studies in Self-Control;* Vol. 3, *Studies in the Organization of Character.* New York: Macmillan Publishing Co.

Hawkins, M.O. (1946), Jealousy and rivalry between brothers and sisters. *Child Study,* 2–5.

Herzog, E., and Sudia, C.E. (1968), Fatherless homes: A review of research. *Children,* Sept.–Oct.: 177–182.

Hoffer, W. (1949), Deceiving the deceiver. In: *Searchlights on Delinquency,* ed. K.R. Eissler. New York: International Universities Press.

Hobson, J.A., and McCarley, R.W. (1977), The brain as a dream state generator: An activation-synthesis hypothesis of the dream process. *Am. J. Psychiatry,* 134:1335–1348.

Johnson, A.M. (1949), Sanctions for superego lacunae of adolescents. In: *Searchlights on Delinquency,* ed. K.R. Eissler. New York: International Universities Press, pp. 225–245.

Jones, E. (1929), Fear, guilt, and hate. *Int. J. Psychoanal.,* 10:383–397.

Kales, A., and Kales, J.D. (1974), Sleep disorders. *N. Engl. J. Med.,* 290:487–499.

Kales, J., Jacobson, A., and Kales, A. (1968), Sleep disorders in children. In: *Progress in Clinical Psychology,* Vol. 8, ed. L. Abt and B.F. Riess. New York: Grune & Stratton, pp. 63–75.

Katan, A. (1946), Experiences with enuretics. *Psychoanal. Study Child,* 2:241.

Kirk, H.D. (1964), *Shared Fate.* Toronto: Collier-Macmillan, The Free Press of Glencoe.

Klein, M. (1955), The psycho-analytic play techniques: Its history and significance. In: *New Directions in Psychoanalysis,* ed. M. Klein, P. Heimann, and R. Money-Kyle. London: Tavistock, pp. 3–22.

Klein, M. (1958), On the development of mental functioning. In: *Melanie Klein: Envy and Gratitude and Other Works, 1946–1963.* London: The Hogarth Press, 1975.

Klein, M. (1960), *Our Adult World and Its Roots in Infancy.* London: Tavistock, p. 9.

Klein, M., and Tribich, D. (1980), On Freud's blindness. *Colloquium,* 3:52–59.

Kohlberg, L. (1964), Development of moral character

and moral ideology. In: *Review of Child Development Research* (Vol. 1), ed. M.L. Hoffman and L.W. Hoffman. New York: Russell Sage Foundation, pp. 383–431.

Kohlberg, L. (1968), Early education: A cognitive developmental view. *Child Dev.,* 39:1013–1062.

Kolvin, I., Taunch, J., Currah, J., Garside, R.F., Nolan, J., and Shaw, W.B. (1972), Enuresis: A descriptive analysis and a controlled trial. *Dev. Med. Child Psychol.,* 14:715–726.

Lemkau, P.W. (1955), *Mental Hygiene in Public Health,* 2nd Ed. New York: McGraw-Hill.

Levy, D.M. (1937), Studies in sibling rivalry. *Research Monograph No. 2.* New York: American Orthopsychiatric Association.

Lewis, H. (1965), The psychiatric aspects of adoption. In: *Modern Perspectives in Child Psychiatry,* ed. J.G. Howells. Springfield, Ill.: Charles C Thomas, pp. 428–451.

Lewis, M. (1971), *Clinical Aspects of Child Development.* Philadelphia: Lea & Febiger.

Lipton, S.D. (1962), On the psychology of childhood tonsillectomy. *Psychoanal. Study Child,* 17:363–417.

Masson, J.M. (1981), The seduction hypothesis in the light of new documents. Presented at the Western New England Psychoanalytic Society, New Haven, Connecticut, June, 1981.

Master, W.H. and Johnson, V. (1966), *Human Sexual Response.* Boston: Little, Brown and Company, pp. 66–67.

Mikkelson, E.J., Rapoport, J.L., Neww, L., Gruneau, C., Mendelson, W., and Gillin, J.C. (1980), Childhood enuresis I. Sleep patterns and psychopathology. *Arch. Gen. Psychiat.,* 37:1139–1145.

Mischel, W., and Mischel, H. (1976), A cognitive social-learning approach to morality and self-regulation. In: *Moral Development and Behavior,* ed. T. Loickona. New York: Holt, Rinehart, and Winston, pp. 84–107.

Musto, D. (1969), The youth of John Quincy Adams. *Proc. Am. Phil. Soc.,* 113:269–282.

Neubauer, P.B. (1960), The one-parent child and his oedipal development. *Psychoanal. Study Child,* 15:286–309.

Peller, L. (1961), Comments on adoption and child development. *Bull. Phila. Assoc. Psychoanal.,* 11:1961.

Peller, L. (1963), Comments on adoption and child development. *Bull. Phila. Assoc. Psychoanal.,* 13:1963.

Piaget, J. (1926), *The Language and Thought of the Child.* New York: Harcourt, Brace & World.

Piaget, J. (1951), *Play, Dreams and Imitation in Childhood,* trans. C. Gattegno and F.M. Hodgson. New York: Norton.

Pierce, C.M., Whitman, R.R., Maas, J.W., and Gay, M.I. (1961), Enuresis and dreaming. *Arch. Gen. Psychiatry,* 4:166–170.

Rapaport, D. (1967), *The Collected Papers of David Rapaport,* ed. M.M. Gill. New York: Basic Books, pp. 589.

Reding, G.R., Rubright, W.C., Rechtshaffen, A., and Daniels, R.S. (1964), Sleep pattern of tooth grinding: Its relationship to dreaming. *Science,* 145:725–726.

Rosenfeld, H. (1955), Psychoanalysis of the superego in an acute schizophrenic. In: *New Directions in Psychoanalysis*, ed. M. Klein, P. Heimann, and R. Money-Kyrle. London: Tavistock, pp. 180–219.

Rubin, K.H., Fein, G.G., and Vandenberg, B. (1983), Play. In: *Handbook of Child Psychology*, Vol. 4, ed. E.M. Hetherington. New York: John Wiley & Sons, Inc., pp. 693–774.

Rutter, M. (1971), Normal psychosexual development. *J. Child Psychol. Psychiatry*, 11:259–283.

Schafer, R. (1974), Problems in Freud's psychology of women. *J. Am. Psychoanal. Assoc.*, 22:459–485.

Schechter, M., Carlson, P.N., Simmons, J.Q., and Work, H.H. (1964), Emotional problems in the adoptee. *Arch. Gen. Psychiatry*, 10:37.

Schwartzman, H.B. (1979), *Transformations: The Anthropology of Children's Play*. New York: Plenum Publishing Corp.

Segal, H. (1964), *Introduction to the Work of Melanie Klein*. London: Heinemann, p. 61.

Shaffer, D. (1985), Enuresis. In: *Child and Adolescent Psychiatry: Modern Approaches*. 2nd Ed., eds. M. Rutter and L. Hersov. London: Blackwell Scientific Publications, pp. 465–481.

Shaffer, D., and Gardner, A. (1981), Classification of enuresis. Presented at the 28th Annual Meeting of the American Academy of Child Psychiatry, Dallas, October 15, 1981.

Sherfey, M.J. (1966), The evolution and nature of female sexuality in relation to psychoanalytic theory. *J. Am. Psychoanal. Assoc.*, 14:28–128.

Sours, J.A., Frumken, P., and Inderwell, R.R. (1963), Somnambulism. *Arch. Gen. Psychiatry*, 9:400–413.

Spitz, R.A. (1962), *The First Year of Life*. New York: International Universities Press.

Toussieng, P.B. (1966), Thoughts regarding the etiology of psychological difficulties in adopted children. *Child Welfare*, February 9.

Triseliotis, J. (1973), *In Search of Origins: The Experiences of Adopted People*. London: Routledge & Kegan Paul.

Vygotsky, L. (1967), Play and its role in the mental development of the child. *Soviet Psychol.*, 5:6–18.

Waelder. R. (1933), The psychoanalytic theory of play. *Psychoanal. Q.*, 2:208–224.

White, R.W. (1960), Competence and the psychosexual stage of development. In: *Nebraska Symposium on Motivation* (Vol. 8), ed. M.R. Jones. Lincoln, Neb.: University of Nebraska Press.

Winston, J. (1985), *Brain and Psyche: The Biology of the Unconscious*. New York: Anchor Press/Doubleday.

Wittenborn, J.R. (1957), *The Placement of Adoptive Children*. Springfield, Ill.: Charles C Thomas, p. 189.

18

THE ELEMENTARY-SCHOOL-AGE CHILD

MATURATION

Something clearly happens in the development of the child between 6 and 11 years of age to suggest that qualitative as well as quantitative qualities have locked into place. The pieces of earlier development seem almost suddenly to fit together and function in a smoother, more integrated fashion. The child not only learns new motor skills, such as balancing on a bicycle, but at some point, perhaps around age 9, does so with ease—the skill has "clicked" and has become an automatic, established, unself-conscious act requiring no effort of concentration. Language skills similarly become better developed and the child becomes more capable of abstract thought. In addition, as noted in Chapter 1, important physiologic maturities are reached at this time.

LATERALITY

Laterality is a measurable, specialized, central function of a paired faculty such as eyes, ears, hands, and feet. *Preference* is the subjective, self-reported experience of an individual and need not be the same as objectively measured laterality. Indeed, the preference of an individual may be related more to the acuity of the peripheral organ (e.g., the ear) than to anything else. *Dominance* is the term used for the concept of cerebral hemisphere specialization, e.g., information processing, language, and speech lateralization.

The term *predominance* has been proposed to take into account the varying degrees of cerebral asymmetry for specific functions (Buffery, 1978). For example, right-handed subjects may have a predominance in the left hemisphere for language functions and a predominance in the right hemisphere for visual-spatial functions.

Hemispheric lateralization appears to proceed sequentially from gross and fine motor skills to sensorimotor skills to speech and language (Leong, 1976). Handedness is commonly consolidated by about age 5, footedness by about age 7, eye preference by about age 7 or 8, and ear preference by about age 9 (Touwen, 1980).

PERSONALITY DEVELOPMENT

Essentially this is a period of consolidation of all earlier developments. All the relatively autonomous, enduring functions that are conceptualized within the structural view of the personality show clear maturation as they become more firmly established. For example, the maturation of certain functions, such as defense mechanisms and reality testing, is more clearly manifested at this stage. Besides the shift from a general phobic organization to a normal obsessional organization characteristic of an elementary-school-age child, there is a much greater capacity for thinking, memory, speech, and conceptualizing. At this stage certain concepts of inevitability (e.g., of death, birth, and sex differences) become established. (The child's reaction to death is discussed in Chapter 21.) Logical secondary-process thinking is clearly dominant, and the child has a far greater capacity to delay and divert the expression of a given impulse. The child is able to take care of his or her body quite well, and now usually thinks of food as food rather than as a symbol. His or her psychologic defenses are greatly strengthened, with the amnesia of earlier infantile urges reinforced by such reaction formations as shame, disgust, and guilt against exhibitionistic, messing, and aggressive urges.

Concomitant with the successful management of impulses, more acceptable forms of gratification become sufficiently satisfying for the child. There is a diminution of *observable* sexuality (see p. 54), the conflicts of the oedipal period are now experienced in a less intense way, and the child is altogether more responsive to his or her environment. There may be occasional, temporary, regressive phenomena, but on the whole the child is more robust at this stage. To the extent that he or she no longer has to consume energy in dealing with impulses, the child is free to pursue activities that are not ordinarily conflict-laden, which allows him or her a greater degree of autonomy (Hartmann, 1955). Thus, energy becomes available for learning and exploring and for widening and deepening relationship with others.

LATENCY

This total complex of phenomena is subsumed under the term latency in psychoanalysis. However, many of the behavioral manifestations that occur during this period of psychosexual and psychosocial change are modified by cultural factors. For example, in some societies overt sexual activity occurs throughout this period of development, particularly when there are no sanctions against such activity. This was seen clearly in the Trobriand Islanders studied by Malinowski (1927). Moreover, in present Western society, the atmosphere of greater freedom permits, for example, a more open expression of sexual interests. Empirical studies (Reese, 1966; Broderick, 1966; Janus and Bess, 1976; Rutter, 1980) have actually shown an *increase* in sexual activities during this period. Lastly, many other complex changes occur at about age 7 (Shapiro and Perry, 1976).

Shapiro and Perry carefully and systematically reviewed three major areas of information about biopsychologic events during this developmental period. Specifically, they reviewed the data on perceptual-postural maturation, temporospatial orientation, and cognitive changes. On the basis of their thoughtful survey, they concluded that the basis for development during this period rests more on processes within the central nervous system, together with increasingly sophisticated and mature cognitive strategies, rather than on the biphasic development of sexual drives. Furthermore, they viewed this maturation as a significant *dis*continuity in behavioral development. Shapiro and Perry then attempted to incorporate all this new multilevel information on the 7-year-old child under the old term of latency. It was a procrustean effort, rather like fitting all the knowledge in modern chemistry under the heading of alchemy. Obviously, psychoanalysts are loath to discard a term.

This discussion suggests that the original meaning of this 75-year-old term, although of historical interest, is no longer sufficient. The term latency, when used at all, should perhaps be confined to the intrapsychic changes that are taking place, particularly with respect to those functions that provide for an increase in internal controls (e.g., mechanisms of defense, increasing capacities for socialization, formation of a sense of moral values, and changes in relationships).

SUPEREGO DEVELOPMENT

Although initially (e.g., at ages 6 to 8) the superego is said to be strict, with signs of a heightened ambivalence and a marked conflict over masturbation, gradually this struggle abates so that in the second half of this period (e.g., ages 8 to 10) the superego is thought to be less strict, sublimation to be more successful, and the child to begin to experience pleasure again from sexual gratification (Bornstein, 1951; Fries, 1957).

RELATIONSHIP WITH PARENTS AND PEERS

In relationships with others at this stage, the child begins to feel somewhat disillusioned with his or her parents, and may even feel they are not as admirable as the parents of his or her friends (Pearson, 1966; see Note 33). Family romance ideas are especially prominent. The child may turn his or her interests to other adults, such as teachers, scout leaders, ministers, and others, whom the child may overvalue. These fantasies and behavioral tendencies are part of the process of increasing separation and autonomy. Most of all, the child needs peers with whom to identify and play (Campbell, 1964). By the beginning of adolescence children will spend nearly half their waking hours with other children (Barker and Wright, 1951). In the elementary school years, friendships are typically formed with members of the same sex. A small number of children, perhaps 10%, tend to be isolated socially; such children are often acutely aware of their lack of friends and lack social skills (Dodge et al., 1983).

IMAGINARY COMPANION

One curious form of "peer" relationship seen in childhood is that of the imaginary companion. In one questionnaire study of 700 adults asked to recall their childhood, approximately one third of the women and one quarter of the men recalled having an imaginary companion during their childhood (Hurlock and Burnstein, 1932). McKellar (1965) described a colleague who recalled having as a companion an imaginary blue fairy called Tinkerbell, who was a friendly figure. At 5 years of age the girl still had Tinkerbell as a companion even though she knew that Tinkerbell did not really exist. Tinkerbell

persisted as a kind of half-belief until the girl was about 9 or 10 years old.

Sometimes the imaginary companion takes the form of a conscious fantasy of having a twin. This fantasy builds up during latency "as the result of disappointment by the parents in the oedipus situation, in the child's search for a partner who will give him all the attention, love and companionship he desires and who will provide an escape from loneliness and solitude" (Burlingham, 1945). In this sense the imaginary companion is a variant of the family romance fantasies and animal fantasies that are prevalent during this period (A. Freud, 1937).

Imaginary companions appear to serve different functions at different levels of development (Nagera, 1969): (1) they may serve as an auxiliary conscience whom the child consults, (2) they may serve as a scapegoat when the child acts upon a forbidden impulse, or (3) they may become the vehicle for some vicarious pleasure. In addition, the imaginary companion may be invoked to ward off regression and to master anxiety, thus serving healthy, adaptive aims.

SOCIAL PREPARATION

While all this development and consolidation is taking place, the child becomes noticeably more pleasant for adults. There is now a pull away from earlier childhood urges, or a strong force to push them down, which is syntonic with the adult position. This is in contrast to the regressive pull of earlier childhood to which young children frequently succumb and which adults often find distinctly annoying. The child has now become in general a more social being.

In terms of social development, the child is also aware at this time that there is a time for play and a time for what is increasingly being called work. The child seems to be aware that he or she must start to prepare more earnestly for adult roles. Erikson calls this the stage of industry versus inferiority, and notes that the child must achieve at this stage the ability to enjoy work, a sense of growing possibilities, and a feeling of capability (Erikson, 1959).

What is of further interest is that the child now begins to experience more directly the impact of the environment outside the family, especially the school and the community. Acculturation still continues to occur mostly through the family, but the family itself is also subject to the influence of society. Hence the role of society must be considered, at least in its broadest terms at this point.

Acculturation and adaptation through this kind of cultural transmission process are, of course, much more rapid than adaptation by means of the survival adaptive traits in the ordinary selective process of evolution. Lorenz put it well when he said, "Within one or two generations a process of ecological adaptation can be achieved which, in normal phylogeny and without the interference of conceptual thought, would have taken a time of an altogether different, much greater, order of magnitude" (Lorenz, 1966). Yet, a certain period of time, perhaps a generation or more, is still necessary to bring about these adaptive changes that will help one make a good adjustment to a slowly evolving and changng society. What if society evolves and changes more rapidly than usual? How is the adaptive process affected, and can it keep up?

Today social and moral values change rapidly. Further, the increasing rate of automation has sometimes caused a skill (or a career) to become obsolescent before it was fully developed by the individual. Moreover, new skills and careers appear more rapidly than even the most thoughtful planning for the future can anticipate. Instantaneous telecommunications and the rapidly increasing rate of technologic development add to the individual's fear of being overwhelmed and out of control. At the same time, the mobility of the American population has at times been associated with family isolation and isolation of the generations. This isolation has been aggravated in large impersonal cities and large impersonal campuses. Moreover, the temporary absolute and relative increase in the adolescent and youth population with respect to the adult population contributed to some of the polarization of viewpoints that has occurred in recent years.

The effect of some of these trends is partly reflected in some of the unrest seen most vividly in adolescents. (Some of the alienation syndromes that have been described will be mentioned later.) The effect of these trends is also beginning to affect preadolescents, partly through the uncertainty and insecurity transmitted to them by parents, teachers, and other adults who are unsettled by the rapid change.

PLAY DEVELOPMENT

Some of the personality characteristics and developments mentioned earlier permeate the play of the child at this stage also (Peller, 1954; see Note 37). The play is typically cooperative play, with team games and board games prominent. The child enjoys special clubs and, especially, making the rules. For example, in deciding to play baseball, boys at this stage may choose the teams, mark out the field, decide on the rules, and have a great time—without ever having thrown the ball! At the same time, some of the intensity with which these games are played, with aggressive attacks and sexual excitement, seem to represent the fears, wishes, and anxieties of the child in relation to parents, brothers, and sisters. Furthermore, having a number of teammates, with the sharing of defense as well as offense, often reassures the individual child. It helps ward off the anxiety of being alone against adults and gives the child a feeling of kinship with others who have the same limitations and frustrations. The play is so gratifying at times that it absorbs some of the longings of the child.

COGNITIVE DEVELOPMENT

The increased capacity at this time for more complex thought has been studied in detail by Piaget, who has called this the stage of concrete operations (from approximately ages 7 to 11) (Inhelder and Piaget, 1958). Two outstanding characteristics of this stage have been noted by Piaget. One is the now permanent possibility of returning to the starting point of a mental operation; e.g., the child can say not only $6 + 4 = 10$ but also $10 - 6 = 4$. This "reversible operation" is an internal action resulting from the integration of other such actions. The other characteristic is that the child is no longer dominated by a configuration he or she perceives at any given moment but can now take into account two or more variables. A well-documented example is the child who can differentiate height and width as variables when an identical quantity of water is poured into a cylinder and a beaker; the child realizes that the amount of water in both beakers is the same (Piaget, 1928). Hitherto the child may have been bound by either the height or the width, and he or she might have said that either the cylinder or the beaker had more water because of either single dimension. Although it is known that conservation of amount of substance appears to precede observation of weight and various other measures, the precise mechanism by which conservation is attained by the child is unclear (Wallach, 1969). Nevertheless, this step in cognitive development is an important factor in the child's capacity for learning at this stage as he or she enters first grade at 6 years of age. (Conservation is discussed in greater detail in Chapter 4.)

PREREQUISITES TO SCHOOL LEARNING

However, the process of learning has been developing long before the child enters elementary school or even nursery school. It is necessary, therefore, to review briefly at this point some of the child's earliest learning experiences. The earliest experiences form the basis for much of the later information-processing patterns, and it is possible that so-called autonomous control processes are laid down and become relatively fixed at an early age (Hebb, 1949). Many workers have demonstrated that the preschool years are of great importance for intellectual as well as social and emotional development (Stevenson et al., 1967; Scott, 1968). However, as Elkind (1970) has pointed out, this is not to say that formal instruction is indicated in the nursery school; rather, preparation for such instruction is what seems to be appropriate. Such nursery-school preparation usually includes (1) fine and gross motor play, to learn about balance, height, and gravity and to acquire the basic perceptual-motor coordination that will be needed later for reading, (2) role playing, to learn about later social roles and adult behavior, and (3) freedom to experiment, through which the child learns the pleasures of discovery and accomplishment. Through these and other kinds of experiences the child in nursery school accumulates the necessary concepts, relationships, attitudes and motivations needed for the learning that is required in elementary school (Elkind, 1970). When the child reaches elementary-school age, the learning process is more complex; it involves many factors, and each factor is affected by a specific cluster of variables, some of which will be described.

LEARNING

In learning, one adapts present behavior to the results of one's previous interaction with the environment. Adequate perception, memory, attention, and motivation are all necessary for learning. General processes for learning include imitation, identification, habituation, sensitization, classical and instrumental conditioning, reinforcement, and generalization. Many specific processes for specific functions are also required, e.g., coding and decoding for reading skills; motor skills may also be important. All these processes involve many areas of the brain and numerous complex neurochemical exchanges. Theoretically, learning may be impaired or interrupted by interference at any point in this complex continuum. The interfering factors may be genetic, prenatal (smoking, drinking, radiation during pregnancy), congenital (birth anoxia), traumatic (head injury), infective (viral encephalitis), immunologic, nutritional, toxic (e.g., lead), maturational, neoplastic, or psychologic. The learning impairment may be pure or may be part of a broader syndrome (e.g., attention deficit disorder). Unfortunately, our clinical and laboratory skills at present are not refined sufficiently to pinpoint the locus of interference, much less recommend a specific remedy. Associated conditions may, obviously, warrant treatment.

READING DIFFICULTIES

Perhaps the single most common difficulty found in school-age children who come to child guidance clinics is some form of school learning difficulty (Rutter, 1974), usually a reading difficulty. In 1983 the United States ranked forty-ninth in the world in literacy level. More than 23 million people in the United States lack elementary reading and writing skills, i.e., they cannot write a check, complete a job application, or take a written driver's license examination. Probably another 40 million people function at or below a level of marginal literacy, and many of these individuals go to great lengths to conceal this inadequacy (Ross, 1983).

Reading is essentially a linguistic skill that requires a comprehension of visual symbols used for communication. Interference with the acquisition of this skill may occur when the child has a visual (e.g., poor fusion) or auditory handicap, a maturational lag, a specific reading or linguistic disability, an attention disorder, mental retardation, a psychologic disturbance, an adverse family environment, or poor teaching.

SPECIFIC READING DISABILITY

Clinical evidence suggests that certain children have a developmental lag in their capacity to understand the written symbols of language that gives rise to the syndrome called developmental dyslexia (Critchley, 1964). The problem usually becomes apparent during first grade, when the child finds reading inordinately difficult. There may be associated speech and language problems, motor awkwardness, some spatial disorientation, and mixed or delayed laterality. Behavior problems may also be observed. Comprehension is poor. The child reads only with much effort, and often makes many omissions and guesses. The child's handwriting is poor, with many rotations, confusions, and transpositions. A family history of slowness in reading development is often present. Parents sometimes recall that something seemed to click for them at a certain age, perhaps as late as age 12, when, more or less suddenly, reading became easy. Unfortunately, the delay in reading, especially when misunderstood, sometimes results in frustration, anger, and a feeling of defeat, causing secondary psychologic difficulties that further impair the capacity to learn and read.

Children with speech retardation and articulation defects are also often delayed in reading (Ingram, 1970). Visual-spatial skills appear to be less important for reading (Robinson and Schwartz, 1973), but may be more important for arithmetic difficulties (Slade and Russell, 1971). Sequencing difficulties in the perception of temporal or spatial ordering may also be associated with reading difficulties.

Sometimes the rare syndrome of hyperlexia is encountered. It occurs most commonly in boys; the child is often described as clumsy and as having a marked apraxia (an inability to copy single figures). The hyperlexic child also has some difficulty in comprehension, with an impaired ability to relate speech sounds to meaning, poor relationships, and such language disorders as echolalia, idioglossia, and pronoun reversal. Because these symptoms are also found in autistic children, a common neuropathology (possibly in the parietal lobe) has been postulated for both conditions (Huttenlocher and Huttenlocher, 1973).

READING AND LATERALIZATION

Lateralization itself appears to follow a logical sequence, with each higher level dependent on the level preceding it. The sequence flows from motor laterality through sensory laterality to lateralization of language (Semmes, 1968). Verbal skills represent the highest level of language differentiation and lateralization (Penfield and Roberts, 1959). Working specifically wth children diagnosed as having developmental dyslexia, Sparrow (1969) found that retarded readers could be differentiated from normal readers on all the higher level perceptual-cognitive measures of lateralization in use at that time, although no differences could be found between dyslexic children and normal children on less complex measures, such as manual dexterity. Sparrow hypothesized that a developmental lag in the process of lateralization, defined as the representation or control of functions by one cerebral hemisphere, frequently resulted in deficits that interfered with learning to read, and in the case of reading-related behaviors it was almost always the left hemisphere. On the other hand, Rutter and his colleagues (1970) found no association between reading difficulties and lateralization other than an association between reading difficulties and *confusion* between right and left. Finally, Buffery (1976) concluded that "the relationship of various patterns of lateral congruity to learning disorders in general remains enigmatic."

LANGUAGE COMPLEXITY AND READING DIFFICULTIES

The specificity of a particular language is a factor that may contribute to certain reading disabilities. The prevalence of reading disability, for example, varies with the language used, being highest in English-speaking countries, lower in German-speaking countries, lower still in Latin-speaking countries (e.g., Italy and Spain), and only 0.98% among Japanese children (Makita, 1968). Makita postulates that this rarity is based upon the fact that in Japanese KANA script there is "almost a key to keyhole" situation in the script-phonetic relationship and that the reading disability of many children in English-speaking

countries might be "more of a philological than a neuropsychiatric problem."

READING AND CENTRAL NERVOUS SYSTEM INTEGRATION

Intactness of both general and specific organic functions is an obvious factor in learning. Thus early brain damage impedes the acquisition of reading skills. Impulsive children also have difficulty in learning to read in part because of their inadequate strategies for learning of any kind (Egeland, 1974). Visual and auditory intactness is a necessary condition for learning in the ordinary school setting. Impairments of any of these special functions require a special adaptation of the environment to enable learning to proceed along an approximately normal course. For example, special intervention is necessary in the case of blind children if learning of the most basic kind is to occur at all (Fraiberg and Freedman, 1964; Fraiberg et al., 1966).

LEARNING PROBLEMS AND ATTENTION DEFICIT DISORDERS

Children with an attention deficit disorder comprise a heterogeneous group who may have (1) a more or less pure disturbance of activity or attention, (2) hyperactivity with developmental delay, (3) hyperkinetic conduct disorder, or (4) "other disorders" (Rutter et al., 1975). The hyperkinetic syndrome, characterized by hyperactivity, impulsivity, distractibility, and excitability, may be associated with learning problems, as well as with aggressive and antisocial behavior and emotional lability (Cantwell, 1975). The syndrome occurred at the rate of about 2 per 2,199 children in Rutter's Isle of Wight study (Rutter et al., 1970). The etiology is varied and in some cases includes brain damage (Werry, 1972), central nervous system arousal disorder (Sutterfield et al., 1974), and genetic factors (Cantwell, 1976). Low academic achievement is common. The learning impairment may result from an interference with attention due to the hyperactivity, a tendency to make impulsive decisions rather than thoughtful ones, or some neurologic deficit.

LEARNING AND INTELLIGENCE

General intelligence is another factor in learning. However, it is important to remember that normal intellectual development is often uneven; children frequently go up or down 10 to 20 points in IQ during their school years (Rutter and Madge, 1976). Similarly, the difficulty of the subject matter waxes and wanes. Consequently, the rate of academic achievement normally may increase and decrease over the years.

Over and above native endowment, functional intelligence is in part determined by the degree of motivation, emotional stability, stimulation, model adequacy, and opportunity. For example, Zigler and Butterfield (1968) have noted that deprived nursery school children suffer from an emotional and motivational deficit that decreases their intellectual performance to a lower level than would be expected from their intellectual potential as measured in an optimizing test situation. The importance of this kind of observation of children in nursery school and kindergarten lies in the possibilities for prediction because most studies of children who appear to develop learning difficulties in elementary school reveal a much earlier onset of problems (Cohen, 1963).

EMOTIONAL FREEDOM TO LEARN

The preceding factor leads to a further general factor, namely, that the environment may either facilitate or hamper learning. A climate of emotional freedom to learn includes the concept that children must have such areas of functioning as attention, memory, and speech sufficiently conflict-free that they can devote themselves to learning. Clearly a large number of factors that cause anxiety may reduce the level of functioning in these areas because of the anxiety aroused.

Some of these factors will be described shortly.

TEMPERAMENT AND LEARNING DISABILITIES

Chess (1968) has drawn attention to the temperament of the child in learning, and has suggested that even in cases in which the cognitive or motivational element is the primary issue in a learning difficulty, the implementation of an appropriate remedial or therapeutic plan may depend on what she terms the child's temperamental individuality. Chess identified and described nine categories that constitute temperament: (1) activity level, (2) rhythmicity of such functions as hunger, elimination, and the sleep-wake cycle, (3) approach or withdrawal in response to, say, a person, (4) adaptability to an altered environment, (5) intensity of any given reaction, (6) threshold of responsiveness, (7) quantity and quality of moods, (8) degree of distractibility, and (9) persistence in the face of obstacles. The therapeutic plan that was devised was appropriate to the temperament as defined by these nine characteristics.

ANXIETY AND SCHOOL UNDERACHIEVEMENT

With this general background it is now profitable to describe some of the more specific psychologic conflicts said to be involved in school learning difficulties. Underachievement in school is found far more often in boys than in girls, and it tends to manifest itself earlier in boys than in girls. For example, in one study boys tended to become chronic underachievers even during the first few grades of elementary school, whereas girls tended to show signs of underachievement in the grades just prior to and at junior high shool (Shaw and McCuen, 1960). Among all the different causes of learning difficulties, anxiety from a number of sources is claimed to be the most common interfering factor (Pearson, 1952). Anxiety may be derived from tension between the parents, sexual conflicts, illness, or problems with siblings. The anxiety may interfere with the capacity to assimilate or utilize new information. Sometimes these conflicts give rise to negativism, delinquency, truancy, or school phobia (Gittelman-Klein and Klein, 1980), with subsequent secondary impairments of learning. At the same time, there is no clearcut relationship between anxiety and underachievement (Rutter, 1974). Most reports of a relationship between reading difficulty and neurotic conflict are based on uncontrolled and highly speculative psychoanalytic studies. (For a discussion of anxiety disorders, see Chapter 30.)

ANXIETY AND AGGRESSION

One speculation about the cause of anxiety is that anxiety arises from a difficulty in controlling aggressive impulses, giving rise to a learning block (Blanchard, 1946). The child may shut himself or herself off from all possibility of having aggressive fantasies stimulated, or the child may experience the act of learning itself as an aggressive act, making nonlearning a counter-aggressive move. Learning difficulties are, of course, usually multidetermined; however, one component may be the hostility the child feels toward parents and his or her unconscious refusal to please them. In failing to perform, the child simultaneously punishes himself or herself, thus warding off guilt.

ANXIETY AND DEPRESSION

Sometimes the anxiety may be part of a more pervasive depressive disorder (Schulterbrandt and Raskin, 1977). Depression in children may be manifested as school failure or by somatic complaints accompanied by feelings of inadequacy, worthlessness, low self-esteem, helplessness, and hopelessness. Temper tantrums, disobedience, running away, truancy and, in adolescents, delinquency, may also be signs of depression in childhood (Glaser, 1967). The depression often consists of a persistent sense of helplessness and/or passive resignation, and the child

feels unable to acquire something that he or she feels is essential to his or her well-being (Sandler and Joffe, 1965). (For a further discussion of depression in children and adolescents, see Chapters 19 and 31 and Epilogue.)

ANXIETY AND THE APPEARANCE OF STUPIDITY

Children may also present themselves as "stupid" when they are trying to maintain a secret, when they are reacting to their frustrated sense of curiosity, when they wish to avoid competition, or when they are caught in a conflict between obeying and rebelling and elect to do neither and both at the same time. Secretiveness and lying on the mother's part, especially when there is a close bond between mother and child, often force the child to appear ignorant and not curious, not only about the forbidden topic but in a more generalized way too (Hellman, 1954). According to Hellman, frequently the mother's secret is that she is having an extramarital love affair.

ANXIETY AND SYMBOLIC ASSOCIATION

Very rarely an unconscious and symbolic association between conflicts and particular words, or even letters, that leads to a reading inhibition is discovered during intensive psychotherapy or psychoanalysis of a child (O'Sullivan and Pryles, 1962).

ANXIETY AND TRUANCY

Truancy may be a further manifestation of anxiety. The act of truancy may represent a wish to escape from an intolerable home situation. Sometimes the truancy represents a flight from reality and a retreat into fantasy. The family ties may be so weak that truancy is facilitated. At other times the truant child may be seeking a lost love object or may be attempting to create a sense of guilt in the parents. Often, the truant child wishes to avoid school because of a primary learning difficulty or a fear of criticism, punishment, or humiliation from his or her classmates or teachers.

ANXIETY AND SCHOOL AVOIDANCE

Separation anxiety may become exacerbated or may make its first appearance during the elementary-school-age stage; separation anxiety may give rise to the symptom of school avoidance (Hersov, 1980). There is often a history of a poorly resolved dependency relationship between mother and child (Waldfogel et al., 1957). Often some acute anxiety is precipitated just prior to the onset of the symptoms. This anxiety may be produced by an illness, an operation such as a tonsillectomy, or an external event so similar to an internal fantasy the child has that the fantasy is intensified to the point that the child fears the fantasy will be realized. Sometimes hysterical or compulsive reactions may be mobilized to deal with the anxiety. In the face of this anxiety, the child may regress and experience an increase in his or her dependency wishes. At the same time, the mother herself may be experiencing anxiety, most often arising from some threat to her security. Such threats might arise from marital unhappiness, economic deprivation, or simply overwhelming demands that the mother resents. She then exploits the child's wish for dependence as a means of gratifying her own frustration, loss, and anxiety. Mother and child then become locked together in a mutual act of regression and dependency, usually combining hostile fantasies that each must hold in check by each keeping close to the other. Often the mother encourages her child to stay home because she has fears for his or her safety (that are based on her own angry wishes toward him). The child, in turn, is afraid to leave the mother for fear something will happen to her in his absence. The absence from school and the anxiety aroused may interfere considerably with the child's learning.

SEXUAL DIFFICULTIES

The expressions of normal sexuality may take a variety of forms during childhood (S. Freud, 1905). Signs of sexual problems may also emerge during this period of adjustment. However, deviant-appearing behavior does not necessarily have the same significance as similar behavior exhibited during adult years, when the individual should have reached sexual maturity. For example, manifest homosexual and heterosexual preferences have different cycles and different meanings during early development. An infant may show affection for an adult, regardless of sex, provided the adult meets the caring and protecting needs of the infant. A preschool-age child begins to show strong feelings, both positive and negative, toward both parents, based in part on the sexual attributes and roles of those parents In this sense, a preschool-age child may show homosexual and heterosexual preferences. During the elementary-school years, a boy may "love" a particular adult who has shown him empathy and understanding. If the adult is a man, the relationship appears to be homosexual; if the adult is a woman, it appears to be heterosexual. In neither case, however, is it necessarily based on the sex of the person; again it is based rather on the function performed by that person. At the same time, the child's relationship with his or her peers may appear singularly homosexual in terms of preferred sex of the playmate yet not represent homosexuality at all. For example, some school-age boys may show a disdain for girls, wishing only to play with other boys. Such boys are not at all destined to become homosexuals; as a matter of fact, boys who at this age prefer to play with girls are thought to be more likely to be vulnerable to later homosexual influences. The key to understanding this paradox lies in the realization that the choice of playmates at this stage is often made largely on the basis of identification and not of actual sexual love for the selected playmate.

HOMOSEXUALITY

Nevertheless, certain influences may turn a child in the direction of homosexuality. Besides any innate bisexual or homosexual tendency that cannot as yet be documented, some children persist in forming narcissistic relationships in which they identify with persons of the same sex. Continuing attachments to adults on the basis of persistent attempts to gratify early needs may also lead to persisting homosexual relationships. Sometimes disguised sexual assaults on children—in the form of activities that have erotic components (e.g., giving enemas, rectal and vaginal douching and temperature taking)—may lead to a persisting passive homosexual longing. In addition, if the oedipal feelings are not adequately resolved, the child may remain fixated at the level of an intense homosexual tie. Last, if the child is unable to mobilize effective defense reactions against homosexuality or if he or she has no satisfactory parent models with whom to identify, there is further likelihood that the homosexual tendencies will outweigh the heterosexual strivings (A. Freud, 1965).

Even so, the balance of factors to be weighed makes prediction of the ultimate sexual outcome difficult. For example, besides the qualities in the parents and their conflicts, numerous conflicts and anxieties may arise in the child that may be aggravated by such external factors as illness, divorce, seduction, incest, and rape (Lewis and Sarrel, 1969), not to mention the myriad opportunities and lost opportunities for satisfactions or frustrations. (Homosexuality will be discussed further in the following chapter.)

TRANSVESTISM

A specific variety of homosexuality seen in children is manifested by transvestite behavior. Boys who dress as girls are regarded with greater concern in our society than are girls who dress as boys. In fact, boys who dress as girls do seem to cope less well with their intrapsychic difficulties. These boys may be trying to win their mother's love, especially if they sense that their mother does not really like them. They may also be attempting to deal with a loss through the normal process of identification. That is, if they somewhat suddenly lose the mother they love (either in reality or in psychic reality), they may attempt to compensate for this loss by identifying with and holding onto the internalized image of the mother. In still other cases, the boy may be acting out hostile, aggressive impulses against the mother by caricaturing how women behave or dress.

The mothers of such children often have a disturbance in their own sexual identity and their object relations (Stoller, 1967). They may dislike men for a variety of reasons and so start their boys off on cross-dressing as soon as they show any signs of developing a masculine identity. They nip the masculine identity in the bud, so to speak. Other mothers may regard their sons as extensions of themselves and may then find themslves unable to tolerate any separation from their sons. Such mothers then so indulge their sons that the boys' gratitude becomes profound enough to lead to a strong identification with the mothers.

Unfortunately, the fathers of such children are usually poor models of masculinity and, furthermore, they fail to protect their sons from the influence of the mothers.

An important clinical point is the degree to which the child becomes sexually excited during the act of dressing in the clothes of the opposite sex. Children who become sexually excited usually find it hard to give up the gratification, and they almost become addicted to cross-dressing. They may resent any interference and may even fly into a rage. Cross dressing is not uniformly associated with later homosexuality.

COMPULSIVE SEXUAL BEHAVIOR IN GIRLS

Homosexuality is not the only risk of such adverse parental influences. Compulsive heterosexual activity may also be an outcome. In some instances, a girl may repeatedly and compulsively act seductively, engage in intercourse, and become pregnant. Some of this compulsion to repeat seductive acts may represent an attempt to work through an earlier traumatic incestuous relationship, as illustrated in the following brief case summary.

When Cathy was a young girl, she lived in a home in which her father was given to violence. When she was about 6 or 7 years of age, her father committed incest with her. When Cathy became an adolescent, she found herself involved again and again with boys who were many years older than herself and who were given to violence. Her particular boyfriend at the time had a criminal record involving robbery with illegal possession of a gun. Eventually, at age 15, Cathy became pregnant by her 24-year-old boyfriend.

Excessively repetitive compulsive behavior may also be part of a larger problem of poor impulse control, resulting from such factors as inadequate models for controls in the parents, overstimulation, or unresolved highly ambivalent child-parent relationships. In some cases the girl may be acting out an unconscious wish of her mother to have an affair or care for a baby again.

STEALING

The significance of stealing depends on whether it is a developmental phenomenon or a neurotic symptom. The infant simply lacks the distinction between self and object, between "what's mine" and "what's not mine." The preschool-age child has a tendency to hoard, and may "acquire" the objects that belong to another child to add to his or her collection. In the nursery school-age period, object relations usually advance to the point of the child's learning what belongs to others, so that taking something that belongs to someone else begins to be called stealing. If the child is delayed in his or her development and continues to be relatively more immature and to have poor impulse control, the impulse to take things that belong to others will continue, especially if there is added stress from any kinds of deprivation.

Once the child is beyond this stage of de-velopment, the act of taking something that belongs to someone else is more properly called stealing. Many motivations may now lie behind the act of stealing. Sometimes it is an expression of a wish to obtain love or to bribe a person into friendship. At other times it is an expression of hostility toward the parents, who are chagrined at the act. Yet, some parents are not chagrined and some may even seem to condone the act, as in the following example. A boy confessed to stealing some table tennis balls from a large department store. His father responded by saying he was not concerned because "the store could stand the loss." The distortion of reality values and the implied condoning of the act were clear. In this case the boy had no more sense of guilt about what he had done than had the father. Such a child may have adequate superego injunctions in other areas, but because the parents are themselves delinquent and provide no taboos against stealing, the child takes in whole this aspect, too, of the parent and as a result has a superego or conscience with noticeable deficits ("lacunae").

Occasionally the act of stealing is a poor sublimation for an intense desire to damage another person. Instead of hurting a part of the other person's body, the stealer takes away his "treasured possession." Sometimes such an unacceptable impulse gives rise to a feeling of guilt, which is then vitiated by the punishment incurred when another "crime" is committed. The act of stealing serves this function when it is performed in such a blatant way that it demonstrates a clear wish to be caught. (Sometimes the item stolen provides a clue to the initial unacceptable impulse.)

Stealing may also be a part of a more general behavior trait. For example, a child may tend to behave in a counterphobic way; that is, the child deals with a fear by repeatedly and increasingly risking the danger he or she most fears. Stealing may be just such a "daring act"; the child defies authority and experiences the thrill of near misses. Sometimes it is an act performed in the service of identification with a group or with a particular leader or in reluctant obedience to the commands of such a person.

LYING

What has been said about stealing can also be said about lying. In infancy, fantasy and reality are not well distinguished. There is throughout childhood a tendency, especially under stress, to revert to the pleasure of fantasy and primary process thinking. The verbal distortion of reality (the untruth) more likely represents the lack of distinction between fantasy and reality or a regression to fantasy than a conscious effort to distort reality. Later, when the distortion of the truth can be more properly called lying, motivations similar to those found in stealing may give rise to lying.

ANTISOCIAL BEHAVIOR

Serious antisocial behavior in children 6 to 11 years of age is a "particularly ominous childhood pattern" (Robins, 1966). Robins compared 524 children seen in a child guidance clinic with 100 matched normal children in a local school. Her study found that children referred to the clinic for such complaints as temper tantrums, learning problems, sleeping and eating problems, and speech problems did not differ much from the control group when they were seen as adults 30 years later; that is, shyness, seclusiveness, nervousness, tantrums, insomnia, fears, tics, speech problems, and similar complaints were *not* related to later psychiatric disorder. However, children referred to the clinic for antisocial behavior *did* differ from the control group seen 30 years later, and the more severe the early antisocial behavior was during childhood, the more disturbed was the later adjustment. Among the children referred to the clinic for antisocial behavior, (1) most had been held back in first grade, (2) their problems had become obvious at the age of 7, and (3) the common referral symptoms had been theft (82%), incorrigible behavior (76%), truancy (75%), running away (71%), having bad

friends (52%), school discipline problems, and sexual activity including promiscuity. (Truancy and poor school performance had been almost universally present in children who later demonstrated antisocial behaviors, and a high percentage of the antisocial children were later diagnosed as being schizophrenic.) Interestingly, in the families of these children referred for antisocial behavior, the father was "sociopathic" or alcoholic, and the homes were impoverished or broken. In short, the best single predictor of adult "sociopathy" was the degree of childhood antisocial behavior, especially in children 6 to 11 years of age.

Poverty, a slum environment, maternal deprivation, foster home or orphanage placement, or even a "sociopathic" mother did not predict adult sociopathy. However, if a child had a sociopathic or alcoholic father and was also sent to a correctional institution, the prognosis for the child was poor. Robins was essentially taking issue with the so-called culture-of-poverty hypothesis of sociopathy. She believed that it was the other way around; that is, that children with antisocial behavior and sociopathic fathers simply fail to rise socioeconomically. Robins concluded that antisocial behavior predicts class status more than class status predicts antisocial behavior.

In a later study of violent juvenile delinquents, Dorothy Otnow Lewis and her colleagues found a greater prevalence of psychotic symptoms, neurologic abnormalities and child abuse in extremely violent delinquents than in their less violent peers (Lewis et al., 1979). Lewis stated that "the combination of trauma to the central nervous system, parental psychopathology . . . and social deprivation . . . creates the kinds of serious, often violent, delinquent acts so prevalent in our society today" (p. 422). Further, Lewis suggested that "the combination of familial vulnerability (e.g., as indexed by the presence of a schizophrenic parent), trauma to the central nervous system (e.g., perinatal trauma, head injury), physical and psychological abuse from a parent, and social deprivation (e.g., failure of a physician to diagnose and treat correctly, or failure of society to provide adequate support systems in the form of community programs or residential treatment) is sufficient to create the violent young offender, and this combination of factors occurs frequently" (p. 423).

Finally, it is important to keep in perspective the prevalence of psychiatric disorders in children in this age group. Rutter et al. (1970) found a prevalence of only 6.8% in a total population studied of 2,199 10- and 11-year-old children (see Note 34).

Note 35

From G.H.J. Pearson (1966), The importance of peer relationship in the latency period. *Bull. Phila. Assoc. Psychoanal.*, 16:109–121.

As we observe children we note that around the age of five and six, the child begins to remove himself from his family and seeks friends of his own age outside the home. . . . Real playing together becomes more definitive from five or six on. By the time he is about six or seven, he gradually spends more and more time with his friends than with his family. He begins to share his interests and ideas more with his friends and less with his parents, and he definitely begins to keep his secrets for his friends and no longer tells them to his parents.

By the time he is eight or nine, this behavior has become quite marked and of course continues into and through adolescence. At the same time he begins to question, both by himself and with his friends, his former concept of his parents as deities who can do no wrong. He begins gradually to recognize that they, like all other adult human beings, are mortal and comes to believe that adults, as a general rule, are not to be trusted. As he finds himself being aware of his parents' and other adults' shortcomings, he relies more and more on the support and cooperation of his peer companions. Somewhere between eight and ten these form a group, tend to gang together against the adults and the adults' authority, and find pleasure in thwarting the adult as much as possible. This turning away from the former worshipful admiration of the parents and other adults and the consequent deprecating of their importance is regarded by the parents, and other adults, with distinct displeasure. . . .

Withdrawal from parents and adults and relating more closely to peers reinforces repression of the oedipal conflict and thus becomes an important factor in personality development. Relationship with peers in itself develops skill in socializa-

tion. . . . this is as necessary an individual step in the total development of the human being as is the relationship with the mother. When there is interference with it or if it does not occur, the later life adjustment of the human being is crippled. . . . This developmental process can be interfered with in two ways: as the result of environmental and adult restrictions; and as the result of inner restrictions which have been produced by frustrations during the pre-oedipal and early oedipal years.

Parents who dislike the incessant activity and use of small and large muscles in the five-, six-, or seven-year-old may insist on less active behavior. As a consequence the child is forced back into the intrapsychic life of daydreaming and fantasy and is prevented from repressing and redirecting the oedipal fantasies. . . . Similarly parents who for whatever reason restrict unreasonably their child's contact with other children or resent bitterly the child's loyalty to his peer group, and the concomitant "disloyalty" to themselves, may interfere with the child's socialization and prevent the (necessary) repression. . . .

External circumstances . . . may restrict the possibility of a child making adequate contact with his peers . . . Sometimes an only child will be sent to a private school from the time he enters school. This school usually is a long distance from his home and no other child from his neighborhood may attend it. His peers may look with contempt on this particular child because he attends a different school. He finds that they don't accept him readily, so he comes more and more to stay by himself on his own property and often within his home. This again forces a difficulty in the solution of his oedipal problems, or at best a delay in their solution. Of course, the opportunity he has for free play with his peers during school hours will help him to some extent.

Very frequent moves from one neighborhood to another during this period also may interrupt old relationships and create difficulties in adjusting to new groups of peers so that the child eventually gives up making further attempts. Long continued illnesses during this period or marked chronic physical disabilities which actively prevent peer contact are a cause in some cases but these are special instances.

Occasionally one sees a child who restricts himself from peer contact because of former painful experiences. . . .

There are a number of cases in which the child during the late prelatent and latency periods restricts himself from peer contact for unconscious reasons, usually the result of traumatic experiences during his pre-oedipal and early oedipal periods. . . .

. . . a child who himself avoids contact with his peers during the late prelatent and latent periods or who is much, much too loyal to his parents in his thinking, must show disturbances in his development.

. . . In short, it is important to remember that the child utilizes a number of methods such as: motor activity, curiosity and interest in the external world, alliance with his peers against adults, increased loyalty to his peers with its accompanying increase in a more realistic appraisal of his parents and other adults, as mechanisms to aid his repressions, to promote separation from parents and to facilitate his own maturing.

Note 36

From M. Rutter, J. Tizard, and K. Whitmore (1970), *Education, Health and Behaviour.* London: Longman Group Limited, pp. 200–201.

Of the total population of 2199 ten- and eleven-year-old children screened, 118 (5.4 per cent) were found to have a clinically significant psychiatric disorder. When this rate was corrected for the number likely to have been missed by the group screening procedures, a prevalence of 6.8 per cent was found. This figure does not include uncomplicated intellectual retardation, monosymptomatic disorders or uncomplicated educational retardation.

The psychiatric disorders were classified into seven main groups: neurotic disorders, antisocial or conduct disorders, mixed neurotic and antisocial disorders, developmental disorders (which were excluded from the prevalence figure given above), hyperkinetic syndrome, child psychosis, and personality disorder. Neurotic disorders and conduct disorders were much the commonest conditions and the two diagnoses were made with about the same frequency. However, whereas neurotic disorders were somewhat commoner in girls, conduct disorders were very much commoner in boys. In addition there was a large group of children who had a mixed conduct and neurotic disorder. This group resembled the antisocial group in many characteristics including sex ratio, family size and associated reading retardation. If it is pooled with the conduct disorder group, the total prevalence of antisocial or conduct disorders is found to be 3.2, or 4.0 per cent when the correction factor is applied. The observed prevalence of neurotic disorders was 2.0 per cent giving a true prevalence of 2.5 per cent.

Only two children showed the hyperkinetic syndrome (although a much larger number showed restlessness or overactivity as part of a conduct or a neurotic disorder); two were psychotic and one girl had a markedly deviant personality.

The largest subgroup of neurotic conditions was anxiety disorders' (30 cases) in which anxiety and worrying were the most permanent symptoms. Many of the children in this group were generally fearful and a third had handicapping specific phobias. Altogether of the 118 children with psychiatric disorder, sixteen had clinically significant phobias (although the phobia was rarely the main and never the only symptom). Specific situational phobias were the most common variety; they were about equally frequent in boys and girls. There was no case of persisting school refusal. Specific animal phobias were only half as common and occurred only in girls. In marked contrast to the type of phobias found in adults, there were no cases of agoraphobia or of handicapping social anxiety.

A smaller number of children (7) had disorders with prominent obsessive features but there were no examples of a fully developed obsessional disorder of an adult type. An overt depressive disorder was found in only three girls and no boys, although a larger number of children in other diagnostic subgroups were to some degree unhappy or miserable. In three further children the most striking feature was the presence of tics. Of the seventeen neurotic boys four were rated as severely impaired, and of the twenty-six neurotic girls thirteen were severely handicapped.

Antisocial disorders were classified according to place, severity and type. Twenty children were antisocial but not delinquent, eight showed a trivial delinquency, in five cases the delinquency was confined to the home, twenty children exhibited 'socialised' delinquency and seventeen 'non-socialised' delinquency. The distinction between 'socialised' and 'non-socialised' delinquency proved to be more difficult than would be judged from the reports of the proponents of this distinction, since the characteristics which were supposed to group together did so only to a very weak extent. In the present study most weight was placed on good peer relationships and an absence of neurotic features in the antisocial acts, in making the diagnosis of "socialised delinquency'. The only difference which could be found between children categorised as 'socialised' and 'non-socialised' was that the latter tended to be eldest children while the former showed no particular ordinal position.

Most of the children with neurotic disorder and most of those with conduct disorder had conditions of at least three years duration.

Note 37

From L.E. Peller (1954), Libidinal phases, ego development, and play. *Psychoanal. Study Child,* 9:178–198.

(See table on page 208)

SURVEY OF PLAY ACTIVITIES

	CENTRAL THEME OF PLAY: OBJECT-RELATIONS:	DEFICIENCIES ANXIETY (DENIED):	COMPENSATING FANTASY:	FORMAL ELEMENTS, STYLE:	SOCIAL ASPECT:	PLAY MATERIAL:	SECONDARY PLAY GAINS:
Group I	Relation to *Body* Anxieties concerning body	My body is no good I am often helpless	My body (its extensions, replicas, variations) is a perfect instrument for my wishes Imagery of grandeurs, of perfect ease	Hallucinations (pos. & neg.) rather than fantasies Imagery increases pleasure, persistence	Solitary	Extensions & variations of body functions & body parts	Increased body skills & mastery Initiation into active search for gratification
Group II	Relation to *Preoedipal Mother* Fear to lose love object	My mother can—desert me; do as she pleases	I can do to *others* what she did to *me* I can go on (or quit)	Short fantasies Endless, monotonous repetitions; few variations No risk, no climax, no real plot Tit-for-tat	Solitary or with mother Other children rank with pets, or things—not as co-players Sporadic mirroring play	Maternal play with dolls, stuffed animals, with other children, and mother herself. Peek-a-boo Earliest tools	Rage, anxiety mitigated. Ability to bear delay, frustration Initiation into lasting object relation
Group III starts about 3 years	*Oedipal* relations & defenses against them Fear to lose love of love object	I cannot enjoy what grownups enjoy	I am big I can do as big people are doing Family romance	Spontaneity Infinite variety of emotions, roles, plots, settings Time is telescoped In later times: Drama, risk	Early co-play Attempts to share fantasy Fantasy always social Activity may be solitary or social	Dollplay; wide variety of events, of father, mother images; (pilot, nurse, magician etc.) Creative play Imaginative play Use of emblems, props, insignia	Preparation for adult roles, adult skills Co-play prepares co-work Initiation into adventure, accomplishment
Group IV starts about 6 years	*Sibling* Relations Fear of superego and superego figures	I am all alone against threatening authority I cannot start all over again	Many of us are united We observed rules conscientiously I can live many lives	Codified plot & roles Importance of rules, program, rituals, *formal* elements Reciprocity (Piaget)	Organized co-play Fantasy tacitly shared	Team games Board games Organized games Games with token armies	Dissolving oedipal ties Co-operation with brothers, with followers & leaders experienced as gratifying

REFERENCES

Barker, R.G., and Wright, H.F. (1951), *One Boy's Day: A Specimen Record of Behavior.* New York: Harper & Row.

Blanchard, P. (1946), Psychoanalytic contributions to the problems of reading disabilities. *Psychoanal. Study Child,* 2:163–187.

Bornstein, B. (1951), On latency. *Psychoanal. Study Child,* 6:279–285.

Broderick, C.B. (1966), Sexual behavior among preadolescents. *J. Soc. Issues,* 22:6–21.

Buffery, A.W.H. (1976), Sex differences in the neuropsychological development of verbal and spatial skills. In: *The Neuropsychology of Learning Disorders,* ed. R.S. Knights and D.J. Bakker. Baltimore, University Park Press, pp. 187–205.

Buffery, A.W.H. (1978), Neuropsychological aspects of language development: An essay on cerebral dominance. In: *The Development of Communication,* ed. N. Waterson and C. Snow. New York: John Wiley & Sons, Inc., pp. 25–46.

Burlingham, D. (1945), The fantasy of having a twin. *Psychoanal. Study Child,* 1:205–210.

Campbell, J.D. (1964), Peer relations in childhood. In: *Review of Child Development Research* (Vol. 1), ed. M.L. Hoffman and L.W. Hoffman. New York: Russell Sage Foundation.

Cantwell, D ̄ (Ed.) (1975), *The Hyperactive child.* New York: Spectrum.

Cantwell, D.F. (1976), Genetic factors in the hyperkinetic syndrome. *J. Am. Acad. Child Psychiatry,* 15:214–223.

Chess, S. (1968), Temperament and learning disability of school children. *Am. J. Public Health,* 58:2231–2239.

Cohen, T. (1963), Prediction of underachievement in kindergarten children. *Arch. Gen. Psychiatry,* 9:444–450.

Critchley, MacD. (1964), *Developmental Dyslexia.* London: Heinemann, p. 104.

Dodge, K.A., Schulndt, D.C., Schocken, I., and Delugach, J.C. (1983), Social competence and children's sociometric status: The role of peer group entry strategies. *Merrill-Palmer Quart.,* 28:309–336.

Egeland, B. (1974), Training impulsive children in the use of more efficient scanning techniques. *Child Dev.,* 45:165–171.

Elkind, D. (1970), The case for the academic preschool: Fact or fiction? *Young Child.,* 25:132–140.

Erikson, E.H. (1959), Industry vs. inferiority. *Psychol. Issues,* 1:65–74.

Fraiberg, S., and Freedman, D.A. (1964), Studies in the ego development of the congenitally blind child. *Psychoanal. Study Child,* 19:113–169.

Fraiberg, S., Siegel, B.L., and Gibson, R. (1966), The role of sound in the search behavior of a blind infant. *Psychoanal. Study Child,* 21:327–357.

Freud, A. (1937), *The Ego and the Mechanisms of Defense.* London: The Hogarth Press, pp. 73–78.

Freud, A. (1965), *Normality and Pathology in Childhood.* New York: International Universities Press.

Freud, S. (1905), *Three Essays on the Theory of Sexuality.* Standard Edition, 7 (1953). London: The Hogarth Press.

Fries, M.E. (1957), Review of the literature on the latency period. *J. Am. Psychoanal. Assoc.,* 5:525.

Gittelman-Klein, R., and Klein, D.F. (1980), Separation anxiety in school refusal and its treatment with drugs. In: *Out of School—Modern Perspectives in School Refusal and Truancy,* eds. L. Hersov and I. Berg. Chichester: John Wiley & Sons, Inc., pp. 321–343.

Glaser, K. (1967), Masked depression in children and adolescents. *Am. J. Psychother.,* 21:565–574.

Hartmann, H. (1955), Notes on the theory of sublimation. *Psychoanal. Study Child,* 10:9–29.

Hebb, D.O. (1949), *The Organization of Behavior: A Neuropsychological Theory.* New York: John Wiley & Sons, Inc.

Hellmann, I. (1954), Some observations on mothers of children with intellectual inhibitions. *Psychoanal. Study Child,* 9:259–273.

Hersov, L., and Berg, I. (Eds.) (1980), *Out of School.* Chichester: John Wiley & Sons, Inc.

Hurlock, R., and Burnstein, A. (1932), The imaginary playmate: A questionnaire study. *J. Genet. Psychol.,* 41:380–391.

Huttenlocher, P.R., and Huttenlocher, J. (1973), A study of children with hyperlexia. *Neurology,* 23:1107–1116.

Ingram, T.T.S. (1970), The nature of dyslexia. In: *Early Experience and Visual Information Processing in Perceptual and Reading Disorders.* ed. F.A. Young and D.B. Lindsley. Washington, D.C.: National Academy of Sciences.

Inhelder, B., and Piaget, J. (1958), *The Growth of Logical Thinking from Childhood to Adolescence.* New York: Basic Books.

Janus, S.S., and Bess, B.E. (1976), Latency: Fact or fiction? *Am. J. Psychoanal.,* 36:339–346.

Leong, Che. K. (1976), Lateralization in severely disabled readers in relation to functional cerebral development and synthesis of information. In: *The Neuropsychology of Learning Disorders,* eds. R.M. Knights and D.J. Bakker. Baltimore, University Park Press, pp. 221–231.

Lewis, D.O., et al. (1979), Violent juvenile delinquents: psychiatric, neurological, psychological and abuse factors. *J. Am. Acad. Child Psychiatry,* 18:307–319.

Lewis, M., and Sarrel, P. (1969), Some psychological aspects of seduction, incest, and rape in childhood. *J. Am. Acad. Child Psychiatry,* 8:609–619.

Lorenz, K. (1966), *On Aggression,* trans. M.K. Wilson. New York: Harcourt, Brace & World, p. 239.

McKellar, P. (1965), Thinking, remembering and imagining. In: *Modern Perspectives in Child Psychiatry,* ed. J.G. Howells. Springfield, Ill.: Charles C Thomas, pp. 170–191.

Makita, K. (1968), The rarity of reading disability in Japanese children. *Am. J. Orthopsychiatry,* 38:599–614.

Malinowski, B. (1927), Prenuptial intercourse between the sexes in the Trobriand Islands, N.W. Melanesia. *Psychonanl. Rev.,* 14:26–36.

Nagera, H. (1969), The imaginary companion. *Psychoanal. Study Child,* 24:165–196.

O'Sullivan, M.A., and Pryles, C.V. (1962), Reading disability in children. *J. Pediatr.*, 60:369.

Pearson, G.H.J. (1952), A survey of learning difficulties in children. *Psychoanal. Study Child*, 7:322–386.

Pearson, G.H.J. (1966), The importance of peer relationship in the latency period. *Bull. Phila. Assoc. Psychoanal.*, 16:109–121.

Peller, L.E. (1954), Libidinal phases, ego development, and play. *Psychoanal. Study Child*, 9:178–198.

Penfield, W., and Roberts, L. (1959), *Speech and Brain Mechanisms*. Princeton, N.J.: Princeton University Press.

Piaget, J. (1928), *Judgement and Reasoning in the Child*. New York: Harcourt, Brace & World, pp. 181–182.

Reese, H.W. (1966), Attitudes toward the opposite sex in late childhood. *Merrill-Palmer Q.*, 12:157–163.

Robins, L. (1966), *Deviant Children Grown Up*. Baltimore: Williams & Wilkins.

Robinson, M.W., and Schwartz, L.B. (1973), Visuo-motor skills and reading ability: A longitudinal study. *Dev. Med. Child Neurol.*, 15:281–286.

Ross Laboratories (1983), Special supplement. April, p. 1.

Rutter, M. (1974), Emotional disorder and educational underachievement. *Arch. Dis. Child.*, 49:249–256.

Rutter, M. (1980), Psychosexual development. In: *Scientific Foundation of Developmental Psychiatry*, ed. M. Rutter. London: Heinemann, pp. 322–339.

Rutter, M., and Madge, N. (1976), *Cycle of Disadvantage: A Review of Research*. London: Heinemann.

Rutter, M., Schaffer, D., and Shepherd, M. (1975), *A Multiaxial Classification of Child Psychiatric Disorders*. Geneva: World Health Organization.

Rutter, M., Tizard, J., and Whitmore, K. (Eds.) (1970), *Education, Health and Behaviour*. London: Longman.

Rutter, M., Tizard, J., and Whitmore, K. (Eds.) (1970), *Education, Health and Behavior: Psychological and Medical Study of Childhood Development*. New York: John Wiley & Sons, Inc.

Sandler, J., and Joffe, W.S. (1965), Notes on childhood depression. *Int. J. Psychoanal.*, 46:88–96.

Schulterbrandt, J.G., and Raskin, A. (Eds.) (1977), *Depression in Childhood: Diagnosis, Treatment and Conceptual Models*. New York: Raven Press.

Scott, J.P. (1968), *Early Experience and the Organization of Behavior*. Belmont, Calif.: Wadsworth.

Semmes, J. (1968), Hemispheric specialization: A possible clue to mechanism. *Neuropsychologia*, 6:11–26.

Shapiro, T., and Perry, T. (1976), Latency revisited: The age of seven plus or minus one. *Psychoanal. Study Child*, 31:79–105.

Shaw, M.C., and McCuen, J. (1960), The onset of academic underachievement in bright children. *J. Educ. Psychol.*, 51:103–108.

Slade, P.D., and Russell, G.F.M. (1971), Developmental dyscalculia: A brief report on four cases. *Psychol. Med.*, 1:292–298.

Sparrow, S.S. (1969), Dyslexia and laterality: Evidence for a developmental theory. *Semin. Psychiatry*, 1:270–277.

Stevenson, H.W., Hess, E.H., and Rheingold, H.L. (1967), *Early Behavior*. New York: John Wiley & Sons, Inc.

Stoller, R.J. (1967), Transvestites' women. *Am. J. Psychiatry*, 124:333–339.

Sutterfield, J., Cantwell, D., and Sutterfield, B. (1974), Pathophysiology of the hyperactive child syndrome. *Arch. Gen. Psychiatry*, 31:839–844.

Touwen, B.C.L. (1980), Laterality. In: *Scientific Foundations of Developmental Psychiatry*, ed. M. Rutter. London: Heinemann, pp. 154–164.

Waldfogel, S., Coolidge, J.C., and Hahn, P.B. (1957), The development, meaning and management of school phobia. *Am. J. Orthopsychiatry*, 27:754–780.

Wallach, L. (1969), On the basis of conservation. In: *Studies in Cognitive Development: Essays in Honor of Jean Piaget*, ed. E. Elkind and J.H. Flavell. New York: Oxford University Press, pp. 191–219.

Werry, J. (1972), Organic factors in childhood psychopathology. In: *Psychopathological Disorders of Childhood*, ed. H.L. Quay and J.S. Werry. New York: John Wiley & Sons, Inc.

Zigler, E., and Butterfield, E.C. (1968), Motivational aspects of changes in IQ test performance of culturally deprived nursery school children. *Child Dev.*, 38:1–14.

19

ADOLESCENCE

PUBERTY AND THE ONSET OF ADOLESCENCE

Puberty is the term used to designate the marked physical maturation that occurs in almost every system of the body in girls at about age 10 and in boys at age 12, although the actual age of onset varies greatly (Tanner, 1962, 1971; Young, 1971). Menarche occurs shortly after girls reach their maximal height sometime between 10 and 16 years of age, and testicular growth between 13 and 17 years. Over the past 150 years there has been a downward trend in the age at menarche at the rate of about 2.3 months per decade related, in part, to better health care and nutrition (Wyshak and Frisch, 1982). Girls, it appears, develop about two years earlier than boys, and some boys have completed their whole physical development of puberty before other boys of the same chronologic age have even begun theirs (Tanner, 1971) (Fig. 19–1 and Table 19–1). Thus the child's age is far too vague a guide to his or her maturational level. Certain of these changes have profound implications for the psychologic development of the individual, who at this time is at some stage of adolescence.

The onset of adolescence, which more or less coincides with puberty, is often influenced by the manifestations of puberty. In one study based on fantasy themes, late-maturing boys were found to be more likely than normally maturing boys to have feelings of personal inadequacy, feelings of rejection and domination by others, prolonged dependency needs, and rebellious attitudes toward their parents (Mussen and Jones, 1957). Early-maturing boys, on the other hand, were more likely to feel self-confident and independent, and they seemed to be more capable of playing a mature role in their social relationships. They also seemed to produce more student body presidents and more athletes (Jones, 1957). Early maturers also seemed to have, on the average, a slightly higher level of intelligence than late maturers (Douglas et al., 1968). (See Note 40.) The young adolescent is still very much a child at this stage—dependent on family, concerned about body changes, and subject to anxiety. The young adolescent brings with him or her whatever sense of trust and certainty he or she acquired during earlier stages of childhood.

Girls who mature early are at greater risk for depressive and anxiety symptoms than are girls who mature at the "normal" time, and are more likely to develop delinquent behavior. In contrast, later maturing girls are more likely than "normal" maturing girls to be more competent and responsible, and more likely to adapt well and function at a higher level in school (Schwab-Stone et al., 1985).

Menarche is usually associated with enhanced self-esteem, a heightened awareness of one's body, and an increase in social maturity (Simmons et al., 1983). Mixed feelings, such as excitement, pleasure, fears, and anxiety, are also present (Petersen, 1983). Being prepared by the mother, and being on time, result in more positive feelings and fewer long-term effects than being unprepared and early.

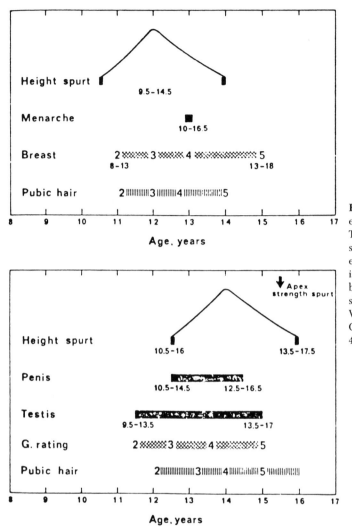

Fig. 19–1. Diagram of sequence of events at adolescence in boys and girls. The average boy and girl are represented. The range of ages within which each event charted may begin and end is given by the figures placed directly below its start and finish. (From Marshall, W.A. and J.M. Tanner (1970), Variations in the Pattern of Pubertal Changes in Boys. *Arch. Dis. Child.*, 45:13.)

Early-maturing females and late-maturing males are more likely to receive negative peer and adult evaluations than on-time females and early-maturing males (Tobin-Richards, Boxer, and Petersen, 1983). Physically attractive adolescents are stereotyped more extensively than unattractive adolescents (Langlois and Stephen, 1981), and unattractive adolescents seem to have more adjustment and behavioral problems than their attractive counterparts (Lerner and Lerner, 1977). Adolescents are likely to be agents in their own development.

ADOLESCENCE: OVERVIEW

Cultural Perspectives

Adolescence as a phase of development existed in some form long before it was recognized and conceptualized in the United States by G. Stanley Hall in 1904. For example, at the time of the Sumerian culture of 4,000 to 3,000 BC, the first case of juvenile delinquency was recorded on clay tablets (Kramer, 1959). The *Oxford English Dictionary* traces the word itself to the fifteenth century. Rousseau, in *Emile* (1762) noted, "We are born,

Table 19–1.   Genital Maturity Stages in Boys and Sexual Maturity Stages in Girls

	Classification of Genitalia Maturity Stages in Boys		
Stage	Pubic Hair	Penis	Testes
1	None	Preadolescent	
2	Slight, long, slightly pig-mented	Slight enlargement	Enlarged scrotum, pink, tex-ture altered
3	Darker, starts to curl, small amount	Penis longer	Larger
4	Resembles adult type, but less in quantity, coarse, curly	Larger, glans and breadth increase in size	Larger, scrotum dark
5	Adult distribution spread to medial surface of thighs	Adult	Adult

	Classification of Sexual Maturity Stages in Girls	
Stage	Pubic Hair	Breasts
1	Preadolescent	Preadolescent
2	Sparse, lightly pigmented, straight, medial border of labia	Breast and papilla elevated as small mound; areolar diameter increased
3	Darker, beginning to curl, increased amount	Breast and areola enlarged, no contour separation
4	Coarse, curly, abundant but amount less than in adult	'Areola and papilla form secondary mound
5	Adult feminine triangle, spread to medial surface of thighs	Mature; nipple projects, areola part of general breast contour

From Daniel, W.A. Jr. (1977) *Adolescents in Health and Disease.* St. Louis, The C.V. Mosby Co., 1977. Adapted from Tanner, J.M. (1962), *Growth at Adolescence,* 2nd Ed. Oxford, England, Blackwell Scientific Publications.

so to speak, twice over; born into existence, and born into life; born a human being and born a man" (pp. 128, 172).

In all cultures and in all times the period has been marked by rites of passage. In simple cultures where young men and women are needed to do adult work, the period of initiation is short. The initiation rites vary from culture to culture, but often involve periods of fasting or other ordeals.

The Australian aborigines and some African peoples circumcise adolescents. Tattooing is used in the South Pacific. Changes in hair style and clothing are common in some Indian tribes of South America. Mixtecan Indians of Mexico begin assuming some parental functions at 6 or 7 years of age and learn to perform adult tasks quite easily, with full parental approval (Phillips et al., 1973). In contrast, the Mundugumor adolescents in the South Seas have a far more unpleasant time, with much hostility from parents of the same sex (Paulson and Lin, 1972). The Chewa of Africa and the Lepcha of India cohabit and copulate early (by 11 or 12 years of age), whereas the Aina of Panama

remain ignorant of adult sexual information until the last stages of the marriage ceremony (Hauser, 1976). Among the Ndembu of Zambia, the boy is painted with white clay and the circumciser dances like a lion. The boy enters manhood during the period of healing and instruction that lasts a month. The Ngatatjara of the Gibson Desert in Australia are reported to perform the circumcision of their pubertal boys by removing the foreskin wth a knife of stone while the boy is straddled across a table made up of the backs of friends who are on their hands and knees; all this apparently takes place amidst dancing round a bonfire. The boy's ability to endure the pain quietly is said to signify his readiness for manhood. Junod, an anthropologist, reported in 1927 that among the Thonga tribe in Africa the 10- to 16-year-old boy is sent to a "circumcision school" where he undergoes severe hazing, including running the gauntlet between two rows of men who beat the boy with clubs, and is then stripped and circumcised. The boy is said to undergo six trials of beatings, exposure to cold, thirst, eating of unsavory foods, punishment, and threats of death (Junod, 1927). Rites of passage for the girl are usually less severe. Among the Cheyenne tribe of North

American Indians, for example, the girl, after her first menstrual period, painted her body red and surrounded herself with smoke from a special incense, after which the girl and her grandmother went into seclusion in a nearby small lodge for four days.

The concept of individuation and the developmental task of separating from the family, so central in our Western view of adolescence, are not universally accepted. The Chinese, for example, see child and adolescent development differently: "The self does not develop in a process of gradual separation and individuation as is often conceptualized in western psychological theories. We see, instead a "little me" maintaining its interdependency within the context of the "big me"—i.e., the family, the state and the world, throughout the life-span" (Dien, 1983).

As our society has become more complex, the duration of adolescence seems to have lengthened and the degree of stress for the adolescent to have increased. As society becomes complex, the law also becomes differentiation when dealing with adolescents. Thus the legal ages for marriage, driving, voting, conscription, compulsory education, and alcohol consumption may vary immensely and are subject to change according to the needs of a given society at a given time. Adolescents in poor families often have to start work early and may have a correspondingly shorter adolescence. Adolescents of more prosperous families tend to stay in school and college longer.

Perhaps what is particularly remarkable about the concept of adolescence is that, while in essence it is comprised of those psychologic processes mobilized to negotiate the change from the biopsychosocial characteristics of childhood to those of adulthood, the actual form and intensity of these characteristics and processes are determined by the interaction of social forces and the individuals' genetically programmed potential of capabilities. Thus, when tremendous changes occur in society over the course of history, astonishing changes emerge in the complex adaptive psychologic mechanism of the individual adolescent. These psychologic changes sometimes produce what amounts to a new stage of psychologic development. Changes in American society illustrate this point.

The great social changes in American society that took place in eighteenth-century America and in the industrial revolution from about the 1880s markedly altered our human social experience. This change in the human social experience in turn necessitated the emergence of different kinds of adaptive mechanisms, which in the aggregate came to be known as the stage of adolescence as we know it today. Changes in society did not stop, however, with the industrial revolution. We are now, for example, in a "high tech" age, characterized in part by a computer technology that is advancing exponentially. Among the demands that these and other social changes make on the individual are the need for more education prolonged over time and the need to solve the new problems for individuals that the social changes pose. Among these new issues is the question, for example, of how we shall conduct our sexual lives when on the one hand contraception is widely available, while on the other hand AIDS represents a growing fatal threat.

As each epoch in social change brings about the emergence of different characteristics that hitherto had only been present as a potential awaiting the appropriate stimulus, the new characteristics in turn may undergo change. Substages may be demarcated. Thus, shortly after the descriptions of adolescence began to appear, the subphases of early, middle, and late adolescence (Blos, 1962) were hypothesized. During middle adolescence (from 15 to 17 years), the adolescent turns intensely toward peers and seems to look for external certainties, presumably to counter feelings of internal insecurity. Such behavior as taking drugs, drinking alcohol, engaging in testing behavior, and becoming infatuated with parent surrogates may appear during this stage. The adolescent may criticize his or her parents, perhaps as a way of reducing their attributed power. But the parents are very much needed as an anchor: the adolescent almost needs the parents to be there to be wrong, so that the adolescent can have at least the illusion of being right, separate, and independent. The adolescent at this stage avoids thinking about his or her past, or the distant future.

In late adolescence the person becomes more adult-like in his or her commitments to work and to other people and in his or her more solid sense of self and internal integration. Some studies report a steady increase in self-esteem as the individual passes through the whole adolescent age range of 13 to 23 years (O'Malley and Backman, 1983).

Subsequently, as the social changes of the 1960s increased in intensity, a whole new "stage" in development was conceptualized—the stage of "youth" (Keniston, 1970). The characteristics of any of these substages or new stages, by the way, are not necessarily homogeneous, and might be found somewhat asynchronously in any of several lines of development, including social behavior, sexual mores, cognitive functioning, and moral reasoning. No doubt more stages and substages lie ahead.

Once the stage of adolescence was conceptualized and subdivided, theories were developed to account for the phenomena described. Hall's theory, for example, seemed to be influenced by Darwin's evolutionary theory and suggested a kind of recapitulation that paralleled the development of the human race (Weiner, 1970). Freud (1905) conceptualized a psychosexual developmental sequence culminating in genital primacy at the conclusion of adolescence. Recapitulation of early phases became a prominent theme in the psychoanalytic writings of Blos (1962) and others. The idea of a normative crisis, with particular emphasis on the development of "identity" vs. "identity diffusion" during adolescence was put forward by Erikson (1963). The stages of cognitive development with the achievement of "formal operations" during adolescence was described by Piaget (1958). Some psychoanalysts thought that disturbance was a normal phenomenon as the ad-

olescent attempted to deal with his or her "developmental tasks" (A. Freud, 1958). Other psychoanalysts sometimes carried this concept of disturbance to extremes: Geleerd, for example, in 1961, stated that she "would feel great concern for the adolescent who causes no trouble and feels no disturbance" (p. 267). Others, such as Rutter et al. (1976), began using the methodologic tools of the day to produce epidemiologic data that seemed to refute the view of adolescence as a pervasive state of storm, stress, and turmoil. Rutter stated that "alienation from parents is *not* common in 14-year-olds" (p. 40) and that most young teenagers in a general population get on rather well with their parents, who in turn continue to have a "substantial influence on their children right through adolescence" (p. 54). Offer (1969), Masterson (1968) and, more recently, Kaplan et al. (1984) have tended to confirm this questioning of the so-called ubiquity of adolescent turmoil.

Do the emergence, prolongation, and subdivision of a developmental phase such as adolescence bring with them a new range of psychopathology?

Few psychiatric illnesses are confined to adolescence, but some, such as depression and attempted suicide, show an increase in prevalence and severity during adolescence (Rutter et al., 1976), and others, such as schizophrenia, may have their onset at this time. What is striking is the increase in social problems that appears as the stage of adolescence becomes stretched over time. These social problems include teenage pregnancy, venereal disease, alcohol and drug abuse, violence, and delinquency. However, the rapidly changing social environment makes prediction hazardous, and it is only safe to say that we do not know what further developmental stages and developmental psychopathology lie ahead, especially for those individuals between 11 and 22 years of age now living in our rapidly advancing society. Much depends on the demands of a given society. Because we cannot predict with certainty what form our society will take, we cannot predict the future of any adolescent stage.

Perhaps therefore we need to keep open multidisciplinary pathways to the understanding and treatment of troubled adolescents in the years ahead.

Does adolescence ever completely end in contemporary society? The phases of development that commonly occupy the years from 18 to 23 may include late adolescence (Blos, 1962), youth (Keniston, 1970), the periods of "Intimacy and Distantiation versus Self-Absorption" and "Generativity versus Stagnation" (Erikson, 1956), and, finally, young adulthood (Lidz, 1968). Indeed, the word "adolescence" means becoming an adult and was first used in the English language in 1430, when it referred to the ages of 14 to 21 years in males, and 12 to 21 years in females. Individuals manifesting what is commonly thought of as adolescent behavior today are often "going on 30."

Just as a stabilization of biologic maturation occurs as epiphyses close and adult stature is achieved, so there should be an increasing stabilization of the personality. Conflict between the self and the changing milieu interieur abates and is displaced by conflict within the self and between the self and the external world. Thus consolidation and integration of one's personality and the adaptation to a changing and unfamiliar society become the pivotal "developmental tasks" at the end of adolescence. Specific developmental tasks include achieving gratifying heterosexual relationships, deciding upon a career, and committing oneself to marriage or an alternative lifestyle. Clearly, these are also the tasks of young adults.

Failure to complete or resolve any of these developmental tasks may occur because of persisting difficulties arising from unresolved earlier conflicts. The result might be persisting adolescence and adolescent psychopathology. Moreover, current conflicts may be heightened by interaction with the existential anxiety that arises when one is confronted with certain challenges of society. These societal challenges, at least in Western society, include the incorporation of advances in technology. For example, the technology of in-

stantaneous mass communication has enabled young people all over the world to realize that they have much in common and that in some societies they constitute the majority.

Another factor influencing the resolution of adolescence is the socioeconomic status of the individual (Esman, 1977). For example, a white, middle-class adolescent has an entirely different experience from that of most native American Indians. Additional factors are sex and parenthood. Psychoanalytic investigations, however, have continued to focus mostly on the affluent individual. For example, Ritvo (1971) has concentrated on a small number of college students and those relatively few who have dropped out of college. Yet even among this group there is change. Thus, the striking difference in the behavior of students in the late 1960s compared to those seen in the early 1970s and 1980s seems to reflect both intrapsychic development and the individual's responsiveness to the particular (historical) social context.

By 18 to 23 years of age, a sufficient history of personality traits and intellectual development has unfolded to provide the individual with the information needed to observe his or her own patterns of behavior in response to internal urges and external demands provided, of course, that the individual has achieved the necessary level of cognitive competence to make these judgments. This conscious identity, including a new decision-making capability, should now be more fully internalized and integrated into the personality and should now be more or less independent of superego reinforcement. Moreover, decisions can now be made in the context of lengthier commitment rather than immediate wishes or superego sanctions. In addition, a greater degree of intimacy now becomes possible as independence from the family is established and a conscious sense of identity is achieved. A new relationship with society emerges as the individual's horizons widen and the inequalities of society are recognized, if not liked. Some young adults experience an acute disillusionment with society, reminiscent of the disillusionment with parents that occurs in the postoedipal phase. Disillusionment with society may be an extension of, or a displacement from, that earlier disillusionment. However, in many, if not most, instances it is a true recognition of human frailty and social reality. Thus, identity is a complex achievement, involving a sense of one's personal identity within a comprehensible social reality and comprising both conscious and unconscious aspects. This identity occurs within the context of a particular historical moment, and is subject to change.

Both males and females who are at the border of adolescence and adulthood are on the threshold of establishing new, long-lasting relationships that are thought to be based primarily on reality considerations rather than fantasy. The short-lived relationships based on replication of original "objects," part-identifications, and overidealization that characterize earlier adolescence are thus now replaced by a fuller sense of identification and the need to form lasting relationships that "fit" the now-consolidated identity. The motivations and forces acting on the formation of long-term heterosexual relationships (including marriage) are early conscious and unconscious need fulfillment, possible unconscious incestuous fantasy wishes, the need for intellectual stimulation, sexual pleasure, self-esteem and narcissistic gratification, the influences of family and peer relationships, social striving, neurotic role interlocking, the wish to have children, and a desire for "complementarity." The degree to which any one of these components overrides the others determines whether the relationship succeeds or fails. Because few, if any, relationships stay the same, a strong conscious commitment is usually required to resolve difficulties and misunderstandings arising from these factors. Older adolescents and young adults are more or less capable of making this kind of commitment, although the high rate of divorce suggests that this is not always the case. A failure to make this kind of commitment or an overriding and interfering unconscious motivation, or even preconscious motivation

that is not allowed recognition or expression, is likely to result in a failure or radical change in such relationships. At the same time, ideas about commitment change as society changes.

During this intermediate adolescent-adulthood phase the individual also become capable of parenthood, during which the individual's own childhood experiences are thought to be reworked (Benedek, 1959). The individual's children act as stimuli and provide opportunities for development. The individual shows a growing capacity for mutuality during what Erikson now calls the stage of "Generativity versus Stagnation." Parenthood, however, is more than a single developmental phase. Some regard it as a series of interconnected subphases, beginning with fantasies of parenthood through the psychologic process for man and woman during pregnancy, labor, and childhood (Bibring et al., 1961), to the identity changes in the parents as their relationships to each other and to their children change as their children move from phase to phase in their development. Historically, societal changes have led to an enormous increase in the number of single adolescent-to-early adult parents, with all the sequelae that affect the child who is being reared by the single young parent.

The period between 18 and 23 years of age is the most common age for the beginning of the experience of being between two generations: that of one's parents and that of one's children. Although one is emancipated from parents, there is a continuing concern that one will be pulled back into the family of origin as a child and not as an adult (Gould, 1972). Consequently, there is a tendency today to intensify peer relationships, provided such relationships, especially in the aggregate, do not in turn threaten one's autonomy and individuality.

An individual at this age is actively involved in setting on a course that involves mastering a work skill, profession, or life-style. Sociocultural and family influences, sex, economic conditions, physical status, cognitive abilities, education, job opportunities, personality type and needs, specific conscious and unconscious motivations, identifications, talents, and skills are some of the factors that determine an individual's work. Sometimes the choice of a particular career provides an environment in which group values can take the place of individually derived moral and ethical values. The individual superego may become dissolved in the group superego or may be reinforced by the group-ego ideal. Repetition compulsion may be another factor in determining not only the individual's choice of work, but the outcome, i.e., the degrees of success or failure in that work. Work may thus be an end in itself, or a means of satisfying old urges, or a force acting upon the young adult—or all three. Adolescence thus should end, and adulthood should begin, but our rapidly changing society and job obsolescence may affect this transition: Adolescence may be prolonged further or may have to terminate abruptly because of a crisis in the family or society.

In overview, the normal individual at the end of adolescence ideally is capable of experiencing for the first time the consolidation of identity, the mastery of drives, the achievement of unfettered true heterosexual object relationships, and a realistic view of the world as he or she enjoys new heights of intellectual activity. Few achieve this ideal state. Indeed, even were this state achieved, it would not last; the next phase of development or societal shifts would once again demand change.

Some of the areas mentioned in this overview will now be discussed in greater detail.

COGNITIVE DEVELOPMENT

Cognitive development during adolescence is characterized by a widening scope of intellectual activity, increased awareness, and a capacity for insight. Piaget has called adolescence a stage of formal operations (Inhelder and Piaget, 1958; Piaget, 1969, see Note 38). The essential cognitive change is that the child begins to be able to grasp highly abstract concepts, such as infinity or irrational numbers, and to reason from hypotheses. The child will now use such propositional phrases as, "if so and so, then such and such" and "either/or."

Egocentrism, a term that essentially refers to a lack of differentiation in some area of human interaction (Piaget, 1962), takes a unique form in adolescence. The extent to which adolescents believe, for example, that other people are as obsessed as they are with their behavior and appearance is one measure of the egocentrism of the adolescent (Elkind, 1967). Based on the (false) premise that others are as admiring or as critical of them as they are of themselves, the adolescent constructs what Elkind calls an imaginary audience, whose reaction the adolescent can of course anticipate. The adolescent constantly feels under scrutiny and often feels shame, self-criticism and self-admiration. But in his or her egocentrism, the adolescent fails, of course, to differentiate between what he or she believes to be attractive and what others actually admire.

Yet at the same time the adolescent also regards his or her own feelings as unique, and he or she develops what Elkind calls personal fables. These fables are stories about himself or herself that the adolescent believes, such as stories that reflect a belief that a boy is immortal or, in the case of a girl, that she will not become pregnant and therefore has no need to take precautions when she has sexual intercourse, or that only the adolescent can feel with extraordinary intensity.

Gradually, by 15 or 16 years of age, the imaginary audience gives way to a perception of the real audience through a process of repeated testing against reality. The personal fable also diminishes as the adolescent discovers in the intimacy of a relationship of mutuality that others have feelings similar to his or her own.

PERSONALITY DEVELOPMENT: UNIVERSAL TASKS

Clear manifestations of personality development are associated with the cognitive changes just mentioned. At least four major groups of universal tasks can be defined: (1) defining one's own self or identity, (2) achieving separation and coming to terms with specific feelings about one's family, (3) developing love relationships, and (4) achieving mastery over one's impulses and body functions and capacities.

REACTIONS TO IDENTITY TASKS

One often sees a young adolescent trying on different roles as he or she struggles with the task of identity (Erikson, 1956, 1963; see Note 37)—as if to see what role fits him or her the best. The adolescent may also keep his or her identity, particularly sexual identity, fluid and ambiguous. Or, again, the choice may be delayed and a psychosocial moratorium declared. The various roles played may also serve to counterbalance feelings of inadequacy. For example, a boy who feels that he is weak may parade as a bully and a girl who is concerned about her femininity may try to play the role of a femme fatale (Galdston, 1967). Occasionally, the role adopted is like a suit of armor, and if the role is too rigid and fixed, occasionally it falls apart under pressure.

SEPARATION FROM AND FEELINGS TOWARD PARENTS

Separation from the family and coming to terms with specific feelings toward one's family and others is another major task of early adolescence. Sometimes, although seeming to be tearing himself or herself from the family abruptly, the young adolescent simultaneously displaces his or her longings onto other people, who either represent the parents or represent their very opposite. At the moment of transfer, the adolescent temporarily feels "free." However, his or her attachment to a leader of a group, gang, or cult may soon undergo the same vicissitudes as do his or her relationships with the parents. (Parents feel quite keenly the sudden loss of the adolescent who attempts to separate so suddenly.)

OTHER REACTIONS TO THE TASK OF SEPARATING

Other adolescents may reverse the tender feelings they have for their family members, and instead feel contempt or hate for them. Such an adolescent presents the picture of an uncooperative and hostile person. Sometimes the adolescent becomes excessively suspicious of others, and at other times he or she feels a sense of depression, depending on whether the hostile feelings are turned outward (projected) or inward (against the self). Depression in adolescents is often manifested by repetitve or frantic activity to ward off boredom, drug taking (see p. 237), and acts of violence or promiscuous sexual behavior (Toolan, 1962). Sometimes the adolescent succeeds in detaching himself or herself from the family but for one reason or another is unable to find a person to love or be loved by. Such an adolescent may then turn his or her love interests inward and become intensely narcissistic or may have difficulty finding someone to love *because* he or she is already too narcissistic. The adolescent either may feel enormously important or, if his or her interests focus on the body, may become inordinately concerned with his or her physical state.

LOVE RELATIONSHIPS

The love relationships of adolescents also seem to follow a developmental sequence (Pearson, 1958), and achieving love relationships can be regarded as a separate developmental task. The pathway outlined here can only be considered as one of many different pathways, each influenced by such factors as socioeconomic status, intelligence, and cultural mores. At the onset of adolescence, a furtive sexual interest in the opposite sex begins to occur in both boys and girls. This interest is soon followed by an at first unconscious desire to attract a person of the opposite sex that is manifested in feats of prowess among boys and, for example, an interest in makeup among girls. Very shortly the desire becomes conscious, and concerns about appearances are manifested. Boys and girls may fall in love with persons of the opposite sex who usually are older—and ineligible. Girls tend to be more romantic in their fantasies and boys are erotic. Parents may resent these new attachments, and in so doing may contribute to the adolescents' conflicts. Gradually both boys and girls become more comfortable with their peers of the opposite sex, and tentative sexual explorations occur. At first, these explorations are somewhat aggressive (e.g., teasing and hair pulling) and seem to be regressive. Eventually, the boy or girl becomes attached to one peer of the opposite sex and experiences a sense of physical excitement in the presence of the person. Often that person is overvalued and exalted as a feeling of love replaces the urge for sexual gratification. At the same time the adolescent may feel unworthy of the object of his or her love. At first the adolescent's love relationships seem to be of limited duration and to consist mostly of talking, with some petting. As the adolescent becomes old and gains experience, a genuine concern for the feelings of the person of the opposite sex emerges, together with an urge for genital sexual experience.

Recent studies suggest that 40% of the 30 million 13- to 19-year-old adolescents in the United States have had sexual intercourse. In fact, by 19 years of age, 80% of boys and 70% of girls have had sexual intercourse. Clearly, these adolescents have a high likelihood of becoming involved in a pregnancy. Indeed, about 1,000,000 adolescent girls become pregnant each year (Marks and Fisher, 1987).

Unresolved Love-Relationship Behavior

Displaced feelings, infatuations, and disappointments are common enough in normal adolescents (A. Freud, 1958). Sometimes an infatuation seems in some ways to evoke the feelings of an earlier love affair; namely, the oedipal attachment of the younger child to the parent of the opposite sex. If the oedipal struggle had been particularly difficult, the young adolescent may experience a great deal of turmoil.

IMPULSE CONTROL AND REGRESSION

Early in development, the child struggles to control his or her impulses. In early childhood, there is the tendency to act on each wish more or less as it arises. This impulsiveness can be seen in the alternating loving, hating, caressing, and kicking behavior of some young children. Later, as more skills (e.g., language skills) become available, the child learns to think about his or her wishes rather than always to act on them. The child also develops the capacity for play, in which he or she can actively work by means of repetition and trial solutions at mastering a problem that is beyond the child's capacity in real life. Of course, he or she is usually reassured by the continuing presence of the parents and by their understanding support and encouragement on the one hand and their avoidance of excessive stimulation on the other hand. The child identifies with the parents and takes over their thoughts and ideals. Their modes of behavior become models for the child. In all these ways (that is, by initial impulsive discharge, by thinking and fantasizing, by trial solutions through play, and by identification), the child learns to cope with his or her strong instinctual urges. If the child is successful he or she is free to learn at school and is prepared more or less for the onset of adolescence.

Many of the child's ways of coping are used again by the adolescent although perhaps in a more complex manner. Some adolescents become almost overwhelmed by the upsurge of their impulses, and they allow themselves to be indiscriminately messy, sloppy, or careless. (Of course, messiness may also be a symptom of depression, oppositional behavior, and anger.) An adolescent who does so may still feel like a young child inside a changing and relatively unfamiliar body, threatened by urges whose strength is also unfamiliar. (Many adults retain an area where they can be messy—the garage, the attic, their study, or their desk drawers.) Occasionally, the normal adolescent will feel overwhelmed and will act in a sexually impulsive manner. In another adolescent, a regression in sexual drive development occurs, leading to behavior in which the adolescent gratifies earlier components of the sexual instinct, including the voyeuristic urge, the urge to explore with the mouth, and the exhibitionistic urge.

INTELLECTUALIZATION AS A DEFENSE

A common mechanism of defense employed by the adolescent to maintain that repression is intellectualization. In intellectualization, the body and its needs are almost totally disregarded and the intellect is exalted in its place. The adolescent calls into service his or her newly acquired cognitive skills. Until recently, intellectualization was regarded as the characteristic defense of adolescence. Today the observation does not appear to be so true. On the contrary, a more common tendency is toward activity or toward what Hartmann (1969) refers to as the fashion of acting out in groups. At the same time, much of the activity of the adolescent is adaptive and devoted to change (Keniston, 1970a).

ALIENATION

Sometimes the so-called syndrome of alienation occurs (Halleck, 1967). Halleck originally described several characteristics of the alienated adolescent, who

1. has a tendency to live in the present and to avoid commitment to people, causes, or ideas,
2. shows an almost total lack of communication with parents or other adults,
3. has an ill-defined self-concept,
4. has a tendency toward sudden severe depression often accompanied by attempts at suicide,
5. has an inability to concentrate or study,
6. shows promiscuous but ungratifying sexual behavior, and
7. uses drugs excessively.

Halleck postulated that the internal mechanisms that lead to the syndrome of alienation include a passive-aggressive rebellion against authority, fears of success or failure, and a feeling of being unloved. In addition, several external forces contribute to the picture. The parents often give ambivalent messages to the child, and the forces and characteristics of society have a specific impact. For example, the increasing rate of social change and social values, the rapid development of automation, and the isolation of the generations are considered by Halleck to be important factors contributing to alienation. The alienated adolescent also appears to have a pervasive distrust of what is said, how power is used, and the motivations of those in power.

It is important to note, however, that not all these characteristics are always present. Indeed, contradictory characteristics are sometimes seen (Noshpitz, 1970; Wise, 1970). For example, far from having a tendency to avoid commitment to people, causes, or ideas, some adolescents who manifest other features of alienation may also have a passionate commitment to causes and ideas. Sometimes the alienation takes specific forms, e.g., the hippie movement of the 1960s (Williams, 1970), while serving the same function. Religious sects, such as the Jesus Movement, Hare Krishna, Children of God, and Sun Myung Moon's "Unification Church," have similarly attracted a number of disillusioned adolescents (Plowman, 1971). At the same time, many adolescents are aware of and concerned about the irrational aspects of the adult world. Keniston (1970a) has made a special plea that more attention be given to the positive, adaptive attempts of the adolescent who is trying "to make the world a more livable place, to create new life styles, to change others."

ADOLESCENT EMOTIONS

Despite the foregoing desciptions of adolescents, most adolescents do *not* have any great psychologic upheaval or disturbance

(Rutter et al., 1976). *Some* adolescents have transitory feelings of misery and self-depreciation and ideas of being laughed at. *Most* adolescents, however, far from being rebellious, are conforming persons, much like most parents. Indeed, most adolescents share the values of their parents (Offer and Offer, 1975; Rutter et al., 1976). In a five-year controlled study of 101 adolescents, Masterson (1968) attempted to distinguish between so-called adolescent turmoil and psychiatric disorder; he regarded the psychiatric effects of adolescent turmoil as the product of the interaction between the turmoil and the personality structure of the adolescent. In the healthy personality, adolescent turmoil, when it occurred at all, produced, at most, subclinical anxiety and depression. Adolescents with a character neurosis suffered psychoneurotic symptoms during the period of adolescent turmoil but retained a residue of pathologic character traits after the turmoil and the accompanying psychoneurotic symptoms subsided. Adolescents with preexisting schizophrenia and personality disorder, however, suffered a worsening of their condition during adolescent turmoil that also persisted into adulthood. Masterson was concerned that a psychiatrist who saw an adolescent with a personality disorder migh attribute the difficulties in diagnosis to the adolescence stage of the patient rather than to the personality disorder. Normal adolescence, as Graham and Rutter (1975) point out, is a period of many psychologic changes, but psychiatric disorder is not one of them.

Psychologic tasks and conflicts in adolescents may sometimes seek expression through an intercurrent event, such as a physical illness. Children with chronic illness, such as diabetes and asthma, often in adolescence unconsciously make use of their condition to express their anxiety over problems involving control of the body and its impulses, and over their need for independence from parental restraints.

Johnny first came to the attention of the pediatrician when, at the age of 10, he had symptoms of diabetes. Initially, the management of the diabetes was not a problem. Then, as Johnny entered adolescence the pediatrician noticed that the diabetes was becoming more difficult to control. Johnny began having attacks of severe acidosis with coma. He also seemed uncooperative and unhappy and showed considerable lassitude. Further, he consistently aroused the antagonism of the medical staff during each of his many hospital stays. Each time his mother went out, Johnny seemed to have an extreme fear that she would desert him.

It soon became evident that there was more to the problem of controlling the diabetes than managing a refractory pancreas, difficult as that was. Attention was therefore focused on other aspects of Johnny's life, and many significant finding came to light.

Johnny's father had died when Johnny was 13, just before the diabetes became difficult to control. His father had also been diabetic and he had died tragically from a staphylococcal infection. Johnny did not believe his father had died when he first heard about it, and for a short while afterward he was angry at almost everyone.

Johnny's mother was hypertensive and obese. She seemed to have conflicts about dependency, but she had remained married to her husband. (She knew when she married him that he had diabetes.) The marriage seemed in some ways to fulfill her need to grapple with a situation that was bristling with difficulties.

After the father's death, the mother seemed to take an immense interest in Johnny's diabetes, to the extent that she herself decided what medication Johnny should have. At times she confused the many doctors she involved in Johnny's care. It appeared that her anxiety about Johnny's life expectancy prevented her from being able to trust doctors. Also, the anxiety seemed related to her own fears and wishes about death, in which, one might say, brinkmanship was constantly involved.

As far as Johnny was concerned, it became clear that the whole matter of "control" of the diabetes was related in part to his ability to "control" his body and his impulses. The illness itself seemed to be experienced as a threat to the integrity toward which he had been striving. The attacks of coma also bore a close affinity to an attempt to test out a self-destructive fantasy; that is, they appeared to be suicidal equivalents. It was as though Johnny was seeking to join his dead father and to identify with him. In addition, Johnny was violently struggling to free himself from his mother's control at the same time that he was acting out what seemed to be an unconscious wish of his mother, namely, to have Johnny replace her husband. (It should be emphasized that these aspects of Johnny's illness were clarified through intensive psychotherapy and are not immediately obvious from the skeleton of the case presented here.)

REACTIONS OF PARENTS

The adolescent is, of course, not behaving in a void; he or she behaves in the context of his or her family and society, who in turn react to the adolescent. For at least three reasons, parents cannot help reacting to the adolescent:

1. The parent is in a sense faced from the other side with the same problems that face the adolescent. For example, in regard to identity choice, the patient may want the adolescent to follow a certain career (possibly one the parent was unable to achieve for himself or herself), while the adolescent may have quite different ideas, and sometimes several at a time, for himself or herself. Involved in this, too, is the narcissistic wound that the parent feels and that often is expressed in a competitive relationship with the daughter or son. For example, a mother may unconsciously try to attract her daughter's date, or a father may do likewise toward his son's date. Some parents may be particularly sensitive to the impending separation of their adolescent and, instead of helping the adolescent make the transition, may actually try to increase his or her tie to family by making the home too comfortable (e.g., by making his or her bed or getting breakfast). Then again, some parents unknowingly may find themselves uncomfortably aroused by the sight, smell, or touch of their adolescent son or daughter.

   A mother once expressed concern, even alarm, that her 15-year-old son, with whom she lived alone, was having violent temper tantrums. When an inquiry was made as to what the temper tantrums were like, it turned out that when the son watched television and saw his team lose at football, he would thown a pencil down on the foor (gently) and say "damn!" (quietly). Subsequently, in the course of psychotherapy, the

mother revealed her own concerns about her sexual and aggressive fantasies. These fantasies were now being displaced and projected onto her 15-year-old son, who was in fact a very subdued adolescent.

Thus parents may unwittingly use an adolescent daughter or son to act out unconscious wishes of their own.

2. Parents react to adolescents because the pattern of behavior of the adolescent arouses discomfort and concern. For example, if an adolescent is careless, messy, unreasonable, sarcastic, unpredictable, alternately affectionate of hostile, sometimes erupting into violent anger in response to an innocuous question, it is not surprising that a parent might react to the adolescent with feelings of anger or guilt or both. However, sometimes the parents so react because the behavior of the adolescent is an uncomfortable invitation to them to act likewise, stirring up in the parents a tendency to regress. Sometimes the parents so react because the parents' own adolescent struggles were not completely mastered and the behavior of the adolescent arouses in the parents memories of conflicts that the parents do not wish to relive. The adolescent often senses this and may turn to a more neutral, less-highly-charged person, such as an uncle or an aunt. (However, it should also be said that some parents may find that the presence of an adolescent offers them an opportunity for further working through of some of their own earlier conflicts.)

3. Parents of an adolescent may be in a period of life that has its own developmental features and corresponding anxieties. For these parents, the troublesome adolescent may be a further source of anxiety. This anxiety is perceived by the adolescent, who in turn feels more insecure, thus creating a vicious cycle.

   Sometimes, a family in crisis may use the adolescent as a scapegoat, perhaps because the adolescent is, for a variety of reasons, a source of great discomfort for the parents. The adolescent may contribute to the scapegoating and may aggravate the situation by his or her provocative behavior. When this interaction occurs, the adolescent is prone to act impulsively (e.g., by committing a petty crime). He or she may do this in part because his or her defenses are impaired and implicit sanction is given for the breakthrough of previous forbidden impulses (Courts, 1967). Sometimes such behavior occurs during a divorce and represents an adolescent's attempt to hold the family together.

SOCIETY AND ADOLESCENTS

Society* in general is also part of the environment with which the adolescent interacts. Society may play a structuring role. Evolving as it does through generation after generation of adults, society has over the years erected structures to channel the problems of adolescence, with varying success. Such structures range from primitive rites and rituals to highly organized systems of apprenticeships and examinations. Television similarly has a shaping effect on adolescents.

By the same token, however, when society itself is in a state of turmoil, unrest, and danger, the adolescent feels less secure and more upset. He or she may then feel impelled toward acts of violence against others or against himself or herself. The adolescent has to learn how to live with the constant and rapid social change that prevails today, as well as with uncertainty, ambiguity, and relativity. Adequate models with whom to identify in deal-

---

* "The term *society* denotes a continuing group of people who have developed certain relatively fixed ways of doing things which express their particular ways of viewing reality, and which employ specific symbols embodying these views. The society creates a whole universe of rules, laws, customs, mores, and practices to perpetuate the commonly accepted values and to cope with the various issues (birth, death, marriage, puberty, etc.) experienced by all members. All of these socially patterned ways of behaving constitute the society's culture." (G.A.P., 1968, p. 763).

ing with complex tasks and roles may not be readily available. Many middle-aged parents today are utterly baffled by the social changes they are witnessing. The current information explosion in the midst of social misery has led some adolescents to seek "relevance" in social action, while others have tried to create a simpler society of their own. Previously held notions of child rearing and education may not meet the needs for the special adaptation to change that is now required. At this point, the question goes beyond the interaction between the adolescent and society and becomes one of priorities in living for the future of mankind.

TROUBLED ADOLESCENTS

Adolescents, who number about 30 million in the 13- to 19-year-old age range, are mostly normal, even though their behavior is sometimes troubling to adults. Nevertheless, disorders do occur during adolescence, and it may be useful to describe briefly some of the more common or important ones. In general, accidents, murders, and suicides account for three out of four deaths among 15- to 24-year-olds (D.H.H.S., 1982). Homicides account for the largest proportion (39%) of deaths among black youth.

DEATH IN AUTO ACCIDENTS

Accidents, particularly auto accidents, are the leading cause of death among adolescents. Twenty-five percent of all auto deaths in the state of Connecticut involve people from 16 to 19 years of age. Accidents may represent suicidal behavior.

SUICIDE AND ATTEMPTED SUICIDE

Suicide now ranks third (after accidents and homicide) as a leading cause of death in adolescence. Further, the number of adolescent suicides is increasing; there are now about 5,000 deaths per year, giving a mortality rate for suicide in the 15- to 24-year-old age group of 12.3 per 100,000, and accounting for 18.8%

of all deaths in this age group. The ratio of boys to girls who commit suicide is 3:1. At the same time, for every reported suicide (and suicides are often not reported), there are between 50 and 200 attempted suicides (Committee on Adolescence, 1980). The ratio of boys to girls who attempt suicide is 1:3. Boys tend to use more fatal means, such as guns and hanging; girls tend to use pills. The ratio of attempted suicide goes up by a factor of 10 between ages 15 and 19 compared with the rate between ages 10 and 14. Thus, attempted suicide as a solution to life's problems has its first peak incidence during adolescence.

Depression, failure of emotional support from the family, despair, and hopelessness are powerful factors that have influenced the dramatic rise in adolescent suicide in the past decade. Many of the common dynamic factors involved in an attempted suicide in adolescents are related to the developmental tasks of adolescents (Lewis and Solnit, 1963), as shown in the following discussion of motivation for suicide attempts:

1. The adolescent may find himself or herself overwhelmed by the task of dealing with sexual and aggressive feelings toward his or her parents, or the persons on whom these feelings have been displaced, and may act impulsively. Sometimes catastrophic social events (e.g., plane crashes, civil disturbances, war) intensify the adolescent's problems and lead to attempted suicide.

2. Occasionally, the adolescent is motivated by an unconscious wish to join a dead relative (e.g., a father who died when the adolescent was a young child).

3. When faced with the identity struggle, the adolescent may fear his or her identity dissolution, and paradoxically may attempt suicide to avoid that fate.

4. Some adolescents are simply desperate and can think of no other solution for dealing with their depression, guilt and anxiety, or their intolerable home situation. Fortunately, in some of these cases there is also a strong wish to be rescued.

5. Occasionally, the adolescent attempts suicide as an act of revenge, or as an attempt to manipulate the family into change.

6. Sometimes the adolescent is schizophrenic; or his or her reality testing may be impaired by brain injury or acute toxic states, caused by infection or drugs.

In short, depression, despair, poor impulse control, and psychosis are some of the major causes of suicide in adolescence. Attention has also been drawn to parental divorce as an immediate cause of suicide attempts in adolescents (Crumley, 1979; Rabin and Swenson, 1981).

DEPRESSION

Depression in adolescents is often the result of the interaction among biologic, psychologic, and social factors at a particular development stage (Lewis and Lewis, 1979). Kashani et al. (1981) have reviewed the biochemical, genetic, psychosocial stress, behavioral reinforcement, and cognitive theories used to understand depression in childhood and adolescence. The normal hormonal changes of puberty have already been mentioned. The lifetime risk for depression in a child of a bipolar parent is about 10%, and the risk for a child of a unipolar parent is about 15% (Cytryn et al., 1980).

McKnew and Cytryn (1979), following a controlled study of nine children 6 to 12 years of age with a diagnosis of chronic depression, suggested that a physiologic counterpart to emotional "detachment" in children may be a suppresison of the general arousal system, mediated through the noradrenergic network and centered on the locus ceruleus. The result is a reduction of urinary 3-methoxy-4-hydroxyphenylethylene glycol (MHPG). Puig-Antich et al. (1979) have demonstrated a cortisol hypersecretion in children diagnosed as suffering from a depressive syndrome. The various feelings of loss that may occur when separation and independence are attempted during adolescence may play an important role in adolescent depression. Many adolescents become depressed when they first go off to college.

Some illnesses that are common during adolescence, such as infectious mononucleosis and other viral illnesses, may precipitate a depression in an adolescent predisposed to depression, as may certain drugs such as barbiturates and alcohol. For further discussion, see Chapter 31.

Depression in children and adolescents also occurs without the classic unhappy, withdrawn picture that makes the diagnosis easy. Although "depressive equivalent" has fallen into disuse, Toolan (1962) coined the term to denote the condition of the adolescent who "may deliberately mask his own feelings by a pretense of happiness and exhibit the picture of a smiling depression" (p. 407). The concept of masked expression described by Glaser (1967) similarly is not a separate entity (Cytryn et al., 1980), but rather simply represents the presenting clinical picture. The cardinal symptoms and signs of depression must still be present to make the diagnosis. Possible presenting symptoms of a depression include enuresis, headache, school failure, school phobia (Agras, 1958; Watts, 1966), hyperactivity, and antisocial behavior. Renshaw (1972) has drawn attention to promiscuity, academic failure, and drug abuse as manifestations of depression. Burks and Harrison (1962) have described how aggressive behavior is used to ward off depression.

Depressed adolescents may lose or gain weight, gorge themselves or starve themselves, boast of their achievements or speak deprecatingly of themselves, become members of groups or isolate themselves, overimmerse themselves in work or refuse to work at all. In fact, the degree of what looks like reaction formation in depressed children and adolescents is quite striking. As stated previously, an early experience of loss or abandonment and ungratified longing are common antecedents of depression in children and adolescents. Whether certain kinds of cognitive, emotional, or sensory deprivation at particular times of development permanently change the biochemical functions of the human organism and result in a chronic or recurrent dysphoric state remains an unanswered question. (For a further discussion of depression, see p. 360.)

JUVENILE DELINQUENCY

The term delinquency is a legal term and the definition is based on age at the time of committing a legal offense. In most states the age limit is 16 to 20 years. Juvenile delinquency is classified into two categories: (1) acts that, if perpetrated by an adult, would be considered criminal, and (2) so-called status offenses, which are acts that only a minor can commit (e.g., truancy, running away, or incorrigibility). The age at which children may be tried as adults is now down to 13 years for certain crimes.

The FBI (1987) has reported that 9% of all murders are committed by juveniles 17 years of age and less. In 1986, for example, 20,613 murders were committed—an increase of 8.6% over the figure for 1985.

Fifteen percent of all rapists are under 18 years of age, and the figures for 1986 again show an increase over those for 1985.

Sixty-two percent of all arrests are for persons under 25 years of age. Arrests for those over 18 years of age have increased 9%, and arrests for those under 18 years of age have increased 4%.

Eleven percent of all robberies are committed by individuals under 18 years of age, given a total of 542,775 for 1986—an increase of 8% over the figure for 1985.

These figures show that delinquency is a frequent occurrence among adolescents. Sometimes the problems of adolescence are part of the multiple causes of delinquent behavior.

THE VIOLENT ADOLESCENT

A simple definition of a physically violent person is "one who acts or has acted in such a way as to produce physical harm or destruction" (American Psychiatric Association, 1974). A more complex definition would address such questions as: Is the violence pathologic? Under what circumstances does it occur? What are the causes of the violence? What is the natural history of the violent behavior? Will it recur, worsen, or subside, and under what conditions are these outcomes likely to take place?

In turn, each of these questions spawns additional questions: Can unprovoked violence ever be truly nonpathologic? What degrees of biologic, environmental, and psychologic factors are necessary to elicit violence? Are there localizable altered brain structures or functions at any level from that of gross anatomy to the level of the brain cell and neurochemistry of the synapse?

Destructive violence, especially that directed at another person, is not a rare phenomenon. From 1971 to 1980 in the United States, arrests of juveniles for violent offenses increased from 62,302 to 86,220—an increase of 38%. Total arrests for all violent crimes committed by adults and adolescents rose 63%, to a total of 446,373 (Hamparian, 1985). Currently, 43.3% of people arrested for serious crimes are under 18 years of age. Recidivism is a serious problem: most serious juvenile offenses are committed by fewer than 10% of juvenile offenders. Fifty percent of all rapes and murders are committed by adolescents; 1,811 adolescents were arrested for murder in 1985. In 1986, nearly 10% of accused murderers were under 18 years of age. Males are arrested for serious violent offenses more often than females. Children and adolescents may physically abuse their parents, perhaps in as much as 10% of families, especially when the family is enmeshed and the parents have abdicated authority to the violent adolescent (Strauss et al., 1980; Harbin and Madden, 1979). Death by violence, including accidents, murders, and suicide, has been responsible for three out of four deaths among 15- to 24-year olds (DHHS, 1982). In 1980 alone, murders of adolescents in the United States cost approximately 98,000 potential years of life (Levine, 1988). Thus, from the point of view of public safety alone, the violent person poses a serious national problem of considerable proportions. Of greater significance, however, is the problem it poses for the individual: How is the violent individual to be understood and treated, and how is violent behavior to be prevented?

First, it is important to note that violence is a symptom, not a diagnosis. Violence may be compared, in medical terms, to a fever: fever is a symptom of many diseases and syndromes each of which requires accurate diagnosis before a rational treatment can be instituted. True, we can apply simple measures to reduce fever (e.g., ice, aspirin)—and these measures may prevent secondary complications—but such measures alone will not eliminate the fever or prevent its recurrence. Similarly, from a medical point of view, accurate diagnosis of violence is essential for effective and specific treatment. A knowledge of the scientific basis of the medical approach is a prerequisite for medical diagnosis. The diagnostician aims to identify each of the multiple causes and how each cause interacts with other causes. There is, after all, virtually no disease with a single cause.

At the same time, some causes are manifestly social and political. Such causes may be prominent in certain forms of violence that are prominent today, e.g., terrorism and organized crime. These will not be discussed. Similarly, such issues as legalized violent acts represented, for example, in capital punishment, or official violence such as that sanctioned in the Vietnam war, will not be discussed.

Nevertheless, some social factors that appear to increase the prevalence of violent behavior should be mentioned. For example, the rise in the number of teenage pregnancies and the greater survival rate among premature infants and children who have suffered head injury appear to correlate, according to some accounts, with an increase in the incidence of violence as a symptom in children and adolescents. Unemployment, drug abuse, ignorance, poor health, peer delin-quest subcultures, inadequate supervision, and psychotic parenting are additional social factors, some of which are discussed shortly.

Genetic Factors

Mednick (1978) noted that adopted children have a higher likelihood of becoming criminal if their biologic parents were criminal. However, there is no single genotype for violence (Rosenthal, 1971). A heterogeneous group of several genetic factors together may create a vulnerability in the child and adolescent that may then contribute toward violent behavior. The vulnerability may arise, for example, when a genetically determined depletion of dopamine contributes to the development of an attention deficit disorder hyperactivity syndrome, which in turn might lead to antisocial behavior.

Similarly, differences in skin conductance (Mednick, 1978), or hypoarousability leading to disobedient behavior (Wender, 1972), have been suggested as possible contributing factors. Abnormalities in neurotransmitters have also been postulated to have a relationship to human aggression (Greenberg and Coleman, 1976).

In some cases the vulnerability caused by genetic factors might be more indirect, acting perhaps through the parents who may have a serious psychopathologic condition leading to disordered parenting.

Although these ideas are speculative, they have important clinical implications: For example, the treatment of an associated attention deficit in the child or adolescent, or the treatment of a psychosis in the parent, may be an important part of the total treatment plan. This knowledge, of course, may be used in a preventive program.

Societal Factors

Environmental and social factors almost always influence the expression of genetic factors. We will discuss two current social phenomena: The United States legal system response to violent children and adolescents, and the effects of television on aggression and violence in children.

Juvenile Justice System. The response of society to the violent child has largely been one of extrusion and punishment. Over the years, for example, the proceedings of the Juvenile Justice System have tended to become more like those of adult courts, and more and more adversarial. Some have lowered the age at which a child may be waived to the adult court for prosecution, and the Juvenile Justice Standards Project (1977) recommended fixed sentences rather than flexible dispositions. The object primarily seems to be "just" punishment. Issues of diagnosable cognitive, emotional, and neurologic impairment, issues of treatment for certain conditions, and issues of preventive measures directed at known etiologic factors do not seem to be addressed or are not effectively addressed.

In the United States, 30 states permit the execution of minors and, in 1987, there were 30 inmates on death row for crimes they had committed when they were under 18 years of age (Levine, 1988). The wait between the death sentence and actual execution appears to be deliberate, i.e., apparently juveniles sentenced to death are executed after they have reached majority, presumably to avoid the distasteful practice of actually killing children.

Seventy-five percent of executed juveniles whose race is known have been black, and all the juveniles executed for rape have been black. Only 9 girls have been executed: 8 were black and 1 was American Indian (Streib, 1987).

In contrast to these figures, Streib notes that all European countries have revoked the death penalty for crimes committed by children or adolescents who are less than 18 years of age.

Television. By the time a child has finished high school, he or she will have seen depicted on television approximately 18,000 murders, and uncountable incidents of beatings, robbery, arson, and other forms of violence (Rothenberg, 1983). A report released by the

National Coalition on Television Violence (NCTV, 1983) compared the amount of violence shown on cable television with that shown on network television, including Saturday morning cartoons for children. The violence that was monitored was confined to what the coalition called "interpersonal violence," defined as "the deliberate and hostile use of overt force or the immediate and direct threat thereof by one individual, or agent, coercively against another individual, or victim." The NCTV found that during a three-month monitoring period (June 28 to September 26, 1982) NBC showed 7.2 violent acts per hour and CBS similarly had 6.8 violent acts per hours. During August and September of that same year, however, the Movie Channel has 19.3 violent acts per hour, HBO has 20.8, and Showtime had no less that 27.2 violent acts per hour!

As Dr. George Gerbner, Dean of the Annenberg School of Communications at the University of Pennsylvania, has noted, when people are watching an average of 6.5 hours a day (which is the current national average), what they see is largely the responsibility of the producer, and not the consumer. Gerbner (1983) also noted that, at their worst, the violence in films on cable does not begin to compare with what young children have encountered on the cartoon shows aired by the networks on Saturday morning, which formerly averaged a staggering 27 violent acts per hours. This average has now declined somewhat.

Extensive research has been done to assess the effects of this tremendous amount of visual input of violence. Murray (1980) reviewed all this research, most of which has been compiled since 1975, and came to the following conclusions with respect to violence:

1. Children *are* likely to learn and remember certain forms of aggressive behavior from the violence they witness on television.

2. A *decrease* in sensitivity to violence seen on television *does* occur in response to the exposure to repetitive violence. This decrease in turn increases the likelihood of a decrease in emotional sensitivity to real aggressive behavior in actual life situations.

3. A *heightening* of aggressive charge occurs when aggression on television is watched, rather than the draining off of aggression that many producers would like us to believe occurs.

4. At the same time, an awareness of the appalling aftermath of aggression can *sometimes* inhibit aggression.

As a result of this research, at least two professional associations, the American Academy of Child Psychiatry (1976) and the American Academy of Pediatrics (1977), have suggested that child psychiatrists and pediatricians raise questions with the children and families they work with about the individual's television viewing habits.

Psychologic Factors

Between the early genetic and biochemical responses on the one hand and the environmental or social influences, including television, on the other hand, lies the actual psychologic experience of *being* a violent adolescent. We tend nowadays to lose sight of what a violent adolescent thinks and feels as research focuses on what might be occurring either at the level of the synapse or at the level of what social factors contribute to the etiology of violence. Yet the psychologic experience is where the research started, beginning with the vivid and detailed descriptions of such pioneers as Healy and Bronner (1926) in Chicago and Boston, through Aichhorn's descriptions in *Wayward Youth* (1935), onto such concepts as Johnson and Szurek's "super-ego lacunae" (Johnson, 1949: Johnson and Szurek, 1952). One lasting contribution of these descriptions is that they remind us of the need for humane treatment of these adolescents who are often themselves the victims of incredible physical abuse, trauma, neglect, and/or psychotic child rearing.

Many of these violent adolescents are enraged adolescents: enraged against the parents who abused them and society who neglects them. Many of these adolescents are delusional and paranoid individuals who perceive the world as a dangerous place as they themselves add to the actual danger. Many of these adolescents are barely in control of their confused and frightening feelings and affects, often the result of the brain damage or brain-dysfunction they suffer. Many of these adolescents are depressed and without hope. Whatever else they have or impose on the rest of society, they suffer.

Clinical Characteristics

Lewis and colleagues (Lewis, 1981) at New York University Medical Center conducted a series of studies that revealed a number of important clinical characteristics of violent children and adolescents. Of 97 serious juvenile offenders 11 to 17 years of age, average age 15, who were incarcerated at a correctional facility, Lewis found that of the 89 who were actually violent, 76% has paranoid symptoms, 57% were illogical and rambling in their thought processes, 41% had auditory hallucinations, 28% had visual hallucinations, 42% had major neurologic signs, and 69% had symptoms of psychomotor epilepsy (Lewis et al., 1979).

Lewis then divided this cohort of 97 children into two groups: one more and the other (relatively) less violent. She then found that 78.6% of the more violent juveniles were known to have witnessed extreme violence, compared to 20% of the less violent group (p<.001%). The violence was extreme. For example, several children had witnessed their fathers, stepfathers, or mother's boyfriends slash their mothers with knives. They saw their siblings tortured with cigarette burns, chained to beds, and thrown into walls.

The children who became extremely violent had also themselves suffered incredible violence: 75.4% compared to 33.3% (p = .003). One parent broke her son's legs with a broom, another broke his fingers and his sister's arm, another chained and burned his son, and yet another threw his son down stairs, causing head injury in the boy and subsequent epilepsy. This kind of abuse, besides causing central nervous system damage with subsequent learning disabilities and attention disorders, engenders enormous rage against the abusing parent, a rage that could subsequently be displaced onto other "authority" figures. At the very least, these children had poor models with whom to identify.

In addition, serious delinquents often had a history of head and face trauma. The percentage of abuse, head injury, and neurologic symptoms in incarcerated delinquents was twice as high as that among nonincarcerated delinquents, and three times as high as that among nondelinquents.

Interestingly, the violent males and females were remarkably alike in all respects, including medical histories, neurologic damage, and violent capabilities. What varied was the dispositions that were made: Violent, disturbed females were more likely to be hospitalized, whereas violent, disturbed males were more likely to be incarcerated.

A disturbing finding was that the white psychiatrically disturbed violent adolescents were likely to be hospitalized, whereas the black psychiatrically disturbed violent adolescents were likely to be incarcerated. This trend suggests that correctional facilities in the United States are being asked to function as the mental hospitals of the lower socioeconomic class black population.

Lewis also found that the more violent children showed significantly more paranoid symptomatology (81.8%), significantly more loose rambling associations (59.6%), and more auditory hallucinations (43.3%).

Moreover, 99% of the more violent delinquents had one or more minor neurologic signs, and almost 30% had grossly abnormal EEGs. The more violent delinquents also had a more severe reading grade discrepancy (4.4 years versus 2.3 years).

These findings are startling and well worth considering because they have never before been so well documented. In summary, Lewis and her colleagues suggest:

that a single factor (e.g., brain damage, social deprivation, vulnerability to psychosis) is insufficient to engender violent delinquency. Unfortunately, often the combination of familial vulnerability (e.g., as indexed by the presence of a schizophrenic parent), trauma to the central nervous system (e.g., perinatal trauma, head injury), physical and psychological abuse from a parent, and social deprivation (e.g., failure of a physician to diagnose and treat correctly, or failure of society to provide adequate support systems in the form of community programs or residential treatment) is sufficient to create the violent young offender, and this combination of factors occurs frequently (p. 13 ff.).

Predicting Violence

A previous history of violence often predicts future violence (Monahan, 1981), and juvenile violence predicts adult violence (Wolfgang, 1978). Recidivists, as noted earlier, are responsible for most juvenile violence.

Serious antisocial behavior in the 6- to 11-year-old group is another "particularly ominous childhood pattern," and can be a predictor of violence in adolescence (Robins, 1966). Robins compared 524 children seen in a child guidance clinic with 100 matched normal children in a local school. Her study found that children referred to the clinic for such complaints as temper tantrums, learning problems, sleeping and eating problems, and speech problems did not differ much from the control group when they were seen as adults 30 years later; that is, shyness, seclusiveness, nervousness, tantrums, insomnia, fears, tics, speech problems, and similar complaints were not related to later psychiatric disorder. However, children referred to the clinic for antisocial behavior did differ from the control group seen 30 years later, and the more severe the early antisocial behavior was during childhood, the more disturbed was the later adjustment. Among the children referred to the clinic for antisocial behavior, (1) most of them had been held back in first grade, (2) their problems had become obvious at the age of 7, and (3) the common referral symptoms had been theft (82%), incorrigible behavior (76%), truancy (75%), running away (71%), school discipline problems, and sexual activity, including promiscuity. (Truancy and poor school performance had been almost univer-

sally present in children who later demonstrated antisocial behaviors, and a high percentage of the antisocial children were later diagnosed as having schizophrenia.) Interestingly, in the families of these children referred for antisocial behavior, the father was "sociopathic" or alcoholic, and the homes were impoverished or broken. In short, the best single predictor of adult "sociopathy" was the degree of childhood antisocial behavior, especially in the 6-to-11 age group.

Interestingly, poverty, a slum environment, maternal deprivation, foster home or orphanage placement, or even a "sociopathic" mother did not predict adult sociopathy. However, if a child had a sociopathic or alcoholic father and was also sent to a correctional institution, the prognosis for the child was poor. Robins was taking issue with the culture-of-poverty hypothesis of sociopathy. She believed that it was the other way around; that is, the children with antisocial behavior and sociopathic fathers simply fail to rise socioeconomically. Robins concluded that antisocial behavior predicts class status more than class status predicts antisocial behavior.

Beyond that, all the risk factors associated with (1) genetic transmission of adverse psychiatric traits and conditions, (2) adverse fetal environment (e.g., alcohol, drugs), (3) birth trauma, (4) child abuse, (5) head injury, and (6) slum environments add to the risk for subsequent violence and should serve to signal out an individual thus exposed. Recently, Lewis et al. (1989) postulated a theory of the genesis of violence that might help predict which juvenile delinquents are most likely to go on to violent criminality as adults. The theory also has implications for treatment and prevention. Essentially, the combination of certain potentially treatable psychiatric, neurologic, and cognitive vulnerabilities, together with having been brutally abused and/or raised in extremely violent households, strikingly increases the risk for continuing violence as adults. The interactive effect might derive from the special vulnerability of the modelling effect of family violence, the engendered rage that is then so difficult to control, and the secondary neurologic, psychiatric, and cognitive impairments caused by the abuse, which is then sometimes invited by these very impairments.

Etiology

Some of the general etiologic factors for violence in children and adolescents are shown in Table 19–2.

Some of the syndromes in children and adolescents that may have violence as a symptom are shown in Table 19–3.

The miniml diagnostic workup for a violent child or adolescent is shown in Table 19–4.

Table 19–2. Etiology of Violence in Children and Adolescents

1. Genetic factors (e.g., in attention deficit hyperactivity disorder)
2. Brain damage (anoxia, head injury)
3. Disordered parenting (alcoholism, paranoid ideation, psychosis)
4. Physical and sexual abuse
   witnessing abuse
   suffering abuse
5. Environmental influences and stressors

Table 19–3. Syndromes in Childhood and Adolescence in Which Violence May Be a Symptom

Affective disorder
Antisocial personality disorder
Asperger's syndrome
Attention deficit hyperactivity disorder
Brain damage (e.g., from genetic disorders, trauma, infections, neoplasms, degenerative diseases, and vascular, toxic, and metabolic disorders)
Complex partial seizure and temporal lobe dysfunction
Conduct disorder
Explosive disorder
Hemangioma
Hyperparathyroidism
Insulinemia with hypoglycemia
Lupus erythematosus
Mental retardation
Pervasive developmental disorders
Premenstrual syndrome
Psychosis
Schizophrenia
Subdural hematoma, chronic
Substance abuse (alcohol; amphetamine; PCP; barbiturates; glue)

Table 19–4. Minimal Diagnostic Workup for Violence in Children and Adolescents

1. History
     comprehensive pediatric and child psychiatric history
     specific history of violence, violent events, and the ecologic context in which these events occurred
2. Physical examination
     general pediatric examination
     specific neurologic evaluation, including visual fields
3. Mental status examination
4. Laboratory tests
     EEG, including standard, sleep-derived EEG, and 24-hour monitored EEG
     CT scan
     PET scan
     MRI
     Evoked potentials
     Psychologic tests, including the WISC(R)
     Metabolic function tests, including glucose tolerance, thyroid function, and calcium levels
     Toxic substance screen, especially for cocaine, PCP, amphetamines, and alcohol

Management and Treatment of Acute Violence in Children

The general management of the acutely violent child or adolescent consists of the following steps:

1. The first requirement is to remove all weapons, including knives and guns.
2. The violent child or adolescent is often a paranoid individual. It is therefore of paramount importance to be absolutely clear with him or her about one's intentions and actions. This includes informing the child or adolescent that one *will* notify others if the child or adolescent says he or she is about to hurt someone, i.e., hospitalization is always available if the adolescent is in imminent danger of harming himself or herself, or others.
3. When outpatient management is attempted, it is important to offer 24-hour telephone availability. At the same time, one must inform the adolescent and his or her parents that they are responsible for the adolescent unless hospitalization takes place.

4. The adolescent may also be helped in various specific ways:
   a. by heightening the adolescent's awareness of premonitory symptoms (auras), including such sensations as irritability, a feeling that something is "coming on," and dysphoria;
   b. by avoiding or dampening precipitating stimuli, including violence seen on movies or television; and
   c. by identifying the most vulnerable target of an adolescent's aggression, and instructing that person on how to be as unprovocative as possible, and how to recognize the early warning signs of violence in the adolescent.
5. The child or adolescent who exhibits pathologic aggression nearly always requires therapy. The therapy often focuses on such issues as anger and shame, and feelings of inadequacy and low self-esteem. Power struggles often occur, and the adolescent is often filled with sadistic fantasies. Interestingly, many violent adolescents also fear they may commit suicide. (Conversely, about 1 in 6 suicide hot-line calls are homicide calls.) The therapist must also deal with powerful countertransference feelings, including anger and fear of doing harm. The therapist must feel safe and must have available the capability for limit setting and, if necessary, inpatient settings for restraint.
6. Medication is also useful in the management and treatment of children and adolescents with pathologic aggression (Campbell et al., 1982; Ballenger and Post, 1980). Medications that may be helpful include haloperidol (Haldol), propranolol (Inderal), carbamazepine (Tegretol) and lithium (Lithobid). The dosage ranges that have been used for these medications are shown in Table 19–5.

Prevention

The prevention of violence in children and adolescents requires attention to primary, secondary, and tertiary areas.

Primary prevention is directed at each of the biopsychosocial risk factors shown in Table 19–2. This means that adequate treatment of parents who are at risk for disordered parenting is essential. Furthermore, diagnosis and a vigorous effort at treatment for the child who shows early evidence of the symptoms or signs of any of the disorders associated with violence must be instituted promptly.

Secondary prevention requires immediate and effective management of the initial violent crisis, followed by a comprehensive treatment plan designed to shorten the duration of the violent episode.

Tertiary treatment requires the availability of ongoing opportunities to prevent complications and to facilitate optimum adaptation. Such treatment may include any of the dynamic psychotherapies (individual, group, family), behavior therapies, cognitive (didactic) therapies, pharmacotherapy, remedial education, medical treatments for medical conditions, and socioenvironmental interventions. The settings for these treatments may include outpatient clinics under the auspices of community agencies of the state, residential treatment centers, or psychiatric hospitals (full service or partial hospitalization). Multiple personnel are almost always required, including physicians (psychiatrists, neurologists, pediatricians), nurses, social workers, educators, psychologists, child care workers, and support staff (occupational therapists, child life specialists, and dieticians).

Treatment Outcome

What is the prognosis? Obviously, much depends on the extent or seriousness of the diagnoses, the degree of symptomatology present, and the availability of treatment in suitable treatment facilities. Studies of these variables are needed before anything definite can be said.

Marohn (1982) has described the violent end of the violent adolescents he has followed:

A 14½-year-old white female was murdered after she had run away from the treatment program;
A 23-year-old white youth hanged himself in a

Table 19–5.   Medication Dosages for Violent Children and Adolescents

Haloperidol (Haldol)	
for agitation	0.3 to 0.7 mg/kg im.
maintenance:	3 mg/day (0.5 mg/kg day to 0.75 mg/kg day)
median range:	0.5 to 5.0 mg b.i.d. or t.i.d.
Propranolol (Inderal)	
dosage range:	50 to 960 mg/day
median dosage:	160 mg/day
Carbamazepine (Tegretol)	
dosage range:	200 mg to 800 mg/day
	(blood level: 8 to 12 μg/ml)
Lithium (Lithobid)	
dosage range:	150 to 300 mg/day
	(blood level 0.6 to 1.2 mEq/L)

correctional facility some 10 years after discharge from the program,

A 24-year-old black woman was found raped and strangled in an alley about 8 years after her discharge,

An 18-year-old black youth was shot under questionable circumstances by a security guard 3⅓ years after his discharge from the program,

And a 23-year-old white male was killed in an auto accident some 8 years after his discharge from the program (p. 359).

Marohn characterized the world of these adolescents as being "fraught with violence—violent behavior, violent feelings, violent experiences, and violent death" (p. 359).

Need for Research

Additional research is clearly needed to answer the questions that might enable us to have a more rational response to the violent child and adolescent. Why is it, for example, that violent incarcerated delinquents have more hospital visits, emergency room contacts, clinic visits and ward admissions, and more accidents, injuries, and signs of neurologic impairment than nonincarcerated children? (Lewis and Shanok, 1977; Lewis et al., 1979). Why do they have a history of more prenatal maternal illness, prematurity, and traumatic deliveries than nondelinquents? Which comes first: does the central nervous system dysfunction lead to accidents, or do the head injuries lead to CNS dysfunction? Or is it both?

Many other questions remain unanswered.

For example, what is the significance of differences in physiologic functions in skin conductance, noted earlier, that have been found in children of criminal fathers compared to children of noncriminal fathers (Mednick, 1978)? What is the significance of such findings as an apparent association between aggression and low levels of 5-hydroxyindole in a group of retarded human subjects (Greenberg and Coleman, 1976), or the association between violence and androgen levels (Mattsson, 1982), or the premenstrual increase in antisocial acts that occurs in women (Dalton, 1961)?

Then again, what can we learn from research in other fields, such as cultural anthropology, that may help us understand violence and aggression in children and adolescents in our own culture? Freeman (1982), for example, has taken issue with Margaret Mead on her observations and hypothesis about aggression in the children in Samoa.

UNWED MOTHERHOOD IN ADOLESCENCE

Adolescent girls who become unwed mothers are not rare in our society and come from every social class. In an early study, 18% of 2,000 single females who had premarital intercourse became pregnant (Kinsey, 1953). In 1971, 46% of unmarried 19-year-old women reported having had intercourse (Zelnik and

Kantner, 1978), and in 1975, 69% of adolescent males were reported to be sexually experienced (Finkel and Finkel, 1975). Of approximately 1,000,000 adolescents who became pregnant, 570,622 gave birth and 370,000 had abortions (McAnarney and Greydanus, 1979). Of the 1,000,000 or more adolescents who become pregnant each year in the United States, about 300,000 are girls under 15 years of age (Lipsitz, 1979). Out-of-wedlock births among 14- to 17-year-olds increased by 75% between 1961 and 1974. In the District of Columbia, the number of out-of-wedlock births exceeded those in wedlock. More pregnant girls 14 years of age have abortions than give birth. Of the babies born to 15-year-olds, 13% weighed less than 2,500 g, compared to 6% born to mothers who were 25 to 29 years of age.

However, it is important to note that these statistics are changing. Sexual activity among teenage girls in cities is increasing; e.g., for adolescents 15 to 18 years old (ninth to twelfth grade), from 14.4% in 1971 to 22.5% in 1979 (Zelnik and Kantner, 1980). However, in 1976, two thirds of all 16-year-old women and half of all 18-year-olds were still virgins (Zelnik et al., 1979). Further, although there was an increase in the number of births to young adolescents in the early 1970s, there is now a decline because of the reduced birth rate and smaller number in this age group (NCHS, 1978). In 1978, 10.9% of all births were to women 18 years of age and under, and only 2% of all births to teenagers occurred in women 15 years of age or younger (Dreisbach and Kasun, 1981). In 1977 there were 570,609 births and about 400,000 abortions in women under the age of 20, whereas for women under 15 years of age, a pregnancy is more likely to be terminated by an abortion than by a live birth (Forrest et al., 1979). The birth rate for girls at 14 years of age increased in the late 1970s (Hollingsworth and Kreutner, 1981).

One report (Alan Guttmacher Institute, 1981) predicts that, if current trends continue, 4 in 10 of today's 14-year-old girls will have at least 1 pregnancy, 2 in 10 will have at least 1 birth, and more than 1 in 7 will have at least 1 abortion while still in their teens.

One of every ten adolescent girls becomes pregnant each year and, of these pregnancies, the vast majority are unintended (Trussel, 1988). The high pregnancy rate reflects the failure to use appropriate methods for contraception which in turn relates, in part, to both failures to anticipate intercourse and denial of the risks involved.

For the adolescent, the event of pregnancy may be related to an attempt to cope with any of the developmental tasks described earlier. In many instances there is an unconscious or even a conscious wish to become pregnant. The wish may be derived from a number of sources. Some girls believe that by producing a baby they will be able to rid themselves of the feeling that they are defective (Bonan, 1963). In others, there are a depression and a fear of loss of the tie to the mother, which are dealt with in part by an attempt to identify strongly with the mother and to produce a child whom the adolescent can mother as she herself wished to be mothered. Occasionally, the wish to have a baby is an attempt to satisfy the adolescent's urge to give a baby to someone, often her mother. Indeed, the adolescent may be acting out the unconscious wish of her mother to have another baby. Often, pregnancy is the accidental result of a wish for closeness with a boy. Rarely is the unwed pregnant teenager promiscuous in the common sense of the word.

The wish of the adolescent's mother for a baby may arise because she is menopausal and feels particularly in need. Her wish may be conveyed to the adolescent, for example, in the mother's turning a blind eye to the adolescent's late nights, by engaging in stimulating sexual conversation with the adolescent, by misplaced "permissiveness," or by providing the young adolescent with contraceptives. Sometimes a pregnancy results through a prophecy-fulfillment mechanism: the parents "expect the worst" of their child, and the child obligingly lives up to this expectation (Bowman, 1958). This phenomenon is sometimes seen in adopted girls who have assumed, as have their parents, that they were born out of wedlock.

Rarely, an adolescent will impulsively become pregnant in an attempt to rid herself of what she feels to be an intolerably bad wish, somewhat along the lines of Oscar Wilde's dictum that "the only way to get rid of a temptation is to yield to it." The conflict is then externalized as the parents and social agencies struggle to help the adolescent decide what to do about her pregnancy: whether the outcome will be abortion, adoption, marriage, or keeping the baby. For some deprived adolescent unwed mothers, the baby is a source of gratification (Khlentzos and Pagliaro, 1965).

During an out-of-wedlock pregnancy, the adolescent girl may experience feelings of shame, guilt, or helplessness and may not take adequate care of herself (perhaps in the hope of inducing an abortion). She usually has considerable fears about her parents' reactions. Parents in most cases find it hard to accept the pregnancy, no matter what their social class (Malinowski, 1966). There may also be much conflict about making suitable plans. Rarely does the unwed pregnant minor see her pregnancy as a symptom of emotional conflict.

Again, a striking aspect of such a pregnancy is its relationship to the adolescent's struggles with impulse control, concerns about the body, striving for a sense of integrity and identity, and regressive pull in the face of the demands of reality—all of which are part of the "normal disturbance" of adolescence.

ALCOHOL USE

Alcohol use (O'Connor, 1977), smoking, and drug taking in the 1970s showed a steady increase among adolescents. In one study, 63% of boys and 53% of girls between 11 and 13 years of age were reported to have tried alcohol, and one in seven 17-year-olds were reported to become drunk once a week. Nearly all (93%) high-school seniors in 1977 were reported to have tried alcohol, and 6%

drank daily (*The Status of Children, Youth and Families*, 1980).

In 1985, 66% of high-school seniors in one survey had consumed alcohol within the preceding month. Thirty-nine percent had indulged in binge drinking (i.e., five or more drinks in a row) within the previous two weeks, and 5% had reported daily drinking (Marks and Fisher, 1987). Alcohol use is more prevalent among boys than among girls. Children of alcoholic parents, particularly alcoholic fathers, may inherit a genetic factor for predisposition to alcoholism (Goodwin, 1984). The psychologic sequelae in both boys and girls include instability, memory lapses, and failing school work.

In our society drinking is a socially and culturally defined pattern of behavior that increases with age (Maddox, 1964). In general, the average age at which a child has his or her first drink is between 14 and 15 years. In a study of alcohol and drug use among public school students, Palmer and Ringwalt (1988) reported that almost 20% of 11th and 12th grade students reported coming to school drunk during the year previous to the survey. The first drink is usually taken in the home, with the parents, and is usually a beer. The reasons for starting to drink usually center around three themes: celebrating a holiday or special occasion, being offered a drink by the family, and curiosity about drinking. Peer pressure becomes an important determinant of alcohol use during adolescence (Brook and Brook, 1988).

The dangers are twofold: habituation and short- and long-term effects of drunkenness. The earlier the onset of alcohol abuse, the poorer the prognosis. The risk of relapse is also greater for those with a history of several episodes of drunkenness. Nylander and Rydelius (1973) showed that boys who had recurring offenses were more likely to have alcoholic or mentally ill fathers and a higher incidence of psychiatric problems at school. "Problem" drinkers are very likely to have problems in other areas (Plant, 1976). If both parents take a drink, the probability is high that their children will also drink. At the same time, peer group support is a powerful factor.

One serious consequence of drinking is the car accident. Accidents, mostly car accidents, are the leading cause of mortality among old adolescents, and intoxication is an important factor in many of these deaths. Death from risk-taking behavior while intoxicated is a real danger in the United States today. Fifty percent of the people who die in car accidents in which drinking is involved are adolescents. Raising the legal age for alcohol consumption in some states is only a partial answer. A national policy is required.

SMOKING

Although there has been a 25% decline in smoking in adults, there was a 43% rise in smoking in adolescents between 1965 and 1975. The number of adolescents who smoke dropped, however, from 15.6% in 1974 to 11.7% in 1979, especially among males (*The Status of Children, Youth and Families*, 1980). In 1985, 12% of high-school seniors were smoking at least half a pack a day, and 30% had smoked within the last month. More girls than boys were regular smokers (Marks and Fisher, 1987). Adolescents are more likely to smoke if their parents smoke. The adolescent may start smoking because smoking makes him or her feel more adult, less anxious and, in some instances, more accepted by peers. Other motivations are curiosity and rebellion.

The health risks of smoking include chronic productive cough, wheezing, prolonged respiratory infection, shortness of breath and, ultimately, lung cancer.

DRUG USE

Drug use among adolescents changes with each generation. Nevertheless, some of the studies done when drug use was on the increase are relevant to the present-day habits of adolescents. In one study, it was reported that approximately 50% of the students enrolled in large universities or colleges near urban centers had tried marijuana and that many high-school students had also tried it (Cohen, 1969). Blum and his colleagues (1969), in a survey of four high schools in the San Francisco Bay area, emphasized how rapidly the use of drugs seemed to have spread, especially marijuana but also LSD and the amphetamines; and they predicted that the use of opiates would also spread rapidly, a prediction that was subsequently confirmed (Kleber, 1970).

In another survey of 26,000 college students, 26% were reported to have used marijuana, 14% to have used amphetamines, and 5% to have used LSD (Mizner et al., 1970). Almost all LSD users had also tried marijuana, and most had used amphetamines. There is no evidence at present that all or most users of marijuana progress to heroin, and nothing to suggest that dependence on marijuana creates any kind of physiologic need for heroin (Stafford-Clark, 1969).

Drug use in 1980, with the exception of stimulants and methaqualone (Quaaludes), declined, as did general cigarette smoking. The decline has been attributed to peer disapproval and heightened health consciousness (Institute for Social Research, 1981).

Marijuana, the most widely used drug, is still used by 26% of high school seniors, and is used daily by 5%. Two thirds of all American students have tried a drug before leaving high school. The percentage for different drugs reported taken in 1985 are listed in Table 19–6.

Lastly, it should be noted that smoking marijuana compared to smoking tobacco results

Table 19–6. Percentages for Drugs Taken in 1985

Drugs	%
Marijuana	41
Stimulants	16
Cocaine	13
Hallucinogens	8
Inhalants	7
Sedatives	6
Tranquilizers	6
Opiates	6

From Marks and Fisher, 1987.

in five times as much carboxyhemoglobin caused by carbon monoxide and three times as much tar inhalation (the amount of smoke inhaled per puff is increased and the length of time the puff is held in the lungs is longer in marijuana smoking than in tobacco smoking) (Tzu-Chin Wu, et al., 1988). The consequences in terms of health hazards (respiratory disease and lung cancer) are obvious.

GLUE SNIFFING

A curious form of inhalation drug taking is seen in young adolescents, particularly 11- to 17-year-old-boys—and usually boys of normal intelligence (Sourindohin, 1985). The striking feature here is that almost any substance that can be vaporized is used (e.g., model-airplane glue, lighter fluid, paint, and gasoline), and the substance is inhaled in all kinds of ingenious methods (Glasser, 1966). The inhaled substance is used with tobacco and alcohol but not usually with other narcotics. The homes of some of these young adolescents have been broken by death, abandonment, or divorce. In some adolescents, the inhalation facilitates wish-fulfilling fantasies (Fawcett and Jensen, 1952), whereas in others it appears to be related to an erotic sensation derived during the act of sniffing, which itself may be a compulsive symptom. This symptom is often part of a regressive tendency during early adolescence. Sometimes it serves to ward off anxiety, boredom, and depression.

NARCOTICS USE

The use of narcotics among adolescents is partly the result of the ready availability in high schools of such drugs as heroin at a time when the adolescents are curious and wish to experiment (Kleber, 1970). Chein and his colleagues (1964) found that 16 seemed to be the age at which most experimentation starts. Many observers now find that 14-year-olds are experimenting with narcotics. If narcotics were not so readily available, drug use might end with experimenting, but with the ready

availability of narcotics, the experimenter may go on to occasional use, then to regular or habitual use, and then he or she may try to break the habit. A user may go through all these stages, but he or she may also stop at any stage (Chein et al., 1964). Heroin is usually started by inhaling ("snorting") a mixture of heroin and quinine water. Subcutaneous injection ("skin popping") is then tried. Later, the adolescent may give himself or herself intravenous injections ("main line"). The adolescent reaches a "high" very quickly, perhaps in less than a minute, and then experience a reversible drowsiness and sensual itching that may last from two to four hours. During the next 4 to 12 hours the individual may experience no particular sensations but neither does he or she yet feel a need to take another dose. From 12 to 15 hours after taking a dose, the adolescent begins to show withdrawal signs. He or she begins to feel anxious, the eyes and nose starts running, he or she gets gooseflesh, and the muscles twitch. During the next day or two, the withdrawal symptoms become worse, with abdominal cramps and chills. The adolescent then often huddles in a blanket to keep warm. Usually, the withdrawal symptoms subside after four or five days, leaving the adolescent feeling exhausted and achy.

Cocaine ("coke," "snow") is now widely used among young adolescents, having increased dramatically in use between 1975 and 1979. Some observers estimate that 10 to 15% of high-school students in some communities use cocaine (Woolston, 1981). Thirty percent of all college students use cocaine at least once before they graduate. The drug, in the form of a white powder, is usually "snorted" through the nostrils, although it may also be smoked in a water pipe, or a solution of cocaine may be injected intravenously. A recent trend is the smoking of an alkaline extraction of cocaine ("crack," free-base), which produces rapid, high concentrations and leads to compulsive use.

Cocaine appears to block reuptake of dopamine, giving rise to continued nerve stimulation and increased receptor activity for norepinephrine and dopamine. The drug gives rise to a feeling of confidence, euphoria, and hyperarousal, often followed by a letdown that leads to the urge for another "hit." Addiction occurs with just six weeks of steady use. Chronic use may cause insomnia, depression, paranoid thinking, and physical debilitation. Repeated use may also destroy the nasal mucous membrane. Adverse effects of the drug include hypertension, tachycardia, ischemia, and angina.

Overdose may cause headaches, nausea, convulsions, and cardiovascular collapse. Juveniles who need money to buy cocaine may become involved in delinquent acts.

Cocaine use by a mother, often a teenager, may result in preterm labor, a small-for-gestational-age baby, fetal and neonatal arrhythmias, perinatal cerebral infarction, and the sudden-infant-death syndrome (SIDS). About one third of infants exposed to cocaine in utero become passively addicted and have withdrawal symptoms within the first three or four days after birth. Because cocaine in the mother crosses over into breast milk, continuing toxic effects may be experienced by the breast-fed infant.

Cocaine-related emergency room admissions rose 300% between 1981 and 1985, amounting to about 9,946 per year. In 1985 at least 613 deaths resulted from cocaine use, up from 169 in 1980. Numerous complications have followed intravenous use, including sepsis, hepatitis, and AIDS.

Amphetamine ("speed") is popular, although it is usually taken for a short time. Euphoria is the usual sought-after effect, but the drug can also cause insomnia, overtalkativeness, and excitement, sometimes accompanied by hypertension and a rapid pulse rate. If an overdose is taken, the adolescent has hallucinations and becomes suspicious of others, and he or she may become wildly violent. After an amphetamine high, there is often a prolonged period of fatigue and depression that sometimes lasts for a week or two. Adolescents soon discover that heroin counteracts this aftereffect, and that discovery is often the first step in heroin addiction.

Psychedelic drugs, such as LSD, mescaline, and STP, may also be taken by the adolescent. Besides their hallucinogenic effects, these drugs may cause excitement and unpredictable aggressive behavior. The complex etiology of adverse reactions ("bad trips") to LSD have been described elsewhere (Ungerleider et al., 1968). Phencyclidine (PCP, "angel dust") is rapidly becoming more popular. Unfortunately, PCP is a dangerous drug because it is unpredictable, associated with violence (Fauman and Fauman, 1979), and may result in death if an overdose is taken.

MOTIVATION FOR DRUG USE

The motivations of adolescents for taking drugs are multiple; some motivations seem to be relatively superficial ones, others to have complex roots. Mizner and his colleagues (in the study mentioned earlier) found that (1) 38% of those who used marijuana for the first time said they did so out of curiosity, (2) 60% of those who used amphetamines said they took the drug to help study or get through exams, and (3) 45% of first-time users of LSD felt it would be a worthwhile experience. At the same time, psychiatric problems are often associated with drug use. However, these psychiatric problems are comparable to the kinds of problems that beset students who avoid drugs. Paulsen (1969) has distinguished three prevailing elements in these problems: (1) disturbances of intellectual functioning (thinking), (2) anxiety, phobic, panic, or depressive episodes (feelings), and (3) behavioral disturbances (action). Other investigators have observed social factors in the motivation for drug use. Thus adolescents in the lower social classes tend to take drugs to suppress their awareness of the squalor in which they live, whereas adolescents from the upper social classes tend to take drugs for the sensual experience.

Findings from studies of adolescents who had taken drugs during psychoanalytic treatment revealed a wide range of psychopathology, none of which could be called pathognomonic for drug users or drug addicts (Hartmann, 1969). However, Hartmann did note that the young adolescents she studied had little tolerance of frustration and tension. Some of the adolescents who had a healthy earlier development had used drugs in defiance of their parents or out of "experimental curiosity." Others had allowed themselves to be seduced into using drugs simply to avoid discomfort. "They remain in a group of other drug users in a pseudoclose relationship, without much emotional commitment; their sexual gratifications are on the level of masturbation; therefore they are as often homosexual as they are heterosexual; the more passive they were to begin with, the greater is the danger of their being seduced by this kind of gratification."

Attempts have been made to relate the adolescent's choice of drug to his or her specific psychologic needs, even to the extent of hypothesizing that "different drugs induce different regressive states that resemble specific phases of early childhood development." The user is said to harbor wishes or tendencies for a particular regressive conflict situation, which the pharmacology of a particular drug is though to facilitate; the repeated experience of "satisfaction" is then said to establish a preference for the specific drug (Wieder and Kaplan, 1969). For example, Wieder and Kaplan assert that (1) LSD states are comparable to the autistic phase, (2) opiate effects have similarities to the narcissistic regressive phenomena of the symbiotic state, and (3) amphetamine effects are reminiscent of the separation-individuation phase. Alcohol is said to be experienced by the younger adolescent as releasing too much drive, leading to fears of loss of control—and marijuana to be preferred because it is shorter acting, less diffuse, and more comfortable: the healthier adolescent will "use alcohol or marijuana only casually and intermittently, in the manner of the healthier adult." What can be said with a little more certainty is that the adolescent's personality determines in large measure how he or she experiences the pharmacologic effects of the drug used. For example, an ad-

olescent with an emotionally unstable personality may experience feelings of profound depersonalization, depression, and ideas of reference that may recur spontaneously for several weeks, all following a single marijuana cigarette (Klein and Davis, 1969).

In many instances, drugs are taken to ward off depression or feelings of inadequacy. For some, drug taking is a form of rebellion. For example, in the 1960s the hippies in part expressed their antiestablishment feelings through drug taking. Other adolescents say that they take drugs because they like them and because they reject what they think are the hypocrisies of society, such as keeping marijuana illegal but allowing the use of tobacco and alcohol. Others are convinced that the drugs they take are helpful to them. Blum and his colleagues (1969) are careful to point out that there is no simple, universal motivation for the use of drugs in the young. Furthermore, they note that drug use among students is prevalent enough that it must be considered within the "normal range of behavior, at least on some campuses." Chein and his colleagues (1964) go farther and note that motivational factors change over time, so that analyses of caused reported at one time may be at another time "hardly more than an historical curiosity rather than germane to pressing contemporary problems."

Because most of the drugs taken are obtained illegally, the meaning that breaking the law has for some adolescents is often intrinsic to the motivation. Some adolescents take drugs as part of a wish to be caught and punished. Others take drugs as a relatively safe and private means of defiance and ridicule.

In general, over time, adolescents seem to prefer sedative drugs to stimulants. Class factors figure in the choice of certain drugs, but they are less clearly defined. Until recently, for example, heroin was rarely taken among the middle class, but that is no longer true. It is rare that an adolescent believes that he or she takes drugs because of an emotional disorder, and he or she rarely comes for treatment with the purpose of being weaned off a drug. Yet it seems so often that the drug taking, pleasurable as it may be, is still part of the adolescent's attempts to deal with the turmoil he or she feels at this stage of development.

RUNNING AWAY

In 1976, about 733,000 youths (10 to 17 years of age) left home without their parents' consent for at least overnight (*The Status of Children, Youth and Families*, 1980). Running away, like attempting suicide, is often an expression of despair, anger, and the wish to be loved (Lewis and Lewis, 1973). The runaway child often is a child who is running away from a hostile environment (Balser, 1939; Foster, 1962; Lowrey, 1941; Riemer, 1940; Robey et al., 1964; Staub, 1943; Wylie and Weinreb, 1958). The hostile environment may be in the home, the school, or the community—or in all three places (Shellow et al., 1967). The parents, as well as the child, may be psychologically disturbed or mentally retarded (Armstrong, 1937; Leventhal, 1964). A child who has not been enabled to work through the death of a parent earlier in his life may run away in an unconscious search for the lost love object. An adopted child who has not been enabled to work through his fantasies about his biologic parents may run away in an unconscious search for his fantasized "true" parents. Children may run away from a family environment that aggravates the conflict surrounding a particular developmental task, such as the struggle for independence, which is accompanied by the child's feelings of helplessness and neediness. Sometimes the child is fleeing from the fantasized or real sexual or aggressive behavior of a parent. Many parents consciously or unconsciously wish that a child would leave home. In such cases, the runaway child is responding to the parents' message.

SEXUALITY

The achievement of an appropriate sexual identity and a heterosexual relationship are primary concerns of the adolescent. Adolescence is the major point for consolidation of final sexual identity. Dating typically begins earlier in girls than in boys, perhaps because girls, on average, mature somewhat earlier; it serves an important function in providing experiences in intimacy and social skills. Sexual activity is, increasingly, a major aspect of this experience (Zelnik and Kanter, 1977). Differences in perceived sexual roles persist with boys, on average, viewing their role as persuading the girl to have sex while girls, on average, view their role as postponing intercourse (La Plante et al., 1980). By middle and late adolescence dating implies some form of emotional commitment. The impact of sexual activity varies, of course, from individual to individual. Loss of virginity may be associated with feelings of accomplishment or pride, or feelings of loss and sadness, or with mixed emotions. The capacity to engage in sexual intercourse does not imply that adolescents engage in this activity responsibly; sexual activity in adolescents may include important aspects of denial or ignorance that lead to pregnancy (Dreyer, 1982).

A homosexual orientation may also be established during adolescence. It is important to realize that a wide variety of homosexual experiences is normal during childhood and adolescence (Fraiberg, 1961) (see also p. 202). The following activities are normal during adolescence:

1. visual comparison of the size of one another's penises
2. group exhibitionism and grabbing of one another's penises
3. mutual masturbation
4. occasional fellatio, and
5. in girls, comparison of the size of breasts, hand holding, kissing, fondling of one another's breasts, and petting one another's genitals.

These kinds of behaviors are almost age appropriate among adolescents, provided they are sporadic, not persistent, and not pervasive. Usually the behavior represents a temporary defense against the anxieties associated with heterosexual relationships. The adolescent may feel considerable guilt or anxiety about feelings of affection toward members of the same sex.

On the other hand, a homosexual identity may become entrenched under certain conditions. For example, persistent homosexual behavior, particularly in late adolescence, with the beginnings of an exclusive preference in that direction, is an indication of such an entrenchment. Prolonged halting of heterosexual explorations because of anxiety may help consolidate adolescent homosexuality. When less common homosexual activities are engaged in (e.g., anal intercourse), heterosexual relationships are less likely to occur. If the adolescent forms a love relationship with an adult of the same sex, it is difficult for the adolescent to relinquish that relationship.

ANOREXIA NERVOSA

Occasionally, the challenges of adolescence uncover the immaturity of the adolescent who is still dealing with conflicts that appear to arise from a much earlier period of development. The conflicts may represent, for example, fixation at earlier points in the sexual development of the child. Further, the child's level of object relations may be such that he or she still leans heavily on the need to be cared for, and unresolved earlier separation difficulties may persist. Sometimes these conflicts express themselves directly as a somatic illness. For example, among many girls who exhibit some form of the anorexia nervosa syndrome, there seems to be a regression as puberty approaches, with a recrudescence of oedipal and preoedipal conflicts.

Descriptively, the anorexia nervosa syndrome consists essentially of disturbances in the body image and the perception of the bodily state, along with a paralyzing sense of ineffectiveness (Bruch, 1962). An eating disturbance is prominent; it may include such symptoms as aversion to all food, strange diets, or eating at times to relieve anxiety. The girl (anorexia nervosa usually affects girls) may deny she is thin, and she seems unaware of fatigue. She may have feelings of shame

and guilt and she avoids the sexual function of the mouth (i.e., kissing). Most adolescents who have anorexia nervosa are perfectionistic, even obsessive-compulsive, with the thought of food as an obsession and the avoidance of food as a compulsion. At the same time, these adolescents are usually somewhat infantile, dependent, and tense, and they easily feel unwanted. In their object relations they are usually shallow, lacking in warmth, and have an ambivalent relationship with their mothers. Their self-concept is often unrealistic: although they wish to be independent, they are, in fact, quite incapable of taking care of themselves. Last, in their sexual adjustment there are marked conflicts, with disgust of sex as a prominent reaction formation.

The symptoms seem to represent in part the adolescent's attempt to escape adult sexual roles. They may also serve to regain control of the body, the self, and the parents (Sours, 1969). More common than the girl with anorexia nervosa is the pubescent girl who attempts to reject her sexual role through milder food fads and diets that alter her body.

CONVERSION REACTION

Another example of how earlier unresolved difficulties and the onset of adolescence can join to produce a clinical syndrome is a conversion reaction, another disorder that occurs predominantly in girls. The syndrome in childhood consists essentially of massive loss of functions without organic cause (Proctor, 1958; Rock, 1971). The most common symptoms are blindness, deafness, inability to walk (astasia), inability to stand (abasia), great pain or no pain, and inhibition of movement or grossly excessive movements, often resembling seizures. Prazar and Friedman (1978) and Friedman (1973) have suggested the following diagnostic features of a conversion reaction: (1) a dramatic description of the symptom, (2) a symbolic meaning to the symptom, (3) the presence of so-called *la belle indifference*, (4) a family whose communication centers on health issues, (5) an adult model who has similar symptoms, and (6) a physical examination whose results are inconsistent with the presenting symptoms.

The symptoms of a conversion reaction may be part of a general hysterical personality, which usually consists of marked immaturity and labile emotions. The adolescent's emotional ties usually seem to be shallow, and the adolescent is often seductive and loves to be the center of attention. Often the adolescent imitates others. She may show an apparent lack of concern for the conversion symptom itself. Most adolescents who have a conversion reaction have a need to maintain a fiction of excellence and to control others, often in a demanding dependent way. It should be emphasized that these needs or wishes are unconscious and that the adolescent does indeed feel pain or does believe she cannot walk.

What is again of interest is that the conversion reaction commonly occurs at puberty. Problems and anxieties in these adolescents often arise from what the adolescent experienced in his or her childhood as seductions and repressed sexual conflicts. Excessive sexual stimulation of the child by immature parents, who at the same time imposed excessve taboos, may have contributed to the conflicts. All remains more or less quiescent until adolescence. At that point, a rekindling of the earlier conflicts occurs, with resultant florid symptom formation. The conversion reaction persists until the anxiety can be successfully resolved or repressed again. Perhaps the similarity of the developmental problems of adolescence to the developmental problems of earlier childhood arouses the earlier conflicts and leads to anxiety and symptom formation.

SUMMARY

After this discussion of some of the troubling behavior that may occur in adolescents, it is important to emphasize once again that most adolescents are essentially normal. Ninety-eight percent of unmarried girls 15 to 17 years of age do not become pregnant; and arrests of persons under 18 years of age for violent crimes are less than 1% of arrests for all ages (Lipsitz, 1979). One large study (Offer, Ostrov, and Howard, 1988) showed that 80% of adolescents adapt well to their psychologic world, have good interpersonal relationships both inside and outside their families, are free from psychopathologic symptoms, do not have mood swings and, in general, enjoy life, and make the most of what life has to offer. In short, most adolescents cope with this time in their lives remarkably well, and they are not at all homogeneous.

Psychiatric disorders do occur in adolescence, but when they do they have much in common with either conduct disorders and emotional disturbances of younger children or the psychoses and depressions of adults (Rutter and Hersov, 1976). In addition, when psychiatric disorders in adolescence are discussed, it is important to keep in mind the order of magnitude. In a survey of the general population of adolescents on the Isle of Wight, Rutter and his colleagues (1976) found that the prevalence of psychiatric disorders, both those continuing from childhood into adolescence and those starting for the first time in adolescence, was from about 10 to 21%, depending on the criteria used. Of the adolescents with psychiatric disorders, about 40% were diagnosed as having anxiety, depression, or some kind of affective disorder, and 40% as having a conduct disorder. Twenty percent had a mixture of antisocial behavior and emotional disturbance. Obsessive-compulsive disorder, conversion reaction, phobias, and tics, although they affected a few of the adolescents with emotional disorders, were much less common, and psychoses were rare (less than 1 per 1,000). Depression, either alone or associated with anxiety, is more common during adolescence than in childhood. School refusal also increases in prevalence again, although when it occurs during adolescence it is more often part of a psychiatric disorder and carries a worse prognosis (Rodriguez et al., 1959). Other conditions that are rare before puberty (e.g., schizophrenia, manic-depressive psychosis, anorexia nervosa, and drug dependence) are more common during later adolescence.

Last, during adolescence some preexisting disorders show important changes. Thus autistic children may develop seizures (Rutter, 1970), and hyperactive children may develop severe social problems.

In short, again few, if any, disorders are specific to adolescence; rather, psychiatric disorders during adolescence resemble those that occur either more commonly in childhood (e.g., conduct disorders and emotional disturbances) or more commonly in adulthood (e.g., depression and psychoses), with particular features associated with the developmental changes seen in adolescence (Graham and Rutter, 1976). Psychiatric disturbance does occur in about 20% of adolescents, but this incidence is similar to that found in adults. Depression, anxiety, phobic symptoms, and drug and alcohol abuse are seen in this group of adolescents. In absolute terms, this 20% amounts to 3.2 million adolescents in the United States, which currently has a total adolescent population of 16 million. Unfortunately, of the 3.2 million in need, only about 800,000 (25%) receive help at any one time.

Adolescence is a time of physical, cognitive, and emotional changes. Most adolescents seem to have little trouble coming to a satisfactory resolution of the problems they face. For them, reality and good judgment rule the day. Psychiatric disorders do occur during adolescence, and they should be diagnosed as such; they should not be confused with normal adolescent behavior and given the misleading label of adolescent turmoil.

Normal adolescents clearly can be sources of great pleasure. A good example was described by Calandra (see Guttman, 1965):

. . . a physics student who was fed up with college instructors trying to teach him how to think instead of "showing him the structure of the subject matter" . . . had been given a zero for his answer to a question on a physics examination. The question was "Show how it is possible to determine the height of a tall building with the aid of a barometer." The student's answer: "Take the barometer to the top of the building, attach a long rope to it, lower the barometer to the street, and then bring it up, measuring the length of the rope. The

length of the rope is the height of the building." Dissatisfied with this solution but conceding that it was not strictly incorrect, the physics teacher gave the student another chance to answer, this time in a way that would show some knowledge of physics. Having selected what he said was the best of many answers he had in his head, the student dashed off the following: "Take the barometer to the top of the building and lean over the edge of the roof. Drop the barometer, timing its fall with a stopwatch. Then, using the formula $S = \frac{1}{2}gt^2$, calculate the height of the building" ($S =$ distance fallen, $g =$ gravitational acceleration of the barometer, and $t =$ time). This apparently satisfied the letter, if not the spirit, of the examination question, and the student received almost full credit for the answer. He was then asked what other answers he had had in mind and responded, in part, with the following: "You could take the barometer out on a sunny day and measure the height of the barometer, the length of its shadow, and the length of the shadow of the building, and, by the use of a simple proportion, determine the height of the building. Or, if not limited to physics, you could take the barometer to the basement and knock on the superintendent's door. When he answers you say: "Here, I have a very fine barometer. If you will tell me the height of this building, I will give you this barometer."

Note 38

From J. Piaget (1969), The intellectual development of the adolescent. In: *Adolescence: Psychosocial Perspectives*, ed. G. Caplan and S. Lebovici. New York: Basic Books, pp. 22–26.

Now, the great novelty that characterises adolescent thought and that starts around the age of 11 to 12, but does not reach its point of equilibrium until the age of 14 or 15—this novelty consists in detaching the concrete logic from the objects themselves, so that it can function on verbal or symbolic statements without other support. Above all the novelty consists in generalising this logic and supplementing it with a set of combinations. . . .

The great novelty that results consists in the possibility of manipulating ideas in themselves and no longer in merely manipulating objects. In a word, the adolescent is an individual who is capable (and this is where he reaches the level of the adult) of building or understanding ideal or abstract theories and concepts. . . . the adolescent is capable of projects for the future. . . . of nonpresent interests, and of a passion for ideas, ideals, or ideologies.

. . . it is apparent how these intellectual transformations typical of the adolescent's thinking enable him not only to achieve his integration into the social relationships of adults, which is, in fact, the most general characteristic of this period of development, but also to conquer a certain number of fundamental intellectual operations which constitute the basis for a scientific education at high school level. The problem that remains unresolved, however, is the generality of these intellectual transformations. . . . It is probable that in underdeveloped societies which still have a tribal organization the individual remains throughout his entire life at the level of concrete operations, without ever reaching the level of formal or propositional operations that are characteristic of adolescents in our cultural environment. But in these societies the younger generations remain under the authority of the "elders" of the tribe, and the elders in turn remain subject to the conservative traditions of their ancestors. . . .

Note 39

From E.H. Erikson (1962), *Childhood and Society*, 2nd Ed. New York: W.W. Norton & Co., Inc., pp. 261–263.
. . . 5. IDENTITY VS. ROLE CONFUSION. With the establishment of a good initial relationship to the world of skills and tools, and with the advent of puberty, childhood proper comes to an end. Youth begins. But in puberty and adolescence all samenesses and continuities relied on earlier are more or less questioned again, because of a rapidity of body growth which equals that of early childhood and because of the new addition of genital maturity. The growing and developing youths, faced with this physiological revolution within them, and with tangible adult tasks ahead of them are now primarily concerned with what they appear to be in the eyes of others as compared with what they feel they are, and with the question of how to connect the roles and skills cultivated earlier with the occupational prototypes of the day. In their search for a new sense of continuity and sameness, adolescents have to refight many of the battles of earlier years, even though to do so they must artificially appoint perfectly well-meaning people to play the role of adversaries; and they are ever ready to install lasting idols and ideals as guardians of a final identity.

The integration now taking place in the form of ego identity is, as pointed out, more than the sum of the childhood identifications. It is the accrued experience of the ego's ability to integrate all identifications with the vicissitudes of the libido, with the aptitudes developed out of endowment, and with the opportunities offered in social roles. The sense of ego identity, then, is the accrued confidence that the inner sameness and continuity prepared in the past are matched by the sameness and continuity of one's meaning for others, as evidenced in the tangible promise of a "career."

The danger of this stage is role confusion.* Where this is based on a strong previous doubt as to one's sexual identity, delinquent and outright psychotic episodes are not uncommon. If diagnosed and treated correctly, these incidents do not have the same significance which they have at other ages. In most instances, however, it is the inability to settle on an occupational identity which disturbs individual young people. To keep themselves together they temporarily overidentify, to the point of apparent complete loss of identity, with the heroes of cliques and crowds. This initiates the stage of "falling in love," which is by no means entirely, or even primarily, a sexual matter—except where the mores demand it. To a considerable extent adolescent love is an attempt to arrive at a definition of one's identity by projecting one's diffused ego image on another and by seeing it thus reflected and gradually clarified. This is why so much of young love is conversation.

Young people can also be remarkably clannish, and cruel in their exclusion of all those who are "different," in skin color or cultural background in tastes and gifts, and often in such petty aspects of dress and gesture as have been temporarily selected as *the* signs of an in-grouper or out-grouper. It is important to understand (which does not mean condone or participate in) such intolerance as a defense against a sense of identity confusion. For adolescents not only help one another temporarily through much discomfort by forming cliques and by stereotyping themselves, their ideals, and their enemies; they also perversely test each others' capacity to pledge fidelity. The readiness for such testing also explains the appeal which simple and cruel totalitarian doctrines have on the minds of the youth of such countries and classes as have lost or are losing their group identities (feudal, agrarian, tribal, national) and face world-wide industrialization, emancipation, and wider communication.

The adolescent mind is essentially a mind of the *moratorium*, a psychosocial stage between child-

---

*See "The Problem of Ego-Identity," *J. Am. Psa. Assoc.*, 4:56–121.

hood and adulthood, and between the morality learned by the child, and the ethics to be developed by the adult. It is an ideological mind—and, indeed, it is the ideological outlook of a society that speaks most clearly to the adolescent who is eager to be affirmed by his peers, and is ready to be confirmed by rituals, creeds, and programs which at the same time define what is evil, uncanny, and inimical. In searching for the social values which guide identity, one therefore confronts the problems of *ideology* and aristocracy, both in their widest possible sense which connotes that within a defined world image and a predestined course of history, the best people will come to rule and rule develops the best in people. In order not to become cynically or apathetically lost, young people must somehow be able to convince themselves that those who succeed in their anticipated adult world thereby shoulder the obligation of being the best. We will discuss later the dangers which emanate from human ideals harnessed to the management of super-machines, be they guided by nationalistic or international, communist or capitalist ideologies. In the last part of his book we shall discuss the way in which the revolutions of our day attempt to solve and also to exploit the deep need of youth to redefine its identity in an industrialized world.

Note 40

From P.H. Mussen, and M.C. Jones (1957), Self-conceptions, motivations, and interpersonal attitudes of late and early-maturing boys. *Child Dev.*, 28:252–255.

The results of the study support the general hypothesis that, in our culture, the boy whose physical development is retarded is exposed to a sociopsychological environment which may have adverse effects on his personality development. Apparently, being in a disadvantageous competitive position in athletic activities, as well as being regarded and treated as immature by others, may lead to negative self-conceptions, heightened feelings of rejection by others, prolonged dependent needs, and rebellious attitudes toward parents. Hence, the physically retarded boy is more likely than his early-maturing peer to be personally and socially maladjusted during late adolescence. Moreover, some of his attitudes are likely to interfere with the process of identifcation with his parents, which is generally based on perceptions of them as warm and accepting. . . . This, in turn, may inhibit or delay the acquisition of mature char-

acteristics and attitudes which are ordinarily established through identification with parents. Fortunately for the late-maturers' subsequent adjustments, they seem more willing and able to face their feelings and emotions. This may be a result of their awareness of others' attitudes toward their immaturity or their feelings of personal inadequacy and dependency.

The physically accelerated boys, on the other hand, are likely to experience environmental circumstances which are much more conducive to good psychological adjustment. Hence, their psychological picture, as reflected in their TAT stories, is much more favorable. By the time they were 17, relatively few early-maturers harbored strong feelings of inadequacy, perceived themselves as rejected or dominated by parents or authorities, or felt rebellious toward their families. As a group, they appeared to have acquired more self-confidence and had probably made stronger identifications with mature adults. Hence, they perceived themselves as more mature individuals, less dependent and in need of help, and more capable of playing an adult male role in interpersonal relationships . . . It seems clear that many attributes of adolescent personality (patterns of motivation, self-conceptions, and attitudes toward others) characteristic of late- and early-maturing boys are relatively stable and durable rather than situational and transitory. This may be attributable to the fact that in our culture adolescence is generally a critical and difficult period of adjustment. Within a relatively brief interval of time, the child must work out numerous complex and vitally important personal problems—e.g., adaptation to his changed biological and social status, establishment of independence, vocational adjustment. In dealing with these problems, he may acquire new behaviors and personality attributes which have broad ramifications, not only on his current adjustment, but also on his subsequent development. If the adolescent can cope with his problems without too much inner stress and turmoil, his self-esteem, feelings of adequacy, and consequently his subsequent adjustment, are likely to be enhanced. On the other hand, if his problems induce great tension and anxiety, he is likely to feel frustrated and inadequate, and, if these feelings are maintained, to adjust less satisfactorily as an adult.

Obviously, the adolescent's success or failure, as well as ease or tension, in handling his problems will be determined to a large degree by the sociopsychological forces to which he is subjected during this time, and these, as we have seen, may be significantly related to his rate of maturation. Thus, physical status during adolescence—mediated through the sociopsychological environment—may exert profound and lasting influences on personality. For this reason, many aspects of the adult's behavior and personality seem consistent with his adolescent adjustments, attitudes and motivations . . .

In conclusion, it should be noted that, although rate of maturing and associated factors may affect personality development, the relationship between physical status and psychological characteristics is by no means simple. A vast number of complex, interacting factors, including rate of maturation, determine each adolescent's unique personality structure. Hence, in any specific instance, the *group* findings of the present study may not be directly applicable, for other physical, psychological, or social factors may attenuate the effects of late- or early-maturing. For example, an adolescent boy who is fundamentally secure and has warm, accepting parents and generally rewarding social relationships may not develop strong feelings of inadequacy even if he matures slowly. Analogously, the early-maturing boy who has deep feelings of insecurity, for whatever reasons, will probably not gain self-confidence simply because he matures early. In summary, in understanding any individual case, generalizations based on the data of the present study must be particularized in the light of the individual's past history and present circumstances.

REFERENCES

Agras, S. (1958). The relationship of school phobia to childhood depression. *Am. J. Psychiatry*, 116:533–536.

Aichhorn, A. (1935), *Wayward Youth*. New York: Viking Press.

Alan Guttmacher Institute (1981), *Teenage Pregnancy: The Problem That Hasn't Gone Away*. The Alan Guttmacher Institute, 360 Park Ave. So., New York, NY, 10010.

American Academy of Child Psychiatry (1976), Statement of the President, December 21, 1976.

American Academy of Pediatrics (1977), Position paper, January 8, 1977.

American Psychiatric Association (1980), DSM-III (*Diagnostic and Statistical Manual of Mental Disorders*, 3rd Ed.). Washington, D.C.

American Psychiatric Association (1974), *Task Force Report 8, Clinical Aspects of the Violent Individual*. Washington, D.C.

Armstrong, C.P. (1937), A psychoneurotic reaction of delinquent boys and girls. *J. Abnorm. Soc. Psychol.*, 32:329.

Ballenger, J., and Post, R. (1980), Carbamazepine in manic-depressive illness: A new treatment. *Am. J. Psychiatry*, 137:782–790.

Balser, B.H. (1939), A behavior problem: Runaways. *Psychiatr. Q.*, 13:539.

Bender, L. (1953), *Aggression, Hostility and Anxiety in Children*. Springfield Il.: Charles C Thomas, p. 94.

Benedek, T. (1959), Parenthood as a development phase. *J. Am. Psychoanal. Assoc.*, 7:389–407.

Bennet,I. (1960), *Delinquent and Neurotic Children: A Comparative Study*. London: Tavistock.

Berger, B.M. (1969), The new stage of American man—Almost endless adolescence. *The New York Times Magazine*, Nov. 2, 1969, p. 32.

Bibring, G.L., Dwyer, T.F. Huntington, D.S., and Valenstein, A.F. (1961), A study of the psychological processes in pregnancy and of the earliest mother-child relationship. In: *The Psycoanalytic Study of the Child* (Vol. 16), ed. R.S. Eissler, A. Freud, H. Hartman, and M. Kris. New York: International Universities Press, pp. 9–44.

Blos, P. (1962), Phases of adolescence. In: *On Adolescence: A Psychoanalytic Interpretation*. New York: The Free Press of Glencoe, pp. 52–157.

Blos, P. (1967), The second individuation process of adolescence. *Psychoanal. Study Child*, 22:162–187.

Blum, R.H. (1969), *Students and Drugs*. San Franciso: Jossey-Bass, p. 399.

Bonan, A.F. (1963), Psychoanalytic implications in treating unmarried mothers with narcissistic character structure. *Soc. Casework*, 44:323–339,

Bowman, L.A. (1958), The unmarried mother who is a minor. *Child Welfare*, 37:13–19.

Brooks, J.E., and Brooks, J.S. (1988), A developmental approach examining social and personal correlates in relation to alcohol use over time. *J. Genet. Psychol.*, 149:93–110.

Bruch, H. (1962), Perceptual and conceptual disturbances in anorexia nervosa. *Psychosom. Med.*, 24:187–194.

Burks, H., and Harrison, S. (1962), Aggressive behavior as a means of avoiding depression. *Am. J. Orthopsychiatry*, 32:416–422.

Butterfield, F. (1982), *China. Alive in the Bitter Sea*. London: Hodder and Stoughton.

Campbell, M., Cohen, I., and Small, A.M. (1982), Drugs in aggressive behavior. *J. Am. Acad. Child Psychiatry*, 21:107–117.

Campbell, M., Small, A., Green, W., Jennings, S., Perry, R., Bennett, W., Padron-Gayol, M., and Anderson, I. (1982), Lithium and haloperidol in hospitalized aggressive children. *Psychopharmacol. Bull.*, 18:126–129.

Chein, L., Gerard, D.I., Lee, R.S., and Rosenfeld, E. (1964), *The Road to H.: Narcotics, Delinquency and Social Policy*. New York: Basic Books.

Cohen, A.K. (1955), *Gang*. New York: Free Press, p. 129.

Cohen, S. (1969), Drug Abuse. In: *Psychiatry Medical World News*. New York: McGraw-Hill Book Company.

Committee on Adolescence, American Academy of Pediatrics (1980), Teenage suicide. *Pediatrics*, 66:144–146.

Courts, R.M. (1967), Family crises and the impulsive adolescent. *Arch. Gen. Psychiatry*, 17:64–71.

Crumley, F.E. (1979), Adolescent suicide attempts. *JAMA*, 241:2404–2407.

Cytryn, L., McKnew, D.H., and Bunney, W.E. (1980), Diagnosis of depression in children: A reassessment. *Am. J. Psychiatry*, 137:22–25.

Dalton, M. (1961), Menstruation and crime. *Br. Med. J.*, 2:1752–1753.

Daniel, W.A., Jr. (1970), *The Adolescent Patient*. St. Louis: C.V. Mosby Company.

DHHS (1980), *That Status of Children, Youth and Families, 1979*. Washington, D.C.: DHHS Publ. No. (OHDS) 80-30274.

DHHS (1982), *Health, United States*, 1982.

Dien, D.S. (1983), Big me and little me: A Chinese perspectve on self. *Psychiatry*, 46:281–286.

Doublas, J.W.B., Ross, J.M., and Simpson, H.R. (1968), *All Our Future: A Longitudinal Study of Secondary Education*. London: Peter Davies.

Dreisbach, P.B., and Kasun, J.R. (1981), Teen-age pregnancy (letter). *N. Engl. J. Med.*, 304:121.

Dreyer, P.H. (1982), Sexuality during adolescence. In: *Handbook of Developmental Psychology*, ed. B.B. Wolman. Englewood Cliffs: Prentice Hall.

Eissler, K.R. (1955), Some problems of delinquency. In: *Searchlights on Delinquency*, 2nd Ed. ed. K.R. Eissler. New York: International Universities Press.

Elkind, D. (1967), Egocentrism in adolescence. *Child Dev.*, 38:1025–1034.

Erikson, E.H. (1956), The problem of ego identity. *J. Am. Psychoanal. Assoc.*, 4:56.

Erikson, E.H. (1959), Growth and crises of the healthy personality. *Psychol. Issues*, 1:50–100.

Erikson, E.H. (1963), *Childhood and Society*, 2nd Ed., New York: Norton, pp. 261–263.

Esman, A.H. (1977), Changing values: Their implications for adolescent development and psychoanalytic idea. In: *Adolescent Psychiatry* (Vol. 5), ed. S. Feinstein and P. Giovacchini. New York: Jason Aronson, pp. 18–34.

Fauman, M.A., and Fauman, B.J. (1979), Violence associated with phencyclidine abuse. *Am. J. Psychiatry*, 136:1584–1586.

Fawcett, R.L., and Jensen, R.A. (1952), Addiction to the inhalation of gasoline fumes in a child. *J. Pediatr.*, 41:364–368.

FBI (1987), Crime in the United States. Uniform Crime Report, July 25, 1987.

Finkel, M., and Finkel, D. (1975), Sexual and contraceptive knowledge, attitudes and behavior of male adolescents. *Fam. Plann. Perspect.*, 7:256.

Forrest, J.D., Sullivan, E., and Tietze, C. (1979), Abortion in the United States, 1977–1978. *Fam. Plann. Perspect.*, 11:329–341.

Foster, R. (1962), Intrapsychic and environmental factors in running away from home. *Am. J. Orthopsychiatry*, 32:486.

Fountain, G. (1961), Adolescent into adult: An inquiry. *J. Am. Psychoanal. Assoc.*, 9:417–433.

Frailberg, S.H. (1961), Homosexual conflicts. In: *Adolescents*, ed. S. Lorand and H.I. Schneer. New York: Paul Hoeber, pp. 78–112.

Freeman, D. (1983), Margaret Mead and Samoa: the Making and Unmaking of an Anthropological Myth. Boston: Harvard University Press.

Freud, A. (1946), *The Ego and the Mechanisms of Defense*. New York: International Universities Press, pp. 154–165.

Freud, A. (1958), Adolescence. *Psychoanal. Study Child*, 13:255–278.

Freud, A. (1969), Adolescence as a developmental disturbance. In: *Adolescence*, ed. G. Caplan and S. Lebovici. New York: Basic Books, pp. 5–10.

Freud, S. (1905), Three essays on sexuality. *Standard Edition 7* (1953). London: The Hogarth Press.

Friedman, S.B. (1973), Conversion symptoms in adolescents. *Pediatr. Clin. North Am.*, 20:873–882.

Galdston, R. (1967), Adolescence and the function of self-consciousness. *Ment. Hygiene*, 51:164–168.

G.A.P. Report No. 68 (1968), *Normal Adolescence* (Vol. 6). New York: Group for the Advancement of Psychiatry, pp. 756–758; 841–846.

Geleerd, E.R. (1961), Some aspects of psychoanalytic technique in adolescence. *Psychoanal. Study Child*, 12:263–283..

Gerbner, N. (1983), As quoted in the *New York Times*, January 22, p. 46.

Glaser, K. (1967), Masked depression in children and adolescents. *Am. J. Psychother.*, 21:565–574.

Glasser, F.B. (1966), Inhalation psychosis and related states. *Arch Gen. Psychiatry*, 14:315–322.

Gonnell, C.B. (1923), *The Cheyenne Indians, Their History and Ways of Life* (Vol. 1). New Haven: Yale University Press, p. 120.

Goodwin, D.W. (1984), Studies of familial alcoholism: A review. *J. Clin. Psychiatry*, 45:14–17.

Gould, R.L. (1972), The phases of adult life: A study in developmental psychology. *Am. J. Psychiatry*, 129:521–531.

Graham, P., and Rutter, M. (1976), Adolescent disorders. In: *Child Psychiatry*, ed. M. Rutter and L. Hersov. Oxford: Blackwell, pp. 407–427.

Greenberg, A.S., and Coleman, M. (1976), Depressed 5-hydroxyindole levels associated with hyperactive and aggressive behavior. *Arch. Gen. Psychiatry*, 33:331–336.

Guttmacher, A. (1976), *11 Million Teenagers: What Can Be Done about the Epidemic of Adolescent Pregnancy in the United States?* New York: Planned Parenthood Federation of America. The Alan Guttmacher Institute.

Guttman, S.A. (1965) (Quoting A. Callandra), Some aspects of scientific therapy construction and psychoanalysis. *Int. J. Psychoanal.*, 46:129–137.

Hall, G.S. (1904), *Adolescence: Its Psychology and Its Relation to Physiology, Anthropology, Sociology, Sex, Crime, Religion and Education*. New York: Appleton.

Halleck, S. (1967), Psychosomatic treatment of the alienated college student. *Am. J. Psychiatry*, 124:642–650.

Hamparian, D.M. (1985), Control and treatment of juveniles committing violent offenses. In: *Clinical Treatment of the Violent Person*, ed. C.H. Roth. Rockville, Md., U.S. Department of Health and Human Services, N.I.M.H., p. 165.

Harbin, J., and Madden, D. (1979), Battered parents: a new syndrome. *Am. J. Psychiatry*, 136:1288–1291.

Hartmann, D. (1969), A study of drug-taking adolescents. *Psychoanal. Study Child*, 24:384–398.

Hauser, A. (1977), Drinking patterns of young people. In: *Alcoholism and Drug Dependence: A Multidisciplinary Approach*. Proc. Third Conf. Alcoholism and Drug Dependence. New York: Plenum Publishing Corp.

Hauser, S.T. (1976), Self-image complexity and identity formation in adolescence. *J. Youth Adolescence*, 5:161–178.

Hawker, A. (1977), Drinking patterns of young people. In: *Alcoholism and Drug Dependence: A Multidisciplinary Approach. Proceedings Third Conference Alcoholism and Drug Dependence*. New York: Plenum Publishing Corp.

Healy, W., and Bronner, A.F. (1926), *Delinquents and Criminals, Their Making and Unmaking: Studies in Two American Cities*. New York: MacMillan Publishing Company.

Hollingsworth, D.R., and Kreutner, A.K. (1981), Teen-aged pregnancy (letter). *N. Engl. J. Med.*, 304:321.

Inhelder, B., and Piaget, J. (1959), *The Growth of Logical Thinking from Childhood to Adolescence*. New York: Basic Books.

Institute for Social Research, University of Michigan (1981), Highlights from student drug use in America 1975–1980. DHHS Pub. No. (ADM) 81-1066.

Johnson, A.M. (1949), Sanctions for superego lacunae of adolescents. In: *Searchlights on Delinquency*, ed. K.R. Eissler. New York: International Universities Press, pp. 225–245.

Johnson, A.M., and Szurek, S.A. (1952), The genesis of antisocial acting out in children and adults. *Psychoanal. Q.*, 21:323.

Joint Commission on Juvenile Justice Standards (1977), Juvenile Justice Standards Drafts, 24 Vol. Cambridge, MA.: Ballinger Publishing Co.

Jones, M.C. (1957), The later careers of boys who were early- or late-maturing. *Child Dev.*, 28:113–128.

Junod, H.A. (1927), *The Life of a South African Tribe*. Cited by J.W.M. Whiting, R.C. Khickhonm, and A. Anthony, The function of male institution ceremonies at puberty. In: *Readings in Social Psychology*, eds. E. Maccoby, T. Newcomb, and E. Hartley. New York: Holt, Rinehart, and Winston, pp. 359–370.

Kaplan, S., Hong, G.K., and Weinhold, C. (1984), Epidemiology of depressive symptomatology in adolescents. *J. Am. Acad. Child Psychiatry*, 23:91–98.

Kashani, J.H., Husain, A., Shekim, W.O., Hodges, K.K., Cytryn, L., and McKnew, D.H. (1981), Current perspectives on childhood depression: An overview. *Am. J. Psychiatry*, 138:143–153.

Kaufman, I., MacKay, E., and Zilbach, J. (1959), The impact of adolescence on girls with delinquent character formation. *Am. J. Orthopsychiatry*, 29:130–143.

Keniston, K. (1970a), Youth: A "new" stage of life. *Am. Scholar*, 39:631–653.

Keniston, K. (1970b), Student activism, moral development, and morality. *Am. J. Orthopsychiatry*, 40(4):577–592.

Kestenberg, H.S. (1961), Menarche. In: *Adolescents*, ed.

S. Lorand and H. Schneer. New York: Paul B. Hoeber, pp. 19–50.

Khlentzos, M.T., and Pagliaro, M.A. (1965), Observations from psychotherapy with unwed mothers. *Am. J. Orthopsychiatry*, 35:779.

Kinsey, A.C. (1953), *Sexual Behavior in the Human Female*. Philadelphia: W.B. Saunders Co., p. 842.

Kleber, H. (1970), Personal communication.

Klein, D.F., and Davis, J.M. (1969), *Diagnosis and Drug Treatment of Psychiatric Disorders*. Baltimore: Williams & Wilkins, p. 417.

Kramer, S.N. (1959), *History Begins at Sumer*. New York: Garden City.

Langlois, J.H., and Stephen, C.W. (1981), Beauty and the beast: The role of physical attraction in peer relationships and social behavior. In: *Developmental Social Psychology: Theory and Research*, ed. S.S. Brehm, S.M. Kassin, and S.X. Gibbons. New York: Oxford University Press.

La Plante, M.N., McCormick, N., and Brannigan, G.G. (1980), Living the sexual script: College students views of influences in sexual encounters. *J. Sex. Res.*, 16:338–355.

Laufer, M. (1976), Personal communication.

Lerner, R.M., and Lerner, J.V. (1977), Effects of age, sex, and physical attractiveness on child-peer relations, academic performance, and elementary school adjustment. *Dev. Psychol.*, 13:585–590.

Leventhal, T. (1964), Inner control deficiencies in runaway children. *Arch. Gen. Psychiatry*, 11:169.

Levine, S.R. (1988), Violence and teens: The tragedy of youth. *Facets*, 49:11–12.

Lewis, D.O. (1981), *Vulnerabilities to Delinquency*. New York: Spectrum.

Lewis, D.O., and Balla, D.A. (1976a) Psychiatric and sociological viewpoints: Changing perspectives and emphases: In: *Delinquency and Psychopathology*, ed. D.O. Lewis and D.A. Balla. New York: Grune & Stratton, pp. 7–18.

Lewis, D.O., and Balla, D.A. (1976b), *Delinquency and Psychopathology*. New York: Grune & Stratton.

Lewis, D.O., Klerman, L., Jekel, J., and Curry, J. (1973), Experiences with psychiatric services in a program for pregnant teenage girls. *Soc. Psychiatry*, 8:16–25.

Lewis, D.O., and Shanok, S.S. (1977), Medical histories of delinquent and non-delinquent children. *Am. J. Psychiatry*, 134:1020–1025.

Lewis, D.O., Shanok, S.S., and Balla, D.A. (1979), Perinatal difficulties, head and face trauma, and child abuse in the medical histories of seriously delinquent children. *Am. J. Psychiatry*, 136:419–423.

Lewis, D.O., Shanok, S.S., Pincus, J.H., and Glaser, G.H. (1979), Violent juvenile delinquents: Psychiatric, neurological, psychological and abuse factors. *J. Am. Acad. Child Psychiatry*, 18:307–319.

Lewis, M., and Lewis, D.O. (1973), *Pediatric Management of Psychologic Crises*. Chicago: Year Book Medical Publishers, p. 43.

Lewis, M., and Lewis, D.O. (1979), A psycho-biological view of childhood depression. In: *Clinical Approaches to Childhood Depression*, ed. A.L. French. New York: Human Sciences Press, pp. 29–45.

Lewis, D.O., Lovelly, R., Yeager, C., and Femina, D.D.

(1989), Toward a theory of the genesis of violence: A follow-up study of delinquents. *J. Am. Acad. Child Adolesc. Psychiatry*, 283:431–436.

Lewis, M., and Solnit, A.J. (1963), The adolescent in a suicidal crisis. In: *Modern Perspectives in Child Development* (In Honor of Milton J.E. Senn), ed. A.J. Solnit and S.A. Provence. New York: International Universities Press, pp. 229–245.

Lidz, T. (1968), The young adult. In: *The Person*. New York: Basic Books, pp. 362–367.

Lipsitz, J.S. (1979), Adolescent development. *Child. Today*, 8:2–7.

Lowrey, L.G. (1941), Runaways and nomads. *Am. J. Orthopsychiatry*, 11:775.

Macoby, E.E., Newcomb, T.M., and Hartley, E.L. (Eds.) (1958), *Readings in Social Psychology*. New York: Holt, Rinehart and Winston, p. 360.

Maddox, G. (1964), Adolescence and alcohol. In: *Alcohol Education for Classroom and Community*, ed. R. McCarthy. New York: McGraw-Hill Book Company, pp. 32–47.

Malinowski, B. (1966), Parenthood—The basis of social structure. In: *The Unwed Mother*, ed. R.W. Roberts. New York: Harper & Row, pp. 25–41.

Marks, A., and Fisher, M. (1987), Health assessment and screening during adolescence.. *Pediatrics*, 80:135–138.

Marohn, R.C. (1982), Adolescent violence. *J. Am. Acad. Child Psychiatry*, 21:354–360.

Marshall, W.A., and Tanner, J.M. (1970), Variations in the pattern of pubertal changes in boys. *Arch. Dis. Child.*, 45:13.

Masterson, J.F. (1968), The psychiatric significance of adolescent turmoil. *Am. J. Psychiatry*, 124:1549–1554.

Mattsson, A. (1982), Personal communication.

McAnarney, E.R., and Greydanus, D.E. (1979), Adolescent pregnancy: A multifaceted problem. *Pediatr. Rev.*, 1:123–126.

McKnew, D.H., and Cytryn, L. (1979), Urinary metabolites in chronically depressed children. *J. Am. Acad. Child Psychiatry*, 18:608–615.

Mednick, S.A., and Hutchings, B. (1978), Genetic and psychophysiological factors in asocial behavior. *J. Am. Acad. Child Psychiatry*, 17:209–233.

Mizner, G.L., Barter, J.T., and Werme, P.H. (1970), Patterns of drug use among college students: A preliminary report. *Am. J. Psychiatry*, 127:15–24.

Monahan, J. (1981), *The Clinical Prediction of Violent Behavior*. Rockville, MD: National Institute of Health.

Murray, J.P. (1980), *Television and Youth: 25 Years of Research and Controversy*. Boys Town Center for the Study of Youth Development: Boys Town, NE.

Mussen, P.H., and Jones, M.C. (1957), Self-conceptions, motivations, and interpersonal attitude of late- and early-maturing boys. *Child Dev.*, 28:243–256.

NCHS (1978), National Center for Health Statistics. Advance report: Final natality statistics, 1978. Monthly Vital Statistics Report (Suppl.), April 28,.1980.

NCTV (1985), How much violence do we see on television? *National Coalition on Television Violence*, 6:3.

Noshpitz, J.D. (1970), Certain cultural and familial fac-

tors contributing to adolescent alienation. *J. Am. Acad. Child Psychiatry*, 9:216–223.

Nylander, I., and Rydelius, P. (1973), The relapse of drunkenness in non-asocial teenage boys. *Acta Psychiatr. Scand.*, 49:435–443.

O'Connor, J. (1977), Normal and problem drinking among children. *J. Child Psychol. Psychiatry*, 18:229–284.

Offer, D. (1969), *The Psychological World of the Teenager*. New York: Basic Books.

Offer, D., Marcus, D., and Offer, J.L. (1970), A longitudinal study of normal adolescent boys. *Am. J. Psychiatry*, 126:917–924.

Offer, D., and Offer, J. (1975), *From Teenage to Young Manhood: A Psychological Study*. New York: Basic Books.

Offer D., Ostrov, E., and Howard, K. (1988), *The Adolescent World: Adolescent Self-Image in Ten Countries*. New York: Plenum Publishing Corp.

O'Malley, P.M., and Backman, J.G. (1983), Self-esteem: Change and stability between 13 and 23. *Dev. Psychol.*, 19:257–268.

Palmer, J.H., and Ringwalt, C.L. (1988), Prevalence of alcohol and drug use among North Carolina public school students. *J. Sch. Health*, 58:288–291.

Paulsen, J. (1969), Psychiatric problems. In: *Student and Drugs*, ed. Richard H. Blum and Associates. San Francisco: Jossey-Bass, pp. 291–304.

Paulson, M.J., and Lin, T.T. (1972), Family harmony: An etiologic factor in alienation. *Child Dev.*, 43:591–604.

Pearson, G.H.J. (1958), *Adolescence and the Conflict of Generations*. New York: Norton, pp. 101–126.

Petersen, A.C. (1983), Menarche: Meaning of measures and measuring meaning. In: *Menarche*, ed. S. Golub. Lexington, MA: Lexington Books.

Phillips, E.L., Phillips, E.A., Fexsen, D.C., and Wolf, M.M. (1973), Achievement place: Behavior shaping works for delinquents. *Psychology Today*, 7:75–79.

Piaget J. (1958), *The Growth of Logical Thinking*. New York: Basic Books.

Piaget, J. (1962), Comments on Vygotsky's critical remarks concerning "The language and thought of the child" and "Judgment and reasoning in the child." Cambridge, Mass.: MIT Press, 71:473–490.

Piaget, J. (1969), The intellectual development of the adolescent. In: *Adolescence: Psychosocial Perspectives*, ed. G. Caplan and S. Lebovici. New York: Basic Books.

Plant, M. (1976), Young drug and alcohol casualties compared. A review of 100 patients at a Scottish psychiatric hospital. *Br. J. Addict.*, 71:31–43.

Plowman E.E. (1971), *The Jesus Movement in America*. New York: Pyramid Books.

Prazar, G., and Friedman, S.B. (1978), Conversion reaction. In: *Principles of Pediatrics: Health Care of the Young*, ed. R.A. Hoekelman. New York: McGraw-Hill Book Company, pp. 687–693.

Proctor, J.T. (1958), Hysteria in childhood. *Am. J Orthopsychiatry*, 28:394–407.

Puig-Antich, J., Chambers, W., Halpern, F., Hanlon, C., and Sachar, E.J. (1979). Cortisol hypersecretion in pre-pubertal depressive illness. *Psychoendocrinology*, 4:191–197.

Rabin, P.L., and Swenson, B.R. (1981). Teen-age suicide and parental divorce. *N. Engl. J. Med.*, 304:1048.

Renshaw, D.C. (1972), Depression of the 70's. *Dis. Nerv. Syst.*, 35:241–245.

Riemer, M.D. (1940), Runaway children. *Am. J. Orthopsychiatry*, 10:522.

Ritvo, S. (1971), Late adolescence: Developmental and clinical considerations. *The Psychoanalytic Study of the Child*, 26:241–263.

Robey, A., Rosenwald, R.I., Snell, J.E., and Lee, R.E. (1964), The runaway girl: A reaction to family stress. *Am. J. Orthopsychiatry*, 34:762.

Robins, L.N. (1966), *Deviant Children Grown Up: A Sociological and Psychiatric Study of Sociopathic Personality.* Baltimore: Williams & Wilkins.

Rock, N.L. (1971), Conversion reactions in childhood: A clinical study of childhood neuroses. *J. Am. Acad. Child Psychiatry*, 10:65–93.

Rodriguez, A., Rodriguez, M., and Eisenberg, L. (1959), The outcome of school phobia: A follow-up study based on 41 cases. *Am. J. Psychiatry*, 116:1563–1577.

Rosenthal, D. (1971), *Genetics of Psychopathology.* New York: McGraw-Hill Book Company.

Rothenberg, M. (1983), The role of television in shaping the attitudes of children. *J. Am. Acad. Child Psychiatry*, 22:86–87.

Rousseau, J.J. (1762), *Emile*, trans. Barbara Foxley. New York: Dutton, 1966.

Rutter, M. (1970), Autistic children: Infancy to adulthood. *Semin. Psychiatry.* 2:435–450.

Rutter, M. Graham, P., Chadwick, O., and Yule, W. (1976), Adolescent turmoil: Fact or fiction? *J. Child Psychol Psychiatry*, 17:35–56.

Rutter, M., and Hersov, L. (Eds.) (1976), *Child Psychiatry.* Oxford: Blackwell.

Schwab-Stone, M., Cohen, P., and Garcia, M. (1985), The timing of puberty and the occurrence of psychopathology in adolescent girls. Paper presented at the Annual Meeting of the American Academy of Child Psychiatry, San Antonio, October, 1985.

Scott, P.D. (1965), Delinquency. In: *Modern Perspectives in Child Psychiatry.* ed. J.G. Howells, Springfield, Ill.: Charles C Thomas, pp. 370–402.

Shellow, R., Schamp, J.R., Liebow, E., and Unger, E. (1967), *Suburban Runaways of the 1960's.* Society for Research in Child Development. Chicago: University of Chicago Press.

Simmons, R.G., Blyth, D.A., and McKinney, K.L. (1983), The social and psychological effects of puberty on white females. In: *Girls at Puberty: Biological and Psychosocial Perspectives*, ed. J. Brooks-Gunn and A.C. Petersen. New York: Plenum Publishing Corp., pp. 229–272.

Sourindohin, I. (1985), Solvent misuse. *Br. Med. J.*, 290:94–95.

Sours, J.A. (1969), Anorexia nervosa: Nosology, diagnosis, developmental patterns, and power control dynamics. In: *Adolescence*, ed. G. Caplan and S. Lebovici. New York: Basic Books, pp. 185–212.

Stafford-Clark, D. (1969), Drug dependence. *Guy's Hospital Gazette*, 83:298–305.

The Status of Children, Youth and Families 1979 (1980), Washington, D.C.: DHHS Pub. No. (OHDS) 80-30274.

Staub, H. (1943), A runaway from home. *Psychoanal. Q.*, 12:1.

Strauss, M., Geller, R., and Steinmetz, S. (1980), *Behind Closed Doors. Violence in the American Family.* Garden City: Anchor Books, Doubleday.

Streib, V. (1987), *Death Penalty for Juveniles.* Bloomington: Indiana University Press.

Surgeon General's Report on Health Promotion and Disease Control (1979), *Healthy People.* Washington, D.C.: Dept. of Health, Education, and Welfare, Pub. No. 79-55071, pp. 5:1–5:15.

Tanner, J.M. (1962), *Growth at Adolescence*, 2nd Ed. Oxford: Blackwell.

Tanner, J.M. (1971), Sequence, tempo, and individual variations in growth and development of boys and girls aged twelve to sixteen. *Daedalus*, 100:907–930.

Tobin-Richards, M.H., Boxer, A.M., and Petersen, A.C. (1983), The psychological significance of pubertal change: sex differences in perceptions of self during early adolescence. In: *Girls at Puberty*, ed. J. Brooks-Gunn and A.C. Petersen. New York: Plenum Press, pp. 127–154.

Toolan, J.M. (1962), Depression in children and adolescents. *Am. J. Orthopsychiatry*, 32:404–415.

Trussel, J. (1988), Teenage pregnancy in the United States. *Fam. Plann. Perspect.* 20:262–272.

Tzu-Chin Wu, Tashkin, D.P., Djahed, B., and Rose, J.E. (1988), Pulmonary hazards of smoking marijuana as compared with tobacco. *N. Engl. J. Med.*, 318:347–351.

Ungerleider, J.T., Fisher, D.D., Fuller, M., and Caldwell, S. (1968), The "bad trip"—The etiology of the adverse LSD reaction. *Am. J. Psychiatry*, 124:1483–1490.

Wardrop, K.R.H. (1967), Delinquent teenage types. *Br. J. Criminol.*, 7:371–380.

Watts, C.A.H. (1966), *Depressive Disorders in the Community.* Bristol: John Wright.

Weinberg. W., Rutman, J., Sullivan, L., Renick, E., and Dietz, S. (1973), The ten symptoms of childhood depression and the characteristic behavior for each symptom. *J. Pediatr.*, 83:1072.

Weiner, I.B. (1970), *Psychological Disturbances in Adolescence.* New York: Wiley-Interscience.

Wender, P.A. (1972), The minimal brain dysfunction syndrome in children. 1. The syndrome and its relevance for psychiatry. II. A psychological and biochemical model for the syndrome. *J. Nerv. Ment. Dis.*, 155:55–71.

Wieder, H., and Kaplan, E.H. (1969), Drug use in adolescents. *Psychoanal. Study Child*, 24:399–431.

Williams, D., Mehl, R., Yudofsky, S., Adams, D., and Roseman, B. (1982), The effects of propanolol on uncontrolled rage outbursts in children and adolescents with organic brain dysfunction. *J. Am. Acad. Child Psychiatry*, 21:129–135.

Williams, F.S. (1970), Alienation of youth as reflected in the hippie movement. *J. Am. Acad. Child Psychiatry*, 9:251–263.

Wise, L.J. (1970), Alienation of present-day adolescents. *J. Am. Acad. Child Psychiatry*, 9:264–277.

Wolfgang, M.E. (1978), as quoted in *Violent Delinquents*, by PA Strasburg. New York: Sovereign Books, p. 179.

Woolston, J.L. (1981), Personal communication.

Wylie, D.C., and Weinreb, J. (1958), The treatment of a runaway adolescent girl through treatment of the mother. *Am. J. Orthopsychiatry*, 28:188.

Wyshak, G., and Frisch, R.E. (1982), Evidence for a secular trend in age of menarche. *N. Engl. J. Med.*, 306:1033–1035.

Young, H.B. (1971), The physiology of adolescence. In: *Modern Perspectives in Adolescent Psychiatry*, ed. H.G. Howells. Edinburgh: Oliver & Boyd.

Zelnick, M., and Kantner, J.F. (1977), Contraception and pregnancy: Experience of young unmarried women in the United States: 1976 and 1971. *Fam. Plann. Perspect.*, 5:21–35.

Zelnik, M., and Kantner, J.S. (1978), First pregnancies to women aged 15–19: 1976 and 1971. *Fam. Plann. Perspect.*, 10:11.

Zelnik, M., and Kantner, J.S. (1980), Sexual activity, contraceptive use and pregnancy among metropolitan area teenagers, 1971–1979. *Fam. Plann. Perspect.*, 12:230.

Zelnik, M., Kim, Y.J., and Kantner, J.F. (1979), Probabilities of intercourse among U.S. teenage women, 1971–1976. *Fam. Plann. Perspect.*, 11:177.

Part Three

Developmental Perspectives on Pediatric Disorders

20

PSYCHOLOGIC REACTIONS TO ILLNESS AND HOSPITALIZATION

Illness is perhaps the most common and widespread stress that can befall the developing child. Every child who is ill has a psychologic reaction to his or her illness. Some reactions are general; others are specific to the illness. The general reactions depend on several factors, including (1) the child's developmental stages (his or her emotional and cognitive levels of development and previous adaptive capacity), (2) the degree of pain or mutilation and the meaning the illness has for the child and parents, (3) the parent-child relationship and the child's response to the reaction of the parents, (4) the child's psychologic reaction to medical and surgical procedures, separation, and hospitalization, and (5) the resultant interference with physical, psychologic, and social functions. The specific reactions depend, in part, on the nature and severity of the illness.

BIRTH DEFECTS

Hypospadias. Anomalies of the external genitalia, for example, or hypospadias, may affect the parents' "gender attitude" toward their child who, in turn, may have a heightened difficulty in accepting a clear sexual identification. Parents are often embarrassed about hypospadias and concerned about the surgical operations required and the subsequent effects. Indeed, such children may feel inferior and may avoid competition, and later are less likely to have intercourse, marry, and have children. For these reasons many rec-

ommend early correction (before 2 years of age) and counseling (Schultz, 1983).

Cryptorchism. In the case of cryptorchism, the parents' attitudes seem to induce in the child a preoccupation with his testes, with associated disorders of behavior, including hyperactivity, accident proneness, lying, and learning difficulties (Blos, 1960). When surgical correction is performed sometime between 2 and 8 years of age, the child may become fearful about damage to his penis. However, with adequate preparation, the psychologic outcome can be good (Cytoya et al., 1967).

Cleft Palate. Mothers of children with cleft palate, after an initial period of shock and anxiety (which may be transmitted to the infant and may increase the feeding difficulties that commonly occur), seem to make especial use of the mechanism of denial and later avoid talking with their child about the deformity. Instead, they may point out to others how "bright" the child is (Tisza et al., 1968). At the same time, because cleft palate is a more or less correctable defect, the drive toward restitution is strongly reinforced in these parents.

Congenital Heart Disease. These relatively common birth defects range in severity from a benign murmur to inoperable cardiac defects. Usually the disorder is noted at birth or shortly after birth as a result of cyanosis, feeding problems, associated anomalies, etc.; sometimes diagnosis occurs prenatally and sometimes not for a period of some years after

255

birth. Cardiac defects are more commonly observed with certain conditions (e.g., certain congenital infections or trisomy 21) and other congenital abnormalities may be observed. In instances where an "innocent murmur" is detected, it is important to help parents avoid excessive anxiety and overprotection (Graham, 1986). In cases that require surgical correction, procedures may, understandably, evoke considerable anxiety in parents; careful preparation of the parents, if possible, can be quite helpful in facilitating their appropriate involvement in the child's care and strengthening the parent-child relationship.

Blindness. How complexly the combination of birth defect and the parents' reaction to the birth defect affects the development of the child is well illustrated in the case of children born totally blind. In a series of longitudinal studies of infants born totally blind, Fraiberg and colleagues found that approximately 25% showed motor stereotypes, such as (1) rocking, lateral rotation of the head and trunk, and empty fingering, (2) no definition of body boundaries, and (3) delayed speech (Fraiberg, 1968; Fraiberg and Freedman, 1964; Fraiberg et al., 1966). Adaptive hand behavior (which ordinarily depends on the coordination of eye and hand schemas), gross motor achievements, and the constitution of a body- and self-image were all delayed. Most significant was the absence of or failure to achieve stable human object relations. For most of their 24-hour day, these infants lived in a "sensory desert."

The parents of these infants were markedly upset, often revealing their unconscious conflicts toward the baby by not touching the baby except when it was necessary. Some fathers developed potency problems soon after the birth of the baby. There was also a conspiracy of silence on the part of other family members, who rarely said anything to indicate that the baby was at all attractive.

However, if the parents were able to perceive and interpret the infant's nonvisual signals and respond appropriately to its needs, the disastrous consequences just described could be avoided. For example, blind infants do, in fact, show a smile response to the mother's or father's *voice* at around the same time that sighted babies smile at the sight of the human face. When told that, and with the support and encouragement of a skilled person, the parents were able to avoid feeling rebuffed by the blind infant's failure to respond with a smile to the presentation of the parents' faces. Indeed, the parents felt elated at the infant's smile response to the presentation of the parent's voice, and they then related in a more affectionate way to their now "responsive" infant. Both parents and infant were then mutually responsive instead of mutually repelling.

One particular nonvisual node of communication in the infant that was especially informative was the infant's expressive hand movements. Interventions designed to bring the hands together in the midline prevented empty fingering and promoted useful hand movement. Later, introduction of objects that had a sound as well as texture led to the infant's being able (at 10 months of age) to conceptualize an object with a sound (e.g., a bell). The infant could then search for a bell "out there" on hearing the sound alone. Once the infant was able to reach out on a sound cue, he or she was motivated to propel himself or herself forward. At that point, creeping, which had been delayed, could proceed.

Deafness. Although congenital blindness might initially appear to be a greater handicap, in reality congenital deafness is clearly more commonly associated with both developmental disturbance and psychiatric morbidity (Denmark et al., 1979; Kolvin and Fundudis, 1982; Rutter et al., 1970). This likely reflects the centrality of language in mediating human experience. Carefully designed studies (e.g., Freeman et al., 1975) suggest that many congenitally deaf children exhibit psychiatric disorders and that family members may also be at increased risk for disturbance. The disorder may be delayed in being diagnosed and parents may receive conflicting advice regarding intervention methods (e.g., use of sign language versus speech training, Jenkins and Chess, In Press). Clearly communication between parent and child is severely compromised. Although considerable speculation has centered around the identification of specific personality traits in deaf children, available research has not generally supported this notion (Reivich and Rothrock, 1972) children with deafness associated with some other handicapping condition are, however, at greatest risk for psychiatric disturbance (Chess and Fernandez, 1980).

Mental Retardation. The diagnosis of mental retardation in infants and young children is typically made only in children with severe or profound retardation. Severe mental retardation may also be associated with various medical conditions and physical problems. Parents must cope with a marked shift in their internal image of the child and his or her potential, any associated medical problems, and multiple practical realities. As with other chronic conditions, the process of adaptation for parents can be lifelong. Children with mental retardation are at increased risk for developing psychiatric disorders; clearly, complex interactions between intellectual level, overt brain dysfunction (e.g., seizures), the nature of specific impairments, and the child's personality and temperament are involved (see Chapter 27).

Reaction of Parents

The pregnant woman's concerns and fantasies about possible fetal abnormalities precede her reactions to a birth defect. The actual presence of a live baby with a congenital defect mobilizes these latent fears and stimulates further reactions. The general reactions to a birth defect include feelings of revulsion, anger, and anxiety, as well as a precipitous drop in the self-esteem and sense of integrity of the mother. The parents may feel guilty and resentful. The more visible the defect, the greater the reaction. Equally significant is the sense of loss that both parents experience as they painfully and slowly relinquish their ideal fantasies of the child during the process of adjusting to the sharply differ-

ent realities and establishing new goals (Solnit and Stark, 1961). Because of the continuing presence of the defective child, the process of working through of loss is a continuing, changing process in that at each stage in the child's development the parents' other expectations for him or her may have to be modified or abandoned. At each stage, new, often unanticipated, problems confront the parents. Some defects may not become known until a later stage of development. For example, certain congenital heart defects may be missed initially but may subsequently be discovered either routinely or as a result of a study for the cause of certain symptoms. Other defects may become apparent only at a later period of development. The process of giving up long-held expectations in such cases is often more difficult because of the tenacity with which those expectations are held.

The specific reactions of parents to a birth defect depend, in part, on the type of defect, e.g., its visibility and location, as well as on the personality of the parents.

Reaction of the Child

Psychologic reactions of children to a birth defect are largely related to parental attitudes, but each also has his or her own characteristic reaction. Sometimes the physical defect is the starting point for a widespread interference with development to which the child then reacts. In children born with a cleft palate, for example, the interference with pleasurable sucking and feeding experiences, as well as the imbalance between gratifying and painful experiences, may lead later to speech difficulties and to a view of life as being essentially painful. In addition, the frequent separations and surgical procedures required to correct this defect, especially during the child's first few years, may interrupt the continuity of affection he or she needs to develop the capacity for good relationships. Even when surgical correction has been achieved, previously established self-concepts, including low-esteem, may persist and may make the child more vulnerable at each succeeding developmental period to adolescence and beyond (Schwartz and Landwirth, 1968).

ACUTE ILLNESS

General Reactions

The general reactions of the child to acute illness again depend to a large extent on the child's developmental level and the reaction of the parents, and those reactions may be adaptive or maladaptive. Under the general impact of acute illness, most young children regress. They may return temporarily to bedwetting, thumb sucking, crying, and clinging behavior. In addition, the young child, particularly, tends to interpret the illness as a punishment for something he or she had done wrong, and since the child sometimes has difficulty in distinguishing between fantasy and reality, the wrongdoing could have been imaginary or actual. The young child who is hospitalized, especially the child under 4 years of age, feels abandoned and fears what harm may come to him or her without the love and protection of the parents. The child may also feel confused and anxious about the more or less sudden confrontations with strangers and about the strange routines (e.g., for eating, dressing, sleeping, and toileting), and special procedures (e.g., immobilizations and injections). These observations have been repeatedly documented. In a well-controlled study by Prugh and colleagues, for example, children under 4 years of age screamed, had outbursts of anger when the parents visited, withdrew, and had difficulty eating and sleeping (Prugh et al., 1953; see Note 41). "In general, children with previously limited capacities for adaptation showed the greatest difficulty in adjusting comfortably to the ward milieu and showed as well the most severe reactions to the total experience of hospitalization." Furthermore, problems of adaptation occurred often about three months after the hospitalization, again with persistent signs of emotional disturbance tending to occur in children under 4 years of

age and in children who had relatively unsatisfactory relationships with their parents, who had undergone severe stress in the hospital, and who had shown the greatest difficulty in adapting to the ward environment.

Anxiety is heightened when the special vulnerabilities of a particular developmental struggle are touched on. For example, an infant, who needs a sense of security and trust, may express through fretting and fussing his or her state of tension and insecurity when held by a mother who is anxious because of the baby's illness. The fear of loss of love and loss of autonomy may be reinforced by separation and illness in the young infant. Castration anxiety may be heightened in the young child who is undergoing surgical procedures. Separation from peers may temporarily rob the school-age child of the comfort and sublimation activities he or she had previously enjoyed. The adolescent may find increasing difficulty in dealing with the upset that may accompany such developmental tasks as body mastery, impulse control, and independence.

Adolescents may regard their illness with shame or as a sign of physical weakness, or as a punishment (e.g., for masturbation). They may use illness or its management as an instrument for the expression of rebellion or as a convenient excuse for avoiding close relationships. At the same time, adolescents may fear loss of control. They may withdraw in the face of illness, either to conserve their strength or because they feel hopeless. Anxiety may be heightened if motor activity in particular is prevented by forced immobilization. A lowering of self-esteem may occur, accompanied by psychiatric illness and academic problems (Rutter et al., 1970). Illness may also be used to enlist help (Peterson, 1972). Last, adolescents may be surprisingly ignorant about their bodies and illnesses, and may have unusual ideas about their illnesses (Kaufman, 1972).

The anxiety aroused in children and adolescents may be dealt with in different ways, depending in part on their level of development. The most common reaction—regression—has already been mentioned. On the other hand, some children fight hard to retain their recently acquired skills. They may, for example, resist bed rest when then have only just learned to walk (Freud, 1952). Other children deny their illness and their anxiety. Some children identify with the doctor or the nurse, who seems to them so aggressive. Aggression is particularly mobilized in the face of motor restraint (Wolff, 1969). Still others may withdraw or may become astonishingly compliant. The particular pattern of response is poorly understood but appears to depend on the many factors mentioned earlier. Sometimes the anxiety beomes manifest after the acute episode has passed (Levy, 1945; Langford, 1948; Neill, 1967). Night terrors, dreams about being left alone in the dark, or fear of the dark may occur with increasing frequency. Negativistic behavior toward the parents often occurs on the child's return home.

Pain and Pain Management. Pain is "What the subject says hurts" (Parkhouse et al., 1979). The unpleasant experience called pain is derived from multiple interacting neuroanatomical, neurochemical, experiential, and "gate control" factors (Table 20–1). The experience of pain may have important developmental functions. For example, psychoanalytic theory proposes that pain serves as an organizer of the body image, contributes to self-object differentiation, and may become linked with phase-specific unconscious fantasies (Frances and Gale, 1975). At the same time, pain associated with medical conditions, diagnostic procedures, and treatment is clearly a source of distress to children and adolescents.

Contrary to common belief, infants do experience pain, e.g., related to circumcision. Children as young as age four can usually localize pain if asked to "point to where it hurts" or if asked to point to a part on a doll or body drawing. Young children develop fantasies about pain (e.g., pain as punishment) and consequently need careful preparation for procedures that involve some pain. As the child's cognitive development proceeds, the child increasingly understands the concept of

Table 20–1. Factors Involved in the Pathogenesis of Pain

NEUROANATOMICAL
Multiple interactions occur along the following pathways:
   Pain receptors
   ↓
   Afferent pathways
   ↓
   Dorsal horn
   ⇕
   Spinothalamic tract
   ⇕
   Reticular formation
   ⇕
   Thalamus
   ⇕
   Limbic system
   ⇕
   Cortex

"Gate control" mechanisms (possibly located in the dorsal horn) can inhibit afferent pain with descending control (Wall, 1978)

NEUROCHEMICAL
Monoamines: Dopamine, Norepinephrine, and Serotonin
Endogenous opioids: Endorphins and Enkephalins (Basbaum and Fields, 1984)

EXPERIENTIAL
Emotions, e.g., anxiety and depression, heighten the experience of pain
Meaning, e.g., soldiers withstand pain better than civilians
Cultural, e.g., in some cultures it is more acceptable to be demonstrative whereas in others denial is emphasized (Zyborowski, 1962)

body damage and becomes increasingly apprehensive about pain. Manifest psychologic reactions to pain vary with developmental level. Infants react by social withdrawal and difficulties in eating and sleeping. Children of school age may become aggressive, oppositional, and difficult to control. Adolescents may exhibit depression.

Measures to control pain include the presence of a comforting person (e.g., the parent), psychologic preparation, use of play, exploration of causes and relief of exacerbating stresses over time, reassurance, and stress reduction measures (e.g., biofeedback, relaxation training, and hypnosis). Appropriate use of medication may be indicated although careful assessment of therapeutic response is needed to ensure that pain relief is adequate. Excessive sedation is avoided because it can itself be experienced as disorganizing and unpleasant.

Reactions to Specific Illnesses or Procedures

Certain illnesses and certain treatment procedures tend to produce characteristic reactions in the child.

Burns. Children who suffer burns often experience severe emotional reactions. Jackson said, "An extensive burn is an accident involving thirty seconds of terror, and it is often followed by years of suffering" (Jackson, 1968). Pain, fright, and body mutilation are, in fact, primary sources of psychologic disturbance in the burned child and in a child traumatized in any other way. Additional sources of disturbance in the burned child include (1) the child's guilt over disobeying a parent's admonition not to play with matches, for example, (2) the turmoil characteristic of the period of acute care, (3) the hospitalization and separation from parents, (4) the immobilization, exposure, and repeated immediate and long-term surgical procedures, (5) the metabolic changes induced by the burns, and (6) the reactions of the distressed and guilty parents and the frustrated and angry hospital staff.

Pain in itself is a significant factor in burns, and it often gives rise to anger, hostility, and depression in the child (Long and Cope, 1961). In an unusual study of the psychologic reactions to a leg burn in a 5-year-old boy who had no pain sensation below the waist (because he had a myelomeningocele), Nover (1973) found that the child had a much less adverse reaction to the burn and was more cooperative in the extensive surgical treatments than are most burned children.

Preexisting emotional difficulties often seem to have predisposed the child to the burn "accident." In a study of 13 families of severely burned children, 10 families were found to have major psychologic and social problems that were present prior to the occasion of the burn (Holter and Friedman, 1969).

Fluid loss, medication, anorexia, and sleep interruption are important aggravating factors during the acute period, and may produce changes in mental status that intensify the child's sense of loss of control. It has also been suggested that magnesium deficiency may aggravate the psychologic symptoms associated with burns (Broughton et al., 1968).

Parents, too, may feel guilt and may have difficulty with the scarred appearance. These feelings may be transmitted to the child and may increase the difficulties in the child. The child may regress, become more clinging, and experience a loss of self-esteem. Subsequently, the child may develop antisocial behavior, and—especially during adolescence—may become depressed and suicidal.

Equally important are the long-term reactions. Grafting operations frequently extend over a period of 5 years, and in some cases as long as 15 years. Numerous concerns arise during this period. Jackson (1968) has observed that burned children ask such questions as "Will my breasts develop normally?", "Will boys look at me with these scars?", and "Will I be able to have a baby?" The importance of these questions in the context of adolescent developmental concerns is obvious.

Tonsillectomy. Another type of specific reaction occurs in response to tonsillectomy. Here, the operation is performed on a well child who usually does not have a clear understanding of why he or she needs the operation or what the nature of the operation is. Although the most commonly performed surgical procedure 3 decades ago, indications for the procedure were not well defined, no adequately controlled studies were available (Horstman, 1969), and follow-up studies (Dey, 1952) suggested that only a minority of cases were judged to truly need the operation. With the advent of antibiotics, it was possible to decrease the incidence of recurrent tonsillitis.

The operation is most often performed at

an age when fantasies of injury to body parts and fears of punishment and retribution are prominent. Moreover, for a number of reasons, the child is often inadequately prepared for the operation. Sometimes the sudden availability of a bed in the hospital forces a somewhat precipitous admission on short notice, perhaps following a telegram. Few explanations are given to the child as he or she is separated from the parents, turned over to strangers, and made to submit to routines that seem remote from the sore throat he or she once had and now has almost forgotten.

The psychologic impact of this relatively minor surgical procedure can be enormous (Jessner et al., 1952; Robertson, 1956) because the child often distorts the procedure and uses the distortion as a means of representing fears and fantasies. Demandingness, irritability, aggressive behavior, temper tantrums, fears, and nightmares often are rampant. Defenses mobilized to contain this anxiety may include the mechanisms of denial and psychosomatic symptom formation. According to Lipton (1962), lasting character traits may be formed during such a psychic trauma. Fortunately, much of this harm can be attenuated and even turned into a constructive experience when the child is adequately prepared for, supported through, and helped after the operation (Robertson, 1956).

Failure to Thrive. This condition is defined on the basis of failure to grow or gain weight either from birth or following a period of normal development, and accounts for 1 to 2% of pediatric admissions. The onset is typically within the first 2 years of life (Woolston, 1985). The condition may be associated with some other medical conditions or may result from inappropriate levels of parental care and nutrition or some interaction of the two. Feeding problems are usually observed with regurgitation of food, chronic vomiting, etc. Often the child exhibits some degree of developmental delay. Some degree of environmental deprivation and/or psychosocial adversity is observed in most cases of nonorganic failure to thrive. Occasional children exhibit significant feeding problems in the apparent absence of a medical explanation of inappropriate parenting. Inadequate food intake appears to be responsible for the associated weight loss (Graham, 1986).

Evaluation should include a careful physical examination and history. Observation of the feeding situation and dietary evaluation may be helpful. In severe cases or in cases where there is evidence of significantly underlying organic disease, hospital admission is indicated. Treatment of nonorganic failure to thrive must be directed at the mother-child dyad as well as to the child; a multidisciplinary approach is useful.

CHRONIC ILLNESS

In general, chronic illnesses impose psychologic as well a physical strains on the developing child. The strains arise from a number of sources. For example, a particular treatment regimen (e.g., motor restriction, diet, medication, and surgical procedures) may foster passivity and dependence, against which the normal child struggles. The child's feeling of being different from other children arouses feelings of resentment and then guilt. Young children in particular find the illness and the treatment virtually incomprehensible, and they develop distorted ideas and frightening fantasies about the illness.

A 5-year-old boy with nephrosis was observed by the nurse to be unusually quiet and immobile. He would sit still in his wheelchair and would contrive to not even turn his head. In the course of an interview, the boy revealed his ideas and fantasies about his illness. He knew that there was something wrong with his kidneys, and that this caused "blood pressure." He was aware of everyone's efforts to keep down his blood pressure. He felt sure that if his blood pressure went up, it would blow off the top of his head. Not surprisingly, he avoided any movement that might increase the blood pressure and lead to such a feared disaster.

Children with certain chronic illnesses that are intermittently acute and debilitating and that chronically impose limitations on the child's life may experience a wide range of reactions, depending on the severity of the illness.

Last, children may learn to use their chronic illness in the service of achieving other aims, as seen in the case of Johnny, who used his diabetes to satisfy certain psychologic needs (see pp. 222 and 265).

Recurrent Nonorganic Abdominal Pain. Recurrent nonorganic abdominal pain (RAP) is usually a diffuse pain lasting several hours, recurring at least three times over at least 3 months, and generally found in tense children of school age who may be experiencing stress at school or at home. There may be associated nonorganic headaches or limb pains and, in some instances, low-grade fever and vomiting may occur. Physical examination is normal. Subvarieties have been called *periodic syndrome* (pain, vomiting, headache, and low-grade fever) (Apley and McKeith, 1968) or cyclical vomiting (recurrent abdominal pain and vomiting). The condition may be viewed as part of a spectrum of disorders from transient normal variants to persistent conversion disorders. The prevalence of RAP is about 10% (Apley, 1975; Green, 1967; Faull, 1986). RAP is more common in girls than boys. The age range is 5 to 12 years, peaking at about 9 and then declining.

The onset tends to be gradual, starting with mild or moderate pain. Nausea, pallor, vomiting, dizziness, and headaches may precede or accompany the pain. The site is variable, but the pain is usually poorly localized to the epigastric area or the perineum. The duration of the pain is variable. Chest pain tends to occur more in older children and adolescents (Rowland and Richards, 1986). The child with RAP is often tense, fearful, inhibited, and overcontrolled (Wasserman et al., 1988). Stress may be found in the family. There is sometimes a history of loss. In most cases the pain is multiply determined.

Apley (1975) observed that RAP is often a pattern of reaction to emotional stress in the child and that this is similar to the family's pattern of reaction. Learning experiences within the family have been proposed (Ley-

bourne and Churchill, 1972). Family dynamics are important; for example, pain may evoke nurturant responses and give rise to secondary gain (Minuchin et al., 1978). In addition, family secrets (Karpel, 1980) and myths (Richtsmeier and Waters, 1984) are thought to play a role.

The clinical evaluation should include a careful history which explores each of the three major etiological factors involved in pain—neuroanatomical, neurophysiological, and experiential. Specific information is needed regarding 1) the nature of the pain (onset, frequency, duration, site, localization or radiation, nature and chronicity), 2) factors which precipitate, aggravate, or relieve the pain, 3) effects of various treatments, 4) observed behavioral response of the child, 5) the child's (and family's) understanding of the pain and their particular concerns and stresses, 6) family responses, 7) associated symptoms (e.g., fever, change in appetite, change in bowel and bladder functions, school performance, peer and family relationships), 8) psychiatric diagnoses present (e.g., conversion disorder, generalized anxiety, depressive disorder). Other areas that should be explored include any family history of complaints of pain (family modeling, secondary pain, degree of enmeshment of the child in the family, stress factors.

One good physical examination is required. Dysfunctional pain tends to be diffuse, poorly localized, or peri-umbilical with no rebound tenderness whereas organic pain tends to be constant, well localized, interferes with sleep, and is associated with physical symptoms and signs (fever, jaundice, etc.). Laboratory tests should be performed as indicated by this history. Psychological testing may help in determining unconscious conflicts and in eliciting data in relation to anxiety, guilt, depression, anger, or specific personality traits.

Medical management of secondary effects, e.g., dehydration caused by excessive vomiting, may be necessary. Explanations that no physical disorder is present, and that the child is experiencing tension and perhaps other upsetting emotions, should be offered and the family given every opportunity to express their emotions and concerns. Exploration of psychological stresses and conflicts in the child and family often is necessary. To the extent possible external stressors at home and in the school should be relieved or minimized. Measures to minimize pain should be instituted. Individual psychotherapy and family therapy may be indicated.

The prognosis is generally good. About one third to one half of cases continue to have RAP into adulthood (Apley and Hale, 1973). A family diathesis for psychogenic pain may persist from one generation to the next.

Asthma. First, there appears to be no evidence for a so-called "psychosomatic-type" of mother-child relationship (Gauthier et al., 1977) in producing asthma; neither is there a specific asthma personality (Herbert, 1965). On the other hand, stress and anxiety commonly precipitate and aggravate asthmatic attacks; parents may become anxious and overprotective, or rejecting, which can aggravate attacks. In turn, children, particularly adolescents, with asthma frequently use their asthmatic attacks to express their dependency needs (they may force hospitalization) and their rebellion against dependency (they may not comply with treatment). Some children with asthma may have fewer attacks while their parents are out of the home, even though they may still be exposed to the same allergens. The frequency of attacks then resumes when the parents return (Purcell and Weiss, 1970). Children with asthma tend to have more absences from school than healthy children (Purcell et al., 1979). Severity of the asthma does not predict individual psychopathologic conditions (Steinhausen et al., 1983). In some instances, the severity of psychologic problems in the child, particularly issues of separation anxiety, guilt, and anger, indicates the need for more intensive psychologic help (Pinkerton and Weaver, 1970). In one study, a third of 26 preschool children with severe asthma experienced significant emotional disturbance, including depressive mood, fearfulness, and sleep disturbances. The children were also oppositional and non-compliant, and had temper tantrums (Mrazek, 1985).

Cystic Fibrosis. Children with this illness, which runs a chronic course resulting in death in adolescence or early adulthood, also react to the parents' attitudes and concerns or to their distorted perception of the parents' attitudes (Wolff, 1969). On the other hand, the actual attitudes of the parents are often a real source of anxiety for the child. In a study of family adaptation to cystic fibrosis in children, for example, McCollum and Gibson (1970) found that, first of all, incorrect or incomplete diagnoses generated in parents a mounting mistrust of the medical profession and hostility toward it. In addition, because the infant patients were often unsatisfied by their feeds and had periods of fussiness, the mothers initially had feelings of self-doubt and self-reproach at their inability to nurture their infants. These feelings in the mothers led to feelings of despair and moments of frank hostility toward the infants, often accompanied by guilt. When the diagnosis of cystic fibrosis was confirmed, the threat posed by the child's having a fatal illness stimulated an acute, anticipatory mourning reaction in the parents. Feelings of helplessness aroused anxiety in the parents and stimulated thoughts about their own death. In an effort to avoid these thoughts, parents invoked such defenses as an apparent absence of affect, denial, avoidance, and forgetting. Parents suffered sleep and appetite disturbances. They often displaced their anger at the child onto others. Many other problems connected with the child's illness (e.g., the knowledge that there is a genetic factor, the impact of the illness on other family members, especially siblings, the need for separate accommodations to house a mist tent, the odor of the stool, the high medical expenses, and the parents' efforts to master the technique of postural drainage) contributed to the parents' anxiety. Long-term adaptation by the parent invariably involved some denial of the prognosis, a denial that was constantly challenged by certain intrusive characteristics of the disease, notably the odor and the persistent cough.

The child, in turn, reacted to all these attitudes with anxiety.

Hemophilia. In a study of 28 hemophiliac children and their families, Browne and colleagues (1960) observed that the children tended to feel isolated and different. They often tried to conceal their illness, and they felt constantly watched. The enforced passivity prevented the discharge of tension through activity and led to anxiety about movement and action. Sometimes the children were outwardly docile and passive, although they often showed evidence of subtle rebellion. For example, children might revenge themselves or their parents by deliberately bumping themselves, by threatening to bleed, or by telling the doctor that the parents spanked them. Curiously, however, trauma was not the overriding factor in bleeding. Bleeding was often spontaneous, and it sometimes seemed to be related more to anxiety, especially anxiety about increased activity and independence, than to trauma. The bleeding would then serve to prevent the child from participating in these activities. Many of the boys experienced anxiety around feelings of loss of masculinity. They felt unable to be active the way boys usually are, and they experienced their fathers' withdrawal from them as a denial of their masculinity. Further, the episodes of uncontrolled bleeding were sometimes linked in their fantasies with the bleeding that occurs in females. In addition, most of the boys knew that hemophilia is handed down through the female.

These specific reactions to hemophilia often lead to psychiatric disorders, the most frequent one being the development of passive-dependent characters, a tendency toward risk-taking (accident-prone) behavior, psychophysiologic responses, such as bleeding in relation to anxiety, and sexual identity problems (Agle, 1964).

These reactions are related in part to the interaction with parents, who themselves showed characteristic responses to the illness. For example, Browne and his colleagues (1960) found that the mothers frequently felt guilt and anger at being the carrier. They tended to be ambivalent toward their sick child and overprotective. On the one hand, they saw themselves as the only effective protector of the child; on the other hand, they saw the child as a cross to bear. The child was restricted in his activities because activity was equated with injury. The mothers often selected the child's playmates, and they usually selected younger, smaller, and passive children. Indeed, quiet little girls seemed the most desirable playmates. Markova and colleagues (1980) found that mothers of hemophiliac boys were particularly anxious about their son's absence from school, although differences in child rearing seemed to vary with the degree of severity of the hemophilia.

Many of the fathers of hemophiliac boys seemed to lose interest in the child and were relieved that they were not involved genetically as carriers. They were afraid to play with their sons, saw school as dangerous, and sought desk jobs for their sons. The child resented the father who denied him any physical activity. In another study, the son tended to regard his father as a traitor to his sex because he felt his father prevented him from expressing his masculinity (Goldy and Katz, 1963). Recently, the risk of being infected with acquired immune deficiency syndrome (AIDS) through a blood transfusion has heightened anxiety in both children and parents.

AIDS. HIV infection in children and adolescents is a growing concern. Although presently a low incidence (if highly lethal), disease estimates suggest that as many as 3000 pediatric cases will be observed by 1991 (CDC, 1988). In addition to the same modes of transmission as in adults (i.e., sexual intercourse, IV drug use with shared needles, or administration of contaminated blood products), perinatal transmission also occurs. Infected infants presently account for the majority of pediatric AIDS cases. In addition to the problems associated with AIDS in adults, children are at increased risk because both medical problems (e.g., chronic infections) and psychosocial adversity (e.g., drug abusing mothers, ostracism from school and society) may jeopardize their development as may the infection itself. Various developmental, psychiatric, and ethical problems may arise in such cases (Krener and Miller, 1989). A range of psychologic supports are typically needed; provision of information to at-risk populations and community education are also important.

Diabetes. Although there is no good evidence that suggests that stressful life events are responsible for the development of the condition, it is clear that psychologic factors can assume major importance in its management, particularly in adolescence. In the case of so-called "brittle" diabetes, many factors contribute to the lability of the condition and the difficulty in control. Stress, for example, may increase epinephrine and catecholamines acting on adrenergic beta-type receptors, leading to excess ketone production (Baker et al., 1969). Stress may arise within the family. Anxious parents may become overprotective, overcontrolling, overpermissive, or rejecting (Johnson, 1980; Minuchin, 1978). Instability in the family may contribute to instability in the diabetes (White et al., 1984). Preadolescents in turn may become overly dependent, and subsequently may become depressed when threatened with separation. Such a child may both regress and rebel when he or she reaches adolescence, or may become suicidal. Healthy siblings may resent the attention given to their younger brother or sister with diabetes, and may act out against both their affected sibling and their parents. Peers too may reject a child with diabetes who uses his or her disease to manipulate the adult to avoid disliked activities or to gain favors (Johnson and Rosenbloom, 1982).

Young children are quite capable of learning how to administer their own insulin, but they may not have the emotional maturity to take full responsibility for this task. Adolescents may fight against the restrictions imposed by the diabetes; the most common cause of diabetic ketoacidosis is noncompliance (Wilkinson, 1981). Adolescents need acceptance and understanding of their feelings together with education on the need for reasonable regularity (Tattersall and Lowe, 1981). The parents too need to develop the same understanding and acceptance of their adolescent's feelings and needs.

Children and adolescents who are well informed often fare better than children who have a poor knowledge of diabetes and their own reactions, but the process of knowing has to be continuous, changing with the cognitive and emotional development of the child and adolescent (Sullivan, 1979). Most youngsters in the end cope well (Johnson, 1980). Physicians can play a helpful role through educating the child and family, clarifying with the child and family mutual expectations, gradually increasing the responsibilities for the child and adolescent, and conveying an understanding, accepting, and supportive attitude (Garrity, 1981).

Kidney Disease. Children with chronic renal disease may experience malaise, depression, and denial. Hemodialysis brings relief and hope, but the possibility of renal transplantation again brings apprehension and fear. Following transplantation, the fear of rejection may again cause depression. Chronic, end-stage kidney disease often leads to withdrawal, depression, anxiety, and noncompliance; metabolic changes associated with dialysis may contribute to these symptoms. These children and their parents, who may experience similar feelings of depression, anxiety, and denial, need a great deal of support.

Cancer. Another phenomenon that is seen more and more today is the reaction of pediatric cancer patients to survival. This is a recent historical phenomenon because, in the past, such conditions were generally fatal. Improved treatments have increased survival rates in various malignancies; aspects of treatment and uncertainties about long-term prognosis may have significant psychologic impact. Koocher and his colleagues (1980), in a study of the psychologic adjustment of 115 pediatric cancer survivors, found that in general the younger the child is at the time of diagnosis and treatment and the greater the number of years since the onset of the illness, the less likely the child is to have later adjustment problems or to have anxiety about recurrence, respectively. Children who have poorer socialization and self-help skills and poorer intellectual functioning are more likely than others to have difficulties in psychosocial adjustment (e.g., residual depression, feelings of isolation and anxiety, and poor self-esteem). Developmental disruptions caused by the cancer treatment experience are apparently more marked and persistent when they occur during middle childhood or adolescence than when they occur during infancy.

Leukemia. Improved survival has been particularly noteworthy for children with leukemia. Such children may have similar reactions to other cancer patients, as do their parents. On hearing the diagnosis of leukemia, parents may feel disbelief and shock. They may also feel angry if the diagnosis was not made during the preceding weeks of nonspecific malaise in the child. The parents may not know what to expect: death or cure. The child next has to embark on a prolonged course of chemotherapy and/or radiation therapy, which has such side effects as nausea, vomiting, and hair loss. Irradiation may also lead to loss of cognitive skills (Jannoun, 1984). The course of the disease must then be followed by painful bone marrow biopsies, which some children come to fear and hate. It is not surprising that many parents and children become anxious and depressed (Maguire, 1983). Young children may find concentration on school work difficult, and school refusal may occur.

Yet at the same time the cure rate at present is about 50%. Parents, of course, hope for this outcome, and the family members mobilize their coping mechanisms to deal with all the stresses and strains of the illness and the treatment, and in fact cope well (Kupst et al., 1984).

Seizure Disorders. Epilepsy occurs relatively commonly in childhood, affecting 7 to 8 in 1000 school age children (Rutter, Graham, and Yule, 1970). Although emotional factors do not cause the disorder, they clearly can precipitate seizure activity (Graham, 1986). Children with seizure disorders are at greater risk for developing psychiatric disturbance than children with other chronic conditions (Rutter, Graham, and Yule, 1970). Families of children with seizures may exhibit disturbance (Grunberg and Pond, 1957). Although medications may facilitate medical management, they may also be associated with untoward psychologic effects (Corbett et al., 1985). The child's sense of loss of control may interact with parental patterns of overprotection or rejection to result in lowered self-esteem and isolation.

Usually the acute onset, characteristic EEG changes, and the symptom picture correctly suggests the diagnosis of seizure disorder. However, alterations in behavior, e.g., absence episode or behavioral automatisms, may be mistaken for psychiatric problems. One particular group of seizure disorders, complex partial seizures, are of special significance for development because the symptoms they produce may be largely behavioral and may include aggressive outbursts or apparent forgetfulness. In some instances, psychogenic or "hysterical" seizures may be observed (Volkmar et al., 1984); often such symptoms act to serve both an unconscious need on the part of the child and parents as well as producing some desired result (secondary gain).

FACTITIOUS ILLNESS

Munchausen by Proxy Syndrome

In this condition, signs and symptoms of illness in children are deliberately induced or fabricated by a caregiver, usually the mother. The degree of fabrication and the range of severity is variable (Forsyth, In Press); in some instances severe injury or death can result (Meadow, 1982; Rosenberg, 1987). Diverse methods of fabrication are used, e.g., administration of drugs, deliberate contamination of urine with blood, reports of seizures or apneic episodes. Actual illness may be produced, e.g., as a result of administration of drugs or other agents or contamination of IV lines. Although the diagnosis has been made in children of all ages, its presence in very young children is particularly worrisome. Older children may collude, to some extent, in the deception. Often a considerable period of time elapses between the onset of the condition and the eventual diagnosis. Usually extensive medical investigations (which themselves carry some risk to the child) have been conducted and the diagnosis suggests itself only as it becomes clear that the symptoms are present only as the parent is present. Often the perpetrator has previously appeared to be zealously concerned with the child's welfare and may have resisted attempts to leave the child even for a brief period. As a result, medical staff are often initially impressed with the parent's concern, thus delaying the recognition of the parental contribution to the condition. Often the mother has had previous health care training or has experienced unexplained illness herself or has fabricated parts of her own history (Forsyth, In Press).

Although a form of child abuse, certain aspects of the syndrome distinguish it from other types of child maltreatment. Although certain aspects of the underlying psychopathology in the parent are similar to those reported in adult factitious illness, a range of psychiatric symptomatology in the parent has been reported (Rosenberg, 1987). Often the mother has an overly close relationship with the child while the father is either largely absent or uninvolved. Despite her overzealousness, the mother may appear to be less concerned about the child's condition than would be expected. The needs of the mother interact with the medical care system in complex ways providing, for example, opportunities to interact with a supportive medical staff and a sense of increased importance.

Warning signs of the disorder include inexplicable persistent or recurrent illness, markedly unusual features (particularly of what appears to be a rare illness), history of a previous child who had died under mysterious circumstances, symptoms that are observed only in the mother's presence, a mother who seems less concerned about the child's condition than would be expected but who also never leaves the child's side, and discrepancies between clinical findings and history (Meadow, 1982; Forsyth, In Press). Management can be difficult; the child's well being should be the primary concern. Premature discussion can result in abrupt departure of parent and child from the hospital; in such cases it is best to minimize laboratory and other studies and devote considerable attention to observation of the parent-child dyad. Once the diagnosis has been established, child protective agencies must be involved and the mother (and other family members) be informed of the diagnosis. Psychiatric consultation may be helpful.

EFFECTS OF HOSPITALIZATION

Until relatively recently, the usual practice in the hospitalization of children was to separate the child from his or her parents. Contact was limited to highly circumscribed visiting hours to prevent infection and to avoid having the child upset if parents visited regularly (particularly at times of their departure). As antibiotics and other specific treatments became available, the pattern of hospitalization changed as concerns about the risk of infection were reduced. At the same time, various adverse effects of hospitalization began to be reported. These reports (e.g., Edelston, 1943; Robertson, 1958; Bowlby, 1961) provided eloquent descriptions of the trauma entailed by separation from parents and identified a characteristic pattern of adaptation (from protest to despair to detachment and apathy). Parents were increasingly encouraged to remain with their child during the hospitalization.

Adverse effects of hospitalization can take various forms, e.g., anxiety, regression, eating disturbance, and withdrawal (Vernon et al., 1966). It appears that recurrent hospitalization puts children at even greater risk for developing psychologic disturbances (Breslau, Staruch, and Mortimer, 1982; Douglas, 1975; Quinton and Rutter, 1976; Shannon, Fergusson, and Diamond, 1984). Of children with chronic illness, 12 to 13% have diagnosable emotional problems (Rutter, Tizard, and Whitmore, 1970; Goldberg, Regier, McInery et al., 1979). Given the estimate that about 10 to 20% of children are chronically ill, the extent of emotional problems among the chronically ill is formidably large.

The factors that increase that risk are developmental and cumulative, and begin before the first hospitalization. Some risk factors relate to the child, others to the illness and its experience, and yet others to the parents. Prehospitalization risk factors include: (1) any premorbid psychopathologic condition that might be present in the child, (2) poor parent-child relationships, (3) psychiatric disturbance in either parent, and (4) age. Younger children are more vulnerable than older children. Children under 5 years of age who have had two or more admissions are especially likely to have psychiatric symptoms, learning problems, and symptoms of a conduct disorder than are nonhospitalized controls (Quinton and Rutter, 1976).

Risk factors related to the experience of the illness include (1) the kind and severity of the illness, (2) the amount and kind of preparation for the hospital given to the child, and (3) the hospital experience itself.

The final risk factors relate to the parents' cognitive understanding of the illness separate from their understanding of and reactions to the child's reactions to his or her illness. The parents may have unrealistic expectations, or may feel exceedingly pessimistic and helpless.

During the first hospitalization, the child is at risk as a result of the separation, specific illness effects, any painful interventions that may be required, and the reactions of the parents (concern, support, and collaboration; anxiety, fear, denial, disbelief; guilt and anger; depression and projection).

Some of the signs of both immediate and persisting distress include:

1. biopsychologic symptoms (malaise, pain, irritability, disturbances in appetite and sleep),
2. increased attachment behavior (clinging, demanding, and heightened separation anxiety),
3. regression (thumb sucking, regression in speech and bowel and bladder control),
4. feelings of helplessness and powerlessness,
5. frightening fantasies about the illness and procedures (punishment, fear of mutilation and bodily harm),
6. anxiety and mobilization of defenses (denial, phobic symptoms, conversion symptoms), and
7. precipitation or aggravation of premorbid psychiatric symptoms.

However, the state in which the child emerges from the first hospitalization may also be affected by the kind of care offered before and during the hospitalization (Wolfer and Visintainer, 1979). For example, useful practices that might mitigate untoward reactions include:

1. prehospital preparation,
2. maintenance of familiar routines and playthings,
3. visits of parents,
4. ongoing dialogue between staff and parents,
5. living-in arrangements,
6. special nursing,
7. substitute parents (e.g., grandparents serving as mother surrogates),
8. child care and school programs,
9. child psychiatry consultation, and
10. education, counseling, and therapeutic help for the parents.

The ultimate experience of the initial illness, hospitalization, and posthospital care may range from an enhanced sense of mastery to severe adverse psychologic reactions, depending on the interactions of all the elements just outlined.

Chronic illness and repeated hospitalization may subsequently intensify any or all of these factors.

At the same time, chronic illness may carry with it particular stresses derived from the particular illness or handicap. For example, such experiences as impaired function, disfigurement, or relative immobilization, for example in the enforced use of a wheelchair, add to the risk. The disabled child with a chronic illness requiring repeated hospitalization may also experience an eroding loss of autonomy, perhaps accompanied by increased attachment behaviors and regression. Normal expectable development goals may have to be modified by the child and parents.

The parents of a chronically ill child may also experience feelings of loss and grief. Family plans have to be modified. The parents, like the child, also may find themselves more often than they wish in the hands of the hospital staff to whom they have to adapt. Mothers, in particular, of disabled children often show signs of exhaustion, guilt, depression, and anxiety (Breslau, Staruch, and Mortimer, 1982). All these factors, together with the financial drain, impose much strain on the marriage. The parents have to readjust their perceptions of, and responses to, the child's needs. The loss of control the parents feel may lead to a similar regression in them. As a result, the parents may begin to feel helpless and less competent in dealing with their child. The whole family, indeed, may become isolated, and psychopathologic traits and trends in each member of the family may become intensified.

Sometimes the siblings find they too have to readjust, and they may react with anxiety, resentment, and guilt.

Needless to say, hospital staff who do not recognize or understand these reactions may react with anger and irritation at both child and parent. Sometimes this behavior on the part of the staff represents a transference, or at least a displacement, as the hospital staff themselves sometimes feel discouraged by the slowness, or even absence, of progress.

In short, the psychologic reactions to recurrent pediatric hospitalization derive first from all the risks associated with the initial illness and hospitalization, including the resulting outcome and impact on the child's development; second from the nature of the chronic illness itself and the reactions of both child and parents; and third from the reinforcing effects of each hospitalization.

The treatment and management of the recurrently hospitalized child and his or her family should address all these factors. Each hospitalization should in fact be regarded as a unique experience for the child and parents, i.e., one should not assume that just because the child has been previously hospitalized the child and parents are completely familiar with the hospital and medical or surgical procedures, and have no anxieties. Rather, the treatment and management should in essence follow the same principles that are the basis for all hospital care of children, whether solitary or recurrent, and should include as a minimum:

1. adequate preparation before and during each hospitalization,
2. living-in, especially for the younger child,
3. maintained visiting,
4. special nursing,
5. child care,
6. a receptive and well-functioning ward environment, and
7. psychiatric consultation for all concerned as needed.

SUMMARY

The reactions of children to recurrent illness and hospitalization are multidetermined. Major factors are the reactions in the parents and the care the child receives. Careful attention to all the factors outlined should help the child master the anxiety, depression, and other effects resulting from recurrent hospitalization. Careful attention to all these elements may also prevent untoward reactions and may facilitate the optimum development of the child.

Note 41

From Prugh, D.G. Staub, E.M., Sands, H.H., Kurschbaum, R.M., and Lenihan, E.A., 1953. A study of the emotional reactions of children and families to hospitalization and illness. *Am. J. Orthopsychiatry*, 23:70–106.

. . . Two groups of 100 children each were selected for study, one designated as the *control* and the other, the *experimental* group.

. . . A base-line study of the control group was carried out initially, covering a period of approximately four months. The circumstances under which hospitalization was encountered by children during this period were those involving traditional practices of ward management, existing prior to the experimental nursing program.

. . . Following an interval sufficient to allow complete turnover of patients who had been in the control study, an experimental program of ward management was put into effect. This involved many of the practices employed in other hospitals and included daily visiting periods for parents, early ambulation of patients where medically feasible, a special play program employing a nursery-school teacher, psychological preparation for and support during potentially emotionally traumatic diagnostic or therapeutic procedures, an attempt at clearer definition and integration of the parent's role in the care of the child, and other techniques. Attention was paid to the handling of admission procedures, with parents accompanying the child to the ward to meet the staff and to assist in the child's initial adjustment. As a part of admission routine, parents were given a pamphlet prepared especially to enhance their understanding of their child's needs and their own role in his care.

In order to coordinate the activities of the professional staff in the management of patients, a weekly Ward Management Conference was held, directed by a pediatrician with psychiatric training. In attendance were the ward physician, head nurse, play supervisor, occupational therapist, dietitian, social worker, psychologist, and frequently a public health nurse. An attempt was made to discuss the adjustment of each child on the ward, although children presenting particular difficulties in adaptation received the most attention. Among other measures discussed and implemented in this interdisciplinary conference were: the assignment of one nurse to the principal care of a particularly anxious child; the scheduling of injections or other medical procedures at times other than feeding, nap, or play times; the use of appropriate psychological preparation for forthcoming procedures by physician, nurse, or play supervisor; the selection of particular play activities designed to meet the emotional needs of particular children; the special handling of feeding or other activities; the flexible arrangement of visiting periods or the encouragement of parental participation in ward care; and the provision of special psychological support for particular parents. Psychiatric consultation and psychological appraisal were provided where indicated, but the essential approach was in the direction of the coordination and potentiation of the efforts of all professional personnel involved in the care of the ill child. . . .

Results

Immediate reactions

. . . 92 per cent of the children in the control or unsupported group exhibited reactions of the degree indicating significant difficulties in adaptation. . . . In the experimental group, this figure totaled 68 per cent. . . .

. . . Immediate reactions to hospitalization were noted to be most marked in children from two through five years of age in both groups. . . .

. . . In general, children with previously limited capacities for adaptation showed the greatest difficulty in adjusting comfortably to the ward milieu and showed as well the most severe reactions to the total experience of hospitalization. . . .

Long-range reactions

. . . Children under four years of age and children who had relatively unsatisfying relationships with their parents, who had undergone very severe stress in the hospital, and who had shown the greatest difficulty in adapting to the ward milieu were those who tended to show persistent signs of emotional disturbance at three months following hospitalization. . . .

Types of individual reactions of children in the hospital

. . . The most common manifestation of disturbance in adaptation at any age level or in either group was that of overt anxiety. . . .

. . . (In) children from two to four years of age (in the) control groups . . . anxiety over separation from parents was the most common manifestation and the most intense of any age level, occurring equally in both sexes and to some degree in all children. Anxiety was often associated with fear or anger at the time of departure of the parents. Constant crying, apprehensive behavior, outbursts of screaming, an acute panic when approached by an adult were frequent, together with occasional somatic concomitants of anxiety such as urinary frequency, diarrhea, vomiting, etc. Depression, at times resembling the anaclitic type described by Spitz . . . homesickness and withdrawal were observed in this group more than in older children, particularly at the outset of hospitalization. The need for tangible evidence of home and family, such as dolls, items of clothing, etc., was particularly manifest in this group, as demonstrated by the anxiety of many children over giving them up. At times, shoes and socks, for example, seemed to be incorporated into the body image, with marked anxiety shown whenever they were removed.

Reactions to the experiencing of overwhelming fear or anxiety showed some specificity for the children in this age group . . . Disturbances in feeding behavior, including anorexia, overeating, and refusal to chew food, often combined with regressive smearing of food or the demand for a return to bottle feeding, were more frequent and severe than in any other group. Changes in toilet behavior were next in incidence, involving regressive loss of control of bladder or bowel functions, most marked in the early phases of hospitalization. Fears of the toilet or of the loss of the stool, fear of loss of control of bowel or bladder functions, as well as guilt and fear of punishment over wishes to soil or wet, were handled by mechanisms of denial, projection, and other modes of adaptation available to the child of his age. Fears of the dark or of physical attack were common and were associated with sleep disturbances—insomnia, nightmares and restlessness. Increase of bedtime rituals and other compulsive acts during hospitalization was often seen.

. . . Open acting-out of infantile wishes and aggressive impulses appeared most frequently in this age group, with wild outbursts of frantic aggression and attendant guilt and anxiety. Marked inhibition of aggressive drives was observed in some children, together with turning inward of hostility. Restlessness, hyperactivity and irritability, with associated rocking, thumb-sucking or aggressive behavior, appeared in many children, particularly if they were confined to bed with the use of a "restrainer," as had been the practice for small or acute disoriented children in order to prevent their falling from bed. With ambulation, this behavior often disappeared or diminished markedly.

A variety of primitive gratification of pregenital character . . . were employed to greater degree than prior to hospitalization. Thumb-sucking and rocking were common, associated with withdrawal and with masturbation in one third of the children. Headbanging was relatively infrequent. In many instances, as children established parent-surrogate relationships, often with the play supervisor or one particular nurse, gratifications of this type diminished, no longer interfering with adjustment to the group.

Among the defense mechanisms available to this younger group, regression was the most widespread. Libidinal regression was often uneven, associated with feeding, bowel and bladder symptomatology. Oral components were manifest through enhanced sucking, overeating, and demanding behavior, with occasional biting and other manifestations. Cruelty, sadistic enjoyment of the pain of others, pleasure in handling or smearing feces, and other regressive anal components of behavior were transparently or openly evident, particularly in children isolated for medical reasons.

In some instances, a nearly total regression of the ego to a relatively narcissistic level of psychosexual development, associated with disturbances in reality testing, was manifest. . .

Denial of illness or of the loss of the loved object, the mother, was observed in a number of children of this age. For example, one child, a boy of three and a half, insisted for three days that his mother was "downstairs" and that he was "all well now," in spite of the persistence of his dyspnea from a bronchopneumonia.

(In the) experimental group . . . the same types of disturbances in adaptation were noted as among the control or unsupported group. In general, however, manifestations were less severe and lighter in incidence. . . .

Reactions to specific types of treatment or diagnostic procedures

. . . The impression was gained that any or all . . . procedures seemed to be interpreted by a child at a particular level of libidinal development in terms of the specific anxieties and fears characteristic of that level, and to be dealt with by means of his own previously developed defenses, rather than in terms of the exact nature of the procedure itself. . . .

In the main, the younger children tended to react to such threatening procedures as to hostile attacks, often interpreted as punishment. . . . The impression was gained, however, that a great deal of the small child's fear of unknown procedures, of separation from the parents, of punishment, and of overwhelming attack was displaced much of the time onto such objectively less threatening but directly visible things as needles, tourniquets, etc. In the experimental group, aggressive responses in particular to various procedures were only half as frequent and were less intense than those in the control group. . . .

Post hospitalization reactions

. . . Following discharge, most of the regressive manifestations in the younger age group appeared to subside rather promptly. Behavior of an infantile or demanding nature, together with greater dependence on parent, persisted for several months in a number of children under five years of age. Wetting, soiling, and intensified pregenital gratifications, however, were ordinarily given up within three months' time.

The most common manifestations among children showing continuing disturbances were related to anxiety over separation from parents, appearing most intensely in younger children but arising also in latency children. . . . All of these manifestations appeared to be milder in children in the experimental group (e.g., sleep disturbances were five times as common in the control as the experimental group). . . .

In general, symptoms which persisted were fewer in number and milder for each child at home than in the hospital. Such symptoms appeared to be related more directly to the personality structure and characteristic patterns of adaptation of the child prior to hospitalization. . . .

Reactions of parents and families
. . . Realistic fear in proportion to the severity of the child's illness, overt anxiety, guilt over possible involvement in the causation of illness or over previously hostile feelings toward the child, and other feelings were handled in various ways, dependent upon the character structure of the parent, the nature of the relationship with the child, experiences immediately preceding hospitalization, and other factors.

. . . Marked ambivalence, even on the part of well-adjusted parents, was frequent in the face of behavioral regression on the part of the child, either during or following hospitalization.

. . . In general, the well adjusted parents whose children were hospitalized under the experimental program seemed more satisfied with visiting regulations than those in the control group, where visiting was strongly curtailed. . . .

Problems in ward management
. . . The common conception that crying occurs more frequently among children whose parents visit frequently was found to be erroneous in the experimental phase of the study. . . .
. . . (Moreover) the hazard of cross-infection is not appreciably increased under circumstances involving more frequent contact with parents.

REFERENCES

Agle, D.P. (1964), Psychiatric studies of patients with hemophilia and related states. *Arch. Intern. Med.*, 114:76–82.

Apley, J. (1975), The child with abdominal pains, 2nd Ed. Oxford: Blackwell Scientific Publications.

Apley, J., and MacKeith, R.C. (1968), *The Child and His Symptoms.* Oxford: Blackwell Scientific Publications.

Apley, J., and Hale, B. (1973), Children with recurrent abdominal pain: How do they grow up? *Br. Med. J.*, 3:7–9.

Baker, L., Barcai, A., Kay, R., and Hague, N. (1969), Beta adrenergic blockade and juvenile diabetes:

Acute studies and long-term therapeutic trial. *Pediatrics*, 73:19–29.

Basbaum, A.I., and Fields, H.L. (1984), Endogenous pain control systems: Brainstem spinal pathways and endorphin circuitry. *Ann. Rev. Neurosc.*, 7:309–338.

Blos, P. (1960), Comments on the psychological consequences of cryptorchism: A clinical study. *Psychoanal. Study Child*, 15:395–429.

Bowlby, J., Ainsworth, M.D., Boston, M., et al. (1956), The effects of mother-child separations: A follow-up study. *Br. J. Med. Psychol.*, 2:211–247.

Breslau, N., Staruch, J., and Mortimer, E. (1982), Psychological distress in mothers of disabled children. *Am. J. Dis. Child.*, 136:682–686.

Broughton, A., Anderson, M.B., and Bowden, C.H. (1968), Magnesium deficiency in burns. *Lancet*, 2:1156–1158.

Browne, W.J., Mally, M.A., and Kane, R.P. (1960), Psychosocial aspects of hemophilia. *Am. J. Orthopsychiatry*, 30:730–740.

Centers for Disease Control (1988), Immunization of children infected with human immunodeficiency virus—supplementary ACIP statement. *MMWR*, 37:12.

Chess, S., and Fernandez, P. (1980), Impulsivity in rubella deaf children: A longitudinal study. *Am. Ann. Deaf.*, 125:505–509.

Collins, S.D. (1938), Frequency of surgical procedures among 9,000 families, based on nation-wide periodic canvasses 1928–31. *Public Health Rep.*, 53:587–628.

Corbett, J.A., Trimble, M.R., and Nicol, T.C. (1985), Behavioral and cognitive impairment in children with epilepsy: The long-term effects of anti-convulsant therapy. *J. Am. Acad. Child Psychiatry*, 24:17–23.

Cytoya, L., Cytoya, E.M., and Rieger, E. (1967), Psychlogical implications of cryptorchidism. *J. Am. Acad. Child Psychiatry*, 6:131–142.

Denmark, J.C., Rodda, M., Abel, R.A., et al. (1979), *A word in deaf ears—a study of communication and behaviour in a sample of 75 deaf adolescents.* London: The Royal National Institute for the Deaf.

Dey, D.L. (1952), A survey of 681 children awaiting tonsillectomy and the indications for operation in childhood. *Med. J. Aust.*, 1:510–514.

Douglas, J.W.B. (1975), Early hospital admissions and later disturbances of behavior and learning. *Dev. Med. Child Neurol.*, 17:456–480.

Edelston, H. (1943), Separation anxiety in young children. *Genet. Psychol. Mongr.*, 28:1–95.

Faull, C., and Nicol, A.R. (1986), Abdominal pain in six-year-olds: An epidemiological study in a new town. *J. Child Psychol. Psychiatry*, 27:215–260.

Forsyth, B. (In Press), Munchausen syndrome by proxy. In: *Child and Adolescent Psychiatry: A Comprehensive Textbook*, ed. M. Lewis, Baltimore: Williams & Wilkins.

Fraiberg, S. (1968), Parallel and divergent patterns in blind and sighted infants. *Psychoanal. Study Child*, 23:264–300.

Fraiberg, S., and Freedman, D.A. (1964), Studies in the ego development of the congenitally blind child. *Psychoanal. Study Child*, 19:113–169.

Fraiberg, S., Siegel, B.L., and Gibson, R. (1966), The

role of sound in the search behavior of a blind infant. *Psychoanal. Study Child*, 21:327–357.

Frances, A., and Gale, L. (1975), Proprioceptive body image in self-object differentiation. *Psychoanal. Q.*, 44:107–125.

Freeman, R.D., Malkin, S.F., and Hasting, J.O. (1965). Psychosocial problems of deaf children and their families: a comparative study. *Am. Ann. Deaf.*, 120:391–405.

Freud, A. (1952), The role of bodily illness in the mental life of children. *Psychoanal. Study Child*, 8:69.

Garriety, T. (1981), Medical compliance and the clinician-patient relationship: A review. *Soc. Sci. Med.*, 15:215–222.

Gauthier, Y., Fortin, C., Drapeau, P., et al. (1977), The mother-child relationship and the development of autonomy and self-assertion in young (16–30 months) asthmatic children. *J. Am. Acad. Child Psychiatry*, 16:109–131.

Goldberg, I.D., Reiger, D.A., McInerny, J.K., et al. (1979), The role of the pediatrician in the delivery of mental health services to children. *Pediatrics*, 63:898–909.

Goldy, F.B., and Katz, A.H. (1963), Social adaptation in hemophilia. *Children*, 10:189–193.

Graham, P. (1986), *Child Psychiatry: A Developmental Approach.* Oxford: Oxford University Press.

Green, M. (1967), Diagnosis and treatment: Psychogenic abdominal pain. *Pediatrics*, 40:84–89.

Grunberg, F., and Pond, D. (1957), Conduct disorders in epileptic children. *J. Neurol. Neurosurg. Psychiatry*, 20:65.

Herbert, M. (1965), Personality factors in bronchial asthma: A Study of South African Indian Children. *J. Psychosom. Res.*, 8:353–364.

Hodges, K., et al. (1985), Depressive symptoms in children with recurrent abdominal pain and in their families. *J. Pediatr.*, 107:622–626.

Holter, J.C., and Friedman, S.B. (1969), Etiology and management of severely burned children. *Am. J. Dis. Child.*, 118:680–686.

Horstman, D. (1969), Personal communication.

Jackson, D.MacG. (1968), What the burnt child goes through. *Proc. Royal Soc. Med.*, 61:1085–1087.

Jannoun, L. (1983), Are cognitive and educational development affected by age at which prophylactic therapy is given in acute lymphoblastic leukaemia? *Arch. Dis. Child.*, 58:953–958.

Jenkins, J.R., and Chess, S. (In Press), Psychiatric evaluation of sensory impaired children: Hearing and visual impairment. In: *Child and Adolescent Psychiatry: A Comprehensive Textbook*, ed. M. Lewis. Baltimore: Williams & Wilkins.

Jessner, L., Blom, G.E., and Waldfogel, S. (1952), Emotional implications of tonsillectomy and adenoidectomy on children. *Psychoanal. Study Child*, 7:126–169.

Johnson, S.B. (1980), Psychosocial factors in juvenile diabetes: A review. *Behav. Med.*, 3:95–116.

Johnson, S.B., and Rosenbloom, A.L. (1982), Behavioral aspects of diabetes mellitus in childhood and adolescence. In: *The Psychiatric Clinics of North America: Pediatric Consultation-Liaison*, ed. M. Sherman. Philadelphia: W.B. Saunders Co., pp. 357–369.

Kaplan De-Nour, A. (1977), Adolescents' adjustment to chronic hemodialysis. *Am. J. Psychiatry*, 136:430–433.

Karpel, M.A. (1980), Family secrets. *Fam. Process*, 19:295–306.

Kaufman, R.V. (1972), Body image changes in physically ill teenagers. *J. Am. Acad. Child Psychiatry*, 11:157–170.

Koesch, B.M., et al. (1971), Experiences with children and their families during extended hemodialysis and kidney transplantation. *Pediatr. Clin. North Am.*, 18:625–637.

Kolvin, I., and Fundudis, T. (1982), Speech disorders of childhood. In: *One Child*, eds. J. Apley, and C. Ounsted. London: Heinemann/Spastistic International Medical Publications, p. 1547.

Koocher, G.P., O'Malley, J.E., Gogan, J.L., and Foster, D.J. (1980), Psychological adjustment among pediatric cancer survivors. *J. Child Psychol. Psychiatry*, 21:163–173.

Krener, P., and Miller, F.B. (1989), Psychiatric response to HIV spectrum disease in children and adolescents. *J. Am. Acad. Child Adolesc. Psychiatry*, 28:596–605.

Kupst, M.J., Schulman, J.L., Maurer, H., et al. (1984), Coping with paediatric leukaemia: A two-year follow up. *J. Pediatr. Psychol.*, 9:149–163.

Langford, W.S. (1948), Physical illness and convalescence: their meaning to the child. *J. Pediatr.*, 33:242.

Levy, D.M. (1945), Psychic trauma of operations in children and a note on combat neurosis. *Am. J. Dis. Child.*, 69:7.

Leybourne, P., and Churchill, S. (1972), Symptom discouragement in treating hysterical reactions of childhood. *Int. J. Child Psychother.*, 1:111–114.

Lipton, S.D. (1962), On the psychology of childhood tonsillectomy. *Psychoanal. Study Child*, 17:363–417.

Long, R., and Cope, O. (1961), Emotional problems of burned children. *N. Engl. J. Med.*, 264:1121.

Maguire, P. (1983), The psychological sequelae of childhood leukemia. *Recent Results Cancer Res.*, 88:47–56.

Markova, I., MacDonald, K., and Forbes, C. (1980), Impact of hemophilia on child-rearing practices and parent cooperation. *J. Child Psychol. Psychiatry*, 21:153–162.

McCollum, A.T., and Gibson, L.E. (1970), Family adaptation to the child with cystic fibrosis. *J. Pediatr.*, 77:571–578.

Meadow, R. (1982), Munchausen syndrome by proxy. *Arch. Dis. Child.*, 57:92–98.

Minuchin, S., Rosman, B., and Baker, L. (1978), *Psychosomatic Families.* Cambridge, Mass., Harvard University Press.

Mrazek D. (1985), Child psychiatric consultation and liaison in pediatrics. In: *Child and Adolescent Psychiatry. Modern Approaches*, ed. M. Rutter and L. Herson. Oxford: Blackwell Scientific Publications, pp. 888–899.

Neill, C.A. (1967), The child and his family at home after hospitalization. In: *The Hospitalized Child and His Family*, ed. J.A. Haller, Jr. Baltimore: Johns Hopkins Press, pp. 67–77.

Nover, R. (1973), Pain and the burned child. *J. Am. Acad. Child Psychiatry,* 3:499–505.

Parcel, G.S., Gilman, S.C., Nader, P.R., and Bunce, H. (1979), A comparison of absentee rates of elementary school children with asthma and unasthmatic schoolmates. *Pediatrics,* 64:878–881.

Parkhouse, J., et al. (1979), *Analgesic Drugs.* Blackwell Scientific Publications, p. 15.

Peterson, E.G. (1972), The impact of adolescent illness on parental relationships. *J. Health Soc. Behav.,* 13:428 437.

Pinkerton, R., and Weaver, C.M. (1970), Childhood asthma. In: *Modern Trends in Psychosomatic Medicine,* ed. O.M. Hill. London: Butterworth, pp. 81–104.

Prugh, D.G., Staub, E.M., Sands, H.H., Kirschbaum, R.M., and Lenihan, E.A. (1953), A study of the emotional reactions of children and families to hospitalization and illness. *Am. J. Orthopsychiatry,* 23:70.

Purcell, K., and Weiss, J. (1970), Asthma. In: *Symptoms of Psychopathology,* ed. C. Costello. New York: John Wiley & Sons, Inc., pp. 597–623.

Quinton, D., and Rutter, M. (1976), Early hospital admissions and later disturbances of behavior: An attempted replication of Douglas' findings. *Dev. Med. Child Neurol.,* 18:447–459.

Reivich, R.S., and Rothrock, I.A. (1972), Behavior problems of deaf children and adolescents: A factor-analytic study. *J. Speech Hear. Res.,* 15:93–104.

Richtsmeier, A.J., and Waters, D.B. (1984), Somatic symptoms as family myth. *Am. J. Dis. Child.,* 138:855–857.

Robertson, J. (1956), A mother's observation on the tonsillectomy of her four-year-old daughter, with comments by Anna Freud. *Psychoanal. Study Child,* 11:410–436.

Robertson, J. (1958), *Young Children in Hospital.* London: Tavistock Publications.

Rosenberg, D. (1987), Web of deceit: A literature review of Munchausen syndrome by proxy. *Child Abuse Negl.,* 11:547–563.

Rowland, T.W., and Richard, M.M. (1986), The natural history of idiopathic chest pain in children. *Clin. Pediatr.,* 25:612–614.

Rutter, M., Graham, P., and Yule, W. (1970), *A Neuropsychiatric Study in Childhood.* London: Heinemann.

Rutter, M., Tizard, J., and Whitmore, K. (1970), *Education, Health and Behavior.* London: Longmans, Green.

Schechter, N.L. (1984), Recurrent pains in children: An overview and an approach. *Pediatr. Clin. North Am.,* 31:949–968.

Schultz, J.A. (1983), Timing of elective hypospadias repair in children. *Pediatrics,* 7:347–351.

Schwartz, A.H., and Landwirth, J. (1968), Birth defects and the psychological development of the child: some implications for management. *Conn. Med.,* 32:457–464.

Shannon, P.T., Ferguson, D.M., and Diamond, M.E. (1984), Early hospital admissions and subsequent behavior problems in six-year olds. *Arch. Dis. Child.,* 58:815–819.

Solnit, A.J., and Stark, M. (1961), Mourning and the birth of a defective child. *Psychoanal. Study Child,* 16:523–537.

Steinhauser, H.C., Schindler, H.P., and Stephen, H. (1983), Correlates of psychopathology in sick children: An empirical model. *J. Am. Acad. Child Psychiatry,* 22:559–564.

Sullivan, B.J. (1979), Adjustment in diabetic adolescent girls. II. Adjustment, self-esteem and depression in diabetic adolescent girls. *Psychosom. Med.,* 41:127–138.

Tattersall, R., and Lowe, J. (1981), Diabetes in adolescence. *Diabetologia,* 20:517–523.

Tisza, V., Selverstone, B., Rosenblum, G., and Hanlon, N. (1968), Psychiatric observations of children with cleft palate. *Am. J. Orthopsychiatry,* 28:416–423.

Vernon, D.T., Schulman, J.L., and Foley, M. (1966), Changes in children's behavior after hospitalization. *Am. J. Dis. Child.,* 111:581–593.

Volkmar, F.R., Poll, J., and Lewis, M. (1984), Conversion reactions in childhood and adolescence. *J. Am. Acad. Child Psychiatry,* 23:424–430.

Wall, P.D. (1978), The gate control of pain mechanisms: A re-examination and re-statement. *Brain,* 101:1–18.

Wasserman, A.L., Whitington, P.F., and Rivara, F.P. (1988), Psychogenic basis for abdominal pain in children and adolescent. *J. Am. Acad. Child Adol. Psychiatry,* 27:179–184.

White, K., Koluan, M.L., Wexler, P., Polin, G., and Winter, R.J. (1984), Unstable diabetes and unstable families: A psychosocial evaluation of diabetic children with recurrent ketoacidosis. *Pediatrics,* 73:749–755.

Wilkinson, D.J. (1981), Psychiatric aspects of diabetes mellitus. *Br. J. Psychiatry,* 138:1–9.

Wolfer, J.A., and Visintainer, M.A. (1979), Prehospital psychological preparation for tonsillectomy patients: Effects on children's and parent's adjustment. *Pediatrics,* 64:646–655.

Wolff, S. (1969), *Children Under Stress.* London: Penguin, pp. 53–93.

Woolston, J.L. (1985), Eating disorder in childhood and adolescence. In: *Psychiatry,* Vol. 2, ed. R. Michaels. Philadelphia: J.B. Lippincott Co.

Zborowski, M. (1962), Cultural components in responses to pain. *J. Soc. Issues,* 8:16–30.

21

DYING AND DEATH IN CHILDHOOD AND ADOLESCENCE: CONCEPTS AND CARE*

Dying is a transitional state in which the child and the family may look to the physician for understanding, support, and direction. However, a physician may experience anxiety in the presence of a dying child because of (1) the feelings of impotence, failure, and anxiety that are aroused in the physician when confronted with his or her own limitations and mortality, (2) the regressive pull the child's loneliness, abandonment, neediness, and insecurity evoke in the physician, and (3) the difficulty of dealing with the parents' anxiety, depression, anger, resentment, and denial. It is important that health professionals be aware of these feelings lest they unconsciously act to isolate the child and family.

Yet there is probably almost nothing that the child or parent fears, imagines, feels, or experiences that cannot be discussed with the child in an honest way. The basis for the discussion is a trusting relationship. Children in particular soon learn whom they can trust and hence whom they can open up to. Indeed, the child often senses more accurately what the adult can tolerate than the adult senses how much the child can assimilate, and the child acts accordingly.

*This chapter is modified from M. Lewis and D.O. Lewis (1973), *Pediatric Management of Psychological Crises*. Chicago: Year Book Medical Publishers, and from M. Lewis and D.O. Lewis (1980), Death and dying in children and their families. In: *The Physician and the Mental Health of the Child* (Vol. 2), Chicago: American Medical Association.

CHILDREN'S CONCEPTS OF DEATH

The child's reaction to his or her own dying or to the death of others is related in part to his or her concept of death (Anthony, 1940; Gartley and Bernasconi, 1967; Schilder and Wechsler, 1934; Wolff, 1969), which in turn is related to his or her developmental stage (Table 21–1)

During the first few years, the child ordinarily has virtually no concept of death other than of death as a disappearance. However, when faced with traumatic events, such as the death of a parent, children under 5 years of age may develop what seems to be a precocious understanding of death.

Children between 5 and 10 years of age (approximately) are beginning to clarify their concepts of death but are still at times confused. For example, a child may say, "When I die, my heart stops, I can't see, and I can't hear. But if I'm buried, how will I breathe?" Some of the child's difficulty in thinking clearly about death is developmental, but some of the difficulty is emotional. If the child of this age has a heightened concern about a part of his or her body and its functioning, he or she may tend to think of death in terms of the harm to that part of the body and its functioning, especially since the child also tends to think in concrete terms at this stage.

Somewhere between 10 and 15 years of age, the child acquires a grasp of the meaning

Table 21–1. Death and Childhood

	BEFORE	DURING — Sudden	DURING — Acute	DURING — Chronic	AFTER — Sudden	AFTER — Acute	AFTER — Chronic
Child	Ideas on Death; Death and Stage Anxieties					Anger at M.D., need for follow-up, over-idealizing, fantasy loss	Remorse; Relief and guilt
0–5	Abandonment, Punishment; Fear of loss of love		Avoidance of pain; Need for love	Withdrawal; Separation anxiety			
5–10	Concepts of inevitability, Confusion; Castration anxiety		Guilt (bad); Regression; Denial	Guilt (religious), regression, denial			
10–15	Reality; Control of body and other developmental tasks		Depression; Despair for future	Depression, Despair, anxiety, anger			
Parents	Sudden / Acute: Anxiety, Concern, Hopefulness / Chronic: Premature mourning, anticipatory grief, guilt, reaction formation and displacement, need for information	Disbelief; Displaced rage; Accelerated grief; Prolonged numbness	Desperate concern; Denial; Guilt	Denial; Remorse; Resurgence of love	Guilt; Mourning		
Siblings	Reactions to changes in parents (senses of loss of love and withdrawal)				1. Respond to reaction of parents; 2. Survivor guilt		
0–5							
5–10	Concern re their implication; Fearful for themselves						
10–15	Generally supportive						
Staff	Anxiety; Conspiracy of silence	Reaction: Withdraw. Tasks: 1. correct distortions, e.g., "am I safe?"; "will someone be with me?"; "will I be helped to feel better?" 2. comfort parents 3. allow hope and promote feeling of actively coping 4. protect dignity of patient					Need for aftercare of survivors; Autopsy request tact; Accurate information regarding disposal of body; Delay billing

of mortality (Kastenbaum, 1959). His or her reaction to death at this time is influenced more by emotional struggles than by intellectual capacities. Thus a young adolescent who is concerned with, among other things, sexual performance, control of impulses, physical intactness, and separation from parents may react with anxiety if any one of these sensitive conflict areas is involved in the fatal illness.

THE CHILD'S REACTION TO HIS OR HER OWN DYING

The very young child is mostly preoccupied with the discomfort of the illness, whether acute or chronic, and the separation and withdrawal that occur when hospitalization is necessary. A somewhat older child, although also troubled by pain and separation, interprets his or her illness according to his or her level of cognitive development and emotional conflicts. Thus, the child may interpret the illness as an act of "immanent justice" for the guilt he or she feels about some real or imagined misdeed. Usually the child shows regressive behavior in the face of the illness, hospitalization, treatment techniques, and fear of mutilation. Occasionally he or she shows a denial of discomfort or dread (Solnit and Green, 1959; Solnit, 1963) or may become overly concerned with practical matters in an attempt to avoid confronting these feelings. An older child who is aware of the finality of death may deny his or her own anxiety but may exhibit a depression, occasionally mixed with outbursts of anger and anxiety. This reaction is especially common in adolescents. As many as 40% of dying children and adolescents may exhibit psychiatric problems (Howarth, 1973). On the other hand, some children are astoundingly courageous and steadfast in the face of death.

The range of reactions is great. In a sense, all that has gone before contributes to the child's understanding of death and his or her reaction to it. Each child is an individual, and a myriad of variables influences the behavior of the child, the family, and the helping persons around him or her.

REACTION OF OTHERS TO THE DEATH OF A CHILD

An important determinant of the child's reaction to death is the reaction of those around him to death. Those others may be parents, siblings, or hospital staff members.

Reactions of Parents

General Reactions. The general reactions of parents have a chronologic sequence, starting before and continuing during and after the moment of death. Initial shock and denial of the diagnosis may last from a few seconds to a few months. This stage may be followed by anger ("Why my child?") or guilt ("If only I had. . ."). Sooner or later, the parent starts to bargain ("If he could only live to. . ."). This stage is followed by normal grieving and mourning over the impending loss and by the beginning of separation. Finally, a stage of resignation or acceptance can be reached.

Specific Reactions. *Perinatal and Early Infant Deaths.* Stillbirth often produces severe distress in the parents, leading to a difficulty in accepting that the baby is dead and recurrent thoughts about the dead baby (Forrest et al., 1982). Prolonged mourning may occur, up to a period of a year. Both parents may become depressed. If the sadness continues beyond a year, the marriage may suffer (Bourne and Lewis, 1984).

Sudden infant death syndrome (SIDS) is the most common cause of death in the first year of life. The etiology of the condition (or conditions) is still not clearly established (Brady and Gould, 1983). What is known is the reaction of the parents. The parents experience sudden severe grief, guilt, and bewilderment. The parents often feel that the death is their fault, and this feeling may be reinforced by police who interrogate the parents on the suspicion of child abuse and suffocation. SIDS is not caused by neglect or suffocation. Infants who die from SIDS appear to be well nourished, have no signs of injury, and generally have been in good health. The siblings have no history of being abused, and the reactions of the parents ring true. The siblings of the dead infant may feel guilty, and they may also fear that they too may die.

Rapid Death. When the death has occurred relatively rapidly (e.g., perhaps as a consequence of a brief illness), the period prior to death is filled with anxiety and concern. The parents may be desperately hopeful, but they may also have feelings of guilt and may need to deny the possibility of death as an eventual outcome. After a rapid death of their child, the parents may again feel some diffuse anger, which may be displaced onto the physician. This reaction may occur whether or not the physician has been diligent, but it is more likely to fester and be prolonged if the physician fails (out of his or her own discomfort) to show consideration at the time and to provide the opportunity for a follow-up interview. Over a period of time the parents will then go through their own characteristic mourning process. Their mourning may include some identification with the lost person and, occasionally, an overidealizing of the lost person (particularly in cases in which the parent also experiences the loss of what they had expected for the lost child). Additional possible reactions may include (1) a displacement of attitudes toward the dead child onto one or more of the surviving children, (2) attempts to fill the loss by another pregnancy, or (3) withdrawal for a time. These and other normal reactions should be respected and left alone.

Prolonged Dying. Occasionally, premature mourning may occur, with anticipatory grief and withdrawal of interest in the dying child, perhaps accompanied by the displacement of warm feelings onto an infant child in the family. Often, unacceptable thoughts arise. For example, a parent may find himself or herself wishing that the child would finally die and relieve everyone of the emotional and financial burden and suffering. Such a wish may horrify a parent and lead to the immediate

mobilization of certain defense mechanisms. A common defense mechanism is that of reaction formation: the parent becomes extraprotective in caring for the dying child. The parent may also feel guilty and may express his or her guilt (and anxiety) by asking repetitive questions that require tactful answers.

As a chronically ill child nears death, the parents may be filled with remorse and may experience a resurgence of love. Rarely, a denial that death is imminent may remain in force. After the death of a chronically ill child, parents may feel a mixture of relief and guilt, perhaps with feelings of remorse uppermost.

Reactions of Siblings

Siblings who are very young, especially those under 5 years of age, feel the withdrawal of the parent intensely and consequently feel a loss of love. Young siblings may view the death as an abandonment, as punishment, as the realization of unacceptable wishes—or as all three. Children between about 5 and 10 years of age generally are somewhat more concerned for the dying child and may also be fearful for themselves. Although it is expected that older children usually can muster a supportive attitude and temporarily assume parental roles for the younger siblings at home, even teenagers feel and react to parental withdrawal and may "act up" during such a trying time. They too require special attention. Children as well as adults may experience survivor guilt after the death of a child (Lifton, 1967). Some surviving children suffer serious symptoms and subsequent distortions of character structure (Cain et al., 1964).

Reactions of Hospital Staff

Hospital staff members also experience anxiety in the presence of a dying child or a grieving parent (Solnit and Green, 1959), and they tend sometimes to deal with that anxiety by withdrawal and a conspiracy of silence. The pediatrician should be aware that overly solicitous care may distract him or her from exploring the feelings that the child and parent should be dealing with. These reactions may hamper them from giving the dying child and the family the best care possible and may prevent the staff members from carrying out certain essential psychologic tasks. Besides comforting the parents, such tasks are helping the child feel as active as possible in his or her attempts to cope with anxiety and allowing the child some hope. Furthermore, the privacy and dignity of the child require protection. Last, certain distortions require correction. The child, for example, may show his or her concern by asking such questions as "Am I safe?"; "Will someone be with me when I need them?"; "Will I be helped to feel better?" The continuing need for tact carries through into the period of care for the survivors.

CLINICAL CARE OF THE DYING CHILD

Talking with Parents about Fatal Illness

The hardest task for the physician is to tell the parents that their child is fatally ill. The physician should take the parents into a private office and allow a sufficient time for the interview, uninterrupted by telephone calls or other tasks. He or she can begin by telling the parents the diagnosis and the nature of the illness. He or she might then go on to describe the treatment that is available to offer some relief for the child's symptoms. At some point, the physician will have to tell the parents that there is no treatment that can cure the child of the illness or that the probability of successful treatment is small. Throughout this interview he or she should pause and give the parents every opportunity to express their feelings and ask questions. The physician must resist the understandable impulse to "shut off" their grief. If they ask whether the child will die from the illness, the physician will have to say that he or she will. If they do not ask, the physician should at some point attempt to clarify that the illness is progressive and that the child will die. At the same time, the physician must re-

member that the parents will not necessarily understand or accept what they have been told.

The physician should not end the interview then but should stay with the parents as they experience their shock (and perhaps anger) and grief. The physician might then tell the parents how he or she plans to treat the child and help the parents feel some measure of participation in and control of the treatment.

The physician is obliged to tell the parents what to expect as the illness progresses. This information need not be given in full in the first interview; rather, it should be given in stages over an extended period. The goal is to give the parents information that will enable them to anticipate the child's needs at each stage. The parents usually will indicate by their questions what they need to know.

Regular contact with the parents then should be planned. The contact should take the form not of comments made in passing but of time set aside to talk, review, and listen in the privacy of an office. The physician should resist the natural impulse to avoid the parents or avoid the subject. In order to do this, he or she must recognize the impotence and anger felt in the face of death. The parents will come to trust the physician and feel safe expressing, if they so wish, some of their less acceptable feelings if they are sure that he or she is available and ready to listen. During these planned interviews, the physician can discuss with the parents their child's behavior, their management of the child, what to tell the siblings, and whether and in what way they would like their minister, priest, or rabbi involved. The parents should be reassured about their own handling of the situation, and the physician should feel free to share his or her admiration for how well they are meeting the child's needs.

The physician may be asked for advice about religious rites for the sick. The practice of offering prayer with the child or administering the Sacrament for the Sick, although intended to comfort, may be anxiety arousing. Although it sometimes happens that the Sacrament of the Sick is given without the parents' consent, or even knowledge, most priests prefer to involve the parents and family first, and to have the family present in the room. However, administering the Sacrament of the Sick may cause as much upset in the family as in the child. The 1972 modification* of the Sacrament of the Sick does not significantly alter the way in which the child might experience the ritual. Indeed, there are no specific modifications for children other than those based on the judgment of the particular priest. The physician should discuss with the parents and the priest the child's needs and how the child might experience the praying or the Sacrament before any step is undertaken.

Talking with the Child

In regard to talking about death with the sick child, especially the young sick child, the parents' feelings and wishes must be respected. Some parents, for example, do not wish the child to be told that he or she is going to die, whereas others do. Some families need to use denial as a protective device.

There is no simple answer to the question of whether the particular child should be told. One useful approach is to discuss with the parents how they think they would respond if their dying child asked them whether he or she was going to die. There are several stages of response to such a question that might be suggested.

1. The child's reason for asking the question must be clarified. The child may be responding to the parents' or the hospital staff's anxious behavior, or the child may be concerned about such things as pain, mutilation, loneliness, and the needs of others. The child then can be given repeated opportunities to talk about what he or she is worried about.

2. If the parents decide that they want the child to know that his or her illness is fatal, the process of telling the child

Ordo Unctionis Infirmorum Eorumque Pastoralis Curae. In: *Rituale Romanum.* Rome: Typis Polyglottis Vaticanis, 1972, pp. 10 and 15.

about the illness and impending death should have the characteristics of a dialogue rather than of an announcement. Some children simply cannot understand and do not want to hear the truth; they should not be told. Others have to arrive slowly at the realization of the significance of their illness; it is too much for them to understand and grasp at one time.

3. The child must be given hope. Even when he or she is told that the illness is one that causes death, the child can and should be told that the physicians will do everything they can to fight the illness.

The adults must agree not only on *how* the child should be told but also on *who* should be the first to tell him. Sometimes the physician is not the right person to disclose this information. A parent or a clergyman who is close to the child may have a more sensitive understanding of the child's needs.

A discussion of this kind with parents often helps them to express some of their own concerns. It also promotes in them a feeling of trust and of being understood, as well as a feeling that they have some control over the care of their child. Nothing is so painful to the parents as their feeling of helplessness as their child's life ebbs.

Most important, the physician who has had a dialogue with the parents is prepared to have a dialogue with the child, always keeping in close touch with the parents. The physician, for example, can convey assuredness as he or she imparts to the child as much of the truth as the parents want and the child seems ready to know. There is no blueprint answer.

The ward staff members should be clear about who has the primary responsibility for talking with the parents and child about the seriousness of the illness. If it has been agreed on by the parents that the physician should tell the child, the physician should first establish a relationship of trust with the child. Before talking with the child, the physician should make sure that someone is available to be with the child after he or she has left the room if the child so desires. The involved staff members should know how much the child knows about the illness so that the child does not receive conflicting and therefore puzzling information. Ward staff members also experience anxiety when in the presence of a dying child or the family. Their natural inclination to avoid these feelings may cause them to stay away from both the child and the grieving family. Such inclinations may be better controlled if the ward staff members have the opportunity to explore and share their feelings in meetings (Lewis, 1962).

Specific Management of the Child Who Is Dying

Kübler-Ross (1972) gives a beautiful description of a dying boy's expression of his thoughts and feelings:

[The dying] boy tried to paint what he felt like. He drew a huge tank and in front of the barrel was a tiny little figure with a stop sign in his hand. This to me represents the fear of death, the fear of the catastrophic, destructive force that comes upon you and you cannot do anything about it. If you can respond to him by saying it must be terrible to feel so tiny and this thing is so big, he may be able to verbally express a sense of smallness or impotence or rage. The next picture he drew was a beautiful bird flying up in the sky. A little bit of its upper wing was painted gold. When he was asked what this was, the boy said it was the peace bird flying up into the sky with a little bit of sunshine on its wing. It was the last picture he painted before he died. I think these are picture expressions of a stage of anger and the final stage of acceptance.

This description underscores the importance of one aspect of the care of the dying child: with the parents' permission and in the privacy of his or her own room, the young child should be given the opportunity on different occasions to express concerns through drawings or through play with toys and dolls. If necessary, and if the parents agree, the collaboration of a child psychiatrist should be sought. The opportunity for expressive play enables the child to exercise some control over his or her anxiety. If the child expresses

concern about such problems as pain, loneliness, and fear through this play, this fact should be noted mentally by the physician. At another time, the child could be reassured, without reference to the play session, that the physicians will make sure that he or she does not have pain, that there will always be someone available to help, and that everything will be done to help him or her feel better. (Such a reassurance during the play itself may cause a child to feel tricked and exposed and so may inhibit future play.)

Patients—adults and children alike—feel threatened by the passivity imposed on them by illness. Every effort must be made to give the child a feeling of active participation in his or her treatment. The child should be informed at each stage what is being done, why it is being done, and what to expect. Some feeling of hope needs to be provided. Last, the dignity of the child requires protection, and his or her privacy should be ensured.

Denial of death in a child, as in an adult, is a defense against anxiety, and it should be respected. Each person must be allowed his or her own way of dealing with the dread of death. At the same time, certain distortions should be corrected. For example, the child may require reassurance that the illness was not brought about by anything the child did (or thinks he or she did). Reactions that generate further anxiety, such as regression, should be gently but firmly controlled by the parents as well as by the hospital staff; excessive regressive behavior is uncomfortable for a child as well as for those caring for the child.

Children vary in their capacity to deal with the inevitability of their impending death or with the diagnosis that implies impending death. Some children, particularly older children, want to know, whereas others do not want to know or cannot comprehend.

The Moribund Child

In a situation in which a child has no brain activity and is being kept alive by artificial methods, and there is no hope of spontaneous respiration or recovery of brain function, the physician must proceed with tact. First, before any decision is made to stop artificial life supports, the parents must be fully informed and prepared. The physician first might tell them that the child is being kept alive by machines but that there is no possibility that the child will breathe on his or her own or will recover brain function. The physician should explain why this is so. In some instances, the parents have already considered the issue and will have decided to discontinue artificial life supports. Such parents may also have decided whether they want to be in the room at the time of death. Other parents may experience great anguish at the burden of deciding to discontinue artificial respiration and may also prefer not to know exactly when it will be stopped. In a tactful way, the physician can say to such parents that there is nothing more that can be done. Then when the parents do decide to discontinue life support the physician should ask the parents where they want to be when it is discontinued.

The parents' wishes must be respected at all times; the child is theirs. The parents should not be rushed. It is always their decision to make, and they need all the help they can receive.

It is essential also that the parents feel a sense of unanimity with and security in the entire ward staff. Therefore, before the plan is carried out, the staff physician should discuss with all the ward staff members the steps just outlined and should encourage them to express their thoughts and feelings. Patients tend to seek different answers from different staff members, and it is essential that all the staff members are aware of the way in which an individual case is being handled so that their responses do not conflict.

If the child dies suddenly without the parents' being present, the parents should be informed of the death immediately, no matter what the time of day. The parents' sense of guilt at not being present when their child dies is an enormous one.

Management of Parents During Prolonged Illness in the Child

The many different reactions that parents may have when the period of dying is one of prolonged suffering necessitate sensitive management. Some parents may request other opinions regarding prognosis or treatment. Often they should be given this opportunity. Sometimes, however, a futile search for a magical cure may devastate a family emotionally and financially. The physician then should gently attempt to steer the parents toward a more realistic and helpful way of coping with their feeling of impotence. The physician can help parents by giving them opportunities to talk about their feelings in an accepting, nonjudgmental way. For example, parents often feel relieved when the physician reassures them that they are doing everything they can and that he or she knows how hard it is for them. The physician can also say, "Many parents have told me how at times they had wished it would all finally end, and then felt bad about thinking that. But it's a natural thought to occur. We all have all kinds of thoughts. What is important is that you have done everything that could possibly be done."

Questions may arise about child rearing during the long period of time during which remissions occur and treatment is administered. Although his or her condition is far from normal, there is often a wish on the part of the child to feel normal. Perhaps this represents in part the child's wish that he or she no longer had the disease, that there was no longer a need for painful treatments, and that he or she could talk freely with others about feelings of frustration, anger, and resentment.

At the same time, parents may be in a quandary about how to rear the child, siblings about how to relate to the child and deal with their guilt, and teachers about how to educate and deal with the child and the other children in the classroom. Once again, there is no blueprint answer; indeed, blanket recommendations (e.g., "Treat the child normally") may only burden the parents with more conflicts and guilt. Each situation must be thought out and managed individually, taking into account the many needs of the child, the parents, and the siblings, with respect for all concerned.

Management of Siblings

Good medical management takes into account how the child's dying and death affect the siblings. Siblings of all ages need support and explanations, and the physician can help the parents provide them. The physician may suggest that the parents gather the family together and then give a simple explanation to all the children. The explanation should include the facts that Johnny is very ill, that everyone is trying to make him as comfortable as possible, that the illness Johnny has could not be prevented, that it is no one's fault, and that it is necessary to figure out together how eveyone can help. Later, individual children in the family may be given more information as they give evidence that they require it. If the siblings are told that death is near, they will also need help on how to conduct themselves in the presence of the dying child. The dying child needs their support, and they can give it by doing such things as making drawings for the child, bringing messages from others, and getting things he or she may need. If the dying child asks them whether he or she is going to die, they can say, "I don't know. I know it's a serious illness. Would you like me to ask Mommy and Daddy, or do you want to ask them yourself?"

When the child dies, in order to avoid hurt feelings, all the siblings should be told of the death at the same time if possible. A simple account of the death can be given if the children ask about it. It is better to avoid such statements as, "He died in his sleep," especially when young children are present, because of the danger of engendering in them a fear of sleep.

A visit to the home by the physician is nearly always deeply appreciated by the parents and siblings of the dead child. If the physician has had a longstanding relationship with the family, he or she should ask about the funeral or memorial service, and should attend the service. A physician who had provided extended care for a dying child may be remembered only for a failure to attend the funeral service or to convey his or her condolences.

Sometimes a parent will ask whether a young sibling should attend the funeral. The physician first should decide whether the parent will probably be in control of himself or herself and who else will be present at the funeral who could support the child. For children under 5 years of age, the funeral can be a puzzling experience unless it is explained and unless a great deal of support is given by a familiar and caring adult. Attendance also depends on cultural practices. Children over 5 years of age often can utilize the funeral rite in the same way as adults to, especially if they have adults in attendance who can also explain to them their feelings and describe what is taking place. A child who does not wish to attend the funeral should not be made to feel guilty. Rather, arrangements should be made for him or her to be in the company of an understanding adult during the time of the funeral. Older children should be encouraged to attend the rites and observe the rituals the adults are attending and observing since, again, these practices usually help one to deal with the reality of death. If the older child chooses not to attend the funeral, the reason for the choice should be explored with him or her, but if the child continues to feel that he or she does not want to attend, these wishes should be respected. Each person mourns in his or her own way. In no circumstance should the subject of the dead person be closed off. A wall of silence hampers the child as he or she struggles with the reality of the death and his or her feelings about death. Some of the specific ways of helping children understand the many facets of death have been described by Wolf (1958).

Other questions involving siblings may arise later. A younger sibling may ask to have some of the dead child's toys. The transfer can be done in a helpful way by suggesting that the dead child would have wanted his or her younger brother or sister to have his or her toys. Other decisions, such as rearranging the dead child's room or giving a sibling the dead child's room, might be deferred until most of the work of mourning has been done. Such decisions can probably be made on a rational basis then, when the mourners are less affected by their emotions.

Requesting Autopsy Permission Or Organ Donation

A difficult task for the physician is requesting autopsy permission or organ donation. Because of the difficulties, the request is frequently made in a hasty, tactless manner. The physician must be aware that many families have strong feelings against such procedures. For example, Orthodox Judaism prohibits the permanent removal of organs. Despite the physician's medical curiosity and zeal to learn, he or she must resist pressuring a family into agreeing to a procedure to which it objects. On the other hand, the physician may legitimately describe an autopsy to the parents as a postmortem internal examination that determines the cause of death and the effects of the treatment given. The physician can honestly present to them the possible potential benefits of an autopsy or organ donation to others. If the physician is asked whether the child will be cut open, he must answer honestly, even if he or she knows that the autopsy or donation request may then be refused. Families who refuse to agree to such procedures should not be made to feel guilty about their refusal.

WHEN A PARENT DIES

The Children

When a parent dies, the physician should help the surviving parent anticipate the reactions to be expected from the children. Children, particularly young children, are unable to tolerate—and therefore complete—the painful task of mourning the death of a parent. Sad feelings often are curtailed, and often the child quickly returns to everyday activities as if nothing had changed. Although mourning in extremely young children is brief, it is difficult to assess the impact of a parent's death on the child's future personality development. Occasionally, a child may express hostile feelings toward the surviving parent. The child may actually be angry at—and feel abandoned by—the parent who died. Because such feelings usually are experienced as unacceptable, the child displaces them onto the surviving parent. The expression of hostile feelings toward the surviving parent unfortunately invites punishment when it is misunderstood. Frequently, a child, by virtue of his or her still somewhat primitive way of viewing the world, is convinced that he or she caused the parent's death, either by not being a good child or by having at one time or another wished the parent dead. When the child provokes the surviving parent, he or she may in part be seeking punishment to assuage feelings of guilt. Therefore, it is necessary to prepare a parent for these reactions as well as to attempt to correct the child's fantasies.

The child who has lost a parent is a child at psychiatric risk (Furman, 1974). This is particularly true of the child who loses a mother. Impairments in the child's capacity to form new, lasting relationships may show up later. Shame at being different may be experienced. Impaired sexual identity and conscience formation also may occur (Neubauer, 1969; Bonnard, 1962). In addition, the loss of a parent during childhood may predispose a child to attempted suicide during adolescence.

The family disruption and the reactions of the surviving parent may lead to a depression in the child. The presenting symptom may be a school learning problem or a behavior difficulty. Another hazard that sometimes occurs is a morbid attachment of the surviving parent to a child of either sex, particularly an adolescent. The adolescent in question may have great difficulty in separating from the parent or may develop along homosexual lines.

On the other hand, as development proceeds, the child may be able to continue the work of the mourning on a piecemeal basis. As his or her cognitive capacity matures and his or her reality testing is strengthened, the child may at some later date be able to express some of the feelings that were repressed. These feelings may include yearning and sadness as well as anger and resentment.

The physician can help most if he or she can enable the parent, who is also in a state of mourning and withdrawal, to recognize the needs of the child. The child needs to know that there is someone to depend on to meet his or her needs and to whom he or she can express feelings. In some instances, the physician may appropriately support the parent in this role by being available to the child if the parent agrees. The pediatrician should not hesitate to suggest a consultation with a child psychiatrist if he or she is especially concerned about the child's behavior.

The Surviving Parent

The death of a parent almost always disrupts a family. As far as possible, the physician should help the family to maintain its stability and to avoid making hasty decisions while the family is in a state of acute grief. The services of a relative or a homemaker may be helpful during this acute period. Some tact is required as the physician tries to steer a course that will not be experienced by the parent ether as intrusive or as an abandonment.

The disruption in the family caused by the death of a parent is not confined to the period of mourning. Loss of income, reduction in the amount of time that can be spent with the children, changed roles for the surviving spouse, caretaking responsibilities for the older children in the family, and altered social relationships are some of the repercussions that continue to affect the family. The physician should remain accessible to the members of the family. Sleep difficulties, psychosomatic disturbances, or school learning difficulties are some of the common signs of continuing distress. Psychiatric evaluation of these difficulties may be indicated (see Chap. 24).

REFERENCES

Anthony, S. (1940), *The Child's Discovery of Death*. New York: Harcourt, Brace & World.

Bonnard, A. (1962), Truancy and pilfering associated with bereavement. In: *Adolescents*, ed. S. Lorand and H.L. Schneer. New York: Paul Hoeber Medical Division, Harper & Row.

Bourne, S., and Lewis, E. (1984), Delayed psychological effects of perinatal death: The next pregnancy and the next generation. *Br. Med. J.*, 289:147–148.

Brady, J.P., and Gould, J.B. (1983), Sudden infant death syndrome: The physician's dilemma. *Adv. Pediatr.*, 30:635.

Cain, A.C., Fast, I., and Erickson, M.E. (1964), Children's disturbed reactions to the death of a sibling. *Am. J. Orthopsychiatry*, 34:741.

Forrest, G.C., Standish, E., and Baum, D. (1982), Support after perinatal death: A study of support and counselling after perinatal bereavement. *Br. Med. J.*, 285:1475–1478.

Furman, E. (1974), *A child's parent dies: studies in childhood bereavement*. New Haven: Yale University Press.

Gartley, W., and Bernasconi, M. (1967), The concept of death in children. *J. Genet. Psychol.*, 110:71–85.

Howarth, R.B. (1972), The psychiatry of terminal illness in children. *Proc. Roy. Med. Soc.*, 65:1039–1040.

Kastenbaum, R. (1959), Time and death in adolescence. In: *The Meaning of Death*, ed. H. Feifel. New York: McGraw-Hill Book Co.

Kübler-Ross, E. (1972), On death and dying. *JAMA*, 221:174.

Lewis, M. (1962), The management of parents of acutely ill children in the hospital. *Am. J. Orthopsychiatry*, 30:60.

Lifton, R.J. (1967), *Death in Life*. New York: Random House.

Neubauer, P.B. (1960), The one-parent child and his oedipal development. *Psychoanal. Study Child*, 15:286.

Schilder, P., and Wechsler, D. (1934), The attitudes of children toward death. *J. Genet. Psychol.*, 45:405–451.

Solnit, A.J. (1963), The dying child. *Dev. Med. Child Neurol.*, 7:693.

Solnit, A.J., and Green, M. (1959), Psychologic considerations in the management of deaths on pediatric hospital services. I. The doctor and the child's family. *Pediatrics*, 24:106.

Wolf, A.W.M. (1958), *Helping Your Child to Understand Death*. New York: Child Study Association of America, Inc., pp. 7–44.

Wolff, S. (1969), *Children Under Stress*. London: Penguin.

22

CHILD AND ADOLESCENT PSYCHIATRIC CONSULTATION AND LIAISON IN PEDIATRICS

HISTORICAL BACKGROUND

Pediatricians and child psychiatrists share an interest in fostering the optimal medical care of children and adolescents. The two specialties share important historic links; child psychiatry developed, in part, from the field of pediatrics and many early child psychiatrists were also pediatricians. The need to provide psychiatric services to pediatrics was recognized in the 1930 White House Conference on Child Health and Protection, which recommended that pediatricians, child psychiatrists, child psychologists, and social workers collaborate in the care of the whole child (JCMHC Report, 1970). Since that conference, similar recommendations have been made periodically (Kanner, 1937; Senn, 1946; Lourie, 1962; Eisenberg, 1967; Anders, 1977; Rothenberg, 1979; Anders and Niehans, 1982; Jellinek; 1982), culminating in official statements by the two respective national organizations: the American Academy of Pediatrics published *The Future of Pediatric Education* (1978) and the American Academy of Child Psychiatry published *Child Psychiatry: A Plan for the Coming Decades* (1983). Both consultation (direct service) and liaison (indirect service) have been identified as important needs.

PRESENT NEEDS

Surveys of outpatient pediatric populations suggest that 5 to 15% exhibit behavioral, ed-

ucational, or social problems, and that 8 to 10% have psychosomatic symptoms (Sarfield et al., 1980). Of children with chronic illness, 12 to 13% have diagnosable emotional problems (Rutter et al., 1970; Goldberg et al., 1979). Children who are hospitalized on pediatric wards are in even greater need of child psychiatric consultation. Stocking et al. (1972) have shown that almost two-thirds (63.7%) of children admitted to pediatric wards would have benefited from child psychiatric consultation. Because about 3,750,000 children are hospitalized at least once in a given year (DHHS, 1981), approximately 2,400,000 hospitalized pediatric patients might benefit from a psychiatric consultation. Children under 5 years of age who have had two or more admissions are still more likely to have psychiatric symptoms, learning problems, and symptoms of a conduct disorder than are nonhospitalized controls (Quinton and Rutter, 1976). Thus, the psychologic needs of hospitalized children have been clearly documented, if difficult to satisfy.

SERVICES PROVIDED

Ideally a range of services is available. These include direct evaluation of children and adolescents within the pediatric setting, usually in response to a specific request or concern on the part of the pediatrician. In such instances, the child psychiatrist is typically asked to address a specific question or questions, and the focus of intervention may similarly be highly specific. In addition to consultation regarding management of specific cases, liaison services provide opportunities for integration of more general principles of child development and child psychiatry into pediatric care (Anders and Niehans, 1982). In all these endeavors, the child psychiatrist must develop good working relationships with members of various disciplines (e.g., pediatrics, nursing, and social work) and must have a good working knowledge both of the individuals involved and the system of medical care delivery to be effective. Given the complexity of modern inpatient care, it is particularly important to identify those professionals most centrally involved in the care of the child (Anders and Niehans, 1982).

Although referral patterns vary from service to service (Monelly et al., 1973; Mattson, 1976; Wrate and Kolvin, 1978; Jellinek et al., 1981), direct consultation requests are generally distributed over six broad categories (Lewis, 1978):

1. Psychiatric disorders requiring collaborative care, e.g., attempted suicide, and sexual abuse.
2. Differential diagnosis, e.g., convulsions and conversion reactions, abdominal pain and depression, and failure to thrive and parental deprivation.
3. Pediatric conditions in which the management of psychologic factors is critical to effective care, e.g., asthma, ulcerative colitis, and anorexia nervosa.
4. Serious pediatric conditions in which consequent psychologic reactions dominate the clinical management, e.g., dying patients.
5. Severe psychologic reactions to illness and hospitalization, e.g., stress reactions and separation anxiety.
6. Presence of a symptom that suggests a concomitant psychologic problem, e.g., behavioral problems, learning difficulties, and reactions to such family stresses as divorce. Referral patterns vary from service to service (Monelly et al., 1973; Mattson, 1976; Wrate and Kolvin, 1978; Jellinek et al., 1981).

The psychologic reactions to illness and hospitalization for which children often need help include regression, increased attachment behavior, feelings of helplessness and powerlessness, frightening fantasies, excessive anxiety often manifested by biopsychologic symptoms, and aggravation of premorbid psychologic problems. Parents' reactions include appropriate concern and care, acute anxiety and fear, and feelings of guilt and anger. Specific reactions in children and parents to specific conditions also occur. The specific reactions of a child to illness depend in part on the child's level of development and concept of his or her body, the reactions of the parents, and the nature of the disorder (e.g., birth defects; acute, chronic, or lethal illnesses) (Lewis, 1982). In addition, child psychiatric consultation is especially useful in the pediatric management of psychologic crises (Lewis and Lewis, 1973), including attempted suicide, child abuse, sexual assault, unwed pregnancy, minor issues, school avoidance problems, and both acute and chronic reactions to family disruption and parental divorce.

Consultation may be sought in advance of admission or in relation to specific procedures as an aspect of preparation of the child; it may also be requested to assist in the management of chronic disease. In relation to these services, both pediatricians and child psychiatrists share the assumption of interaction between biologic and psychosocial processes. Despite this shared assumption, it is clear that despite considerable levels of knowledge child psychiatric consultation is underutilized.

IMPEDIMENTS TO COLLABORATION

Unfortunately, the overall referral rate from pediatrics to psychiatry is low (Sack et al., 1977). Pediatricians usually request child psychiatry consultations on only about 10%

of pediatric patients (Stocking et al., 1972). Monelly et al. (1973) found that consultation requests occurred in only 1% of admissions. Thus the need in general is not being met. Part of the difficulty lies with child psychiatry, and part with pediatrics. One source of the difficulty arose when child psychiatry apparently shifted alliance and attention from pediatrics to general psychiatry in the 1950s as child psychiatry became a subspecialty of the American Board of Psychiatry and Neurology rather than a subspecialty of pediatrics. The American Board of Pediatrics, however, insisted that a pediatrician always be a member of the Committee on Certification in Child Psychiatry. Consequently, child psychiatry consultation in pediatrics continues to be a requirement for training and certification in child psychiatry (American Medical Association, 1983). Nevertheless, training in the basics of pediatrics is still not a requirement for child psychiatrists, and neither is training in the basics of child psychiatry a requirement for pediatricians. Pediatric training in child development is often minimal. More recently, child psychologists and other related professionals are becoming readily available in pediatric settings (Houpt, 1985). Child psychologists bring areas of expertise to consultation liaison work, particularly in the areas of psychological and behavioral assessment and treatment; conversely, their knowledge of medical conditions is often limited.

Numerous other impediments to collaboration between pediatricians and child psychiatrists have been cited, including:

1. the failure of child psychiatrists to understand how pediatricians function in practice, and vice versa,
2. the degree of availability of child psychiatrists,
3. professional identity problems in both disciplines,
4. different perceptions of patients (Fritz and Bergman, 1985),
5. different interviewing ("anamnesis" versus "listening") techniques,
6. anxiety among pediatricians in dealing with emotional problems of children and their families,
7. inappropriate reactions based on personal experience (transference and countertransference issues),
8. time constraints in both pediatric rotation training schedules and in-patient load,
9. financial considerations, including inadequate funding for child psychiatry consultation services in pediatrics (Wright et al., 1987),
10. ambivalent support for the concept of coordinated multidisciplinary care for the whole child and his or her family,
11. limited opportunities for continuity of care in pediatric training,
12. compartmentalized disease-oriented research rather than collaborative biopsychosocial research, and
13. inadequate outcome studies.

Because each of several specialists who care for the child, including developmental and behavioral pediatricians, child psychologists, and child neurologists, has its expertise to offer, planning the ideal comprehensive care of the child is sometimes further impeded by competition and confusion. For example, while the behavioral approach has much to offer in pain control, preparation for procedures, and management of eating disorders and toilet training disturbances, the unique contributions of the child psychiatrist probably lie mostly in the areas of diagnosis of psychiatric disorders and in specialized psychiatric treatments utilizing psychopharmacology. Yet these various special skills may not always be appreciated in choosing the best approach to the diagnosis and treatment of the child.

The identity problems in both disciplines may be a special difficulty that affects their professional relationship with each other. Pediatrics, according to some observers (Lantos, 1987) is currently experiencing an identity crisis based in part on the change that is now occurring within the field. Traditional pediatrics, which in the past has included primary care and prevention, is in danger of becoming obsolete. In modern pediatrics, hospital care of the rare and more unusual infant and childhood diseases is emphasized more than ever for pediatric residents, and has virtually ousted longitudinal primary care and prevention as valuable enterprises.

Child and adolescent psychiatry too is experiencing an identity crisis based in part on the tremendous changes that have occurred within the field. From the 1930s through the 1960s psychoanalysis was a central and dominant force in child psychiatry. Then, beginning perhaps in the late 1960s and early 1970s, an astonishing change began to occur in child psychiatry. A surge of methodologically rigorous data-based scientific studies began to be emphasized in the field, and a broad-based biopsychosocial model for understanding psychopathology began to serve as a foundation for multimodal multidisciplinary treatment methods.

This major scientific shift is reflected in the scientific contents of what is now the *Journal of the American Academy of Child and Adolescent Psychiatry*. Beginning in 1975, the *Journal* contents changed from papers that were largely oriented to service delivery issues to scientifically sophisticated papers coauthored by various child specialists and reporting data-based research on such major childhood psychopathologic conditions as attention deficit hyperactivity disorder, childhood autism, and major depressive disorder (Lewis, 1986; AACP, 1983). Much of this change occurred because of the use of (1) the Diagnostic and Statistical Manuals of Disorders (DSM-III and DSM-III-R) (APA, 1980, 1987), which established criteria for diagnoses, (2) structured interviews that improved the reliability and comparability of research data (Young, et al., 1987), (3) advanced statistical techniques, and (4) the technology and knowledge available in such related fields as genetics, neurochemistry, pharmacology, immunology, and diagnostic imaging. In essence, the shift has completely changed the face and substance of child and adolescent psychiatry.

Child psychiatrists trained before the 1960s sometimes feel breathless at this astonishing scientific spurt in their field, as well as beleaguered by their nonmedical colleagues, especially psychologists and social workers, who often are equally competent in the psychotherapeutic skills hitherto cherished by psychiatrists as a treasured possession unique to their field. Nevertheless, modern child and adolescent psychiatry now demands a higher precision in diagnosis than was formerly required, incorporates a broad-based biopsychosocial understanding of psychiatric disorders of childhood and adolescence, and orchestrates a multifaceted, multidiscipline treatment plan for the child and his or her family. Treatment includes ongoing collaboration with child psychologists, social workers, child neurologists, and other specialists.

SOLUTION

How, then, can the disciplines better collaborate for improved psychiatric consultations in pediatrics? We know quite well the *areas* in which they should collaborate: service, teaching (Lewis and Colletti, 1973), and research (Anders, 1979).

Members of the child psychiatric consultation team should function at four levels in the consultation process, particularly on the pediatric wards. They should attend (1) to the intrapsychic life of the child, (2) to the family dynamics, (3) to the relationship between the child and the family and the ward staff, and (4) to the interdisciplinary dynamics among pediatrician, house officer, nurse, and social worker.

What we still have to refine is the *process* of collaboration in a child psychiatric consultation service in pediatrics. On the basis of the foregoing, the following points are essential:

1. There must be ready availability (and visibility) of child psychiatrists and child psychologists as part of a team in every pediatric setting. This can be done through participation in ward rounds, conferences, and meetings. This liaison

work constitutes an important matrix or substrate enabling consultation work to flourish.

2. There might be an awareness or, better still, a familiarity by the pediatrician, child psychiatrist, and child psychologist of the multiple levels of a consultation and of the transference and countertransference issues involved, and the clinical methods of each discipline.

3. A clear definition of the consultation request is necessary, including:
   Who is asking for the consultation?
   What are the consultation questions?
   What is the time frame for the consultation?
   Is there an implicit question or hidden agenda?
   What previous or current workup is available?
   Have the parents been informed?
   Have all the aforementioned been discussed first with the responsible physicians, prior to doing the consultation?

4. The child psychiatrist must develop a technique appropriate to the pediatric setting (Lewis, 1988).

5. The child psychiatric consultant should write a concise and useful report, including the question to be addressed, a summary of the pertinent data, a diagnosis, useful treatment recommendations, and subsequent follow-up plans.

6. Mutual ongoing *verbal* as well as written communication between psychiatric consultant and pediatrician is essential. (They should talk to each other.)

Besides attention to these six basic points, attention could well be paid to each of the other multiple impediments to the collaboration mentioned earlier. Among these items, the following deserve special attention: An empathic understanding and easing of anxiety in the caring staff as well as in the child and his or her family are needed to diminish the desire to act out impulses. Realistic combined teaching and collaborative research opportunities for child psychiatrists and pediatricians should be explored. The departments of pediatrics and child psychiatry should share in some proportionate way the financial cost of child and adolescent psychiatric consultation and liaison services in pediatrics. Finally, a clear understanding and mutual respect for the methods and work styles of the respective disciplines are essential to quality health care.

REFERENCES

American Academy of Child Psychiatry (1983), *Child Psychiatry: A Plan for the Coming Decades.* Washington, D.C.

American Academy of Pediatrics (1978), A report by the Task Force on Pediatric Education: *The Future of Pediatric Education.* Elk Grove, IL.

American Medical Association (1983/1984), Essentials of accredited residency in child psychiatry. In: *Directory of Residency Training Programs.* Chicago, p. 69.

American Psychiatric Association (1980), *Diagnostic and Statistical Manual of Mental Disorders*, 3rd Ed. Washington, DC.

American Psychiatric Association (1987), *Diagnostic and Statistical Manual of Mental Disorders*, 3rd Ed. Washington, D.C.

Anders, T.F. (1977), Child psychiatry and pediatrics: The state of the relationship. *Pediatrics*, 60:616–620.

Anders, T.F. (1979), Child psychiatry and pediatrics: The state of the relationship. *Pediatrics* 60 (Suppl.):616.

Anders, T.F., and Niehans, M. (1982), Promoting the alliance between pediatrics and child psychiatry. In: Pediatric Consultation-Liaison. ed. M. Sherman. *Psychiatr Clin. North Am.*, 5:241–258.

Eisenberg, L.(1967), The relationship between psychiatry and pediatrics: A disputatious view. *Pediatrics*, 39:645–647.

Fritz, G.K., and Bergman, A.S. (1985), Child psychiatrists seen through the pediatricians' eyes: Results of a national survey. *J. Am. Acad. Child Psychiatry*, 24:81–86.

Goldberg, I.D., Regier, D.A., McInery, J.K., et al. (1979), The role of the pediatrician in the delivery of mental health services to children. *Pediatrics*, 63:898–909.

Houpt, J.L. (1985), Introduction: Psychosomatic medicine, consultation-liaison psychiatry, and behavioral medicine. In *Psychiatry* (Vol. 2), ed. R. Michels. Philadelphia: J.B. Lippinott Co.

JCMHC Report (1970), *Crisis in Child Mental Health.* New York: Harper & Row, p. 5.

Jellinek, M.S. (1982), Sounding board: The present status of child psychiatry in pediatrics. *N. Engl. J. Med.*, 306:1227–1230.

Jellinek, M.S., Herzog, D.B., and Selter, L.F. (1981), A psychiatric consultation service for hospitalized children. *Psychosomatics*, 22:29–33.

Kanner, L. (1937), The development and present status of psychiatry and pediatrics. *J. Pediatr.*, 418–435.

Lantos, J. (1987), Baby doe five years later: Implications for child health. *N. Engl. J. Med.*, 317:444–447.

Lewis, M. (1978), Child psychiatric consultation in pediatrics. *Pediatrics*, 62:359–364.

Lewis, M. (1982), *Clinical Aspects of Child Development*, 2nd Ed. Philadelphia: Lea & Febiger, pp 307–341.

Lewis, M. (1986), The Journal 1975–1985. A decade of change. *J. Am. Acad. Child Psychiatry*, 25:1–7.

Lewis, M. (1988), Personal communication.

Lewis M., and Colletti RB (1973), Child psychiatric teaching in pediatric training: The use of a study group. *Pediatrics*, 52:743–745.

Lewis, M., and Lewis, D.O. (1973), *The Pediatric Management of Psychological Crises*. Chicago: Year Book Medical Publishers, Inc.

Lourie, R.S. (1962), The teaching of child psychiatry in pediatrics. *J. Am. Acad. Child Psychiatry*, 1:477–489.

Mattson, A. (1976), Child psychiatric ward records on pediatrics. *J. Am. Acad. Child Psychiatry*, 15:357–365.

Monelly, E.P., Ianzito, B.M., and Stewart, M.A. (1973), Psychiatric consultations in a children's hospital. *Am. J. Psychiatry*, 130:789–790.

Public Health Service, DHHS Panel Report (1981), Select Panel for the promotion of child health. Better health for our children. DHHS (PHS), 79:55–71.

Quinton, D., and Rutter, M. (1976), Early hospital admissions and later disturbances of behavior: An attempted replication of Douglas' findings. *Dev. Med. Child Neurol.*, 18:447–459.

Rothenberg, M.B. (1979), Child psychiatry-pediatric consultation liaison services in the hospital setting: A review. *Gen. Hosp. Psychiatry*, 1:281–286.

Rutter, M., Tizard, J., and Whitmore, K. (eds.) (1970), *Education, Health and Behavior*. London: Longmans.

Sack, W., Cohen, S., and Grout, C. (1977), One year's survey of child psychiatry consultations in a pediatric hospital. *J. Am. Acad. Child Psychiatry*, 16:716–727.

Senn, M.J.E. (1946), Relationship of pediatrics and psychiatry. *Am. J. Dis. Child.*, 711:537–549.

Starfield, B., Gross, E., Wood, M., et al. (1980), Psychosocial and psychosomatic diagnoses in primary care of children. *Pediatrics*, 66:159–167.

Stocking, M., Rothberg, W., Grosser, G., et al. (1972), Psychopathology in the pediatric hospital: Implications for the pediatrician. *Am. J. Public Health*, 62:551–556.

Wrate, R.M., and Kolvin, I. (1978), A child psychiatry consultation service to pediatricians. *Dev. Med. Child. Neurol.*, 20:347–356.

Wright, H.H., Eaton, J.S., Butterfield, P.T., et al. (1987), Financing of child psychiatry pediatric consultation-liaison programs. *J. Dev. Behavioral Pediatr.*, 8:221–226.

Young, J.G., O'Brien, J.D., Gutterman, E.M., and Cohen, P. (1987), Structured diagnostic interviews for children and adolescents. Introduction. *J. Am. Acad. Child Adoles. Psychiatry*, 26:611–612.

Part Four

Introduction to Clinical Psychiatric Diagnosis

23

THE PSYCHIATRIC EVALUATION OF THE INFANT, CHILD, AND ADOLESCENT

The immediate aims of the psychiatric evaluation of the child are to understand and define the child's behavior as accurately as possible, including the context in which it occurs, and to seek its causes. The ultimate aims are to assess normality, strengths, and psychopathologic conditions in order to recommend treatment, to predict the future course, to communicate to others, and to devise preventive interventions.

The methods used in the psychiatric assessment of the child and adolescent include (1) clinical interviews, (2) structured interviews, rating scales, and questionnaires, and (3) standardized tests, including psychologic, developmental, neurologic, educational, linguistic, and biologic studies. This chapter will focus on the clinical interview approach.

For a brief overview of recent studies on selected structured interviews, see Young, O'Brien, Gutterman, and Cohen (1987).

In a screening intake procedure, which may be done by telephone, the clinician obtains the patient's full name and telephone number and the name of the referring person. He or she then attempts to clarify the problem and the appropriateness of the referral (e.g., by asking, "Can you tell me something about the problem?"). The clinician also initiates the evaluation process by outlining briefly the steps and procedures (e.g., the number and kinds of interviews, and the administrative practices for such matters as permission forms and fees).

There are some built-in biases that affect how the clinician approaches the child and the family. For example, the source of the referral may be reflected in the diagnostic label used at the time of referral. Children referred by school officials are often labeled as having "learning difficulties," and the request is to "rule out organic disorder," almost as a ticket of admission. Children referred by juvenile court officials are readily viewed as "delinquent" or "sociopathic," with the bias that they are somehow therefore untreatable. Parents' concerns about a child often reflect their concerns about themselves or some prevailing family attitudes or worries. The clinician also has to assess the reliability of the witness or the history giver. Finally, there may be a hidden agenda, such as a custody suit that is pending.

In addition, clinicians, like other people, all have certain bêtes noirs: deformed children may repel the clinician at first; aggression in children often mobilizes strong defenses in the clinician; children with AIDS may evoke concerns about infection; and the psychiatric problems of mentally retarded children are often overlooked or given inadequate attention.

In approaching a diagnostic evaluation, the clinician should have in the back of his or her mind some idea of the important possibilities, along the lines of a psychiatric sieve or "decision tree." For the sake of simplicity, it can be said clinically that there are seven major basic categories of psychopathology to be screened for and assessed. The italic type in the following questions indicates what those categories are.

1. What is the level of *development* of the child? Is there a *neurodevelopmental delay?*
2. What degree of *organic dysfunction* is present, and to what degree does it affect perception, coordination, attention, learning, emotions, and impulse control?
3. Is there any evidence of a *thought disorder?*
4. What evidence is there of *anxiety, conflict, or neurotic symptoms* (e.g., phobic behavior, obsessive-compulsive behavior, hysterical behavior, or depression)?
5. Is there a *temperament* difficulty or *personality* disorder?
6. Is there a *psychophysiologic disorder?*
7. Is the child *reacting to an unfavorable environment* (family, school, community, or society)?

The categories are not mutually exclusive. In fact, problem behaviors from all categories may be present in some degree. Sometimes the behaviors are a cause of other behaviors; sometimes they are a consequence of a particular behavior. (The particular functions will be discussed in greater detail later in the chapter.)

Also to be kept in mind are possible significant predisposing or causative factors, which can be put into five major groups:

1. *Genetic factors*, as expressed, for example, in developmental dyslexia, attention disorders, mental retardation, autism, and schizophrenia.
2. *Organic causes,* including prenatal factors (e.g., malnutrition, exposure to radiation, the use of drugs during pregnancy, prematurity), traumatic factors (e.g., head injury), infective factors (e.g., encephalitis), neoplastic factors

(e.g., brain tumors), degenerative factors (e.g., cerebromacular degenerations), metabolic factors (e.g., thyrotoxicosis), and toxic factors (e.g., ingestion of amphetamines, steroids, and lead).
3. *Developmental immaturity*, whether due to intrinsic factors or external environmental factors (e.g., stimulus deprivation) or both.
4. *Inadequate parenting*, e.g., parental deprivation, separation, loss, abuse by parents (including sexual and physical abuse), ambivalence in parents, and psychiatric disorders in parents.
5. *Stress factors*, including illness, injury, surgery, hospitalization, school failure, poverty, life-events, and racial discrimination.

Again, all five groups of factors may interact.

THE PARENTS

With these "sets" in mind, the clinician starts usually by interviewing both parents together. Adolescents may prefer to be seen alone first, and they might be given the choice. In some instances, seeing the whole family together may be useful, especially for diagnostic purposes. Each spouse should also be seen individually in addition to being seen together with the other spouse.

In general, historic and factual data such as age, sex, race, legal status, birth history data, developmental milestones, and previous illnesses are best gathered by asking specific questions, whereas data about feelings and relationships are best explored by an open indirect approach. Parents in any case frequently recall historic dates incorrectly, although they may offer comparisons such as "Johnny was much slower in talking than Jane." To offset these shortcomings, data should be gathered from as many objective sources as possible, e.g., hospital records, school reports, previous evaluations, and tests, and from multiple observers (child, brother, father).

There are six parts to the evaluative process as far as the parents are concerned:

1. The clinician strives to get a detailed history of the child, which includes (a) a careful description of the problem and the parents' view of the problem, (b) the personal history, (c) the developmental history, (d) the history of previous illnesses, (e) the social history, (f) the family history, (g) the school history, (h) the history of such biologic functions as appetite, sleep, bladder and bowel control, growth, and menstruation, (i) a description of the child's relationships within the family and with peers, (j) a description of significant events, such as separations and losses, and (k) information about previous psychiatric, psychologic, and neurologic evaluations.

2. The clinician strives also to assess the psychiatric state of each parent, the marriage, and the family relationships, both nuclear and extended.

3. The parents should be given an opportunity to ask questions.

4. The clinician should again outline for the parents both the subsequent procedure and how the parents might prepare the child for it. An open-ended question like "Have you thought about what you will tell your child about coming to see me?" may elicit important information, e.g., do the parents intend to "trick" the child into coming? When necessary, parents should be given guidance on how the child should be prepared for the interview.

5. Various administrative matters (e.g., those regarding the fee, consent forms, and requests for outside information) should be discussed and settled.

6. The clinician must make a final review and recommendation.

THE INFANT

The developmental assessment of the preschool-age child requires a special approach.

Developmental scales and assessment techniques commonly used in the United States include the original Gesell and Amatruda scales as updated by Knobloch and Pasamanick (1974), the Bayley Scale (1969), the Denver Developmental Screening Test (Frankenburg and Dodds, 1967), and the Yale Revised Developmental Schedules (see Volkmar, 1989 for a review of assessment methods). However, for screening purposes, the items listed in Tables 23–1 and 23–2 are useful.

An evaluation of the parents' child rearing skills is particularly important in the psychiatric assessment of the infant. General characteristics to be assessed include the parents' physical health, self-esteem, competence, flexibility, and ability to provide a safe, nurturing, and appropriately stimulating environment. Specific characteristics to be assessed include the parents' perception of, and sensitivity to, the infant' needs, the "goodness of fit" of parent and infant, the parents' ability to respond rapidly on a contingent basis to the infant's expressed needs, the quality of play between parent and infant, and the amount of support, encouragement, and assistance ("scaffolding") the parents can provide for the child. The parents should also be able to provide a "stimulus barrier" to prevent the child from being overwhelmed.

Infants under 18 months of age should also subsequently be observed in spontaneous free play, using such games as peek-a-boo and pat-a-cake.

Children between 18 months and 3 years of age can participate more fully in regular constructed play interviews. The play items should look reasonably realistic because children at this age have a limited capacity for abstraction and symbolic play.

THE CHILD

Before the child is seen, space and time for the appointment should be set aside. The child should have enough space and appropriate equipment to play with such things as a ball, crayons and paper, Play-Doh, a dollhouse, rubber dolls, puppets, toy guns, a doc-

Table 23–1. **Checklist for Assessment by Observation of Developmental Level of Preschool-Age Child**

Age	Historical (or Observed) Items	Items to be Tested
2 years	Runs well Walks up and down stairs—one step at a time Opens doors Climbs on furniture Puts 3 words together Handles spoon well Helps to undress Listens to stories with pictures	Builds tower of 6 cubes Circular scribbling Copies horizontal stroke with pencil Folds paper once
2½ years	Jumps Knows full name Refers to self by pronoun "I" Helps put things away	Builds tower of 8 cubes Copies horizontal and vertical strokes (not a cross)
3 years	Goes upstairs, alternating feet Rides tricycle Stands momentarily on one foot Knows age and sex Plays simple games Helps in dressing Washes hands	Builds tower of 9 cubes Imitates construction of bridge with 3 cubes Imitates a cross and circle
4 years	Hops on one foot Throws ball overhand Climbs well Uses scissors to cut out pictures Counts 4 pennies accurately Tells a story Plays with several children Goes to toilet alone	Copies bridges from a model Imitates construction of a gate with 5 cubes Copies a cross and circle Draws a man with 2 to 4 parts—other than head Names longer of two lines
5 years	Skips Names 4 colors Counts 10 pennies correctly Dresses and undresses Asks questions about meaning of words	Copies a square and triangle Names 4 colors Names heavier of 2 weights

From R.S. Paine, and T.E. Oppé (1966), *Neurological Examination of Children.* New York: Heinemann, p. 40.

tor's bag, and a few games, such as checkers and cards. The list of toys can, of course, be expanded (e.g., to include toy telephones). The space and furniture in the room should be scaled to the child. Some small (one-inch) cubes are needed for the preschool-age child.

Two, three, or more interviews of approximately 30 to 60 minutes each are generally needed to allow for the child's anxiety over the unfamiliar and to get a better sample of his or her behavior.

The areas that will require closest examination are usually suggested in the interview with the child's parents. Thus the clinician might want to pay special attention to, say, organicity, a thought disorder, a developmental delay, mental retardation, or a specfic syndrome, such as Gilles de la Tourette syndrome.

In the organization of the interview with the child, a frame of reference is useful. The interview consists of four parts: (1) the introductory statements, (2) free play, (3) the mental status examination, and (4) the conclusion. In practice, these parts are not distinct; there is considerable overlapping, especially of free

Table 23–2.   Prototypic Age-Adequate Behavior Between 0–36 Months

Age (mo)	Communication	Daily Living	Socialization	Motor Skills
0–6	Listens when spoken to by caregiver; smiles in response to familiar person	Indicates anticipation of feeding on seeing bottle, breast, food; opens mouth when spoon is presented	Looks at face of caregiver; distinguishes caregiver from others; shows affection	Holds head erect for 15 seconds; picks up small object; with hands/thumb and fingers; transfers object
6–12	Raises arms when caregiver says "up," "come"; imitates adult sounds; understands meaning of at least 10 words; gestures appropriately (yes, no, and I want)	Removes food from spoon with mouth; eats solid foods; drinks from cup or glass unassisted	Shows interest in children; reaches for familiar person; plays with toy alone or with others; shows interest in others' activities	Raises self to sitting and stays 1 minute; crawls across floor, stomach up; opens doors by pulling or pushing; rolls ball while sitting
12–18	Listens attentively to instructions; follows instruction requiring action and object; names 20 objects without being asked; uses phrases containing a noun and a verb	Feeds self with spoon; understands hot things are dangerous; indicates wet or soiled clothes or diaper by gesture or sounds; feeds self with fork; removes front opening sweater, shirt by self	Imitates simple adult actions (e.g., clap, wave bye) when shown; laughs or smiles when praised; addresses at least two people by name (e.g., Mommy, Daddy); shows desire to please	Primarily walking; climbs both in and out of adult chair; marks with pencil, crayon on paper; walks up stairs, using both feet
18–24	Listens to story for five minutes; points to all body parts when asked; says 50 recognizable words; relates experience	Urinates in potty-chair; bathes self with assistance; demonstrates interest in changing wet or muddy clothes	Participates in one game or activity; imitates adult phrases heard previously; engages in elaborate make-believe play	Walks down stairs, putting both feet on each step; runs smoothly; opens doors with door knob; jumps over object
24–30	Points accurately to all body parts; says 100 recognizable words; speaks in full sentences	Defecates in potty-chair; asks to use toilet; toilet-trained at night; puts on "pull-up" pants; understands the function of money	Says "please" when asking for something; labels happiness, sadness, fear and anger in self	Screws and unscrews jar lid; pedals tricycle; hops on one foot, while holding on
30–36	States own first and last name when asked; uses "what," "where," "who," "why," and "when" questions	Brushes teeth without assistance; helps with extra chores	Shares toys without being told; follows rules in simple games without being reminded	Walks down stairs alternating feet; opens and closes scissors with one hand

From Carter, A., and Sparrow, S.: Adaptive behavior in infancy. *Sem. Perinatol.*, 13:476.

play and mental status examination, depending on the behavior of the particular child. (For example, some children want to play right away; others will not play or say a word.) The four parts of the interview are discussed separately in the paragraphs that follow.

The Introductory Statements

The clinician should keep a reasonable physical distance from the child in the waiting room in order not to loom too large and forbidding. The physician should introduce himself or herself to the child, and invite the child to accompany him or her to the office, reassuring the child that the parents will be in the waiting room when he or she returns. For a very young child it may be appropriate to evaluate the child in the presence of a parent. Once inside the office, the clinician should ask the child what he or she prefers to be called, and he or she should make sure the child knows the clinician's name. The clinician should clarify what is the child's understanding of why he or she has come and then give his or her own understanding of why the child has come. Next, the clinician should tell the child, in a developmentally appropriate way (e.g., for the school-aged child), what will take place: "It's a time set aside to see if I can help you understand what may be bothering you. We will have 45 minutes together, at the end of which you will return to your parents." The clinician should clarify the extent of the confidentiality: "I *will* be meeting with your parents, but I will *first* discuss with you what I will or will not say to your parents." In some circumstances, e.g., a court-ordered evaluation, there is no confidentiality, and a report must be rendered to the court. The clinician should inform the child of this fact.

It is probably best not to take notes during the interview. Note taking might inhibit the child, and it will inhibit the clinician in observing. The clinician should avoid asking leading questions or any kind of demanding interrogation since that too is unproductive and may inhibit the play and communication. Open-ended questions (e.g., "What happened then?") are better than leading questions or questions that require only a single answer. At least initially the child should be allowed to set the pace for the interaction. (A short bibliography covering the various practical techniques used in psychiatric interviews with children is given in the references for this chapter.)

Free Play

The clinician should invite the child to play (e.g., by saying, "Is there anything you would like to play with?") and should observe the play, perhaps encouraging the child with a word or two if he or she appears interested in playing with a particular toy. If appropriate, the clinician should engage in the play in an accepting, nondirective, and noncompetitive manner.

One need not be rigid about this. One may also begin by asking the child, "Who is in your family?" and may use the child's response as an opportunity to begin exploring the child's relationships with various family members. Aspects of the child's play such as the level of organization, nature of themes expressed, nature of play disruptions, and patterns of engagement with the examiner should be noted.

THE ADOLESCENT

Clinical interviews with adolescents require an even more explicit approach.

The clinician can explain to the adolescent that his or her parents have come to see the clinician and have discussed their concerns, but the clinician would like to learn directly the adolescent's views on what the parents have said, or on what bothers him or her. Sometimes the adolescent may be interviewed before the parents. The clinician should show genuine interest and should not try to deceive or be phony with the adolescent. The clinician should not overidentify with the adolescent's dress or talk, nor should he or she talk down to or belittle the adolescent's views. If the clinician feels bored, rushed, uncertain, or uncomfortable, he or she should think over these feelings, preferably *before* the interview with the adolescent. The clinician should give the adolescent his or her undivided and uninterrupted attention.

If the adolescent talks in terms of a third person ("I have a friend who. . . " or "I read that. . . "), the clinician should answer matter-of-factly, in the same third-person way. The adolescent is not fooling the clinician, and the clinician is not fooling the adolescent, but he or she is allowing the adolescent room to move, and the adolescent then will not feel so much on the spot.

Rejection, even outright hostility, on the first few visits with an adolescent is not uncommon. The clinician should be patient and not jump to conclusions: the anger may turn out to be a test of how much the clinician can be trusted, a defense against anxiety, or a transference phenomenon. The clinician should recognize the anger by saying something such as, "I can seen you're pretty angry at being here. What are you particularly angry about? Perhaps there is some way I can be of help to you."

Silence should not be allowed to go on for too long—it may just start a useless power game to see who can last longest. Similarly it is important not to be rigid about the length of the interview. The 50-minute session is not a sacred rule, and the clinician should feel free to vary the time according to the situation at hand. In some instances an adolescent might also feel more comfortable initially if he or she is invited to go for a walk with the clinician rather than sit face to face in a confined space.

The clinician must be particularly clear with the adolescent about the extent of confidentiality. When appropriate, the adolescent should be informed that a report will be made to a third party, such as a judge. A sense of trust is infinitely preferable to a feeling of betrayal, even at the expense of some tidbit of knowledge.

In general it is better not to give advice, but the clinician should not obsessively deny *any* opinion or advice. An occasional well-judged opinion (if asked) on the color of a lipstick or some well-chosen advice may help an adolescent feel understood and supported.

The clinician interviewing a child or adolescent can also sometimes offer an interpretation of an obvious preconscious feeling or fantasy: it is often eye-opening and clarifying for the child or adolescent, interests him or her, and sets a model for any subsequent psychotherapy that might be reommended. For example, the child's attention can be directed to the content of his or her actions or verbalizations. Sometimes attention can be drawn to a coincidence that the child has perceived but has not, or professes not to have, registered; more frequently, one can draw attention to certain paradoxes. Thus in the course of the child's play, the therapist may provide a verbal counterpart to the action being portrayed, to an affect that might be present, or to the conspicuous absence of certain persons, actions, or affects.

An 8-year-old boy with a severe school phobia repeatedly enacted a war scene in which the general was attacked and almost killed. Many fantasies were contained in this play, but one prominent feature was the absence of any female, not only in this play item but in any other play. After attention was drawn to this "fact," the child recognized his fear of attack from his mother, his wish to attack her, his resentment that his father was often attacked and offered him no protection, the displacement of his aggression toward his mother to his father, and his anxiety about even mentioning his mother.

This kind of interpretation during a diagnostic interview is different from the kind of direct translation of a possible unconscious symbolic representation in the play that may occur in the course of psychoanalytic psychotherapy. The play characteristic to which attention is here drawn is in bold relief, and is capable of being fully recognized and understood by the child.

Eventually the clinician must inquire about such sensitive areas as suicidal thoughts, hallucinations, use of drugs, and sexual relationships. This inquiry should be done in a matter-of-fact, straightforward manner.

Countertransference

During clinical interviews with children and adolescents the clinician should be aware of important countertransference as well as transference phenomena that may occur, i.e., unconscious reactions that affect the interaction. For example, children who are aggressive often tend to mobilize strong defenses in the clinician, the problems of mentally retarded children are often overlooked or inadequately served, and children with physical disabilities may initially repel some clinicians.

Other signs of countertransference include the following:

1. The clinician may fail to recognize where a child or adolescent is in his or her development. Expectations then are not commensurate with the child's or adolescent's maturational and developmental capacities.
2. The regressive pull experienced by the clinician interviewing a child or adolescent may give rise to the temptation to identify and/or act out with the child or adolescent.
3. A misreading by the clinician of the child's or adolescent's relationship to the clinician may occur, in which the relationship is regarded as realistic when in fact it may be a transference from the child's or adolescent's feelings toward his or her parents. Clinicians are usually well aware of a patient's aggressive feelings, but may be less aware of a child's or adolescent's seductiveness toward an adult (parent).
4. When the clinician is exposed to certain specific behaviors in the child or adolescent, old conflicts may be stirred up and may cause anxiety in the clinician. For example, aggressive behavior or disguised masturbation may be upsetting to the clinician.
5. Sometimes the clinician may transfer early feelings from *his* or *her* own childhood onto the parents of the child or adolescent, and may then overidentify with the child or adolescent in his or her struggle with the parents. Residual feelings from the clinician's own childhood relations with his or her brothers and sisters similarly may be an important source of ambivalence toward the child or adolescent.
6. Sometimes the clinician simply cannot understand the meaning of certain behavior in a child or adolescent. Of course, there are times when we all find some item of behavior inexplicable. However, the persistent drawing of a blank in understanding a repeated item of behavior should lead to the suspicion of an interference by one's own conflicts—an emotional blind spot, so to speak.
7. A clinician may find himself or herself feeling depressed or uneasy during work with a child or adolescent. Assuming the clinician is not suffering from a true depression, the possibility exists that emotions from old conflicts have been aroused and are interfering with the clinician's functioning or, of course, that the clinician is responding empathically to the child's affect. Occasionally a clinician may find himself or herself aroused and experiencing great affection for a patient. This too may interfere with his or her work with that child or adolescent.
8. A clinician may feel the wish to encourage acting out in a child or adolescent. For example, a clinician may suggest to a child or adolescent that he or she must stand up for himself or herself and hit back. The wish and the suggestion should be carefully examined.
9. A clinician may need the admiration obtained by having the child or adolescent like him or her. This too may represent a need of the clinician, and may not be in the best interests of the patient.
10. Conversely, repeated arguing with a child or adolescent may suggest that the clinician has not only become involved,

but has become enmeshed with that patient.

11. Recurring countertransference problems commonly arise in relation to specific characteristics of a child or adolescent. For example, a retarded child or adolescent may evoke guilt and defenses against such guilt in the clinician, or omnipotent rescue fantasies that are acted out. Passive, hostile children or adolescents may arouse anger in a clinician. Aggressive children and adolescents may evoke counteraggression. Sexually attractive children and adolescents of the same or opposite sex as the clinician may threaten him or her, leading to either vicarious and excessive "exploitation" of sexual issues, or denial and avoidance.

THE MENTAL STATUS EXAMINATION

What and how the child plays, speaks, and undertakes tasks constitute the raw data for the mental status examination of the child. To bring some order to the understanding of what seems like random play, it is useful to have an outline of things one particularly wants to observe and of why one wants to observe them. When completed, such an outline constitutes the report of the child's mental status.

Some of the data emerge spontaneously, some only after questioning. The categories in the outline that follows are for convenience only; they are composed of behavior items that are not isolated, and the behaviors listed usually do not occur in any special sequence. The child acts as a whole and in the context of a given environment, and the child's present behavior is always continuous with his or her past behavior. It is not necessary to elicit the information in the precise order presented here, and all these categories need not be covered in equal detail or in one sitting. The clinician should use his or her clinical judgment as to how fast and in what detail to proceed and as to what he or she wants to

look for. The clinician should also consider the age and developmental level of the child when assessing a given response.

1. Physical Appearance
   a. Small stature is often associated with a more infantile self-image; the child who is short may also be depressed because of his or her size. The cause of the shortness needs to be determined (e.g., the child may have a pituitary disorder). Conversely, the precociously developed younger adolescent may have inappropriately advanced expectations or may be viewed as more psychologically mature than he or she really is.
   b. Head size may indicate microcephaly and mental retardation, or hydrocephaly.
   c. Physical signs of a chromosomal disorder (e.g., Down's syndrome, fragile X syndrome, or Turner's syndrome) or of prenatal toxicity (e.g., fetal alcohol syndrome) may be present.
   d. Neurologic signs, such as strabismus, may suggest organicity (see the discussion of soft neurologic signs, p. 304).
   e. Bruising may indicate child abuse. An uncared for appearance, particularly in a young child, may suggest some degree of neglect.
   f. Nutritional state may indicate an eating disorder, ranging from anorexia nervosa to obesity.
   g. Level of anxiety may be manifested by hyperalertness, tics, biting of lips or nails, and hair pulling. The activity may have a "driven" quality: the child cannot sit still, has motor overflow as he or she moves from one activity to another, is easily distracted, and has a "short attention span," low frustration tolerance, and labile emotions. All these may suggest an attention deficit disorder as well as anxiety.

h. Momentary lapses of attention (staring, head nodding, eye blinking) may indicate epilepsy or hallucinatory phenomena. The clinician will subsequently inquire about such seizure phenomena as auras (nausea, vomiting, epigastric sensations), micropsia ("Do things seem to get smaller as you look at them?") or macropsia ("Do things seem to get bigger as you look at them?"), or about hallucinations (see 11d).

i. Gait may indicate a particular disorder (e.g., walking on tiptoe may indicate childhood autism; a stiff gait may indicate cerebral palsy).

j. Dress gives some idea of the care the child has received and how much the child cares for himself or herself. Sexual preferences and conflicts may be expressed in attitudes, behavior, and dress.

k. Mannerisms may provide a clue to a disorder (e.g., smelling everything may be a sign of childhood autism, tics a sign of anxiety, thumb sucking or repetitive play a sign of regression).

2. Separation
   Some initial caution is usually appropriate. Too much ease in separating may indicate superficial relationships associated with maternal deprivation. Excessive difficulty in separating may indicate an ambivalent parent-child relationship.

3. Manner of Relating
   The child usually relates to the clinician cautiously at first. However, some children are indiscriminately friendly and are shallow. Autistic children appear to "look through" one.

4. Orientation to Time and Place
   Orientation may be impaired by organic factors, intelligence, anxiety, or a thought disorder.

5. Central Nervous System Functioning
   Child psychiatrists are often particularly interested in the presence of so-called

soft neurologic signs as a possible indication of organicity. The concept of soft neurologic signs was introduced by Paul Schilder, and the term was first used by Lauretta Bender (1956). Soft neurologic signs are those signs that do not in themselves signify a definitive, manifest, specific neurologic lesion but that taken together may indicate organicity. They constitute a statistical association rather than a pathognomonic finding. They are often neurodevelopmental immaturities that have persisted.

There is no completely satisfactory classification of soft neurologic signs. One classification is as follows:

a. Group A signs. A developmental delay in relation to chronologic and mental age is reliably present. The delay may be in such functions as speech, motor coordination, right-left discrimination, and perception; and it may as associated with (1) mental retardation, (2) specific, genetically determined maturational disorders, and/or (3) brain damage.

b. Group B signs. A reliable single sign, such as nystagmus or strabismus, that may or may not have a determinable neurologic cause.

c. Group C signs. Slight unreliably present signs, such as asymmetry of tone or asymmetry of reflexes, which may be associated with various deprivational states or any of the conditions just mentioned.

Soft neurologic signs include deficiencies in:

a. Gross motor coordination. Awkwardness, clumsiness, motor overflow with extraneous movements, and contralateral "minor" movements of the opposite limb seen in posture, gait, balance, skill in climbing stairs, and ball throwing and catching.

b. Fine motor coordination (perceptuomotor capacities). The child is asked to copy the following designs:

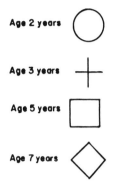

Age 2 years

Age 3 years

Age 5 years

Age 7 years

c. Performance of the Bender gestalt test. Clinically, it is useful to ask the child to copy various Bender designs (Fig. 23–1). Formal testing is required if the child has difficulty copying the designs.
The difficulties may include:
(1) Trouble with angulation and juxtaposition

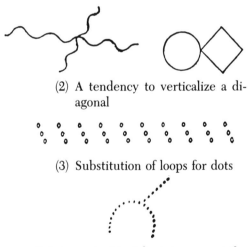

(2) A tendency to verticalize a diagonal

(3) Substitution of loops for dots

It is important to take into account the child's developmental level (Fig. 23–2).
d. Laterality. Handedness is usually consolidated by 5 years of age, footedness by about 7 years of age, eye preference by about 7 or 8 years of age, and ear preference by about 9 years of age. Clinically, these may be tested for as follows:

(1) Eye. The child might be asked to look through a "telescope" (e.g., a rolled-up piece of paper). A more accurate method is to ask the child to look at an object through a small fixed aperture (e.g., made by criss-crossing the fingers of both hands) with each eye in turn. The object in view persists with the dominant eye but disappears with the nondominant eye.
(2) Hand (while the child is writing).
(3) Foot (while the child is kicking a ball).
Laterality, preference, and dominance are not identical. Clinically, one may merely be testing preference, which in turn may depend on the peripheral organ than on any central mechanism (see p. 193).
e. Right/left discrimination. (The child should be asked to put the right hand to the left ear, the left hand to the right knee, etc.) At 5 years of age children can identify right and left hands. At 6 years of age the child has ipsilateral double orientation (i.e., "left hand to left ear") and at 7 years of age, contralateral orientation is achieved (i.e., "left hand to right ear") (Silver and Hagin, 1982).
f. Muscle tone. The clinician should observe how the child handles toys or crayons.
g. Tremors. The child is asked to extend his or her arms and stretch out his or her fingers. The clinician looks for choreiform movements.
h. Eye tracking. The child should be asked to look right or left at a picture on the wall, with just his or her eye. The clinician should observe whether the child turns the entire body.
i. Extension test. The child stands with feet together, eyes closed,

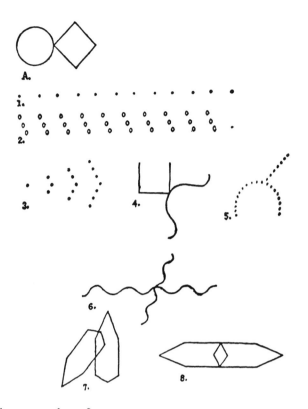

Fig. 23–1. The visual motor gestalt test figures.

From L. Bender, *The Bender Visual Motor Gestalt Test*, published by The American Orthopsychiatric Association, Inc.

arms extended, and torso flexed for 20 seconds. In right-handed children, the right hand is elevated, perhaps reflecting hemispheric dominance. Right-handed children with reading disability elevate the left hand.

j. Rapid alternating movements
   (1) Wrist rotation (pronation and supination)
   (2) Patting back of one hand with middle finger of the other hand (finger tapping)

k. Heel-to-toe walking and hopping on one foot (usually by 7 years of age)

l. Reflex symmetry

m. Short attention span, which may be due to:
   (1) Distractibility or poor discrimination of foreground from background

   (2) Task too difficult
   (3) Fatigue
   (4) Anxiety

n. Hyperactivity. More often than not hyperactivity is disorganized activity that appears to be hyperactive. The "hyperactivity" seems to be more noticeable in the classroom than in one-to-one situations.

o. Motor overflow, especially when excited (e.g., when throwing a ball)

p. Strabismus

q. Nystagmus

r. Convergence difficulties

s. Delayed or absent light reflexes

t. Speech defects (poor modulation of voice) (see below)

u. Reading, writing, and language difficulties (see below)

Rutter, Graham, and Yule describe a

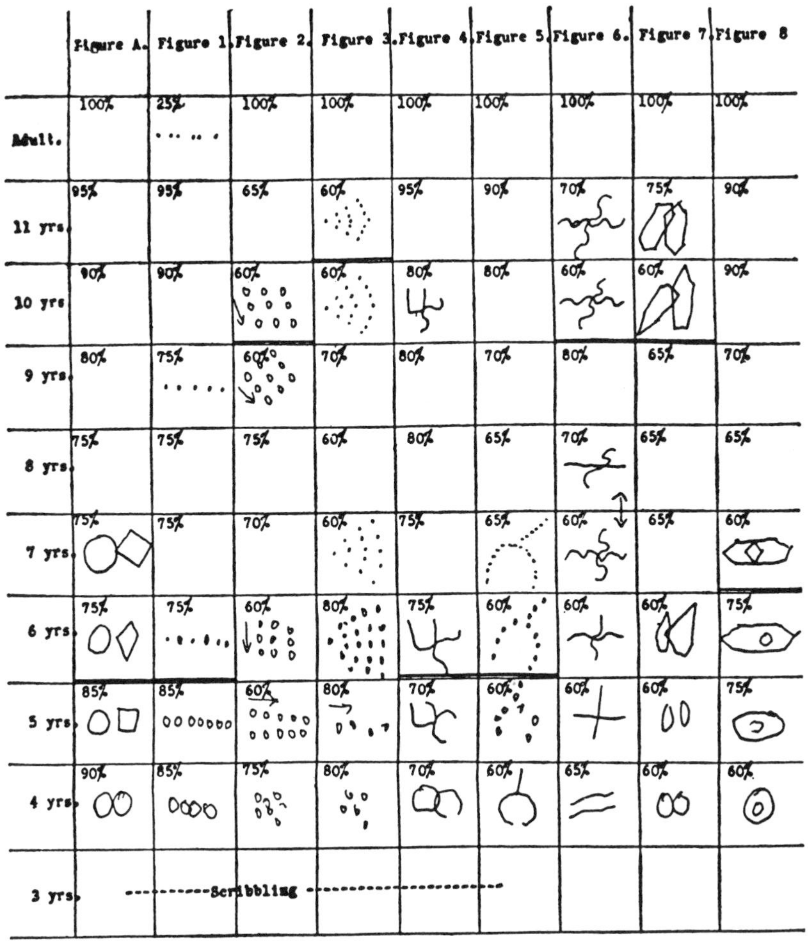

	Figure A	Figure 1	Figure 2	Figure 3	Figure 4	Figure 5	Figure 6	Figure 7	Figure 8
Adult.	100%	25%	100%	100%	100%	100%	100%	100%	100%
11 yrs.	95%	95%	65%	60%	95%	90%	70%	75%	90%
10 yrs	90%	90%	60%	60%	80%	80%	60%	60%	90%
9 yrs.	80%	75%	60%	70%	80%	70%	80%	65%	70%
8 yrs.	75%	75%	75%	60%	80%	65%	70%	65%	65%
7 yrs.	75%	75%	70%	60%	75%	65%	60%	65%	60%
6 yrs	75%	75%	60%	80%	75%	60%	60%	60%	75%
5 yrs	85%	85%	60%	80%	70%	60%	60%	60%	75%
4 yrs	90%	85%	75%	80%	70%	60%	65%	60%	60%
3 yrs	--------Scribbling -------------------------								

Fig. 23–2.   Norms for the visual motor gestalt test.

From L. Bender, *The Bender Visual Motor Gestalt Test*, published by The American Orthopsychiatric Association, Inc.

useful, brief (20-minute) neurologic examination for screening purposes only. If the screening procedures reveal that the child has soft neurologic signs, a comprehensive neurologic examination is required.

6. Reading Difficulties

The child may have one or more of the difficulties shown in Figure 23–3.

The brief screening test depicted in Table 23–3 gives an approximate idea of the child's reading ability.

A more accurate assessment of reading can be obtained through the Gray Oral Reading Tests. The GORT-R yields in-

Table 23–3.   Screening Tests of Reading Ability

First Grade:	40 seconds; 4 errors A little boy had a cat; she ran away; she said, "I want some milk."
Second Grade:	25 seconds; 2 errors A man took me to see his large barn. There was a horse in the yard; its tail was black.
Third Grade:	30 seconds; 2 errors One of our favorite birds is the robin. He is a very useful bird. He eats many insects and worms. The robin is less afraid of people than most birds.

1. **Reversals and inversions**
   Of letters: *d-b, q-p, u-n, W-M, t-f*
   Of sequences of letters: *was-saw, felt-left, oh-ho, plea-peal, blind-build*

2. **Confusions**
   Between letters: *f-l, k-h, m-n*
   Between small words: *of-off, at-it, of-if, me-we*

3. **Omissions**
   Of letters and syllables: *stad (stand), afaid (afraid), perstent (persistent), stike (strike), transportion (transportation), place (palace)*

4. **Substitutions**
   a-the, off-on, pretty-beautiful, house-home, woods-trees, grand-great

Fig. 23–3. Types of reading difficulties. Error patterns in dyslexic persons. From J.S. Osman, and P.D. Rome (1977), Remediation: Procedures for helping the dyslexic. *Psychiatr. Ann.*, 7:75.

formation about (a) oral reading speed and accuracy, (b) oral reading comprehension, (c) total oral reading ability, and (d) oral reading miscues. Grade-equivalent scores are not given because they are virtually useless in assigning students to classroom texts. Instead of grade equivalents, standard scores and percentile ranks are provided (Wiederholt and Bryant, 1986).

Many normal 6-year-old (first-grade) children show reversals. These reversals usually disappear as reading skill matures (Payne, 1930).

Children with reading difficulties often come from large families, and the children may have symptoms of attention deficit hyperactivity disorder or conduct disorder. Children with general reading backwardness usually have a broadly retarded reading level (2 to 2½ years below the predicted level) consistent with their below-average I.Q. Children with developmental reading disorder (dyslexia) are presumed to have some as yet undetermined central nervous system disorder, and the condition clinically is often found to be part of a

multifaceted complex learning disability.

7. Writing and Spelling Difficulties
   Children with writing difficulties (developmental expressive writing disorder) sometimes try to write with reckless speed as if to hide their difficulty. They may have a spelling problem. Many children with dyslexia also have writing and spelling difficulties (Fig. 23–4).

   If a child shows positive findings in any of the aforementioned clinical screening tests for reading, writing, and spelling, more systematic evaluation is usually indicated. Standard tests are available for these purposes (see Table 23–3).

8. Language and Speech
   Children who do not use words by 18 months or phrases by 2½ to 3 years, but who have a history of normal babbling, who understand commands, and who use as well as respond to nonverbal cues are probably developing normally. Delays beyond these ages or disturbances in these other forms of communication are indications for further diagnostic evaluation (see Table 23–4).

   The general signs of a language dysfunction include:

   a. Reduced vocabulary, especially for abstract concepts, such as feelings, and for question words such as when? and where?

   b. Delay in the acquisition of two sentences, usually acquired by 2 years of age.

   c. Overuse of concrete nouns and verbs.

   d. Underuse or omission of abstract word classes (e.g., adjectives, adverbs, prepositions, articles, and conjunctions), giving rise to telegraphic or unintelligible speech. Some children may avoid speaking or may have "interpreters," who speak for them.

   e. A tendency to repeat an utterance, or simply to nod the head, rather

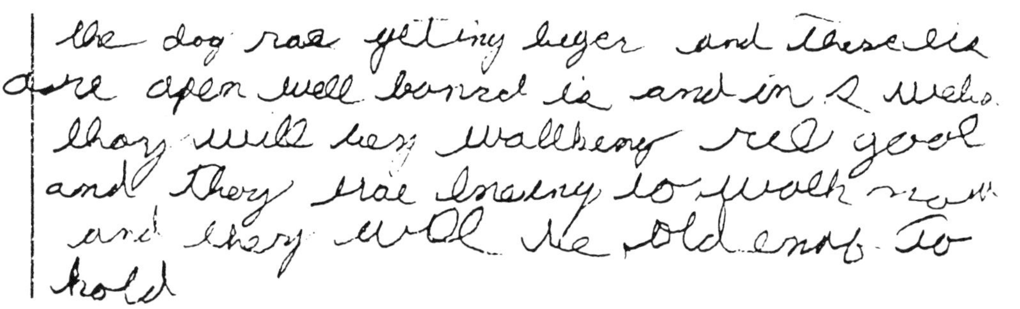

Fig. 23–4. Example of writing difficulty. Writing of a dyslexic 12-year-old seventh-grader. From Rome, R.D., and Osman, J.S. (1979), Procedures for helping the dyslexic child: Remediation. *Pediatr. Ann.*, 8:664.

than to clarify what he or she is trying to say.

Language problems may stem from receptive or expressive difficulties, although clinically both kinds of difficulties commonly occur together.

Receptive language problems include:

a. Sensory impairments such as blindness or deafness. Deafness often gives rise to delayed or unclear speech

b. Neurologic damage, such as cerebral palsy

c. Mental retardation

d. Developmental delay

Receptive abilities in various conditions are illustrated in Table 23–5.

Expressive language problems include:

a. Delayed or impaired expressive abilities, such as quality of babbling (by history), use of gestures to communicate, and delayed developmental level of spoken language

b. Syntax delay. The normal child can make one-word utterances at 18 months, two- to three-word phrases at 30 months, and four-word sentences at 40 months

c. Semantic delays, in which the capacity to differentiate meaning is impaired or stunted, and the child fails to use words correctly in regard to meaning

Delays in syntax and semantic development may first be encountered in a history of limited or poor babbling. The child may then use gestures instead of verbal language to communicate.

Abnormalities of expressive language include:

a. Echolalia

b. Delayed echolalia

c. Neologisms

d. Misuse of pronouns and gender

Speech problems may be due to:

a. Developmental delay

Common speech difficulties consist of delays, omissions, or distortions in the normal acquisition of particular sounds, e.g., *wabbit* instead of *rabbit*. Most uncomplicated common speech acquisition difficulties of this kind resolve by 7 or 8 years of age. Stuttering, which consists of repetitions, hesitations, or blocks in the production of a speech sound, often begins about 3 years of age and follows a fluctuating course that usually ends in adolescence. In some cases (less than 20%) it may persist into adulthood. There is often a family history of stuttering, suggesting a genetic component. Developmental delay due to mental retardation is usually associated with delayed speech.

b. Deafness

The child usually has normal facial expressions, but develops defective speech.

c. Anatomic dysfunction

Dysfunctional speech patterns may reflect the level of integration at

Table 23–4.   An Outline for a Communication Development Interview

Age	Communication Developmental Milestone	Question for Parents
0–2 months	Responsiveness to sounds in the speech frequency range	Does the child turn head or look up at the sound of voices?
	Preference for speech over other rhythmic sounds	Can the child be soothed or made to smile by the sound of voices? Does the child seem to like listening to people talk?
	Tendency to synchronize movements to breaks in speech	Does the child seem aware of when you stopped talking? Does the child wait for a pause to reach or move?
	Categorical perception for speech sounds	
	Preference for human faces over other visual stimuli	Does the child attend to your face? Does the child seem to look at you more often than at others things when you are in the room?
2–8 months	Mother-child "dialogue" in mutual gaze, joint action, babbling	Does the child "talk back" to you when you talk "baby talk"? Can you direct the child's attention to objects? Does the child seem to enjoy playing with you using toys, playing games such as "pat-a-cake" or "So big"?
9–12 months	Expression of nonverbal communicative intents to request, reject, call attention to self and object	Does the child make wants and needs known by gesturing and making sounds? Does the child attempt to get your attention this way? Does the child attempt to get you to play games or comment on his or her activities?
	Understanding a few words in routine contexts	Does the child eventually recognize a few words from games such as peek-a-boo and act spontaneously when he or she hears the word?
12–18 months	Use of first recognizable word	Does the child use any words to express wants and needs?
	Understanding of words outside routine contexts	Does the child understand any words without gesture or facial cues? For example, if you said, "Where's Daddy?" would the child turn and look for him?
18–24 months	Two words combined to form telegraphic sentences expressing a limited range of meanings	Does the child put words together in two-word sentences?
	Understanding of words for absent objects	If you ask for an object in another room, can the child fetch the correct item without gestural clues?
	Understanding of conversational obligation to respond to speech with speech	Does the child attempt to answer questions or respond to your comments in some way, verbal or nonverbal?
	Use of language to request information	Does the child ever either verbally or nonverbally try to get you to say the names of objects?
2–5 years	Average sentence length increases from 2.0 to 4.5 words or more	Does the child gradually add more words to sentences?
	Rules for forming plurals, past tense, etc., are overgeneralized	Does the child ever say words wrong, such as *comed, goed,* or *foots*?
	Mastery of morphological and syntactic rules for simple sentences; emergence of complex sentences	Do the child's sentences eventually sound more like an adult's?

Table 23–4.　An Outline for a Communication Development Interview *Continued*

Age	Communication Developmental Milestone	Question for Parents
2–5 years *Cont.*	Use of linguistic rules for understanding sentences	Does the child ever misunderstand things you say, especially when you use long or complicated sentences?
	Use of language to talk about events remote in time and space	Does the child tell you about things that happened away from home? In the past?
	Use of language for diverse purposes, such as imagining, predicting, interpreting	Does the child talk about things that will happen later? Could happen? Does the child talk about "make-believe" things?
	Increased conversational skills; topic maintenance	Can the child stick to a subject in conversation, say something new about the subject?
	Clarification	If the child doesn't understand you, does he or she ask you to repeat? Can the child repeat or repair a sentence you misunderstand?
	Polite, indirect requests	Can the child use language to "wheedle something out of you"? Can the child "say it nicer" in other ways than just adding *please*?
	Choice of the appropriate speech style for the social situation	Does the child talk differently to younger children? Is the child more polite to grownups than peers?
5-12 years	Use of devices to elaborate and condense information in sentences	Can the child tell stories without stringing sentences together only with *and*?
	Ability to use and understand unusual sentence types in the language, such as *passives*	Does the child sometimes use complex sentence forms in speaking? Writing?
	Development of metalinguistic awareness	Does the child ever make up words, play games with words, make up puns? Could the child tell you his or her favorite word?

From Paul, R. (1982), Communication development and its disorders: A psycholinguistic perspective. *Schizophr. Bull.*, 8:287–290.

Table 23–5.　Receptive Abilities

	Deafness	Mental Retardation	Infantile Autism	Elective Mutism
Sound discrimination	↓	Normal	Normal	Normal
Attentiveness	↓ Watches face	↓	↓ ↓	Normal
Understanding complex orders	↓	↓	↓ ↓ ↓	Normal

which the central nervous system is affected.

(1) *Aphonia* may occur when the neuromuscular level is involved, including such structures as the lips, tongue, palate, nasopharynx, larynx, and medulla oblongata.

(2) *Dysarthria* may occur when the corticobulbar level is involved.

Temporary dysarthria and slurred speech may occur with drug and alcohol intoxication.

(3) *Scanning, explosive, and monotonous* speech may occur when the cerebellum is affected.

(4) *Agnosia* (failure to understand symbols) and *aphasia* (failure to understand the spoken word or

to speak) may occur when the cerebral level is affected.

d. Psychologic states

During regressive episodes, infantile speech patterns may reappear. Anxiety may give rise to a high-pitched "tight" voice that may inhibit speech, and in "elective mutism" a child may refuse to talk.

Cognitive and psychosocial factors that might be involved are the level of intelligence, the amount and kind of stimulation, the degree of socialization, and the quality of attachments and relationships.

When any of the aforementioned clinical findings are present, a full diagnostic evaluation is usually indicated. This might include a complete physical examination, neurologic examination, hearing assessment, reading assessment, comprehensive language and speech tests (Tables 23–6 and 23–7), and an educational test battery.

Language and/or speech impairments may be present in the following conditions:

a. Childhood autism: echolalia, delayed echolalia, neologisms, misuse of pronouns and gender; lack of nonverbal communication behavior, including lack of direct eye gaze and lack of facial expression

b. Mental retardation: delayed language and speech

c. Organic brain damage: scanning speech

d. Deprivation: too many concrete words; too few abstract words

e. Anxiety: high-pitched, "tight" voice

f. Drug intoxication: dysarthria

g. Regression: infantile speech

(The reader who wishes a more comprehensive assessment of language and its disorders is referred to Cantwell and Baker [1987] and Rutter [1972].) See also Tables 23–6 and 23–7.

9. Intelligence

A rough idea of the child's intelligence may be assessed by an evaluation of the following:

a. General vocabulary, responsiveness, and level of comprehension and curiosity.

b. Ability to identify the parts of his or her body. For example, at 5 years of age the normal child can identify the jaw, temples, forearms, and shins.

c. Drawing ability.

d. Performance on the Wechsler Intelligence Scale for Children (revised version) or other standardized instrument.

e. Ability to subtract serial 7s or serial 3s.

10. Memory

a. At 8 years of age the normal child can count five digits forward and two or three digits backward; at 10 years of age he or she can count six digits forward and four digits backward. Very poor performance on the digit span test may indicate brain damage (particularly left-hemisphere damage) or mental retardation. Minor difficulties may simply reflect anxiety.

b. The child can repeat three items five minutes after having been told them.

11. Thinking Processes

a. Disorder of speed (e.g., retardation and push of thinking and speaking)

b. Disorder of flow (e.g., blocking and excessive repetition of words and sentences)

c. Disorder of content including:

   (1) Neologisms

   (2) Idiosyncratic logic or reasoning (e.g., transductive reasoning in which things that are related in time and space are believed to be related causally)

   (3) Excessive concreteness

   (4) Difficulty in discerning similar-

Table 23–6.   Assessment of Speech and Language Sources of Data

A. *General*
  1. Comprehensive pediatric and psychiatric history
  2. Child observations in multiple settings
  3. Standardized interviews (play)
  4. Documentation (e.g., home movies)

B. *Specific*	Informal Techniques	Typical Formal Tests
1. Hearing	by history/responses to sound	audiometry
2. Language comprehension	name body parts, follow commands	Peabody Picture Vocabulary Test
3. Speech production	by history/imitation of sounds	Goldman-Fristoe Test of Articulation
4. Expressive language	by history/observations	Developmental Sentence Analysis
5. Auditory processing		
a) attention	"Simon Says"	Goldman-Fristoe-Woodcock Auditory Selective Attention Test
b) discrimination	repeat "bat," "pat"	1) Wepman Auditory Discrimination Test 2) Goldman-Fristoe-Woodcock Test of Auditory Discrimination
c) memory	digit span	DiSimoni Token Test for Children
d) other (blending, auditory association, auditory closure)		Illinois Test of Psycholinguistic Abilities
6. Thought disorder		
7. Nonlanguage developmental levels		

ities and differences and in discerning what is relevant and what is irrelevant

  d. Disorder of perception. For example, the clinician should ask about auditory and visual hallucinations as though he or she were taking a medical history of the eyes and ears (Lewis, 1981). He might ask, "Do you have any trouble with your ears?" "Do your ears ever hurt you?" "Do your ears ever play tricks on you?" "Do you ever think you hear something, but nothing is there?" A similar sequence can be designed for inquiring about visual hallucinations. In younger children, hallucinations may be poorly described and the examiner must infer their presence on the basis of various behaviors, e.g., appearance of responding to internal stimuli by head turning or verbalizations apparently directed at a person or figure not actually present. It is particularly difficult to establish the presence of hallucinations in the preverbal child and almost nothing is known about such experiences.

  e. Paranoid ideation. There may be an associated disorder of mood (depression, elation, inappropriate mood, or paranoid rage) and behavior (disorganized, regressive, aggressive, withdrawn, or bizarre behavior).

 12. Fantasies and Inferred Conflicts
  The clinician might evaluate:

  a. The child's response to the following: "Do you have good dreams or

Table 23–7.   Language and Speech Tests

Analysis of Spontaneous Speech Samples
Developmental Sentence Scoring (Lee)
Assigning Structural Stages (Miller)
Linguistic Analysis and Remediation Procedure (Crystal)
Systematic Analysis of Language Transcripts (Miller and Chapman)

Language

Preschool Language Scale (Zimmerman)
Language Screening Test (Bankson)
Test for Auditory Comprehension of Language (Woolfolk)
Sequenced Inventory of Communicative Development (Hedrik, Prather, and Tobin)
Reynell Developmental Language Scales
Miller Yodor Language Comprehension Test
Clinical Evaluation of Language Functions (Seimel-Mintz, Wiig, and Merrill)
Illinois Test of Psycholinguistic Abilities (Kirk)
Detroit Tests of Learning Aptitude
Test of Early Language Development (Hresko, Reid, and Hamill)
Test of Language Development (Newcomer and Hamill)

Vocabulary Tests

Peabody Picture Vocabulary Tests, Revised Edition (Dunn)
Expressive One-Word Picture Vocabulary Test (Gardner)

Articulation Tests

Goldman-Fristoe Test of Articulation
The Assessment of Phonological Processes (Hodson)

Auditory Discrimination

Goldman-Fristoe-Woodcock Test
Wepman Auditory Discrimination Test

---

bad dreams?" "Tell me one of your dreams."

b. The child's response to the question, "If you could have three wishes, what would you wish for" (Winkley, 1982)?

c. The child's drawings of (1) a person, or (2) whatever the child wants to draw.

d. The child's squiggles (Winnicott, 1971; Berger, 1980).

e. The child's spontaneous play.

f. A story the child makes up in response, for example, to a question about his or her drawing of a person; e.g., "Suppose that the person has just finished doing something, is doing something now, and is going to do something soon; what do you think he or she is doing?"

g. The child's response to the request, "Tell me about a TV program you watch."

h. The child's description of specific fantasy figures.

13. Affects

Observe affects such as anxiety, depression, apathy, guilt, and anger, which may be caused by such factors as withdrawal, mental retardation, the deprivational syndromes, substance intoxication, depression, and neurotic conflicts.

Depression is a particularly important effect that must not be overlooked. Depressive affect is often accompanied by low self-esteem ("I can't do that," "I'm no good at drawing") as well as fatigue, loss of interest and pleasure, guilt, difficulty in concentrating, and disturbances in sleep, appetite, and motor activity. These symptoms constitute a diagnosis of major depressive disorder. The child may be asked: "Do you ever feel sad, upset, or bad?" "Do you ever feel unloved or uncared for?" "Do you feel you're not very good?" "Do you cry a lot?" "Do you have trouble making or keeping friends?" "Do you prefer to keep by yourself?" "Do you blame yourself a lot?"

Suicidal risk may be part of a major depressive disorder and should be explored by asking the following questions:

a. *Suicidal fantasies or actions*
"Have you ever thought of hurting yourself?" "Have you ever threatened or attempted to hurt yourself?" "Have you ever wished or tried to kill yourself?" "Have you ever wanted to or threatened to commit suicide?"

b. *Concept of what would happen*
"What did you think would happen if you tried to hurt or kill yourself?" "What did you want to have happen?" "Did you think you would die?" "Did you think you would have severe injuries?"

c. *Circumstances at the time of the child's suicidal behavior*
"What was happening at the time you thought about or tried to kill yourself?"

d. *Previous experiences with suicidal behavior*
"Have you ever thought about or tried to kill yourself before?" "Do you know of anyone who either thought about, attempted, or committed suicide?" "How did this person carry out his (her) suicidal ideas or action?" "When did this occur?" "Why do you think that this person wanted to kill himself (herself)?" "What was happening at the time this person thought about or tried to kill himself (herself)?"

e. *Motivation for suicidal behaviors*
"Why do you want to kill yourself?" "Why did you try to kill yourself?" "Did you want to frighten someone?" "Did you want to get even with someone?" "Did you wish someone would rescue you before you tried to hurt yourself?" "Did you feel rejected by someone?" "Were you feeling hopeless?" "Did you hear voices telling you to kill yourself?" "Did you have very frightening thoughts?" "What else was a reason for your wish to kill yourself?"

f. *Experiences and concept of death*
"What happens when people die?" "Can they come back again?" "Do they go to a better place?" "Do they go to a pleasant place?" "Do you often think about people dying?" "Do you often think about your own death." "Do you often dream about people or yourself dying?" "Do you know anyone who has died?" "What was the cause of this person's death?" "When did this person die?" "When do you think you will die?" "What will happen when you die?"

g. *Depression and other affects*
"Do you ever feel sad, upset, angry, bad?" "Do you ever feel that no one cares about you?" "Do you ever feel that you are not a worthwhile person?" "Do you cry a lot?" "Do you get angry often?" "Do you often fight with other people?" "Do you have difficulty sleeping, eating, concentrating on school work?" "Do you prefer to stay by yourself?" "Do you often feel tired?" "Do you blame yourself for things that happen?" "Do you often feel guilty?"

h. *Family and environmental situations*
"Do you have difficulty in school?" "Do you worry about doing well in school?" "Do you worry that your

parents will punish you for doing poorly in school?" "Do you get teased by other children?" "Have you started a new school?" "Did you move to a new home?" "Did anyone leave home?" "Did anyone die?" "Was anyone sick in your family?" "Have you been separated from your parents?" "Are your parents separated or divorced?" "Do you think that your parents treat you harshly?" "Do your parents fight a lot?" "Does anyone get hurt?" "Is anyone in your family sad, depressed, very upset?" "Who?" "Did anyone in your family talk about or try to kill himself?"

A useful checklist for suicide assessment in children is the Corder-Haizlip Child Suicide Checklist (Table 23–8).

14. Object Relations
   a. With the family. The clinician might ask the child (1) who is in his or her family and (2) what family members the child gets along with best and least.
   b. With peers. The clinician might ask the child (1) who his or her friends are and (2) whom the child likes best and least.
   c. With teachers. The clinician might ask the child what teachers he or she likes and dislikes.

15. Drive Behavior
   a. Sexual: Is the child seductive? Autoerotic?
   b. Aggressive: Is the child violent? Destructive?

16. Defense Organization
   a. Is the child phobic (e.g., is he or she afraid of something in the room, such as a radiator)?
   b. Is the child obsessive (e.g., are his or her drawings too neat)?
   c. Does the child show denial (e.g., does the child say that he or she has no problems)?

   d. Does the child show a reaction formation (e.g., could he or she be described as too good to be true)?

17. Judgment and Insight
   To evaluate the child's judgment and insight, the clinician should try to assess:;
   a. what the child thinks caused the problem
   b. how upset the child appears to be about the problem
   c. what the child thinks might help solve the problem
   d. how the child thinks the clinician can help him or her

18. Self-Esteem
   The child who has low self-esteem often makes such remarks as "I can't do that" and "I'm no good at all."

19. Adaptive Capacities
   The child is adept at many different kinds of problem-solving activities.

20. Positive Attributes
   The following description of a child who has many positive attributes might help the clinician decide what positive attributes the child he or she is examining has:
   The child is attractive, is of normal height, and has normal vision and hearing; is a likeable person and seems to be happy; relates to peers and adults easily, and has formed a number of suitable and lasting friendships; plays well (e.g., is imaginative, has themes, and is sustained in his or her play); is active and has sustained attention; draws well and is good at ball play (he or she is well coordinated); enjoys playing on teams; has healthy concepts (e.g., of a person or his or her body), and is of normal intelligence; emotional responses are appropriate, and he or she does not have extreme mood swings; is in touch with his or her feelings and fantasies; has a good command of language, and can verbalize his or her thoughts and feelings; is not easily made anxious, nor

Table 23–8.   The Corder-Haizlip Child Suicide Checklist

Questions Addressed to Parents
1. Has your child seen a physician over a period of months for a series of physical complaints for which there was no recognizable physical basis?
2. Has your child been treated by a physician for a series of minor accidents or injuries?
3. Has any serious change occurred in your child's life during the past few months or year?
4. Has your child experienced a specific loss in the past months or year?
5. Has your child shown any significant difficulties or unexpected problems with school, sports, or other areas of achievement?
6. Has your child been very self-critical?
7. Has your child made any unusual statements about death or dying?
8. Do you as parents perceive your child as more adult-like, special, talented, sensitive, or intelligent than other children?
9. Do you as parents expect adult-type speech and behavior from your child?
10. Does your child have easy access to medication and firearms?
11. Has there been any noticeable change in your child's behavior or mood in the past few months?
12. Do you describe yourselves as being closer to each other than you perceive the average family?
13. Have there been any unusual changes in your family in the past few months?
14. Have members of your extended family been especially close and attentive to your child?
15. Have you been disappointed lately in your child's performance?
16. Have stresses or recent changes left you with less time to focus on your child?
17. Have there been friends or relatives who have attempted suicide?

Questions Addressed to the Child
1. Have you had some sad and mad feelings that you have had trouble telling about or letting people know about?
2. Do you feel that things are going to get better or does it seem they will stay the same or get worse?
3. Do you ever think that things would be better if you were dead?
4. What do you think it would be like to be dead?
5. What do you think would happen with your mother and father if you were dead?
6. Have you thought about how you could make yourself die?

is he or she rigid (i.e., he or she is not obsessional, phobic, or denying); does not shirk problems; feels good about himself or herself; does well at school, both academically and socially.

CONCLUSION

In the course of the evaluation of the child, the clinician establishes a trusting relationship with the child and the parents. Consequently, the clinician considers the feelings of the child and the parents during the conclusion phase of the evaluation. For example, the clinician informs the child ahead of time when the last session will take place. Then, during the final interview, the clinician ensures that the child knows what will take place next. This can be done by asking the child: "Are there any things you would particularly

like me to tell your parents?" "Are there any things you don't want me to say to your parents?" "This is what I plan to say to your parents" (see below); "How does that sound to you?" "Do you have any questions?" Sometimes a child will express feeings about the ending. These feelings should be recognized, acknowledged, and dealt with sympathetically and realistically.

At the final review meeting with the parents, the clinician may start by asking how the child reacted to coming for his or her interviews. Sometimes information comes to light that may help the clinician in assessing the child's capacity to make a relationship and engage in psychotherapy. The clinician can then give the parents an account of the child's strengths. Every child has some strengths (the child may be attractive, intelligent, delightful to be with, well coordinated, able to

Table 23–9.   Selected Developmental and Psychological Tests*

Test Category	Age Range	Test Description
Adaptive Behavior		
Vineland Adaptive Behavior Scales (Survey and Expanded Forms)	0–Adult	Interview with parent or caregiver on use of communication, daily living, social, and for younger chidren, motor skills
Vineland Adaptive Behavior Scales (Classroom Edition)	3–13	As above but teacher completed
Developmental Assessments		
Brazelton Newborn Behavior Assessment Scale	Newborn	Infant state, reflexes, and interaction
Uzgiris-Hunt Ordinal Scales	0–2	Assessment of Piagetian stages of sensorimotor development
Gesell Infant Scale	8 wks–3½ yrs	Mostly motor developmental in the first
Catell Infant Scale		year, with some social and language assessment
Bayley Infant Scale of Development	8 wks–2½ yrs	Motor and social
Denver Developmental Screening Test	2 mos–6 yrs	Screening
Yale Revised Developmental Test	4 wks–6 yrs	Gross motor, fine motor, adaptive, personal/social, language
Individual Intelligence Tests		
Stanford-Binet (4th Ed.)	2 yrs–24 yrs	Verbal reasoning, abstract visual, reasoning, quantitative reasoning, short-term memory. Composite score (IQ equivalent)
Wechsler Preschool and Primary Scale of Intelligence (WPPSI)	4–6½	Verbal, performance, and full-scale IQ
Wechsler Intelligence Scale for Children Revised (WISC-R)	6–17 yrs	Verbal performance and full-scale IQ
McCarthy Scales of Children's Abilities	2½–8 yrs	General cognitive index (IQ equivalent) Score for: verbal quantitative memory motor laterality
Kaufman Test of Children's Achievement	2½–12½ yrs	Sequential processing Simultaneous process Achievement Mental processing Composite (IQ equivalent)
Leiter International Performance Scale (Arthur adaptation)	2–18	Nonverbal Intelligence
Motor Skills		
Bruininks-Oseretsky Test of Motor Proficiency	4½–14½ yrs	Eight subtests; gross and fine motor and balance
Perceptual and Perceptuomotor Skills		
Bender Visual-Motor Gestalt Test	4–12 yrs	
Draw-A-Person	All ages	
Benton Visual Retention Test (BVRT)	8 yrs–adult	
Beery Test of Visual Motor Integration (VMI)	2:11–16 yrs	

Table 23–9. Selected Developmental and Psychological Tests* *Continued*

Test Category	Age Range	Test Description
Personality		
Rorschach Test	3 yrs–adult	
Thematic Apperception Test (TAT)	6 yrs–adult	
Children's Apperception Test (CAT)	2½ yrs–adult	
Roberts Apperception	Latency age	
Personality Inventory for Children (PIC)	6–16	
School Grade Level Skills		
Wide Range Achievement Test (WRAT-R)	5 yrs–adult	Reading, spelling, math
Peabody Individual Achievement Test	5:4–18:3 yrs	Word identification spelling math reading comprehension general information
Kaufman Test of Educational Achievement	Grades 1–12	Reading decoding Spelling Reading comprehension Math application Math computation
Gray Oral Reading Test-Revised (GORT-R)	Grades 1–12	Oral reading and comprehension

*We are grateful to Sara Sparrow, Ph.D. for her assistance in the preparation of this table.

think clearly), and it is important that the parents be told about such qualities by the clinician.

Next, the clinician talks with the parents about his or her assessment of the child's difficulties. The assessment should be discussed in clear language and documented with vignettes from the clinical interviews and/or any of the special tests that help to illustrate and make clear the nature of the difficulty. If psychologic tests have been performed, the psychologist may wish to participate in the review meeting with the parents.

The parents should be given every opportunity to ask questions. Reactions on the part of the parents should be recognized and understood; the parents need the support of the clinician. The parents will need an explanation of the possible causes for the child's condition. They should also be reassured about all the good things they have done to help the child. Finally, treatment options and recommendations should be discussed with the parents. The parents should not be rushed,

and they may be invited to telephone or return if they so wish.

Documentation of the basis for the findings is particularly important when a written report has to be submitted, for example, to a court for evidence in a custody conflict (Lewis, 1974). When appropriate and with the parents' permission, the clinician should also send a report to the referring person. The limits of the confidentiality must be clearly understood by the child, the parents, and the clinician, and the clinician must exercise special care to safeguard this confidentiality.

Taking the history, performing the mental status examination, and observing during the clinical interviews are problem-solving exercises for the diagnostician. He or she observes, asks questions, and elicits responses for the purpose of confirming or refuting the presence of a symptom or sign that may be pathognomonic, cardinal, or important for a particular condition. Obviously he or she must be selective, since it is not practical to ask every imaginable question (Cox, Rutter, and Holbrook, 1981). Each observation, question, or special test should have a purpose and should have been selected carefully on the bases of priority and probability. Because troubled children and their families are often anxious or even distraught, the diagnostician asks his or her questions tactfully and thoughtfully.

The many practical techniques for history taking and interviewing have been described elsewhere (see the references for this chapter). Experience is an important ingredient. Psychologic tests have been reviewed elsewhere (Gittelman, 1980) (Table 23–9), as have neurologic examinations (Paine and Oppé, 1966) and EEG examination (Solomon, 1975).

Finally, it is important to remember that the psychiatric evaluation of the child and his or her family goes beyond the diagnosis. Each child and family member has his or her own private experience of life. In a good psychiatric evaluation, the clinician is privileged to enter that private experience momentarily, and to empathize with that person's feelings, hopes, and fears. We try to capture this aspect of an individual's life in the descriptive diagnostic formulation that follows the formal diagnosis.

REFERENCES

Bayley, N. (1969), *Bayley Scales of Infant Development Manual*. New York: The Psychological Corporation.

Bender, L. (1956), *Psychopathology of Children with Organic Brain Damage*. Springfield, Ill.: Charles C Thomas.

Cox, A., Rutter, M., and Holbrook, D. (1981), Psychiatric interviewing techniques. V. Experimental study. Eliciting factual information. *Br. J. Psychiatry*, 139:29–37.

Frankenburg, W.K., and Dodds, J.B. (1967), The Denver Developmental Screening Test. *J. Pediatr.*, 71:181–191.

Gittelman, R. (1980), The role of psychological tests for differential diagnosis in child psychiatry. *J. Am. Acad. Child Psychiatry*, 19:413–438.

Knobloch, H., and Pasamanick, B. (Eds.) (1974), *Gesell and Amatruda's Developmental Diagnosis*, 3rd Ed. New York: Harper & Row.

Lewis, D.O. (1981), Personal communication.

Lewis, M. (1974), The latency child in a custody conflict. *J. Am. Acad. Child Psychiatry*, 13:635–647.

Paine, R.S., and Oppé, T.E. (1966), *Neurological Examinations of Children*. Clinics in Developmental Medicine, Vols. 20, 21. London: Heinemann, p. 40.

Rutter, M. (1972), Clinical assessment of language disorders in the young child. In: *The Child with Delayed Speech*, ed. M. Rutter and J.A.M. Martin. Clinics in Developmental Medicine, No. 43. London: SIMP/Heinemann.

Solomon, S. (1975), Neurological evaluation. In: *Comprehensive Textbook of Psychiatry*, Vol. 2, ed. A.M. Freedman, H.I. Kaplan, and B.J. Sadock. Baltimore: Williams & Wilkins, pp. 188–212.

Volkmar, F.R. (1989), Developmental Assessment. *Sem. Perinatol.*, 13:467–473.

Winnicott, D.W. (1971), *Therapeutic Consultation in Child Psychiatry*. New York: Basic Books.

Child Psychiatric Interviewing Techniques

Anthony, E.J., and Bene, E. (1957), A technique for the objective assessment of the child's family relationships. *J. Ment. Sci.*, 103:541–555.

Beiser, H.R. (1979), Formal games in diagnosis and therapy. *J. Am. Acad. Child Psychiatry*, 18:480–491.

Beiser, H.R. (1962), Psychiatric diagnostic interviews with children. *J. Am. Acad. Child Psychiatry*, 1:652–670.

Bender, L. (1952), *Child Psychiatric Techniques*. Springfield, Ill: Charles C Thomas, p. 335.

Berger, L.R. (1980), Winnicott squiggle game. *Pediatrics*, 66:921–924.

Cantwell, D.P., and Baker, L. (1987), *Developmental Speech and Language Disorders*. New York: The Guilford Press.

Conn, J.H. (1939), The play interview: A method of studying children's attitudes. *Am. J. Dis. Child.*, 58:1199–1214.

Cox, A., and Rutter, M. (1976), Diagnostic appraisal and interviewing. In: *Child Psychiatry*, ed. M. Rutter and L. Hersov. Oxford: Blackwell.

Despert, J.L. (1937), Technical approaches used in the study and treatment of emotional problems in children. 5. The playroom. *Psychiatr. Q.*, 11:677–693.

DiLeo, J.H. (1970), *Young Children and Their Drawings*. New York: Brunner/Mazel, p. 386.

DeLeo, J.H. (1973), *Children's Drawings as Diagnostic Aids*. New York: Brunner/Mazel, p. 227.

Felice, M., and Friedman, S.B. (1978), The adolescent as a patient. *J.C.E. Pediatr.*, October, 15–28.

G.A.P. Report of No. 38 (1957), The diagnostic process in child psychiatry. New York: Group for the Advancement of Psychiatry, p. 44.

G.A.P. Report No 87 (1973), From diagnosis to treatment: New York: Group for the Advancement of Psychiatry, p. 139.

Goodman, J., and Sours, J. (1967), *The Child Mental Status Examination*. New York: Basic Books, p. 134.

Gubbay, S.S., Ellis, E., Walton, J.N., and Court, S.D.M. (1965), Clumsy children: A study of apraxic and agnosic defects in 21 children. *Brain*, 88:295–312.

Levy, D.M. (1933), Use of play technic as experimental procedure. *Am. J. Orthopsychiatry*, 3:266–277.

Lowe, M. (1975), Trends in the development of representational play in infants from one to three years: An observational study. *J. Child Psychol. Psychiatry*, 16:33–47.

MacCarthy, D. (1974), Communication between children and doctors. *Dev. Med. Child Neurol.*, 16:279–285.

MacDonald, P.F. (1965), The psychiatric evaluation in children. *J. Am. Acad. Child Psychiatry*, 4:569–612.

Paine, R.S. and Oppé, T.E. (1966), *Neurological Examination of Children*. Clinics in Developmental Medicine, Vols. 20, 21. London: Heinemann, p. 40.

Payne, C. (1930), The classification of errors in oral reading. *Elementary School J.*, 31:142–146.

Reisman, J.M. (1973), *Principles of Psychotherapy with Children*. New York: John Wiley & Sons, Inc.

Rutter, M. (1972), Clinical assessment of language disorders in the young child. In: *The Child with Delayed Speech*, ed. M. Rutter and J.A.M. Martin. Clinics in Developmental Medicine. No. 43. London: SIMP/Heinemann.

Rutter, M., Graham, P., and Yule, W. (1970). *A Neurological Examination: Description*. London: SIMP/Heinemann, pp. 27–39.

Rutter, M., Graham, P., and Yule, W. (1970), *A Neuropsychiatric Study in Childhood*. Clinics in Developmental Medicine, Nos. 35, 36. London: SIMP/Heinnemann.

Silver, A.A., and Hagin, R.A. (1982), A unifying concept for the neuropsychological organization of children with reading disability. *Dev. Behavioral Pediatr.*, 3:122–132.

Simmons, J.E. (1974), *Psychiatric Examination of Children*, 2nd Ed. Philadelphia: Lea & Febiger, p. 239.

Werkman, S.C. (1965), The psychiatric diagnostic interview with children. *Am. J. Orthopsychiatry*, 35:764–771.

Wiederholt, J.L., and Bryant, B.R. (1986), *GORT-R Gray Oral Reading Tests Revised*. Austin, Texas: Pro-ed, pp. 4, 5.

Winkley, L. (1982). The implications of children's wishes—research note. *J. Child Psychol. Psychiatry*, 23:477–483.

Winnicott, D.W. (1971), *Therapeutic Consultations in Child Psychiatry*. New York: Basic Books.

Yarrow, L.J. (1960), Interviewing children. In: *Handbook of Research Methods in Child Development*, ed. P.H. Mussen. New York: John Wiley & Sons, Inc. pp. 561–602.

Young, J.G., O'Brien, J.D., Gutterman, E.M., and Cohen, P. (1987), Structured diagnostic interviews for children and adolescents. *J. Am. Acad. Child Adolesc. Psychiatry*, 26:611–675.

24

DIFFERENTIAL DIAGNOSIS*

From all the information that has been gathered, it should be possible to narrow the possibilities down for a differential diagnosis. The differential diagnosis aims at distinguishing among the various conditions that may have similar symptoms in order to arrive at an accurate diagnosis as a basis for specific treatment and preventive measures, communication, and research.

Difficulties arise in child psychiatry because symptoms, the conditions from which they arise, and the causes of these conditions are not well defined (Zigler and Phillips, 1961). In practice, the term symptom in child psychiatry may mean almost any behavioral manifestation that comes to the attention of the observer. When certain traits, signs, or behaviors are particularly prominent and occur together frequently, conventional labels are commonly applied to define a condition or syndrome; for example, the symptom cluster of short attention span, hyperactivity, labile emotions, and clumsiness is conventionally represented by the label attention deficit disorder. These labels in turn, may imply an etiology, a treatment, or a prognosis (Rutter, 1978). However, often the causes are many, the treatment is untested, and the prognosis is unknown. In the example given, genetic, congenital, traumatic, infective, neoplastic, metabolic, psychodynamic, and environmental factors may

give rise to the same behavioral manifestations. The treatment is also generally nonspecific, and the prognosis is wide-ranging. In many instances, each factor in such a symptom cluster is in itself complex and it interacts with the other factors in the cluster in a complex manner. Finally, the validity of any such grouping ultimately depends on the accuracy with which each symptom was defined initially.

A second class of difficulties arises because there is no satisfactory or universally accepted classification of diagnostic entities. In addition to the categoric diagnostic approach, various rating scales, checklists, etc. have been used to provide dimensional assessments of psychopathology (see Appendix B). Many attempts have been made to improve the definition and classification of diagnoses (Feighner et al., 1972; G.A.P., 1966; Rutter et al., 1975; Spitzer and Cantwell, 1980). However, the problem remains unsolved. Changes in syndrome expression over the course of development pose additional difficulties for development of diagnostic schemes. The classification currently used in the United States is that given in the *Diagnostic and Statistical Manual of the American Psychiatric Association* (DSM-III-R). The relevant DSM-III-R categories of disorders that arise during childhood and adolescence are given in Appendix A. (Rutter and Schaffer [1980] provided an excellent critique of DSM-III.)

Yet a third class of difficulties arises because methods of eliciting data are either inadequate or not standardized (Rutter and Schaffer, 1980). This defect leads to a loss of

---

*Material for this chapter was drawn largely from the chapter "Differential Diagnosis" in *Basic Handbook of Child Psychiatry*, edited by J.D. Noshpitz, and we gratefully acknowledge the permission of Basic Books, Inc., to use this material.

reliability and, consequently, of validity (Rutter and Graham, 1968). Reliability in this sense is measured by the degree of agreement between independent, trained observers and refers to the consistency with which disorders are classified. Attempts have been made to improve reliability through meticulous and standardized interview structures and rating scales (Chambers, Puig-Antich, and Tabrizi, 1978; Carlson and Cantwell, 1980; Goodman and Sours, 1967; Kovacs and Beck, 1977; McKnew and Cytryn, 1979; Orvashel, Sholomskas, and Weissman, 1980; Petti, 1978; Simmons, 1974; Spitzer et al., 1970; Rutter and Schaffer, 1980). The skill of the observer and the setting in which the observations are made must also be taken into account. Observer bias is particularly troublesome (see Chapter 23). Although sophisticated data analytic techniques have facilitated research, their ability to discern valid diagnostic categories is highly limited, i.e., diagnostic categories emerge from clinical experience. At present there is no universally agreed-on method of data collection.

Perhaps a fourth class of difficulties arises from the fact that the same maladaptive behavior may have arisen out of different factors (Rubin et al., 1972), including (1) intrinsic defects or immaturities in the child that render him or her vulnerable to normal demands in the family, school, and society; and/or (2) such factors as deprivation, rejection, hostility, inconsistencies, and bizarre parental behavior acting upon a child at specific stages in development. Concerns have been raised about the possibility that children will be stigmatized through use of diagnostic labels (Hobbs, 1975); in this regard it is important to note that it is *disorders* not children who are categorized (Rutter and Gould, 1985).

The immediate tasks in differential diagnosis are to define as carefully as possible the behavior in question and to assess its significance. This raises the question of normality. Normal behavior is behavior that conforms to the expectations of the majority in a given society at a given time. Normality is not an absolute; it is a function of the prevailing historical, cultural, and social factors. By the same token, disorder behavior in a child is behavior that the majority of adults judge inappropriate either in form, frequency, or intensity in the particular circumstances in which the behavior occurs.

Unfortunately, the criteria for such judgments are often nebulous (Helzer and Coryell, 1983). The reliability of the witnesses, the tolerance of the child, family, school, and community, and the context of the psychiatrist's observations, as well as the psychiatrist's biases and thresholds, must all be taken into account by the psychiatrist in reaching a judgment. Further, as Ross (1974) has pointed out, "behavior that is observed at any point in time represents the end point of the interaction of four variables: genetic constitutional endowment, past learning, the individual's current physiological state, and his current environmental conditions." The practical question then is, Under what conditions does the so-called abnormal behavior appear? For example, even when a definite organic condition such as psychomotor epilepsy is present, a seizure may occur only under certain conditions such as stress, anxiety, fatigue, rage, and excitement.

Assessments of the nature, sources, and conditions under which a problem arises need to be made systematically. As described in Chapter 23, the work-up should include information about the pediatric and psychiatric history, the child's mental status, the parents' and the family's relationships, the school and community environments, and the confirmatory studies, such as the neurologic examinations, EEGs, psychologic tests, and educational tests. Data from such an exploration should enable a diagnosis to be made.

However, a considerable number of cases remain in which the data do not fit neatly into the diagnostic categories suggested by the classifications. Indeed, most of the descriptions of syndromes depict a more or less typical or prototypical clinical picture. In practice, most cases either lack all the diagnostic features of a given syndrome or include diagnostic features that are not ordinarily considered part of that syndrome. An additional problem is posed by the fact that certain conditions are commonly observed in association with each other, e.g., problems of conduct and attention. Further, there appears to be a gradient of exactitude in syndromes, extending from certain clear-cut conditions, such as the Gilles de la Tourette syndrome and autism, to increasingly amorphous categories, such as "atypical child" or "borderline child." The more amorphous a category is, of course, the less useful it is, particularly for research purposes. Nonetheless, it may have some limited communication value for clinicians, particularly those in a specific setting.

Thus diagnosis is a means, not an end, and differential diagnosis begins with a differentiation of symptoms. In childhood, the range of behavior is wide but not infinite.

When clusters of these behavior items occur with some regularity, they give rise to the so-called syndromes. Besides the small, subtype clusters that constitute the syndromes, larger correlations of symptoms may also occur. For example, in a factor-analysis study by Achenbach (1966), phobias, stomach aches, fearfulness, and pains had a high correlation with one another, constituting a group of so-called internalizing symptoms. Other symptoms found in this group include shyness, worrying, seclusiveness, withdrawal and apathy, headaches, nausea and vomiting, obsessions, and compulsions, crying, and preoccupation with fantasy. In this internalizing group, the number of girls was twice that of boys.

At the other end of the pole, symptoms such as disobedience, stealing, lying, fighting, cruelty, destructiveness, vandalism, firesetting, inadequate guilt feelings, swearing, temper tantrums, showing off, hyperactivity, truancy, and running away constituted a group of so-called externalizing symptoms. Externalizers tended to move often, have poor school performance, and a history of psychiatric, school, and police problems. Aggression, in fact, was more poorly controlled in this group. In this externalizing group, the number of boys was twice that of girls. In-

terestingly, the parents of children in this externalizing group tended to more often have psychiatric and criminal records. The family histories spoke of alcoholism, divorce, neglect, desertion, and illegitimacy.

This categorization, of course, is too global for clinical purposes. Many of the symptoms subsumed under either category may have multiple causes. Such symptoms as daydreaming, impulsiveness, nervous movements, including twitching, frequent dizziness, staring blankly, sudden changes in mood or feelings, sleepwalking, and talking while asleep, may have a variety of causes.

Nevertheless, it should be possible to construct an index of differential diagnosis of symptoms in child psychiatry. To illustrate, an introductory partial index follows of just a few of the symptoms or symptom disorders that commonly require a differential diagnosis. A more comprehensive index may be found elsewhere (Lewis, 1989).

SYMPTOMS THAT COMMONLY REQUIRE DIFFERENTIATION

Attention Difficulties: Short Attention Span; Hyperactivity

These terms are usually descriptive rather than truly quantitative. In any case, there is little agreement on what is meant by attention (Taylor, 1980). Short attention span is frequently a result of fatigability, which in turn is a function of the amount of effort the child has to expend to overcome any difficulty he or she has in discriminating background from foreground or in trying to hold onto more units of data than he or she can manage. Similarly, so-called hyperactivity is often a form of disorganized motor activity that becomes worse in a 1:30 classroom situation rather than an excess of normal, organized behavior. Anxiety may account for this behavior. However, in addition the child may have signs of clumsiness, extraneous movements, confusions of right and left, front and back, before and after, together with so-called soft neurologic signs, particularly asymmetries of reflexes or of fine finger and hand movements. In such instances, attention deficit disorder may be present.

Psychiatric interviews, classroom observations, psychologic tests including the Bender gestalt test, neurologic examination and, if necessary, an EEG will help in deciding among these possibilities.

Bed-Wetting

Bed-wetting may be maturational, organic, or psychologic. Diurnal as well as nocturnal enuresis, and dysuria, may indicate the presence of an organic disorder, such as posterior urethral valve obstruction, a double ureter, or cystitis. Psychologic causes are likely when the child had been successfully toilet trained. After a dry interval, enuresis begins, following psychologic stress associated with, for example, the birth of a sibling, the loss of a parent, or illness.

Developmental aspects of bed wetting are prominent (see pp. 186–187). By age three, about 75% of children will achieve nighttime bladder control and by age 7, over 90% of children will have achieved such control. The differential diagnosis of this condition includes a careful evaluation of associated factors (maturational, physiologic, and psychologic) and associated conditions (e.g., developmental delays, attention problems, and stress reactions).

Hallucinations

Hallucinations in childhood are almost always pathologic, although the literature is confusing (Rothstein, 1981). The following clinical categories should be considered.

Drug Intoxication. Many drugs are potentially hallucinogenic; they include marijuana, mescaline, psilocybin, LSD, STP, amphetamines, barbiturates, bromides, MAO inhibitors, antihistamines, and atropine-like drugs. At the same time, children and adolescents who take drugs may have an antecedent psychiatric disturbance (Paulsen, 1969). Sometimes the timing and form of the hallucinations suggest the possibility of drug ingestion. Other symptoms of drug ingestion may be present, including drowsiness, paranoid behavior, confusion, restlessness, excitement, violence, dilated pupils, ataxia, dysmetria, tremor, dysarthria, dyskinesia, akathisia, and hypotensive signs. The clinician must ask about drug ingestion.

Urine and blood samples must be tested when drug ingestion is suspected.

Seizure Disorder. Hallucinations, particularly hypnagogic hallucinations, may occur in narcolepsy and other seizure disorders. Hallucinations may be the first symptoms of degeneration following previous encephalitic illness. A neurologic examination and an EEG are required.

Metabolic Disorders. The metabolic disorders that may give rise to hallucinations include adrenal cortical hypofunction, thyroid and parathyroid disease, hepatolenticular degeneration, porphyria, beriberi, hypomagnesemia (secondary to prolonged parenteral fluid replacement therapy, diuretic therapy, excess vitamin D intake, or diabetic acidosis). Signs of the primary metabolic disorder are usually present.

Infection. Encephalitis, meningitis, and acute febrile illnesses (especially in young children) may give rise to hallucinations.

Immaturity and Stress. Acute grief reactions following the death of a parent may give rise to hallucinations. Usually these hallucinations are auditory and consist of admonitions and prohibitions attributed to the dead parent.

Hallucinations following severe anxiety may occur when the anxiety overwhelms the child. Young children who are under severe stress and resort to the defense mechanisms of repression, projection, and displacement may also have hallucinations. The hallucinations appear to be part of a regressive phenomenon, in which the distinction between fantasy and reality is temporarily lost. Often the stress is sexual, and the child may have been exposed to too much stimulation. The content of the hallucination may suggest the underlying psychologic conflict.

In older children, external conflicts rarely, if ever, give rise to hallucinations. However, if the stress is massive and overwhelms the child, it can lead to profound regression. The circumstances in which this occurs include severe and sudden illness. For example, a previously healthy 15-year-old girl suddenly developed hemolytic uremic syndrome, with acute renal shutdown that necessitated immediate hemodialysis. While undergoing hemodialysis, the girl began to hallucinate. For another example, an active child who is suddenly immobilized to treat a fractured limb may hallucinate during moments of acute anxiety.

In some instances, severe cultural deprivation, *together* with a disturbed parent-child relationship, may determine the prevalence and the form of the hallucinations. The hallucinations in this setting are said to be localized, orderly, and related to reality, consisting of forbidding voices and overt wish fulfillments (Wilking and Paoli, 1966). Often the hallucinations in this setting are consistent with the superstitions of the parents. The child may appear to be well organized in other ways. However, there is usually evidence of a personality disturbance in the child and psychosis in the parent, suggesting at least the possibility of a genetic or organic component as well as powerful sociocultural influences (Esman, 1962). In fundamentalist sects, a high value is placed on being possessed by the spirit. Hysterically inclined children and youths may lend themselves to this experience and may "hear voices."

Schizophrenia. When hallucinations are more fragmented, incoherent, and bizarre in content, there is a greater likelihood that schizophrenia is present (Bender, 1954). Bodily complaints and paranoid delusions may be associated with the psychosis. The child is often frightened and secretive about the hallucinations. There are usually other signs of a thought disorder, including disordered, illogical thought processes and inappropriate affect. A history of psychiatric disturbance in the family and maternal deprivation during infancy are often present. Sometimes the child presents with delinquent behavior

(Lewis, 1975). Psychologic tests, particularly projective tests, are indicated.

Language and Speech Dysfunction

The general signs of a language dysfunction includes (1) a reduced vocabulary, especially for abstractions, such as feelings, (2) a delay in the acquisition of two-word sentences (usually acquired by 24 months of age), (3) an overuse of concrete nouns and verbs, (4) an underuse or lack of use of abstract word classes (e.g., adjectives, adverbs, prepositions, articles, and conjunctions), which gives rise to telegraphic or unintelligible speech, and (5) difficulties in social use of language (pragmatics) may be present. Subsequently, some children may also avoid speaking and tend to have "interpreters," who speak for them.

Language dysfunction may arise as a result of a hearing loss, understimulation, mental retardation, a psychosis, a central nervous system impairment, a developmental language disorder (developmental aphasia), or an anatomic defect in any of the apparatuses serving speech. These are the major categories the psychiatrist must consider. In screening for specific conditions within these categories, the minimal requirements are a detailed history, a physical examination, a psychiatric evaluation, and communication and psychologic tests. Depending on what condition seems most probable, more specific studies are then required.

Children with a developmental language disorder may have receptive, expressive, or mixed language disorders. Receptive language disorders are usually characterized by a difficulty in (1) understanding language at one or more of the various stages of decoding (including auditory or visual perception of particular sounds or pictures), (2) integration, (3) storage, and (4) sequence recall. Children with an expressive language disorder have a normal and appropriate level of understanding language and concepts but have difficulties in articulation and in "getting the words out." Their vocabulary and grammar are usually below age level. It often is the case that receptive and expressive problems occur together.

Certain associated speech patterns may reflect the level of integration at which the central nervous system is affected. For example, (1) aphonia may occur when the neuromuscular level is involved, including involvement of such apparatuses as the lips, tongue, larynx, and medulla oblongata, (2) dysarthria may occur when the corticobulbar level is involved, (3) scanning, explosive, and monotonous speech may occur when the cerebellar level is affected, and agnosia (failure to understand symbols) and aphasia (failure to understand the spoken word and/or to speak) may occur when the cerebral level is affected. Dysrhythmias, such as cluttering, stuttering, and/or stammering, and rapid speech may be exaggerations of normal errors of speech. Idioglossia occurs typically among twins.

Specific language dysfunctions, such as echolalia, idioglossia, and pronoun reversal, may occur in childhood autism and hyperlexia.

Reading Difficulty

Children who have difficulty in learning to read may be suffering from visual or auditory perceptual handicaps, mental retardation, psychologic disturbances, maturational lags, poor teaching, adverse family environments, linguistic problems, or specific reading disabilities. The etiology of a specific reading disability may include those factors associated with attention deficit disorders. It is obvious that each of these factors must be considered and investigated. The workup must therefore include tests for hearing and vision, a careful neurologic examination, the Wechsler Intelligence Scale for Children, the Rorschach and TAT tests, the Bender visual-motor test, an evaluation of the child, the family, and the school, and specific reading tests, such as the Wide Range Achievement Test. Psychiatric interviews alone are rarely sufficient.

Pure (but by no means simple) developmental dyslexia usually becomes apparent after the first grade. Many of the children with this problem have to repeat first grade. Clinically, reading is an effort for the child, and he or she makes many omissions and guesses. Comprehension is poor and handwriting is poor, with many rotations, confusions, and transpositions. All-around frustration, anxiety, and anger are almost inevitable. There are usually no convincing neurologic findings.

The rare syndrome of hyperlexia is occasionally encountered, predominantly in boys (Silberberg and Silberberg, 1967). Children with hyperlexia are often clumsy, and have a marked apraxia (an inability to copy simple figures). They also have some difficulty in comprehension, with an impaired ability to relate speech sounds to meaning, poor relationships, and such language disorders as echolalia, idioglossia, and pronoun reversal. These symptoms are also found in childhood autism; in fact, a common neuropathologic condition, possibly one involving the parietal lobe, has been postulated for both disorders (Huttenlocher and Huttenlocher, 1973).

Seizure Behavior

A frequent and important differential diagnosis is that between a paroxysmal epileptic disorder and a conversion reaction. In a conversion reaction there is rarely any aura, and consciousness is impaired but not lost. Sequential movements are uncommon. Loss of bladder or bowel control and tongue biting do not usually occur. The attack may end suddenly, and there is no postictal confusion. The EEG is normal. Conversion symptoms usually have some secondary gain for the child who may also exhibit indifference to the symptom. In difficult cases, induction of seizures with saline solution and suggestion during EEG monitoring may help in diagnosing hysterical seizures (Cohen and Suter, 1982).

Breath-holding spells may sometimes be confused with seizures. Children under 6 years of age may hold their breath during a crying spell, become cyanotic, and then lose consciousness. In epilepsy, the cyanosis follows the seizure. In hysterical adolescents, hyperventilation may give rise to fainting, presenting as a transient loss of consciousness. Actual loss of consciousness, especially if prolonged, suggests epilepsy. Syncope, of course, may precipitate a seizure in an epileptic child.

Sleep Disturbances

Sleep disturbances are primary or secondary. The major primary sleep disorders include somnambulism, nightmares and night terrors, delta wave disturbance with enuresis, narcolepsy, and hypersomnia (Kales and Kales, 1974).

Secondary sleep disturbances are associated with pain, physical discomfort, anxiety, excitement, depression, neurosis (particularly obsessive-compulsive neurosis), and psychosis (including borderline disturbances and schizophrenia).

Sleepwalking, found more often in boys than in girls, usually occurs in stage 3 or stage 4 sleep and lasts for a few minutes. There is often some awareness during the episode but usually no memory of the event once the child is awakened.

Children who are sleepwalkers also commonly have night terrors, which consist of intense anxiety, outbursts of screaming and thrashing, rapid heart rate, and deep, rapid breathing. All these phenomena last for a few minutes, but again, the child has little or no memory of the event after he or she has awakened. Night terrors, like sleepwalking, occur early in stage 4 sleep. Both conditions have been considered to be arousal disorders, consisting of delayed or impaired arousal out of stage 3 or stage 4 sleep, perhaps as a result of delay in maturation (Broughton, 1968).

Spontaneous remission usually occurs as the child grows older. It is comparatively unusual to find any pathognomonic psychopathologic condition in these children. However, of those who remain sleepwalkers during young adulthood, approximately one third are schizophrenic (Sours et al., 1963).

Unlike children who sleepwalk and who have night terrors, children who have anxiety dreams ("bad dreams") may have psychologic problems. Essentially, these easily remembered frightening dreams occur during REM sleep from which the child is easily aroused.

Some adolescents are prone to sudden irresistible brief attacks of shallow sleep (narcolepsy), often accompanied by sudden fleeting attacks of loss of muscle tone (cataplexy). Narcolepsy and cataplexy are especially likely to occur during strong emotional states, such as anger. The child is easily aroused from sleep and has no postictal confusion. Consciousness is not lost in cataplexy.

Spelling Difficulties

When spelling difficulties are accompanied by reading difficulties, there is often a common basic language deficit (Nelson and Warrington, 1974). The workup then is identical to that for the differential diagnosis of a reading or language difficulty. However, sometimes there is a specific problem unrelated to reading. The causes are virtually unknown in these cases (Frith, 1980).

Stealing

The symptom of stealing may have many causes. Sometimes the symptom is due to a failure in distinguishing between "what's mine" and "what's not mine." That failure in turn may be due to immaturity. If there is also an organic component, the compulsive defenses that are usually prominent in such children will lead to an exaggeration of the "hoarding" tendency of young children. This development may prepare the ground for the child, who subsequently feels unloved and ungratified, to then steal to obtain love. If the child is also frustrated and enraged at the ungiving adult, he or she will steal specifically from that person, representing in part the mixed dependency and hostility the child feels toward that person. (Such ambivalence is not uncommon.) When the child's personality development has been considerably distorted, the child may steal because there have been no parental sanctions against stealing. In such cases the child rarely feels guilty.

Indiscriminate repeated stealing is often a sign of poor impulse control, particularly true in children who have poor parental models, who are deprived, or who live in a subculture in which stealing has other meanings. Sometimes the stealing is an attempt to find a place in and identify oneself with a peer group of equally deprived children who roam and steal.

The child who feels guilty about stealing may steal in such a way that he or she is likely to be caught and punished. In such a child, the punishment assuages the feelings of guilt, and the basic (unconscious) motivation for stealing may escape detection.

Stealing may first appear or may become aggravated when the child is under stress; in this sense, it is a regressive phenomenon, much as enuresis is sometimes a regressive phenomenon.

Temper Tantrums

Temper tantrums are most commonly observed in toddlers, i.e., at a time before expressive language is well developed. In these younger children the motor discharge is accompanied by screaming, obvious distress, and the appearance of loss of behavioral control. Sometimes such behaviors arise within the context of problems in parent-child interaction; at other times such behaviors may represent a normal phase in the process of developing autonomy and individuation.

Children with infantile autism may also have temper tantrums. However, the child with infantile autism is almost certainly markedly deviant in other ways, whereas the normal infant is not.

Anger and frustration are frequent causes of temper tantrums. When the tantrums give rise to violent and aggressive behavior with destructive components, they become clinical issues. The frustrations may be the normal frustrations encountered in growing up, but they may also be chronic frustrations arising out of a feeling of being unloved or deprived or out of too much stimulation. A search for these sources of frustration is the first step toward solving the problem.

Panic or anxiety may be manifested as temper tantrums (or, in a sense, "terror tantrums"). Usually other signs associated with the cause are present (e.g., decompensating phobic or obsessional symptoms, signs of an attention deficit disorder, or signs of a pervasive developmental disorder).

In some cases, the parents' tolerance level may be too low, leading them to describe an item of their child's behavior as maladaptive when, in fact, the behavior is normal—or at any rate, characteristic of the particular child or other children at the same age.

In addition, even when the behavior is so severe that it suggests a problem, the behavior may still be adaptive. For example, a child may be appropriately enraged at a frustrating social situation although not mature enough to change the situation. In such a circumstance, the behavior (the rage) is adaptive if it secures what the child needs (e.g., attention).

The Socially Isolated Child

The role of social relationships in facilitating various aspects of development has been increasingly recognized (Cairns, 1979). The formation of stable relationships, initially with parents and siblings, and subsequently with peers, is an important developmental task that provides opportunities for learning rules of interaction and culturally appropriate behavior, for integrating other aspects of knowledge within a social context, and for developing a coherent self-concept. Differences in sociability are noted from infancy, apparently reflecting both inborn temperamental differences (Chess and Thomas, 1986) and early experience. Behavioral inhibition at 21 months has been noted to predict social avoidance at age 5 and to correlate with heart rate and cortisol level (Kagan et al., 1988); similarly, patterns of attachment have been observed to be relatively stable from infancy to age 6 (Main and Cassidy, 1988).

Children with problems in developing peer relationships are more likely to exhibit psychopathology (Hartup, 1983). Various factors appear to contribute to social isolation (e.g., psychopathology in the child, physical appearance, presence of handicapping conditions, lack of friendliness in the child, and intelligence). Unfortunately, much of the available research is correlational in nature and it is difficult, in reality, to disentangle the often complicated series of events and interactions that produce the socially isolated child.

Shyness is appropriate, to some extent, in certain developmental periods and in some contexts and the shy child need not, necessarily, exhibit any psychiatric disturbance. However, numerous psychiatric conditions of childhood are associated with serious disturbances in social relationships. Apart from autism (perhaps the prototypic disturbance of social relatedness) there are few specific syndromes that are primarily defined by disturbances in social development. Problems in the development of peer or family relations can be observed in a number of conditions, e.g., attention deficit-hyperactivity disorder, conduct problems, elective mutism, various personality problems (e.g., borderline personality and schizoid personality), anxiety disorders, and depression (Rutter and Garmezy, 1983; Hartup, 1983). The concept of reactive attachment disorder has been used to describe children who develop deviant patterns of social interaction as a result of neglect and or abuse; these children form social relationships but these are often deviant in either of two ways, i.e., either the child is overly indiscriminate or overly inhibited.

Thought Disorder

The process of thinking has three major clinical dimensions: actual thought content, speed of thinking, and ease of flow. A variation in any of these dimensions may be of such a degree and duration as to constitute a thought disorder (see Chap. 23).

Disordered thought content may take the form of neologisms and idiosyncratic logic, including transductive reasoning (things that are related in time or space are believed to be related causally), difficulty in discerning differences and similarities, difficulty in distinguishing the relevant from the irrelevant, and excessive concreteness.

Disordered speed of thinking may take the form of retardation or a push of thinking and speaking. Disorders of flow may take the form of blocking, muteness, and excessive repetitions of words and sentences.

A child may experience any of these manifestations subjectively as being alien, out of his or her control and, sometimes, frightening.

There may be an associated disorder of (1) mood (depression, elation, inappropriateness, or paranoid rage), (2) behavior (disorganized, regressive, aggressive, withdrawn, or bizarre behavior) or (3) perception (delusions or hallucinations).

Thought disorder is another example of a cluster of symptoms that is not in itself a diagnosis. The possible causes of the thought disorder cluster may be classified clinically as follows:

1. psychologic (e.g., acute and massive psychologic stress reaction),
2. genetic (e.g., inborn errors of metabolism, such a Hartnup's disease and Kufs' disease, and schizophrenia),
3. traumatic (e.g., postconcussion syndrome),
4. infective (e.g., viral encephalitis and brain abscesses),
5. neoplastic (e.g., brain tumor),
6. toxic (e.g., amphetamines, steroids, bromism),
7. deficiencies (e.g., pellagra),
8. endocrine (e.g., thyrotoxicosis), and
9. multiple (e.g., pervasive developmental disorder, schizophrenia).

The aforementioned examples are illustrative rather than comprehensive. The important point here is to think of the classes of possible causes.

The symptoms, or rather the cluster of symptoms, that constitute a thought disorder should lead to a systematic review of these possible causes. Obviously, some causes will be easily ruled out, whereas others will immediately appear to be more likely possibilities. Once the field has been narrowed in this way, a more detailed study can lead to a further narrowing. For example, the associated presence of hallucinations (see p. 313) may give a cross-differential diagnosis of specific syndromes.

Violent Behavior

Important psychiatric and neurologic factors may give rise to delinquent behavior (Lewis, 1975). The severity of the offense is not a reliable guide. An inability to remember violent acts should raise the possibility of some form of seizure disorder, including psychomotor epilepsy or episodic dyscontrol. A history of birth difficulty, cerebral infection, or head injury may be an important forerunner of an organic condition resulting in poor impulse control or a seizure disorder. Early child abuse, interpersonal difficulties, and behavior problems at school may be important harbingers of later psychotic symptoms, including hallucinations and paranoid thinking associated with violent acts (Lewis et al., 1973). A history of psychiatric disturbance in the family is significant. Living with a psychiatrically impaired relative may be a contributing factor. Antisocial behavior is sometimes the child's way of calling attention to the parent's disturbance. Poor socioeconomic conditions (Cloward and Ohln, 1960; Cohen, 1965; Merton, 1938; Matza, 1964; Shaw and McKay 1969), as well as psychodynamic factors (Aichorn, 1935; Glueck and Glueck, 1970; Jenkins and Hewitt, 1944; Johnson, 1949; Schmideberg, 1953), must also be evaluated as possible causes of violent delinquent behavior. Depression may be an important component of the child's antisocial behavior. The label sociopathic should be avoided (Lewis and Balla, 1975). Rather, a specific psychiatric and/or neurologic diagnosis is required.

THE DIAGNOSTIC FORMULATION

Even a differential diagnosis of symptoms or symptom clusters does not lead directly to a diagnosis. Such an approach merely opens up possibilities to be considered. The actual diagnosis ultimately depends on a careful and meticulous assessment of all the available data. The data must be judged in the context of the child's equipment, vulnerabilities, and developmental level; his or her family and other environmental factors; and the circumstances of the evaluation process itself. Actually, an accurate description of an individual child goes beyond the assigned stereotyped diagnostic category. Each child requires an individual diagnostic formulation. It is here that the various metapsychologic profiles have their best use (see Appendix C).

REFERENCES

Achenbach, T. (1966), The classification of children's psychiatric symptoms: A factor-analytic study. Psychol. Monog., 80(615).

Aichorn, A. (1935), *Wayward Youth*. New York: Viking Press.

Bender, L (1954), Imaginary companion: Hallucinations in children. In *A Dynamic Psychopathology of Childhood*. Springfield, Charles C Thomas.

Broughton, R.J. (1968), Sleep disorders: Disorders of arousal. *Science*, 159:1070–1078.

Cairns, R.B. (1979), *Social Development: The Origins and Plasticity of Interchanges*. San Francisco: Freeman, Cooper & Co.

Carlson, G.A., and Cantwell, D.P. (1980), A survey of depressive symptoms, syndromes and disorders in a child psychiatric population. *J. Child Psychol. Psychiatry*, 21:19–25.

Chambers, W., Puig-Antich, J., and Tabrizi, M.A. (1978), The ongoing development of the Kiddie-SADS (Schedule of Affective Disorders and Schizophrenia for School-Age Children). Paper read at Annual Meeting of American Academy of Child Psychiatry, San Diego, CA.

Chess, S., and Thomas, A. (1986), *Temperament in Clinical Practice*. New York: Guilford Press.

Cloward, R.A., and Ohln, L.E. (1960), *Delinquency and Opportunity: A Theory of Delinquent Gangs*. New York: Free Press.

Cohen, A.K. (1965), The sociology of the deviant act: Anomie theory and beyond. *Am. Soc. Rev.*, 30:5–14.

Cohen, R.J., and Suter, C. (1982), Hysterical seizures: Suggestion as a provocative EEG test. *Ann. Neurol.*, 11:391–395.

Esman, A.H. (1962), Visual hallucinosis in young children. *Psychoanal. Study Child*, 17:334–343.

Feighner, J.P., et al. (1972), Diagnostic criteria for use in psychiatric research. *Arch. Gen. Psychiatry*, 26:57–63.

Frith, U. (1980), Reading and spelling skills. In: *Scientific Foundations of Developmental Psychiatry*, ed. M. Rutter. London: Heinemann, pp. 220–229.

G.A.P. Report No. 62 (1966), Psychopathological disorders in childhood: Theoretical considerations and a proposed classification. New York: Group for the Advancement of Psychiatry.

Glueck, S., and Glueck, E. (1970), *Toward a Typology of Juvenile Offenders: Implications for Therapy and Prevention*. New York: Grune & Stratton.

Goodman, J.E., and Sours, J.A. (1967), *The Child Mental Status Examination*. New York: Basic Books.

Hartup, W. (1983), Peer relations. In: *Handbook of Child Psychology*, Vol. 4, ed. E. M. Hetherington. New York: John Wiley & Sons, pp. 103–196.

Helzer, J.E. and Coryell, W. (1983), More on DSM III: How consistent are precise criteria. *Biol. Psych.*, 18:1201–1203.

Hobbs, N. ed. (1975), *Issues in the Classification of Children*, Vols. 1 and 2. San Francisco: Jossey-Bass.

Huttenlocher, P.R., and Huttenlocher, J. (1973), A study of children with hyperlexia. *Neurology*, 23:1107–1116.

Jenkins, R.L., and Hewitt, L. (1944), Types of personality structure encountered in child guidance clinics. *Am. J. Orthopsychiatry*, 14:84–94.

Johnson, A.A. (1949), Sanctions for superego lacunae of adolescents. In: *Searchlights on Delinquency*, ed. K.R. Eissler. New York: International Universities Press.

Kagan, J., et al. (1988), Childhood derivatives of inhibition and lack of inhibition to the unfamiliar. *Child Dev.*, 59:1580–1589.

Kales, A., and Kales, J. (1974), Sleep disorders. *N. Engl. J. Med.*, 290:487–499.

Kovacs, M., and Beck, A.T. (1977), An empirical approach toward a definition of childhood depression. In: *Depression in Childhood*, ed. J.G. Schulterbrandt and A. Raskin. New York: Raven Press, pp. 21–25.

Lewis, D.O. (1975), Diagnostic evaluation of the juvenile offender. *Child Psychiatry Hum. Dev.*, 6:198–213.

Lewis, D.O., and Balla, D. (1975), "Sociopathy" and its synonyms: Inappropriate diagnoses in child psychiatry. *Am. J. Psychiatry*, 132:720–722.

Lewis, D.O., et al. (1973), Psychotic symptomatology in a juvenile court clinic population. *J. Am. Acad. Child Psychiatry*, 124:660–675.

Lewis, M. (1989), *An Index of Differential Diagnosis in Child Psychiatry.*

McKnew, D.H., and Cytryn, L. (1979), Urinary metabolites in chronically depressed children. *J. Am. Acad. Child Psychiatry*, 18:608–615.

Main, M., and Cassigy, J. (1988), Categories of response to reunion with the parent at age 6: Predictable from infant attachment classifications and stable over a 1-month period. *Child Dev.*, 24:415–426.

Matza, D. (1964), *Delinquency and Drift*. New York: John Wiley & Sons, Inc.

Merton, R.K. (1938), Social structure and anomie. *Am. Soc. Rev.*, 3:672–682.

Nelson, H.E., and Warrington, E.K. (1974), Developmental spelling retardation and its relation to other cognitive abilities. *Br. J. Psychol.*, 65:265–274.

Orvaschel, H., Sholomskas, D., and Weissman, M.M. (1980), The Assessment of Psychopathology and Behavioral Problems in Children: A Review of Scales Suitable for Epidemiological and Clinical Research (1967–1979). Mental Health Service System Reports. Series AN, No. 1, U.S. Department of Health and Human Service, Rockville, MD.

Paulsen, J. (1969), Psychiatric problems. In: *Students*

and Drugs, ed. R.H. Blum and Associates. San Francisco: Jossey-Bass.

Petti, T.A. (1978), Depression in hospitalized child psychiatry patients. *J. Am. Acad. Child Psychiatry*, 17:49–59.

Ross, A.O. (1974), *Psychological Disorders of Children*. New York: McGraw-Hill Book Company.

Rothstein, A. (1981), Hallucinatory phenomena in childhood. *J. Am. Acad. Child Psychiatry*, 20:623–635.

Rubin, E.Z., et al. (1972), *Cognitive Perceptual Motor Dysfunction*. Detroit: Wayne State University Press.

Rutter, M. (1978), Diagnostic validity in child psychiatry. *Adv. Biol. Psych.* 2:2–22.

Rutter, M., and Gould, M. (1985), Classification. In: *Child and adolescent psychiatry: Modern approaches*, eds. M. Rutter and L. Hersov. Oxford: Blackwell Scientific Publications.

Rutter, M., and Garmezy, N. (1983), Developmental Psychopathology. In: *Handbook of Child Psychology*, Vol. 4, ed. E.M. Hetherington. New York: John Wiley and Sons, pp. 775–911.

Rutter, M.L., and Graham, P.J. (1968), The reliability and validity of the psychiatric assessment of the child. I. Interview with the child. *Br. J. Psychiatry*, 114:563–579.

Rutter, M.L., and Schaffer, D. (1980), DSM-III: A step forward or back in terms of the classification of child psychiatric disorders? *J. Am. Acad. Child Psychiatry*, 19:371–394.

Rutter, M.L., Schaffer, D., and Shepherd, M. (1975), *A Multi-Axial Classification of Child Psychiatric Disorders*. Geneva: World Health Organization.

Schmideberg, M. (1953), The psychoanalysis of delinquents. *Am. J. Orthopsychiatry*, 23:13–19.

Shaw, C.R., and McKay, H.D. (1969), *Juvenile Delinquency and Urban Areas*. Chicago: University of Chicago Press.

Silberberg, N.E., and Silberberg, M.D. (1967), Hyperlexia: Specific word recognition skills in young children. *Except. Child.*, 34:41–42.

Simmons, J.E. (1974), *Psychiatric Examination of Children*. Philadelphia, Lea & Febiger.

Sours, J.A. Frumken, P., and Inderwell, R.R. (1963), Somnambulism. *Arch. Gen. Psychiatry*, 9:400–413.

Spitzer, R.L., and Cantwell, D.P. (1980), The DSM-III classification of the psychiatric disorders of infancy, childhood, and adolescence. *J. Am. Acad. Child Psychiatry*, 19:356–370.

Spitzer, R.L., Fleiss, J.C., and Cohen, J. (1970), Psychiatric status schedule: A technique for evaluating psychopathology and impairment in role functioning. *Arch Psychiatry*, 23:41–55.

Taylor, E. (1980), Development of attention. In: *Scientific Foundation of Developmental Psychiatry*, ed. M. Rutter. London: Heinemann, pp. 185–197.

Wilking, V.N., and Paoli, C. (1966), The hallucinatory experience. *J. Am. Acad. Child Psychiatry*, 5:431–440.

Zigler, E., and Phillips, L. (1961), Psychiatric diagnosis: A critique. *J. Abnorm. Soc. Psychol.*, 63:607–618.

Part Five

Historic and Developmental Perspectives in Child and Adolescent Psychopathology

25

HISTORIC PERSPECTIVE ON VIEWS OF CHILD AND ADOLESCENT PSYCHOPATHOLOGY

A brief overview of the history of child and adolescent psychiatry reveals astonishing changes in our viewpoints of childhood psychopathology. In part, these reflect the diverse origins of the field in pediatrics, developmental psychology, the Mental Hygiene Movement, the juvenile justice system, and in adult psychiatry (Musto, 1989). By and large, six major perspectives can be discerned: descriptive, nature-nurture, psychoanalytic, biologic, developmental, and interactional. Usually one of these perspectives is dominant at a particular moment in history. Sometimes the change from one perspective to the next is precipitated by the genius of a new conceptual approach, sometimes by the discovery of a technologic advance, and sometimes by the prevailing economic and political climate. Occasionally we seem to go in circles or swing like a pendulum from one extreme to another. Yet on the whole the increase in our knowledge of psychopathology is immense and has perhaps increased exponentially in recent years.

DESCRIPTION AND MEASUREMENT

When child psychiatry as a professional field began to emerge in the late nineteenth and early twentieth century, the most impressive studies on childhood psychopathology were found in the work done on mentally retarded children. Studies by such pioneers

as Lightner Witmer (see Sears, 1975) at the University of Pennsylvania, HH Goddard (1912) in Vineland, New Jersey, and Walter Fernald in Boston achieved great strides in describing, defining, and measuring the kinds and degrees of mental retardation in children. In addition, as so often happens in the history of ideas, the investigators first used tests that had first serendipitously been developed elsewhere, in this case by Binet and Simon for schoolchildren in Paris. This early goal of describing, defining, and measuring represents an important basic theme in the history of the conceptualization and subsequent scientific study of childhood psychopathology and the first substantial appearance of the prescriptive and measuring perspective.

Mental retardation has undergone major shifts in prevailing attitudes throughout recorded history ranging from demonic contempt to holy adoration (Rosen, Clark, and Kivitz, 1976). The distinction between emotional problems and mental retardation was first recognized during the eighteenth century in the writings of Locke (Doll, 1962). It was not until the turn of the nineteenth century, however, that a more humane and modern era in the field was influenced by the work of a French psychiatrist, Itard, who was successful in educating the "Wild Boy of Aveyron" through a system of sensory input and allied habit training. Toward the middle of

335

the nineteenth century Seguin, who was inspired by Itard, continued a progressive influence by establishing schools and residence centers for the humane care of "idiots and other feebleminded persons." This trend continued throughout the nineteenth century as the American Association of Mental Deficiency was founded (1876) and major attempts were made toward educating and improving the lives of the mentally retarded. However, at the end of the nineteenth century the Parisian school of psychiatry and neurology focused its efforts on etiologic factors and the identification of a common cerebral defect. This "defect theory" accounted for a tragic shift in attitudes toward the mentally retarded population. The approach was largely limited to education, and efforts were made to encourage institutionalization of even the mildly retarded for the protection of society. Sexual segregation and forced sterilization were commonly recommended (Zigler and Hodapp, 1985). This trend, paradoxically, was supported by the popularity of the Binet test of intelligence along with the emphasis on inherited factors, all of which focused on the defects of a person.

THE NATURE-NURTURE CONTROVERSY

Shortly after this early work on retarded children, what were to become classic studies of juvenile delinquents began to appear. William Healy (see Sears, 1975), a neurologist at the Juvenile Psychopathic Institute in Chicago and cofounder of the first juvenile court clinic, in 1909 published many of these studies of delinquents. At that time the prevailing view suggested that the adolescent's antisocial behavior was organic in nature, although Healy, a neurologist, was more concerned about environmental factors that were being overlooked. Healy in effect served as a counterbalance to the views of others, such as Lombroso, who believed that criminal tendencies were derived mainly from heredity. Thus in Healy's studies of juvenile delinquency, a second major debate or theme in

the study of childhood psychopathology began to form: the relative roles of organic factors and environment. These two factors were seen initially mostly as an either/or proposition (the so-called "nature-nurture" controversy) rather than as two interacting factors. Protagonists for each side of the equation were often forceful in their views. Subsequently in psychology too, Arnold Gesell (1952) at Yale, for example, was primarily a maturationist who largely ignored the environment, whereas John B. Watson (see Kessen, 1965) was essentially a behaviorist who largely ignored biologic factors.

PSYCHOANALYSIS

Meanwhile a third major perspective in the history of the study of childhood psychopathology began to emerge, again in 1909, when Sigmund Freud published his account of the psychopathology and treatment of Little Hans (Freud, 1909). The basic concepts of psychoanalysis, especially the concepts of an unconscious functioning of the mind and psychosexual phases of development, became a rich source of "explanation" of almost every symptom and behavior (as well as a popular hope for a universal cure for all psychologic disorders).

Although psychoanalysis as a method of research and as a form of treatment has changed little* in its fundamental aspects since Freud first devised the method of free association, psychoanalysis as a theory has undergone a number of changes, from the early topographic model through to the structural model, ego psychology, object relations theory and, more recently, self theories. Nevertheless, in spite of these changes, certain basic concepts, including psychic determinism, a dynamic unconscious, sexual and aggressive drive development, psychic conflicts, mechanisms of defense, and transference, have remained more or less in-

*". . . a contemporary psychoanalysis is more similar to one of twenty-five or even fifty years ago than is true of almost any other form of treatment in psychiatry or medicine" (Michaels, 1988, p. 168).

tact. These concepts and the findings from which they were derived provided useful clinical explanations for a wide range of psychopathologic conditions in infants, children, and adolescents. Indeed, almost every psychiatric symptom has in the past been "explained" in part by various combinations of these basic concepts. Symptoms such as infant feeding and sleep difficulties, failure to thrive, bed-wetting, encopresis, separation anxiety, learning and reading difficulties, phobias, compulsions, conversion symptoms, depression, and psychoses were all understood, at least in part, in psychodynamic terms through the 1930s, 1940s, and even 1950s.

BIOLOGIC RESEARCH

A change then occurred: scientific research began to focus increasingly on the biologic processes involved in these disorders. Quite dramatically almost every symptom and disorder now could be understood, again at least in part, in biologic terms. Some examples of this change in our understanding are described below. This blossoming of biologic research, particularly during the past 10 years, has overtaken the virtual standstill of scientific research in psychoanalysis, and has led to a more comprehensive biopsychosocial understanding of major psychiatric disorders in children and adolescents. The psychoanalytic constructs mentioned previously continue to play a useful role.

DEVELOPMENTAL PERSPECTIVES

The developmental perspective was highlighted in the efforts of early developmental psychologists, particularly G. Stanley Hall who applied questionnaire and other techniques in the study of common psychologic problems and issues. Hall and his students, e.g., Terman at Stanford and Gesell at Yale, had a profound influence on the development of child psychology as an academic discipline. They emphasized the importance of studying normal development for understanding developmental deviation. Hall himself was initially sympathetic to psychoanalytic theory and arranged for Freud's only visit to this country. During the 1920's and 1930's developmental psychologists became particularly interested in longitudinal studies of development as well as in attempts to experimentally investigate psychoanalytic concepts. Subsequently, academic child psychology has experienced a tremendous growth as various diverse influences (e.g., the work of Piaget) have been incorporated in the rigorous experimental approach to the study of child development.

MULTIPLE INTERACTIONS

Subsequently, a sixth theme in childhood psychopathology emerged in which *all* the previously mentioned perspectives were viewed as useful contributory theories or models that individually might explain some behaviors, some symptoms, and some syndromes better than any one of the other existing theories. No single theory was sufficient, however, to explain all behavior. That is, until a comprehensive theory was found, we needed to utilize many different theories.

Subsequent attempts were made to formulate an interactive model for the multiple theories. One such model was the "goodness of fit" framework proposed by Stella Chess, Alexander Thomas, and Herbert Birch (1968) in their New York Longitudinal Study of temperament in children. Temperament was first assessed through the evaluation of nine categories of behavior. Three common groups of temperament were found: the "easy" child (40%), the "slow-to-warm-up" child (20%), and the child with a "difficult" temperament (10%). Each of these patterns was then examined in the context of the child's family, giving rise to many different final expressions, depending upon whether there was a "goodness of fit" or a "poorness of fit."

This interactional model has widespread implications. Thus, although developmental processes may begin with genetic coding, the phenotypic expression is continuously modulated by interactions with the environment at each stage of development (Eisenberg, 1977). For example, environmental variables may determine which identical twin develops schizophrenia (Kety, 1976), which children with neurologic deficits at 1 year of age subsequently will show signs of an attention deficit disorder (Rutter, et al., 1970), or which child who experiences a separation from parents subsequently will show a disturbance (Rutter, 1972). Even the temperament of the child does not remain fixed, but varies with the successive environments in which he or she develops (Chess, 1978; Graham, et al., 1973). In short, at present we attempt to see the child in his or her biologic and social context as well as intrapsychically, and to see this whole within a developmental frame of reference.

Violence in Children and Adolescents. An example of an interactional model can be seen in Lewis's studies of violence in children and adolescents. Early views on the psychopathology of aggressive behavior in children and adolescents included Lombroso's presumed (but unproved) theory of genetic transmission, psychoanalytic theories such as the "superego lacunae" concept (Johnson and Szurek, 1952), sociologic theories including role models (Shaw and McKay, 1942), social frustration (Merton, 1957), and a deprivation model describing a core of minority delinquents from socioeconomically deprived backgrounds (Wolfgang, Figlio and Cellin, 1972). More recently, attention has been paid to neurobiologic factors, including norepinephrine (Alpert, 1981) and 5-hydroxytryptamine (Valzelli, 1974) metabolism, hyporesponsive autonomic activity (Mednick and Christiansen, 1977), and elevated testosterone levels (Mattsson et al., 1980).

Gradually, the following viewpoint has emerged: many instances of aggressive and violent behavior in children and adolescents may be a symptom that represents a final common pathway brought about by the confluence of multiple psychosocial vulnerabilities (neurologic, psychiatric, and cognitive) and severe physical abuse (both witnessed and suffered) (Lewis, 1979, 1981, 1989). Thus, a contemporary viewpoint of violent children is that the aggressive behavior is frequently caused by the interaction of multiple etiologic factors, and that there is rarely one simple cause for the violence. (For a further discussion of violence in children and adolescents, see pp. 205 and 226.)

DISCUSSION

One final historical note is the oscillation between each of the viewpoints just outlined. One example is the debate that apparently still continues between maturationists and developmentalists. Gesell, of course, was an early ardent proponent of the maturational viewpoint. Freud, Erikson, and others are obvious examples of early proponents of the developmental viewpoint.

More recently, a maturational approach has reappeared in the form of a new concept called "discontinuities." The leading proponent is Kagan who noted, for example, an enhancement of memory between 8 and 12 months of age and a shift from a perceptual mode to a symbolic-linguistic mode at about 17 months (Kagan, 1979). Kagan hypothesized that this shift was essentially a *discontinuity* that occurred almost entirely on the basis of CNS maturation. One consequence of this maturational viewpoint (revisited) was the suggestion that not *all* the experiences of the average infant with his or her parents necessarily have a long-lasting or cumulative effect, since new maturational phenomena might add to the plasticity of the infant and in effect supersede previous behaviors and experiences. Kagan in fact suggested that problems seen during the first year or two of life may linger for two or three years but may then diminish and eventually disappear. At the same time, Hunt (1979) has noted that "A major share of early losses can be made up if the development-fostering quality of experience improves, and a great deal of early gain can be lost if the quality of experience depreciates."

This historical overview of different perspectives in the study of childhood psychopathology reveals different degrees of emphasis at any given time on each of the six major themes: descriptive, environmental, psychoanalytic, biologic, developmental, and interactive. Some of the different emphases can be clearly seen in our changing views on the psychopathology of particular disorders.

REFERENCES

Alpert, J.E., et al. (1981), Disorder of attention, activity, and aggression. In: *Vulnerabilities to Delinquency*, ed. D.O. Lewis. New York: Spectrum Publications.

Chess, S. (1978), The plasticity of human development. *J. Am. Acad. Child Psychiatry*, 17:80–91.

Doll, E.E. (1962), A historical survey of research and management of mental retardation in the United States. In: *Readings on the Exceptional Child*, ed. E.P. Trapp and P. Himelstein. New York: Appleton-Century-Crofts.

Eisenberg, L. (1977), Development as a unifying concept in psychiatry. *Am. J. Psychiatry*, 133:225–237.

Freud, S. (1966–1972). Analysis of a phobia in a five-year-old boy. In *Standard Edition* (Vol. 10), ed. J. Strachey. London: Hogarth Press, pp. 3–152.

Gesell, A. (1952), Arnold Gesell. In: *History of Psychology in Autobiography* (Vol. 4), ed. E.G. Boring, H.S. Langfeld, H. Werner, et al. Worcester MA: Clark University Press, pp. 123–142.

Glaser, K. (1967), Masked depression in children and adolescents. *Am. J. Psychother.*, 11:565.

Goddard, H. (1912), *The Kallikak Family*. New York: Macmillan Publishing Co.

Graham, P., Rutter, M., and George, S. (1973), Temperamental characteristics as predictors of behavior disorders in children. *Am. J. Orthopsychiatry*, 43:328–339.

Hunt, J. (1979), Psychological development: Early experience. In: *Annual Review of Psychology* (Vol. 30), ed. L.W. Porter, M.R. Rosenzweig. Palo Alto, CA: Annual Review.

Johnson, A.M., and Szurek, S.A. (1952), The genesis of antisocial acting out in children and adults. *Psychoanal. Q.*, 21:323.

Kagan, J. (1979), The form of early development. *Arch. Gen. Psychiatry*, 36:1047–1054.

Kanner, L. (1943), Autistic disturbances of affective contact. *Nerv. Child.*, 2:217–250.

Kessen, W. (1965), *The Child*, New York: John Wiley & Sons, Inc., pp. 230–231.

Kety, S.S. (1976), Studies designed to disentangle genetic and environmental variables in schizophrenia. *Am. J Psychiatry*, 133:1134–1137.

Lewis, D.D., et al. (1979), Violent juvenile delinquents: Psychiatric, neurological, psychological and abuse factors. *J. Am. Acad. Child Psychiatry*, 18:307–319.

Lewis, D.D., Lovely, R., Yeager, C., and Femina, D.D. (1989), Toward a theory of the genesis of violence: A follow-up study of delinquents. *J. Am. Acad. Child Adolesc. Psychiatry*, 28:431–436.

Lewis, D.O. (Ed.) (1981), *Vulnerabilities to Delinquency*. New York: Spectrum Publications.

Mattsson, A. et al. (1980), Plasma testosterone, aggressive behavior, and personality dimensions in young male delinquents. *J. Am. Acad. Child Psychiatry*, 19:476–491.

Mednick, S.A., and Christiansen, K.O. (Eds.) (1977), *Biosocial Bases of Criminal Behavior*. New York: Gardner Press.

Merton, R.K. (1957), *Social Theory and Social Structure*. New York: Free Press.

Michaels, R. (1988), The future of psychoanalysis. *Psychoanal. Q.*, 57:167–185.

Musto, D.F. (1985), Child Psychiatry: An Historical Perspective. In: *Psychiatry*, Volume 2, ed. R. Michels. Philadelphia: J.B. Lippincott Co.

Rochlin, C. (1959), The loss complex: A contribution to the etiology of depression. *J. Am. Psychoanal. Assoc.*, 7:299–316.

Rosen, M., Clark, G., and Kivitz, M. (1976), *The History of Mental Retardation* (Vol. 1). Baltimore: University Park Press.

Rutter, M. (1972), *Maternal Deprivation Reassessed.* Harmondsworth: Penguin.

Rutter, M. (1984), Cognitive deficits in the pathogenesis of autism. *J. Child Psychol. Psychiatry*, 24:513.

Rutter, M., Tizard, J., and Whitmore, K. (1970), *Education, Health and Behavior.* London: Longmans. (?).

Sears, R.R. (1975), *Your Ancients Revisited: A History of Child Development.* Chicago: University of Chicago Press.

Shaw, R.C., and McKay, H.D. (1942), *Juvenile Delinquency and Urban Areas.* Chicago: University of Chicago Press.

Thomas, A., Chen, S., and Birch, H.G. (1968), *Temperament and Behavior Disorders in Children.* New York: New York University Press.

Toolan, J.M. (1962), Depression in children and adolescents. *Am. J. Orthopsychiatry*, 32:404.

Valzelli, L. (1974), 5-Hydroxytryptamine in aggressiveness. In: *Advances in Biochemical Psychopharmacology*, ed. E. Costa, G. Gessa and M. Sandler. New York: Raven Press.

Wolfgang, M.E., Figlio, R.M., and Cellin, T. (1972), *Delinquency in a Birth Cohort.* Chicago: University of Chicago Press.

Zigler, E., and Hodapp, R.M. (1985). Mental retardation. In: *Psychiatry* (Vol. 2), ed. J.O. Cavenar. Philadelphia: Lippincott, pp. 1–9.

26

DEVELOPMENTAL PERSPECTIVE ON PSYCHOPATHOLOGY: INTRODUCTION

Some psychiatric disorders, such as autism, typically have their onset in early childhood, whereas others, such as depression and suicide, typically occur more frequently and in more severe form at or after puberty. Is the young child protected in some way from depression? Some symptoms, such as separation anxiety during early childhood, seem to be exaggerations of developmentally appropriate phenomena, whereas others, such as agoraphobia or the onset of school refusal during adolescence, have no obvious relationship to normal phenomena.

Symptoms related to and concurrent with developmental phenomena seem to have a better prognosis than those that are not so related. For example, simple problems in articulation tend to resolve with maturation whereas early onset (before age 6) of antisocial behavior does not augur well for the child. Some psychiatric illnesses, such as obsessive-compulsive disorder, persist into adult life, whereas others such as enuresis generally remit and disappear before adulthood. Here, outcome in some cases is in part a function of development. In some disorders, such as sadness and depressive disorder, the distinction between normal and abnormal is often clinically blurred. In schizophrenia and the schizophrenic spectrum of disorders, however, the array of symptoms that usually characterize the disorder may be incomplete, leaving one in doubt as to whether the condition is a forme fruste (due, perhaps, to weak penetrance of the gene or special environ-

mental circumstances), a related but not identical disorder, or a prodromal or subthreshold state that will express itself more fully at a later stage of development. In all these ways, developmental considerations may affect diagnosis. Sometimes a disorder emerges as a result of changing interactions over time between child and parent. For example, depression may occur in the child when a "goodness of fit" between the child's temperament and the parent's tolerance or understanding changes to a "poorness of fit." In this situation, the child's behavior changes as a result of development and the parent's behavior changes as a result, for example, of marital discord and divorce. Thus, the course of a disturbance may vary with development and this interaction proceeds in complex ways. Finally, most children with emotional disorders grow up to be normal adults without any specific psychiatric disorder. Developmental factors serve to fortify the child against the possible harmful effects of prolonged anxiety.

Each of these considerations deserves further exploration. Surprisingly, there is not at present a well-developed coherent body of knowledge of the role of development in the determination of onset, epidemiology, psychopathology, diagnosis, severity, response to treatment, and natural history of disorders seen during infancy, childhood, and adolescence. Fortunately, there is great interest in this developmental perspective (Rutter, 1988).

The purpose of the chapters that follow,

340

then, is to illustrate some of the development issues in the psychopathology of children and adolescents in the context of the historical shifts in emphasis noted in the previous chapter. Selected categories of psychopathology are briefly summarized and some developmental perspectives specific for each category are outlined. Neither the categories selected nor the developmental issues outlined are intended to be comprehensive; rather, they are used to highlight the developmental approach.

The selection consists of an example from some of the major categories of psychopathology listed on page 296:

1. general developmental delay (mental retardation)
2. pervasive development disorder (infantile autism)
3. psychosis (childhood onset schizophrenia)
4. anxiety disorders, separation disorder, anxiety disorder, avoidant disorder, overanxious disorder)
5. affective disorder (major depressive disorder and suicide)
6. mixed disorder (attention deficit-hyperactivity disorder)
7. personality disorder (borderline personality disorder)

Case vignettes are included at the conclusion of each chapter to illustrate developmental aspects of the disorders.

These additional disorders have obvious developmental implications: reactive attachment disorder of infancy or early childhood, developmental language and learning disorders, eating disorders, elimination disorders (enuresis and encopresis), gender identity disorders (homosexuality and transsexualism), tic disorders, organic brain disorder, somatiform disorders (conversion disorder and somatization disorder), sleep disorders, impulse control disorder, and stress disorders. Some of these conditions, as well as those selected for this section, are mentioned in other sections in the context of particular developmental phases.

REFERENCE

Rutter, M. (1988), Epidemiological approaches to developmental psychopathology. *Arch. Gen. Psychiatry*, 45:486–495.

27

MENTAL RETARDATION

Definition. Mental retardation is defined on the basis of intellectual functioning (IQ less than 70) with concurrent deficits in adaptive functioning, i.e., in the capacity to meet expected demands for personal independence and self-sufficiency. Intellectual level should be assessed on the basis of an individually administered IQ test; for most tests an IQ of 70 is two standard deviations from the population mean of 100 (Fig. 27–1).

Historical Note. Mental retardation has been recognized since antiquity; it became an important area of study in the late nineteenth and early twentieth centuries when Binet and Simon in 1905 devised intelligence tests for schoolchildren in Paris. Numerous other tests were subsequently developed (p. 318). Syndromes that caused mental retardation were rapidly identified. At present more than 200 syndromes have been described; however, these syndromes only account for about 20 to 25% of cases of mental retardation and usually such conditions are found in association with more severe levels of retardation.

Prevalence. The prevalence of mental retardation at any point in time is about 1% (Baird and Sadovnick, 1985), i.e., several million persons in the United States exhibit mental retardation. The prevalence of the disorder varies over the life cycle as a result of various factors: (1) given that IQ tests are designed to assess skills important for school performance it is not surprising that the diagnosis is most commonly made in school age children, (2) some individuals, particularly those with milder degrees of retardation,

make sufficient improvement so that they are no longer classified as mentally retarded, and (3) individuals with more severe retardation and associated physical disorders have a higher mortality rate. The disorder is about 1.5 times as common in males as in females. Some of this distribution may be accounted for by genetic factors, social role expectations, and possibly a reduced tolerance for deviance among males. The curve for intelligence generally follows a normal distribution pattern except for a higher prevalence of more severe retardation among the early preschool group.

Only about 5% of retarded children are severely retarded and cannot learn. About 20% of children who are retarded can learn, although symbolic functions such as reading, writing, or arithmetic cannot be performed.

About 75% of children who are retarded have no identifiable disorder, are normal in appearance, have an IQ in the range of 50 to 70 and can do almost everything except more abstract thinking. The retardation in this largest group with so-called familial retardation is the result of a combination of factors, including genetic inheritance and limited environmental stimulation. Often limited environmental support is associated with factors such as poor medical care and greater family disruption. Central nervous system dysfunction is not common in this group, but when brain damage is present the incidence of psychopathologic and behavioral problems increases.

Although the distinction between "organic" and "familial" retardation has historically been used, it is obviously the case that

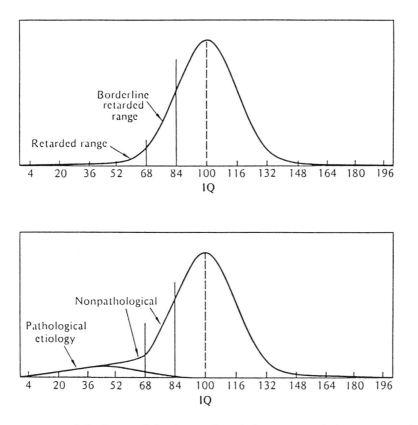

Fig. 27–1. Comparison of the theoretical distribution of Stanford-Binet IQs with the approximate form of the distribution actually found. Reprinted with permission from Achenbach, T.M. (1974), *Developmental Psychopathology*, New York: The Ronald Press Company.

failure to find organic factors does not necessarily mean they are not present.

Clinical Features. Children who have familial retardation often have a general delay in development, especially in motor and language development. Because deafness and blindness may have initial similar effects on early development, these sensory problems should be specifically ruled out. The more severe and early the retardation, the more likely it is that an identifiable disease is present.

Etiology. A large number of syndromes are associated with mental retardation (Table 27–1).

Psychopathology. In general, children who are retarded experience the same range of emotional conflicts and psychopathology as do normal children. However, they are more likely to experience failure and consequent rejection when the demands for socialization, education, relationships, and training are felt as excessive stresses. Indeed, society often fails to adapt to the specific needs and the modified expectations required by the child who is retarded in order for the child to experience success and feelings of being loved and secure. For this reason alone, the child who is mentally retarded is vulnerable to the development of behavior disorders (Penrose, 1949; Chess, 1970, 1977). The presence of neurologic damage not only increases the risk for a psychopathologic condition, but worsens the prognosis. Available research suggests that the prevalence of mental disorders in individuals with retardation is high (Corbett, 1985).

Laboratory Studies. To confirm the diagnosis, psychologic tests that measure IQ and adaptive behavior (see p. 318) are used. Other

Table 27–1. Causes of Mental Retardation

A. *Genetic Disorders*

Genetic disorders account for nearly 50% of children who are severely mentally retarded (Crandall, 1977), and include:

    I. Chromosomal abnormalities . . . . Trisomy 21 (Down's syndrome), trisomy 18 (Edwards syndrome), X-linked syndromes (e.g., fragile-X syndrome)

    II. Single gene mutations

        Enzymatic disorder (nonstorage) . . . . Phenylketonuria, tyrosinemia, methylmalonic aciduria, galactosemia

        Storage diseases . . . . Sphingolipidoses (e.g., Tay-Sachs disease), mucolipidoses (e.g., Hurler's syndrome), mucopolysaccharides (e.g., Hunter's syndrome), polysaccharides (e.g. Pompe's disease)

        Transport defects . . . . Wilson's disease, Hartnup's disease, Menkes syndrome

        Structural disorders . . . . Tuberous sclerosis, multiple neurofibromatosis

        Multiple congenital abnormalities . . . . Smith-Lemli-Opitz syndrome, DeSanctis-Cacchione syndrome, Seckel syndrome, Cockayne syndrome, Sjögren-Larsson syndrome, congenital myotonic dystrophy, cranial synostoses, multiple lentigines

        Central nervous system malformations . . . . Spina bifida, hydrocephalus, encephalocele

B. *Environmental Hazards*

During pregnancy any insults to the fetus may cause abnormalities and mental retardation, including:

    Drugs . . . . Alcohol (fetal alcohol syndrome), trimethadione, hydantoin, progesterone, warfarin

    Infections . . . . Rubella, AIDS, cytomegalovirus, toxoplasmosis

Toxins

Radiation

Trauma, birth trauma, and anoxia

studies are needed to rule out any of the known medical syndromes that are associated with retardation, many of which have specific morphologic or anatomic stigmata.

Differential Diagnosis. Differential diagnosis of the many conditions that cause mental retardation is usually made on the basis of the history and physical examination before proceeding with laboratory tests. Some disorders (e.g., autism) are commonly observed in association with mental retardation. A clinical classification (Table 27–2) following an early developmental framework for onset may suggest which laboratory studies are needed (Packman, 1987).

Prenatal diagnosis may be made in some cases by amniocentesis. The presence of abnormalities at birth may provide immediate knowledge of retardation (e.g., in trisomy 21).

Having eliminated any of the aforementioned conditions that are pertinent, one arrives at the largest group of children who are retarded: those with so-called familial retardation. These children frequently have an IQ in the 50 to 70 range and usually show no evidence of CNS dysfunction (Zigler and Balla, 1977).

Treatment. Treatment first involves the sensitive discussion with the parents about the diagnosis. The parents are usually anxious and need a great deal of support to enable them to absorb the information they will require to anticipate the child-rearing problems that lie ahead. Many parents experience a series of reactions (denial, anger, guilt) before they eventually cope. The child will need an enriched environment and special education. A team approach of different specialists is of-

Table 27–2.   Clinical Classification of Mental Retardation

Prenatal onset......	Environmental causes affecting the fetus, primary CNS developmental defects, multiple malformations, chromosomal syndromes
Perinatal onset.....	Hypoxia, kernicterus, hypoglycemia, sepsis, intracranial hemorrhage
Postnatal onset.....	Environmental: e.g., trauma (head injury), infections (encephalitis), toxins (lead), cerebrovascular accidents
	Familial and multifactorial causes, inborn errors of metabolism, other (e.g., congenital hypothyroidism)

ten helpful. Psychotherapy for emotional problems and appropriate management of assorted medical conditions are, of course, indicated as needed. Genetic counseling for the parents is required when a genetic disorder is present. Recent legislation and court decisions have significantly expanded the rights of affected individuals to services (Zigler and Hodapp, 1986).

Developmental Perspective. The developmental issues in mental retardation begin with environmental influences that may have their impact at any point in development from the fetal period onward. The subsequent development of the child with mental retardation continues to depend to a considerable extent on this continuing interaction between the child and his or her environment. A child who has an IQ below 70 and is less able to deal with the ordinary unmodified environmental stresses of everyday life may experience more failure and may consequently be at greater risk for developing behavior problems than a child with an IQ of 100. At the same time, the child who is mentally retarded experiences the same developmental stages, faces the same developmental tasks, and has the same needs as a child who is of normal intelligence. Thus, if the environment is modified for that child, one might predict fewer behavior problems.

One way to view this process in nonorganic cultural-familial retardation is through the use of a model (Fig. 27–2) proposed by Zigler (1980).

Here progression through developmental phases in the child with familial retardation and an IQ of 66 is depicted as a continuous spiral having the same invariant sequence of developmental stages as that of the child with an IQ of 100 or 150. Progression occurs at a slower rate, however, and has a more limited end point compared to that in the child with an IQ of 100 or an IQ of 150. Thus the child with an IQ of 50 can be thought of as simply being at the lower end of the normal distribution curve. Such a child should then be regarded in the same way one regards every other child within the normal distribution curve: that is, all children, regardless of where they fall on the normal distribution curve for intelligence, need to be loved, stimulated, educated, and reared in a similar way.

The model also demonstrates why physical abnormalities are not found with any greater frequency in this group of children at the lower (but not extreme) end of the distribution curve compared with those at the upper end of the curve. Finally, the model illustrates how the interactions between the child and his or her environment might affect the final end point. Positive environmental influences and success experiences enhance development, whereas adverse environmental influences and failure experiences restrict development and give rise to behavior problems in all children.

Case Vignette

Nancy was the first of two children born to middle-class parents. She was a difficult and fussy baby; her developmental milestones were significantly delayed. Although her parents consulted her pediatrician about her delayed speech at 18 months they were reassured. As a toddler Nancy's behavior was difficult to manage because of her oppositional behaviors and limited attention span. When she was 30 months old her parents realized that her 15-month-old sister was talking more than Nancy. They sought a comprehensive evaluation that revealed marked

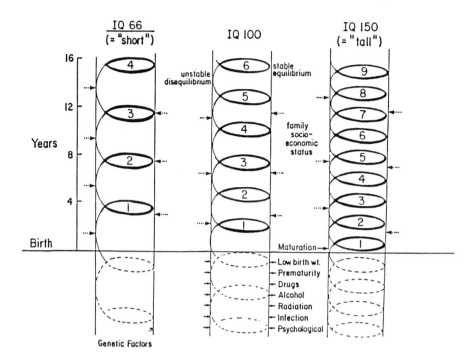

Fig. 27–2. Continuity and maturation in a stage model for cognitive development. Modified from Zigler, E., and Cascione, R. (1980), Overview of cognitive, behavioral and communicative disorders. In: *The Physician and the Mental Health of the Child.* II. *The Psychological Concomitants of Illness,* ed. H.J. Grossman and R.L. Stubblefield. Monroe, WI: American Medical Association.

deficits in intellectual and adaptive skills; various medical studies failed to reveal any specific condition that might be responsible for her developmental delay. Although her parents were shocked when the possibility of retardation was raised, they acknowledged the need for intervention. Nancy was subsequently enrolled in an early intervention program where she made noteworthy gains, particularly in the area of behavioral control. In elementary school Nancy was placed in various special education classes; although she made progress academically she felt stigmatized and was sometimes depressed. Partial mainstreaming appeared to increase her self-confidence. Psychologic testing at age 10 revealed a full scale IQ score of 55 with commensurate deficits in adaptive behavior. In high school Nancy exhibited more behavior problems as she entered adolescence and became acutely jealous of her younger sister. A period of counseling with a social worker was

helpful to Nancy and her family. As an adult Nancy continues to exhibit moderate mental retardation. She lives semi-independently in a group home for the retarded and attends a local sheltered workshop. She is pleased by her personal self-sufficiency and accomplishments and is active in the community.

Comment. This case illustrates several important features in the care of individuals with mental retardation. Individuals like Nancy can make good use of various services (educational and psychotherapeutic). Early intervention and special educational efforts can foster acquisition of important basic skills that optimize adult outcome.

REFERENCES

Baird, P.A., and Sadovnick, A.D. (1985), Mental retardation in over half-a-million consecutive livebirths: An epidemiological study. *Am. J. Ment. Defic.,* 89:323–330.

Binet, A., and Simon, T. (1905), New methods for the

diagnosis of the intellectual level of subnormalcy. *L'Annee Psychologique,* tr. and reprinted in: *The Development of Intelligence in Children,* ed. A. Binet and T. Simon. Baltimore: Williams & Wilkins (1916), pp. 37–90.

Chess, S. (1970), Emotional problems in mentally retarded children. In: *Psychiatric Approaches to Mental Retardation,* ed. F.J. Menolascino. New York: Basic Books, pp. 55–67.

Chess, S. (1977), Evolution of behavior disorders in a group of mentally retarded children. *J. Am. Acad. Child Psychiatry,* 16:4–18.

Corbett, J.A. (1985), Mental Retardation: Psychiatric Aspects. In: *Child and Adolescent Psychiatry: Modern Approaches,* eds. M. Rutter and L. Hersov. Oxford: Blackwell Scientific Publications, pp. 661–678.

Crandall, B.F. (1977), Genetic disorders and mental retardation. *J. Am. Acad. Child Psychiatry,* 16:88–108.

Packman, S. (1987), Diagnostic evaluation of the child with mental retardation. In: *Pediatrics,* ed. A.M. Rudolph and J.I.E. Hoffman. Norwalk: Appleton & Lange, pp. 378–381.

Penrose, L.S. (1949), *The Biology of Mental Defect.* London: Sidgwick & Jackson.

Zigler, E., and Balla, D. (1977), Personality factors in the performance of the retarded. *J. Am. Acad. Child Psychiatry,* 16:19–37.

Zigler, E., and Cascione, R. (1980), Overview of cognitive, behavioral and communicative disorders. In: *The Physician and the Mental Health of the Child. II. The Psychological Concomitants of Illness,* ed. H.J. Grossman and R.L. Stubblefield. Monroe, WI: American Medical Association.

Zigler, E., and Hodapp, B. (1986), *Understanding Mental Retardation.* Cambridge: Cambridge University Press.

28

AUTISTIC DISORDER

Definition. Autistic disorder is a pervasive development disorder characterized by marked deviance in social and language development, with accompanying stereotyped behaviors and a desire for sameness in routines. It is commonly associated with mental retardation.

Historical Note. Our view of infantile autism has undergone several changes since Kanner's original description in 1943 of 11 cases of "inborn autistic disturbance of affective contact" (Kanner, 1943). Kanner stressed the biologic roots of the disorder but noted an apparent association with higher social class that now appears to have been an artifact. Subsequently, psychoanalysts such as Bettelheim (1967) blamed "refrigerator mothers" for the condition, causing much guilt and further suffering among parents of autistic children. Then, beginning perhaps in the 1960s, it became clear through research that the type of parenting the child received did *not* account for the condition, although parents surely react to an autistic child, often with depression and social isolation. Today, most of the research findings point to neurobiologic factors as being of primary etiologic importance in infantile autism. Unfortunately, numerous anatomic and biochemical studies have not revealed any consistent ultimate causes for the disorder (Rutter, 1985). Linguistic, cognitive, and social deficits are current areas of intense investigation.

Prevalence and Epidemiology. The prevalence of autism is about 2 to 4 cases per 10,000 (Lotter, 1966). The sex ratio is about 3 boys to 1 girl; girls are more severely affected. Siblings are affected at a rate of 50 times that of the general population (Rutter, 1985). There is often a family history of speech delay. The concordance rate in monozygotic twins is higher as compared with dizygotic twins (Folstein and Rutter, 1977). There are no significant class differences.

Clinical Features. The onset is early, often within the first 6 months and usually before the child is 3 years of age.

The marked deviant social development is manifest in the child's lack of social responsiveness and failure to establish attachments (Volkmar, 1987). Attachment behaviors, such as anticipatory posturing or following behavior, are absent. The child seems to "look through" another person rather than relate to another person. Empathy is lacking, and the child seems unable to perceive or respond to the feelings of others. In addition, the child appears to be unable to modulate any kind of emotional expression, giving rise to a somewhat unexpressive, bland face.

The deviant language development is seen in the child's difficulties in both understanding and communicating with other people. In addition, there may be echoing, idiosyncratic language, and pronomial (I-you) reversal.

Stereotyped behaviors include whirling, hand flapping, finger movements at the periphery of vision, and preoccupations with various smells, colors, or textures. The child seems to have an inordinate desire for sameness, with a need for rigid unchanging routines. If the routines are changed, the child becomes extraordinarily upset.

The subsequent development of a child with autism is variable. Very few achieve normal adulthood; those who do are usually children with a high IQ. Approximately 15% are able to work and have some kind of social life. However, the majority (75%) remain severely impaired through to adulthood and require care. This group of children often tests low in IQ (below 50). Generally, if there is no useful language by 5 years of age, a poor outcome is likely. In fact, only about 50% acquire useful speech. At adolescence, about 25% develop seizures, and this occurrence also is more likely among those who are severely retarded.

Etiology. The ultimate cause of autism is not known, but a genetic component for at least the language and cognitive deviance is strongly suspected. The role of other biologic factors is suggested by the frequency of various neurologic abnormalities and seizure disorder in autistic children. In some instances autism occurs secondary to congenital rubella, tuberous sclerosis, infantile spasms, and perhaps other neurologic conditions.

Psychopathology. Neurobiologic factors are thought to be involved in most cases of autism. There is no evidence that parents cause the condition. On the other hand, families are emotionally drained in caring for an autistic child.

Laboratory Studies. There are no specific biologic markers for autism. Laboratory studies may be needed to rule out any of the conditions considered in the differential diagnosis and any other possible primary disorder that may have caused the autism.

Differential Diagnosis. Autism is a pervasive developmental disorder of early onset characterized by ritualistic behavior and deviance in social relationships and language. Because there is no evidence for thought disorder (e.g., hallucinations), autism is not considered to be a psychosis.

Schizophrenia. On the other hand, schizophrenia is a psychosis characterized in children by a later onset, usually later than 8 years of age, with clear evidence of a thought disorder, including hallucinations and any of the other features of a thought disorder.

Developmental Language Disorder. Usually confined to the specific language prob-

lem, developmental language disorder does not affect the development of the capacity to form relationships in any major way. The child with language disorder may become avoidant and shy, but he or she will not "look through" the other person and usually is nonverbally communicative.

Mental Retardation. Mental retardation per se in children is not usually associated with all the characteristic features that are present in autism. Social development is less impaired than in autism.

Elective Mutism. This condition is indeed elective, and the child can usually speak quite normally and relate well to certain people with whom he or she has formed satisfactory attachments. In addition, the other features of autism are absent.

Disintegrative Disorder (Heller's disease). This rare disorder has a slightly later onset (2 to 4 years of age), preceded by a period of clearly normal development followed by severe, progressive deterioration, including loss of bowel and bladder control.

Treatment. Treatment of the child with autism usually includes special education, behavior therapy, and selective use of drugs. Psychotherapy is sometimes indicated. Counseling and help for the parents are also part of the treatment plan (Howlin and Rutter, 1987). Outcome is difficult to predict, with or without treatment. Generally the level of intelligence does not change and is most strongly related to outcome.

Developmental Perspective. Autism is an example of a condition in which several lines of development, including attachment, language, and sociability, are severely affected in their earlier stages. The developmental failure is characterized by marked deviance. For example, a central problem in autism is the child's inability to understand and react appropriately to the message the other person is trying to communicate through language, voice, and facial expression. In contrast, a normal infant of 14 months of age readily comprehends and responds to the signals and messages being communicated to him or her by the parent. This problem for the child with autism often persists throughout development, through to the adult years.

The prominence and pervasiveness of the developmental failure are the obvious reasons for classifying the disorder as a pervasive developmental disorder.

Case Vignette

Charles was the second of three children born to middle class parents. The pregnancy, labor, and delivery had been problem free and his parents were delighted with this first son who was described as a placid and undemanding baby. Although motor skills initially seemed to develop appropriately, his parents felt that he was hard to reach; they became concerned as language failed to develop. In contrast to their previous child Charles seemed much less interested in social interaction. Stranger anxiety had never really developed and Charles was as comfortable with strangers as with his parents. Charles responded in unusual and idiosyncratic ways to the environment. Although he was exquisitely sensitive to some sounds, e.g., the vacuum cleaner, his pediatrician became concerned about his lack of language at age 2 and obtained hearing testing which revealed normal hearing. He was seen at 3 years of age for developmental examination; at that time motor skills were near age level but communication and social skills were severely delayed. Charles was noted to be intolerant of change, unattached to his parents, and exhibited various self-stimulatory behaviors. A comprehensive medical evaluation failed to reveal any specific medical condition which might account for his developmental difficulties. Family history was negative apart from a history of learning disabilities in several relatives. A diagnosis of autism was made and Charles was enrolled in a special education program at age 4.

Charles gradually acquired some, limited, expressive language skills. His language was remarkable for echolalia, pronoun reversal, and an unusual monotonic voice. He continued to be isolated, preferring to engage in self-stimulatory activities (finger flicking and body rocking) rather than in interaction with peers or family members. By the time he reached primary school his IQ was in the moderately retarded range. Although his language skills were quite impaired he did exhibit some unusual nonverbal problem solving skills, particularly related to memory. As an adolescent Charles developed a seizure disorder. As an adult he lives in a group home and attends a sheltered workshop. He continues to be isolated and has little interest in social interaction.

Comment. Although autism appears to have its origins at, or shortly after, birth it is often the case that parents become seriously concerned about the child's development only as speech fails to develop. It is usually the case that the child responds remarkably to aspects of the nonsocial environment, e.g., to certain sounds. Typically motor skills are relatively preserved initially while communicative and cognitive skills are delayed and unusually scattered. On average, outcome is related to both IQ and the acquisition of communicative skills. Although some, limited, social skills emerge over time, even the highest functioning adults usually remain rather isolated and have difficulties in understanding aspects of social interaction.

REFERENCES

Bettelheim, B. (1967), *The Empty Fortress*. New York: Free Press.

Folstein, S., and Rutter, M. (1977), Infantile autism: A genetic study of 21 twin pairs. *J. Child Psychol. Psychiatry*, 18:297–321.

Howlin, P., and Rutter, M. (1987), *Treatment of Autistic Children*. New York: John Wiley & Sons, Inc.

Kanner, L. (1943), Autistic disturbances of affect contact. *Nervous Child*, 2:217–230.

Lotter, V. (1966), Epidemiology of autistic conditions in young children. I. Prevalence. *Soc. Psychiatry*, 1:124–137.

Rutter, M. (1985), Infantile autism and other child psychoses. In: *Child Psychiatry: Modern Approaches*, ed. M. Rutter and L. Herson. Oxford: Blackwell Scientific Publications, pp. 545–566.

Rutter, M. (1985), Infantile autism and other pervasive developmental disorders. In: *Child and Adolescent Psychiatry*, 2nd Ed., ed. M. Rutter and L. Herson. Oxford: Blackwell Scientific Publications.

Volkmar, F.R. (1987), Social development. In: *Handbook of Autism*, ed. D. Cohen and A. Donnellan, New York: John Wiley & Sons, pp. 41–60.

29

SCHIZOPHRENIA

Definition. Schizophrenia is diagnosed in the same way in children and adults. The disorder is characterized by the presence of symptoms of a thought disorder, which include hallucinations and delusions accompanied by abnormal affects and relationships.

Historical Note. After the adult syndrome of schizophrenia was described, attempts were made to extend the concept to children. For many years the term childhood schizophrenia was synonymous with childhood psychosis. However, schizophrenia was first clearly separated from autism in England by Rutter (1967) and Kolvin (1971). An early-onset condition, beginning before 3 years of age, (called at that time "infantile psychosis") appeared to have all the characteristics of autism, whereas a later-onset condition, beginning after 8 years of age (called at that time "late-onset psychosis") appeared to have all the characteristics of schizophrenia seen in adults. In effect, what was then called "late-onset psychosis" is now considered to be early-onset or childhood-onset schizophrenia, a psychosis quite separate and different from autism, which is now considered to be a pervasive developmental disorder.

Prevalence and Epidemiology. Childhood-onset schizophrenia is a rare disorder, occurring perhaps at the rate of 0.08 to 0.32 per 10,000 (Kramer, 1978). Recent studies suggest a slight predominance of this disorder in boys (Volkmar, In Press). Parents of children with schizophrenia have a higher rate of schizophrenia than parents of nonschizophrenic children.

Clinical Features. The onset is rarely before age 5 and is usually after 8 years of age, and typically occurs during adolescence. Prior to onset the child may have been described as a hypotonic infant with some developmental delay (Zetlin, 1986), and may have had soft neurologic signs. Usually the onset of the disorder is insidious, with a gradual deterioration in functioning. Occasionally the onset is abrupt.

The thought disorder that characterizes schizophrenia includes the presence of hallucinations and delusions, and looseness of association and concrete thinking. Schneiderian "first-rank symptoms" (Schneider, 1959; 1971) may be present: (1) hearing of one's thoughts spoken aloud, (2) auditory hallucinations that comment on the patient's behavior, (3) somatic hallucinations, (4) the experience of having one's thoughts controlled, (5) the spreading of one's thoughts to others, (6) delusions, and (7) the experience of having one's actions controlled or influenced from the outside. The child often has a low frustration tolerance, may be hypochondriacal, and may have temper tantrums, or the child may have episodes of anxiety, sometimes accompanied by stereotypies and obsessional features. The child is often emotionally aloof, with a blunt, flattened affect. Violent fantasies may be present, and the child's behavior may be bizarre, sadistic, and even murderous. The earlier the onset, the poorer the outcome (Eggers, 1978).

Etiology. The cause of childhood-onset schizophrenia is unknown. The contribution of genetic factors is suggested by the increased rate of the disorder in first-degree

351

relatives (Kolvin, 1971; Kallman and Prugh, 1971) and the higher concordance in monozygotic as compared to fraternal twins. The adopted-away monozygotic twin child of schizophrenic parents develops schizophrenia at the same rate as his or her sibling reared by the schizophrenic biologic parent (Fischer, Harvald and Hauge, 1969). The onset of the disorder in childhood might relate to increased genetic loading or a complicated interaction between biologic vulnerability and the environment. Affected children have been noted to exhibit signs of neurologic immaturity (e.g., "soft" signs and hypotonia) (Cantor, 1988). Similarly, electrophysiologic studies provide nonspecific evidence of central nervous system dysfunction (Waldo, Cohen, Caparulo, et al., 1978). Neuropsychologic studies have revealed deficits in attentional capacities and the processing of information. Studies of neurotransmitter systems have not been common and have produced conflicting results, e.g., Cantor et al. (1980) reported depressed cholinergic functioning while Walker et al. (1986) noted possibly lowered levels of catechol-o-methyl-transferase (COMT).

Although some studies have posited a theoretic relationship between disturbed patterns of family communication and schizophrenia, available evidence suggests that parents do not cause schizophrenia. Disturbed patterns of family interaction might well reflect the impact of a disturbed child. Conversely, stress may facilitate the expression of the disorder or exacerbate it.

Laboratory Studies. No biologic markers have been found. Psychologic testing, using projective and other unstructured techniques, may provide evidence regarding the presence of thought disorder.

Differential Diagnosis. *Conduct Disorder.* Children diagnosed initially as having a conduct disorder are often later diagnosed as having schizophrenia. The presence of symptoms and signs of a thought disorder is essential in making the diagnosis of schizophrenia, and should be carefully looked for whenever one is tempted to make a diagnosis of conduct disorder (Lewis et al., 1984).

Major Affective Disorder. Some children who have a major affective disorder such as manic depression may sometimes mistakenly be regarded as having schizophrenia. Usually the history and subsequent mood swings will clarify the diagnosis.

Language Disorder. Occasionally a child with a severe language disorder may appear to be psychotic. Usually language tests can help resolve this difficulty.

Hallucinations. The greatest difficulty lies in deciding whether a child, particularly a young child under 8 years of age, actually has hallucinations or any of the other expressions of a thought disorder. Interpreting the responses of the child to inquiries made in the course of the mental status examination is not an easy task. Sometimes the preoperational level of cognitive development itself mimics a thought disorder and blurs the distinction the child makes between fantasy and reality. The younger the child, the greater the difficulty in deciding whether the child is experiencing an hallucination. Many very young children are simply illogical and difficult to follow in their language and play. For a further discussion of hallucinations, see Chapter 23.

Treatment. For the child, treatment consists of a combination of psychotherapy and antipsychotic medication, together with special education. The parents often need support, psychotherapy, and genetic counseling.

Developmental Perspectives. The important developmental perspectives on this condition are in the areas of diagnosis, treatment, and outcome. The younger the child, i.e., under 8 years of age, the more difficult it is to make the diagnosis. The young child's cognitive development and ability to give an accurate history are too immature.

One of the treatment problems lies in the serious hazard of increasing the lifetime risk for tardive dyskinesia. The risk is heightened when phenothiazines are given on a maintenance basis to a very young child.

Developmental factors appear to affect the

outcome. The younger the child at the time of onset, the worse the prognosis. Individuals who have an onset of schizophrenia late in adolescence may have only one such episode. In some children the disorder appears to be chronic, whereas in others it runs an episodic course (Kydd and Werry, 1982).

Case Vignette

Edward was the second of two children born to a lower class family. His mother was a native of Eastern Europe who had immigrated to this country as a child; his father was employed as a laborer. The pregnancy with Edward had been unremarkable; he had been born at term after a normal labor and delivery. Edward's early development appeared to proceed appropriately. He was enrolled in head start at age 3 and subsequently in regular kindergarten and primary school classes. Apart from being noted to be somewhat shy, no concerns were expressed about his cognitive or emotional development. At age 9 he appeared to become somewhat more withdrawn and preoccupied; he was observed talking to himself and became overly engaged with fantasy figures. His parents consulted their priest who recommended psychiatric evaluation. Prior to his first outpatient visit, Edward experienced an episode of acute behavioral disorganization that required emergency psychiatric hospitalization. During examination in the emergency room Edward was noted to be preoccupied with internal stimuli. He voiced concerns that a radio transmitter had been implanted in his head and in the heads of parents and sibling; his drawings of himself (Fig. 29–1) included radio attennae that he felt served as "message receivers." Edward voiced concerns that he was about to be kidnapped and sexually molested. No history of exposure to pharmacologic or other agents was elicited, although the mother noted that one of her siblings as well as her mother had been hospitalized for similar psychiatric disturbance. Because of Edward's poor reality testing and obvious behavioral disorganization, he was admitted to a psychiatric unit on an emergency basis.

Fig. 29–1.

While hospitalized he became more overly anxious and complex rituals and compulsive behaviors were observed. Extensive investigation failed to reveal a specific medical explanation for his difficulties. Low doses of major tranquilizer led to partial remission of the hallucinations and delusions although he remained quite withdrawn and preoccupied. After a 2 month hospitalization, he was returned to the care of his family and began twice weekly psychotherapy. Because of his difficulties attending regular classes, special education intervention was provided. At follow-up at age 12 psychological testing revealed an IQ score in the low average range; projective testing revealed continued problems with reality testing. On psychiatric examination Edward was noted to use irrelevant language, and neologisms; his associations were somewhat loose with tangential thinking. Exacerbation of his difficulties in late adolescence led to placement in a long-term psychiatric facility.

Comment. In contrast to autism, the early

development of children who develop schizophrenia appears to be relatively normal. Although the behavioral disorganization was relatively abrupt, it had been preceded by a prodromal phase (withdrawal and preoccupation). Hallucinations and delusions were unequivocally present in this case; in younger children their presence may be more difficult to establish.

REFERENCES

Cantor, S. (1988), *Childhood Schizophrenia*. New York: The Guilford Press.

Cantor, S., Trevemen, C., Postum, R., et al. (1980), Is childhood schizophrenia a cholinergic disease? I. Muscle Morphology. *Arch. Gen. Psychiatry*, 37:658–667.

Eggers, C. (1978). Course and prognosis of childhood schizophrenia. *J. Autism Child. Schizophrenia*, 8:21–36.

Fischer, M., Harvald, P., and Hauge, M. (1969), A Danish twin study of schizophrenia. *Br. Med. J.*, 115:981–990.

Kallman, F.J., and Prugh, D.G. (1971), Genetic aspects of pre-adolescent schizophrenia. *Am. J. Psychiatry*, 112:599–606.

Kolvin, I. (1971), Late onset psychoses. *Br. Med. J.*, 3:816–817.

Kolvin, I. (1971), Studies in the childhood psychoses: I. Diagnostic criteria and classification. *Br. J. Psychiatry*, 118:381–386.

Kramer, M.C. (1970–1975; 1978), Population changes and schizophrenia. In: *The Nature of Schizophrenia: New Approaches to Research and Treatment*, ed. J.C. Wynne, R.L. Cromwell, and S. Matthysse. New York: John Wiley & Sons, Inc.

Kydd, R.R., and Werry, J.S. (1982), Schizophrenia in children under 14 years. *J. Autism Dev. Disord.*, 12:343–357.

Lewis, D.O., Lewis, M., Unger, L., and Goldman, C. (1984), Conduct disorder and its synonyms: Diagnosis of dubious validity and usefulness. *Am. J. Psychiatry*, 141:514–519.

Lotter, V. (1974), Factors related to outcome in autistic children. *J. Autism Child Schizophrenia*, 4:263–277.

Rutter, M., and Lockyer, L. (1967), A five to fifteen year follow-up study of infantile psychosis: I. Description of sample. *Br. J. Psychiatry*, 113:1169–1182.

Rutter, M., and Lockkyer, L. (1967), A five to fifteen year follow-up study of infantile psychosis: II. Social and behavioral outcome. *Br. J. Psychiatry*, 113:1183–1199.

Schneider, K. (1959), *Clinical Psychopathology* (English translation of 1950 edition). New York: Grune & Stratton.

Schneider, K. (1971), *Klinische Psychopathologie*. Stuttgart: Thieme.

Volkmar, F.R. (In Press), Childhood Schizophrenia. In: *Child and Adolescent Psychiatry: A Comprehensive Textbook*, ed. M. Lewis. Baltimore, Williams & Wilkins.

Waldo, M.C., Cohen, O.J., Caparulo, B.K., et al. (1978), EEG profiles of neuropsychiatrically disturbed children. *J. Am. Acad. Child Psychiatry*, 17:656–670.

Walker, H.A., Danielson, E., and Levitt, M. (1976), Catechol-a-methyltransferase activity in psychotic children. *J. Autism Child. Schizophrenia*, 6:263–268.

Zetlin, H. (1986), *The Natural History of Psychiatric Disorder in Childhood*. Maudsley Monographs. London: Oxford University Press.

30

ANXIETY DISORDERS

Definition. Transient feelings of anxiety are experienced and usually mastered by every child and adolescent in the course of normal development. Anxiety disorders in children and adolescents are characterized by a persistent, prominent, and more or less disabling unpleasant sense of apprehension or dread that the child or adolescent is unable to master. Anxiety may be focused around certain issues or situations (e.g., separation from parents or fears of certain animals) or it may be more generalized or related to social situations. This feeling may be accompanied, to a greater or lesser extent, by physiologic responses, mostly autonomic responses such as sweating, trembling, dryness of the mouth, rapid pulse rate, pupillary dilatation, and gastrointestinal or urogenital upsets. Behavioral manifestations include restlessness, inattention, hyperactivity, compulsions, and shyness. The symptoms of anxiety may also be present in many, if not all, the common psychiatric disorders seen in children and adolescents.

Historical Note. The classification of anxiety disorders in children and adolescents has undergone many changes, and it is still unsatisfactory. Difficulties in definition of these disorders reflect the emphasis on delineation of discrete behavioral criteria for phenomena which are, to a considerable extent, internal and covert. Additional problems are posed in clarifying the exact point at which anxiety related symptoms become sufficiently severe and persistent as to constitute an anxiety disorder. DSM-III-R (1987) lists three types of anxiety disorders of childhood or adolescence: separation anxiety, avoidant disorder of childhood or adolescence, and overanxious disorder.

At the same time many of the other anxiety disorders listed in DSM-III-R do occur in childhood and adolescence, including panic disorder, social phobia, simple phobia, obsessive-compulsive disorder, post-traumatic stress disorder, and generalized anxiety disorder.

Etiology. Genetic factors are suggested by an increase in anxiety disorders among first-degree relatives, particularly female relations, and by a higher concordance rate in monozygotic twins compared with dizygotic twins (Carey and Gottesman, 1981).

Neuroendocrine correlates stemming from the pituitary-adrenal axis have been demonstrated, including an elevation of plasma cortisol (Ko et al., 1983).

Neurophysiologic mechanisms that stimulate the locus ceruleus, leading to excitation of the noradrenergic system and consequent anxiety, have been postulated (Charney, Heninger, and Redmond, 1983).

Ethologic patterns, notably anxiety generated in the infant when separation from the caregiver threatens the child's security and leads to the activation of attachment behaviors, have been postulated as a model for separation anxiety disorder (Bowlby, 1969).

Psychoanalytic theory postulates modal evolutionary danger situations that automatically elicit signal anxiety. This signal anxiety becomes the stimulus for the mobilization of defense mechanisms to repress the unpleasurable affect. The resulting clinical picture may take different forms, depending on the defense mechanisms used, e.g., phobias or obsessive-compulsive symptoms (Kandel, 1983).

Learning theory derives from the classic conditioning model of Pavlov (Shaffer, 1986).

Prevalence and Epidemiology. In general, anxiety symptoms are probably common in childhood and adolescence (Orvaschel and Weissman, 1986). In one study, anxiety disorders among a general population of 10- and 11-year-old children were diagnosed in about 1% of the population (Rutter, Tizard and Whitmore, 1970). There are few, if any, consistent findings about sex, social class, or family size differences. However, some age-of-onset differences seem related to developmental findings. Those will be described below.

Clinical Features. The clinical features of the three anxiety disorders that typically have their onset during childhood and adolescence are described separately in the following sections.

Separation Anxiety Disorder. Anxiety on separation from parents to whom the child is attached is normal in the preschool child. However, when the anxiety on separation is severe or persistent, and impairs social functioning, a separation anxiety disorder is likely to be present. Often the child worries about harm (e.g., an accident) to the parent, or fears that he or she may get hurt in some disastrous manner. The child's fear of being alone and need to stay close to the parents may result in refusal to sleep over at a friend's house or to go to school. A need to sleep close to the parents may arise. The child may have bad dreams about being separated, and when the child is separated, he or she may experience such symptoms as stomach ache, nausea and vomiting, or headache. The child may become fearful of even the thought of separation, and may develop anticipatory anxiety manifest by temper tantrums, tearfulness, sleep difficulties, withdrawal, and depression. Sometimes the child has fears of dying and death. The disorder follows an intermittent course, but may continue as a separation

anxiety diathesis into adulthood. Separation anxiety disorder often occurs in families (Noyes, Clancy, Crowe et al., 1978).

According to Gittleman-Klein and Klein (1971, 1973), some agoraphobic adult patients suffer from a disruption of biologic processes that regulate separation anxiety. During childhood, these patients experienced panic and severe clinging, dependent behavior associated with separation. Both propranolol and imipramine appear to block the unpredictable and spontaneous attacks, apparently associated with an outpouring of catecholamines, in such adults. Consequently, imipramine was used in children with severe separation anxiety, e.g., "school phobia," with some startling, if transient, success.

Avoidant Disorder of Childhood or Adolescence. In this disorder the child persistently and excessively shrinks from any social contact with unfamiliar people, to the extent that social functioning is impaired. Thus the child is less concerned about separation than about new social contacts with unfamiliar people. A child who is often timid, fearful, and unassertive (a "slow-to-warm-up" child) may, if there is a "poorness of fit," develop the disorder in social situations and may become electively mute. In infants the disorder may represent an abnormal continuation of stranger anxiety. Children who have a language or speech disorder may develop avoidant disorder as well.

Overanxious Disorder. In overanxious disorder the child, most often a boy, is a persistent and chronic worrier. For example, the child worries about getting hurt, about not meeting the expectations or approval of others, about examinations, or about visits to the doctor. The child may worry as much about past performance as future performance. The worry is often severe, and may be accompanied by such vegetative symptoms as abdominal pain, nausea, dizziness, headache, or a lump in the throat. The child's thinking may at times seem obsessive and self-doubting, and the child seems to need a lot of reassurance. Usually the condition is seen at the stage of early adolescence.

Treatment. In general, children with anxiety disorders are treated with some form of psychotherapy (individual, family). The psychotherapy may be psychodynamic or, especially in the case of phobias, behavioral. Antianxiety medication is not commonly effective, but treatment of some children with severe separation anxiety and school refusal with imipramine, a tricyclic antidepressant, combined with psychotherapy may be useful (Gittelman, 1986).

Obsessive-Compulsive Disorder. Although not strictly a variety of anxiety disorder, obsessive-compulsive disorder is frequently associated with conscious and unconscious anxiety.

Some studies suggest a neurobiologic hypothesis for obsessive-compulsive disorder in children. The evidence includes twin studies, association with Tourette's disorder, neuropsychologic test data, psychosurgery reports, association with certain kinds of brain damage, and psychopharmaclogic effects, especially the response to clonidine (Elkins, Rapoport, and Lipsky, 1980).

More specifically, a serotonin hypothesis has been suggested by the finding that clomipramine response correlates with changes in the cerebrospinal fluid levels of 5-hydroxyindoleacetic acid (a serotonin metabolite), and L-tryptophan (a serotonin precursor) (Insel et al., 1982).

At the same time, certain social situations clearly precipitate or aggravate the symptoms, whereas others relieve them. The exact epidemiology and psychopathology of the disorder have yet to be determined.

Developmental Perspectives. Transient feelings of anxiety occur throughout normal development. In the infant, anxiety may appear when the infant is insecure in the hands of an anxious adult, or when the infant is in a state of acute need (e.g., of food, sleep, physical relief). Young infants also normally become upset and look afraid when they experience sudden loud noises. As the infant develops memory, discrepant stimuli, such as a new face, may cause anxiety, so-called stranger anxiety, at about 8 months of age.

During the development of normal attachment, separation anxiety commonly occurs. The young child between, for example, 3 and 6 years of age often exhibits a fear of the dark, of animals, of imaginary monsters and ghosts, or of bad dreams. School-age children may fear bodily harm, or lightning and thunder. Adolescents may become anxious in social situations, or may fear loss of prestige or failure.

Most of these fears disappear with cognitive and emotional development. When they persist, they may appear to be the forerunner of an anxiety disorder. Thus, a persistent stranger anxiety might be the basis for an avoidant disorder; a persistent separation anxiety may develop into a separation disorder; or the common fears of a young child may persist and develop into a phobic disorder (Abe, 1972). During adolescence, the normal fears and anxieties associated with the physical, emotional, and cognitive changes that occur at puberty may become exacerbated and may be experienced as hypochondriacal bodily concerns and preoccupations, identity diffusion, existential dread, and a fear of leaving home.

This range from normal to pathologic in the specific kinds of anxiety seen during each developmental phase poses difficult diagnostic problems. When is an anxiety or fear normal, and when is it a sign of a disorder? In arriving at this distinction the clinician makes judgments along several dimensions: the age of onset of the fear or anxiety; the peculiar features of the anxiety; its persistence, severity, or bizarreness; the degree to which it interferes with functioning and ongoing development; whether it is isolated or one of many fears; whether other symptoms and signs are present; the duration, persistence, and courses of the anxiety over time; what factors relieve or increase the anxiety; and how much the fear is tolerated by others. A knowledge of normal developmental fears and anxieties is an essential baseline for these clinical judgments.

Case Vignette

Jonathan, an 11 year old, was referred for child psychiatric evaluation because of persistent concerns with failure in school despite receiving good grades. His parents, who had separated when Jonathan was 10 years old, were concerned that he appeared chronically tense and restless. His early history had been remarkable only for the chronic marital tension that had eventually resulted in the parents' separation. His mother described him as an alert, inquisitive baby. His development of speech had been precocious. He had entered school without difficulty and had done well academically. His father had strongly encouraged Jonathan to excel in sports where his abilities appeared to be only at the average level. Approximately 7 months before the evaluation Jonathan's mother had been injured in an automobile accident and the onset of his difficulties was, the parents believed, related to this event because he subsequently had experienced excessive concerns about her safety. Jonathan's younger sister was developing normally. There was no family history of psychiatric disturbance other than the chronic marital difficulties and a mild depression in the mother following her auto accident.

On examination, Jonathan complained of persistent feelings of tension and anxiety that were exacerbated by minor frustrations. Despite his awareness of getting good grades and being a reasonable athlete, he was concerned that he was not, and had not been, performing at his highest possible level. He was markedly self-conscious during the evaluation and appeared chronically tense and anxious. He complained of various physical symptoms (particularly headaches) for which no physical explanation had been determined. He complained of no specific fears other than those related to his performance and competence. He was socially competent and generally related well with his peers. During his evaluation he reported various nightmares and voiced some concern that his lack of achievement was responsible for the parent's marital problems. A diagnosis of overanxious disorder was made. A period of individual psychotherapy with periodic parent counseling was associated with substantial improvement.

Comment. The pattern of persistent and chronic worries is typical for overanxious disorder. The preoccupation with performance and competence arises even in the face of reasonable academic and personal success and involves worries about past, as well as future, performance. Psychotherapy is often effective in such cases.

REFERENCES

Abe, K. (1972), Phobias and nervous symptoms in childhood and maturity: Persistence and associations. *Br. J. Psychiatry*, 120:275–283.

Berg, I. (1970), A follow-up study of school phobic adolescents admitted to an in-patient unit. *J. Child Psychol. Psychiatry*, 11:37–47.

Bowlby, J. (1969), *Attachment and Loss* (Vol. I). New York: Basic Books.

Cary, G., and Gottesman, I.I. (1981), Twins and family studies of anxiety, phobic and obsessive disorders. In: *Anxiety: New Researh and Changing Concepts*, ed. D.F. Klein and J.G. Rabkin. New York: Raven Press, pp. 117–135.

Charney, D.S., Heninger, G.R., and Redmond, D.E.J. (1983), Clonidine induced anxiety and increased noradrenergic function in humans: Effects of diazepam and clonidine. *Life Sci.*, 33:19–29.

Elkins, R., Rapoport, J.L., and Lipsky, A. (1980), Obsessive-compulsive disorder of childhood and adolescence. A neurobiological viewpoint. *J. Am. Acad. Child Psychiatry*, 19:511–524.

Gittelman, R. (1986), Childhood anxiety disorders: Correlates and outcome. In: *Anxiety Disorders of Childhood*, ed. R. Gittelman. New York: Guilford Press, pp. 101–125.

Gittelman-Klein, R. (1973), School phobia: Diagnostic considerations in the light of imipramine effects. *J. Nerv. Ment. Dis.*, 156:199–215.

Gittelman-Klein, R., and Klein, D. (1971), Controlled imipramine treatment of school phobia. *Arch. Gen. Psychiatry*, 25:204–207.

Insel, T.R., Alterman, I., and Murphy, D.L. (1982), Antiobsessional and antidepressant effects of clomipramine in the treatment of obsessive-compulsive disorder. *Psychopharm. Bull.*, 18:115–117.

Kandel, E.R. (1983), From metapsychology to molecular biology: Explorations into the nature of anxiety. *Am. J. Psychiatry*, 140:1277–1293.

Ko, G.N., et al. (1983), Panic-induced elevation of plasma MHPG levels in phobic-anxious patients: Effects of clonidine and imipramine. *Arch. Gen. Psychiatry*, 40:425–430.

Marks, I.M., and Gelder, M.G. (1966), Different ages of onset in varieties of phobias. *Am. J. Psychiatry*, 123:218–221.

Noyes, R., Clancy, J., Crowe, R., et al. (1978), The familial prevalence of anxiety neurosis. *Arch. Gen. Psychiatry*, 35:1507–1559.

Orvaschel, H., and Weissman, M.M. (1986), Epidemiology of anxiety disorders in children: A review. In: *Anxiety Disorders of Childhood*, ed. R. Gittelman. New York: Guilford Gress. pp. 58–72.

Rutter, M., Tizard, J., and Whitmore, K. (1970), *Education, Health and Behavior*. London: Longmans.

Shaffer, D. (1986), Learning theories of anxiety. In: *Anxiety Disorders of Childhood*, ed. R. Gittelman. New York: Guilford Press, pp. 157–167.

31

DEPRESSIVE DISORDER

Definition. Depressive disorders in childhood are defined essentially as they are in adults with minor modifications that reflect developmental level. Essential features include depressed mood, loss of interest or pleasure, vegetative signs (sleep or eating disturbance), psychomotor agitation or retardation, fatigue, and inappropriate sense of guilt.

Historical Note. Until the 1960s several prominent psychoanalysts declared that depression in children did not exist (Rochlin, 1959). The presumption was that children did not have well developed superegos and thus could not experience a sense of guilt. Subsequent studies suggested not only that depression did exist in childhood, but that it was isomorphic with depression in adults (Carlson and Cantwell, 1982; Puig-Antich, Chambers and Halpern, 1979; McKnew and Cytryn, 1979). More recent studies have examined developmental differences in depression at different stages of childhood and adolescence (Kovacs et al., 1984a; Garber, 1984).

Prevalence and Epidemiology. Rates of depression vary depending on the definition used and the samples studied. Current prevalence rates of major and minor depression among 9-year-old New Zealand children are 1.7% and 3.6%, respectively. In the Isle of Wight study, depression in children in the general population occurred in 3 out of 2,193 10-year-olds and 35 out of 2,303 14-year-olds (Rutter, Tizard, and Whitmore, 1970). Depression increases with age, and increases most markedly in both prevalence and se-

verity during adolescence. Depression is equally common in the two sexes in young children, perhaps more common in boys before puberty, but more common in girls after puberty onward into adulthood (Kovacs et al., 1984a,b; Weissman, 1988). There is an increased risk of depression in the child when depression is present in young parents, when both parents are psychiatrically ill, or when many first-degree relatives of the parents have major depressive disorder or any psychiatric disorder (Weissman et al., 1984). If one parent has a mood disorder, there is a 30% chance the child also will have a mood disorder. If both parents have a mood disorder, there is a 50 to 70% chance the child will have this disorder.

Clinical Picture. The manifestations of depression vary with the developmental level of the child.

Infants who are depressed, e.g., as a result of the loss of their caregiver, appear listless, apathetic, and withdrawn, and seem to be unresponsive (Spitz, 1946). Sometimes the infant has a sleep difficulty, cries a great deal, and may exhibit the features of a failure-to-thrive syndrome, with weight loss.

School-age children appear sad, show loss of interest, cry, and feel rejected. They may also have temper tantrums, aggressive behavior, and symptoms resembling a so-called conduct disorder. Somatic symptoms, such as stomach aches, are common.

Adolescents show more typical symptoms. In particular, they may have suicidal thoughts and will attempt suicide.

The cardinal symptoms of depression in

360

children and adolescents are a persistent depressed mood and an apathetic loss of interest or pleasure. Sleep difficulties such as an inability to fall asleep, loss of appetite, and psychomotor retardation may occur. The child may feel unloved and unworthy. School work may become more difficult for the child, and he or she may begin to fail academically. Suicidal ideation and behavior may be present.

In some children these symptoms may be defended against by what appear to be reaction formations, so that the child may then have almost the opposite symptoms. For example, instead of looking sad, the child or adolescent (usually an adolescent) may have a fixed grin—a "smiling depression." Instead of experiencing loss of appetite, the child or adolescent may overeat and become obese, as if to fill a sense of emptiness. Far from being slowed down, adolescents in particular may engage in activity, sometimes taking risks, trying in this way to ward off the depression. Instead of not sleeping, some adolescents sleep inordinately long—all morning, or even longer. Finally, instead of seeming depressed, the child may feel irritable. These symptoms have sometimes been called "depressive equivalents," or have been referred to as a "masked depression" because the symptoms appear to mask the underlying cardinal ones. Other symptoms include bedwetting, soiling, and phobias.

Depression may be present in children who have other diagnoses, including so-called conduct disorder, separation anxiety, attention deficit hyperactivity disorder, anorexia nervosa, and bulimia. Children who are abused may also be depressed.

The average length of a depressive episode is about 8 months; most children recover within 18 months. However, the relapse rate over a 5-year period is about 70% [Kovacs et al., 1984(a) and (b)]. Younger children take longer to recover.

Etiology. Genetic factors are postulated on the basis of the aforementioned family findings. Family history findings suggest a high risk for major depressive disorder, alcoholism, and antisocial personality in first-degree relatives of prepubertal children who are depressed. Psychologic theories include psychoanalytic and cognitive concepts (see below).

Loss, deprivation, and rejection experiences may be contributory. Young children of divorced parents may become depressed. Repeated failure experiences may precipitate or aggravate depression. Adverse home environment may exacerbate a depression. Viral illnesses, particularly infectious mononucleosis, may be followed by a prolonged depression, suggesting a psychoimmunologic response (Hamblin, Hussain, Akbar et al., 1983). It is possible that an interaction of biologic (genetic) and experiential factors is involved in some cases.

Psychopathology. Biologic findings suggest alterations in neurotransmitter and T-cell function. For example, McKnew and Cytryn (1979), in a controlled study of nine children 6 to 12 years of age with diagnosed cases of depression, suggested that a physiologic counterpart to emotional "detachment" in children may be a suppression of the general arousal system, mediated through the nonadrenergic network and centered on the locus ceruleus, resulting in a reduction in the level of 3-methoxy-4-hydroxyphenylethylene glycol (MHPG). Puig-Antich et al. (1979) demonstrated hypersecretion of cortisol in children suffering from a depressive syndrome. Puig-Antich essentially demonstrated that prepubertal children who fit the Research Diagnostic Criteria (RDC) for major depressive illness have a disturbance of the circadian rhythm of cortisol excretion similar to that of depressed adults: In the evening and early morning, secretion ceases in control subjects but continues in depressed patients. Brumback and Station (1981) hypothesized that dysfunctional aminergic neurotransmission associated with depression may unmask previously subclinical neurologic signs. Signs of left hemiparesis (including pronation drift of the outstretched left arm, hyperactive left-sided tendon reflexes, and left extensor plantar responses), found during a major depressive disorder suffered by the two children studied, disappeared when the depression was temporarily relieved by treatment with tricyclic antidepressant medication (Staton, Wilson, and Brumback, 1981). They also observed, in 21 children with major depressive illness, that treatment with amitriptyline was associated with improvement in the results of right-hemisphere and frontal-lobe tests, including improvement in IQ on the WISC(R) Performance Scale (Brumback, Staton, and Wilson, 1980).

Psychoanalytic findings derive from Freud's work and extend to the present day. For example, Freud (1917) suggested that unconscious feelings of self-reproach were turned against an internalized partially lost love-object, leading to feelings of guilt. Abraham (1924) similarly suggested that depression and suicide ideation were related to unconscious internalized hostility and ambivalence turned against the self, leading to self-punitive behavior and self-injury. Bibring (1953) thought that some experiences lead to loss of self-esteem, feelings of helplessness, and resignation. Sandler and Joffe (1965) thought that children felt they had lost, or were unable to acquire, something that was essential to their well-being; they felt helpless and resigned. The pain the children suffered was thought to be the result of the child's perceived discrepancy beween the actual self and an ideal state of well-being.

Learned helplessness (Seligman, 1975) has been suggested as a cognitive explanation for depression in children.

Laboratory Studies. Numerous studies have shown that the biologic findings in children who are depressed are similar to those found in adults who are depressed, although in some instances the results may not be quite as specific or sensitive as they are in adults. These differences may be due to developmental factors, but may also be due to the confounding presence of associated conditions. Or possibly the differences may be a result of the presence of more than one kind of syndrome of depression in children.

The biologic correlates include:

1. cortisol hypersecretion, especially during the acute stage;
2. a positive dexamethasone suppression test in which cortisol is not suppressed after giving dexamethasone in prepubertal children with endogenous depression;
3. growth hormone hyporesponsivity to insulin-induced hypoglycemia;
4. decrease in melatonin circadian rhythms; and
5. sleep studies.* These studies, however, do not show the decreased delta sleep and sleep efficiency, or the increased REM density or shortened REM latency as well as abnormal REM sleep distribution typically found in adults who are depressed. One possible explanation for these different sleep study results in children compared to adults in the immaturity and developing nature of sleep during childhood. As the normal child grows older, REM latency and sleep efficiency progressively decrease, which may affect the results of polysomnography performed on children who are depressed.

One interesting psychobiologic hypothesis has been offered by Mandell (1978), who suggested that the developing central nervous system in infants is vulnerable to any impingement on its biochemical balance. Psychologic loss might lead to a depletion of monoamine neurotransmitters, and an altered biochemical state might then become the new "normal" baseline or "thermostat level" for that individual throughout life. Any subsequent experience that was pleasurable or gratifying might temporarily change the biochemical balance, but the prevailing tendency would always be to return to this new

---

REM density is the number of eye movements per unit of time.

Sleep latency is the time required to fall asleep.

Sleep efficiency refers to the amount of time it takes to fall asleep, how often the child awakes during the night, and the total amount of sleep and percentage of sleep obtained.

Delta waves are high-voltage activity at 0.5 to 2.5 cycles per second that occurs during stages 3 and 4 of sleep.

"normal" but, in fact, depressive baseline state.

Differential Diagnosis. *Mourning and grief* following the death of a loved one have many of the features of depression. However, the precipitating event is clear, and the period of bereavement has its own course and is self-limited. Preadolescent children may not show all the typical signs of bereavement. Instead, there may be an initial denial, followed by feelings of guilt and shame, especially in young children, and subsequent intermittent periods of grieving as the child is able to tolerate on a piecemeal basis more of the feelings of loss. Such intermittent, piecemeal grieving also occurs in bursts at times when the loved one is most missed, e.g., birthdays, Christmas, vacation time, or special anniversaries. The intermittent grieving may sometimes manifest itself in a temporary falling off of school work, bursts of anger, temper tantrums, or episodic bed-wetting.

Nevertheless, in some instances the bereavement may not resolve and may leave the child with a depression.

Dysthymia may be present in children who do not meet the full criteria for depressive disorder, but who seem to be sad and have a low self-esteem.

Mania and *cyclothymia* may be observed in children (Dwyer and DeLong, 1987). Mania can be difficult to diagnose because of symptom overlap with other disorders such as attention deficit hyperactivity disorder (Coll and Bland, 1979). It is possible that children who present with major depressive episodes are at risk for developing bipolar disorder. Cyclothymia, as in adults, is characterized by recurrent hypomanic and depressive episodes.

Psychoses, including schizophrenia, may be the primary disorder, accompanied by secondary symptoms of depression. The presence of persisting signs of schizophrenia (hallucinations and delusions) is the key differentiating feature.

Treatment. Treatment of children with major depressive disorder includes psychotherapy and the use of antidepressant medications, particularly tricyclic drugs such as imipramine and desipramine (Ambrosini, 1982). Cognitive therapy has been used for some older children and adolescents.

Outome is generally good, although relapses are common.

Developmental Perspectives. The developmental issues in childhood depression are found at several levels. First, young children are especially vulnerable to depression following a major loss, yet they may be protected by family support. At the same time, the clinical picture of depression is different at various stages of development. For example, crying is frequent during infancy, irritability is common during 5 to 15 years of age, and mood swings increase in adolescence (Shepherd, Oppenheim, and Mitchell, 1971). Because a major increase in prevalence and severity of depression occurs in adolescence, it is possible that the hormonal, cognitive, and emotional changes at puberty are important etiologic factors. In addition, because the personality structure changes throughout development, the psychodynamics of the depression are presumably different at each stage, and may warrant an as yet undetermined subcategorization of depression in children; e.g., depressive disorder of infancy, depressive disorder of childhood, depressive disorder of adolescence. The treatment may also vary according to the developmental level of the child. Certainly the metabolism of drugs changes throughout childhood, necessitating special dosages and monitoring procedures. The prognosis may be different, depending on the age of onset, the severity of the disorder, and the support the child receives, especially for the very young child.

These development issues need further exploration, and are now receiving increasing attention in research literature.

Case Vignette

Tommy was a 10 year old admitted on an emergency basis to a child psychiatry inpatient service after voicing concerns that he might hurt himself. He had been born after a normal pregnancy, labor, and delivery to a single mother who herself had a history of substance abuse and conduct problems. She had periodically abandoned Tommy to the care of her own parents and he was in the custody of child protective services at the time of his admission. He had a history of school difficulties and was performing nearly 2 years below age level on standard test of achievement despite normal levels of intelligence. He had previously been evaluated as an outpatient on several occasions; diagnoses of attention deficit disorder and conduct disorder had been made. However, treatment with stimulant medications had had no effect and these had been discontinued. At the time of the emergency admission he was residing in his third foster home; foster placement had resulted after the death of his grandmother some 6 months previously. Subsequent to admission he had begun to eat and sleep excessively.

During his admission Tommy was noted to be a mildly obese, overtly depressed boy. He had difficulties concentrating and had little interest in activities. He was often quite agitated and was preoccupied with the notion that he had caused his grandmother's death (as a result of overwork taking care of him) or had been responsible for the separation from his mother. Tricyclic antidepressants were begun and produced significant remission in depressive symptoms.

Comment. Several losses preceded the development of overt depression in this case; however, the degree of depression appeared more severe and prolonged than in a normal grief reaction. This case illustrated the development of characteristic reactions associated with depression. In addition to the affective experience of depression, other signs of the disorder included psychomotor agitation, excessive sleep and appetite, difficulties in concentration, and apathy. In other cases, psychomotor retardation, diminished appetite and weight loss, and decreased sleep are observed.

REFERENCES

Abraham, K. (1924), A short study of the development of the libido, viewed in the light of mental disorders. In: *Selected Papers on Psychoanalysis* (1927), pp 480–502. London: Hogarth.

Ambrosini, P.J. (1987), Pharmacotherapy in child and adolescent major depressive disorder. In: *Psychopharmacology: The Third Generation of Progress*, ed. H.Y. Meltzer. New York: Raven Press, pp. 1247–1254.

Bibring, E. (1953), The mechanisms of depression. In: *Affective Disorders*, ed. P. Greenacre. New York: International Universities Press.

Brumback, R.A., and Staton, R.D. (1981), Depression-induced neurological dysfunction. *N. Engl. J. Med.*, 355:642.

Brumback, R.A., Staton, R.D., and Wilson, H. (1980), Neuropsychological study of children during and after remission of endogenous depressive episodes. *Percept. Mot. Skills*, 50:1163–1167.

Carlson, G.A., and Cantwell, D.F. (1982), Diagnosis of childhood depression: A comparison of the Weinberg and DSM III criteria. *J. Am. Acad. Child Psychiatry*, 21:247–250.

Coll, P.G., and Bland, R. (1979), Manic-depressive illness in adolescence and childhood. *Can. J. Psychiatry*, 24:255–263.

Dwyer, J.T., and DeLong, G.R. (1987), A family history study of twenty probands with childhood manic-depressive illness. *J. Am. Acad. Child Adolesc. Psychiatry*, 26:176–180.

Freud, S. (1917), *Mourning and Melancholia. Standard Edition* (Vol. 14), pp. 243–258. London: Hogarth Press, 1957.

Garber, J. (1984), The developmental progression of depression in female children. In: *Childhood Depression*, ed. D. Cicchetti and K. Schneider-Rosen. San Francisco: Jossey-Bass, pp. 29–58.

Hamblin, T.J., et al. (1983), Immunological reason for chronic ill health after infectious mononucleosis. *Br. Med. J.*, 287:85–88.

Kovacs, M., Feinberg, T., Crouse-Novak, M.A., Paulauskas, S., and Finkelstein, P. (1984a), Depressive disorders in childhood: I. A longitudinal prospective study of characteristics and recovery. *Arch. Gen. Psychiatry*, 411:229–237.

Kovacs, M., Feinberg, T., Crouse-Novak, M.A., Paulauskas, A., Pollock, M. and Finkelstein, R. (1984b), Depressive disorders in childhood: II. A longitudinal study of risk for subsequent major depression. *Arch Gen. Psychiatry*, 41:643–649.

Kovacs, M., and Paulauskas, S. (1984a), Developmental stage and the expression of depressive disorders in children: An empirical analysis. In: *Childhood Depression*, ed. D. Cicchetti and K. Schneider-Rosen. San Francisco: Jossey-Bass, pp. 59–80.

Mandell, A.J. (1976), Neurobiological mechanisms of adaptation in relation to models of psychobiological development. In *Psychopathology and Child Development*, ed. E. Schopler and R.J. Reichler. New York: Plenum Publishing Corp., pp. 21–22.

McKnew, D.H., and Cytryn, L. (1979), Urinary metabolites in chronically depressed children. *J. Am. Acad. Child Psychiatry*, 18:608–615.

Puig-Antich, J., Chambers, W., Halpern, F., et al. (1979), Cortisol hypersecretion in prepubertal depressive illness. *Psychoneuroendocrinology*, 4:191–197.

Rochlin, G. (1959), The loss complex: A contribution to the etiology of depression. *J. Am. Psychoanal. Assoc.*, 7:299–316.

Rutter, M., Tizard, J., and Whitmore, K. (1970), *Education, Health and Behavior.* London: Longmans.

Sandler, J., and Joffe, W.S. (1965), Notes on childhood depression. *Int. J. Psychoanal.*, 46:88–96.

Seligman, M. (1975), *Helplessness.* San Francisco: Freeman, Cooper & Co.

Shepherd, M., Oppenheim, B., and Mitchell, S. (eds.) (1971), *Childhood Behavior and Mental Health.* London: University of London Press.

Spitz, R.A. (1946), Anaclitic depression. *Psychoanal. Study Child*, 2:213–241.

Staton, R.D., Wilson, H., and Brumback, R.A. (1981), Cognitive improvement associated with tricyclic antidepressant treatment of childhood major depressive illness. *Percept. Mot. Skills.*, 53:219–234.

Weissman, M.M. (1988), Psychopathology in the children of depressed and normal parents: Direct interview study. In: *Relatives at Risk for Mental Disorders*, ed. D.L. Dunner and E.S. Gershon. New York: Raven Press.

Weissman, M.M., Prusoff, B.A., Gammon, G.D., et al. (1984), Psychopathology in the children (age 6–18) of depressed and normal parents. *J. Am. Acad. Child Psychiatry*, 23:78–84.

32

SUICIDE AND ATTEMPTED SUICIDE

Definition. Attempted suicide and suicide are the terms used when the child or adolescent intends in part or in full to bring about his or her death through self-imposed acts.

Historical Note. The most striking historical point about suicide, particularly among adolescents, is the 150% increase that has occurred in the past 20 years. Although better reporting is a factor, the increase is, for the most part, as real as it is substantial.

Prevalence and Epidemiology. Suicide is now the third most common form of death in adolescents, following accidents and homicide. Many so-called accidents are the results of suicidal wishes. In the United States more than 5,000 adolescents and young adults die every year from suicide. Thus the mortality rate is 12.3 per 100,000 in this age group, accounting for 18.8% of all deaths in adolescents (15- to 24-year-olds). A survey of "normal" high-school students 14 to 18 years of age revealed that almost 9% reported at least one suicidal attempt. More than half (52%) of these adolescents did not visit a mental health professional (Letter, 1985). Suicide is uncommon in children under the age of 12, but it does occur (Shaffer, 1974). The male:female ratio of completed suicide is 3:1. The male:female ratio of attempted suicide in adolescents over the age of 12 is 1:3. Under the age of 12, more boys than girls attempt suicide (Pfeffer, 1986). Methods include drug ingestion, hanging and carbon monoxide poisoning, shooting, etc. (Shaffer, 1974). Suicide and attempted suicide occur in all classes. Researchers predict that by the year 2,000 there will be a 94% increase in suicide rates

in the 15- to 19-year-old age group, notwithstanding the recent trend toward a slightly lower rate for all ages.

Clinical Features. The following stable risk factors have been identified:

1. male sex
2. increasing age or advanced pubertal development
3. impaired ability to communicate with others, including the child's or adolescent's therapist
4. presence of major depressive disorder
5. a detailed knowledge and understanding of the lethality of various methods
6. availability of cash to buy the means to commit suicide
7. extremes (high or low) of intelligence
8. a history of violent or aggressive behavior
9. previous attempts

Precipitating factors include some kind of disciplinary crisis in the home, or a humiliating crisis outside the home. Such an incident may highlight the discrepancy between the child's or adolescent's performance and his or her expectations (or family's expectations).

Common changes in behavior that may presage a suicidal attempt include veiled statements of intent: "There's nothing to look forward to," "I can never be happy," "Others will be better off without me," "I guess I won't be seeing you again," "I'm just a burden to you," "I'm not going to put up with it anymore," or saying "goodbye" instead of "good night." Sometimes the child or adolescent begins to give away possessions. A sudden period of calm after a period of agitation may be ominous, suggesting that the adolescent has now made up his or her mind, and the depression has now lifted enough to enable him or her to act. Occasionally an adolescent makes clear statements of suicidal intent, and may seek help prior to the attempt. At least 40% of adolescents who have either attempted or completed suicide will have visited medical or psychiatric services in the week prior to the suicidal act. A family history of suicide or suicide attempts is observed in many cases; such a history increases risk of suicide, in part by breaking the taboo associated with suicide.

Etiology and Psychopathology. Depression is a common cause of suicidal ideation and behavior. Suicide and attempted suicide may also be observed in association with other psychiatric conditions, e.g., psychosis or substance abuse. Feelings of helplessness and of being overwhelmed may give rise to a wish to escape from life. In some instances a manipulative intent may serve to bring about an environmental change, e.g., to bring together divorcing parents. In others there is a fantasy of revenge ("now you'll be sorry"), or a wish to bring back some emotionally important person. Often a high level of parent-adolescent conflict is present. Complex unconscious conflicts have been described, including aggressive wishes toward the mother, fears of abandonment and rejection, and a feeling of being unable to change things (Laufer, 1975). Some adolescents perceive themselves as a "suicidal person" and read the literature of authors who have committed suicide, such as Sylvia Plath. Sometimes "outbreaks" of suicide occur in a school or a community, and the attendant publicity in the media may engender additional incidents. Suicide rates have been noted to increase temporarily following televised depictions of suicide and attempted suicide (Gould and Shaffer, 1986) although subsequent research (Kessler et al., 1989) has questioned this observation.

Work-up. The work-up should include a detailed assessment of the degree of depression present. How extensively feelings of hopelessness, parent-adolescent conflicts, and manipulativeness contribute to the despair of the adolescent should also be evaluated (Pfeffer, 1986).

Other areas of inquiry include the specific suicidal fantasies and the adolescent's concepts of what he or she expected would happen. The circumstances at the time of the adolescent's attempt might provide clues to the motivation for the suicidal behavior. Previous attempts, or experiences with others who have been suicidal, may have weakened the suicide taboo and made it easier for repeated attempts to occur. The adolescent's concept of death and experiences with dying persons may be important. The ready availability of medications used in the household may have facilitated the attempt. The response of the parents is important.

Differential Diagnosis. This is rarely in doubt. The so-called "suicidal gesture" should be taken seriously. Occasionally, especially in older adolescents, unusual forms of suicide such as sexual asphyxia occur.

Treatment. Treatment is directed first at saving life, then at the cause of the attempt (Lewis and Lewis, 1973; Pfeffer, 1986). If nothing changes as a result of the suicide attempt, the likelihood of repeated attempts remains high. Preventive programs in schools have been tried (Holden, 1987).

Developmental Perspectives. Several important developmental issues arise in relation to the suicide rates in different age groups. Suicide among the very young is rare; suicide in adolescents is all too common. What accounts for the difference? Differences in cognitive development play some part. Very young children have an incomplete concept of death (see p. 275), and the preoperational child cannot easily take distance on himself or herself. The need for a dependent relationship is also more syntonic for the younger child. Depressive affective states may also be less intense and of shorter duration in very young children, and these children elicit more nurturing responses from adults in the child's environment. Some of these factors may therefore serve as a protection against suicidal fantasies and behavior. Suicide in older children is usually associated with despair over the current life situation and the worry that things will never improve.

In adolescents the hormonal upset may give rise to profound and prolonged depression. Depression, we know, becomes more frequent and more severe at adolescence. The struggle around issues of dependency and autonomy is also more intense during adolescence. In addition, the capabilities of the adolescent are greatly increased, making suicidal behavior more accessible.

Case Vignette

Deborah was a 15-year-old girl who ingested an overdose of her mother's prescription barbiturates followng a fight with the mother. She was the middle of three children born to a lower middle-class couple with a stormy marital relationship. Her mother had a history of depressive episodes and her father was an alcoholic who had occasionally been abusive to Deborah and her siblings. Deborah had a history of chronic school problems and truancy. She had once been arrested for shoplifting although charges had been dropped. Prior to the current attempt she had made one suicide gesture in relation to terminating a relationship with a boyfriend. Past psychiatric evaluations had suggested that Deborah was chronically depressed. Her ambivalence about treatment and the disorganization of her family had prevented her from engaging in sustained psychotherapy.

Her relationship with her present boyfriend had lasted for nearly 9 months. It had ended when Deborah discovered that she was pregnant. Her boyfriend and mother insisted she have an abortion. After the abortion she became more overtly depressed and irritable.

Her relationships with both her mother and boyfriend deteriorated. She voiced suicidal ideation on several occasions; immediately prior to the current attempt she had had an angry confrontation with her mother who threatened to turn her out of the house. Deborah wrote a long suicide note in which she indicated the disposition of various treasured belongings. This note was left in a prominent place in the family kitchen but Deborah's mother was unexpectedly delayed in returning home and discovered it only after Deborah was comatose.

Comment. The age at which suicide was attempted in this case is relatively typical. Suicidal behavior is associated with a range of psychiatric problems and premorbid conditions not simply limited to depression. In this case Deborah had a history of ambivalent relationships which made it more difficult for her to seek help in the face of multiple losses (both her boyfriend and the pregnancy). Even when suicide is apparently carefully planned, the wish to be rescued is often observed.

REFERENCES

Gould, M.S., and Shaffer, D. (1986), The impact of suicide in television movies: Evidence of imitation. *N. Engl. J. Med.*, 315:690–694.

Harkavy, J.M., and Asnis, G. (1985), Suicide attempts in adolescence: Prevalence and implications (letter to the editor). *N. Engl. J. Med.*, 313:1290–1291.

Holden, C. (1987), Romeo and Juliet and youth suicide. *Science*, 235:21.

Kessler, R.C., Downey, G., Stipp, H., and Milavsky, J.R. (1989), Network television news stories about suicide and short-term changes in total U.S. suicides. *J. Nerv. Ment. Dis.*, 177:551–555.

Laufer, M. (1975), Preventive intervention in adolescence. *Psychoanal. Study Child*, 30:511–528.

Lewis, M., and Lewis, D.O. (1973), The management of attempted suicide. In *The Pediatric Management of Psychologic Crises* (monograph). Chicago: Yearbook Medical Publishers, Inc.

Pfeffer, C.R. (1986), *The Suicidal Child*. New York: Guilford Press.

Schaffer, D. (1974), Suicide in childhood and early adolescence. *J. Child Psychol. Psychiatry*, 15:275–291.

33

ATTENTION-DEFICIT HYPERACTIVITY DISORDER

Definition. Attention-deficit hyperactivity disorder (ADHD) is characterized by motor restlessness, inattention, and impulsivity.

Historical Note. Clinicians have been aware of the behavioral manifestations of this condition since the 1800s. In 1908, Tredgold coined the term "minimal brain damage," one of a succession of many terms to label children who appear to be impulsive, inattentive, and hyperactive. This term seemed particularly apt when it appeared that children with obvious brain damage, e.g., postencephalitis, exhibited problems in activity and attention. The present term was coined for DSM-III-R (1987). In spite of numerous studies, no specific brain lesion for all children with ADHD has ever been reliably documented. Similarly, a wide range of etiologic factors, including genetic abnormalities, perinatal insult, infections, lead poisoning, head injury, metabolic disorders, neurotransmitter disorders, dietetic problems, and psychosocial factors, have at one time or another been implicated in the cause of ADHD. Because the disorder now appears to have a complex cause, the prevailing view suggests a more complex interactional model of pathogenesis. This interactional model has also served as a basis for the multimodal treatment approach that is now recommended for children with the disorder.

Whether one ascribes to a categorical (i.e., syndromal) or dimensional model of ADHD, stimulants appear to be effective in controlling the symptoms of restlessness and inattention, and certain immature behaviors. The first successful use of a stimulant drug (Benzedrine) was reported by Bradley in 1937. Interestingly, long-term effects on educational achievement have been less clearly documented.

Catecholamine and norepinephrine metabolism is probably involved at some level in the pathogenesis and treatment of ADHD. The catecholamine hypothesis for the disorder was first suggested by Kornetsky in 1970. There may also be some modifications in noradrenergic function, but not in serotonin metabolism. Currently, researchers are looking at frontal lobe function and its relation to the corpus striatum.

Prevalence and Epidemiology. The disorder affects 3 to 5% of school-age children (Lambert et al., 1981), and occurs in boys more commonly than in girls. Children from all social classes may be affected. The condition is seen more often in first-born children than in those born subsequently. Diagnostic practice differs in other countries, for example, in Great Britain other diagnostic labels, such as conduct disorder, are more commonly used.

Clinical Features. Although usually not diagnosed until the time the child enters school, the onset is typically between 3 and 7 years of age, but may be earlier. The child is restless and unable to sit still. Hands and feet may be in constant motion. Easily distracted by fleeting stimuli, the child has difficulty awaiting turns, seems disorganized, and often has difficulty following through on a task. The child may be very talkative, and may have difficulty modulating his or her voice. Relationships are sometimes difficult, owing in part to the child's frequent, impulsive interruptions and intrusions. The child also seems not to listen and does poorly at school work. Sometimes the child is careless and loses things, or dashes heedlessly into the street. Accident-proneness is frequent. The child, in short, seems "on the go," "driven," and "immature." The symptoms are worse in a large classroom situation, and may not be apparent at all in a 1:1 situation. Soft signs and minor physical abnormalities are frequently present. The child may also have an associated learning difficulty or conduct disorder, with features of depression and anxiety.

Adolescents may have difficulty organizing their work, and are often late with assignments. The symptoms persist into adulthood in about half the cases (Weiss et al., 1985). About one quarter (23%) of the adults show signs of an antisocial personality disorder.

Etiology. Multiple factors have been implicated. There is some evidence for polygenetic factors. Monozygotic twins are affected more often than dizygotic twins. Family studies indicate a high prevalence of psychiatric disorder among the adult relatives of children seen in psychiatric clinics (Cantwell, 1972). Food sensitivities, particularly sensitivity to food additives as well as a sensitivity to carbohydrates, are possibly present in a subgroup (Weiss, 1982). Brain damage is not found in the majority of children with the disorder. However, the symptoms of the disorder may occur secondarily to insults to the brain, including fetal alcohol syndrome, birth trauma, head injury, encephalitis, toxic substance (lead) poisoning, and Reye's syndrome. Adverse socioeconomic conditions, family stress, and psychiatric disorder in the family increase the risk for the emergence of symptoms. At the molecular level, a complex model involving catecholamine modulation, norepinephrine metabolism, and frontal lobe

inhibition has been proposed (Zametkin and Rapoport, 1987).

Psychopathology. The psychopathology in a given individual derives from an interaction among the biologic, psychologic, family, and social factors mentioned previously.

Laboratory Studies. There is no single pathognomonic test for attention-deficit hyperactivity disorder. However, a review of the etiology and differential diagnosis will suggest which investigations are needed. The history might indicate likely causes, or at least the causes that are of most concern to the child and parents. Thus, concerns about brain damage, impaired neurologic function, intelligence, learning difficulties, and diet and lead poisoning may require a systematic study. Beyond such categorical assessments, a careful evaluation of the child's level of functioning in the family, in school, and with peers is needed as a basis for treatment planning.

Differential Diagnosis. Differential diagnosis includes anxiety disorders, affective disorders, conduct disorder, antisocial personality disorder, borderline personality disorder, severe learning difficulties, and mental retardation. Most of these conditions, particularly learning difficulties and conduct disorder, frequently coexist with attention-deficit hyperactivity disorder. A careful review for the cardinal symptoms of each of these disorders will facilitate differentiation.

Treatment. Treatment is multimodal (Satterfield, Satterfield and Cantwell, 1981), and includes discussions with the child and family, counseling, psychotherapy (individual, group, or family), school consultation, environmental changes, medication and, in selected cases, diet management. Medications commonly used include stimulants such as methylphenidate and tricyclic antidepressants such as imipramine and desipramine.

Developmental Perspectives. Development considerations play a large role in the disorder. First, in the development of attention, perception, and memory (see Chap. 2), the child normally makes a shift from the compelling interest in a salient or discrepant feature of a stimulus to a more systematic, logical, and flexible searching. This change is similar to the shift, in Piagetian terms, from the stimulus-bound cognition of the preoperational child to the relative independence from the stimulus of the moment (decentering) that characterizes the thinking of the child in the stage of concrete operations. It is usually coincident with the blossoming of language. If a child is delayed in making this shift, he or she remains vulnerable to being distracted by whichever is the more powerful stimulus of the moment. Such a child may also have a relatively limited reservoir of strategies for exploring and learning. In addition, the child may appear impulsive, or at least inattentive, because he or she will continue to flit from stimulus to stimulus. Again, a child who remains stimulus-bound may also persevere in a task, e.g., copying a row of dots.

Developmental issues also arise in the problems of clinical diagnosis. The disorder is usually recognized by 3 years of age, yet earlier signs may presage the condition. For example, the preschool child may appear to be generally immature with, for example, a delay in language and motor development. On developmental assessment, the infant may show the "hot potato" or "hot cube" sign: the infant on grasping a cube will instantly let it go as though it would a hot potato, instead of exploring the cube's properties. When holding a cube in each hand, the child drops them, instead of exploring their relationships with one another. The child thus misses out on important steps in exploration and learning.

Later, when the child enters nursery school, an astute nursery teacher may observe that the child has difficulty in staying with a task and needs a great deal of repetition before he or she will learn something new.

These early developmental clues may be missed if one only looks for the signs present in the full-blown syndrome, especially since some time is required for the maturational and developmental gap to reveal itself. In addition, the social, educational, and psychologic expectations for the 1- 2- or 3-year-old

are such that the child's difficulties may be overlooked.

Sometimes the signs are observed, but are called by some other term that does not immediately associate with what will later be an attention-deficit hyperactivity syndrome. Thus the child may be thought of as accident-prone (e.g., in a case of accidental poisoning) or as having a difficult temperament. Symptoms such as head banging or rocking may be part of a more general restlessness. Immaturity and language and motor delay may be noted, but not followed.

Once the condition is established, any further delay in recognition may lead to increasing difficulties as the behavior of the child is misunderstood and thought of as willfull. The child is then punished instead of treated. If this persists, the child's self-esteem falls, and a depression occurs. Some children react with aggressive behavior, and learning in school is affected.

Case Vignette

Leonard, an 8-year-old boy, was referred at the request of his teacher for evaluation. Presenting complaints included disruptive behavior in the classroom, high activity levels, and poor academic performance. Leonard was the fourth child, and only boy, in the family. His parents reported that he had always seemed "full of energy" and "on the go" and had not been particularly concerned about his development until he had entered primary school. In the classroom he was described as unable to sit still, having poor attention skills, and possessing noteworthy impulsivity. Psychologic testing had been performed in the school and had revealed an IQ in the normal range with lower than expected achievement scores. As a result of his behavior problems, he tended to be a "loner" in the class.

His birth and early developmental history were unremarkable apart from several episodes of otitis media. His hearing had been tested and found to be within the normal range. His parents reported that he had been involved in several accidents. On examination, Leonard's behavior became more disorganized as he became more comfortable with the examiner and the setting. His motor skills were poor; his writing skills were significantly delayed. In highly structured settings, he was able to attend to tasks for more extended periods of time. He was aware of being isolated in the school setting. A trial of stimulant medications, in conjunction with family counseling and behavior procedures, resulted in significant symptomatic improvement. During the course of treatment it emerged that his father had had similar symptoms as a child. As an adolescent he continued to have some difficulties in impulse control and attending to tasks.

Comment. Several features of this case are typical of attention-deficit hyperactivity disorder. Although the presenting complaint related to classroom behavior, there was an earlier history of high activity levels and recurrent accidents. Although the symptoms responded to treatment with stimulant medications, they persisted into adolescence. The family history of the disorder is also relatively common.

REFERENCES

Bradley, C. (1937), The behavior of children receiving Benzedrine. *Am. J. Psychiatry*, 94:577–585.

Cantwell, D. (1972), Psychiatric illness in the families of hyperactive children. *Arch. Gen. Psychiatry*, 27:414–417.

Kornetsky, C. (1970), Psychoactive drugs in the immature organism. *Psychopharmacologia*, 17:105–136.

Lambert, M.N., Sandoval, J., and Sasone, D.M. (1981), Prevalence of hyperactivity and related treatments among elementary school children. In: *Psychosocial Aspects of Drug Treatment for Hyperactivity*, ed. K.D. Gadow and J. Looney. Boulder CO: Westview Press.

Satterfield, J., Satterfield, B., and Cantwell, D. (1981), Three-year multimodality treatment study of 100 hyperactive boys, *Behav. Pediatrics*, 98:650–655.

Weiss, B. (1982), Food additives and environmental chemicals as sources of childhood behavior disorders. *J. Am. Acad. Child Psychiatry*, 21:144–152.

Weiss, G., Hechtman, L., Milroy, T., and Perlman, T. (1985), Psychiatric status of hyperactives as adults: A controlled prospective 15-year follow-up of 63 hyperactive children. *J. Am. Acad. Child Psychiatry*, 24:211–220.

Zametkin, A.J., and Rapoport, J.L. (1987), Neurobiology of attention deficit disorder with hyperactivity: Where have we come in 50 years? *J. Am. Acad. Child Adolesc. Psychiatry*, 26:676–686.

34

BORDERLINE PERSONALITY DISORDER*

Definitions. A personality trait, which is equivalent to a character trait, may be defined as an enduring pattern of perceiving, relating to, and thinking about the enviroment and oneself. A personality trait becomes a personality disorder when the trait becomes inflexible and maladaptive and causes either subjective distress or impairment in social or occupational functions.

Classification. In 1987 the *Diagnostic and Statistical Manual of Mental Disorders, DSM-III-R*, broadly classified personality disorders into three clusters: (1) an "eccentric" group that includes paranoid, schizoid, and schizotypal personality disorders; (2) a group that appears dramatic, emotional, or erratic and includes antisocial, borderline, histrionic, and narcissistic personality disorders; (3) a group that seems to be excessively fearful and anxious and includes such personality disorders as avoidant, dependent, obsessive compulsive, and passive-aggressive. Other unclassified disorders include sadistic, impulsive, immature, and self-defeating disorders (DSM-III-R, 1987).

Children under 18 years of age who seem persistently, over a long time, to have the essential characteristic features (albeit modified by developmental considerations) of any of the aforementioned personality disorders described for adults may be so diagnosed. However, more often the child is given a diagnosis appropriate for his or her age that is

not a personality disorder diagnosis but that often continues as a personality disorder in an adult (Table 34–1).

Prevalence. Borderline personality disorder is the most frequently diagnosed personality disorder seen in severely disturbed children who are in residential treatment.

Clinical Features. The behavior of a child or adolescent with a borderline personality disorder is characterized by unpredictability and marked fluctuations in mood and identity. Such an individual has immature and poor social relationships. He or she may have severe temper tantrums during which the child or adolescent is out of contact with reality and acts as if he or she were warding off an attacker; in essence, that is, the child or adolescent becomes paranoid and regressed. The behavior is like that of a younger child; when the adolescent feels unloved, he or she either withdraws or becomes hostile and aggressive. Such an adolescent has a small "reality span." The adolescent tries to control the person he or she is struggling to stay attached to, in part to maintain his or her hold on reality. Such a child or adolescent is often obsessional and has difficulty in thinking abstractly. In fact, the presence of a thought disorder, however fluctuating, may be central in treatment planning. Often there is an associated disorder of mood (especially depression), of behavior (which may be disorganized, aggressive, withdrawn, or bizarre), or of perception (delusions, hallucinations). Interestingly, one

*Modified from Cavenar, J. (Ed.) (1985), *Psychiatry*, Philadelphia: J.B. Lippincott Company.

373

Table 34–1.   Correspondence of Childhood Disorders and Adult Personality Disorders

Childhood or Adolescent Disorder (under 18 years of age)	→	Adult Personality Disorder (over 18 years of age)
Avoidant disorder of childhood or adolescence	→	Avoidant personality disorder
Conduct disorder	→	Antisocial personality disorder

often finds signs of organicity in these children and adolescents.

The level of anxiety in these children is often quite high. Anxiety seems to be experienced as an overwhelming threat rather than as a signal for the utilization of defenses. Important functions, such as establishing and maintaining object relations, mobilizing defenses, and developing reality testing, are tenuously and only intermittently maintained. As if to compensate for this precarious state, omnipotent fantasies are often prominent.

Many of the children also appear to be depressed. They have a low self-esteem, their motivation to succeed in relationships or learning may virtually disappear, and they feel unloved. In many of the families of borderline children there is a pathologic infantilization of the child, which sometimes cannot be halted without the use of an actual separation (e.g., through residential treatment).

Etiology. The prevailing contemporary thrust for conceptualizing the development of a personality disorder is that of a complex model involving psychologic, polygenetic, organic (including brain damage), cognitive, developmental, and social-environmental factors. There appears to be an interactional effect between individual genetic-psychologic vulnerabilities and environmental stresses or varying degrees of intensity or duration. Other factors in the interactions include the presence of brain damage, the degree of intelligence, perceptual abilities, and success or failure experiences within the family or in other extrafamilial social settings.

Psychopathology. There appears to be an instability of inner representation in the child or adolescent with a borderline personality disorder, and as a result the inner world appears to invade, color, and even at times obliterate a true perception of the external world as far as the child or adolescent is concerned. Reality testing is lost at these times. Unstable primitive defenses (such as projection and identification) and impaired reality testing prevail. The child or adolescent with a borderline personality disorder also manages to make the therapist feel a regressive pull toward a similar chaotic and archaic level of functioning.

The child or adolescent with a borderline personality disorder in essence has failed to develop an adequate, stable level of functioning in such major areas as impulse control, affect modulation, attention, cognition, and object relations. The failure in personality development is such that the person usually has not even reached the relatively stable level of organization found in dependent, histrionic, compulsive, or passive-aggressive personality disorders, much less the level of organization required for the development of such symptom neuroses as a phobic disorder or an obsessive-compulsive disorder. The marked and prominent lability of affective discharge has led some observers to place borderline personality disorder within the broad category of affect disorders, much as the prominent features of disordered thinking in the paranoid personality have led the same observers to place that disorder within the broad category of schizophrenic disorders (Millon, 1981).

Diagnosis and Differential Diagnosis. Paradoxically, although the roots of many of the personality disorders described for adults are thought to stem from disturbances during certain phases of development during infancy and childhood, the diagnosis of a personality disorder during childhood is often difficult because the personality as a relatively stable organization may not occur until after late adolescence or early adulthood.

Another reason for caution in making a diagnosis of a personality disorder in a child is that certain behaviors that appear consistent with a personality trait or disorder may subsequently turn out to have been the antecedents of a genetically and/or environmentally determined psychiatric disorder of later onset. For example, girls who seem shy, withdrawn, and excessively compliant, or boys who seem aggressive, irritable, oppositional, and defiant, may be exhibiting the prodromal behavior of a later adult schizophrenic disorder (Rutter, 1980).

At the same time, certain items in the history and qualities discerned in the clinical interviews may help in the differential diagnosis of a borderline personality disorder. The general qualities of a personality disorder include, for example, a characteristic maladaptive style of response to an environmental stress, sometimes accompanied by a disagreeable reaction in others who have to deal with such a person's response.

The narrow, rigid, maladaptive defenses that constitute the behavior seen in a child with a personality disorder may arise from an unfortuate combination of genetic and environmental factors, including disordered parenting characterized by psychotic child-rearing practice and child abuse. The resulting disorder of personality usually includes a pervasive and persistent difficulty in forming and maintaining satisfactory and satisfying relationships and in establishing stable work patterns. Furthermore, the anticipated and actual consequent life experiences of such a child or adolescent only add to the depression, despair, and anxiety that may accompany a personality disorder, especially a borderline personality disorder. Moreover, the striking lack of empathy that is often present in the child with a borderline personality disorder in particular paves the way for a repetitious reinforcement that may take place in every social interaction in which the child is involved.

The differential diagnosis of personality disorders may include schizophrenia, somatization disorder, conduct disorder, mental retardation, cyclothymic disorder, or partial complex seizure-type disorders. Anxiety, depression, and symptoms and signs of an attention-deficit hyperactivity disorder may also be present.

Treatment. Treatment of the child with a borderline personality disorder is almost by definition multimodal, and includes psychotherapy (Lewis and Brown, 1979), behavior therapy, and medication aimed at the specific target symptoms present. Outcome is varied. In many instances the child and family remain vulnerable to stress and often have a tendency to exhibit paranoid behavior under stress.

Developmental Perspectives. *Biologic Origins.* One root of personality development and its disorders lies in genetic factors. For example, the temperament of a child, which in effect constitutes a personality style or trait (Thomas, Chess and Birch, 1968), is thought to derive in part from genetic factors (Torgersen and Kringlen, 1978). At the same time, there is considerable plasticity as the child develops and experiences different life events (Chess, 1978).

Other genetic evidence from the study of developmental psychopathology at present is suggestive rather than conclusive. For example, Schulsinger (1972) has suggested a group of genetic factors for antisocial personality disorder. Similarly, Cantwell (1976) and Rapoport and Zametkin (1980) have suggested a polygenic model for the syndrome of attention-deficit disorder, the behavioral manifestations of which often seem to have the characteristics of a personality disorder. (Retrospective, clinical reviews of adults diagnosed as having borderline personality disorder have sometimes revealed childhood symptoms consistent with the diagnosis of attention-deficit hyperactivity disorder.)

Other more general genetic and biologic factors that may contribute to personality development include the genetic programming and biologic and hormonal factors that support the survival of the newborn and determine in part the infant's level of activity, attachment behavior, intelligence, and sexual and aggressive behavior, as well as factors that offer a biologic guarantee for the semiotic function. In addition, later myelination and hormonal changes, both of which are partially under the influence of genetic factors and continue to occur through and during adolescence, affect personality development.

Psychologic Origins. Most of the developmental psychologic theories of personality disorders imply a concept of a "sleeper," or delayed, effect of early psychologic trauma, since the effects are not readily apparent either at the time of the trauma or during early childhood. Sometimes the delayed effect is though to occur because of a heightened, or induced, vulnerability caused by the trauma, which then makes the child more susceptible to later social-environmental stresses.

Psychologic theories of the formation of character (or personality) and the development of disorders of personality have particularly strong roots in psychoanalysis. Yet, surprisingly, Freud wrote little about character; in fact, his most important statements can be easily summarized. They include the following ideas: First, the "formula for the way in which character in its final shape is formed out of the constituent instincts [was simply that] the permanent character traits are either unchanged prolongations of the original instincts, or sublimations of those instincts, or reaction formations against them" (Freud, 1908, p. 175). What Freud described as a person's character, or personality, was built up to a considerable extent "from the material or sexual excitations and is composed of instincts that have been fixed since childhood, or constructions achieved by means of sublimation, and of other constructions, employed for effectively holding in check perverse impulses which have been recognized as being unutilizable" (Freud, 1905, pp. 238–239). In the case of some character (personality) traits, Freud thought he could trace a connection with particular erotogenic components. Thus, obstinacy, thrift, and orderliness arose from an "exploitation of anal eroticism," while ambition was determined by a

"strong urethralerotic disposition" (Freud, 1905, p. 239).

Freud drew a sharp distinction between character and neurosis, stating flatly that "the failure of repression and the return of the repressed, which are peculiar to the mechanism of neurosis, are absent in the formation of character. In the latter, repression either does not come into action or smoothly achieves its aim of replacing the repressed by reaction-formations and sublimations" (Freud, 1913, p. 323). What created character was "first and foremost . . . the incorporation of the former parental agency as a superego, which is no doubt its most important and decisive portion, and, further, identifications with the two parents of the later period and with other influential figures, and similar identifications formed as precipitates of abandoned object-relations . . . [Other] contributions to the construction of characters . . . [include] the reaction-formations which the ego acquires" (Freud, 1933, p. 91). In essence, Freud summarized his views by saying that "the character of the ego is a precipitant of abandoned object-cathexes and that it contains the history of those object-choices" (Freud, 1923, p. 29).

Today we believe that this psychoanalytic concept of fixed derivatives from defenses against early drives is no longer sufficient to account for character, or personality, even in the domain of psychologic factors. Nor is Reich's later description (1949) of "character armor" sufficient. Interestingly, Reich himself still thought that "the continuing actual conflicts between instinct and outer world give the character armor its strength and continued reason for existence" (p. 146), meaning essentially that it still continued to have the exclusively defensive function from which he thought it derived.

More recent ideas on the psychologic component of the development of personality disorders, for example, are related to more recent concepts of child development. Thus, Kohut (1971; 1980) viewed the patient with a narcissistic disorder as having a disorder of his or her sense of self, arising during the separation-individuation phase (especially the so-called rapprochement phase) of development when the parents responded to the child inadequately. The disordered sense of self may be perpetuated either as a draining and persistent regressive need to seek a kind of accepting, affirming mirror of the child's sense to omnipotence or grandiosity or as a tendency to overidealize another person and merge with that person. Such persons have little tolerance either for the less than ideal nature of others or for their own defects. They require perfection in others. They are easily overwhelmed and are often chronically enraged, a rage that may be projected in the course of a projective identification. They may turn to drugs or other kinds of self-stimulating activities. Recurrent bouts of depression, low self-esteem, and preoccupation with bodily functions are common. Separations are difficult. Kernberg (1975) also saw the same disorders as arising during the separation-individuation phase but as a defense against early splitting of rage and envy directed toward internalized object representations. This splitting may persist, seen often as rapid shifts between overidealization and devaluation of the object, with the consequent development of a grandiose sense of self.

Neither of these more recent concepts has been reliably documented or validated, and in neither view, it should be noted, is there sufficient attention paid to biologic and social environmental factors. However, they do represent an arresting developmental perspective, placing the psychologic origin of the disorder at particular phases of early infant development.

Although personality development and its disorders may originate in these phases or stages, the personality does continue to develop throughout the successive stages of the life cycle (Erikson, 1959). The rate of change does slow down during the periods of adulthood, giving an impression of stability of personality organization. Yet we know that important personality changes can still occur at midlife, or at retirement, or indeed at any time in response to major life stresses, including divorce, illness, and severe personal loss.

Because in general the rate of change during childhood and adolescence is relatively higher than during later periods of development, clinicians have adopted the convention that personality is "not yet formed" during childhood and adolescence and exists only in adults. This, of course, is an oversimplification. A more accurate statement would be that the personality is always changing and subject to modification (indeed, that is the rationale for many forms of psychotherapy), but that the rate of change in the preadult period makes diagnosis and prediction more hazardous. Practically speaking, the longer the "track record" of a personality trait or symptom, the more likely it is that the clinician can be confident in the diagnosis. In the case of children and adolescents, a flexible, adaptive personality fails to develop, leading to the syndrome of a so-called borderline personality disorder.

Case Vignette

Lauren was born to a single teenaged mother who had a history of recurrent psychiatric hospitalizations and substance abuse. She was born nearly a month prematurely and was noted to be difficult to comfort. Early motor and communicative milestones were somewhat delayed. Lauren's early history was marked by repeated episodes of relative neglect and one of actual abandonment on the part of her biological mother. During most of the first 5 years of her life, she had lived with her mother who had entered into a masochistic relationship with an alcoholic man who physically abused both Lauren and the mother, and Lauren often witnessed her mother being beaten. The mother's eventual abandonment of Lauren led to her placement in a series of foster homes. Lauren was noted to be a difficult child who had trouble in school both academically and relating to peers. During her multiple foster home placements she was noted to exhibit various behavior problems including severe temper tantrums and aggression, poor impulse control, and periods of depression with occasional suicidal ideation. Reunification with her mother was attempted when Lauren was 14 years old. However, Lauren developed feelings of unreality and paranoid ideation that led to emergency psychiatric admission.

During her hospitalization, Lauren was noted to exhibit a pervasive pattern of instability in mood, interpersonal relationships, and self-concept. She would characteristically develop intense relationships with other patients and staff but these relationships were highly unstable; splitting of staff members (pitting one against another) was often an issue. Her mood was unstable with periods of depression alternating with anxiety and irritability. She often became involved in fights and engaged in impulsive, self-defeating behaviors. She complained of episodes of depersonalization (a sense of loss of personal reality) accompanied by feelings of emptiness, and she was preoccupied with the possibility that her mother would once again abandon her. Suicidal ideation became prominent when she was stressed. She was eventually discharged to a long-term psychiatric facility where she profited from intensive psychotherapy, educational intervention, and a highly structured program. However, she impulsively left this placement in an apparent attempt to rejoin her mother. Follow-up information from the mother indicated that this plan had quickly proven unworkable and, when she had last contacted her mother, Lauren was engaging in prostitution.

Comment. This case illustrates the complex range of symptoms usually seen in borderline personality disorder. Problems in mood, in identity, and in social relationships are usual. Similarly, the apparently complicated interaction of psychological, genetic, and social-environmental factors is typical. Often such children achieved their highest levels of functioning in highly structured treatment programs; gains made may, however, be lost when children return to unsupportive or chaotic family environments.

REFERENCES

American Psychiatric Association (1987), *Diagnostic and Statistical Manual of Mental Disorders*, 3rd ed. Washington, DC, APA, pp. 65–67.

Andrulonis, P.A., Glueck, B.C., Stroebel, C.F., et al. (1981), Organic brain dysfunction and the borderline syndrome. *Psychiat. Clin. North Am.*, 4:61–66.

Cantwell, D.P. (1976), Genetic factors in the hyperkinetic syndrome. *J. Am. Acad. Child Psychiatry*, 15:214–223.

Chess, S. (1978), The plasticity of human development. *J. Am. Acad. Child Psychiatry*, 17:80–91.

Chess, S., and Thomas, A. (1977), Temperamental individuality from childhood to adolescence. *J. Am. Acad. Child Psychiatry*, 16:218–226.

Cohen, D.J., Shaywitz, S.E., Young, G., et al. (1983), Borderline syndromes and attention deficit disorders of childhood. In: *The Borderline Child*, ed. K.S. Robson. New York: McGraw-Hill Book Co., pp. 197–222.

Erikson, E.H. (1959), Identity and the life cycle. *Psychol. Issues*, 1:101–172.

Freud, S. (1905), Three essays on sexuality. In: *The Complete Works of Sigmund Freud (Vol. 7) Standard Edition*, ed. J. Strachey. London: Hogarth Press, 1953.

Freud, S. (1908), Character and anal eroticism. In: *The Complete Works of Sigmund Freud (Vol. 9) Standard Edition*, ed. J. Strachey. London: Hogarth Press, pp. 167–175, 1957.

Freud, S. (1913), The disposition to obsessional neurosis. In: *The Complete Works of Sigmund Freud (Vol. 12) Standard Edition*, ed. J. Strachey. London: Hogarth Press, pp. 313–325, 1958.

Freud, S. (1923), The ego and the id. In: *The Complete Works of Sigmund Freud (Vol. 19) Standard Edition*, ed. J. Strachey. London: Hogarth Press, pp. 12–59, 1961.

Freud, S. (1933), New introductory lectures on psychoanalysis. In: *The Complete Works of Sigmund Freud (Vol. 22) Standard Edition*, ed. J. Strachey. London: Hogarth Press, pp. 3–184, 1964.

Kernberg, O. (1975), *Borderline Conditions and Pathological Narcissism*. New York: Jason Aronson.

Kohut, H. (1971), *The Analysis of the Self*. New York: International Universities Press.

Kohut, H. (1980), Self psychology: Reflections on the present and future. Presented before the Boston Psychoanalytic Association Symposium on Reflections on Self Psychology.

Lewis, M., and Brown, T.E. (1979), Psychotherapy in the residential treatment of the borderline child. *Child Psychiatry Hum. Dev.*, 9:181–188.

Millon, T. (1981), *Disorders of Personality. DSM III, Axis II*. New York: John Wiley & Sons.

Rapoport, J., and Zametkin, A. (1980), Attention deficit disorder. In: *Child Psychiatry*, ed. B.J. Blinder. Philadelphia: W.B. Saunders Co.

Reich, W. (1949), *Character Analysis*. New York: Orgone Institute Press.

Rutter, M. (1980), *Scientific Foundations of Developmental Psychiatry*. London: Heinemann.

Schulsinger, F. (1972), Psychopathology, heredity and environment. *Int. J. Ment. Health*, 1:190.

Thomas, A., Chess, S., and Birch, H. (1968), *Temperament and Behavior Disorders in Children*. New York: New York University Press.

Torgersen, A.M., and Kringlen, E. (1978), Genetic aspects of temperamental differences in infants: A study of same-sexed twins. *J. Am. Acad. Child Psychiatry*, 17:433–444.

35

RESEARCH TRENDS IN CHILD AND ADOLESCENT PSYCHOPATHOLOGY

In addition to the expanding interest in the scientific investigation of the biologic aspects of child and adolescent psychiatric disorders, research has also blossomed in the areas of methodology (especially in the use of structured interviews), epidemiology, stress disorders, and neurobiologic studies. In addition, new techniques are increasingly becoming available and are enhancing the level of sophistication in research.

STRUCTURED DIAGNOSTIC INTERVIEWS

One important trend in research is in the methodology of research in child and adolescent psychiatry. In particular, research on structured interviews is noteworthy (Young et al., 1987).

Currently, five structured interviews are keyed to DSM III criteria and, in some instances, such as the DISC, to DSM-III-R.

These interviews, which are undergoing revisions, are:

1. Child Assessment Schedule (CAS)
2. Diagnostic Interview for Children and Adolescents (DICA)
3. Diagnostic Interview Schedule for Children (DISC)
4. Schedule for Affective Disorders and Schizophrenia for School-Age Children (present episode version) (K-SADS-P)
5. Interview Schedule for Children (ISC)

Some of the characteristics of these structured interviews are shown in Table 35–1.

Structured interviews have many advantages:

1. They systematically and comprehensively cover important areas for clinical inquiry.
2. They encourage greater precision and facilitate comparable data.
3. They may be administered by a technician who can be rapidly trained for the task.

On the other hand, structured interviews also have some disadvantages:

1. They are unreliable and often inappropriate for preschool children.
2. Sometimes they have long lists of questions (e.g., the DICA has 207 items, which may exhaust the child if not the interviewer).
3. They sometimes cluster items around symptoms, thus focusing too much on negative behavior. This focus may interfere with the development of rapport.
4. They lack flexibility.
5. They do not require much judgment.
6. They lack normative data.
7. They rarely focus on father-child interaction.
8. They may not always correspond to the clinical diagnosis.
9. They sometimes need a support system, such as computers and staff.
10. They are generally nontherapeutic.

On balance, what one trades off in depth,

Table 35–1.   Considerations in Selection of Structured Diagnostic Interviews for Children and Adolescents

	CAS*	DICA	DISC	L-SADS-P†	ISC
Primary application	Clinical research	Epi/clin	Epi	Clin	Clin
Time to administer‡	C 60 P 60	C 40 P 45	C 45–60 P 60–90	C 60–90 P 60–90	C 45–90 P 90–150
Age range (yr)	7–17	6–17	8–17	6–18	8–17
Format§					
Introduction	Structured	Structured	Structured	Unstructured	Unstructured
Dx assessment	Structured	Structured	Structured	Semistructured	Semistructured
Organization	Functional domains	Functional domains	Functional domains	Diagnostic complexes	Diagnostic complexes
Time frame for inquiry	Present	Lifetime: past, present	Present: past year/6 mos.	Present: sx most severe this episode; past week	Present: 2 wk/6 mos.
Severity ratings	N	N	N	Y	Y
Interviewer observations	Y	Y	N	Y	Y
Informants	Parent/child, parallel forms	Parent/child, parallel forms	Parent/child, parallel forms	Parent/child, single form	Parent/child, single form
Level of clinical skills advised	Clinicians	Clinicians	Lay interviewers	Clinicians	Clinicians
Computer algorithm	Y	Y	Y	Y	N

*CAS, Child Assessment Schedule; DICA, Diagnostic Interview for Children and Adolescents; DISC, NIMH Diagnostic Interview Schedule for Children; K-SADS-P, Schedule for Affective-Disorders and Schizophrenia for School-Age Children (present episode version); ISC, Interview Schedule for Children: Y, yes; N, no; epi, epidemiologic; clin, clinical research.

†The K-SADS-E (epidemiologic version) differs from the K-SADS-P in the following respects: its primary application is both epidemiologic and clinical. The time frame for inquiries includes the current episode and the most severe past episode of any symptom. Severity of symptoms is not recorded.

‡Estimated time in minutes to administer to child (C) and parent (P).

§Level of structure of introductory section and queries to assess diagnostic criteria (Dx Assessments).

Reprinted with permission from Gutterman, E.M., O'Brien, J.D., and Young, J.G. (1987). Structured diagnostic interviews for children and adolescents: current status and future directions. *J. Am. Acad. Child Adolesc. Psychiatry*, 26:622.

Table 35–2. Psychiatric Interview Instruments*

Diagnostic Interview for Children and Adolescents (Herjanic and Welner)
Parent Interview (Herjanic and Welner)
Mental Health Assessment Form (Kestenbaum and Bird)
Interview Schedule for Children (Kovacs and co-workers)
Screening Inventory (Langner and co-workers)
Kiddie—SADS (Pulg–Antich and Chambers)
A Behavioral Screening Questionnaire (Richman and Graham)
Isle of Wight Survey (Rutter and Graham)

*Reprinted with permission from Cavenar, J.O. (ed.) (1985), *Psychiatry.* Philadelphia: J.B. Lippincott Co., Ch. 20, p. 13.

one gains in coverage of the signs of disorder at least at the level of initial screening, e.g., epidemiologic studies. Interestingly, children report more thoroughly about feelings, but parents report more thoroughly about behavior.

Rating scales, like the scales of a thermometer, are often a measure of severity rather than a litmus test of diagnostic sensitivity and reliability.

The number of schedules and scales now available is formidable. A preliminary classification of some of the more commonly used scales may be found in Tables 35–2 through 35–5.

EPIDEMIOLOGIC RESEARCH

Epidemiologic research constitutes an important sector of the research effort in child and adolescent psychiatry today.

Epidemiology, the study of the distribution (including incidence* and prevalence†) of disease in the population, is also concerned with the distribution of factors that are important for prevention, and with the distribution and delivery of health services in the population.

$$* \quad \text{incidence rate} = \frac{\text{number of cases observed in a year}}{\text{population at risk}} \times 1{,}000$$

$$† \quad \text{prevalence rate} = \frac{\text{number of cases observed at a given time}}{\text{population at risk}} \times 1{,}000$$

Table 35–3. General Psychopathology Scales*

Child Behavior Checklist (Achenbach)
Children's Behavior Checklist for Parents (Arnold and Smeltzer)
Child Behavior Characteristics Scale (Borgatta and Fanshel)
Children's Behavior Diagnostic Inventory (Burdock and Hardesty)
Childhood Personality Scale (Cohen and co-workers)
Connors' Rating Scales (Connors)
 Parent Questionnaire
 Teacher Questionnaire
Teacher's Behavior Rating Scale (Cowen)
Children's Assessment Package (Cytrynbaum and Snow)
Adolescent Life Assessment Checklist (Gleser and co-workers)
The Minnesota Child Develpment Inventory (Ireton and Thwing)
The Symptom Checklist (Kohn and Rosman)
Louisville Behavior Checklist (Miller)
Louisville School Behavior Checklist
Behavior Problem Checklist (Quay and Peterson)
The Quincy Behavior Checklist (Reinherz and Kelfer)
Behavior Checklist (Richman and Graham)
Children's Behavior Questionnaire for Teachers (Rutter)
Devereux Elementary School Behavior Rating Scale (Spivack and Swift)
Devereux Child Behavior Rating Scale (Spivack and Swift)
Devereux Adolescent Behavior Rating Scale (Spivack and co-workers)

*Reprinted with permission from Cavenar, J.O. (ed.) (1985), *Psychiatry.* Philadelphia: J.B. Lippincott Co., Ch. 20, p. 13.

Table 35–4. Specific Syndrome Scales*

Hyperactivity
 Hyperactivity and Withdrawal Rating Scale (Bell and co-workers)
 Parent–Teacher Questionnaire (Conners)
 Hyperkinetic Rating Scale (Davids)
Anxiety
 Manifest Anxiety Scale—Children's Form (Castaneda and co-workers)
Fear
 Louisville Fear Survery for Children (Miller and co-workers)
Depression
 Children's Affective Rating Scale (Cytryn and McKnew)
 Children's Depression Inventory (Kovacs and co-workers)

*Reprinted with permission from Cavenar, J.O. (ed.) (1985), *Psychiatry.* Philadelphia: J.B. Lippincott Co., Ch. 20, p. 13.

Table 35–5. Assessment Techniques for Childhood Depression*

Self-report measures (rate severity of depression in children)

Children's Depression Inventory (CDI), which consists of 27 items, each rated on a three-point scale and based essentially on the Beck Depression Inventory (BDI; Kovacs and Beck, 1977)

Short Children's Depression Inventory (SCDI; Carlson and Cantwell, 1980, which has 13 items, including mood, self-esteem, hopelessness, anhedonia, guilt, suicide, relationship with others, motivation, fatigability, sleep, appetite, and others from the original adult short BDI, all scored from 0 to 3

Interview techniques, which include

Kiddie—SADS (Schedule for Affective Disorders and Schizophrenia for School Age Children; Chambers, Puig-Antich and others, 1978)

Interview Schedule for children (ISC); Kovacs and co-workers, 1977)

Bellevue Index of Depression (BID; Petti, 1978)

Children's Depression Rating Scale (CDRS; Poznanski and co-workers, 1979)

Children's Affective Rating Scale (CARS; McKnew and Cytryn, 1979)

Diagnostic Interview for Children and Adolescents (DICA; Herjanic and Campbell, 1977)

*Reprinted with permission from Cavenar, J.O. (ed.) (1985), *Psychiatry.* Philadelphia: J.B. Lippincott Co., Ch. 20, p. 13.

Most epidemiologic studies today use multiple methods of study.

Shaffer (1987) presented a useful overview of what the epidemiologic method can bring to our understanding of childhood disorders. Gould et al. (1981) summarized the findings from all 35 of the important epidemiologic studies of psychiatric disorders in the United States and Western Europe up to that time. They found that the overall rate of clinical maladjustment in the United States is "probably no lower than 11.8%" (with specific rates ranging across age, social class, ethnic group, and geographic region).

Child psychiatrists are familiar with at least two classic epidemiologic studies: that of Lee Robins in her book *Deviant Children Grown Up* (1966) and that of Michael Rutter and his colleagues in the Isle of Wight Study who reported in two books, *A Neuropsychiatric Study in Childhood* (1970a) and *Education, Health and Welfare* (1970b).

Epidemiologic studies since these classics have provided us with a wealth of information and constitute an important trend in research in child and adolescent psychiatry (Earls, 1980; Links, 1983; Rutter, 1985; Yule, 1981). Following DSM-III and the advent of structured interviews, additional epidemiologic studies, particularly in regard to depressive disorders in children, have been published (see below).

STRESS AND DISORDERS

Another important research trend is found in the attempts to study children's reactions to severe stress. What has become clear from this research is the complexity of children's reactions, the variety of models used to understand the child's responses, and the need to develop more sophisticated methodologies for the research (Anthony, 1986; Garmezy, 1986).

Among the theoretical constructs, the following have been proposed:

1. proneness to helplessness or hopelessness (Schmale, 1972);
2. competence and coping in relation to the locus of control along an internal-external dimension (Rutter, 1966);
3. the adaptive and prophylactic aspects of denial (Goldberger, 1983); and
4. the role of the family as a support system (Caplan, 1976).

Children who are overwhelmed with anxiety resulting from stress may first experience confusion, disorientation, disorganization, numbness, hopelessness, and helplessness, and then may develop a full-blown post-traumatic stress disorder, the common symptoms of which are a tendency (1) to reexperience the stressful event, (2) to detach oneself from the environment, (3) to be apprehensive about further exposure, and (4) to show exaggerations of attachment behavior, especially toward family members (Bowlby, 1973).

In addition, the psychologic stress of remembering is a particularly disturbing factor, which sometimes affects rescuers as much as it does victims of disasters.

At the same time, different kinds of stresses may give rise to differences in the clinical picture. For example, (1) survival after a disaster in which many others die may induce survival guilt, (2) personal loss may give rise to feelings of protest, despair, and detachment, and (3) uprooting and relocation may give rise to feelings of alienation, homesickness, and projection of persecutory anxieties on to the new host.

These severe stresses also evoke complex biologic responses that follow a tripartite response sequence of (1) alarm and mobilization of defenses, (2) resistance and maintenance, and (3) exhaustion and even death, constituting what Hans Selye (1946) called the general adaptation syndrome. Almost every system and organ in the body is involved, including the pituitary-adrenocortical system, hormones (such as prolactin, melatonin, and endorphins), the immune system, the sympathetic and autoimmune nervous systems, epinephrine metabolism, and cardiovascular regulation.

Among the more recent studies of children's reactions to stress are those of Lenore Terr (1979; 1981) and Pynoos et al. (1987). Terr studies 26 schoolchildren, 5 to 14 years of age, in Chowchilla, California, who were kidnapped and buried in their school bus for 16 hours. The children subsequently experienced a great deal of anxiety, manifest in part by bad dreams about their own death, and engaged in play that was repetitive and compulsive.

Pynoos et al. (1987) were able to study children 5 to 13 years of age who were exposed to a fatal sniper attack in their elementary school playground. One hundred and fifty-nine children were interviewed using a post-traumatic stress disorder reaction index to elicit symptoms of a post-traumatic stress disorder. They found significant differences in children grouped according to the degree of exposure to the attack.

A *severe* reaction was most frequent in those who were in the playground at the time of the attack.

A *moderate* reaction was more frequent in those who were at school, but not on the playground.

Those not at school at the time of the attack usually showed no reaction in terms of symptoms.

The symptoms include intrusiveness, emotional constriction, and avoidance. Even among those children who had only mild reactions, there were symptoms of increased fear and anxiety subsequent to the event. Those children with severe reactions had such symptoms as difficulty in concentrating at school and disturbed sleep.

In summary, Pynoos et al. found strong evidence for a post-traumatic stress disorder in the children, with a correlation between proximity to the violence and the type and number of post-traumatic stress disorder symptoms.

Some children—especially those in closely knit, healthy families—nevertheless may emerge unscathed. We need to learn more about the various protective and noxious factors at work.

NEUROBIOLOGIC STUDIES

Bax (1980) has reviewed some of the technologies in research that are now available. For example, using a sophisticated combination of radioactive labeling of oxygen, carbon dioxide, and glucose with a computerized scanning technique called proton emission tomography (PET), Lassen (1977) has reported fascinating studies of cerebral blood flow during a whole range of normal cerebral activities. Phelps et al. (1981) have shown how "positron computed tomography can map the distribution of local cerebral metabolic functions in humans in a safe and noninvasive manner that is not possible by any other technique" (p. 1447).

Computerized tomography (CT) also has revealed such abnormalities as cerebral atrophy and asymmetry in 32% of children 4 to 15 years of age who had a diagnosis of "minimal brain damage" (Bergstrom and Bille, 1978). Evoked potentials combined with computer technology have similarly given rise to a new technique of "neurometrics" (John et al., 1977) for the study of children with learning disorders. These techniques offer the opportunities for potential advances in the understanding of conditions such as learning disorders.

Magnetic resonance imaging (MRI) may yield information on tissue chemistry and may provide useful images of brain anatomy. The measure used is the "relaxation" time required for atomic nuclei to lose the energy gained after being placed in a strong magnetic field. A tentative finding is that relaxation times in the brains of manic-depressive patients are longer than normal and return to normal with lithium treatment. Abnormalities in the cerebellums of autistic individuals using MRI scans have also been reported (Courchesne et al., 1988).

PSYCHOANALYSIS

Finally, we must consider the status of research in child psychoanalysis. A serious problem now confronting child psychoanalysis is sometimes stated in its most general form: is psychoanalysis a science? Not surprisingly, psychonanalysts themselves staunchly defend psychoanalysis as a science (Arlow & Brenner, 1988; Wallerstein, 1986). On the other hand, many scientists and philosophers fault psychoanalysis for its lack of scientific credibility (Hook, 1959; Popper, 1963; Holt, 1981; Grunbaum, 1984; Laor, 1985). Sometimes the debate seems at cross purposes, reminding one of the story told by Medawar (1982) of the Reverend Sydney Smith, a famous wit: Smith and a friend were walking "through the extremely narrow streets of old Edinburgh when they heard a furious altercation between two housewives from high-up windows across the street. 'They can never agree,' said Smith to his companion, 'for they are arguing from different premises' " (p. 103). Thus before one can judge whether psychoanalysis is a science, one must declare one's premise, i.e., one's definition of science.

However, whatever one's definition, we can all probably agree with Sherwood (1969) who stated that "in perhaps no other field has so great a body of theory been built upon such a small public record of raw data" (p. 70). Even Wallerstein (1986) had to note that ". . . to date, grossly insufficient efforts have been directed toward . . ." (p. 446) the rededication of this almost intolerable situation noted by Sherwood. Wallerstein laconically observed that "the cadre of serious psychoanalytic researchers . . . is . . . pitifully small" (p. 447). Arlow (1982) agreed that any future confidence in psychoanalysis "will have to rely on solid observation data, meticulously gathered in the analytic situation and *objectively evaluated*, for it is upon this set of procedures that the claim of psychoanalysis to a place among the empirical sciences is based" (p. 18, italics added). Kaplan (1981), in his Presidential Address to the American Psychoanalytic Association, similarly emphasized that the fundamental challenge to psychoanalysis was still "a much needed *validation* of . . . basic theoretical and clinical concepts" (p. 23, italics added). More specifically, he told analysts that "any progress in psychoanalysis must include an evaluation of the psychoanalytic process which involves making *all* of the data *public* by *notes, tape recordings*, etc, . . " (p. 19, italics added)

Even the context of the practice of psychoanalysis is facing some important challenges in today's society. At present, psychoanalysis is available mostly to an elite, educated, and affluent few, many of whom are themselves mental health professionals (Panel, 1978). Few persons suffering from mental disorders have these features (Michels, 1988), and there is little, if any, valid scientific evidence about the outcome of psychoanalytic treatment, even for this small group of analysands. This situation may eventually become intolerable in our society and may force psychoanalysis to become equally available to the poor and, at the same time, more open to review by nonanalysts and to regulation by those powers that subsidize and govern much of health care today. Such a choice may not be unanimously welcomed by psychoanalysts.

Meanwhile, in terms of research, some psychoanalysts have provided data that challenge certain traditional psychoanalytic beliefs. For example, Emde (1981) reviewed a large corpus of child development research (Clarke and Clarke, 1976; Bell and Harper, 1977; Clark-Stewart, 1977; Kagan, Kearsley, and Zelazo, 1978; Sameroff, 1978; Osofsky, 1979) and noted a number of challenges to clinical theory in psychoanalysis:

1. The infant constructs his or her own reality, and what analysts "reconstruct" for the patient in fact may never have happened. Analysts therefore should renew their emphasis on recent and current experience and should not be so concerned with understanding or modifying early experiences. Analysts have identified, as it were, too much with the "helpless infant" who, it turns out, is not as helpless as we formerly believed.

2. Discontinuities are prominent in development, suggesting too that we modify the theory of so-called reorganization of experience that is said to take place, for example, at puberty. Discontinuities may occur not only during infancy, but also during so-called "latency" and, indeed, at puberty, when new myelination arcs occur (Yakovlev and Lecours, 1967).

3. Because there is a strong self-righting tendency after deflection from a developmental pathway, a single traumatic episode is unlikely to be pathogenic.

4. The concept of irreversibility of adverse effects, such as major maternal deprivation, should be modified, because it has been shown that environmental changes can offer major compensation for early environmental deficits.

5. The term "object relations" is unfortunate in light of two recent findings of social reciprocity and mutual interaction and change between infant and caregiver; the "object" is not simply the "target" of drives.

6. Psychoanalysts have not given sufficient attention to transaction within the family that determines which opportunities prevail and what early experience endures. Psychoanalysts now should look to the environment as well as to the individual, to the interface as well as to the intrapsychic.

7. Developmental phases other than infancy are equally important, and subsequent experiences continue to modify early ones.

Having posed these challenges, we must also stress that psychoanalysts doing research in psychoanalysis have formidable problems in establishing reliability and validity. Nevertheless, some sophisticated work is being done, such as the research on object relations by Blatt and others (Blatt and Lerner, 1982). Such work is rare, however.

One consequence of this relative sterility in child psychoanalytic research is that many of the concepts in psychoanalysis are now considered by many analysts to be metaphor rather than true theory. Yet we should not throw out the baby with the bathwater. Although relatively little in psychoanalysis has been proved, much remains to be tested. The wealth of accumulated clinical experience still awaits objective evaluation, and this should be the highest priority for research in child analysis.

Another challenge for psychoanalysis is to locate itself within and relate itself to the spectrum of biologic sciences that form part of the foundation for human behavior. Neither psychoanalysis nor the neurochemistry of the synapse alone, nor perhaps even both together, is sufficient to explain all human behavior. Behavior that may appear to have (and that may indeed have) strong psychodynamic determinants may also be associated with significant biologic origins.

At the very least, a rapprochement between the psychologic and biologic sciences is needed. Better still, we need a superordinate general developmental theory that will incorporate knowledge from many different fields. For that we may have to wait for the next genius of the order of magnitude of Darwin or Freud to appear.

REFERENCES

Anthony, E.J. (1986), The response to overwhelming stress: Some introductory comments. *J. Am. Acad. Child Adolesc. Psychiatry,* 25:299–305.

Arlow, J.A., and Brenner, L. (1988), The future of psychoanalysis. *Psychoanal. Q.,* 57:1–14.

Bax, M.C.O. (1980), Future trends and problems. In: *Scientific Foundations of Developmental Psychiatry,* ed. M. Rutter. London: Heinemann.

Beitchman, J.H., Nair, R., Clegg, M., Ferguson, B., and Patel, P.G. (1986), Prevalence of psychiatric disorders in children with speech and language disorders. *J. Am. Acad. Child Adolesc. Psychiatry,* 25:528–535.

Bell, R.Q., and Harper, L.V. (1977), *Child Effects on Adults.* New York: Halsted.

Bergstrom, K., and Belle, B. (1978), Computed tomography of the brain in children with minimal brain damage: A preliminary study of 46 children. *Neuropediatrics,* 9:378–384.

Blatt, S.J., and Lerner, H. (1982), Investigations in the psychoanalytic theory of object relations and object representations. In: *Empirical Studies on Psychoanalytic Theories,* ed. J. Masling. New York: Halsted.

Bowlby, J. (1973), *Attachment and Loss: Separation Anxiety and Anger* (Vol. 21), New York: Basic Books.

Caplan, G. (1976), The family as a support system. In: *Support Systems and Mutual Help: Multidisciplinary Explorations,* ed. G. Caplan and M. Kallilea. New York: Grune & Stratton, pp. 19–36.

Clark-Stewart, A. (1977), *Child Care in the Family: A Review of Research and Some Propositions for Policy.* New York: Academic Press.

Clarke, A.M., and Clarke, A.D.B. (1976), *Early Experience: Myth and Evidence.* London: Open Books.

Courchesne, E., Yeung-Courchesne, R., Press, G., Hesseling, J.R., and Jernigan, T.L. (1988), Hypoplasia of cerebellar vermal lobules VI and VII in autism. *N. Engl. J. Med.,* 318:1349–1354.

Earls, F.A. (1980), Epidemiological child psychiatry: An American perspective. In: *Psychopathology of Children and Youth: A Cross Cultural Perspective,* ed. E.F. Purcell. New York: Macy Foundation.

Emde, R.N. (1981), Changing models of infancy and the nature of early development: Remodeling the foundation. *J. Am. Psychoanal. Assoc.,* 29:179–219.

Garmezy, N. (1986), Children under severe stress: Critique and commentary. *J. Am. Acad. Child Psychiatry,* 25:384–392.

Goldberger, L. (1983), The concept and mechanisms of denial: A selective review. In: *The Denial of Stress,* ed. S. Brezwitz. New York: International Universities Press, pp. 83–102.

Gould, M.S., Wimsch-Hitzig, R., and Dohrenwena, B.

(1981), Estimating the prevalence of childhood psychopathology. *J. Am. Acad. Child Psychiatry,* 20:462–476.

Grunbaum, A. (1984), *The Foundation of Psychoanalysis: A Philosophical Critique.* Berkeley: University of California Press.

Gutterman, E.M., O'Brien, J., and Young, J. (1987), Structured diagnostic interviews for children and adolescents: Current status and future direction. *J. Am. Acad. Child Adolesc. Psychiatry,* 26:621–630.

Holt, R.R. (1981), The death and transfiguration of metapsychology. *Int. Rev. Psychoanalysis,* 8:129–143.

Hook, S. (ed.) (1959), *Psychoanalysis, Scientific Method and Philosophy.* New York: New York University Press.

John, E.R., et al. (1977), Neurometrics: Numerical taxonomy identifies different profiles of brain functions within groups of behaviorally similar people. *Science,* 196:1393–1410.

Kagan, J., Kearsley, R.B., and Zelazo, P.R. (1978), *Infancy: Its Place in Human Development.* Cambridge: Harvard University Press.

Kaplan, A.H. (1981), From discovery to validation: A basic challenge to psychoanalysis. *J. Am. Psychoanal. Assoc.,* 29:3–26.

Klaus, M.H., and Kennell, J.H. (1982), *Parent-Infant Bonding.* St. Louis: C.V. Mosby Co.

Korsch, B.M. (1983), More on parent-infant bonding. *J. Pediatr.,* 102:249–250.

Krull, M. (1986), *Freud and His Father* (English Edition). New York: W.W. Norton.

Lamb, M.E. (1982), The bonding phenomena: Misinterpretations and their implications. *J. Pediatr.,* 101:555.

Laor, N. (1985), Psychoanalysis as science: The inductivist's resistance revisited. *J. Am. Psychoanal. Assoc.,* 33:149–166.

Lassen, N.A. et al. (1977), Cerebral function, metabolism and circulation. *Acta Neurol. Scand.* (Suppl.), 64.

Links, P.S. (1983), Community surveys of the prevalence of childhood psychiatric disorders: A review. *Child Dev.,* 54:531–548.

Medawar, P. (1982), *Pluto's Republic.* New York: Oxford University Press.

Michels, R. (1988), The future of psychoanalysis. *Psychoanal. Q.,* 57:167–185.

Osofsky, J. (ed.) (1979), *Handbook of Infant Development.* New York: John Wiley & Sons.

Panel, (1978), Survey of psychoanalytic practice 1976; some trends and implications. S.E. Pulver, Reporter. *J. Am. Psychoanal Assoc.,* 26:615–631.

Phelps, M.E., Kuhl, D.E., and Mazziotta, J.C. (1981), Metabolic mapping of the brain's response to visual stimulation: Studies in humans. *Science,* 221:1445–1448.

Popper, K.R. (1963), *Conjectures and Refutations: The Growth of Scientific Knowledge.* New York: Basic Books.

Pynoos, R.S., Frederick, C., Nader, K., et al. (1987), Life threat and post-traumatic stress in school age children. *Arch. Gen. Psychiatry,* 44:1057–1063.

Robins, L.N. (1966), *Deviant Children Grown Up.* Baltimore: Williams & Wilkins.

Rutter, J.B. (1966), Generalized expectancies for internal

versus external control of reinforcement. *Psychol. Monogr.*, 80:609.

Rutter, M. (1988), Epidemiological approaches to developmental psychopathology. *Arch. Gen. Psychiatry*, 45:486–495.

Rutter, M., Graham, P., and Yule, W. (1970a), *A Neuropsychiatric Study in Childhood*. Clinics in Developmental Medicine. Philadelphia: J.B. Lippincott Co.

Rutter, M., Tizard, J., and Whitmore, J. (1970b), *Education, Health and Welfare*. London: Longmans.

Sameroff, A. (ed.) (1978), Organization and stability of newborn behavior. *Monogr. Soc. Res. Child Dev.*, 43:5–6.

Schmale, A.H. (1972), Giving up as a final common pathway to changes in health. *Adv. Psychosom. Med.*, 8:20–40.

Selye, H. (1946), The general adaptation syndrome and the diseases of adaptation. *J. Clin. Endocrinol.*, 6:117–120.

Shaffer, D. (1981), Epidemiology and child psychiatry.

Introduction. *J. Am. Acad. Child Adolesc. Psychiatry*, 20:439–443.

Sherwood, M. (1969), *The Logic of Explanation in Psychoanalysis*. New York: Academic Press.

Terr, L. (1979), Children of Chowchilla. *Psychoanal. Study Child*, 34:552–623.

Terr, L. (1981), Forbidden games: Post-traumatic child's play. *J. Am. Acad. Child Adolesc. Psychiatry*, 20:741–759.

Wallerstein, R.S. (1986), Psychoanalysis as a science: A response to the new challenges. *Psychoanal. Q.*, 55:414–451.

Yakovlev, P.I., and Lecours, A.R. (1967), The myelogenetic cycles of regional maturation of the brain. In: *Regional Development of the Brain*. ed. A. Kinkonski. Oxford: Blackwell Scientific Publications.

Young, J.G., O'Brien, J.D., Gutterman, E.M., and Cohen, P. (1987), Introduction. *J. Am. Acad. Child Adolesc. Psychiatry*, 26:611–612.

Yule, W. (1981), The epidemiology of child psychopathology. In: *Advances in Clinical Child Psychology* (Vol. 4), ed. B.B. Lahey and A.E. Kazdin. New York: Plenum Publishing Corp., pp. 1–51.

Part Six

Developmental Perspectives on Treatment

36

DEVELOPMENTAL PERSPECTIVES ON PSYCHOTHERAPY FOR CHILDREN AND ADOLESCENTS*

Each major form of psychotherapy is based on its unique theoretical base. For example, psychodynamic psychotherapies (individual, group) are based on psychoanalytic theory. Behavior therapies are based on behavior theories, and family therapies are based on behavior systems theory and communication theory. In all types of therapy, the developmental level of the child must be taken into account in implementing the specialized techniques of that therapy. In this chapter the prototype for individual psychodynamic psychotherapy is described in some detail because individual developmental considerations are clearest in this form of treatment. At the same time, developmental considerations are important in behavior and family therapies. For example, in behavior therapy the type of program designed must take into account the developmental level of the child. In family therapies, the development of the child is seen almost entirely in the context of the development of the family.

INDIVIDUAL PSYCHODYNAMIC PSYCHOTHERAPY

A developmental perspective on individual psychodynamic psychotherapy reveals several differences between child and adult therapy. First, the child rarely presents sponta-

neously on his or her own accord; generally, it is a parent who brings the child for treatment and provides the history. Then again, children do not ordinarily have the concept of treatment that an adult might have in seeking help. The child may draw more on his or her experience with "seeing the doctor," which may include such things as needle pricks. Nevertheless, the child can easily be appropriately prepared. Few, if any, children or adolescents tolerate the use of a couch or the so-called rule of abstinence (i.e., refraining from life decisions or acting out while in treatment). On the contrary, the play of children is often motorically active, and sometimes demanding.

During treatment a certain level of cognitive development is required for the child to grasp various kinds of interventions, including "attention statements" (see below). Usually a child in the second phase of the stage of concrete operations can grasp the essence of interpretive statements. Children who are at the preoperational level of cognitive development can understand statements made in the context of their play more readily than they can direct statements. Children as a rule have a tendency to act rather than think, which sometimes gives a misleading impression of excessive aggression. A child in the later phases of concrete operations can think about thinking, and can exercise some self-observing function. Adolescents may exercise

*Material for this chapter was drawn in part from Lewis M. (1974), *J. Am. Acad. Child Psychiatry*, 13:32–53.

an excessive self-referring kind of thinking, a reflection of their egocentrism. Children in treatment may still have certain age-appropriate expectations of the adult therapist, including the wish or expectation for birthday gifts. School-age children may strongly resist looking inward, whereas older adolescents are increasingly able to shift their attention from attributed external "causes" (e.g., society, school) to internal anxieties and conflicts. Children who are in the midst of a developmental change may be especially vulnerable and may exhibit an increased resistance in their own defense. Massive symbolic interpretations of unconscious features often pass by the child and are heard only as noise rather than as something that provides insight and relief; indeed, such massive interpretations when given to a young child may simply lead to play disruption or, worse, play inhibition.

Despite these developmental differences, the principles and goals of the psychotherapeutic treatment of children are remarkably similar, if not identical. Thus, the general goal of intensive individual psychotherapy is the same in children and adolescents as it is in adults: "to make the best of him [or her] that his [or her] inherited capacities will allow and so to make him [or her] as efficient and as capable of enjoyment as is possible" (Freud, 1928/1955, p. 251).

Specific aims may include reduction of anxiety, improvement in self-esteem, increased frustration tolerance, disappearance of symptoms, better coping strategies, appropriate independence, good relationships with peers and adults, satisfactory and satisfying schoolwork, feelings of pleasure and joy, and a sense of resumption of development.

The method essentially involves a trusting, confidential, real relationship between a trained, motivated, caring, and accepting person who offers help and a person who needs that help. Usually the therapist and the child's parent agree about the type of therapy used. Generally, opportunities are provided for the verbal expression of feelings, increasing self-knowledge, and improving self-mas-

tery (Karasu, 1977; Langs, 1982; Paolino, 1981). The therapy is divided into periods of 30 to 50 minutes given 1 to 4 times a week in a suitable office setting. Although numerous methods, techniques, and theories have been categorized (London and Klerman, 1982) and described (Varma, 1974), unequivocal superiority of any one method has not been established (Luborsky, Singer, and Luborsky, 1975; McDermott and Harrison, 1977; Schaefer and Millman, 1977; Wolman, Egan, and Ross, 1978).

How does one become a child therapist? First, neither the amount nor the kind of training is a reliable guide to the eventual effectiveness of a therapist; indeed, highly trained psychotherapists often achieve no more with their patients than do those with much less experience (Strupp and Hadley, 1979). Victor Raimy once observed that "psychotherapy is an undefined technique applied to unspecified cases with unpredictable results. For this technique, rigorous training is required" (quoted in London, 1964, p. 155). Supervision and continuous case conferences with acknowledged experts seem to be the generally accepted methods of acquiring psychotherapy skills. The amount required varies with the endowment and needs of the individual psychotherapist. In a brief (8-month) longitudinal study of 12 beginning psychiatric residents, Buckley et al. (1982) found that appropriate use of clarification, confrontation, management of resistance, and the ability to deal with negative transference could be learned with supervision and experience, whereas the capacity for empathy and awareness of countertransference did not change during the period of the study. There is some evidence that ordinary communication skills and empathic understanding can be taught quickly (Bird, 1980; Ivey, 1980; Matarazzo, 1978; MacGuire, 1980) and that the rest is experience. There is no evidence that a personal analysis must be a part of psychotherapeutic training (Marks, 1982).

The question of when intensive individual psychoanalytic psychotherapy in childhood is the treatment of choice today often resolves into the question of what other forms of therapy are available and indicated for a particular child with a particular diagnosis. Diagnosis is thus an essential prerequisite and, for this purpose, must go beyond DSM-III-R (American Psychiatric Association, 1987) to an assessment of the personality structure (A. Freud, 1968). Rarely does a single form of treatment for the child suffice. In most instances, various combinations of treatment are necessary, including pharmacotherapy, behavior therapy, family therapy, educational remedies, environmental changes, and concomitant work with the parents. For example, multimodality treatment including various combinations of individual therapy, group therapy, parent training, and medication brings about significant improvement in children with attention deficit hyperactivity disorder (Satterfield, Satterfield, and Cantwell, 1980). An account of the steps in the process of planning treatment for children and adolescents is given by Looney (1984).

Anxiety is present in almost all psychiatric conditions of childhood and, to the extent that anxiety is either unrecognized or evokes earlier infantile anxieties, psychoanalytic psychotherapeutic treatment for that anxiety may be indicated. Anxiety disorders in childhood by definition may require a special focus or emphasis. The principles of treatment for anxiety as defined previously are still operative, however, no matter what other treatments are required for diagnosis in which the other, primarily biologic, causes are present.

Pure intensive individual psychoanalytic psychotherapy alone is thus rarely indicated. It is only used with confidence when the child's problem is internal, confined to the so-called infantile neurosis of the past, and there is no other known factor amenable to treatment of any other kind. Such is rarely the case. Conversely, when the child's problems are more external than internal or internalized, and other etiologic factors are recognized, one becomes less confident in the solitary use of intensive individual psychotherapy. Thus, there may also be present various current conflicts and frustrations, losses,

physical illness, and other stresses, as well as other psychiatric diagnoses that may require the addition of one or more of the previously mentioned measures.

Yet, no matter what accompanying treatments are necessary, when individual psychotherapy is used, the same essential elements of the process unfold, albeit modified by the age, diagnosis, and presence of these other factors, with or without the other forms of treatment. The basic requirements for psychotherapy for children, together with a broad description of the stages and various components of the ongoing clinical work, have been described by McDermott and Chan (1984). Brief psychotherapy with children, adolescents, and their families has been described by Dulcan (1984). This chapter focuses on the particular essential elements of intensive individual psychoanalytic psychotherapy.

Intensive individual psychoanalytic psychotherapy specifically places great importance on interpretation (making the unconscious or preconscious conscious), particularly interpretation of the transference, as the principal therapeutic agent (Lewis, 1974). This emphasis holds true whether one is treating a preschool child (Neubauer, 1972), school-age child (A. Freud, 1946/1950, 1968), or an adolescent (Blos, 1962) and applies to a wide range of diagnoses (Witmer, 1946).

For purposes of discussion, intensive individual psychoanalytic psychotherapy can be approached as a process with three major phases: initial phase, middle phase, and termination phase.

INITIAL PHASE

The major goal of the initial phase is to foster the therapeutic alliance between therapist and child. This general goal is usually achieved by enabling the child to experience a nonjudgmental, understanding response to his or her behavior. The actual relationship itself is, in fact, a therapeutic agent in its own right, as well as the soil upon which the seed of an interpretation may flourish. A positive actual relationship therefore is encouraged.

The child must first be given some understanding by the parents of why he or she is being brought to a therapist and what therapy is like. Essentially, the child can be told that, in addition to himself or herself, others such as parents or teachers are concerned about how the child is feeling and/or behaving and that the child's parents believe the child may be troubled or upset, possibly by something he or she is not aware of.

Next, the parents may tell the child that talking with someone who understands children may help them and the child understand what may be troubling the child. The child can be told that the parents know of such a person, and the parents can describe the person, the setting, and the arrangements. The child should then be encouraged to ask any questions, and the parents should be prepared to answer truthfully and accurately.

The child will feel understood if he or she is offered an interpretation that provides some insight, yet does not arouse undue anxiety. The therapist can do this by using a range of preliminary interpretive statements (Lewis, 1974), culminating in the interpretation of the transference, which is discussed shortly. Such preliminary interpretations include setting statements, attention statements, reductive statements, and situational statements.

Setting Statements

A child may first be told in language appropriate to the developmental level that this is a time set aside so that the child can allow himself or herself to think freely and begin to understand why he or she sometimes feels troubled. The child should also be told that sometimes the therapist will intervene but with the understanding that it will always be in the interest of helping the child understand himself or herself better.

Attention Statements

Next, the child's attention can be directed to the content of her or her actions or verbalizations. Sometimes attention is drawn to a coincidence that the child has perceived but has not, or professes not to have, registered; more frequently, attention is drawn to certain paradoxes. The immediate aim is to free the child to produce new material and to consolidate existing gains (Devereux, 1951). In the course of the child's play, the therapist may, for example, provide a verbal counterpart to the action being portrayed, to an affect that might be present, or to the conspicuous absence of certain persons, actions, or affects.

An 8-year-old boy with a severe school phobia repeatedly enacted a war scene in which the general was attacked and almost killed. Many fantasies were contained in this play, but one prominent feature was the absence of any female, not only in this play item, but in any other play. After attention was drawn to this "fact," the child recognized his fear of attack from his mother, his wish to attack her, his resentment that his father was often attacked and offered him no protection, the displacement of his aggression toward his mother to his father, and his anxiety about even mentioning his mother.

This interpretation is quite different from any kind of direct translation of possible symbolic representation in the play. The play characteristic to which attention is drawn is in bold relief, and is capable of being understood by the child. This fact is emphasized to draw the distinction from more subtle paradoxes, which are not readily perceived, at least not by the younger child.

Reductive Statements

Certain statements reduce apparently disparate behavioral patterns to a common form that hitherto has not been noticed by the child. Thus, a child may manifest certain kinds of behavior whenever he or she is angry. The child may not have been aware of this anger.

In the course of the treatment of a 10-year-old boy, it was noticed that there were recurring episodes of mocking, insulting, or denigrating behavior toward the therapist. Each of these episodes was related in time to one of the frequent trips away from home that the boy's mother would take. His resentment at being left behind, together with his anxiety at being left alone with his father, led to the behavior just described. This type of behavior could be reduced to a single behavioral reaction to underlying rage and anxiety precipitated by the temporary loss of his mother. When the child was told of this relationship, he reacted first of all by an intensification of the behavior pattern, but subsequently was able to recognize for the first time his underlying feelings when he stated, "My parents are always nice to me when we do fun things, but they don't help me with the serious things when I'm unhappy."

The child here was manifesting a fixed defense which, in the example given, was brought into sharper relief. A certain level of cognitive development, including some capacity to take distance from and observe affects, must be available to the child for this reaction to occur.

Situational Statements

Situational statements naturally follow from those previously described. For example, the child now aware of his or her anger can be shown the situations that give rise to this anger and how in certain instances he or she has repeatedly brought about such situations, either in current relationships or in the transference. However, the degree of directness with which such situational statements may be made varies with the cognitive and developmental levels of the child. Children who are at the stage of concrete operations and in latency can usually be approached directly. Children who are at the preoperational stage of cognitive development or in oedipal or preoedipal phases probably need to have these statements made to them in the context of the play, either through dolls and puppets, or indirectly through some other hypothetical child or children.

MIDDLE PHASE

The essence of the middle phase of psychotherapy is the interpretation of the transference and "working through." Notwithstanding the difficulties of the initial phase, a child soon understands one of the goals of

psychotherapy: the attempt to understand the way he or she feels and behaves. After the initial phase of treatment, the child realizes that everything he or she says and does is subject to use by the therapist. Consequently, the child's play that follows is part of the associative process in the context of therapy. In certain respects, however, the developmental difference between the child and the adult influences the form of these associations. The child is more susceptible to current reality, which exerts a powerful influence on his or her play. The play is often goal-directed and not freely associative. Again, the child tends to act rather than think, giving at least the impression of an overemphasized aggressive transference (A. Freud, 1965, p. 36). In addition, in school-age children especially, the play is often characterized by organization, reflecting a developmental shift. Lastly, the child may become totally absorbed in his or her play and may then be unable to exercise an observing function.

At the same time, in addition to play, a child also communicates through most of the other elements that constitute "free association." That is, the child talks, pauses, shows affects, exhibits mannerisms, and portrays attitudes. This total picture, viewed as a whole over the course of several hours, enables the therapist to discern an associative thread. This overall connection can also often be grasped by the child.

Transference

In the course of discerning this total picture, one can usually observe a true transference neurosis—that is, those previously fixed conflicts and neurotic symptoms of the child that are now being experienced currently by the child in relation to the therapist (Harley, 1967). Again, the developmental differences between child and adult modify, but do not eradicate, this emerging transference neurosis in three ways: (1) To the extent that the child is normally dependent, the parents with whom the original conflict was concerned are still with the child and continue to exert their influence on the child. (2) The child is not an equal with the therapist; he or she is still a child relating to an adult as well as a patient relating to a therapist. Thus, besides the mutual respect that should exist between patient and therapist, the child also has certain expectations of the adult, such as appropriate birthday and holiday greetings. (3) The continuing development of the child continues to modify the transference, especially during shifts from the oedipal period to latency and from latency to adolescence. In addition, fixations that occurred earlier may be modified with the increased range, flexibility, and shifts of defenses that occur with the development of the child.

For all these reasons, the transference neurosis in child psychotherapy is incomplete and more unstable than the transference neurosis in the therapy of an adult. Nevertheless, to the extent that there is a transference neurosis, however modified, it is available for interpretation. The more common situation in work with children is one in which a relatively simple current displacement from parent to therapist is recognized and interpreted. Even within such apparently simple displacements, however, elements of a transference neurosis can be found, and when they are interpreted, they throw light on the child's current behavior.

Reconstruction

An etiologic link between the complexities of the child's current behavior and his or her earlier fantasies may be offered to the child. Such earlier material is derived from the personal myth of the child or from reconstruction. The striking aspect of a reconstruction is that it helps the child "make sense" out of what was previously discomforting and/or perplexing. It also occasionally helps a child by confirming what was probably an essentially correct perception by the child at the time, but which has since undergone distortion. The conceptual abilities of the child are such that he or she often attributes affects he or she perceives in the parents as resulting from thoughts or wishes of his or her own. In

addition, the child frequently projects his or her own fantasies and affects onto the parents, and subsequently acts against the parents whom the child now regards as perhaps dangerous or angry. The preoperational child also has difficulty distinguishing fantasies from reality (Piaget, 1929).

Process of Interpretation

Some additional general points on the process of interpretation may be considered. Loewenstein (1951), whose account would be more complete had he placed greater emphasis on the interpretation of unconscious, or at least preconscious, material, described the following steps: (1) Show the patient that certain common elements exist in a series of events. (2) Point out the similar behavior of the patient in each of these situations. (3) Demonstrate that such behavior was manifested in circumstances that all involved, for example, competitive elements and where rivalry might have been expected. (4) Point out, as in the example given, that rivalry does exist unconsciously, but is replaced by another kind of behavior, such as avoiding competition. (5) Show that this behavior originates in certain critical events of the patient's life and encompasses reactions and tendencies that can be grouped together.

In the stages just outlined, the interpretation of mechanism, as opposed to that of content or affect, is significant. A gradual transition from preparatory intervention, through confrontation, to an interpretation containing a genetic component is also evident. Ferenczi once described his own experiences as he proceeded in the steps just outlined:

One allows oneself to be influenced by the free association of the patient; simultaneously one permits one's own imagination to play on these associations; intermittently one compares new connections that appear with previous products . . . without, for a moment, losing sight of, regard for, and criticism of one's own biases. Essentially, one might speak of an endless process of oscillation between empathy, self-observation, and judgment. This last, wholly spontaneously, declares itself intermittently as a signal that one naturally immediately evaluates for what it is; only on the basis of further evidence may one ultimately decide to make an interpretation (quoted in Kris, 1961, p. 29).

The description given by Erikson (1940) is remarkably similar. Speculations are first derived from the observer's impressions, associations, and recollections; for example, "It was as if . . ." The observer also associates past impressions in the same child, from other children, or from data derived from the parents. The therapist reflects on the latent possibilities, that the associations may possibly correspond to a genetic or associative connection in the child's mind, and pictures what the child is doing under the observer's eyes and what the child is said to have done in other situations. This speculation all leads up to the interpretation. Erikson then describes three steps in making the interpretation. First, there are observations, feelings, and reflections that lead to interpretational hints. For example, a symbolic equation or metaphor may make it possible to recognize a play act as alluding to and standing for an otherwise manifestly avoided item (a person, an object, an idea). Or a play arrangement may prove to represent a special effort on the part of the child to rearrange in effigy his or her psychologic position in an experienced or expected danger situation. Such an arrangement usually corresponds to the child's defense mechanisms. Second, these hints are then subject to further observations and reflections and emerge as a conviction in the observer's mind in the form of the reconstruction of a genetic sequence or of a dynamic configuration pertaining to the patient's inner or outer history. Finally, the therapist may proceed to convey part of these reconstructions to the child at an appropriate time. Erikson considers the last step to be the therapeutic interpretation.

The significant point here is the step-by-step progression in working with children implied in Erikson's statement that "The observer may proceed to convey parts of these reconstructions to the child whenever he feels the time has come to do so" (1940, p.

589). However, it is important to remember the developmental level of the child, since massive interpretations given to a young child are more likely to be heard as interfering noises than helpful statements, with a consequent heightening of resistance and play disruption or, worse, a play inhibition.

In short, the therapist, while still engaging with the child, takes mental distance from the immediate transaction and tries to place the immediate observations into the context of what has previously occurred. The therapist does this by means of a mental "play back." Material from previous sessions is not only "played back" mentally, but is also translated to a higher level of abstraction, which enables the therapist to formulate to himself or herself "what is going on" as a basis for formulating an interpretation. The therapist then mentally translates this back to the level of the child and the immediate situation and makes his or her interpretation at that level.

General Guidelines for Interpretation

Multiple Appeal. As a rule, interpretations are probably more effective when they have "multiple appeal" (Hartmann, 1951). The therapist also describes clinically when to interpret the past, the current reality, and the transference—or all three.

Sequence. A number of other guidelines for the order of interpretation have been suggested. Resistances or defenses should be interpreted before the instinctual derivatives (Loewenstein, 1951). One should avoid interpreting an important neurotic symptom at the beginning, and one should start with interpretation of still-mobile defense traits in preference to rigid characterologic defenses.

An 8-year-old boy wanted to take along some tracing paper belonging to his therapist on the eve of a car trip with his mother and father, the anticipation of which had already aroused considerable anxiety. What were the possibilities here for interpretation?

1. The therapist could simply have confronted the child with his wish to take something along. At the particular stage in the therapy of this child, however,

this approach would have been redundant.

2. The therapist could have shown the child how anxious he was about the trip with his parents, but doing so might have forced the child to face abruptly his anxiety without the therapist's support.

3. The therapist might conceivably have tried to link this wish with the boy's reactions in other similar situations in which he had become anxious, but this could not be done without the previous steps.

4. The therapist could have interpreted the patient's wishes toward the therapist for protection, but in this patient such a move might have left the child feeling stripped and defenseless.

5. The therapist might have made the connection for the child between this coming event and earlier events in his life, but this intervention might have had little use for this particular patient, since he did not yet have a clear idea of his feelings about the coming event.

6. One might ask whether anything should be said at all. Something should be said, but something that would temporarily buttress the child and offer support, at the same time that both the defense and the fear were being interpreted. For example, the therapist could say to the child, "How nice it will be to have something to take along, especially if you are worried about the trip." There would be no need to interpret the positive transference aspect at this point, since the movement is in a forward direction; or the therapist might also decide to include an aspect of the transference, but in a supportive way. The therapist might say, for example, "I think you would like to have something of mine with you on this trip." He or she might then allow the child to keep the paper and reserve for a latter date any further exploration of the act: "Why don't you take the paper with you?

When you come back we can talk again about how you feel when you have to take a trip with your mother and father."

These examples are not meant to be recommendations of specific things to say, but rather illustrations of underlying principles. The choice of level and wording depends on such factors as the diagnosis, the stage of the therapy, and the developmental level of the child. A 6-year-old child at the beginning of psychotherapy might experience his or her anxiety on the eve of such a trip as ego-syntonic and fail to understand an interpretation of the anxiety. On the other hand, a 10-year-old who was more advanced in therapy might well experience such anxiety as inappropriate and ego-alien, and might find such an interpretation useful.

Timing. An interpretation is probably well timed when the therapist thinks that the statement at that moment will help to consolidate existing gains and elicit new material (Devereux, 1951). Devereux described an interpretation as being "timely" when it is capable of being utilized by the patient, and this in turn can occur only if the patient understands it.

Focus of Interpretation. When should an interpretation be made in the play, and when should it be taken out of the play? When attention statements are made, the interpretations are clearly made "in the play." Reductive statements imply that the child is receptive to statements about himself or herself, that is, "out of play," whereas transference interpretations in their most effective form are made distinctly "out of the play," given the earlier steps of preparation. The use of play in psychotherapy with children has been extensively described (Buxbaum, 1954; Haworth, 1964; Winnicott, 1971; McDermott and Harrison, 1977; Beiser, 1979).

Tact. Tact is required when significant developmental differences are considered. A young child may have great difficulty in tolerating ambivalence and may find it especially difficult to accept a hostile or aggressive wish or fantasy. This reluctance may be overcome by placing within a fuller context the emotion that is to be interpreted. For example, one might more tactfully say to a child: "It is very hard to be angry at someone you love."

Glover (1930) tried to be more specific with regard to tact, stating that the interpretation should be delivered as a plain statement in terms devoid of active emotional stress. The purpose apparently was to prevent an immediate, overwhelming conscious conviction on the patient's part that his or her therapist was in a state of countertransference.

Glover also cautioned about the use of wit, the exploitation of the comic, and the shelter provided by technical expressions. It is usually preferable to refer to the child's parents as "mother" or "father." Only with a very young child would one use such terms as "mommy" and "daddy," and then only because these terms are developmentally and age appropriate.

Wording. Wording should be specific and concrete; the interpretation should also be worded to fit the individual situation. Again, the therapist is cautioned to avoid the same defense mechanism as the patient, for example, laughing things off and minimizing them. Interpretations appear to gain when they contain an element of time, for example, "now," "before," "at the age of," or "after this happened."

Wording becomes particularly critical with children, not only in terms of the level of cognitive development, but also in terms of what the child can accept in his or her dependent position with respect to the parents and in terms of the child's own struggle against regressive pulls or progressive pushes. The child attaches greater meaning to certain words than does the adult, and it becomes necessary for the therapist to understand these special meanings.

Inexact and Incomplete Interpretation. Glover (1930) distinguished between inexact and incomplete interpretations. Glover termed an incomplete interpretation a "preliminary interpretation." For example, one would interpret a genital fantasy before an anal fantasy. He contrasted this with an inexact interpretation when one might never interpret the anal fantasy at all. That is, if the interpretation of the genital fantasy were regarded as the complete interpretation, then the interpretation was ipso facto inexact.

An interpretation is never complete until the immediate defensive reactions following on the interpretations are subjected to investigation. The complete interpretation is really the complete treatment: ". . . every construction is an incomplete one . . . As a rule he (the patient) will not give his assent until he has learnt the whole truth—which often covers a very great deal of ground" (Freud, 1937/1964, pp. 263, 265 ff.).

In the case of the child, one rarely achieves a state of completion, and neither is it necessary. Often, all that is necessary is to bring about a reduction of anxiety sufficient to enable development to proceed.

Countertransference

In work with children, the therapist is particularly prone to countertransference phenomena, i.e., the only partly conscious attitudes and feelings of the therapist toward the patient that are based on the therapist's own, earlier, life experiences. For example, there is a much greater "regressive pull" (Bornstein, 1948). The therapist must learn to recognize the feelings aroused in himself or herself so that he or she can deal with the child in a way that is helpful. Feelings are a vital instrument for understanding. At the same time, if the therapist is not aware of, or is not clear about, the nature of his or her aroused feelings and their sources (both external and internal), he or she may be hampered in working effectively with the child. Indications that countertransference feelings may be at work include the following:

1. The therapist may fail to recognize where a child is in his or her development. Expectations then will not be commensurate with the child's maturational and developmental capacities. Unrealistic goals, alternating with de-

spair, may then be experienced by the therapist.

2. The regressive pull experienced by the therapist playing and working with a child may give rise to the temptation to identify with and/or act out with the child, or infantilization of the child may occur.

3. A misreading of the child's relationship to the therapist may occur, in which the relationship is seen as realistic when in fact it may be a transference from the child's feelings toward his or her parents. Therapists are usually well aware of a child's aggressive feelings, but may be less aware of a child's seductiveness toward an adult (parent).

4. Remnants of the therapist's own childhood relations with his or her brothers and sisters may be an important source of the therapist's ambivalence to the child. For example, excessive concern—or lack of concern—for a child climbing a chair or approaching a tall column of heavy building blocks may mask an underlying wish that the child will hurt himself or herself and may be associated with guilt feelings when the child does stumble or fall. This feeling of guilt may come about because of the partial unsuspected fulfillment of the unacceptable wish.

5. The stirring up of old conflicts within the therapist, when exposed to certain behavior in the child, may cause anxiety in the therapist. For example, uncontrolled aggression, sex play, or masturbation may be upsetting to the therapist.

6. The therapist may transfer old feelings from his or her own childhood onto the parents of the child. One may thus identify with the child in his or her struggle with the parents. Rescue fantasies may then occur. Conversely, the therapist may erroneously identify with the parents (perhaps through an identification with the aggressor mechanism) and consequently may exercise unnecessary, even punitive, controls against the child who is acting too aggressively or sexually for the therapist's comfort.

7. Sometimes the therapist simply cannot understand the meaning of certain behavior in a child. Of course there are times when all therapists find some item of behavior inexplicable. However, the persistent drawing of a blank in understanding a repeated item of behavior should lead to the suspicion of an interference by one's own conflicts—an emotional blind spot, so to speak.

8. A therapist may find himself or herself feeling depressed or uneasy during work with children. Assuming the therapist is not suffering from a true depression, the possibility exists that emotions from old conflicts have been aroused and are interfering with the therapist's functioning. Occasionally, a therapist may find himself or herself aroused and experiencing great affection for a child. This too may interfere with his or her work with the child.

9. It sometimes happens that a therapist will permit, or even encourage, acting out in the child. For example, a therapist may suggest to a child that he or she must stand up for himself or herself and hit back. On occasion a therapist may even feel the impulse to act out with a child.

10. A therapist may need the admiration obtained by having the child like him or her. This too many represent a need of the therapist and may not be in the best interests of the child.

11. Conversely, repeated arguing with a child may suggest that the therapist has not only become involved, but has become enmeshed with the child.

12. Recurring countertransference problems commonly arise in relation to specific characteristics of a child. For example, a retarded child may evoke guilt and defenses against such guilt with the therapist, or omnipotent rescue fantasies, which are acted out. Passive, hos-

tile children may arouse anger in a therapist. Aggressive children may evoke counteraggression. Sexually attractive children and adolescents of the same or opposite sex as the therapist may threaten the therapist, leading to either vicarious and excessive "exploitation" or sexual issues or denial and avoidance.

Working Through

It is clear that working through is necessary to sustain any therapeutic effect (Greenacre, 1956). The defensive conflicts remain somewhat structured unless they are dealt with repetitively in relation to various behaviors, events, and feelings. Historically, working through was first stressed from the point of view of being of educative value and compared with mourning and the progressive detachment of the individual libido from the organized tensions and aims that permeated the later life.

The concept of the corrective emotional experience is really an aspect of working through, at least in its more modern construction. Originally, the idea involved replenishment of earlier deficiencies through the current relationship. This appealing idea unfortuately proved to be too simplistic. It failed to take into account the power of the unconscious repetition compulsion. The concept has some merit, however, if it is modified to provide the child in the here-and-now with a reaction different from his or her previous experiences, a reaction that is now more appropriate and does not perpetuate the malignant interactions to which he or she has become accustomed. The concept then is also a different idea, however, and one that is more in keeping with the concept of working through. With the rise of ego psychology, the recognition of the need for consistent work with the patterns of defense and the affects related to them once more becomes paramount (Bornstein, 1948).

From a developmental point of view, working through with children poses a special problem. The chief difficulty is that the parents are usually present and may continue to exert a reinforcing influence upon the child's original conflicts. Sometimes this interference can be alleviated by concomitant work with the parents, through some form of psychotherapy, or through regular meetings between the parents and the child's therapist. Occasionally, it becomes clear that the child cannot work through a conflict while in the home, and an alternative plan may become necessary, such as boarding school in the case of an older child. Sometimes the difficulty is insuperable at the time, and the therapy must be interrupted until the child is in a more advantageous situation for therapy. Occasionally, it is possible to hold the child in therapy until such a situation occurs. In some instances the child can be helped to understand the repetitive and reinforcing behavior of the parents and his or her involvement in precipitating or responding to their behavior. If the influence of the parents is not too strong, the child can be helped to modify his or her own behavior in this regard and to interrupt the vicious cycle.

TERMINATION PHASE

The criteria for termination ideally include some actual achievement (as opposed to a "flight into health," Train, 1953) of the goals of therapy: reduced anxiety, improved self-esteem, increased frustration tolerance, disappearance of symptoms, better coping strategies, relative independence, good relationships with peers and adults, satisfying schoolwork, feelings of pleasure and joy, and a sense of resumed developmental progress.

In almost every instance these achievements are judged clinically rather than measured scientifically. Clinically, there is no such thing as a perfect therapy (or a perfect patient or therapist). Every therapy eventually stops, and when it does the child should be progressing toward these laudable goals. A child may even have gained a better understanding of himself or herself and may no longer need to act out so many of the infantile longings, frustrations, and feelings, and may have learned instead more adaptive ways, say, to love and be loved. In some cases, however, the therapy simply stops because there is a sense of diminishing returns, the resistances are too great, the treatment is inappropriate, or for various other reasons the treatment is a failure. In one survey of terminated analytic cases (n = 49), only 14% terminated by mutual agreement among parent, therapist, and child (A. Freud, 1971).

The actual phase of termination is a useful period to explore issues of separation, reactions to loss, dependency versus independence, and anxiety about progressive developmental movements. Some children undergo a temporary regression, manifested by a reappearance of their presenting symptoms, in the face of leaving the therapist and returning, as it were, to the family. Others are able to "reconstruct" and recall the beginning of their treatment rather than reenact it through regressive behavior. Depending on the frequency, duration, and intensity of the psychotherapy, a reasonable period of time is required to deal with these issues. Thus, when the question whether to terminate has been decided, preferably by mutual agreement, a termination date is set that will allow a suitable amount of time for the termination phase. This period may vary from 6 weeks to 3 months.

Follow-up communication is often helpful in consolidating the work of the termination phase.

THERAPEUTIC ACTION
AND THEORY

Many attempts have been made to describe the therapeutic effects of interpretation in terms of the insight achieved. The particular type of interpretation that will produce a therapeutic insight, that is, a structural change, has been given different names, as has the actual therapeutic insight. For example, "transference" (Fenichel, 1945) or "mutative" (Strachey, 1934) interpretations may produce "emotional," "psychological," "ostensive" (Richfield, 1954), or "dynamic" insights as opposed to "intellectual," "descrip-

tive," or "neutral" (Reid and Finesinger, 1952) insights. The significant point is that shifts from unconscious to conscious awareness are thought to occur only after derivatives of the original feeling are recognized with an experiential sense of conviction and worked through. Bergler (1945) considered that the whole process of working through is centered chiefly in the correct handling and mobilization of the feeling of guilt. Devereux (1951) felt that an interpretation (which consists of supplying an unconscious closure element) is effective when practically all conscious and preconscious material pertaining to the neurotic gestalt has been produced. Loewenstein (1951) believed that the therapeutic effect is due to a psychic process in which each of the following parts has its respective place: (1) the overcoming of resistances, (2) the working through, (3) the remembering and reliving of repressed material, and (4) the effect of the reconstruction.

Anticipated changes resulting from psychotherapy are also to some extent a function of normal development. Therefore, all the factors that facilitate normal development will also facilitate the desired change in psychotherapy.

The experience with the psychotherapist not only is a corrective one, but also represents an oasis phenomenon for the child who now finds himself or herself, at least temporarily, in a relatively protected facilitating environment that enables development to proceed by reducing the impact of trauma and the acting-out tendencies in the child. That is, the child in psychotherapy finds himself or herself at least momentarily at a distance from the acute upset of the current developmental turmoil, whether it be a too exciting, sexualized relationship with a parent, a sadomasochistic relationship with a parent, a grief reaction at the birth of a sibling, or frightening fantasies of bodily harm.

The child is also afforded an opportunity for confirmation of his or her essentially correct perception of the parents, leading to a strengthening of reality testing and an increase in self-esteem. The play of the child, as well as the use of words, inasmuch as they represent an intermediate stage between action and thought, provides a handle by which the child grasps affects and is enabled to delay. Most important, the play itself undergoes a development that carries with it a significant shift from primary process to secondary process. The dyadic therapeutic relationship provides an introspective opportunity for the child, and also serves to foster an identification with an appropriate adult model. Indeed, the child may "borrow" from the psychotherapist as the child struggles to deal with an acute developmental crisis. Concomitant work with other family members also leads to shifts in the dynamic equilibrium within the family, releasing the child and parents from their locked-in, fixed positions and allowing development to proceed. A further significant therapeutic force is the change from despair to hope, leading to a therapeutic optimism. Lastly, the extended moment of time, the opportunity to examine in detail, itself contributes to clearer, more direct communications.

EVALUATION OF OUTCOME OF PSYCHOTHERAPY

Evaluation of the effectiveness of psychotherapy is in general a complex phenomenon (Strupp and Hadley, 1977), and research is plaqued by methodologic problems (Hine, Werman, and Simpson, 1982). Parloff (1982) reviewed nearly 500 rigorous controlled studies providing research evidence on outcome. Parloff concluded that all forms of psychologic treatment are comparably effective in producing therapeutic benefits, and such benefits are reliably superior to those found in controls. Ultimately, outcome in psychotherapy is a value judgement, requiring that we recognize the multiple values, criteria, and factors that enter into such judgments. Research on psychotherapy with children, in particular, is especially sparse (Levitt, 1971; Shaffer, 1984).

BEHAVIOR THERAPIES

Behavior therapies emphasize current environmental factors that influence target behaviors, make no assumptions about the past or presumed unconscious mechanisms, and use objective measurements of change in the behavior of the child. The child is viewed as an active learner, and the approach is problem-oriented. Many different subtypes of behavior therapies have been developed since the original work of Pavlov, Watson, and Skinner (Kazdin, 1978), including the use of respondent (classic Pavlovian) conditioning, operant conditioning, biofeedback, desensitization, implosive therapy, flooding, cognitive therapies, learning techniques, and token economies. In several, positive outcomes are reported, particularly with reference to highly circumscribed symptoms or problems such as phobias although further research is needed. The child's level of development is taken into account in devising a suitable behavior treatment program. The behavior therapist who uses any of the many behavior techniques must, of course, be well trained for success to occur.

FAMILY THERAPIES

Family therapies emphasize dysfunction within the family as the focus for change. What are presented as the child's problems are located within the complexity of the developing family's structure, organization, and relationships, and the multiple types of interactions that recur. The techniques then used are aimed at changing any identified dysfunctional patterns in the family. The techniques include, but are not limited to, structural family therapy (Minuchin, 1974) and strategic family therapy (Haley, 1976). The basic concepts of all family therapies have been well outlined by Goldner (1985). Child development and family development are interwoven, making developmental factors vital, if not complex, considerations in the skillful application of family therapy techniques.

REFERENCES

American Psychiatric Association (1987), *Diagnostic and Statistical Manual of Mental Disorders,* 3rd Ed. Washington, DC.

Beiser, H.R. (1979), Formal games in diagnosis and therapy. *J. Am. Acad. Child Psychiatry,* 18:480–491.

Bergler, E. (1945), "Working through," in psychoanalysis. *Psa Rev,* 32:449–480.

Bird, J. (1980), Teaching medical intervewing skills: A comparison of medical and non-medical tutors. In: *Research in Medical Education: Proceedings of the Association of American Medical Colleges.* Washington, DC: Association of American Medical Colleges.

Blos, P. (1962), *On adolescence: A psychoanalytic interpretation.* New York: Free Press.

Bornstein, B. (1948), Emotional barriers in the understanding and treatment of young children. *Am. J. Orthopsychiatry,* 18:691–697.

Buckley, P., Conte, H.R., Plutchik, R., et al. (1982), Learning dynamic psychotherapy: A longitudinal study. *Am. J. Psychiatry,* 139:1607–1610.

Buxbaum, E. (1954), Technique of child therapy. *Psa Study Child,* 9:297–333.

Devereux, G. (1951), Some criteria for the timing of confrontations and interpretations. *Intl. J. Psa,* 32:19–24.

Dulcan, M.K. (1984), Brief psychotherapy with children and their families: The state of the art. *J. Am. Acad. Child Psychiatry,* 23:544–551.

Erikson, E.H. (1940), Studies in the interpretation of play. *Genetic Psychology Monographs,* 22:557–671.

Fenichel, O. (1945), *The Psychoanalytic Theory of Neurosis.* New York: Norton.

Freud, A. (1950), *The Psychoanalytic Treatment of Children.* New York: International Universities Press (originally published 1946).

Freud, A. (1965), *Normality and Pathology in Childhood.* New York: International Universities Press.

Freud, A. (1968), Indications and contraindications of child analysis. *Psa Study Child,* 23:37–46.

Freud, A. (1971), Termination of child analysis. In: *The Writings of Anna Freud* (Vol. 7). New York: International Universities Press, pp. 3–31.

Freud, S. (1955), Two encyclopedia articles. In: *The Standard Edition of the Complete Psychological Works of Sigmund Freud* (Vol. 18), ed. and trans. J. Strachey. London: Hogarth Press, pp. 235–263 (originally published 1928).

Freud, S. (1964), Constructions in analysis. In: *Standard Edition* (Vol. 23), ed. and trans. J. Strachey. London: Hogarth Press, pp. 257–269 (originally published 1937).

Clover, E. (1930), The "vehicle" of interpretations. *Intl. J. Psa,* 11:340–344.

Goldner, V. (1985), Family therapy. In: *The Clinical Guide to Child Psychiatry,* ed. D. Shaffer, A.A. Ehrhardt, and L.L. Greenhill. New York: The Free Press, pp. 539–553.

Greenacre, P. (1956), Re-evaluation of the process of working through. *Intl. J. Psa,* 37:439–444.

Haley, J. (1976), *Problem Solving Therapy.* San Francisco: Tossey-Bass.

Harley, M. (1967), Transference developments in a five-

year-old child. In: *The Child Analyst at Work,* ed. E.R. Geleerd. New York: International Universities Press, pp. 115–141.

Hartmann, H. (1951), Technical implications of ego psychology. *Psa Q.,* 20:31:43.

Haworth, M.R. (Ed) (1964), *Child Psychotherapy.* New York: Basic Books.

Hine, F.R., Werman, D.S., and Simpson, D.M. (1982), Effectiveness of psychotherapy: Problems of research on complex phenomena. *Am. J. Psychiatry,* 139:204–208.

Ivey, A.E. (1980), *Counselling and Psychotherapy: Skills, Theories and Practice.* Englewood Cliffs, N.J.: Prentice-Hall.

Karasu, T.B. (1977), Psychotherapies: An overview. *Am. J. Psychiatry,* 134:851–863.

Kazdin, A.E. (1978), *History of Behavior Modification: Experimental Foundations of Contemporary Research.* Baltimore: University Park Press.

Kris, E. (1951), Ego psychology and interpretation in psychoanalytic therapy. *Psa Q.,* 20:15–30.

Langs, R. (1982), *Psychotherapy.* New York: Jason Aronson.

Levitt, E.E. (1971), Research on psychotherapy with children. In: *Handbook of Psychotherapy and Behavior Change.* ed. A.E. Bergin and S.L. Garfield. New York: Wiley-Interscience, pp. 474–494.

Lewis, M. (1974), Interpretation in child analysis: Developmental considerations. *J. Am. Acad. Child Psychiatry,* 13:32.

Loewenstein, R.M. (1951), The problem of interpretation. *Psa Q.,* 20:1–14.

London, P. (1964), *The Modes and Morals of Psychotherapy.* New York: Holt, Rinehart & Winston.

London, P., and Klerman, G.L. (1982), Evaluating psychotherapy. *Am. J. Psychiatry,* 139:709–717.

Looney, J.G. (1984), Treatment planning in child psychiatry. *J. Am. Acad. Child Psychiatry,* 23:529–536.

Luborsky, L., Singer, B. and Luborsky, L. (1975), Comparative studies of psychotherapies: Is it true that "Everyone has won and all must have prizes?" *Arch. Gen. Psychiatry,* 32:995–1008.

MacGuire, P. (1980), Teaching medical students to interview psychiatric patients. *Bull. R. Coll. Psychiatry,* 4:188–190.

Marks, I. (1982), Personal psychotherapy in the training of a psychiatrist? *Bull. R. Coll. Psychiatry,* 6:39–40.

Matarazzo, R. (1978), Research on the teaching and learning of psychotherapeutic skills. In: *Handbook of Psychotherapy and Behavior Modification,* 2nd Ed., ed. S. Garfield and A.R. Bergin. New York: John Wiley & Sons, Inc., pp. 941–966.

McDermott, J.F., and Chan, W.F. (1984), Stage-related models of psychotherapy with children. *J. Am. Acad. Child Psychiatry,* 23:537–543.

McDermott, J.F., and Harrison, S.I. (Eds.) (1977), *Psychiatric Treatment of Children.* New York: Jason Aronson.

Minuchin, S. (1974), *Families and Family Therapy.* New York: Basic Books.

Neubauer, P.B. (1972), Psychoanalysis of the preschool child. In: *Handbook of Child Psychoanalysis,* ed. B.B. Wolman. New York: Van Nostrand Reinhold, pp. 221–252.

Paolino, T.J. (1981). *Psychoanalytic Psychotherapy.* New York: Brunner/Mazel.

Parloff, M.B. (1982), Psychotherapy research evidence and reimbursement decisions: Bambi meets Godzilla. *Am. J. Psychiatry,* 139:718–727.

Piaget, J. (1929), *The Child's Conception of the World.* New York: Harcourt Brace.

Reid, J.R., and Finesinger, J.E. (1952), The role of insight in psychotherapy. *Am. J. Psychiatry,* 108:726–734.

Richfield, J. (1954), An analysis of the concept of insight. *Psa Q.,* 23:390–408.

Satterfield, J., Satterfield, B. and Cantwell, D. (1980), Multimodal treatment: A two-year evaluation of 61 hyperactive boys. *Arch. Gen. Psychiatry,* 37:915–919.

Schaefer, C.E., and Millman, H.L. (1977), *Therapies for Children.* San Francisco: Jossey-Bass.

Shaffer, D. (1984), Notes on psychotherapy research among children and adolescents. *J. Am. Acad Child Psychiatry,* 23:552–561.

Strachey, J. (1934), The nature of the therapeutic action of psychoanalysis. *Intl. J. Psa.,* 15:127–159.

Strupp, H.H., and Hadley, S.W. (1977), A tripartite model of mental health and therapeutic outcomes. *Am. Psychol.,* 32:187–196.

Strupp, H., and Hadley, S. (1979), Specific vs. nonspecific factors in psychotherapy. *Arch. Gen. Psychiatry,* 36:1125–1136.

Train, G.F. (1953), Flight into health. *Am. J. Psa,* 7:463–486.

Varma, V. (Ed.) (1974), *Psychotherapy Today.* London: Constable.

Winnicott, D.W. (1971), *Therapeutic Consultations in Child Psychiatry.* New York: Basic Books.

Witmer, H.L. (Ed.) (1946), *Psychiatric Interviews with Children.* Cambridge: Harvard University Press.

Wolman, B.B., Egan, J., and Ross, A.O. (Eds.) (1978), *Handbook of Treatment of Mental Disorders in Childhood and Adolescence.* Englewood Cliffs, NJ: Prentice-Hall.

37

DEVELOPMENTAL PERSPECTIVES ON DRUG TREATMENT FOR CHILDREN AND ADOLESCENTS

Developmental factors influence the rate at which children at different ages absorb and metabolize drugs. The child's longer gastric emptying time and increased intestinal motility frequently lead to faster absorption. The liver:body weight ratio of a 6-year-old child is greater than that of an adult, and the liver enzymes are more active, leading to a relatively higher dose requirement on a dose-per-weight basis, sometimes as much as 50% greater. Liver metabolism of drugs decreases early in puberty, giving rise to a temporary increase in the plasma level of a particular drug at a given dose, but the subsequent increase in body weight may then require a further dose increase. Kidney clearance for some drugs, such as lithium, is greater during childhood. There may also be differences between children and adults in neuronal sensitivity and the blood-brain barrier. In some instances, e.g., with methylphenidate, the therapeutic effects in children do not seem to correlate closely with the plasma level. Sometimes, as in the case of methylphenidate, the initial phase of relatively rapid rise of blood level during the first 30 minutes is the time when the drug is most effective. In other drugs, especially neuroleptics, the peak blood level may not be reached for several hours. It is important to keep in mind that the most common reason medications don't work is that they are not taken. Given that the child is often not the person complaining, compliance may be a problem. For this reason, it is important to carefully explain the expected benefit and potential side effects and risks carefully to both the child (in an appropriate way) and the parent.

The side effects of some drugs (Table 37–1) may be particularly troublesome at different phases of development. Thus, neuroleptics given to adolescents may make their acne worse, and they may easily become sunburned. Many drugs must be started at a low dose, increased gradually, and then tapered slowly before being discontinued. Some drugs can be given in a single dose; others require divided doses. (For dosages of commonly used drugs, see Table 37–2.)

For all these reasons, drug treatment of children and adolescents requires a careful preparatory work-up, careful monitoring, a thorough knowledge of the pharmacology and pharmacokinetics of the drug being considered, an understanding of the variations encountered during the different developmental phases throughout childhood and adolescence, and a knowledge of the indications, contraindications, and side effects for each drug, as well as possible drug interactions. Suggested introductory readings for these considerations are included in the references.

Table 37–1.   Groups of Drugs Commonly Used for Children and Adolescents, with Commonly Associated Side Effects

A. NEUROLEPTIC DRUGS
Phenothiazines
   aliphatics
      chlorpromazine (Thorazine)
   piperidines
      thioridazine (Mellaril)
   piperazines
      perphenazine (Trilafon)
      trifluoperazine (Stelazine)
Thioxanthines
   thiothixene (Navane)
   chlorprothixene (Taractan)
Butyrophenones
   haloperidol (Haldol)
Dibenzoxazepines
   loxaprine (Loxitane)
Side Effects
   General: lassitude, listlessness and drowsiness (which often disappear after a few days), increased appetite, decreased appetite, weight gain (especially with Mellaril), stomach upset
   Agranulocytosis: acute onset of sore throat, fever, and ulcerations (during the first 6 to 8 weeks)
   Akathisia: inability to sit still; agitation, restlessness, and pacing, within first 5 weeks (early onset)
   Allergic reactions: jaundice, sensitivity to sunlight, skin rashes
   Autonomic reactions: dry mouth, blurred vision, constipation, urinary retention, frequency, urgency, enuresis, low blood pressure (fainting, dizziness), miosis, mydriasis, impotence
   Dyskinesia: loss of voice (aphonia), spasm of neck muscles, with involuntary turning of head to one side (torticollis), facial tics, blinking, lip smacking, chewing movements, tongue movements, shoulder shrugging, pedaling with legs—all of early onset; inability to swallow (dysphagia)
   Dystonic reactions, acute: oculogyric crises, opisthotonus, torticollis, spasm of the tongue, lasting from a few minutes to several hours, usually with early onset
   Endocrine problems: breast engorgement, menstrual changes, retrograde ejaculation
   Eye abnormalities: corneal opacities, retinitis pigmentosa
   Parkinsonism: tremors, of the hands (pill-rolling), muscle stiffness (cogwheel rigidity), inability to sit or stand still, jumpiness (akathisia), mask-like face and drooling, emotional blunting, shuffling gait, early onset
   Tardive dyskinesia: slow, rhythmical, atypical, involuntary movements of lips, mouth, tongue, hands, and feet; may be athetoid, choreiform, dystonic, myoclonic, or tic-like; "fly-catching" movements of tongue, tongue thrusting, smacking of lips, lateral jaw movements; stumbling, drunken gait, loss of balance, falling; Late onset, usually emerging after discontinuation; often irreversible

B. ANTIANXIETY AGENTS
      chlordiazepoxide (Librium)
      diazepam (Valium)
      flurazepam (Dalmane)
      meprobamate (Miltown, Equanil)
   Side Effects: drowsiness, slurred speech, ataxia, "paradoxical reactions," including anxiety, aggression, insomnia, rage, and hallucinations, following initial use or dose increase

C. ANTIDEPRESSANTS
Tricyclics
      imipramine (Tofranil)
      desipramine (Norpramin; Pertofrane)
      amitriptyline (Elavil)
      nortriptyline (Aventyl)
      trazodone (Desyrel)
   Side Effects: fainting and dizziness due to low blood pressure (hypotension), blurring of vision, dry mouth, palpitations, constipation, tremors, allergic skin rashes, sensitivity to sunlight, jaundice, blood disorders, tachycardia, increased P–R interval on EKG

Table 37–1. Groups of Drugs Commonly Used for Children and Adolescents, with Commonly Associated Side Effects *Continued*

D. STIMULANTS
      amphetamine (Benzedrine)
      dextroamphetamine (Dexedrine)
      methylphenidate (Ritalin)
      pemoline (Cylert)
      Side Effects: anxiety, insomnia, loss of appetite, growth inhibition (usually mild), hallucinations

E. SEDATIVES AND SLEEP MEDICATION
      chloral hydrate (Noctec)
      diphenhydramine (Benadryl)
      sodium pentobarbital (Nembutal)
      Side Effects: depression or withdrawal, paradoxical excitement

F. ANTIMANIC DRUGS
      lithium carbonate
      Side Effects:
      Early: nausea, diarrhea, stomachache, thirst, urinary frequency, muscle weakness, irritability, dizziness, tremor, weight gain, sedation, headache
      Later: diabetes insipidus (polydypsia, polyuria), interstitial renal fibrosis
      Toxicity: hyperirritability, sluggishness, slurred speech, ataxia, anorexia, EEG changes, coma

G. ANTICONVULSANTS

Major Epilepsy	*Petit.Mal*	*Psychomotor Epilepsy*	*Minor Seizures*
phenobarbital	Zarontin	Dilantin	clonazepam
Dilantin	clonazepam	Tegretol	Valium
Mysoline	Tridione	Mysoline	Mysoline
Tegretol		phenobarbital	
Mesantoin			

Table 37–2. Alphabetical List by Brand Name of Drugs Commonly Used in Children and Adolescents, With Commonly Used Dosages*

Anfaril (clomipramine)
    Dose not established for children. Dose range of 100 to 200 mg/day has been used in childhood obsessive-compulsive disorder.
Aventyl (nortriptyline) 20–50 mg/day
Benadryl (diphenhydramine)

Age		Minimum Dosage	Maximum Dosage
3–6 years		25 mg	150 mg
6–12 years		50 mg	300 mg
	average:	2 mg/lb/day	
		5 mg/kg/day	
		1–5 mg/lb/day	

Catapres (clonidine) 0.15–0.30 mg/day (2–3 µg/kg)
Cogentin
    1–2 mg p.o. or i.m.; repeat in 30 minutes, if necessary
Cylert (pemoline)
    0.5–3 mg/kg/day in one daily dose, maximum 112.5 g
Dexedrine (dextroamphetamine)
    2.5–40 mg/day in divided doses
Dilantin
    1.5–4.5 mg/lb/day
    5 mg–10 mg/kg/day
    Side Effects: fever, rash, and enlarged lymph nodes, nystagmus, ataxia, lethargy, gum hyperplasia, anemia

Table 37–2. Alphabetical List by Brand Name of Drugs Commonly Used in Children and Adolescents, With Commonly Used Dosages* *Continued*

Elavil (amitriptyline) 45–110 mg/day

Haldol (haloperidol)

Age	Minimum Dosage	Maximum Dosage
3–6 yrs	.01 mg/kg/day	.03 mg/kg/day
6–11 yrs	2.0 mg	16.0 mg

Typical dose: 0.5 mg–5.0 mg b.i.d. or t.i.d.

NOTE: Haldol lowers the threshold for seizures, and potentiates the effects of imipramine. Therefore, it should be given with care to children with seizures or to those who are taking imipramine. It is used in the treatment of Tourette's disorder and in agitated states associated with psychosis.

Inderal (propranolol)

Dose not established for children. Dosages for adolescents have ranged from 50 to 960 mg/day, with a median dosage of 160 mg/day given in one study (Williams, 1982).

Klonopin (clonazepam)

Begin at 0.01 to 0.05 mg/kg/day in 3 to 4 divided doses

Increase every fifth to seventh day up to 0.1 to 0.25 mg/kg.

Side Effects: ataxia, drowsiness, dysarthria, irritability, weight gain

Librium (chlordiazepoxide)

5 mg b.i.d. or q.i.d. (may be increased occasionally to 10 gm b.i.d. or t.i.d.)

Lithium (lithium carbonate)

150–300 mg/day (blood levels: 0.4–1.2 mEq/L

Lithium dosage (mg) Schedule

Wt (kg)	8 am	12 noon	6 pm	Total Daily Dose
<25	150	150	300	600
25–40	300	300	300	900
40–50	300	300	600	1,200
50–60	600	300	600	1,500

Therapeutic range 0.6–1.2 mEq/L.

Do not exceed 1.4 mEq/L.

Draw blood level 12 hours after last dose.

Mellaril (thioridazine)

Age	Minimum Dosage	Maximum Dosage
3–6 yrs	.5 mg/kg/day	3.0 mg/kg/day
6–12 yrs	2 mg/lb/day	8 mg/lb/day

Typical doses:

mild:	10 mg b.i.d. or t.i.d.
moderate:	25 mg b.i.d. or t.i.d.
maximum:	200 mg/day

NOTE: Has sedating effect. Postural hypotension prominent.

Mesantoin (mephenytoin)

>6 years: 100 mg t.i.d.

Side Effects: blood disorders, fever, rash, enlarged lymph nodes

Mysoline (primidone)

Start at 50 mg/day, given in two divided doses.

Average dose: 150–500 mg/day

Navane (thiothixene) 4.8–42.6 mg/day (mean 16.2)

Noctec (chloral hydrate)

5–15 mg/lb at night, not to exceed 1 g dose

(1 tsp [5 ml] = 500 mg)

Norpramin (see Pertofrane)

Pertofrane (desipramine)

75 mg at bedtime for enuresis

Table 37–2. Alphabetical List by Brand Name of Drugs Commonly Used in Children and Adolescents, With Commonly Used Dosages* *Continued*

Phenobarbital
   Start at 5 mg/kg/day (1–3 mg/lb/day), given in two divided doses
   Side Effects: drowsiness, hyperkinetic behavior
Prolixin (fluphenazine)
   Initial dose 0.025–0.05 mg/kg. Average dose 0.15–0.3 mg/kg. (Average total daily dose 3–6 mg.)
Ritalin (methylphenidate)
   0.3 to 1.0 mg/kg/day

Age	Minimum Dosage	Maximum Dosage
3–6 yrs	5 mg/day increase every 3 days to 10 mg/day	20 mg/day
6–10 yrs	10 mg/day	60 mg/day

Stelazine (trifluoperazine)
   .025–.3 mg/lb/day   0.1–0.5 mg/kg/day
   6–12 yrs   1–20 mg/day
   12 yrs or older   4–40 mg/day
   NOTE: Marked extrapyramidal symptoms (parkinsonism), fidgetiness, restlessness (akathisia).
Tegretol (carbamazepine)
   6 yrs   100 mg/day
   6–12 yrs   200 mg/day–800 mg/day
   Side Effects: double vision, white cell depletion, liver damage, skin reactions
Thorazine (chlorpromazine)
   3–6 mg/kg/day
   Children: 0.5–4 mg/lb/day
   Adolescents: 2–8 mg/lb/day, up to a maximum of 800 mg/day for adolescents
      Increase every 3 days up to 200 mg
   Ages 6–12 yrs: 50–200 mg/day, in divided doses, or as a single night-time dose
   NOTE: Has high sedating effect. Dryness of mouth, blurred vision, and constipation commonly occur. Lowers convulsive threshold.
Tofranil (imipramine)
   <3.5 mg/kg/day

Age	Minimum	Maximum
6–12 yrs	25 mg/day	75 mg/day

Treatment regimen for depression (Ambrosini, 1987)
   Initial dose 1.0–1.5 mg/kg/day
   Increase gradually, every 4 or 5 days, over 2 to 3 weeks

   day #1: 1.5 mg/kg/day
   day #4: 3   mg/kg/day
   day #7: 4   mg/kg/day
   day #10: 5   mg/kg/day

   FDA maximum: 5 mg/kg/day
   Monitor: EKG (P-R interval <0.21 msec; QRS complex <130% of baseline)
      Blood pressure (<145/95)
      Pulse rate (<130/min)
Treatment regimen for enuresis
   (1) imipramine 25 mg at bedtime for 3 months (Martin, 1971)
      or
   (2) imipramine 25 mg at bedtime for 4 days, up, if necessary, to 50 mg at bedtime for 4 days, up, if necessary, to 75 mg at bedtime for 4 days
   Give for 8 weeks, then taper: first every other, then every third day over a one-month period.
Treatment regimen for school phobia (Gittelman-Klein and Klein, 1972)

Table 37–2.   Alphabetical List by Brand Name of Drugs Commonly Used in Children and Adolescents, With Commonly Used Dosages* *Continued*

(Medication given in two daily doses: morning and evening.)
  25 mg/day for the first 3 days
  50 mg/day for the next 4 days
  75 mg/day during the second week.
  Therafter, dosage adjusted weekly for remainder of 6-week period of treatment. Maximum:
    200 mg/day.
Trexan (naltrexone)
  0.5–2.0 mg/kg/day
Tridione (replaced by Zarontin)
  300 mg b.i.d. up to 600 mg t.i.d.
  Side Effects: photophobia
Trilafon (perphenazine)
  General range: .01–1 mg/lb/day   0.1–0.5 mg/kg/day

Age	Minimum Dosage	Maximum Dosage
3–6 yrs	.05 mg/day	.1 mg/day
6–16 yrs	2 mg/day	16 mg/day

Typical doses:	mild:	2–4 mg t.i.d.
	moderate:	4–8 mg t.i.d.
	maximum:	8–16 mg t.i.d.

NOTE: Less sedating, more parkinsonian.
Valium (diazepam)
  1–25 mg b.i.d., t.i.d., or q.i.d., up to a maximum of 20 mg in adolescents.
  Increase gradually as needed and tolerated.
  Typical range: 2–10 mg daily
NOTE: (1) onset ½ to 1 hour
      (2) for seizures: 5–10 mg daily
  Side Effects: drowsiness, ataxia, double vision
Xanax (alprazolam)
  0.5–6 mg daily has been reported, but not established.
Zarontin (ethosuximide)
  Start at 250 mg b.i.d. or t.i.d.

		Daily	
Drug	*Dose Equivalent (mg)*	*Dose Range (mg)*	*Maximum Dosage (mg/kg)*
Thorazine	100	10–200	2
Mellaril	100	10–200	3
Stelazine	5	1–20	
Haldol	2	0.5–16	.02–2

*Every effort has been made to ensure that the information on drugs in this book was accurate at the time of writing. However, new information may supersede that provided here. The most recent package information should be reviewed for any recent changes that have occurred.

REFERENCES

Ambrosini, P.J. (1987), Pharmacotherapy in child and adolescent major depressive disorder. In: *Psychopharmacology: The Third Generation of Progress*, ed. H.Y. Meltzer. New York: Raven Press, pp. 1247–1254.

Biederman, J., and Jellinek, (1984), Psychopharmacology in children. *N. Engl. J. Med.*, 310:968–972.

Campbell, M., Green, W.H., and Deutsch, (1985), *Child and Adolescent Psychopharmacology*. Beverly Hills: Sage Publications.

Campbell, M., and Spender, E.K. (1988), Psychopharmacology in child and adolescent psychiatry: A review of the past five years. *J. Am. Acad. Child Adolesc. Psychiatry*, 27:269–279.

Gittelman-Klein, R., and Klein, D.F. (1972), School phobia; diagnostic considerations in the light of imipramine effects. In: *Drugs, Development and Cerebral Function*, ed. W.L. Smith. Springfield: Charles C Thomas, pp. 200–223.

Martin, G.I. (1971), Imipramine pamoate in the treatment of childhood enuresis. *Am. J. Dis. Child.*, 122:42–47.

Popper, C.W. (1985), Child and Adolescent Psychopharmacology. In: *Psychiatry*, (Vol. 2), ed. J.O. Cavenar, Jr. Chpt. 59, Philadelphia: J.B. Lippincott, Co., pp 1–23.

Schatzberg, A.E. and Cole, J.O. (1986), *Manual of Clinical Psychopharmacology*. Washington, DC: American Psychiatric Press, Inc.

Shaffer, D., Erhardt, A.A., and Greenhill, L.L. (Eds.) (1985), *The Clinical Guide to Child Psychiatry*. New York: The Free Press.

Werry, J.S. (Ed.) (1978), *Pediatric Psychopharmacology: The Use of Behavioral Modifying Drugs in Children*. New York: Brunner/Mazel.

Wiener, J.M. (Ed.) (1977), *Psychopharmacology in Childhood and Adolescence*. New York: Basic Books.

Williams, D., Mehl, R., Yudofsky, S., Adams, D., and Roseman, B. (1982), The effects of propranolol on uncontrolled rage outbursts in children and adolescents with organic brain dysfunction. *J. Am. Acad. Child Psychiatry*, 21:129–135.

Epilogue

SOCIETY, DEVELOPMENT, AND PSYCHOPATHOLOGY

ROOTS OF SOCIETY'S RELATIONSHIP WITH CHILDREN IN AMERICA

The relationship between the child and contemporary society in America has its roots in the early development of the United States. The first recorded relationship is that of the Puritans, who regarded children as inherently sinful, to be saved only by strict rules enforced by the kind of severe punishment that was in vogue in society at that time. The child identified with this perception, and perpetuated the relationship. Locke (1632–1704) subsequently conceived of the child as a tabula rasa (a blank slate), upon whom various experiences would act and, in that way, would mold the child's development. Parents were then to be ardent teachers rather than martinets, signaling a change in the relationship between society and the child as mediated through the parents.

Rousseau (1712–1778), who lived at the time of Mozart and Jefferson and published *Emile* in 1762, then came to the realization that children were not just little adults, but were different psychologically as well as physically from adults. The child was seen as a separate person who actively discovered the world and constructed his or her own knowledge—a forerunner of modern Piagetian views on the construction of reality in children. Rousseau in essence was the first to introduce the concept of development and

developmental stage, thus paving the way for another change in the way in which society conceptualized the child and later legislated on behalf of the child.

In more recent times, Gesell (1880–1961) in the 1930s and 1940s introduced the term "maturation," or unfolding, which he thought was only slightly influenced by the environment or society. Watson (1878–1958) took the opposite view: that environment and social experiences were the major forces in the development of the child, thereby giving birth to "behaviorism" and all that followed in the work of Dollard, Miller, Sears, Hull, and Skinner. Meanwhile, Freud (1856–1939) looked inward at the independent inner life of the child, while Erikson elaborated a psychosocial perspective on childhood and society.

Yet very few of these giants addressed the specific problems and trends in their contemporary society and the effects of these problems and trends upon the developing child. The purpose, then, of this epilogue is to draw attention to certain current problems and trends in American society and their effects upon the children of our time. In order to present a coherent account, some of the material presented earlier is repeated here for the convenience of the reader.

DIVORCE

A major contemporary social phenomenon in the United States today is the high rate of divorce. Current projections suggest that about two-thirds of first marriages are now likely to end in divorce (Martin and Bumpass, 1989). The effects upon children of the whole divorce process, including the predivorce failing marital relationship, the events during the separation and the divorce itself, the accompanying custody conflicts, and the subsequent rearing by a single parent, are staggering (Hetherington et al., 1985; Wallerstein, 1985). Divorce produces a prolonged psychologic and social imbalance that stresses the child. Young boys are especially vulnerable, and as much as 6 or 7 years after the divorce latency-age boys are significantly less well adjusted than their male counterparts in intact families (Guidubaldi and Perry, 1985). Girls from divorced families may experience reactions during adolescence, which may take the form of precocious sexual activity, substance abuse, and running away (Kalter et al., 1985). Wallerstein (1980) has demonstrated the fear of betrayal in heterosexual relationships in young women who experienced divorce and continuing sadness. In short, the modulation of sexuality and aggression in the child is at risk for impairment.

Parenthood, unlike marriage, cannot be easily dissolved. Benians et al. (1983) have clearly shown that children whose parents separate and divorce do not themselves believe or feel they have only one parent, even though 40% of children of divorce do lose contact with the noncustodial parent within two years of the divorce. Prior to divorce the child has a bilateral network of relatives. Indeed, knowledge of this extended family is important to the child's developing sense of identity. Loss of contact with one parent often leads to the loss of connections with all the aunts, uncles, cousins, and grandparents form that side of the family.

We should conclude that access to the noncustodial parent is a necessity. Unfortunately, we often do not; instead, current practice seems to regard access as a privilege for which the disputing parent, usually the father, must strive. This focus on the parents rather than on the child is wrong. Many divorced parents need a great deal of help in maintaining the focus on the needs of the child. Very young children, for example, need frequent access. Many factors must be taken into account in custody decisions. Although joint custody would appear ideal in this regard, such custodial arrangements can serve as a vehicle for the continuation of bitter marital relationships. We need studies that will provide us with data on which to make rational recommendations in the face of this massive national phenomenon.

SINGLE PARENTHOOD

Single parenthood, often a result of divorce, is another growing trend in the United States today (see also p. 96). More single adolescents as well as single older women are giving birth to children. In the last 20 years the proportion of births among unmarried women rose from 5% in 1960 to 19% in 1982.* Looked at another way, the majority of poor families with children are headed by women (Moynihan, 1985). There has in fact been a major growth in families headed by women with no husband present—nearly 10 million households, amounting to almost 12% of all households. Beyond that, the Bureau of Labor Statistics reported in 1985 that 46% of all mothers with children under 3 years of age are in the work force. The likelihood is that more and more families will be headed by a single parent who has to go to work. When a mother is employed, 40 or 50 hours of work are added to the family system (Hunt and Hunt, 1977), and when she is a single parent, few, if any, other adults are available to share this extra allotment of work.

Who, then, takes care of the children?

Sometimes a young preadolescent sibling, maybe 12 or 14 years of age is the caregiver; sometimes the children are just left to fend for themselves. The best estimates are that there are between 2 and 5 million "latchkey" children 6 and 13 years of age, and probably as many as 8 to 10 million children altogether

*National Center for Health Statistics, Washington, D.C., 1985.

under 18 years of age who are "latchkey" children.

Unfortunately, scarcely any controlled data are available on the safety, health, education, or welfare of these children as they grow up, much less on their emotional health. The variables are many: much depends on the needs of the children, the strengths and weaknesses of the families, and the support system available. The issue is large enough for society as a whole to consider. For one thing, some of this significant group of children may be at risk for subsequent disorders, including the risk for violence and delinquency.

At present we have no solutions for this problem, which means that we, in the United States, are a nation at risk as far as the next generation is concerned. National attention, therefore, must be paid to these children now.

DAY CARE

Is day care the answer? At present a wide range of standards exists among day-care centers. The outcome for the children is immensely variable. Clarke-Stewart (1982) noted, for example, that physical development is accelerated in children of poor families who use day care, but not in middle class children. At the same time, children in day care do as well as, and in some cases better than, children at home. Day-care children are usually well attached to their mothers. Because different children have different needs, thought needs to be given to the match between child and day-care center, beyond the basic issue of adequate minimal standards for all day-care centers. Some programs, like Head Start, are outstanding, but Head Start can handle only 20% of the eligible children.

Day care is an important alternative for these children, but it is not the full answer and, in any case, has many problems of its own to be solved, among them the issues of safety and minimal standards.

Until recently only $25 million in federal child-care training funds were shared among participating states. If as a society we decide not to spend the money needed for quality day care, we will have to accept the responsibility too for mental health problems that will follow in children who have suffered poor care.

HOMOSEXUAL PARENTS

There are about 1.5 million homosexual parents in the United States (Hunter and Polikoff, 1976). What is known about the effects upon the child of such parenting? The question is important because, in the absence of knowledge, myth prevails. Such myths include notions that homosexuality is necessarily pathologic, that homosexuals will act out sexually in front of or with children, that the child will become confused in his or her gender identity, and that the child will become homosexual.

Lesbian mothers in fact are perfectly successful in maternal roles (Hoeffer, 1981; Kirkpatrick, Smith and Roy, 1981). Lesbian mothers, like heterosexual mothers, are greatly concerned about the care of their children (Pagelow, 1980), and are also concerned that their children have adequate male figures with whom to identify (Kirkpatrick et al., 1981). The lesbian partner is often viewed as an aunt or big sister, and household chores are shared equally (Hall, 1978).

Lesbian mothers are similar to heterosexual mothers too in their encouragement of non-sex type toys for both boys and girls (Hoeffer, 1981). There is no evidence that lesbian mothers prefer their children to become homosexual. Rather, acceptance of a child's object choice seems to be more common.

In general, the rearing of children in all-female households does not in itself lead to disorders of gender identity or homosexuality. In particular, Green (1978) in a study of 37 children raised by homosexual and transsexual parents suggested that the children in general develop appropriate sexual identities and assume usual heterosexual attitudes, as do children reared in heterosexual mother households. Golombok, Spencer, and Rutter

(1983), in a controlled study of 37 children 5 to 17 years of age, found no evidence that lesbianism causes any risk of incestuous advances to children and no evidence of inappropriate gender identity. All the children reported that "they were glad to be the sex that they were and none would prefer to be the opposite sex" (p. 562). In essence, the study found no differences in gender identity, sex role behavior, or sexual orientation between children brought up in lesbian households and those brought up in heterosexual single-parent households, and that "rearing in a lesbian household per se did not lead to atypical psychosexual development or constitute a psychiatric risk factor" (p. 571).

Interestingly, a much publicized case in Boston* was that of a male homosexual couple who applied to become foster parents. They were an openly gay, working couple who had lived together for almost 10 years. The State of Massachusetts Social Service, after a year of study, finally decided to give them two little boys, one 3 years of age and the other not quite 2 years of age. The children had been abused, and the boys' mother gave approval. It seemed to be a good arrangement for all concerned. Then the Boston Globe publicized the placement and TV crews descended on the family. The State immediately took the children back. There was, incidentally, no legal issue involved. When the children had to leave that home, they were "angry, confused and in tears." It is clear that the issue of homosexual men caring for children still remains unresolved and unstudied.

On the basis of these findings, the rise of homosexuality, per se in our society does not appear to lead to disturbance in the child. Whether these findings will dispel myths is another matter. At the same time, policies and legal decisions based on myths should be discarded.

HOMOSEXUALITY

A related social trend today is the increasing recognition and tolerance of homosexu-

*New York Times, May 19, 1985, p. 24.

ality, at least in some communities (see also pp. 97 and 241). In most children and adolescents who exhibit homosexuality, we do not have enough data to support any one cause as explaining all homosexual orientation and behavior. The causes in fact are probably multiple, and often unknown. This led the American Psychiatric Association in 1974 to delete "homosexuality" as a mental disorder, and to regard instead the individual's choice in most instances as simply an alternative choice of sexual expression. More recently, in 1983, the American Academy of Pediatrics' Committee on Adolescence promulgated four assertions about homosexuality during the teenage years; (1) that some homosexual experimental behavior is experienced by many adolescents; (2) that homosexual characteristics appear to be established before adolescence; (3) that some previously heterosexually oriented adolescents will become involved in homosexual activities if circumstances reinforce this behavior or if heterosexual alternatives are not available (so-called facultative homosexuality) and that most of these individuals will revert to heterosexual practices when circumstances change; and (4) that the majority of behaviors should not be characterized as "male" or "female" since most are common to all young people.

The medical consequences of homosexual activity, on the other hand, are serious. Sexual practices such as fellatio, cunnilingus, and anal intercouse may result in gonorrhea, hepatitis B, *Giardia lamblia*, and AIDS.

The social consequences of homosexual orientation in an adolescent include difficulties in peer group acceptance, family rejection, harrassment in school, limited employment opportunities, legal difficulties, and social isolation. Although homosexual orientation in itself does not appear to predispose to mental illness, the social consequences of this lifestyle in a teenager may engender secondary psychologic problems.

DRINKING

Yet another rising social phenomenon is the increase in drinking, and its possible relation to morbidity and even mortality in adolescents.

In our society drinking is a socially and culturally defined pattern of behavior that increases with age (Maddox, 1964). The average age at which a child has his or her first drink is between 14 and 15 years, although some studies in the United States show that between the ages of 11 and 13 years, 63% of boys and 53% of girls had tried alcohol (Hawker, 1977). Bruun and Hauge (1963) found in the Scandinavian countries that, at the age of 18, it is unusual for a boy not to have consumed alcohol. The first drink is usually taken in the home, with the parents, and is usually a beer. Studies in the United States have found that one in seven 17-year-olds was becoming intoxicated once a week (Hawker, 1977). The reasons for starting to drink usually center around three themes: (1) celebrating a holiday or special occasion, (2) being offered drink by their families, and (3) curiosity about drinking.

The dangers are twofold: habituation and short- and long-term effects of drunkenness. The earlier the onset of alcohol abuse, the poorer the prognosis. The risk of relapse is also greater for those with a history of several episodes of drunkenness. Nylander and Rydelius (1973) showed that boys who had recurring offenses were more likely to have alcoholic or mentally ill fathers and to have a higher incidence of psychiatric problems and disciplinary problems at school. "Problem" drinkers are likely to have problems in other areas (Plant, 1976). If both parents take a drink, the probability is high that their children will also drink. At the same time, peer group support is a powerful factor.

One serious consequence of drinking is the car accident. Accidents, mostly car accidents, are the leading cause of mortality among older adolescents, and intoxication is an important factor in many of these deaths. Death from risk-taking behavior while intoxicated is a real danger in the United States today.

In order to make this point more strongly, The Center for Disease Control (CDC) in Atlanta revised its Morbidity and Mortality Weekly Report to include "Potential Years of Life Lost by Cause of Death." This information is derived for persons 1 to 65 years of age at the time of death by taking the number of deaths in each age category (as reported by the National Center for Health Statistics, Monthly Vital Statistics Report) multiplied by the difference between 65 years and the age of the midpoint of each category.

Using this new way of looking at causes of death produces the staggering figure of more than 665,497 potential years of life lost to children and teenagers from automobile accidents in only one year. This figure was higher than the number of potential years of life lost, for all ages, in the United States in 1980 due to any of the following: chronic liver disease and cirrhosis, cerebrovascular diseases, pneumonia and influenza, diabetes mellitus, or chronic obstructive pulmonary diseases and allied conditions (Table E–1).

The problem of prevention remains unsolved. Raising the legal age for alcohol consumption in some states is only a partial answer. A national policy is required.

CHILD ABUSE

An undercurrent of violence begins to emerge in this review of the relationship between society and the child. In fact, another growing social trend and problem in our sometimes violent society is the increase in child abuse. In 1985 1 out of 33 children 3 to 17 years of age living with two parents at

Table E–1.　Deaths and Potential Years of Life Lost for Children and Adolescents in United States, 1975*

Age (yr)	No. of Deaths from Auto Accidents	Potential Years of Life Lost Before Age 65 from Auto Accidents
1	225	14,400
1–4	1,321	82,563
4–9	1,576	91,408
10–14	1,710	90,630
15–19	8,052	286,496
Total	12,884	665,497

*Adapted from L. S. Robertson (1982).

home was the victim of severe violence, giving rise to a total of one million or more children each year who are abused. Of these one million children, between 2,000 and 5,000 die each year as a result of the abuse (AMA, 1986; Gelles and Straus, 1985). Some violence occurs in 62% of all families. In Connecticut, as in many other states, the number of reported cases has been increasing every year, with a 35% rise in reported sexual abuse. Among reported child abuse cases, 48% are in poor, single-parent households.

By and large the outlook for many abused children and their families is not good. Lynch and Roberts (1982), among others, have noted a high incidence of abnormality in follow-up of abused children, and a failure to thrive that often accompanies child abuse. Martin et al. (1974) found 53% of their children to have some neurologic abnormalities as well. Martin and Beezley (1977) studied the behavior of 50 children 4½ years after abuse, and found that over half were described as having low self-esteem and types of behavior that made peers, parents, and teachers reject them. Often by the time they reach primary school these children are socially isolated and identified as "hostile" by their teachers (Roberts et al., 1978). Even if the abused child is placed outside his or her biologic family, he or she is still in a high-risk group for both fostering and adoption breakdown.

A study by Vitulano et al. (1986) documented the need for improved initial assessment of all abused children, particularly in the areas of developmental, psychologic, and social assessment. Only then can an appropriate set of multiple treatment recommendations be made for a particular child. Moreover, a method of follow-up documentation of the results of any recommendations actually implemented needs to be built into any plan for a successful treatment and prevention program for abused children. We need to move beyond our understandable concern for the physical safety of the child to the equally important concern for the subsequent emotional development, and we need a national plan for such an approach (Helfer, 1985).

SEXUAL ABUSE

Currently in our society we are seeing an increase in the number of reports of sexual abuse of children. In fact, reported cases have increased more than 600% in the last 7 years. Sexual abuse reports increased an average of 35% across the country last year. The incidence is estimated at 100,000 to 250,000 cases per year (AMA, 1986).

What do we know about sexual abuse? Eighty percent of sexual abuses of children occur in the middle class. In most instances the abuser is known to the child, and uses enticement or bribery to get the child to comply. This way of taking advantage of the child's immaturity and vulnerability has an important aftermath for the child, who at a later time may feel guilty and may realize that he or she has been tricked or betrayed. In cases where there is a use of force, or even just an accompanying threat of violence, the child also feels his or her body has been damaged, and this is followed by a loss of self-esteem, with subsequent depression and anxiety. Such a child needs an opportunity to talk to a skilled person, alone. The therapist can get a sense of the validity of the child's account when the child begins to describe multiple episodes, perhaps each escalating in degree over a period of time, with explicit detail. There is usually an initial period of secrecy to which the child has been sworn or instructed by the abuser, and this also later engenders guilt in the child. Such children need psychotherapeutic intervention. Yet surprisingly, the child's complaints are often ignored, and treatment is not given. Again, we must now pay particular attention to the psychologic needs of these children.

TELEVISION VIOLENCE

By 16 years of age the average American child has watched about 20,000 hours of television and will have seen 200,000 acts of violence and 50,000 attempted murders. Of these murder attempts, 33,000 will have been with guns (NCTV, 1985). Guns appear in television shows an average of 9 times per hour during prime time. Handguns are involved in 50% of all murders in the United States (Schetky, 1985). Children's television programs are six times as violent as adult television programs, and despite yearly fluctuations the average amount of violence has essentially remained stable from 1967 (Signorielli et al., 1982). If anything, the network prime-time violence has increased over the past five years (Table E–2). Cable television shows even more violent acts per hour (Table E–3). The cartoon shows aired by the network on Saturday morning have averaged 27 violent acts per hour.

In addition to the programs, the average child watches more than 20,000 television commercials each year (Choate, 1976). Two thirds of these commercials are for high-sugar foods. Young children have difficulty distinguishing the commercials from the programs and, in any event, tend to assume that the commercial provides accurate information.

Research conducted over the past 10 years (Murray, 1980; Zuckeman and Zuckerman, 1985) provides the following facts:

1. Children *are* likely to learn and remember new forms of aggressive behavior from the violence they witness on television.

2. A *decrease* in sensitivity to violence seen on television *does* occur in response to the exposure to repetitive violence, and this decrease in turn makes a decrease in emotional sensitivity to real aggressive behavior more likely in actual life situations.

3. If anything, a *heightening* of aggressive behavior occurs when aggression on television is watched, rather than any draining off of aggression.

4. Sometimes an awareness of the aftermath of aggression can inhibit aggression.

In addition, children learn the stereotypes presented on television. Such stereotypes include the depiction of nonwhites as smaller and less important than whites, as criminals or victims, or as subordinate to whites. Women are usually dominated by men, and single women are more likely to be portrayed as victims of violence than are married women. Finally, employed women are more likely to be portrayed as villains than are full-time housekeepers.

Violence and its distortions on television are harmful to the developing child. Our society should take steps to reduce the amount of violence shown on programs. Viewers should be warned of the harmful effects of television violence on children at the beginning of each program that presents violence. Parents should be encouraged to question their children's viewing habits, set limits, and educate their children on the ill effects of violent behavior in real life. Parents should also correct for their children the misinformation and distortions that are presented on television. Perhaps we need a national policy on the presentation of violence on television.

Table E–2. Violent Acts per Hour

		ABC	NBC	CBS
Fall-Winter	1980–1981	5.8	4.9	6.1
Winter	1982	9.8	6.7	7.6
Winter	1983	11.2	9.4	7.1
Winter	1984	9.5	10.4	6.3
Winter	1985	14.6	14.2	13.0

Adapted from NCTV Monitoring (1985), 6:6.

Table E–3. Violent Acts per Hour on Cable Television

(June 28–September 26, 1982)	
Movie Channel	19.3
HBO	20.8
Showtime	27.2

Adapted from NCTV Monitoring (1985), 6:6.

VIOLENCE IN ADOLESCENCE

Currently in the United States about half of those arrested for serious crimes are under the age of 18. Fifty percent of all rapes and murders are committed by adolescents. As the juvenile increases in age, the likelihood of court involvement increases. Boys are arrested for serious violent offenses more often than girls. At the same time, arrests for violent crimes among girls under 18 years of age have recently increased.

Accidents, murders, and suicides are responsible for three out of four deaths among 15- to 24-year-olds (DHHS, 1982). The death rate for young men is three times higher than that for young women, and the mortality rate among blacks is 20% higher than among whites.

Many violent adolescents are enraged adolescents—enraged against the parents who abused them and society who neglects them. Many of these adolescents are delusional and paranoid individuals who perceive the world as a dangerous place as they themselves add to the actual danger. Many of these adolescents are barely in control of their confused and frightening feelings and affects, often the result of the brain damage or brain dysfunction they suffer. Many of them are depressed and without hope. Whatever else they have or impose on the rest of society, they suffer.

In one study of juvenile offenders 11 to 17 years of age, average age 15, who were incarcerated at a correctional facility, among the 89 who were actually violent, 76% had paranoid symptoms, 57% were illogical and rambling in their thought processes, 41% had auditory hallucinations, 28% had visual hallucinations, 42% had major neurologic signs, and 69% had symptoms of psychomotor epilepsy (Lewis et al., 1979).

The children who were to become extremely violent had also themselves suffered severe violence. In addition to causing CNS damage with subsequent learning disabilities and attention disorders, this kind of abuse engenders enormous rage against the abusing parent, a rage that could subsequently be displaced onto other "authority" figures. At the least, these children had poor models with whom to identify.

In addition, serious delinquents often had a history of head and face trauma. The percentage of abuse, head injury, and neurologic symptoms in incarcerated delinquents was twice as high as that among nonincarcerated delinquents, and three times as high as that among nondelinquents.

Interestingly, the violent boys and violent girls were remarkably alike in all respects, including medical histories, neurologic damage, and violent capabilities. What varied were the dispositions that were made: violent disturbed girls were more likely to be hospitalized, whereas violent disturbed boys were more likely to be incarcerated.

Race was another factor accounting for differences in dispositions. White psychiatrically disturbed violent adolescents were likely to be hospitalized, whereas black psychiatrically disturbed violent adolescents were likely to be incarcerated. This finding suggests that correctional facilities in the United States are being asked to function as the mental hospitals of the lower socioeconomic class black population. This trend can hardly lead to satisfactory treatment, much less prevention. The problem of violence by adolescents needs to be addressed more comprehensively at a national level.

ILLITERACY

One third of our adult population—60 million men and women—cannot usefully read; for example, they cannot read a note sent home with their children from the public schools, or the instructions on a bottle of medication. Illiterate adults often remain unemployed, cannot attract political attention, and cannot help their children rise out of the appalling despair they suffer. Among adults in the United States who are either total, functional, or marginal nonreaders, 16% are white, 44% are black, and 56% are Hispanic. Young black and Hispanic women are the single highest group of illiterate adults. With more than half of nonwhite infants growing up in single-parent, female-headed homes, it is reasonable to assume that it is *their* children who are in greatest jeopardy of perpetuating this illiteracy from one generation to the next. This illiterate underclass in the United States represents a serious problem affecting our children and future generations. A national policy for the education of these children is needed.

THE BLACK CHILD IN AMERICA

Finally attention must be paid to social factors and attitudes that continue to have an important effect on the development of the black child in America. In order to understand these attitudes we must remember the history of the black family in this country. During the critical time when the initial primary wealth was being distributed, slavery existed in America and continued as American social policy for about 250 years. One unfortunate consequence of these juxtaposed social phenomena is that today one out of every two black children compared to one out of every seven white children still lives in poverty (Comer and Hill, 1985). (In 1984 more than 40% of all children in the United States were living below the poverty level.) The subsequent disproportionate numbers of black children with social, emotional, cognitive, and psychologic problems have given rise to an over-representation of black adults with social problems and mental illnesses.

Many blacks have had to endure repeated exclusion from the mainstream of society and its major institutions, giving rise to an increasing sense of frustration. One consequence of this frustration has been a rise in sexual and social acting out, rage, and anger, and a tendency in some toward denial, avoidance, and dependency.

Thus much of what affects the black child and black adult today has important historic roots and antecedents (Comer, 1985). Clearly we now need a national social policy that redresses and continues to address all these long-term causes and effects that have resulted in the disproportionate representation of blacks among those with economic and psychologic problems.

DISCUSSION

How may we evaluate all these particular trends among others that affect children? Perhaps we are neither better nor worse than any previous generation—who is to decide? Yet it is important that we address those social issues of our day that manifestly are affecting our children.

Some of the more salient issues discussed previously include: divorce, single parenthood, lesbian parents, homosexuality, drinking, child abuse, sexual abuse, television violence, street violence, illiteracy, poverty, and the effects of a devastating past social policy on a large sector of the United States population. Much needs to be done. We need more data, but that will probably always be true. Meanwhile we must act on the best information we have available; surely we cannot afford to wait for scientific purity before we act. This task requires the collaboration of mental health professionals, health care professionals, educators, and politicians at all levels. Although we may point at times with pride at our past performance, we could better serve children by implementing programs we believe will more adequately address the problems to be tackled. This approach will require a comprehensive national policy for children to provide the necessary coordination and drive.

Lastly, the problems that face American society in its relationship to children may not be peculiar to America, and may occur to some extent and in modified ways in all civilized societies in the world today. We may require an International Policy for Children, perhaps under the auspices of the World Health Organization.

REFERENCES

AMA Council on Scientific Affairs (1986), AMA diagnostic and treatment guidelines concerning child abuse and neglect. Conn. Med., 50:122.

Benians, R., Berry, T., Gouling, D., and John, P. (1983), *Children and Family Breakdown—Custody and Access: Guideliness—The Need for a New Approach.* Discussion document prepared for "Families Need Fathers." London.

Bruun, K., and Hauge, R. (1963), *Drinking Habits Among Northern Youth.* The Finnish Foundation for Alcohol Studies, Helsinki.

Choate, R. (1976), Testimony before the Federal Trade Commission in the matter of a trade regulation rule on food nutrition advertising. Washington, D.C., Council on Children, Media and Merchandising.

Clarke-Stewart, A. (1982), *Day Care.* Boston: Harvard Univerisity Press.

Comer, J. (1985), Black children and child psychiatry, introduction. *J. Am. Acad. Child Psychiatry,* 24:129–133.

Comer, J., and Hill, H. (1985), Social policy and the mental health of black children. *J. Am. Acad. Child Psychiatry,* 24:175–181.

DHHS (1982), Statistical Report.

Gelles, R.J., and Straus, M.A. (1985), National Family Violence Surveys. Presented at the National Conference on Child Abuse and Neglect. Chicago, November 11, 1985.

Golombok, S., Spencer, A., and Rutter, M. (1983), Children in lesbian and single-parent households: Psychosexual and psychiatric appraisal. *J. Child Psychol. Psychiatry,* 24:551–572.

Green, R. (1978), Sexual identity of 37 children raised by homosexual or transsexual parents. *Am. J. Psychiatry,* 135:692–697.

Guidubaldi, J., and Perry, J.D. (1985), Divorce and mental health sequelae for children: a two-year follow-up of a nationwide sample. *J. Am. Acad. Psychiatry,* 24:531–537.

Hall, M. (1978), Lesbian families: Cultural and clinical issues. *Soc. Casework,* 23:380–385.

Hawker, A. (1977), Drinking patterns of young people. In: *Alcoholism and Drug Dependence: A Multidisciplinary Approach. Proceedings Third Conference Alcoholism and Drug Dependence.* New York: Plenum Publishing Corp.

Helfer, R. (1985), Where to now, Henry? A commentary on the battered child syndrome. *Pediatrics,* 76:993–997.

Hetherington, E.M., Cox, M., and Cox, R. (1985), Long-term effects of divorce and remarriage on the adjustment of children. *J. Am. Acad. Child Psychiatry,* 24:518–530.

Hoeffer, B. (1981), Children's acquisition of sex-role behavior in lesbian mother families. *Am. J. Orthopsychiatry,* 51:536–544.

Hunt, J.G., and Hunt, L.L. (1977), Dilemmas and contradictions of status; the case of the dual career family. *Soc. Problems,* 24:407–416.

Hunter, N., and Polikoff, N. (1976), Custody rights of lesbian mothers: Legal theory and litigation strategy. *Buffalo Law Rev.,* 25:691.

Kalter, N., Riemer, B., Brickman, A., and Chen, J.W. (1985), Implications of parental divorce for female development. *J. Am. Acad. Child Psychiatry,* 24:538–544.

Kirkpatrick, M., Smith, K., and Roy, R. (1981), Lesbian mothers and their children: A comparative study. *Am. J. Orthopsychiatry,* 51:545–551.

Lewis, D.O., Shanok, S.S., Pincus, J.H., and Glaser, G.H. (1979), Violent juvenile delinquents. Psychi-atric, neurologic, psychological and abuse factors. *J. Am. Acad. Child Psychiatry,* 18:307–319.

Lynch, M.A., and Roberts, J. (1982), *Consequences of Child Abuse.* London: Academic Press.

Maddox, G. (1964), Adolescence and alcohol. In: *Alcohol Education for Classroom and Community,* ed. R. McCarthy. New York: McGraw-Hill Book Co., pp. 32–47.

Martin, H.P., and Beezley, P. (1977), Behavioral observations of abused children. *Dev. Med. Child Neurol.,* 19:373–387.

Martin, H.P., Beezley, P., Conway, E.F., and Kempe, C.H. (1974), The development of abused children. In: *Advances in Pediatrics* (Vol. 21), ed. I. Schulman. Chicago: Year Book Medical Publishers.

Martin, T.C., and Bumpass, L.L. (1989), Recent trends in marital disruption. *Demography,* 26:37–51.

Moynihan, D.P. (1985), *Family and Nation.* New York: Harcourt Brace Jovanovich.

Murray, J.P. (1980), *Television and Youth: 25 Years of Research and Controversy,* Nebraska: Boys Town Center for the Study of Youth Development.

NCTV (1985), How much violence do we see on television? *National Coalition on Television Violence,* 6:3.

Nylander, I., and Rydelius, P (1973), The relapse of drunkenness in non-asocial teenage boys. *Acta Psychiatr. Scand.,* 49:435–443.

Pagelow, M. (1980), Heterosexual and lesbian single mothers: A comparison of problems, coping and solutions. *J. Homosex.,* 5:189–204.

Plant, M. (1976), Young drug and alcohol casualities compared. Review of 100 patients at a Scottish psychiatric hospital. *Br. J. Addict.,* 71:31–43.

Roberts, J. (1978), Social work and child abuse. In: *Violence and the Family,* ed. J.P. Martin. New York: John Wiley & Sons, Inc.

Robertson, L.S. (1982), Present status of knowledge in childhood injury prevention, In: *Preventing Childhood Injuries,* ed. A.B. Bergman. Report of the Twelfth Ross Roundtable on Critical Approaches to Common Pediatric Problems. Columbus, OH, Ross Laboratories.

Schetky, D.H. (1985), Children and handguns: A public health concern. *Am. J. Dis. Child.,* 139:229–231.

Signorielli, N., Gross, L., and Morgan, M. (1982), Violence in television programs: Ten years later. In: *Television and Behavior: Ten Years of Scientific Progress and Implications for the Eighties: Technical Reviews,* (Vol. 2), ed. D. Pearl, L. Bouthilet, and J. Lazar. US DHHS, National Institute of Mental Health (NIMH).

Vitulano, L., Lewis, M., Doran, L., Nordhaus, B., and Adnopoz, J. (1986), Treatment recommendation, implementation and follows up in child abuse. *Am. J. Orthopsychiat.,* 56:478–480.

Wallerstein, J.S. (1985), Children of divorce: Preliminary report of a ten-year follow-up of older children and adolescents. *J. Am. Acad. Child Psychiatry,* 24:545–553.

Wallerstein, J.S., and Kelly, J.B. (1980), *Surviving the Breakup: How Children and Parents Cope with Divorce.* New York: Basic Books.

Zuckerman, D.M., and Zuckerman, B.S. (1985), Television's impact on children. *Pediatrics,* 75:233–240.

Appendix A

DSM-III-R CLASSIFICATION OF DISORDERS USUALLY FIRST EVIDENT IN INFANCY, CHILDHOOD, OR ADOLESCENCE*

DSM-III-R, and its predecessor DSM-III, reflect the significant advances in diagnosis and classification made over the past decade. A multiaxial approach to diagnosis is used in recognition of the fact that multiple kinds of information are relevant to psychiatric diagnosis. This approach has proven particularly valuable for child psychiatry (Rutter et al., 1975). Five separate Axes are used: Axis I includes clinical syndromes and "V codes" (conditions that do not constitute a mental disorder but may be an important focus of attention or treatment, e.g., parent-child problems). Axis II includes developmental disorders (e.g., mental retardation, autism, specific developmental disorders) and personality disorders; these disorders arise in childhood and are presumed to be relatively stable, persistent conditions. Axis III includes any physical disorders or conditions. Axis IV provides for ratings of the severity of psychosocial stressors and Axis V for ratings of global assessment of functioning (see Table A–1). Information on Axes IV and V is intended to supplement the diagnostic information provided on Axes I, II, and III.

It is possible (and indeed is often the case)

Table A–1.	Multiaxial Evaluation
Axis I	Clinical Syndromes and V Codes
Axis II	Developmental Disorders and Personality Disorders
Axis III	Physical Disorders and Conditions
Axis IV	Severity of Psychosocial Stressors
Axis V	Global Assessment of Functioning

that children and adolescents receive multiple psychiatric diagnoses, e.g., problems of attention and impulsivity are often associated with disturbances in conduct. Similarly, diagnoses may be made on different axis, for example, a child with mental retardation may exhibit separation anxiety disorder. In instances where multiple diagnoses are given the principle diagnosis should be specified; diagnoses should be listed within each Axis in terms of the order of their priority for treatment. It is possible to note that a diagnosis is made only provisionally, that a diagnosis is deferred, or (for nonpsychotic disorders) to indicate that an unspecified disorder is present. Some diagnostic categories are, by definition, mutually exclusive, e.g., autism and of attention deficit-hyperactivity disorder. Disorders classified elsewhere in DSM-III-

---

*Abstracted from the Diagnostic and Statistical Manual of Mental Disorders, 3rd Ed., revised. With permission of the American Psychiatric Association.

423

R, e.g., schizophrenia, may be appropriately applied to children and adolescents.

DIAGNOSTIC CRITERIA FOR MENTAL RETARDATION

A. Significantly subaverage general intellectual functioning: an IQ of 70 or below on an individually administered IQ test (for infants, a clinical judgment of significantly subaverage intellectual functioning, since available intelligence tests do not yield numerical IQ values).
B. Concurrent deficits or impairments in adaptive functioning, i.e., the person's effectiveness in meeting the standards expected for his or her age by his or her cultural group in areas such as social skills and responsibility, communication, daily living skills, personal independence, and self-sufficiency.
C. Onset before the age of 18.

DIAGNOSTIC CRITERIA FOR AUTISTIC DISORDER

At least eight of the following sixteen items are present, these to include at least two items from A, one from B, and one from C. **Note:** Consider a criterion to be met *only* if the behavior is abnormal for the person's developmental level.

A. Qualitative impairment in reciprocal social interaction as manifested by the following:
(The examples within parentheses are arranged so that those first mentioned are more likely to apply to younger or more handicapped, and the later ones to older or less handicaped persons with this disorder.)
   (1) marked lack of awareness of the existence or feelings of others (e.g., treats a person as if he or she were a piece of furniture; does not notice another person's distress; apparently has no concept of the need of others for privacy)
   (2) no or abnormal seeking of comfort at times of distress (e.g., does not come for comfort even when ill, hurt, or tired; seeks comfort in a stereotyped way, e.g., says "cheese, cheese, cheese" whenever hurt)
   (3) no or impaired imitation (e.g., does not wave bye-bye; does not copy mother's domestic activities; mechanical imitation of others' actions out of context)
   (4) no or abnormal social play (e.g., does not actively participate in simple games; prefers solitary play activities; involves other children in play only as "mechanical aids")
   (5) gross impairment in ability to make peer friendships (e.g., no interest in making peer friendships; despite interest in making friends, demonstrates lack of understanding of conventions of social interaction, for example, reads phone book to uninterested peer)
B. Qualitative impairment in verbal and nonverbal communication, and in imaginative activity, as manifested by the following: (The numbered items are arranged so that those first listed are more likely to apply to younger or more handicapped, and the later ones to older or less handicapped, persons with this disorder.)
   (1) no mode of communication, such as communicative babbling, facial expression, gesture, mime, or spoken language
   (2) markedly abnormal nonverbal communication, as in the use of eye-to-eye gaze, facial expression, body posture, or gestures to initiate or modulate social interaction (e.g., does not anticipate being held, stiffens when held, does not look at the person or smile when making a social approach, does not greet parents or visitors, has a fixed stare in social situations)
   (3) absence of imaginative activity, such as playacting of adult roles, fantasy characters, or animals; lack of interest in stories about imaginary events

(4) marked abnormalities in the production of speech, including volume, pitch, stress, rate, rhythm, and intonation (e.g., monotonous tone, questionlike melody, or high pitch)

(5) marked abnormalities in the form or content of speech, including stereotyped and repetitive use of speech (e.g., immediate echolalia or mechanical repetition of television commercial); use of "you" when "I" is meant (e.g., using "You want cookie?" to mean "I want a cookie"); idiosyncratic use of words or phrases (e.g., "Go on green riding" to mean "I want to go on the swing"); or frequent irrelevant remarks (e.g., starts talking about train schedules during a conversation about sports)

(6) marked impairment in the ability to initiate or sustain a conversation with others, despite adequate speech (e.g., indulging in lengthy monologues on one subject regardless of interjections from others)

C. Markedly restricted repertoire of activities and interests, as manifested by the following:

(1) stereotyped body movements, e.g., hand-flicking or -twisting, spinning, head-banging, complex whole-body movements

(2) persistent preoccupation with parts of objects (e.g., sniffing or smelling objects, repetitive feeling of texture of materials, spinning wheels of toy cars) or attachment to unusual objects (e.g., insists on carrying around a piece of string)

(3) marked distress over changes in trivial aspects of environment, e.g., when a vase is moved from usual position

(4) unreasonable insistence on following routines in precise detail, e.g., insisting that exactly the same route always be followed when shopping

(5) markedly restricted range of interests and a preoccupation with one narrow interest, e.g., interested only in lining up objects, in amassing facts about meteorology, or in pretending to be a fantasy character

D. Onset during infancy or childhood.

Specify if childhood onset (after 36 months of age).

DIAGNOSTIC CRITERIA FOR DEVELOPMENTAL ARITHMETIC DISORDER

A. Arithmetic skills, a measured by a standardized, individually administered test, are markedly below the expected level, given the person's schooling and intellectual capacity (as determined by an individually administered IQ test).

B. The disturbance in A significantly interferes with academic achievement or activities of daily living requiring arithmetic skills.

C. Not due to a defect in visual or hearing acuity or a neurologic disorder.

DIAGNOSTIC CRITERIA FOR DEVELOPMENTAL EXPRESSIVE WRITING DISORDER

A. Writing skills, as measured by a standardized, individually administered test, are markedly below the expected level, given the person's schooling and intellectual capacity (as determined by an individually administered IQ test).

B. The disturbance in A significantly interferes with academic achievement or activities of daily living requiring the composition of written texts (spelling words and expressing thoughts in grammatically correct sentences and organized paragraphs).

C. Not due to a defect in visual or hearing acuity or a neurologic disorder.

DIAGNOSTIC CRITERIA FOR DEVELOPMENTAL READING DISORDER

A. Reading achievement, as measured by a standarized, individually administered test, is markedly below the expected level, given the person's schooling and intellectual capacity (as determined by an individually administered IQ test).

B. The disturbance in A significantly interferes with academic achievement or activities of daily living requiring reading skills.

C. Not due to a defect in visual or hearing acuity or a neurologic disorder.

DIAGNOSTIC CRITERIA FOR DEVELOPMENTAL ARTICULATION DISORDER

A. Consistent failure to use developmentally expected speech sounds. For example, in a three-year-old, failure to articulate p, b, and t, and in a six-year-old, failure to articulate r, sh, th, f, z, and l.

B. Not due to a Pervasive Developmental Disorder, Mental Retardation, defect in hearing acuity, disorders of the oral speech mechanism, or a neurologic disorder.

DIAGNOSTIC CRITERIA FOR DEVELOPMENTAL EXPRESSIVE LANGUAGE DISORDER

A. The score obtained from a standardized measure of expressive language is substantially below that obtained from a standardized measure of nonverbal intellectual capacity (as determined by an individually administered IQ test).

B. The disturbance in A significantly interferes with academic achievement or activities of daily living requiring the expression of verbal (or sign) language. This may be evidenced in severe cases by using a markedly limited vocabulary, by speaking only in simple sentences, or by speaking only in the present tense. In less severe cases, there may be hesitations or errors in recalling certain words, or errors in the production of long or complex sentences.

C. Not due to a Pervasive Developmental

Disorder, defect in hearing acuity, or a neurologic disorder (aphasia).

DIAGNOSTIC CRITERIA FOR DEVELOPMENTAL RECEPTIVE LANGUAGE DISORDER

A. The score obtained from a standardized measure of receptive language is substantially below that obtained from a standardized measure of nonverbal intellectual capacity (as determined by an individually administered IQ test).

B. The disturbance in A significantly interferes with academic achievement or activities of daily living requiring the comprehension of verbal (or sign) language. This may be manifested in more severe cases by an inability to understand simple words or sentences. In less severe cases, there may be difficulty in understanding only certain types of words, such as spatial terms, or an inability to comprehend longer or more complex statements.

C. Not due to a Pervasive Developmental Disorder, defect in hearing acuity, or a neurologic disorder (aphasia).

DIAGNOSTIC CRITERIA FOR DEVELOPMENTAL COORDINATION DISORDER

A. The person's performance in daily activities requiring motor coordination is markedly below the expected level, given the person's chronological age and intellectual capacity. This may be manifested by marked delays in achieving motor milestones (walking, crawling, sitting), dropping things, "clumsiness," poor performance in sports, or poor handwriting.

B. The disturbance in A significantly interferes with academic achievement or activities of daily living.

C. Not due to a known physical disorder, such as cerebral palsy, hemiplegia, or muscular dystrophy.

DIAGNOSTIC CRITERIA FOR ATTENTION-DEFICIT HYPERACTIVITY DISORDER

Note: Consider a criterion met only if the behavior is considerably more frequent than that of most people of the same mental age.

A. A disturbance of at least six months during which at least eight of the following are present:

(1) often fidgets with hands or feet or squirms in seat (in adolescents, may be limited to subjective feelings of restlessness)

(2) has difficulty remaining seated when required to do so

(3) is easily distracted by extraneous stimuli

(4) has difficulty awaiting turn in games or group situations

(5) often blurts out answers to questions before they have been completed

(6) has difficulty following through on instructions from others (not due to oppositional behavior or failure of comprehension), e.g., fails to finish chores

(7) has difficulty sustaining attention in tasks or play activities

(8) often shifts from one uncompleted activity to another

(9) has difficulty playing quietly

(10) often talks excessively

(11) often interrupts or intrudes on others, e.g., butts into other children's games

(12) often does not seem to listen to what is being said to him or her

(13) often loses things necessary for tasks or activities at school or at home (e.g., toys, pencils, books, assignments)

(14) often engages in physically dangerous activities without considering possible consequences (not for the purpose of thrill-seeking), e.g., runs into street without looking

Note: The above items are listed in descending order of discriminating power based on data from a national field trial of the DSM III R criteria for Disruptive Behavior Disorders.

B. Onset before the age of seven.

C. Does not meet the criteria for a Pervasive Developmental Disorder.

Criteria for Severity of Attention-deficit Hyperactivity Disorder

Mild. Few, if any, symptoms in excess of those required to make the diagnosis *and* only minimal or no impairment in school and social functioning.

Moderate. Symptoms or functional impairment intermediate between "mild" and "severe."

Severe. Many symptoms in excess of those required to make the diagnosis *and* significant and pervasive impairment in functioning at home and school and with peers.

DIAGNOSTIC CRITERIA FOR CONDUCT DISORDER

A. A disturbance of conduct lasting at least six months, during which at least three of the following have been present:

(1) has stolen without confrontation of a victim on more than one occasion (including forgery)

(2) has run away from home overnight at least twice while living in parental or parental surrogate home (or once without returning)

(3) often lies (other than to avoid physical or sexual abuse)

(4) has deliberately engaged in fire-setting

(5) is often truant from school (for older person, absent from work)

(6) has broken into someone else's house, building, or car

(7) has deliberately destroyed others' property (other than by fire-setting)

(8) has been physically cruel to animals

(9) has forced someone into sexual activity with him or her

(10) has used a weapon in more than one fight

(11) often initiates physical fights

(12) has stolen with confrontation of a vic-

tim (e.g., mugging, purse-snatching, extortion, armed robbery)

(13) has been physically cruel to people

Note: The above items are listed in descending order of discriminating power based on data from a national field trial of the DSM III R criteria for Disruptive Behavior Disorders.

B. If 18 or older, does not meet criteria for Antisocial Personality Disorder.

Criteria for Severity of Conduct Disorder

Mild. Few if any conduct problems in excess of those required to make the diagnosis, *and* conduct problems cause only minor harm to others.

Moderate. Number of conduct problems and effect on others intemediate between "mild" and "severe."

Severe. Many conduct problems in excess of those required to make the diagnosis, *or* conduct problems cause considerable harm to others, e.g., serious physical injury to victims, extensive vandalism or theft, prolonged absence from home.

DIAGNOSTIC CRITERIA FOR OPPOSITIONAL DEFIANT DISORDER

Note: Consider a criterion met only if the behavior is considerably more frequent than that of most people of the same mental age.

A. A disturbance of at least six months during wich at least five of the following are present:

(1) often loses temper

(2) often argues with adults

(3) oten actively defies or refuses adult requests or rules, e.g. refuses to do chores at home

(4) often deliberately does things that annoy other people, e.g., grabs other children's hats

(5) often blames others for his or her own mistakes

(6) is often touchy or easily annoyed by others

(7) is often angry and resentful

(8) is often spiteful or vindictive

(9) often swears or uses obscene language

Note: The above items are listed in descending order of discriminating power based on data from a national field trial of the DSM III R criteria for Disruptive Behavior Disorders.

B. Does not meet the criteria for Conduct Disorder, and does not occur exclusively during the course of a psychotic disorder, Dysthymia, or a Major Depressive, Hypomanic, or Manic Episode.

Criteria for Severity of Oppositional Defiant Disorder

Mild. Few, if any, symptoms in excess of those required to make the diagnosis *and* only minimal or no impairment in school and social functioning.

Moderate. Symptoms of functional impairment intermediate between "mild" and "severe."

Severe. Many symptoms in excess of those required to make the diagnosis *and* significant and pervasive impairment in functioning at home and school and with other adults and peers.

DIAGNOSTIC CRITERIA FOR SEPARATION ANXIETY DISORDER

A. Excessive anxiety concerning separation from those to whom the child is attached, as evidenced by at least three of the following:

(1) unrealistic and persistent worry about possible harm befalling major attachment figures or fear that they will leave and not return

(2) unrealistic and persistent worry that an untoward calamitous event will separate the child from a major attachment figure, e.g., the child will be lost, kidnapped, killed, or be the victim of an accident

(3) persistent reluctance or refusal to go to school in order to stay with major attachment figures or at home

(4) persistent reluctance or refusal to go to sleep without being near a major

attachment figure or to go to sleep away from home

(5) persistent avoidance of being alone, including "clinging" to and "shadowing" major attachment figures

(6) repeated nightmares involving the theme of separation

(7) complaints of physical symptoms, e.g., headaches, stomachaches, nausea, or vomiting, on many school days or on other occasions when anticipating separation from major attachment figures

(8) recurrent signs or complaints of excessive distress in anticipation of separation from home or major attachment figures, e.g., temper tantrums or crying, pleading with parents not to leave

(9) recurrent signs of complaints of excessive distress when separated from home or major attachment figures, e.g., wants to return home, needs to call parents when they are absent or when child is away from home

B. Duration of disturbance of at least two weeks.

C. Onset before the age of 18.

D. Occurrence not exclusively during the course of a Pervasive Developmental Disorder, Schizophrenia, or any other psychotic disorder.

DIAGNOSTIC CRITERIA FOR AVOIDANT DISORDER OF CHILDHOOD OR ADOLESCENCE

A. Excessive shrinking from contact with unfamiliar people, for a period of six months or longer, sufficiently severe to interfere with social functioning in peer relationships.

B. Desire for social involvement with familiar people (family members and peers the person knows well), and generally warm and satisfying relations with family members and other familiar figures.

C. Age at least 2½ years.

D. The disturbance is not sufficiently per-

vasive and persistent to warrant the diagnosis of Avoidant Personality Disorder.

DIAGNOSTIC CRITERIA FOR OVERANXIOUS DISORDER

A. Excessive or unrealistic anxiety or worry, for a period of six months or longer, as indicated by the frequent occurrence of at least four of the following:

(1) excessive or unrealistic worry about future events

(2) excessive or unrealistic concern about the appropriateness of past behavior

(3) excessive or unrealistic concern about competence in one or more areas, e.g., athletic, academic, social

(4) somatic complaints, such as headaches or stomachaches, for which no physical basis can be established

(5) marked self-consciousness

(6) excessive need for reassurance about a variety of concerns

(7) marked feelings of tension or inability to relax

B. If another Axis I disorder is present (e.g., Separation Anxiety Disorder, Phobic Disorder, Obsessive-Compulsive Disorder), the focus of the symptoms in A are not limited to it. For example, if Separation Anxiety Disorder is present, the symptoms in A are not exclusively related to anxiety about separation. In addition, the disturbance does not occur only during the course of a psychotic disorder or a Mood Disorder.

C. If 18 or older, does not meet the criteria for Generalized Anxiety Disorder.

D. Occurrence not exclusively during the course of a Pervasive Developmental Disorder, Schizophrenia, or any other psychotic disorder.

DIAGNOSTIC CRITERIA FOR ANOREXIA NERVOSA

A. Refusal to maintain body weight over a minimal normal weight for age and height, e.g., weight loss leading to main-

tenance of body weight 15% below that expected; or failure to make expected weight gain during period of growth, leading to body weight 15% below that expected.
B. Intense fear of gaining weight or becoming fat, even though underweight.
C. Disturbance in the way in which one's body weight, size, or shape is experienced, e.g., the person claims to "feel fat" even when emaciated, believes that one area of the body is "too fat" even when obviously underweight.
D. In females, absence of at least three consecutive menstrual cycles when otherwise expected to occur (primary or secondary amenorrhea). (A woman is considered to have amenorrhea if her periods occur only following hormone, e.g., estrogen, administration.)

DIAGNOSTIC CRITERIA FOR BULIMIA NERVOSA

A. Recurrent episodes of binge eating (rapid consumption of a large amount of food in a discrete period of time).
B. A feeling of lack of control over eating behavior during the eating binges.
C. The person regularly engages in either self-induced vomiting, use of laxatives or diuretics, strict dieting or fasting, or vigorous exercise in order to prevent weight gain.
D. A minimum average of two binge-eating episodes a week for at least three months.
E. Persistent overconcern with body shape and weight.

DIAGNOSTIC CRITERIA FOR PICA

A. Repeated eating of a non-nutritive substance for at least one month.
B. Does not meet the criteria for either Autistic Disorder, Schizophrenia, or Kleine-Levin syndrome.

DIAGNOSTIC CRITERIA FOR RUMINATION DISORDER OF INFANCY

A. Repeated regurgitation, without nausea or associated gastrointestinal illness, for at least one month following a period of normal functioning.
B. Weight loss or failure to make expected weight gain.

DIAGNOSTIC CRITERIA FOR GENDER IDENTITY DISORDER OF CHILDHOOD

For Females:
A. Persistent and intense distress about being a girl, and a stated desire to be a boy (not merely a desire for any perceived cultural advantages from being a boy), or insistence that she is a boy.
B. Either (1) or (2):
  (1) Persistent marked aversion to normative feminine clothing and insistence on wearing stereotypical masculine clothing, e.g., boys' underwear and other accessories
  (2) persistent repudiation of female anatomic structures, as evidenced by at least one of the following:
    (a) an assertion that she has, or will grow, a penis
    (b) rejection of urinating in a sitting position
    (c) assertion that she shoes not want to grow breasts or menstruate
C. The girl has not yet reached puberty.

For Males:
A. Persistent and intense distress about being a boy and an intense desire to be a girl, or more rarely, insistence that he is a girl.
B. Either (1) or (2):
  (1) preoccupation with female stereotypical activities, as shown by a preference for either cross-dressing or simulating female attire, or by an intense desire to participate in the games and pastimes of girls and rejection of male

stereotypical toys, games, and activities

(2) persistent repudiation of male anatomic structures, as indicated by at least one of the following repeated assertions:

(a) that he will grow up to become a woman (not merely in role)

(b) that his penis or testes are disgusting or will disappear

(c) that it would be better not to have a penis or testes

C. The boy has not yet reached puberty.

DIAGNOSTIC CRITERIA FOR TRANSSEXUALISM

A. Persistent discomfort and sense of inappropriateness about one's assigned sex.

B. Persistent preoccupation for at least two years with getting rid of one's primary and secondary sex characteristics and acquiring the sex characteristics of the other sex.

C. The person has reached puberty.

Specify history of sexual orientation: **asexual, homosexual, heterosexual,** or **unspecified.**

DIAGNOSTIC CRITERIA FOR GENDER IDENTITY DISORDER OF ADOLESCENCE OR ADULTHOOD, NONTRANSSEXUAL TYPE (GIDAANT)

A. Persistent or recurrent discomfort and sense of inappropriateness about one's assigned sex.

B. Persistent or recurrent cross-dressing in the role of the other sex, either in fantasy or actuality, but not for the purpose of sexual excitement (as in Transvestic Fetishism).

C. No persistent preoccupation (for at least two years) with getting rid of one's primary and secondary sex characteristics and acquiring the sex characteristics of the other sex (as in Transsexualism).

D. The person has reached puberty.

Specifiy history of sexual orientation: **asexual, homosexual, heterosexual,** or **unspecified.**

DIAGNOSTIC CRITERIA FOR TOURETTE'S DISORDER

A. Both multiple motor and one or more vocal tics have been present at some time during the illness, although not necessarily concurrently.

B. The tics occur many times a day (usually in bouts), nearly every day or intermittently throughout a period of more than one year.

C. The anatomic location, number, frequency, complexity, and severity of the tics change over time.

D. Onset before age 21.

E. Occurrence not exclusively during Psychoactive Substance Intoxication or known central nervous system disease, such as Huntington's chorea and postviral encephalitis.

DIAGNOSTIC CRITERIA FOR CHRONIC MOTOR OR VOCAL TIC DISORDER

A. Either motor or vocal tics, but not both, have been present at some time during the illness.

B. The tics occur many times a day, nearly every day, or intermittently throughout a period of more than one year.

C. Onset before age 21.

D. Occurrence not exclusively during Psychoactive Substance Intoxication or known central nervous system disease, such as Huntington's chorea and postviral encephalitis.

DIAGNOSTIC CRITERIA FOR TRANSIENT TIC DISORDER

A. Single or mulitple motor and/or vocal tics.

B. The tics occur many times a day, nearly every day for at least two weeks, but for no longer than 12 consecutive months.

C. No history of Tourette's or Chronic Motor or Vocal Tic Disorder.

D. Onset before age 21.

E. Occurrence not exclusively during Psychoactive Substance Intoxication or known central nervous system disease, such as Huntington's chorea and postviral encephalitis.

Specify: single episode or recurrent.

DIAGNOSTIC CRITERIA FOR FUNCTIONAL ENCOPRESIS

A. Repeated passage of feces into places not appropriate for that purpose (e.g., clothing, floor), whether involuntary or intentional. (The disorder may be overflow incontinence secondary to functional fecal retention.)
B. At least one such event a month for at least six months.
C. Chronologic and mental age, at least four years.
D. Not due to a physical disorder, such as aganglionic megacolon.

Specify primary or secondary type.

Primary type: the disturbance was not preceded by a period of fecal continence lasting at least one year.

Secondary type: the disturbance was preceded by a period of fecal continence lasting at least one year.

DIAGNOSTIC CRITERIA FOR FUNCTIONAL ENURESIS

A. Repeated voiding of urine during the day or night into bed or clothes, whether involuntary or intentional.
B. At least two such events per month for children between the ages of five and six, and at least one event per month for older children.
C. Chronologic age at least five, and mental age at least four.
D. Not due to a physical disorder, such as diabetes, urinary tract infection, or a seizure disorder.

Specify primary or secondary type.

Primary type: the disturbance was not preceded by a period of urinary continence lasting at least one year.

Secondary type: the disturbance was pre-

ceded by a period of urinary continence lasting at least one year.

Specify nocturnal only, diurnal only, or nocturnal and diurnal.

DIAGNOSTIC CRITERIA FOR CLUTTERING

A disorder of speech fluency involving both the rate and the rhythm of speech and resulting in impaired speech intelligibility. Speech is erratic and dysrhythmic, consisting of rapid and jerky spurts that usually involve faulty phrasing patterns (e.g., alternating pauses and bursts of speech that produce groups of words unrelated to the grammatical structure of the sentence).

DIAGNOSTIC CRITERIA FOR STUTTERING

Frequent repetitions of sounds or syllables that markedly impair the fluency of speech.

DIAGNOSTIC CRITERIA FOR ELECTIVE MUTISM

A. Persistent refusal to talk in one or more major social situations (including at school).
B. Ability to comprehend spoken language and to speak.

DIAGNOSTIC CRITERIA FOR IDENTITY DISORDER

A. Severe subjective distress regarding uncertainty about a variety of issues relating to identity, including three or more of the following:
  (1) long-term goals
  (2) career choice
  (3) friendship patterns
  (4) sexual orientation and behavior
  (5) religious identification
  (6) moral value systems
  (7) group loyalties
B. Impairment in social or occupational (in-

cluding academic) functioning as a result of the symptoms in A.

C. Duration of the disturbance of at least three months.

D. Occurrence not exclusively during the course of a Mood Disorder or of a psychotic disorder, such as Schizophrenia.

E. The disturbance is not sufficiently pervasive and persistent to warrant the diagnosis of Borderline Personality Disorder.

DIAGNOSTIC CRITERIA FOR REACTIVE ATTACHMENT DISORDER OF INFANCY OR EARLY CHILDHOOD

A. Markedly disturbed social relatedness in most contexts, beginning before the age of five, as evidenced by either (1) or (2):

(1) persistent failure to initiate or respond to most social interactions (e.g., in infants, absence of visual tracking and reciprocal play, lack of vocal imitation or playfulnes, apathy, little or no spontaneity; at later ages, lack of or little curiosity and social interest)

(2) indiscriminate sociability, e.g., excessive familiarity with relative strangers by making requests and displaying affection

B. The disturbance in A is not a symptom of either Mental Retardation or a Pervasive Developmental Disorder, such as Autistic Disorder.

C. Grossly pathogenic care, as evidenced by at least one of the following:

(1) persistent disregard of the child's basic emotional needs for comfort, stimulation, and affection. *Examples:* overly harsh punishment by caregiver; consistent neglect by caregiver.

(2) persistent disregard of the child's basic physical needs, including nutrition, adequate housing, and protection from physical danger and assault (including sexual abuse)

(3) repeated change of primary caregiver so that stable attachments are not pos-

sible, e.g., frequent changes in foster parents

D. There is a presumption that the care described in C is responsible for the disturbed behavior in A; this presumption is warranted if the disturbance in A began following the pathogenic care in C.

Note: If failure to thrive is present, code it on Axis III.

DIAGNOSTIC CRITERIA FOR STEREOTYPY/HABIT DISORDER

A. Intentional, repetitive, nonfunctional behaviors, such as hand-shaking or -waving, body-rocking, head-banging, mouthing of objects, nail-biting, picking at nose or skin.

B. The disturbance either causes physical injury to the child or markedly interferes with normal activities, e.g., injury to head from head-banging; inability to fall asleep because of constant rocking.

C. Does not meet the criteria for either a Pervasive Developmental disorder or a Tic Disorder.

COMMENTS

Diagnostic classification in child psychiatry should serve various functions, e.g., it should facilitate communication among clinicians and should enhance both research and clinical service. Additionally, diagnostic classification schemes should provide important information about treatment, course, prognosis, etc. (Rutter, 1978). In contrast to the categorical approach adopted in DSM-III-R, other approaches examine dimensions of function or dysfunction (Werry, 1985). Although a psychiatric diagnosis should provide important information relevant to patient management, it is important to realize that diagnosis, *per se*, should be one of many factors taken into account in planning for clinical care. It is also the case that disorders, rather than individuals, are classified (Rutter and Gould, 1985); this is a common source of misunderstanding among parents and professionals alike. The implication of this view is that definitions and disorders may be expected to change over time as a result of clinical experience and research.

Our understanding of the underlying pathophysiology of most disorders remains limited. The approach adopted in DSM-III-R is, accordingly, largely atheoretical. It relies heavily on the provision of detailed diagnostic criteria; this approach stems from the relatively recent emphasis on providing detailed diagnostic criteria for research purposes (Spitzer et al., 1978).

As a practical matter, diagnostic systems like DSM-III-R are periodically reevaluated

and updated; it is likely, for example, that major changes will be made in some categories in DSM-IV (Shaffer et al., 1989). For example, the validity of some categories presently included in DSM-III-R is somewhat questionable (e.g., identity disorder), whereas other categories or conditions are not presently included in this diagnostic system (e.g., there is no provision for noting that child abuse is present).

Despite its limitations, the systematic approach adopted in DSM-III-R has proven useful. The decision tree provided in Table A-2 provides a helpful method for psychiatric diagnosis in children and adolescents.

Table A–2. Disorders Usually First Evident in Infancy, Childhood, or Adolescence*

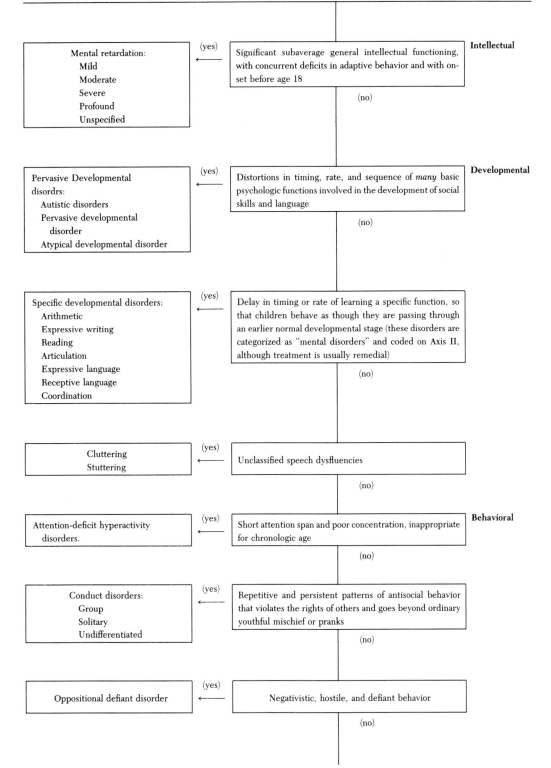

Table A-2.   Disorders Usually First Evident in Infancy, Childhood, or Adolescence*

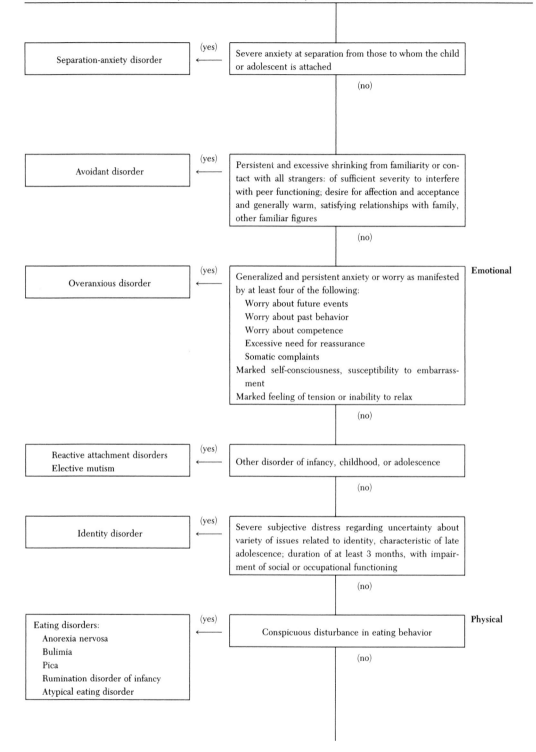

Separation-anxiety disorder — (yes) ← Severe anxiety at separation from those to whom the child or adolescent is attached

(no)

Avoidant disorder — (yes) ← Persistent and excessive shrinking from familiarity or contact with all strangers: of sufficient severity to interfere with peer functioning; desire for affection and acceptance and generally warm, satisfying relationships with family, other familiar figures

(no)

Overanxious disorder — (yes) ← Generalized and persistent anxiety or worry as manifested by at least four of the following: **Emotional**
Worry about future events
Worry about past behavior
Worry about competence
Excessive need for reassurance
Somatic complaints
Marked self-consciousness, susceptibility to embarrassment
Marked feeling of tension or inability to relax

(no)

Reactive attachment disorders
Elective mutism — (yes) ← Other disorder of infancy, childhood, or adolescence

(no)

Identity disorder — (yes) ← Severe subjective distress regarding uncertainty about variety of issues related to identity, characteristic of late adolescence; duration of at least 3 months, with impairment of social or occupational functioning

(no)

Eating disorders:
Anorexia nervosa
Bulimia
Pica
Rumination disorder of infancy
Atypical eating disorder — (yes) ← Conspicuous disturbance in eating behavior   **Physical**

(no)

Table A–2.   Disorders Usually First Evident in Infancy, Childhood, or Adolescence*

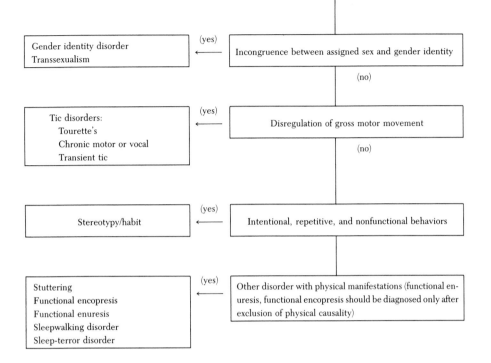

N.B.   Any appropriate adult diagnosis can be used for diagnosing a child or adolescent.

*Original, here modified and updated for DSM-III-R, was reprinted with permission from Janicak, P.G., and Andriukaitis, S.M. (1980), DSM-III: Seeing the Forest Through the Trees. *Psychiatric Annals*, 10:284–297.

REFERENCES

Rutter, M. (1978), Diagnostic validity in child psychiatry. *Adv. Biol. Psychiatry.*, 2:2–22.

Rutter, R., and Gould, M. (1985), Classification. In: *Child and Adolescent Psychiatry: Modern Approaches*, ed. M. Rutter and L. Hersov. Oxford: Blackwell Scientific Publications, pp. 304–321.

Rutter, M., Shaffer, D., and Shepherd, M. (1975), A multiaxial classification of child psychiatric disorders. Geneva: World Health Organization.

Shaffer, D., et al. (1989), Child and adolescence psychiatric disorders in DSM IV. *J. Am. Acad. Child Adolesc. Psychiatry.*, 28:830–835.

Spitzer, R.L., Endicott, J.E., and Robbins, E. (1978), Research diagnostic criteria. *Arch. Gen. Psychiatry*, 35:773–782.

Werry, J.S. (1985), ICD 9 & DSM III classification for the clinician. *J. Child Psychol. Psychiatry*, 26:1–6.

Appendix B

CHILD BEHAVIOR CHECKLIST FOR AGES 4–16*

CHILD'S NAME

PARENT'S TYPE OF WORK (Please be specific—for example: auto mechanic, high school teacher, homemaker, laborer, lathe operator, shoe salesman, army sergeant, even if parent does not live with child.)

SEX
☐ Boy
☐ Girl

AGE

RACE

FATHER'S TYPE OF WORK: _____

MOTHER'S TYPE OF WORK: _____

TODAY'S DATE

Mo. _____ Day _____ Yr. _____

CHILD'S BIRTHDATE

Mo. _____ Day _____ Yr. _____

THIS FORM FILLED OUT BY:
☐ Mother
☐ Father
☐ Other (Specify)

I. Please list the sports your child most likes to take part in. For example: swimming, baseball, skating, skate boarding, bike riding, fishing, etc.
☐ None

Compared to other children of the same age, about how much time does he/she spend in each?

	Don't Know	Less Than Average	Average	More Than Average
a. _____	☐	☐	☐	☐
b. _____	☐	☐	☐	☐
c. _____	☐	☐	☐	☐

Compared to other children of the same age, how well does he/she do each one?

	Don't Know	Below Average	Average	Above Average
a.	☐	☐	☐	☐
b.	☐	☐	☐	☐
c.	☐	☐	☐	☐

II. Please list your child's favorite hobbies, activities, and games, other than sports. For example: stamps, dolls, books, piano, crafts, singing, etc. (Do not include T.V.)
☐ None

Compared to other children of the same age, about how much time does he/she spend in each?

	Don't Know	Less Than Average	Average	More Than Average
a. _____	☐	☐	☐	☐
b. _____	☐	☐	☐	☐
c. _____	☐	☐	☐	☐

Compared to other children of the same age, how well does he/she do each one?

	Don't Know	Below Average	Average	Above Average
a.	☐	☐	☐	☐
b.	☐	☐	☐	☐
c.	☐	☐	☐	☐

III. Please list any organizations, clubs, teams, or groups your child belongs to.
☐ None

Compared to other children of the same age, how active is he/she in each?

	Don't Know	Less Active	Average	More Active
a. _____	☐	☐	☐	☐
b. _____	☐	☐	☐	☐
c. _____	☐	☐	☐	☐

IV. Please list any jobs or chores your child has. For example: paper route, babysitting, making bed, etc.
☐ None

Compared to other children of the same age, how well does he/she carry them out?

	Don't Know	Below Average	Average	Above Average
a. _____	☐	☐	☐	☐
b. _____	☐	☐	☐	☐
c. _____	☐	☐	☐	☐

*Reprinted with permission of T. Achenbach, University of Vermont, Burlington, VT 05404.

V. 1. About how many close friends does your child have? ☐ None ☐ 1 ☐ 2 or 3 ☐ 4 or more

  2. About how many times a week does your child do things with them? ☐ less than 1 ☐ 1 or 2 ☐ 3 or more

VI. Compared to other children of his/her age, how well does your child:

		Worse	About the same	Better
a.	Get along with his/her brothers & sisters?	☐	☐	☐
b.	Get along with other children?	☐	☐	☐
c.	Behave with his/her parents?	☐	☐	☐
d.	Play and work by himself/herself?	☐	☐	☐

VII. 1. Current school performance—for children aged 6 and older:

☐ Does not go to school

	Failing	Below average	Average	Above average
a. Reading or English	☐	☐	☐	☐
b. Writing	☐	☐	☐	☐
c. Arithmetic or Math	☐	☐	☐	☐
d. Spelling	☐	☐	☐	☐
e. _____	☐	☐	☐	☐
f. _____	☐	☐	☐	☐
g. _____	☐	☐	☐	☐

Other academic subjects: for example: history, science, foreign language, geography.

2. Is your child in a special class?

☐ No   ☐ Yes—what kind?

3. Has your child ever repeated a grade?

☐ No   ☐ Yes—grade and reason

4. Has your child had any academic or other problems in school?

☐ No   ☐ Yes—please describe

When did these problems start and end?

VIII.   Below is a list of items that describe children. For each item that describes your child *now* or *within the past 6 months*, please circle the *2* if the item is *very true* or *often true* of your child. Circle the *1* if the item is *somewhat* or *sometimes true* of your child. If the item is *not true* of your child, circle the *0*.

0 1 2	1.	Acts too young for his/her age	16
0 1 2	2.	Allergy (describe): _____	
		_____	
0 1 2	3.	Argues a lot	
0 1 2	4.	Asthma	
0 1 2	5.	Behaves like opposite sex	20
0 1 2	6.	Bowel movements outside toilet	
0 1 2	7.	Bragging, boasting	
0 1 2	8.	Can't concentrate, can't pay attention for long	
0 1 2	9.	Can't get his/her mind off certain thoughts; obsessions (describe): _____	
		_____	
0 1 2	10.	Can't sit still, restless, or hyperactive	25
0 1 2	11.	Clings to adults or too dependent	
0 1 2	12.	Complains of loneliness	
0 1 2	13.	Confused or seems to be in a fog	
0 1 2	14.	Cries a lot	
0 1 2	15.	Cruel to animals	30
0 1 2	16.	Cruelty, bullying, or meanness to others	
0 1 2	17.	Day-dreams or gets lost in his/her thoughts	
0 1 2	18.	Deliberately harms self or attempts suicide	
0 1 2	19.	Demands a lot of attention	
0 1 2	20.	Destroys his/her own things	35
0 1 2	21.	Destroys things belonging to his/her family or other children	
0 1 2	22.	Disobedient at home	
0 1 2	23.	Disobedient at school	
0 1 2	24.	Doesn't eat well	
0 1 2	25.	Doesn't get along with other children	40
0 1 2	26.	Doesn't seem to feel guilty after misbehaving	
0 1 2	27.	Easily jealous	
0 1 2	28.	Eats or drinks things that are not food (describe): _____	
		_____	
0 1 2	29.	Fears certain animals, situations, or places, other than school (describe): _____	
		_____	
0 1 2	30.	Fears going to school	45

0 1 2	31.	Fears he/she might think or do something bad	
0 1 2	32.	Feels he/she has to be perfect	
0 1 2	33.	Feels or complains that no one loves him/her	
0 1 2	34.	Feels others are out to get him/her	
0 1 2	35.	Feels worthless or inferior	50
0 1 2	36.	Gets hurt a lot, accident-prone	
0 1 2	37.	Gets in many fights	
0 1 2	38.	Gets teased a lot	
0 1 2	39.	Hangs around with children who get in trouble	
0 1 2	40.	Hears things that aren't there (describe): _____	
		_____	55
0 1 2	41.	Impulsive or acts without thinking	
0 1 2	42.	Likes to be alone	
0 1 2	43.	Lying or cheating	
0 1 2	44.	Bites fingernails	
0 1 2	45.	Nervous, highstrung, or tense	60
0 1 2	46.	Nervous movements or twitching (describe): _____	
		_____	
0 1 2	47.	Nightmares	
0 1 2	48.	Not liked by other children	
0 1 2	49.	Constipated, doesn't move bowels	
0 1 2	50.	Too fearful or anxious	65
0 1 2	51.	Feels dizzy	
0 1 2	52.	Feels too guilty	
0 1 2	53.	Overeating	
0 1 2	54.	Overtired	
0 1 2	55.	Overweight	70
0 1 2	56.	Physical problems without known medical cause:	
0 1 2	a.	Aches or pains	
0 1 2	b.	Headaches	
0 1 2	c.	Nausea, feels sick	
0 1 2	d.	Problems with eyes (describe): _____	
0 1 2	e.	Rashes or other skin problems	75
0 1 2	f.	Stomachaches or cramps	
0 1 2	g.	Vomiting, throwing up	
0 1 2	h.	Other (describe): _____	
		_____	

0 1 2	57.	Physically attacks people		
0 1 2	58.	Picks nose, skin, or other parts of body (describe): _____		
		_____ 80		
0 1 2	59.	Plays with own sex parts in public 16		
0 1 2	60.	Plays with own sex parts too much		
0 1 2	61.	Poor school work		
0 1 2	62.	Poorly coordinated or clumsy		
0 1 2	63.	Prefers playing with older children 20		
0 1 2	64.	Prefers playing with younger children		
0 1 2	65.	Refuses to talk		
0 1 2	66.	Repeats certain acts over and over; compulsions (describe): _____		
0 1 2	67.	Runs away from home		
0 1 2	68.	Screams a lot 25		
0 1 2	69.	Secretive, keeps things to self		
0 1 2	70.	Sees things that aren't there (describe): _____		
0 1 2	71.	Self-conscious or easily embarrassed		
0 1 2	72.	Sets fires		
0 1 2	73.	Sexual problems (describe): _____ 30		
0 1 2	74.	Showing off or clowning		
0 1 2	75.	Shy or timid		
0 1 2	76.	Sleeps less than most children		
0 1 2	77.	Sleeps more than most children during day and/or night (describe): _____		
0 1 2	78.	Smears or plays with bowel movements 35		
0 1 2	79.	Speech problem (describe): _____		
0 1 2	80.	Stares blankly		
0 1 2	81.	Steals at home		
0 1 2	82.	Steals outside the home		
0 1 2	83.	Stores up things he/she doesn't need (describe): _____ 40		

0 1 2	84.	Strange behavior (describe): _____	
0 1 2	85.	Strange ideas (describe): _____	
0 1 2	86.	Stubborn, sullen, or irritable	
0 1 2	87.	Sudden changes in mood or feelings	
0 1 2	88.	Sulks a lot 45	
0 1 2	89.	Suspicious	
0 1 2	90.	Swearing or obscene language	
0 1 2	91.	Talks about killing self	
0 1 2	92.	Talks or walks in sleep (describe): _____	
0 1 2	93.	Talks too much 50	
0 1 2	94.	Teases a lot	
0 1 2	95.	Temper tantrums or hot temper	
0 1 2	96.	Thinks about sex too much	
0 1 2	97.	Threatens people	
0 1 2	98.	Thumb-sucking 55	
0 1 2	99.	Too concerned with neatness or cleanliness	
0 1 2	100.	Trouble sleeping (describe): _____	
0 1 2	101.	Truancy, skips school	
0 1 2	102.	Underactive, slow moving, or lacks energy	
0 1 2	103.	Unhappy, sad, or depressed 60	
0 1 2	104.	Unusually loud	
0 1 2	105.	Uses alcohol or drugs (describe): _____	
0 1 2	106.	Vandalism	
0 1 2	107.	Wets self during the day	
0 1 2	108.	Wets the bed 65	
0 1 2	109.	Whining	
0 1 2	110.	Wishes to be of opposite sex	
0 1 2	111.	Withdrawn, doesn't get involved with others	
0 1 2	112.	Worrying	
0 1 2	113.	Please write in any problems your child has that were not listed above:	
0 1 2		_____ 70	
0 1 2		_____	
0 1 2		_____	

PLEASE BE SURE YOU HAVE ANSWERED ALL ITEMS.   UNDERLINE ANY YOU ARE CONCERNED ABOUT.

Appendix C

THE DEVELOPMENTAL PROFILE

In 1945, Anna Freud pointed out the hazard of making assumptions on the basis of manifest childhood symptomatology. She directed attention instead to the child's development and the need to assess those factors that might threaten that development (A. Freud, 1945). In 1962, she began to formulate a psychoanalytic "profile of development" (A. Freud, 1962). Part of this profile was subsequently elaborated in her "Concept of Developmental Lines" (A. Freud, 1963). Two years later, her *Outline of the Developmental Profile* was published (A. Freud, 1965).

The purposes of the profile are to assess the development of the child as a basis for deciding on the indication for child psychoanalysis and to assess the child's readiness for certain experiences, such as entering nursery school. In practice, both kinds of assessments are usually made on much simpler information.

In its general form, the profile consists of a number of headings under which data can be organized (see *General Child Metapsychologic Profile*, p. 444). It attempts to combine clinical observations with metapsychologic considerations. Over the years, this general profile has been elaborated and modified into profiles for different developmental periods: a baby profile (W.E. Freud, 1967), a latency profile (Meers, 1966), the adolescent profile (Laufer, 1965), and a profile for adulthood (A. Freud et al., 1965). Within these categories, the profile has been applied to the study of borderline and psychotic children, blind children, and children with impulse character disorders (see *References*).

The major differences between the general profile and the baby profile, besides the obvious detailed description of the pregnancy, labor, and perinatal period, are that the baby profile provides opportunities to describe the mother and father, and aspects of the infant's behavior under various conditions. The aims of the baby profile are (1) to permit thinking metapsychologically about the infant, (2) to convey a global, overall picture of the infant's personality, (3) to point to phenomena that might otherwise be overlooked, and (4) to provide a systematic schema for monitoring normal development and early recognition of pathologic conditions.

The major differences in the adolescent profile are in its elaboration of ego development, particularly in regard to defenses, affects, and identifications. Special attention is also given to superego development and the development of the total personality.

Although the literature on the profile has grown (see *References*), most of the work on the profile has been confined to the Hampstead Child Therapy Clinic in London. Few other centers use the profile in a systematic way. Indeed, the profile is now used almost exclusively by only a small number of the relatively few child psychoanalysts, each of whom sees only a few children in psychoanalysis.

Perhaps part of the reason for this limited application is that the profile is only as good as the experience of the investigator and is sometimes time-consuming to use. In addition, the profile is not standardized within a given setting, much less from institution to institution. There are no criteria or units for measurement, and categories within the profile are at different levels of abstraction and inference. Nevertheless, it is reproduced here because it is one of the few attempts to provide an in-depth picture of an individual child, a picture that goes beyond the diagnostic level.

GENERAL CHILD METAPSYCHOLOGIC PROFILE

I. Reason for referral
II. Description of child
III. Pediatric history, including family, personal, developmental, social, and history of previous illnesses
IV. Environmental influences
V. Assessments of development
  A. Drives
    1. Libido
      a. Level and dominance of phase development
      b. Distribution to self, object
      c. Level, quality, and dominance of object libido
    2. Aggression
      a. Quantity
      b. Quality; i.e., correspondence with libido development
      c. Direction (self; object world)
  B. Ego and superego
    a. Ego functions—perception, memory, motility, reality testing, synthesis, speech, secondary process
    b. Defense organization—against which drive? age adequate? balance? effectiveness? dependence on object world?
    c. Secondary interference of defense activity with ego achievements
    d. Consider developmental lines here (see Chap. 7)

VI. Genetic assessments (regression and fixation points)
  a. By manifest behavior
  b. By fantasy activity
  c. By symptomatology
VII. Dynamic and structural assessments
  a. External (fear)
  b. Internalized (guilt)
  c. Internal conflicts (unsolved ambivalence, activity vs. passivity, masculinity vs. passivity)
    i. Assess level of maturity (relative independence)
    ii. Assess severity of disturbance
    iii. Assess intensity of therapy needed for alleviation or removal of disturbance
VIII. Assessment of some general characteristics
  a. Frustration tolerance
  b. Sublimation potential
  c. Overall attitude to anxiety (retreat or mastery)
  d. Progressive vs. developmental forces
XI. Diagnosis
  a. Variations of normality
  b. Transitory symptoms as by-products of developmental strain
  c. Permanent drive regression and fixation → neurotic conflicts → infantile neuroses and character disorders
  d. Drive regression and ego and superego regression → infantilisms, borderline, delinquent, or psychotic disturbances
  e. Primary deficiencies of an organic nature, or early deprivations that distort development and structuralization → retarded, defective, and nontypical personalities
  f. Destructive processes at work (organic, toxic, psychic—known or unknown)

REFERENCES
Normality
Diagnostic Profile

Freud, A. (1962), Assessment of childhood disturbances. *Psychoanal. Study Child*, 17:149–158.

Freud, A. (1945), Indications for child analysis. *Psychoanal. Study Child*, 1:127–149.

Freud, A. (1963), The concept of developmental lines. *Psychoanal. Study Child*, 18:245–265.

Freud, A. (1965), *Normality and Pathology in Childhood*. New York: International Universities Press.

Nagera,* H. (1963), The developmental profile: Notes on some practical considerations regarding its use. *Psychoanal. Study Child*, 18:511–540.

Babies

Freud, W.E. (1967), Assessment of early infancy. *Psychoanal. Study Child*, 22:216–238.

Latency

Meers, D.R. (1966), A diagnostic profile of psychopathology in a latency child. *Psychoanal. Study Child*, 21:483–526.

Adolescents

Laufer, M. (1965), Assessment of adolescent disturbances. *Psychoanal. Study Child*, 20:99–123.

Adults

Freud, A., Nagera, H., and Freud, W.E. (1965). Metapsychological assessment of the adult personality. *Psychoanal. Study Child*, 20:9–41.

*First published case.

Pathology

Blind Children

Burlington, D. (1975), Special problems of blind infants. Blind Baby Profile. *Psychoanal. Study Child*, 30:3–14.

Colonna, A. (1968), Discussion (The re-education of a retarded blind child). *Psychoanal. Study Child*, 23:386–390.

Nagera, H., and Colonna, A. (1965), Aspects of the contribution of sight to ego and drive development: A comparison of the development of some blind and sighted children. *Psychoanal. Study Child*, 20:267–287.

Impulsive Psychopathologic Character

Michaels, J.J., and Stiver, I.P. (1965), The impulsive psychopathic character according to the Diagnostic Profile. *Psychoanal. Study Child*, 20:124–141.

Psychotic Children (4), aged 7 to 10

Thomas, R., et al. (1966), Comments on some aspects of self and object representation in a group of psychotic children: An application of Anna Freud's Diagnostic Profile. *Psychoanal. Study Child*, 21:527–580.

Borderline Twin, aged 14

Maenchen, A. (1968), Objective cathexis in a borderline twin. *Psychoanal. Study Child*, 23:438–456.

Borderline States

Frijling-Schreuder, E.C.M. (1969), Borderline states in children. *Psychoanal. Study Child*, 24:307–327.

Index

Page numbers in *italics* refer to figures; page numbers followed by *t* refer to tables; page numbers followed by *n* refer to notes.

447

physician interview and role with, 279-280

specific management of, 281

See also Death

"easy"

temperamental constellation of, 113*n*-114*n*

elementary-school-age. *See* Elementary-school-age children

institutionalized

IQ scores of, 163-164

latchkey

family development and, 96-97

single parenthood and, 414-415

moribund

management of, 281-282

mother's latent expectations of, 119

positive attributes of, 316-317

preschool

checklist for psychiatric testing of, 298*t*

psychiatric evaluation of. *See* Evaluation

reactions of

to acute illness, 258

to birth defects, 257-258

roles of in family, 99

runaway, 241

sexual instinct in

Freud on, 56*n*-58*n*

"slow-to-warm-up"

temperamental constellation of, 113*n*-114*n*

socially isolated, 329-330

violent

clinical characteristics of, 230-231

medication dosages for, 233, 234*t*

See also Childhood

Children's Act of 1975, 177-178

Cholinergic pathway(s)

development of, 5

Chomsky, N.

generative transformational grammar theory of, 45-46

Circular reaction(s)

primary, 136

secondary, 137, 148*n*

secondary and tertiary, 32

of sensorimotor stage, 31

tertiary, 137, 148*n*-149*n*

Cleft palate

child's reaction to, 257

parental reaction to, 255

Clinging

infant, 21

preoedipal ambivalence and, 77*n*

in presence of stranger, 22

Clinician

choice of

for sexual abuse cases, 102*n*

countertransference in, 302-303

Cluttering

classification of, 435*t*

diagnostic criteria for, 432

Cocaine

exposure to in utero, 239

use of during adolescence, 238-239

Cogentin

dosage of, 408*t*

Cognitive defect

in infantile autism, 140

Cognitive deprivation, 128

Cognitive development, 31-42, *34, 36, 38, 39, 40, 42n*

during adolescence, 218

during ages 1 to 3, 155-156, 179-180

concrete operations stage of, *36,* 36-37

defective

in infantile autism, 140

early signs of, 136

in elementary-school-age child, 196-197

formal operations stage of, 37-41, *38, 39, 40*

moral judgment and, 81, 84*n*

preoperational stage of, 32-36, *34*

sensorimotor stage of, 31-32

two concepts of, 137-138

Commercial(s)

television

violence and, 419

Committee on Adoption and Dependent Care

on birth record access, 178

Communication

impaired

in autistic disorder, 424-425

Communication development interview

outline for, 310*t*-311*t*

Companionship

after egocentricity, 75

Computerized tomography (CT)

use of with stress disorders, 383-384

Concentration

preoperational

defined, *34,* 34-35

Concrete operations stage

child's goal during, *40*

of cognitive development, *36,* 36-37, 196-197

defined, 138

delay in

in attention-deficit hyperactivity disorder, 371

formal operations stage vs., 37-38

moral development and, 81

Condensation mechanism, 138

Conduct disorder(s)

classification of, 435*t*

diagnostic criteria for, 427

differential diagnosis of, 352

in elementary-school-age child, 207*n*

as sign of anxiety, 180

Conflict(s)

inferred

assessment of, 313-314

"Congenital activity types," 20

Conservation

child's mastery of, 197

types of, 37

Constraints

morality of, 81